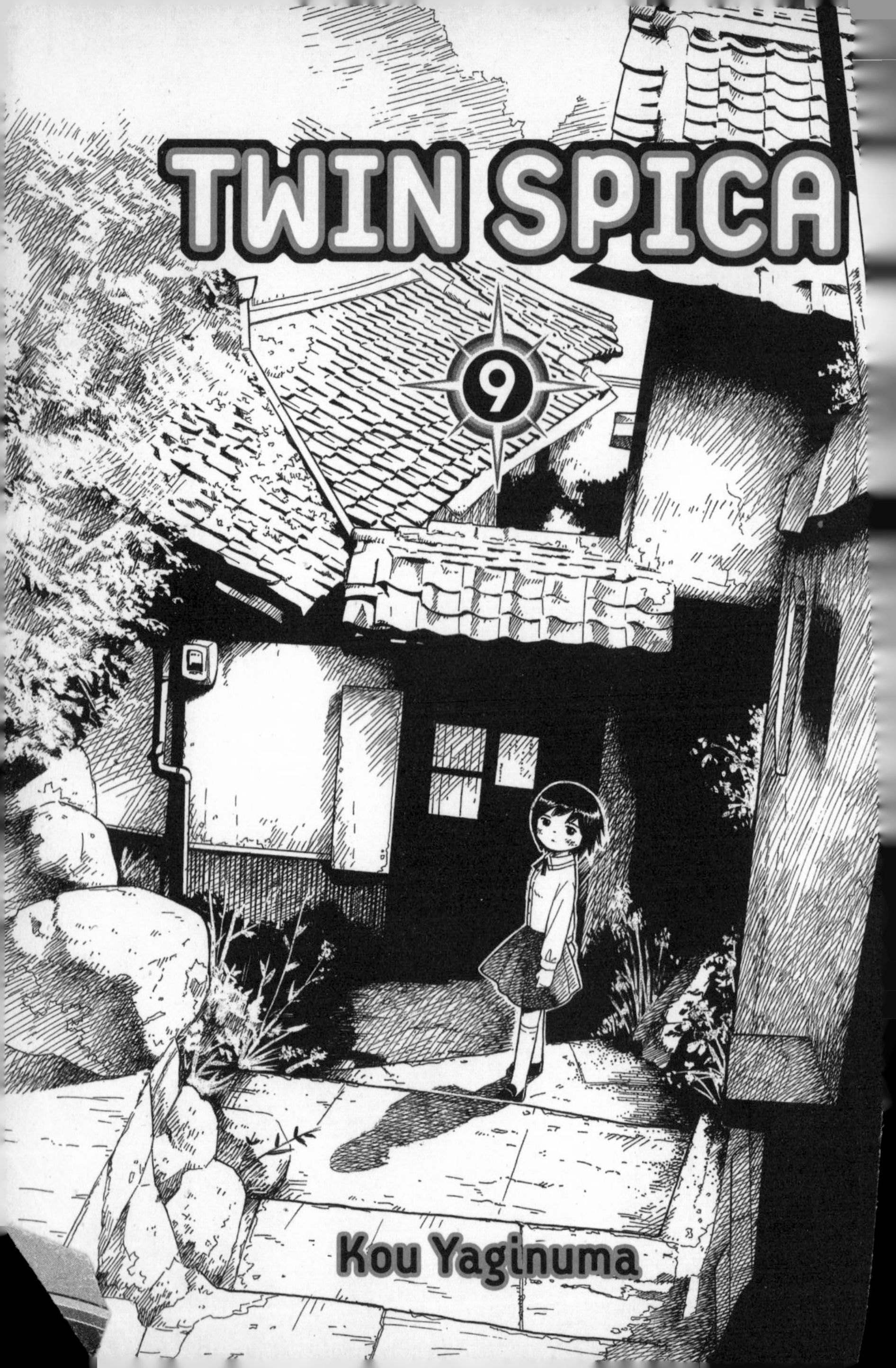TWIN SPICA
9
Kou Yaginuma

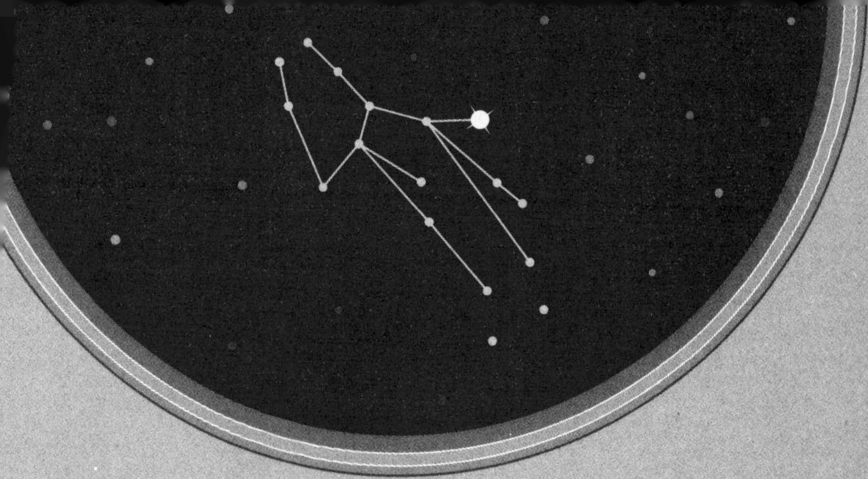

CONTENTS

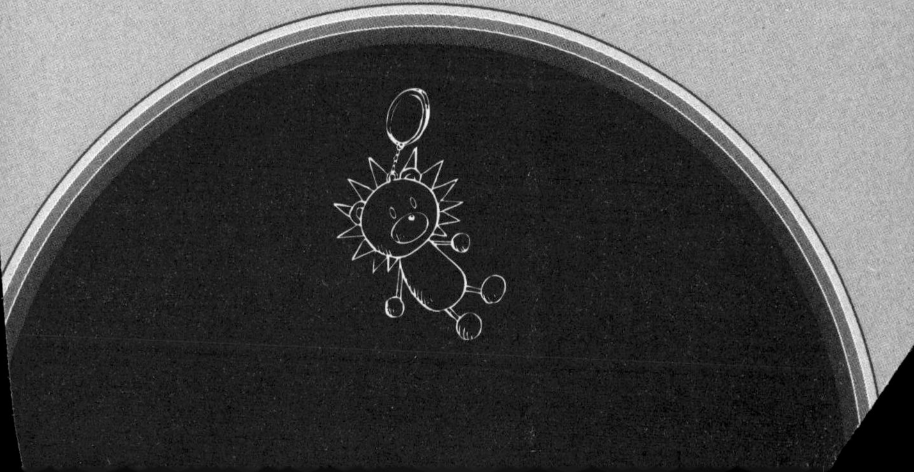

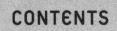

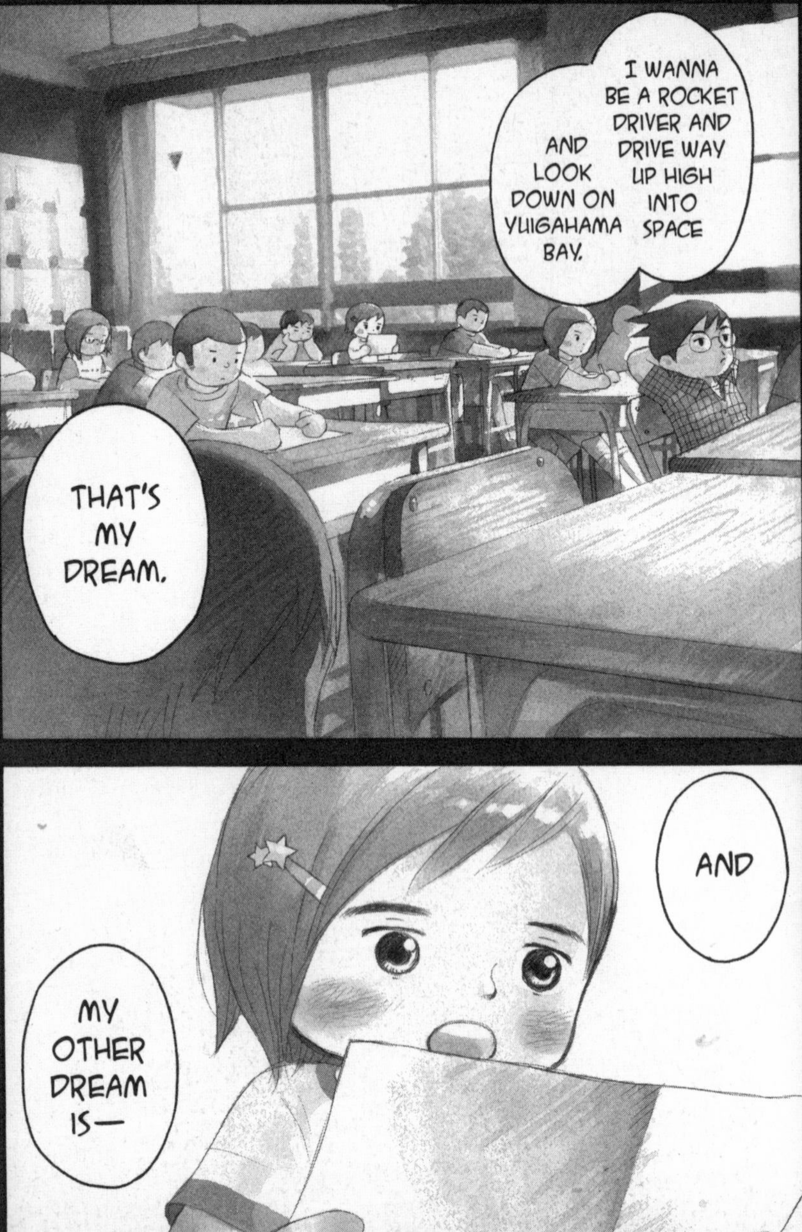
I WANNA BE A ROCKET DRIVER AND DRIVE WAY UP HIGH INTO SPACE
AND LOOK DOWN ON YUIGAHAMA BAY.
THAT'S MY DREAM.
AND
MY OTHER DREAM IS—

MISSION:47

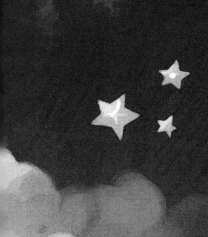

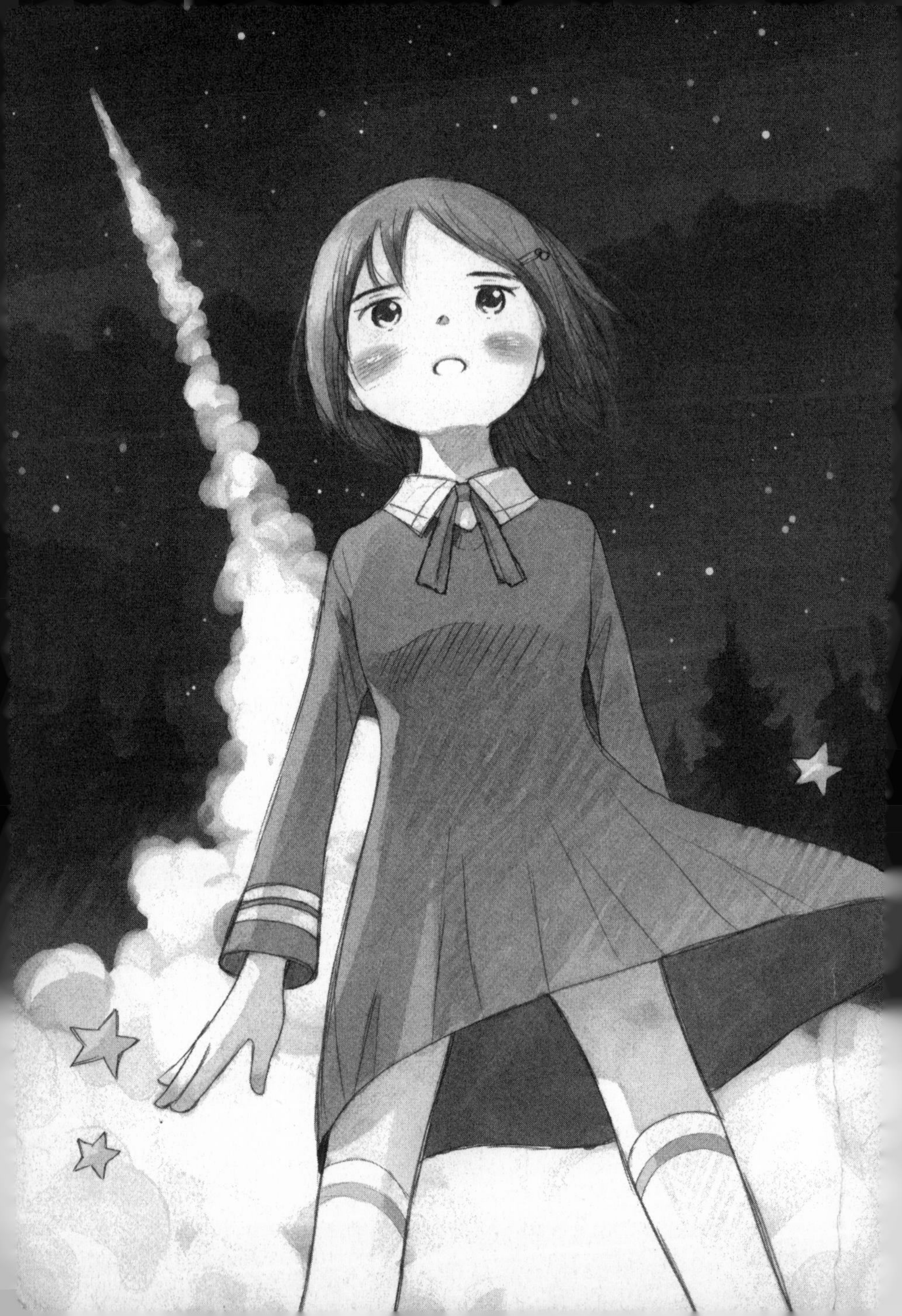

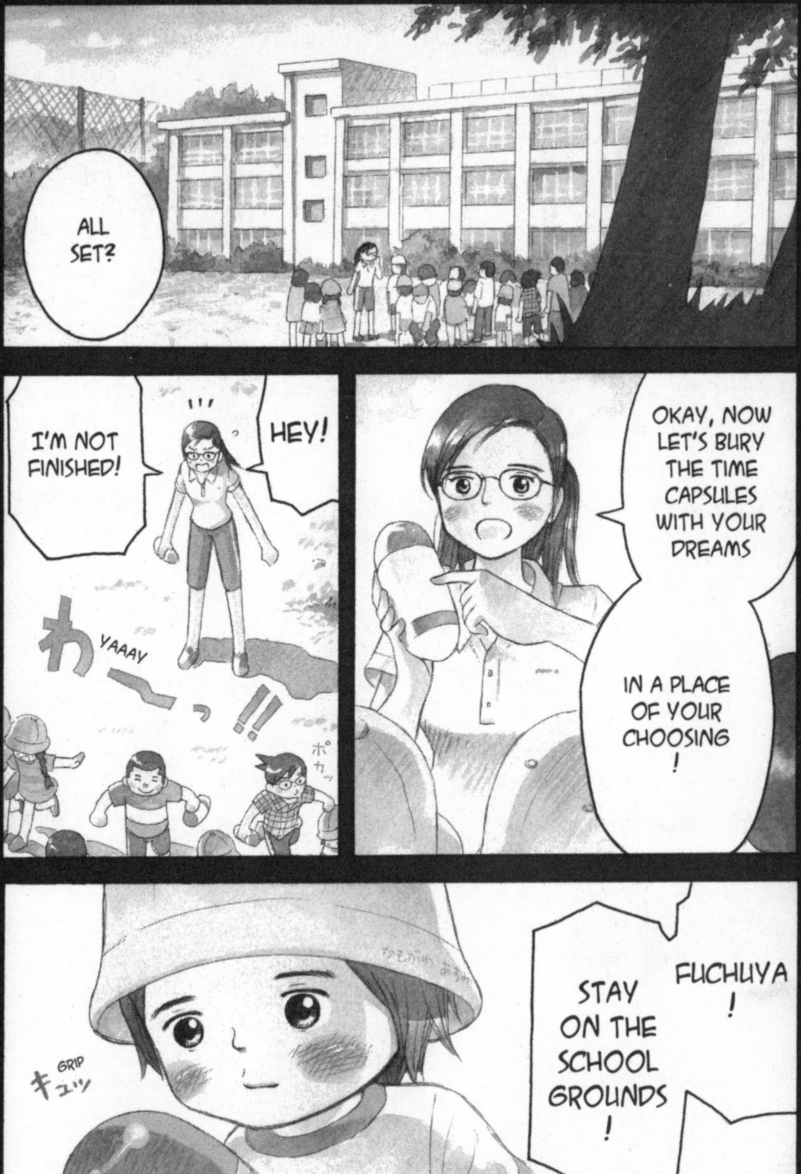
ALL SET?
OKAY, NOW LET'S BURY THE TIME CAPSULES WITH YOUR DREAMS
IN A PLACE OF YOUR CHOOSING!
HEY!
I'M NOT FINISHED!
わーっ!!
YAAAY
ポカッ
FUCHUYA!
STAY ON THE SCHOOL GROUNDS!
キュッ
GRIP

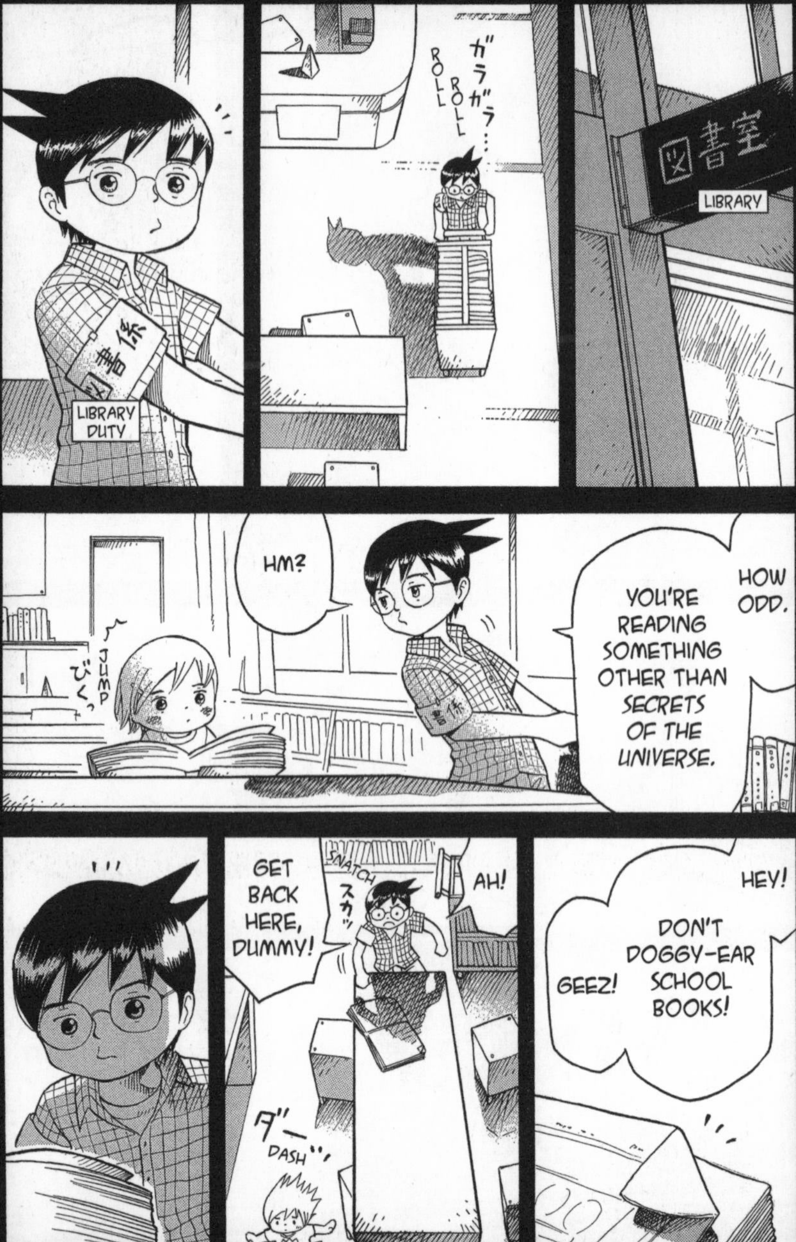
図書室
LIBRARY
ガラガラ…
ROLL ROLL
図書係
LIBRARY DUTY
HOW ODD.
YOU'RE READING SOMETHING OTHER THAN SECRETS OF THE UNIVERSE.
HM?
びくっ
JUMP
HEY!
DON'T DOGGY-EAR SCHOOL BOOKS!
GEEZ!
AH!
スカッ
SNATCH
GET BACK HERE, DUMMY!
ダー
DASH

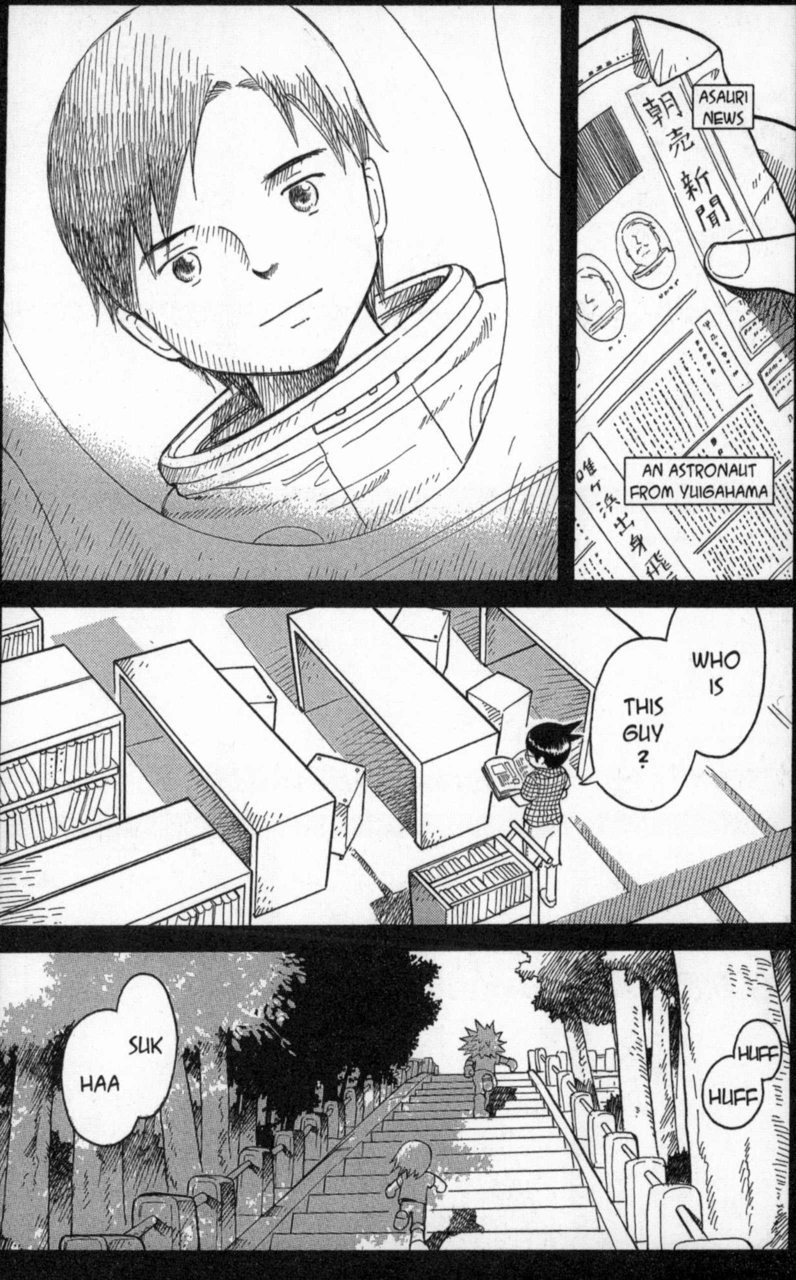
朝売新聞
ASAURI NEWS
AN ASTRONAUT FROM YUIGAHAMA
WHO IS THIS GUY?
HUFF
HUFF
SUK
HAA

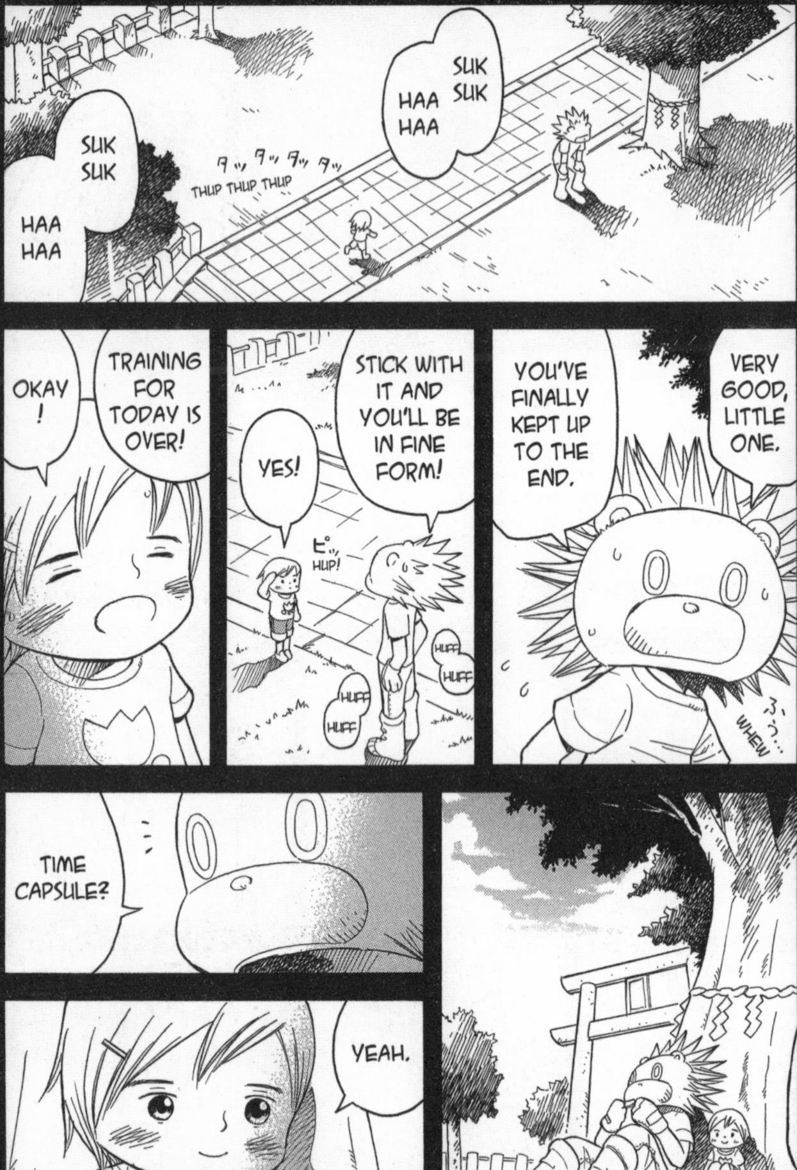
SUK SUK
HAA HAA
タッ タッ タッ タッ
THUP THUP THUP
SUK SUK
HAA HAA
VERY GOOD, LITTLE ONE.
YOU'VE FINALLY KEPT UP TO THE END.
ふぅ…
WHEW
STICK WITH IT AND YOU'LL BE IN FINE FORM!
YES!
ピッ
HUP!
HUFF
HUFF
HUFF
HUFF
TRAINING FOR TODAY IS OVER!
OKAY!
TIME CAPSULE?
YEAH.

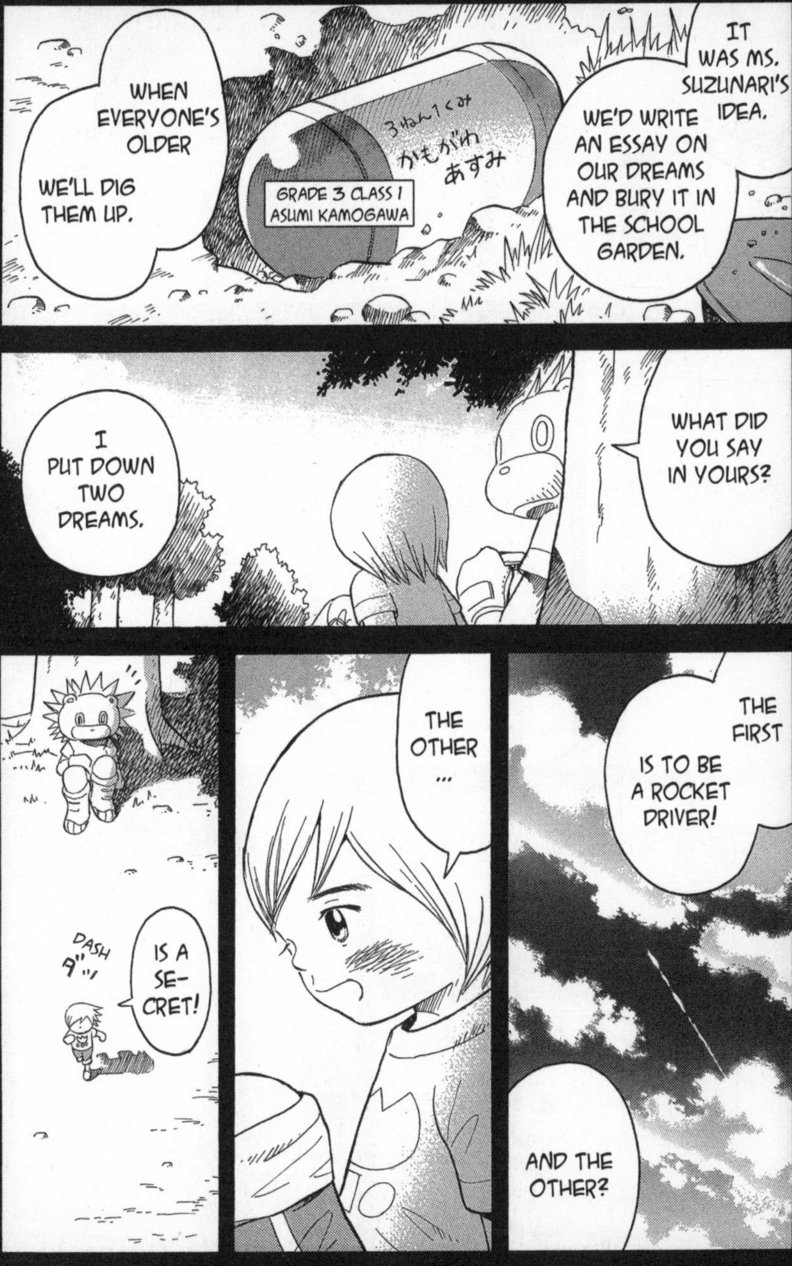
IT WAS MS. SUZUNARI'S IDEA.
WE'D WRITE AN ESSAY ON OUR DREAMS AND BURY IT IN THE SCHOOL GARDEN.
3ねん1くみ かもがわ あすみ
GRADE 3 CLASS 1 ASUMI KAMOGAWA
WHEN EVERYONE'S OLDER
WE'LL DIG THEM UP.
WHAT DID YOU SAY IN YOURS?
I PUT DOWN TWO DREAMS.
THE FIRST
IS TO BE A ROCKET DRIVER!
AND THE OTHER?
THE OTHER ...
DASH
IS A SE-CRET!

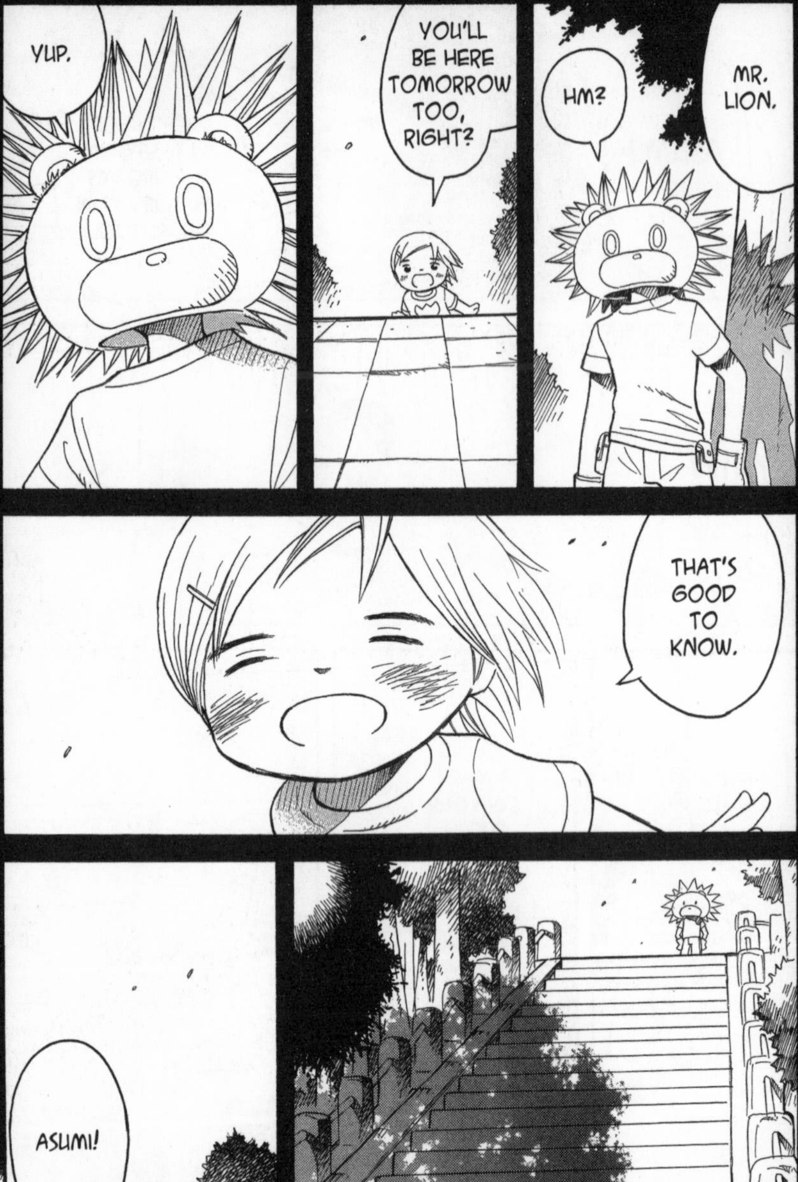
MR. LION.
HM?
YOU'LL BE HERE TOMORROW TOO, RIGHT?
YUP.
THAT'S GOOD TO KNOW.
ASUMI!

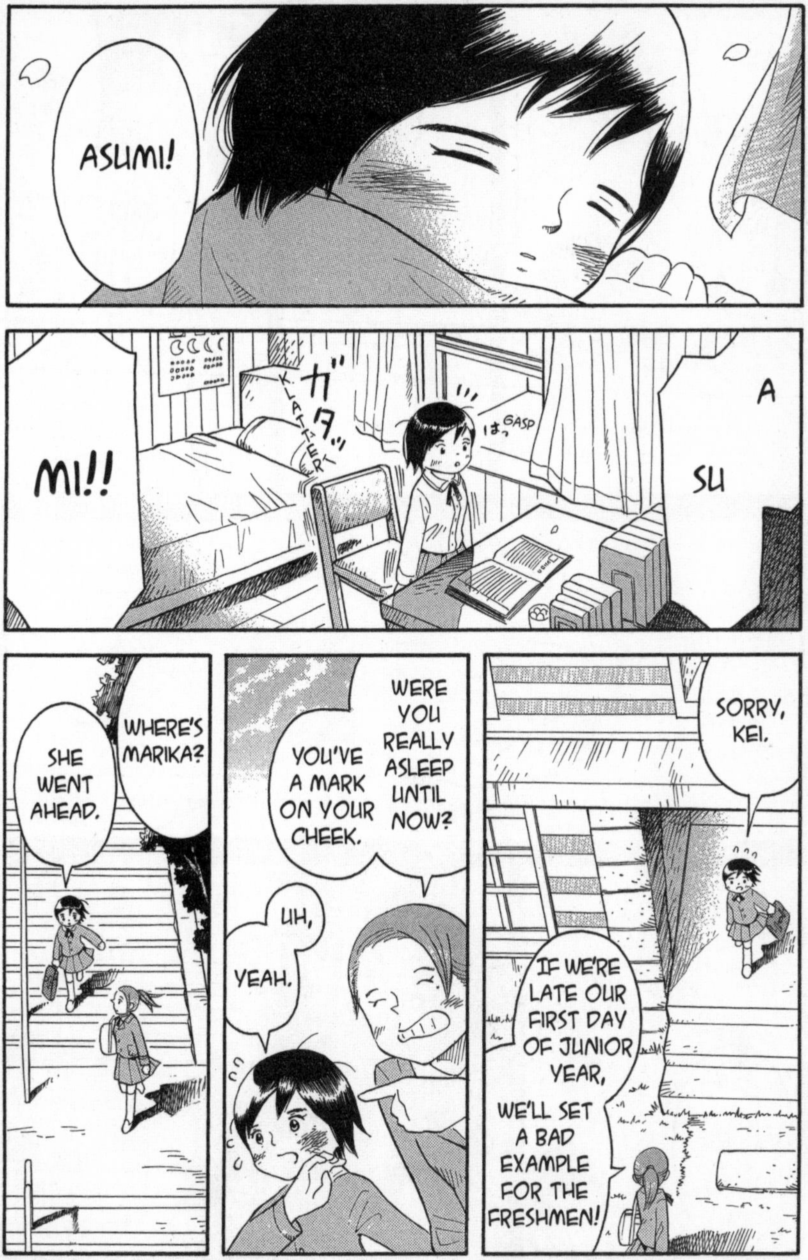
ASUMI!
A
SU
MI!!
ガタッ KLATTER
はっ GASP
SORRY, KEI.
IF WE'RE LATE OUR FIRST DAY OF JUNIOR YEAR,
WE'LL SET A BAD EXAMPLE FOR THE FRESHMEN!
WERE YOU REALLY ASLEEP UNTIL NOW?
YOU'VE A MARK ON YOUR CHEEK.
UH,
YEAH.
WHERE'S MARIKA?
SHE WENT AHEAD.

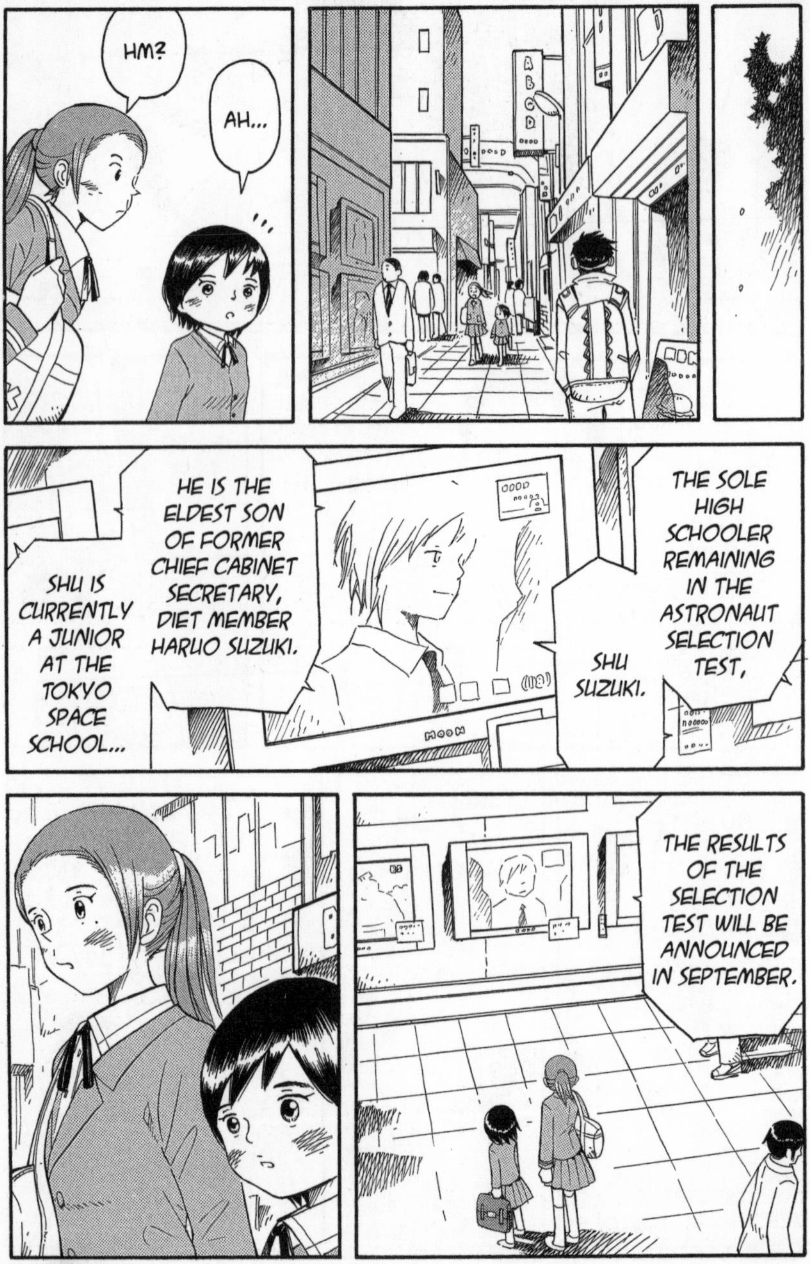
HM?
AH...
THE SOLE HIGH SCHOOLER REMAINING IN THE ASTRONAUT SELECTION TEST,
SHU SUZUKI.
HE IS THE ELDEST SON OF FORMER CHIEF CABINET SECRETARY, DIET MEMBER HARUO SUZUKI.
SHU IS CURRENTLY A JUNIOR AT THE TOKYO SPACE SCHOOL...
THE RESULTS OF THE SELECTION TEST WILL BE ANNOUNCED IN SEPTEMBER.

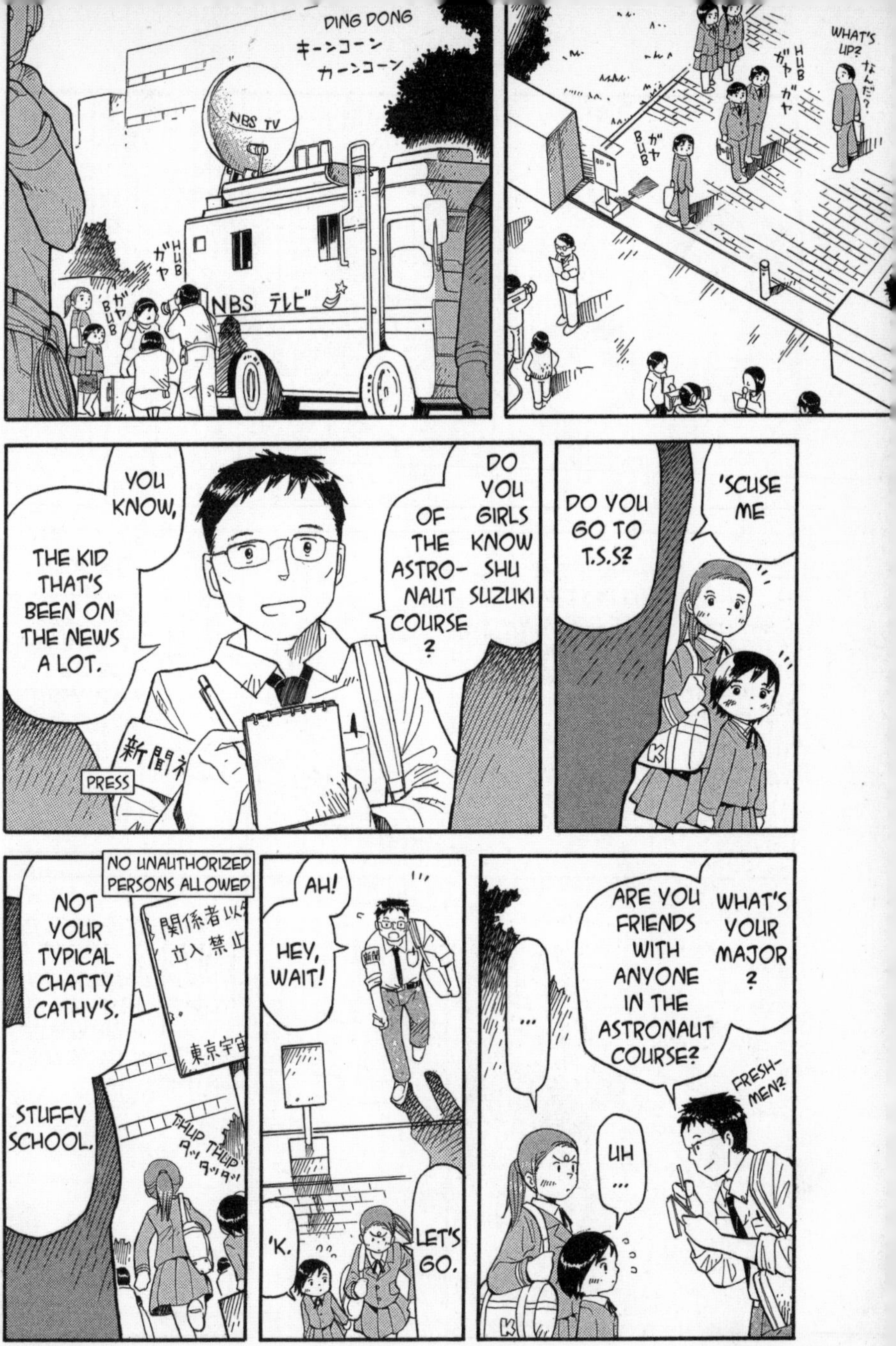
WHAT'S UP?
なんだ?
HUB ガヤ
ガヤ
BUB ガヤ
DING DONG
キーンコーン
カーンコーン
NBS TV
HUB ガヤ
BUB ガヤ
NBS テレビ
'SCUSE ME
DO YOU GO TO T.S.S?
DO YOU GIRLS KNOW SHU SUZUKI OF THE ASTRONAUT COURSE?
YOU KNOW, THE KID THAT'S BEEN ON THE NEWS A LOT.
PRESS
WHAT'S YOUR MAJOR?
ARE YOU FRIENDS WITH ANYONE IN THE ASTRONAUT COURSE?
...
FRESHMEN?
UH ...
AH!
HEY, WAIT!
LET'S GO.
'K.
NO UNAUTHORIZED PERSONS ALLOWED
立入禁止
NOT YOUR TYPICAL CHATTY CATHY'S.
STUFFY SCHOOL.
THUP THUP
タッタッタッ

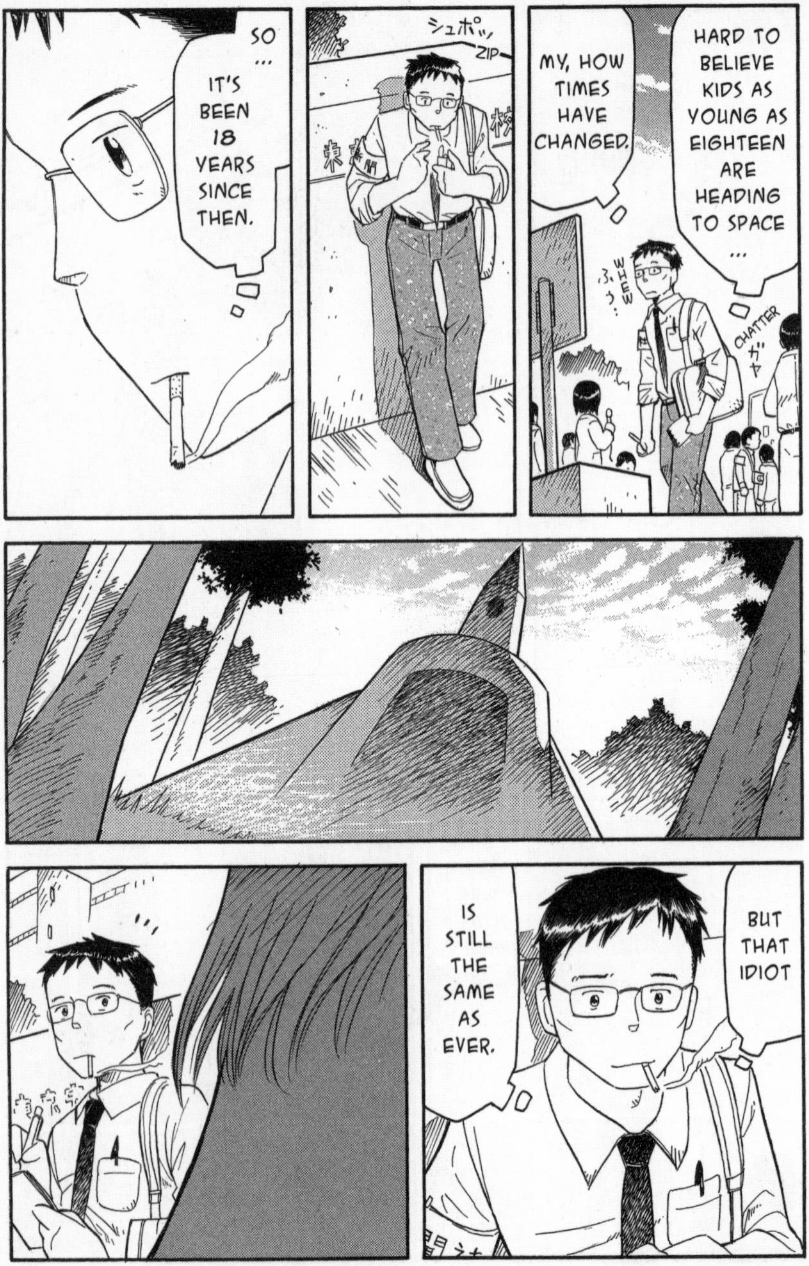
HARD TO BELIEVE KIDS AS YOUNG AS EIGHTEEN ARE HEADING TO SPACE ...
MY, HOW TIMES HAVE CHANGED.
ふぅ… WHEW
ガヤ CHATTER
シュポッ ZIP
SO ...
IT'S BEEN 18 YEARS SINCE THEN.
BUT THAT IDIOT
IS STILL THE SAME AS EVER.
...

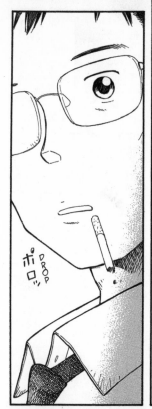

DROP

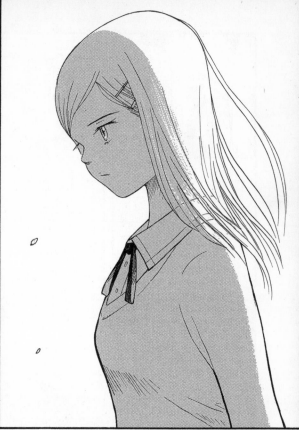

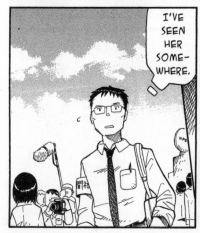

I'VE SEEN HER SOME-WHERE.

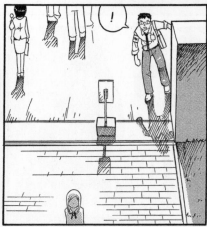

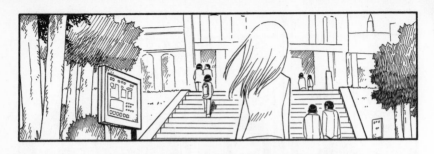

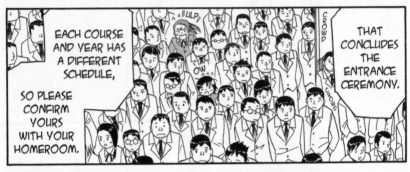

THAT CONCLUDES THE ENTRANCE CEREMONY.
CROWD
CROWD
ULP
OW
EACH COURSE AND YEAR HAS A DIFFERENT SCHEDULE,
SO PLEASE CONFIRM YOURS WITH YOUR HOMEROOM.
THE PRIN-CIPAL'S AS LONG-WINDED AS EVER.
HE TALKED ALL HE WANTED IN THE MORNING, TOO.
CHATTER ガヤ
ガタッ KLAK
HM?!
KRIK
OW...
STILL FEELING THAT BEAR STINT ...
GEEZ
わーっ! YAAY
KICK キーック
THOSE LITTLE BRATS!

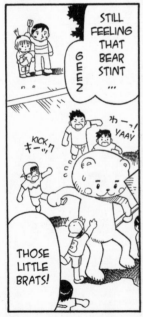

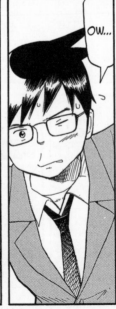

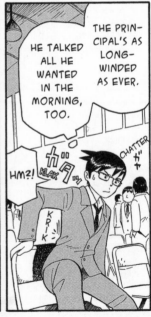

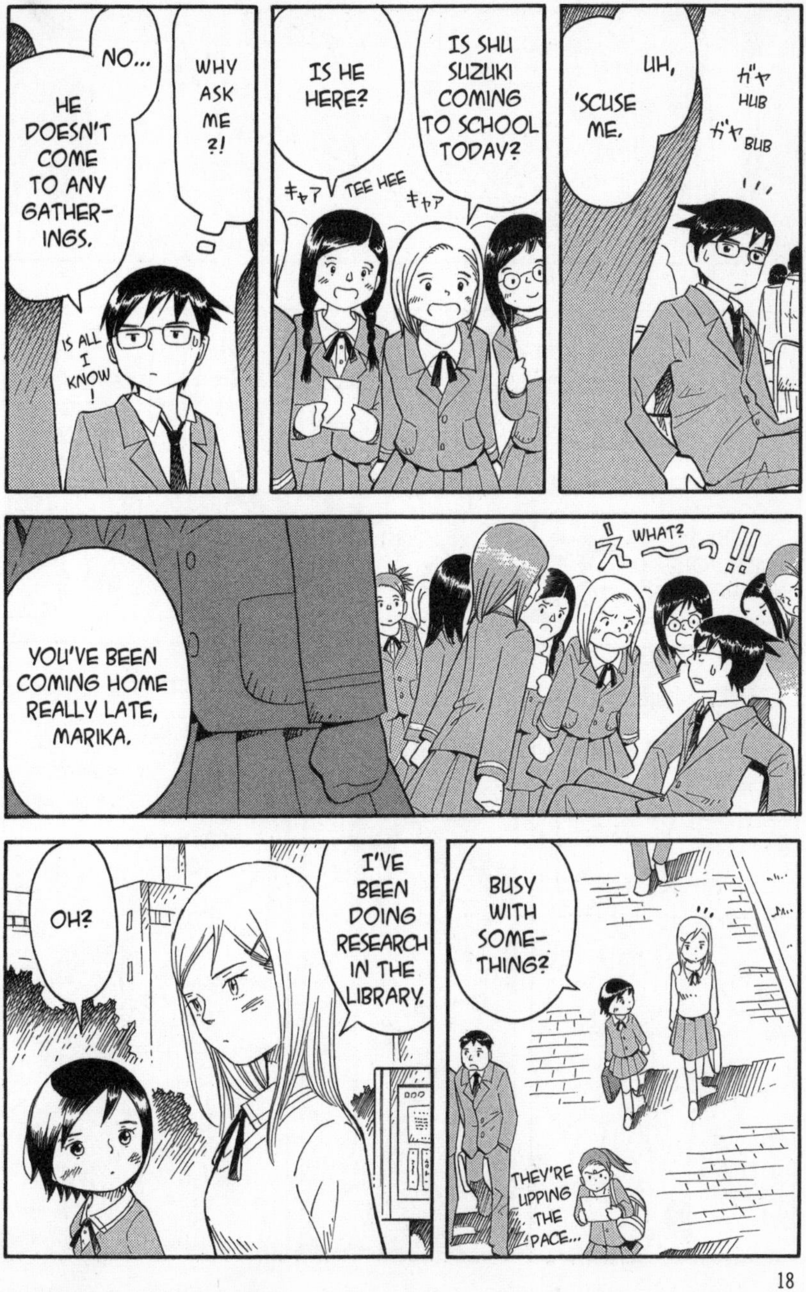
UH, 'SCUSE ME.
ガヤ HUB
ガヤ BUB
IS SHU SUZUKI COMING TO SCHOOL TODAY?
IS HE HERE?
キャア TEE HEE キャア
WHY ASK ME ?!
NO... HE DOESN'T COME TO ANY GATHER-INGS.
IS ALL I KNOW !
え〜っ!! WHAT?
YOU'VE BEEN COMING HOME REALLY LATE, MARIKA.
BUSY WITH SOME-THING?
THEY'RE UPPING THE PACE...
I'VE BEEN DOING RESEARCH IN THE LIBRARY.
OH?

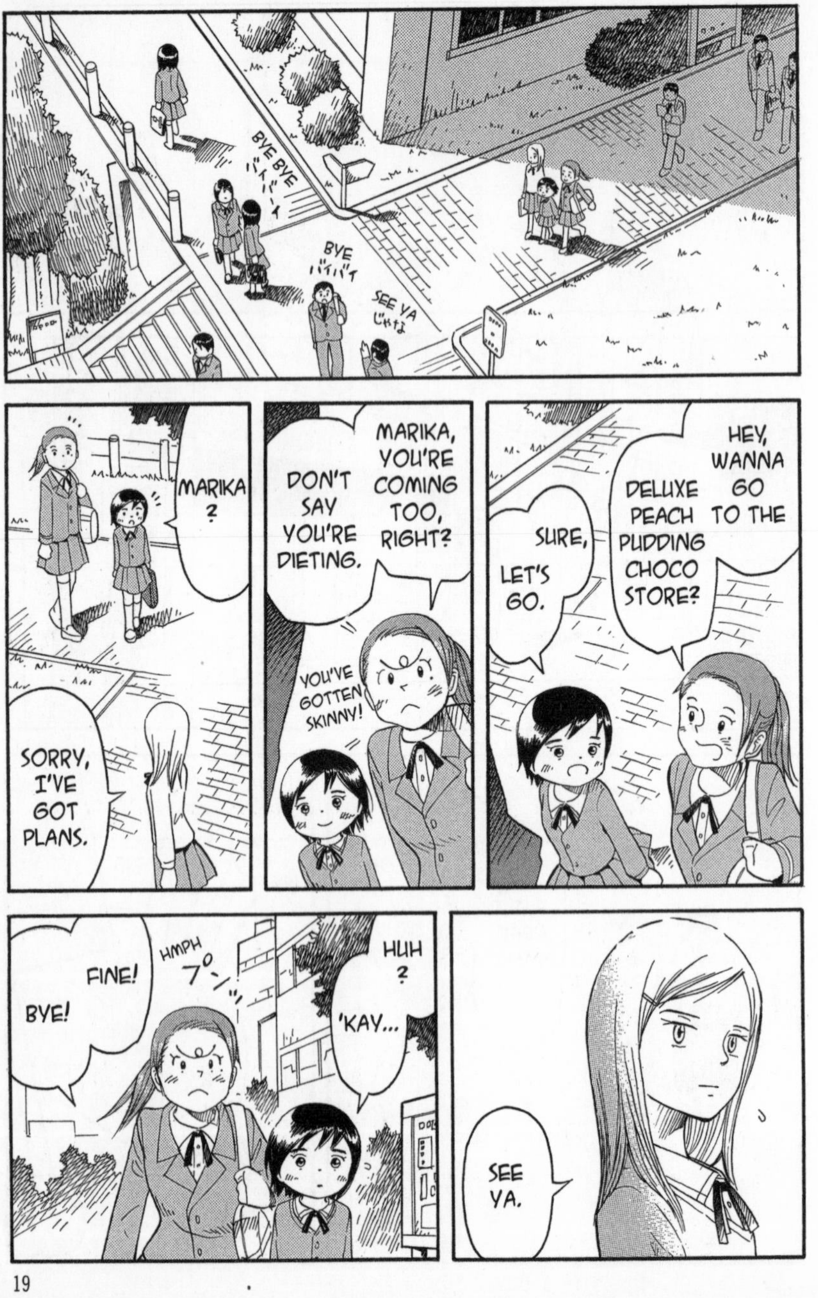
BYE BYE
バイバーイ
BYE
バイバイ
SEE YA
じゃあな
HEY, WANNA GO TO THE DELUXE PEACH PUDDING CHOCO STORE?
SURE, LET'S GO.
MARIKA, YOU'RE COMING TOO, RIGHT?
DON'T SAY YOU'RE DIETING.
YOU'VE GOTTEN SKINNY!
MARIKA?
SORRY, I'VE GOT PLANS.
SEE YA.
HUH?
'KAY...
HMPH
FINE!
BYE!

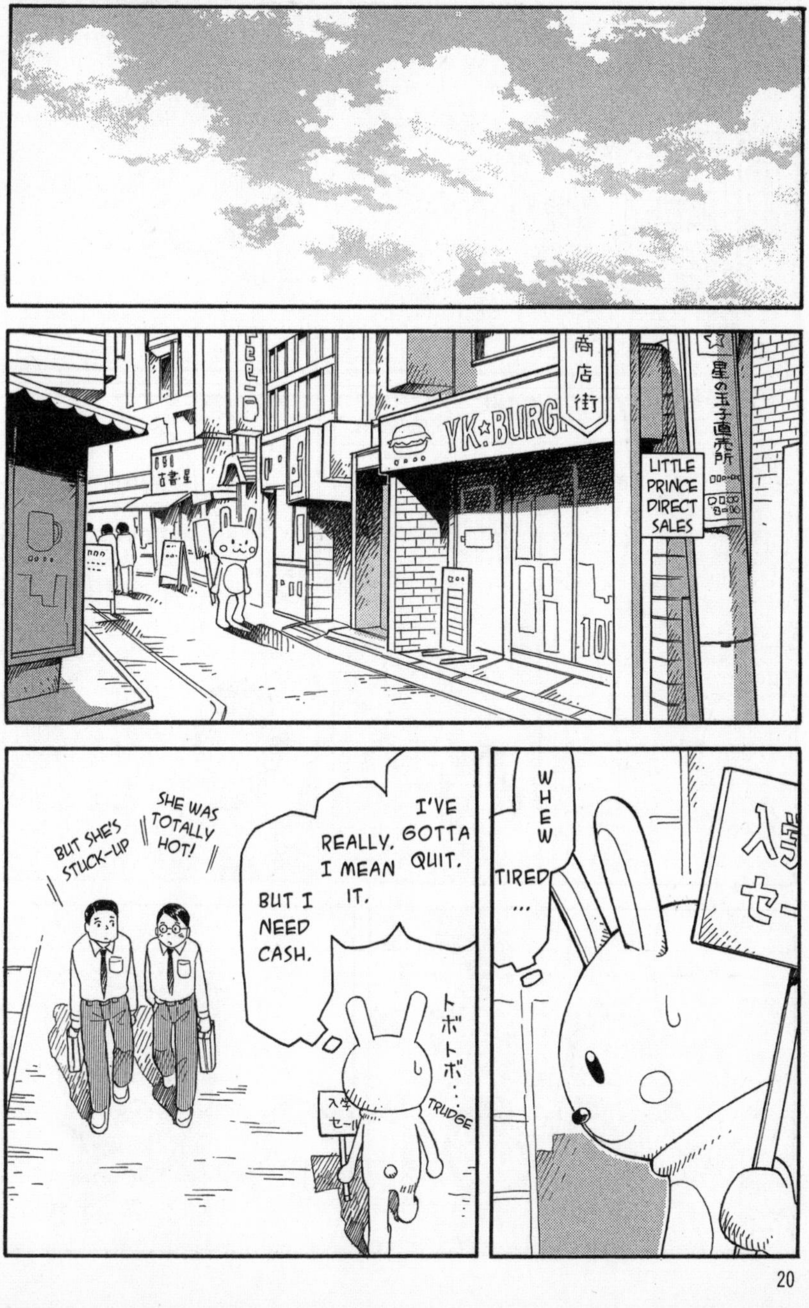

商店街
星の王子直売所
LITTLE PRINCE DIRECT SALES
YK☆BURG
古書・星
WHEW
TIRED...
I'VE GOTTA QUIT.
REALLY. I MEAN IT.
BUT I NEED CASH.
トボトボ…
TRUDGE
入学セール
SHE WAS TOTALLY HOT!
BUT SHE'S STUCK-UP

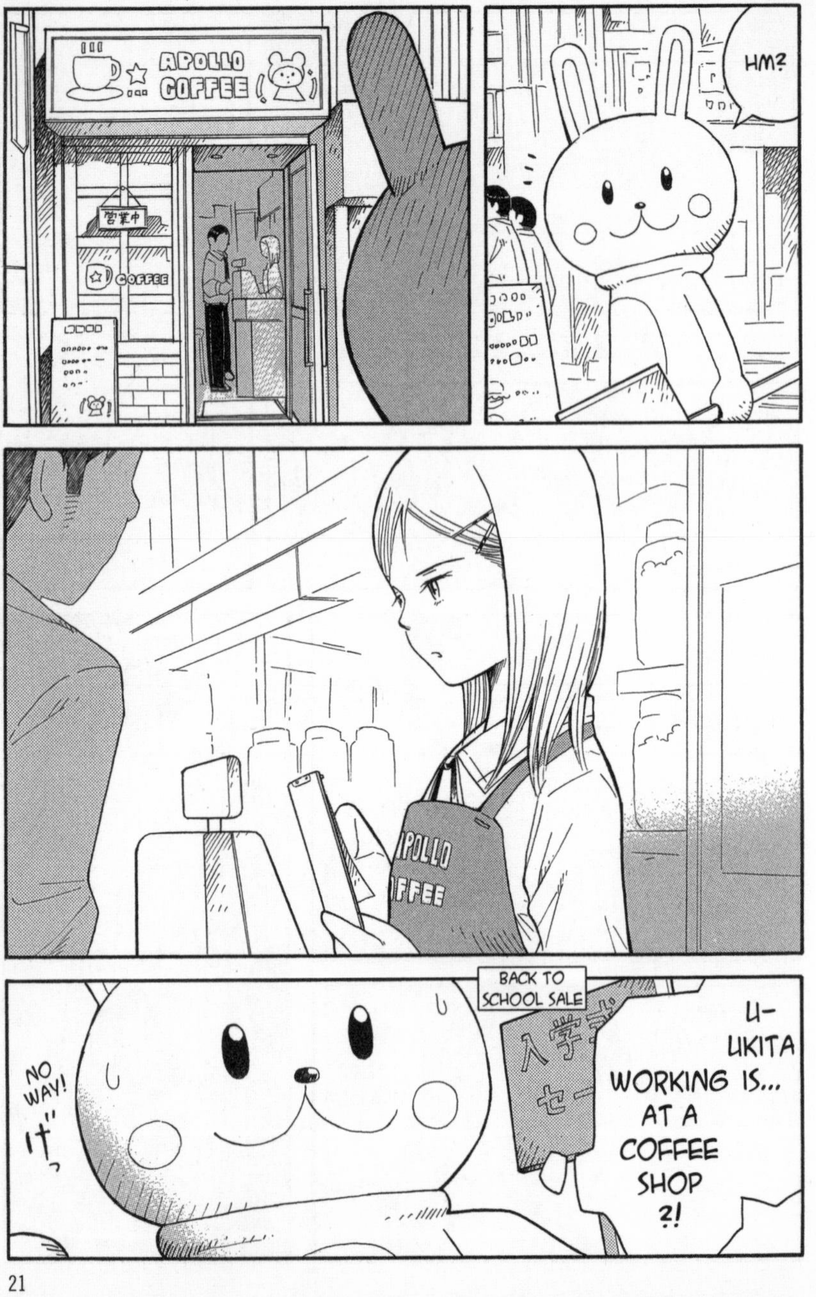
HM?
APOLLO COFFEE
営業中
COFFEE
U-UKITA WORKING IS... AT A COFFEE SHOP ?!
BACK TO SCHOOL SALE
NO WAY!
げっ

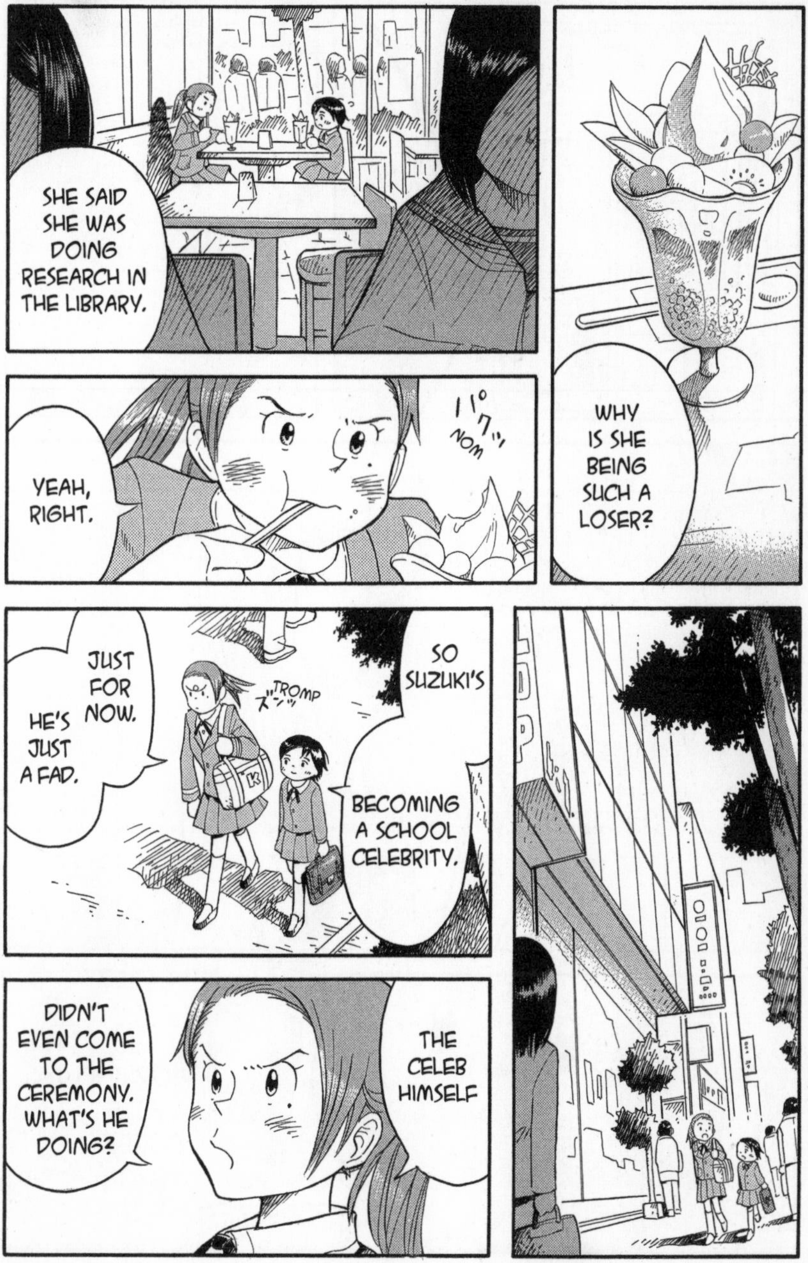
WHY IS SHE BEING SUCH A LOSER?
SHE SAID SHE WAS DOING RESEARCH IN THE LIBRARY.
NOM
YEAH, RIGHT.
SO SUZUKI'S BECOMING A SCHOOL CELEBRITY.
TROMP
JUST FOR NOW.
HE'S JUST A FAD.
THE CELEB HIMSELF
DIDN'T EVEN COME TO THE CEREMONY. WHAT'S HE DOING?

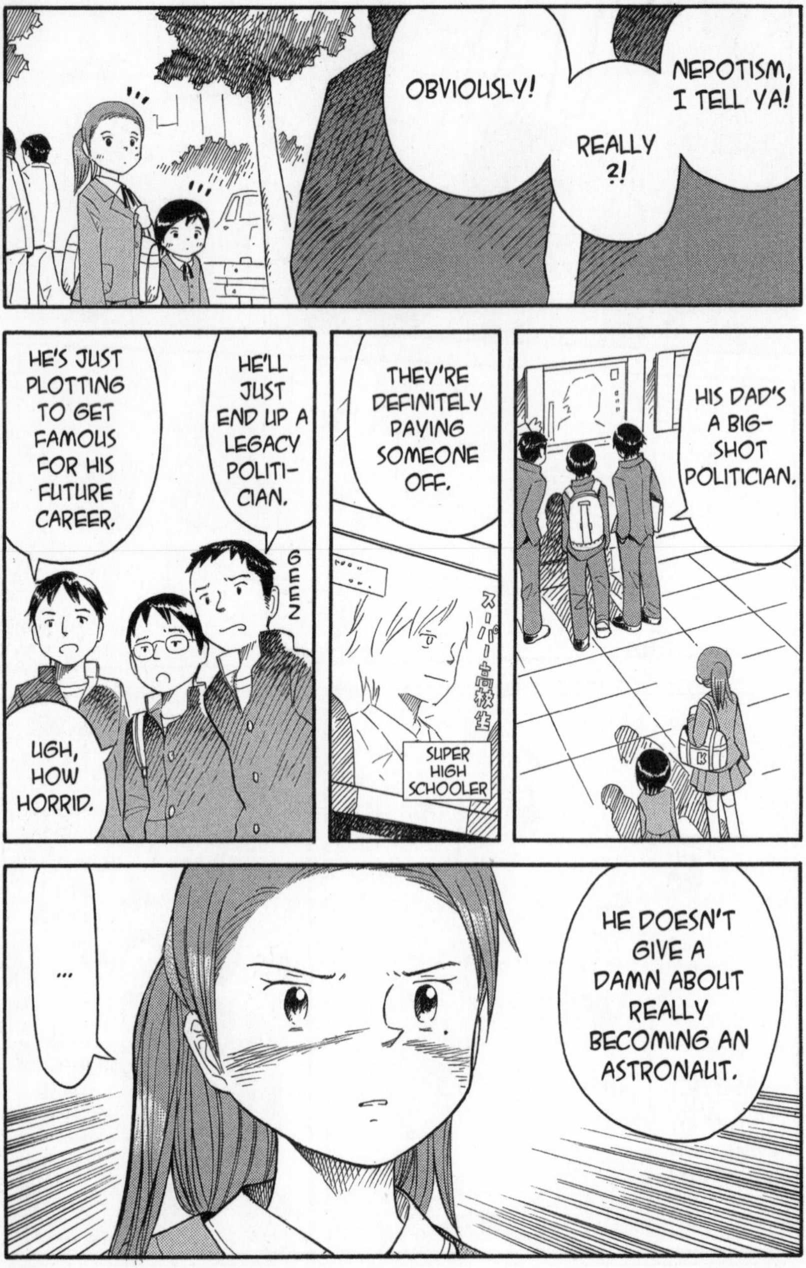

NEPOTISM, I TELL YA!
OBVIOUSLY!
REALLY ?!
HIS DAD'S A BIG-SHOT POLITICIAN.
THEY'RE DEFINITELY PAYING SOMEONE OFF.
スーパー高校生
SUPER HIGH SCHOOLER
HE'LL JUST END UP A LEGACY POLITI-CIAN.
GEEZ
HE'S JUST PLOTTING TO GET FAMOUS FOR HIS FUTURE CAREER.
UGH, HOW HORRID.
HE DOESN'T GIVE A DAMN ABOUT REALLY BECOMING AN ASTRONAUT.
...

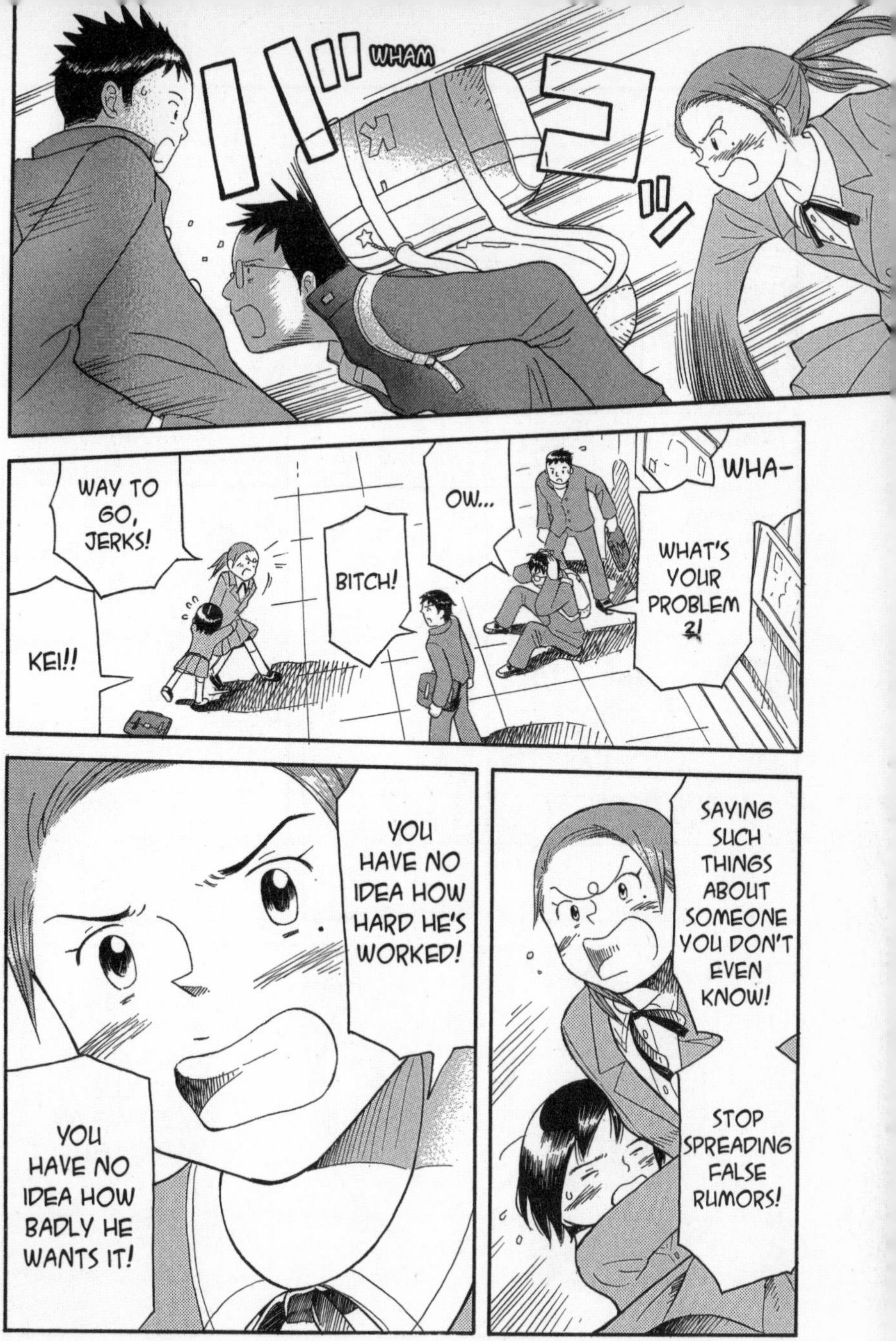
WHAM
WHA-
WHAT'S YOUR PROBLEM ?!
OW...
BITCH!
WAY TO GO, JERKS!
KEI!!
SAYING SUCH THINGS ABOUT SOMEONE YOU DON'T EVEN KNOW!
STOP SPREADING FALSE RUMORS!
YOU HAVE NO IDEA HOW HARD HE'S WORKED!
YOU HAVE NO IDEA HOW BADLY HE WANTS IT!

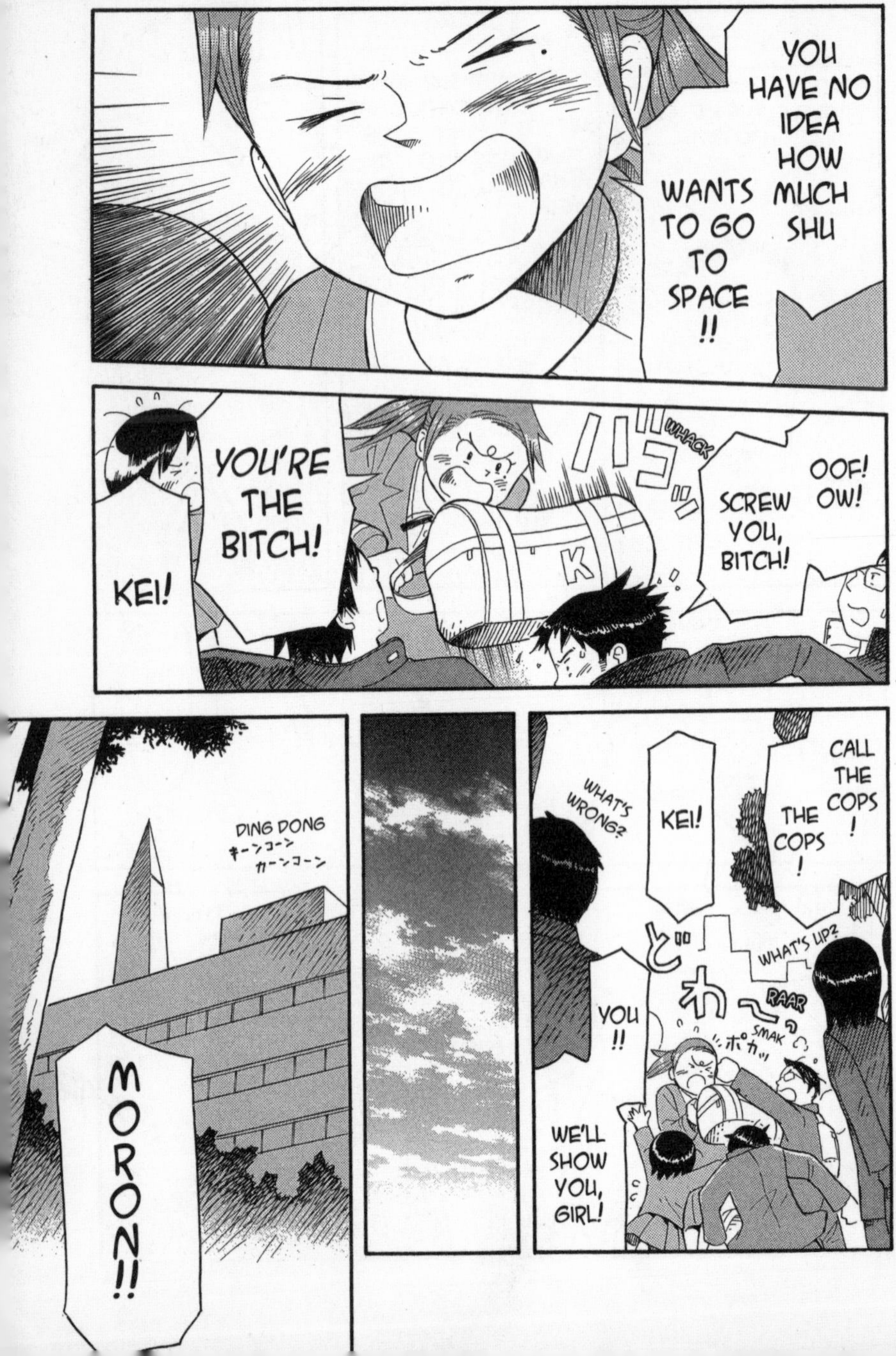
YOU HAVE NO IDEA HOW MUCH SHU WANTS TO GO TO SPACE!!
OOF! OW!
SCREW YOU, BITCH!
WHACK
YOU'RE THE BITCH!
KEI!
CALL THE COPS!
THE COPS!
KEI!
WHAT'S WRONG?
WHAT'S UP?
RAAR
SMAK
ポカッ
YOU!!
WE'LL SHOW YOU, GIRL!
DING DONG
キーンコーン
カーンコーン
MORON!!

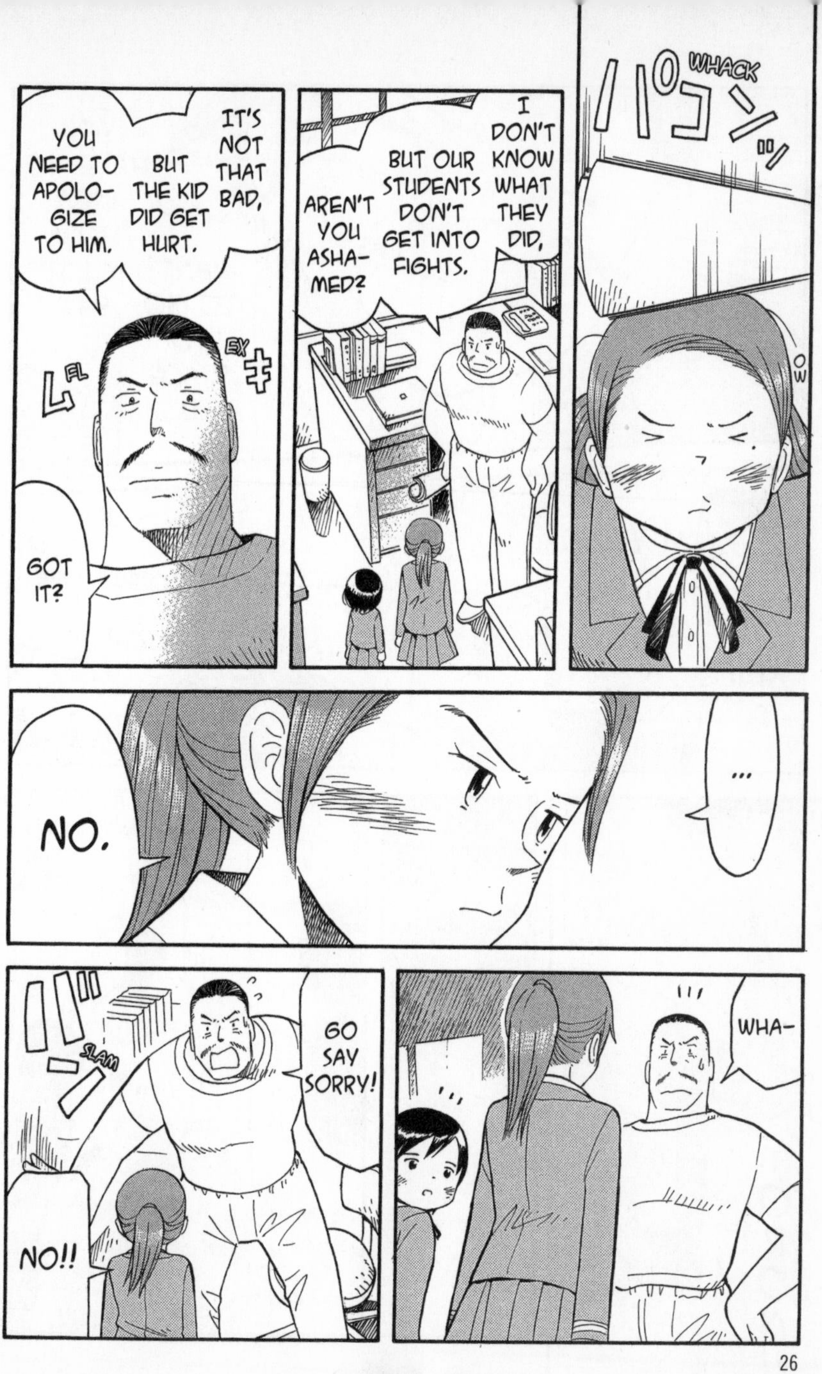
WHACK
OW
I DON'T KNOW WHAT THEY DID,
BUT OUR STUDENTS DON'T GET INTO FIGHTS.
AREN'T YOU ASHAMED?
IT'S NOT THAT BAD,
BUT THE KID DID GET HURT.
YOU NEED TO APOLOGIZE TO HIM.
EX
FL
GOT IT?
...
NO.
WHA-
GO SAY SORRY!
SLAM
NO!!

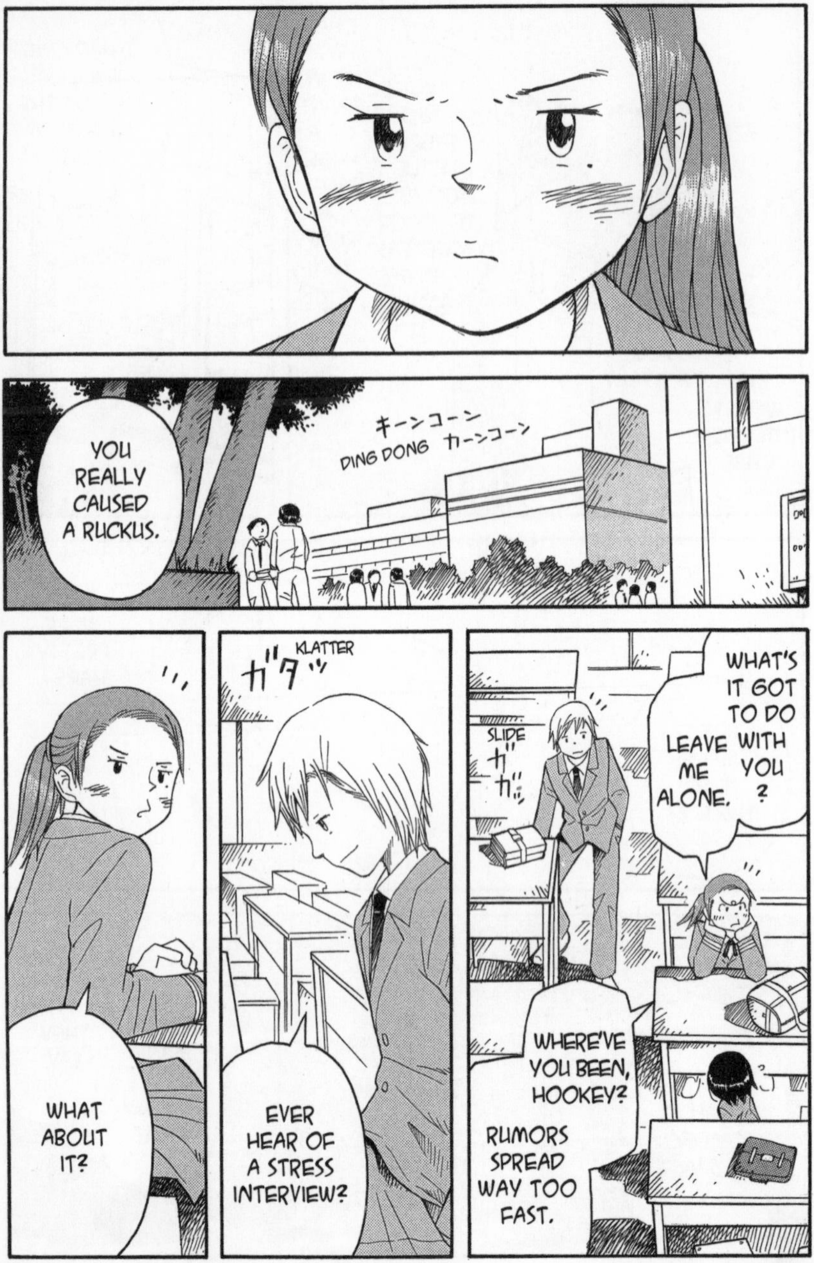
キーンコーン
DING DONG
カーンコーン
YOU REALLY CAUSED A RUCKUS.
WHAT'S IT GOT TO DO WITH YOU?
LEAVE ME ALONE.
SLIDE
ガガ
WHERE'VE YOU BEEN, HOOKEY?
RUMORS SPREAD WAY TOO FAST.
KLATTER
ガタッ
EVER HEAR OF A STRESS INTERVIEW?
WHAT ABOUT IT?

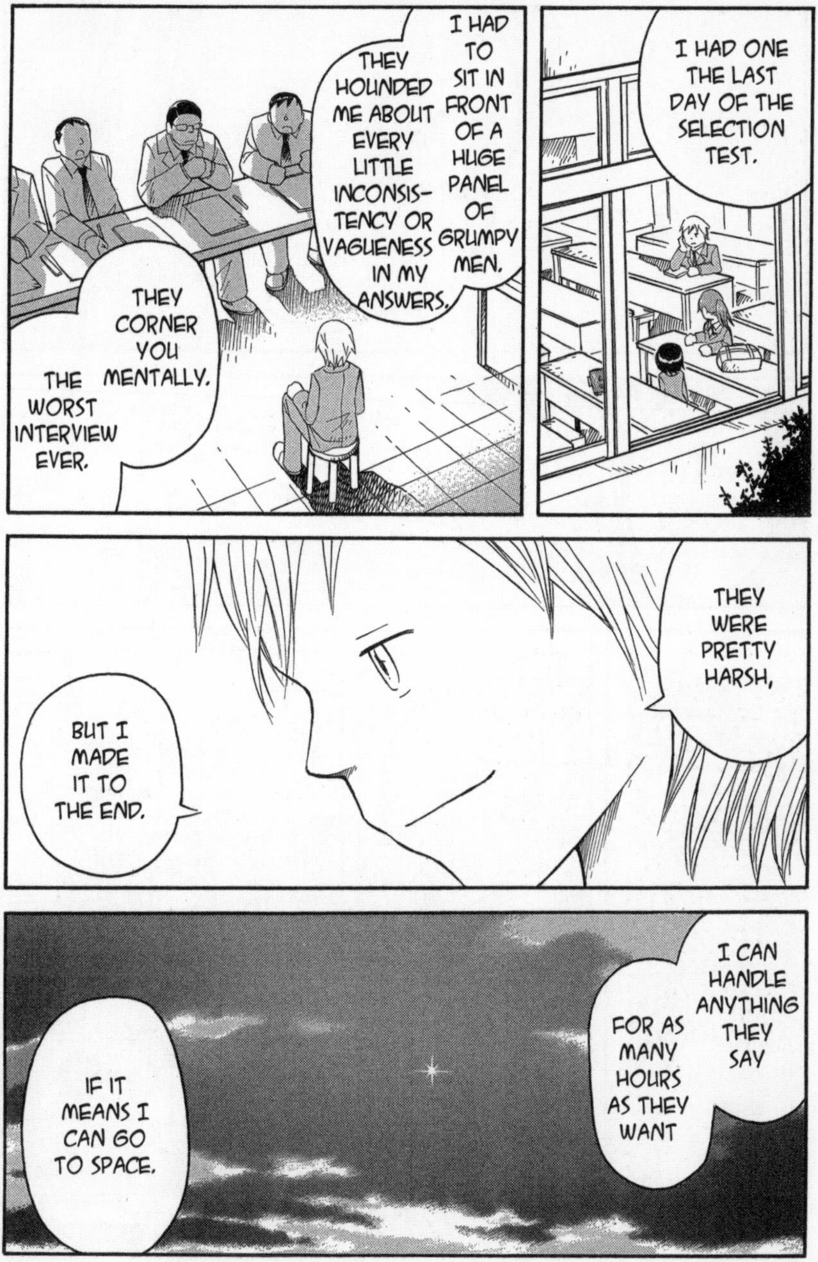
I HAD ONE THE LAST DAY OF THE SELECTION TEST.
I HAD TO SIT IN FRONT OF A HUGE PANEL OF GRUMPY MEN.
THEY HOUNDED ME ABOUT EVERY LITTLE INCONSIS-TENCY OR VAGUENESS IN MY ANSWERS.
THEY CORNER YOU MENTALLY.
THE WORST INTERVIEW EVER.
THEY WERE PRETTY HARSH,
BUT I MADE IT TO THE END.
I CAN HANDLE ANYTHING THEY SAY
FOR AS MANY HOURS AS THEY WANT
IF IT MEANS I CAN GO TO SPACE.

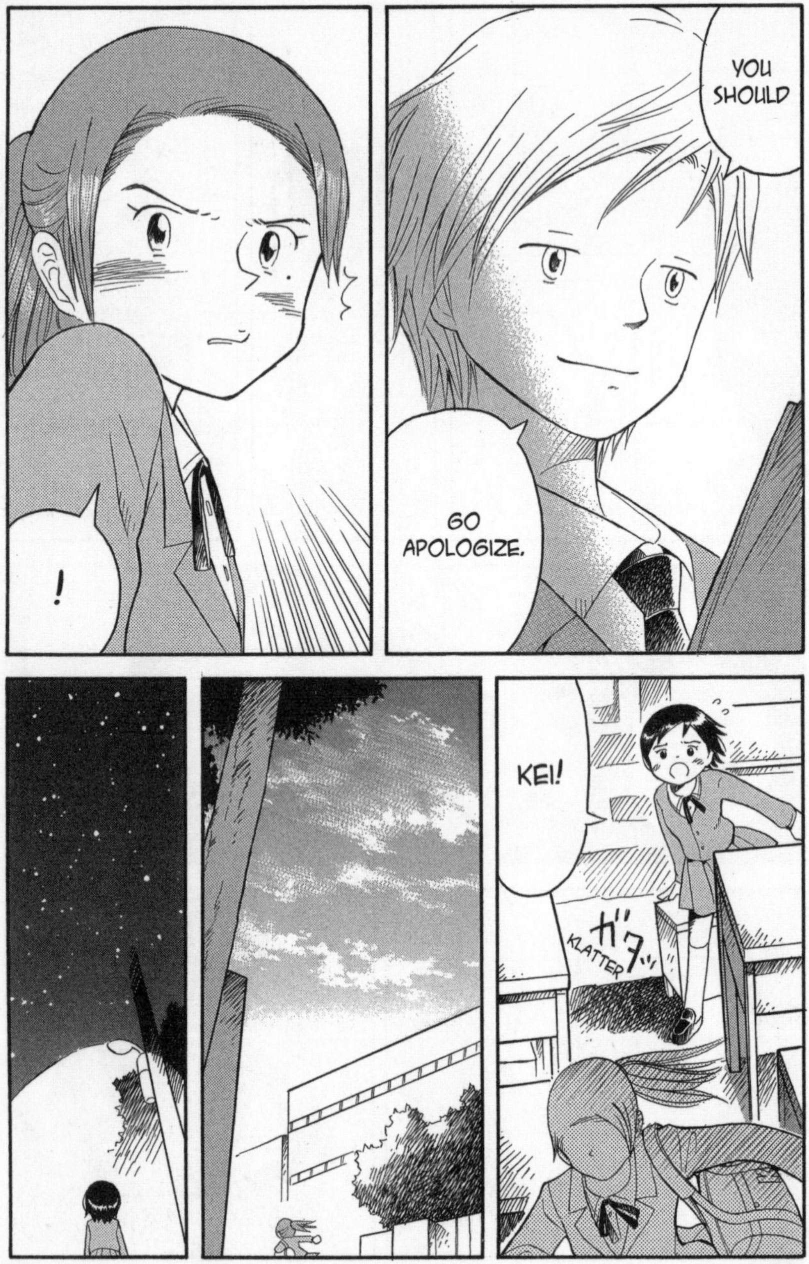
YOU SHOULD
GO APOLOGIZE.
!
KEI!
ガタッ
KLATTER

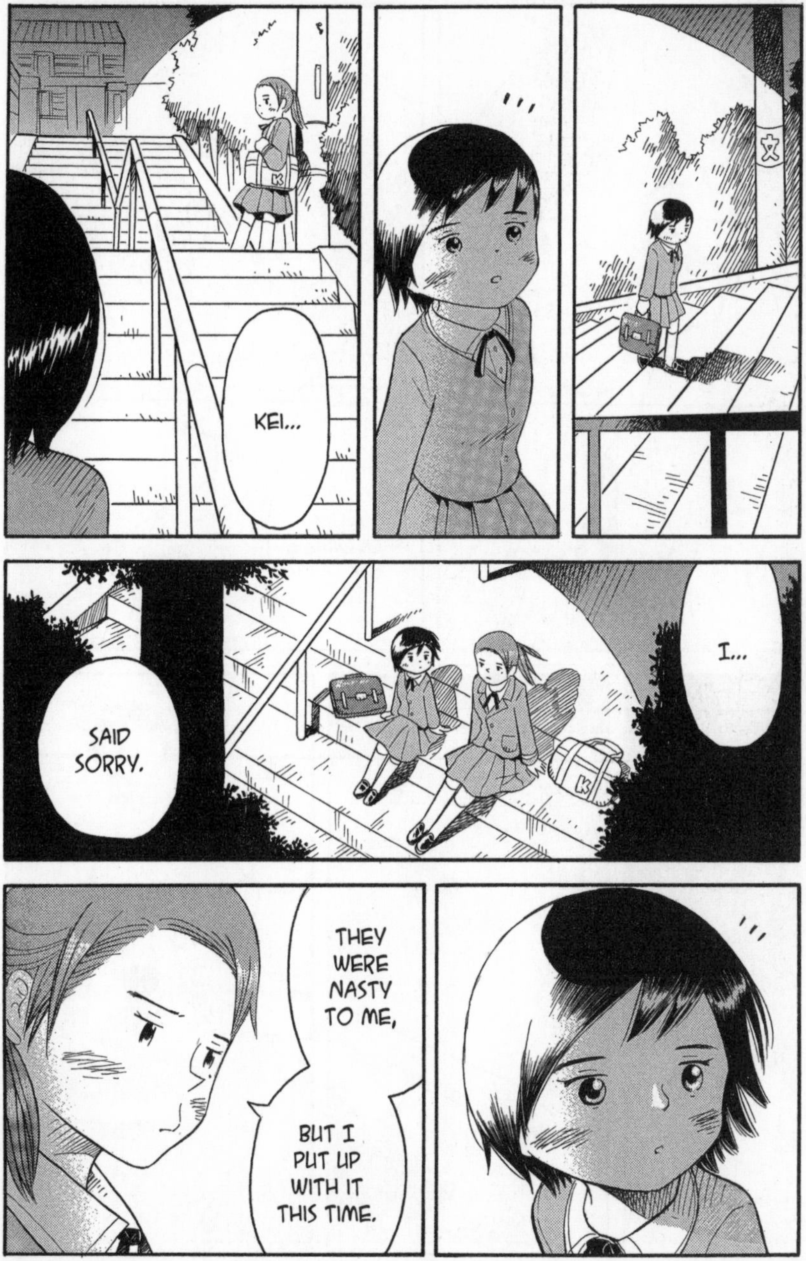
KEI...
I...
SAID SORRY.
THEY WERE NASTY TO ME,
BUT I PUT UP WITH IT THIS TIME.

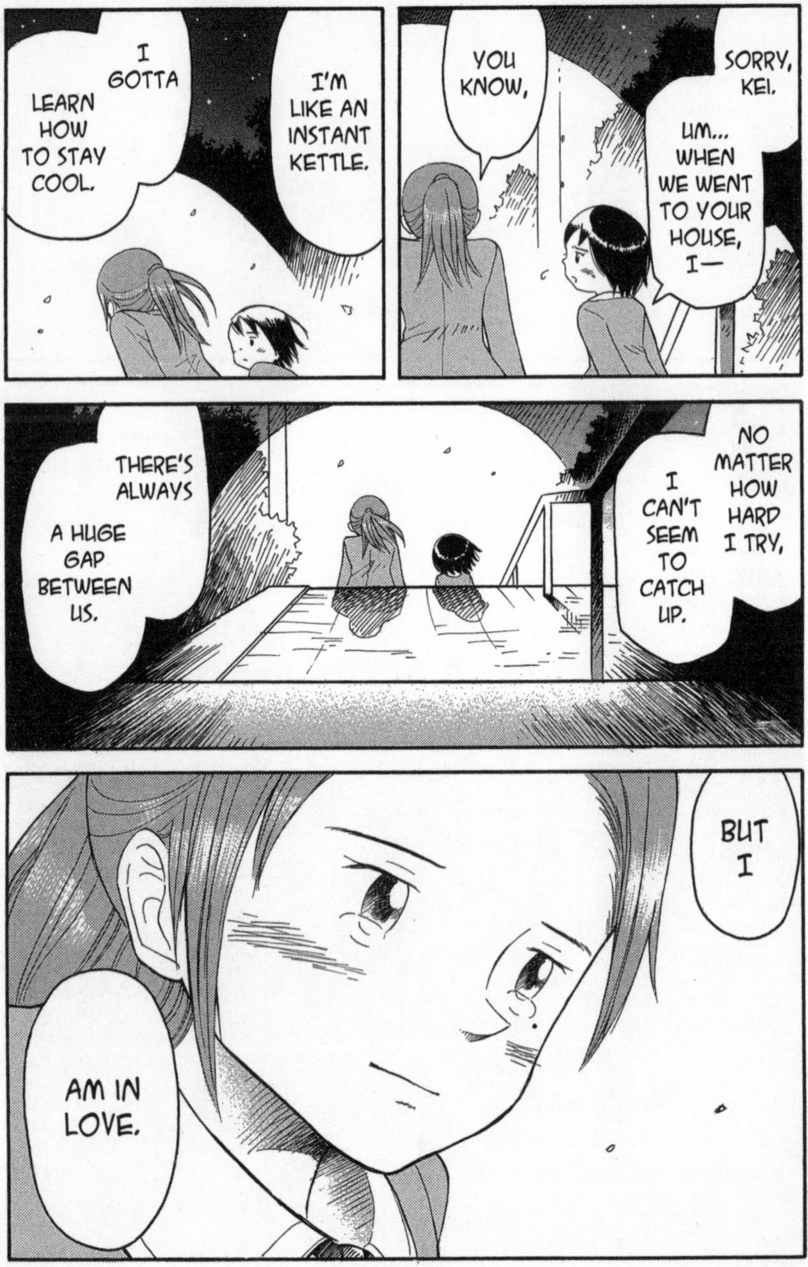
SORRY, KEI.
UM... WHEN WE WENT TO YOUR HOUSE, I—
YOU KNOW,
I'M LIKE AN INSTANT KETTLE.
I GOTTA LEARN HOW TO STAY COOL.
NO MATTER HOW HARD I TRY,
I CAN'T SEEM TO CATCH UP.
THERE'S ALWAYS
A HUGE GAP BETWEEN US.
BUT I
AM IN LOVE.

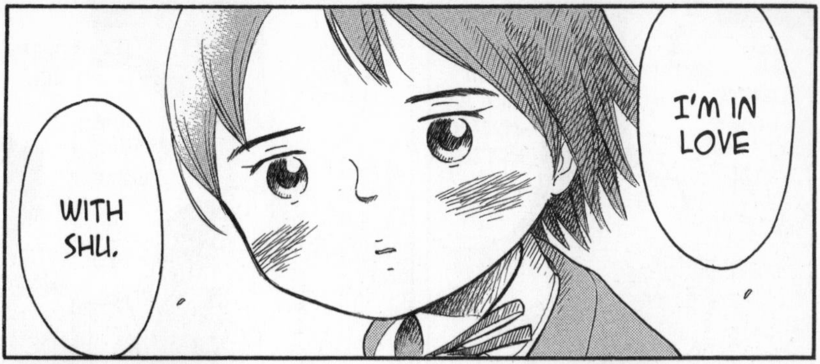
I'M IN LOVE
WITH SHU.

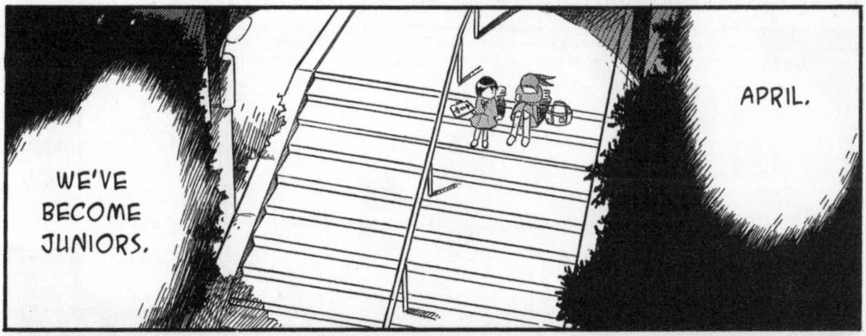
APRIL.
WE'VE BECOME JUNIORS.

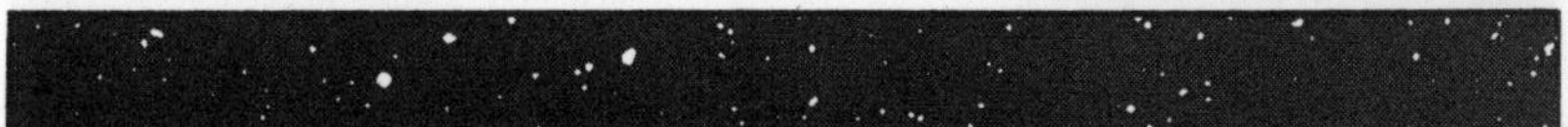
NOW BEGINS
OUR FINAL YEAR.

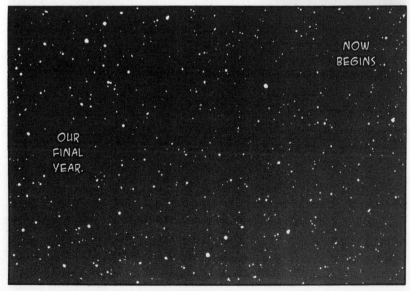

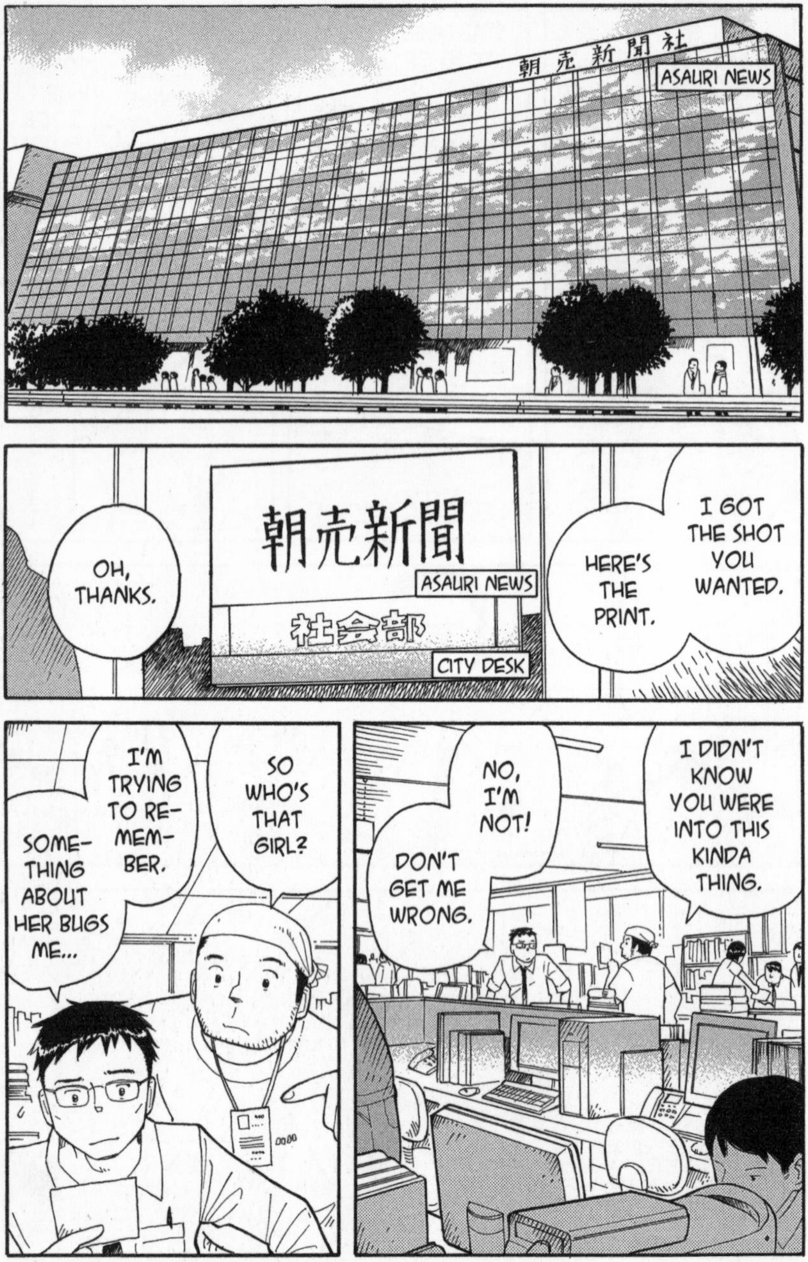
朝売新聞社
ASAURI NEWS
I GOT THE SHOT YOU WANTED.
HERE'S THE PRINT.
朝売新聞
ASAURI NEWS
社会部
CITY DESK
OH, THANKS.
I DIDN'T KNOW YOU WERE INTO THIS KINDA THING.
NO, I'M NOT!
DON'T GET ME WRONG.
SO WHO'S THAT GIRL?
I'M TRYING TO RE-MEM-BER.
SOME-THING ABOUT HER BUGS ME...

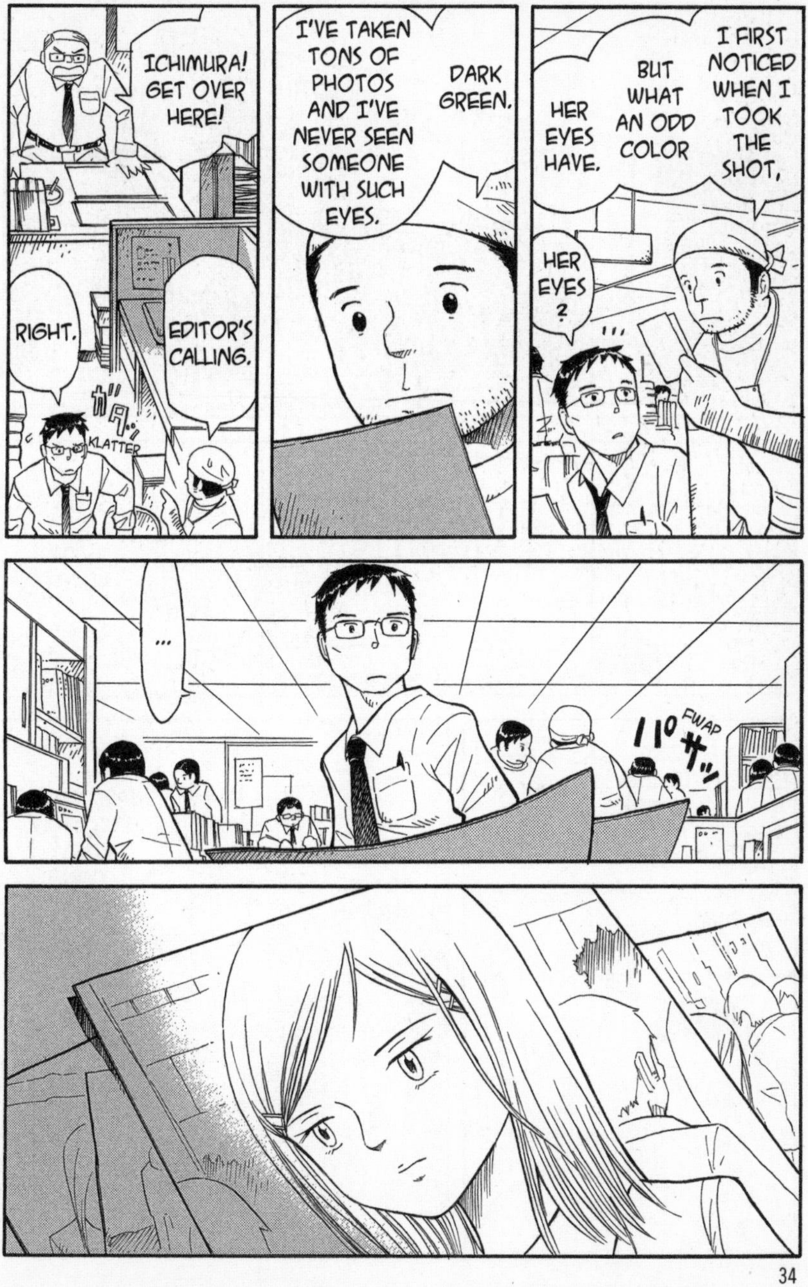
I FIRST NOTICED WHEN I TOOK THE SHOT,
BUT WHAT AN ODD COLOR
HER EYES HAVE.
HER EYES?
DARK GREEN.
I'VE TAKEN TONS OF PHOTOS AND I'VE NEVER SEEN SOMEONE WITH SUCH EYES.
ICHIMURA! GET OVER HERE!
EDITOR'S CALLING.
RIGHT.
KLATTER
FWAP
...

MISSION:48

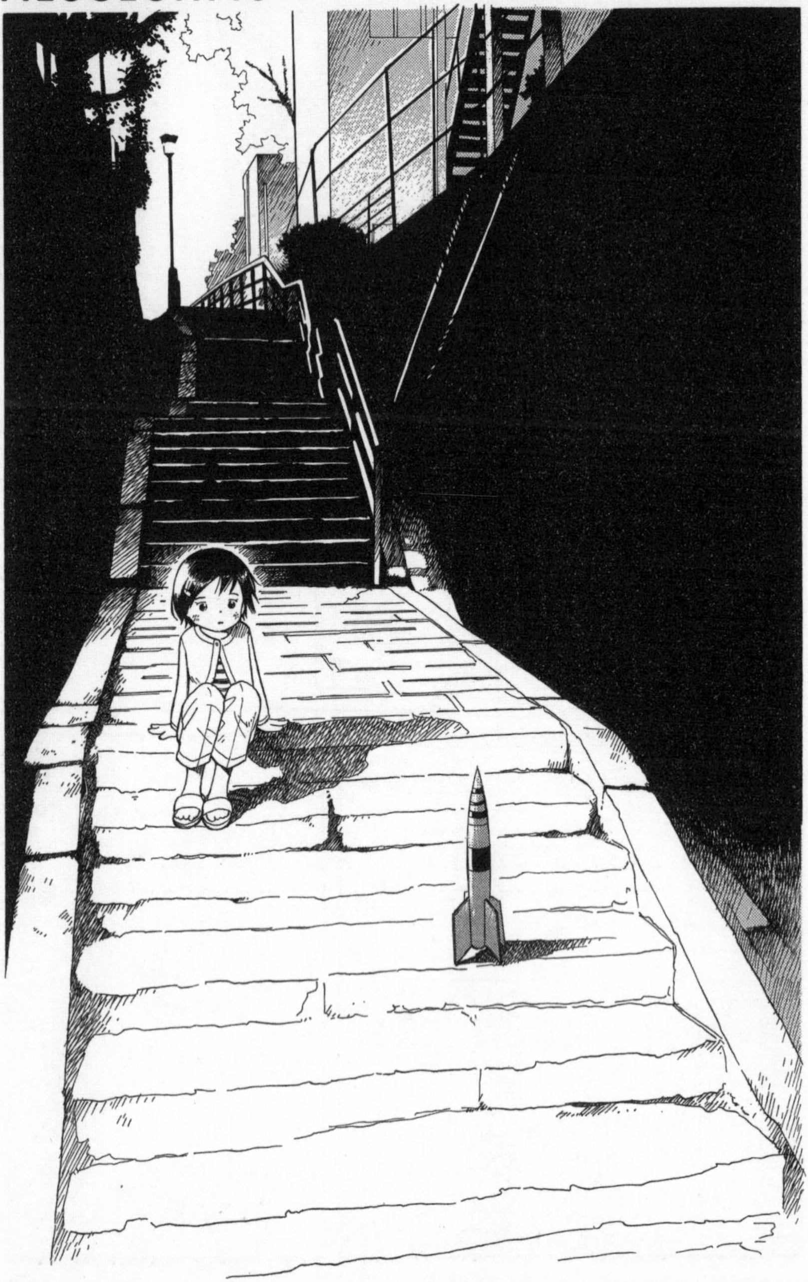

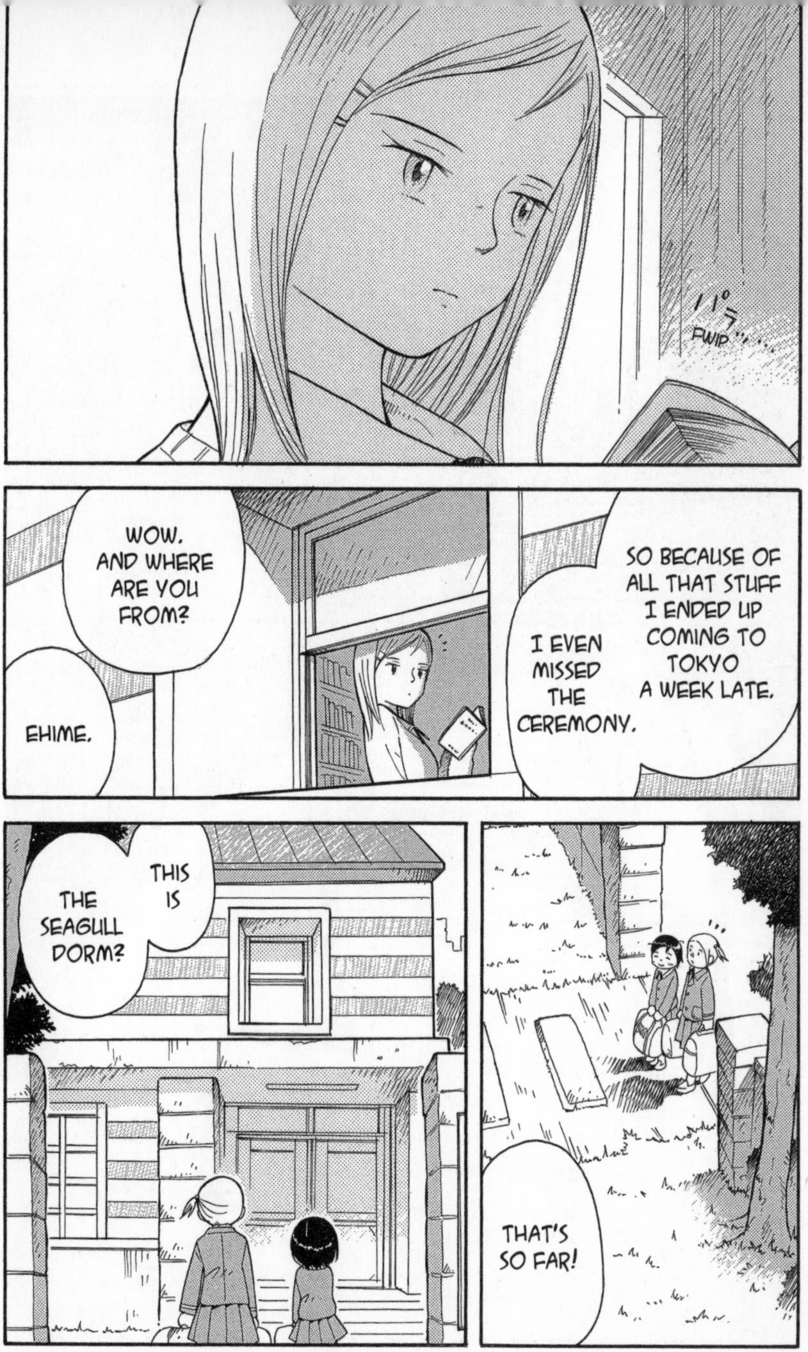
パラ
FWIP...
SO BECAUSE OF ALL THAT STUFF I ENDED UP COMING TO TOKYO A WEEK LATE.
I EVEN MISSED THE CEREMONY.
WOW. AND WHERE ARE YOU FROM?
EHIME.
THAT'S SO FAR!
THIS IS THE SEAGULL DORM?

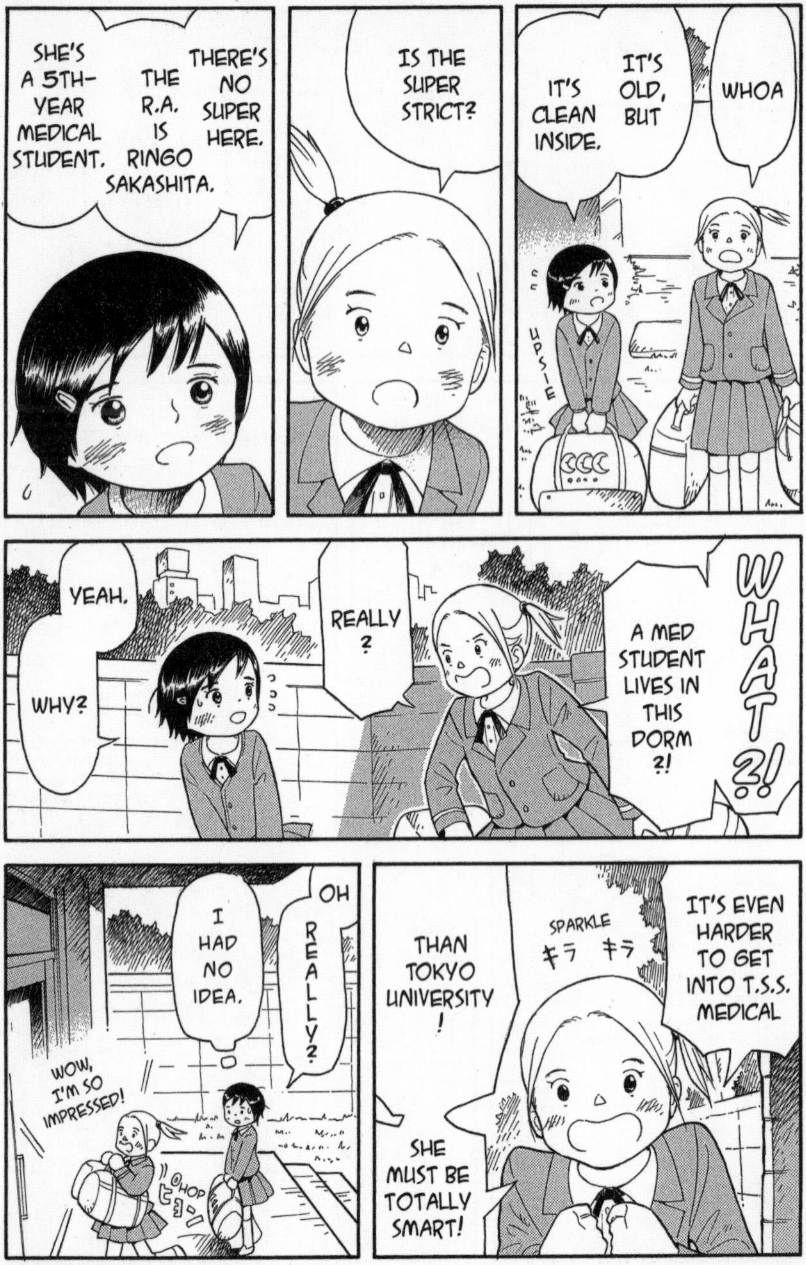
WHOA
IT'S OLD, BUT IT'S CLEAN INSIDE.
UPSIE
IS THE SUPER STRICT?
THERE'S NO SUPER HERE.
THE R.A. IS RINGO SAKASHITA.
SHE'S A 5TH-YEAR MEDICAL STUDENT.
WHAT?!
A MED STUDENT LIVES IN THIS DORM?!
REALLY?
YEAH.
WHY?
IT'S EVEN HARDER TO GET INTO T.S.S. MEDICAL
SPARKLE
キラ キラ
THAN TOKYO UNIVERSITY!
SHE MUST BE TOTALLY SMART!
OH REALLY?
I HAD NO IDEA.
WOW, I'M SO IMPRESSED!
HOP
ピョン

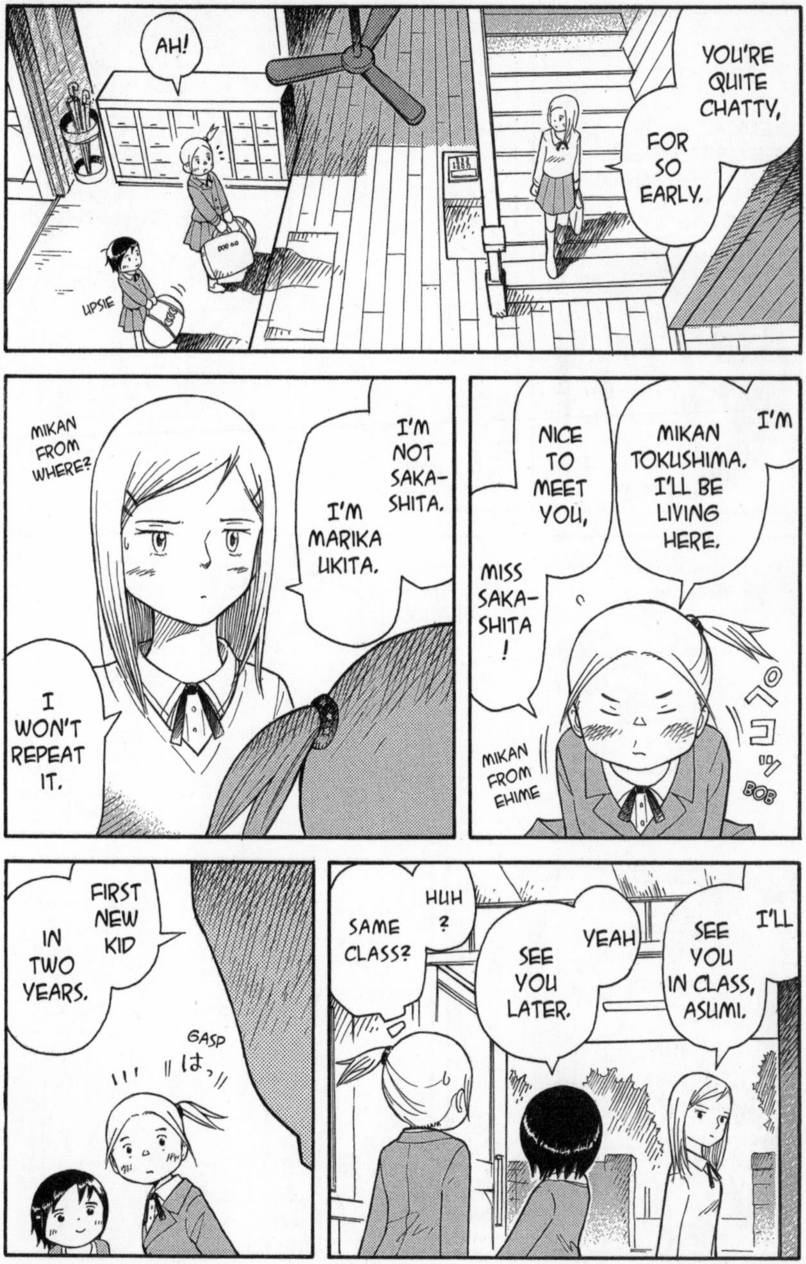
YOU'RE QUITE CHATTY,
FOR SO EARLY.
AH!
UPSIE
I'M MIKAN TOKUSHIMA. I'LL BE LIVING HERE.
NICE TO MEET YOU, MISS SAKA-SHITA!
ペコッ
BOB
MIKAN FROM EHIME
I'M NOT SAKA-SHITA. I'M MARIKA UKITA.
MIKAN FROM WHERE?
I WON'T REPEAT IT.
I'LL SEE YOU IN CLASS, ASUMI.
YEAH SEE YOU LATER.
HUH? SAME CLASS?
FIRST NEW KID IN TWO YEARS.
GASP
はっ

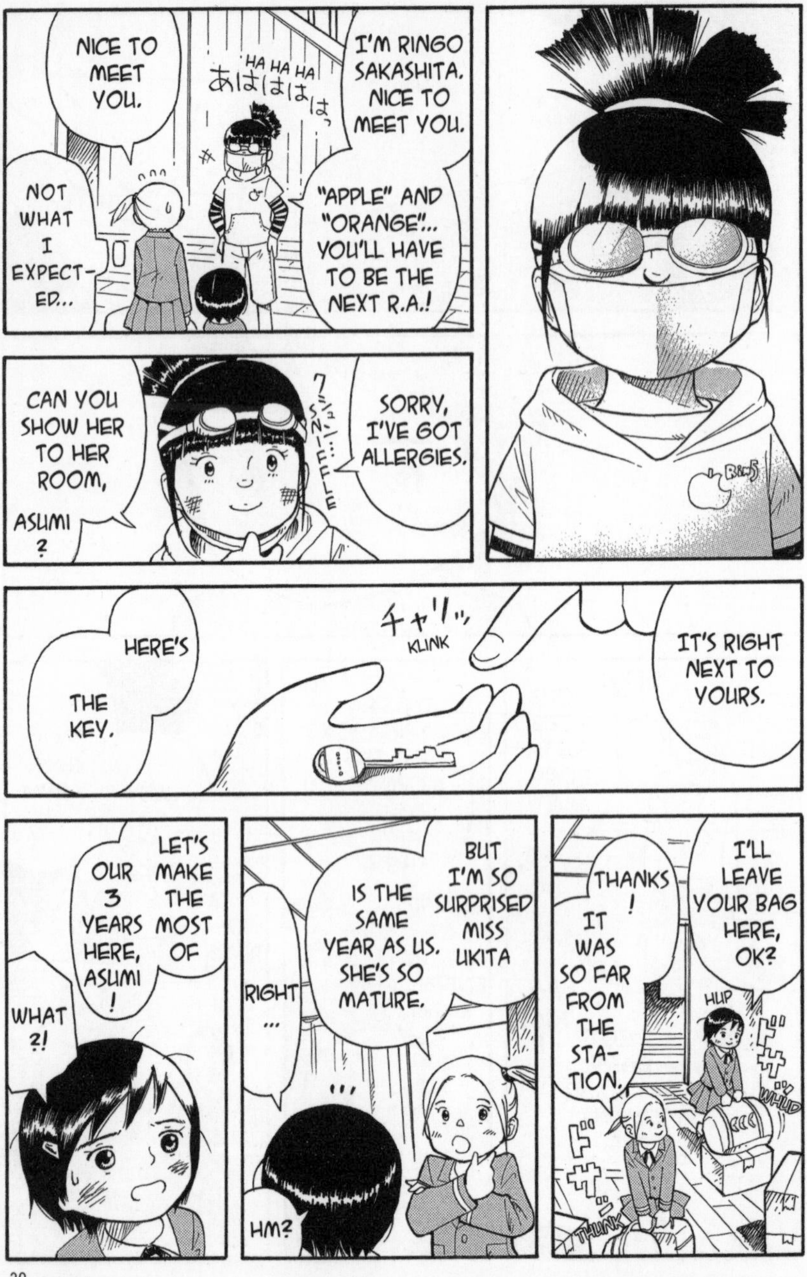
I'M RINGO SAKASHITA. NICE TO MEET YOU.
HA HA HA
あはははっ
NICE TO MEET YOU.
"APPLE" AND "ORANGE"... YOU'LL HAVE TO BE THE NEXT R.A.!
NOT WHAT I EXPECTED...
SORRY, I'VE GOT ALLERGIES.
SNIFFLE
CAN YOU SHOW HER TO HER ROOM, ASUMI?
IT'S RIGHT NEXT TO YOURS.
チャリッ
KLINK
HERE'S THE KEY.
I'LL LEAVE YOUR BAG HERE, OK?
HUP
WHUD
THANKS! IT WAS SO FAR FROM THE STATION.
THUNK
BUT I'M SO SURPRISED MISS UKITA IS THE SAME YEAR AS US. SHE'S SO MATURE.
RIGHT...
...
HM?
LET'S MAKE THE MOST OF OUR 3 YEARS HERE, ASUMI!
WHAT?!

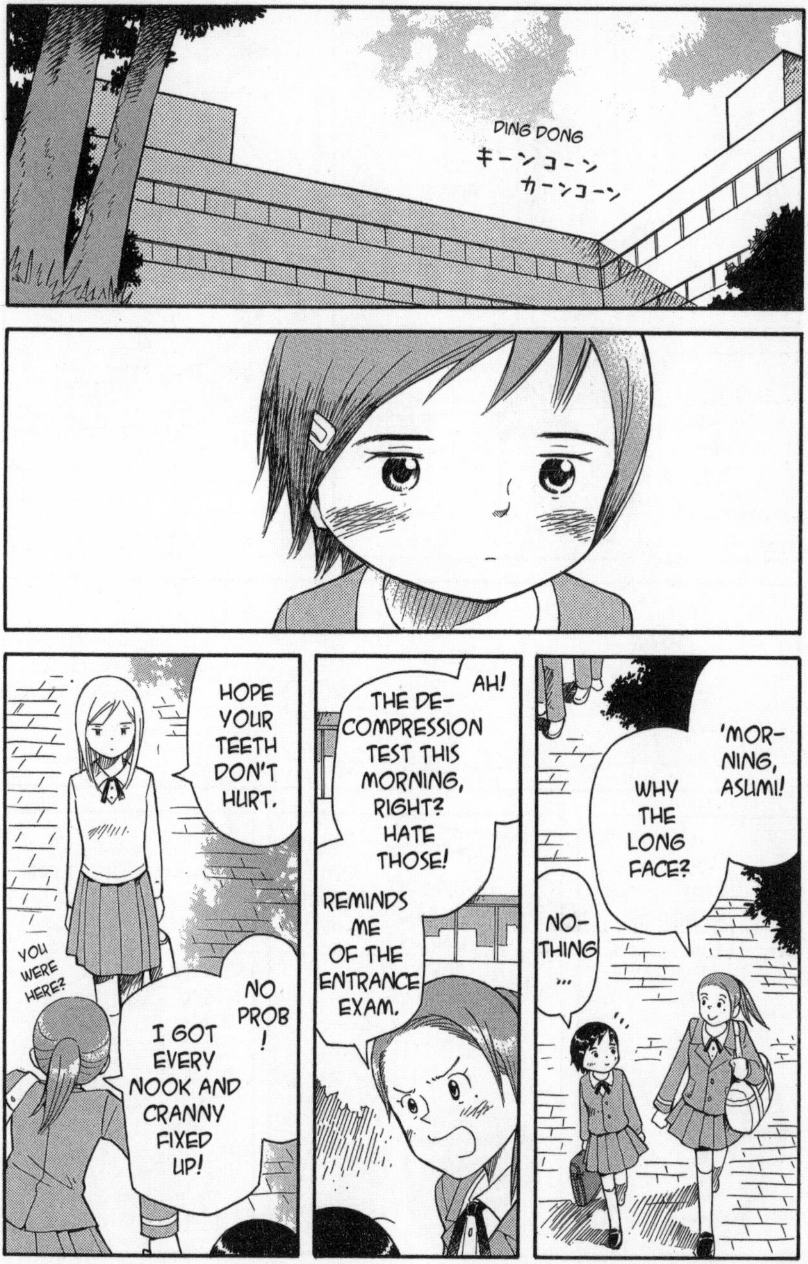
DING DONG
キーンコーン
カーンコーン
'MOR-NING, ASUMI!
WHY THE LONG FACE?
NO-THING...
AH!
THE DE-COMPRESSION TEST THIS MORNING, RIGHT? HATE THOSE!
REMINDS ME OF THE ENTRANCE EXAM.
HOPE YOUR TEETH DON'T HURT.
NO PROB!
I GOT EVERY NOOK AND CRANNY FIXED UP!
YOU WERE HERE?

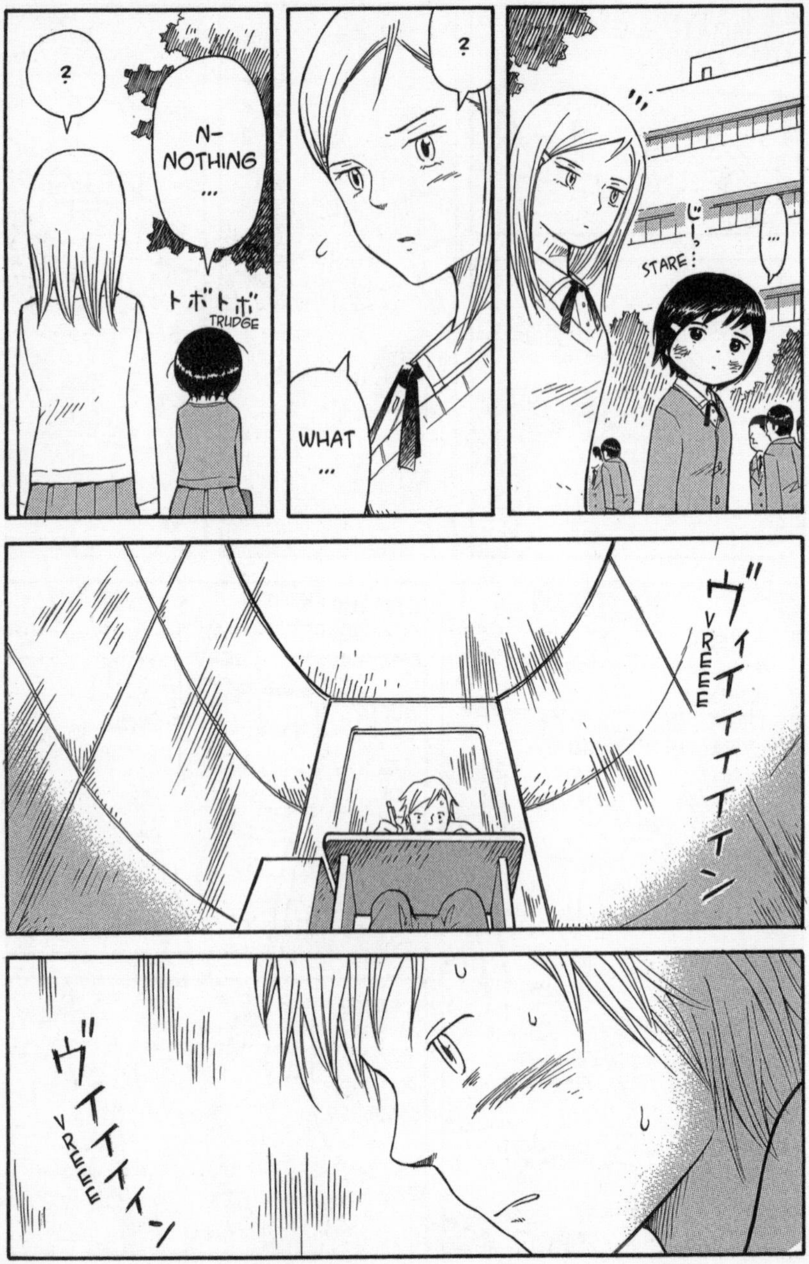
...
じーっ
STARE
?
WHAT ...
N-NOTHING ...
?
トボトボ
TRUDGE
ヴィイイイイイイン
VREEE
ヴイイイイイーン
VREEE

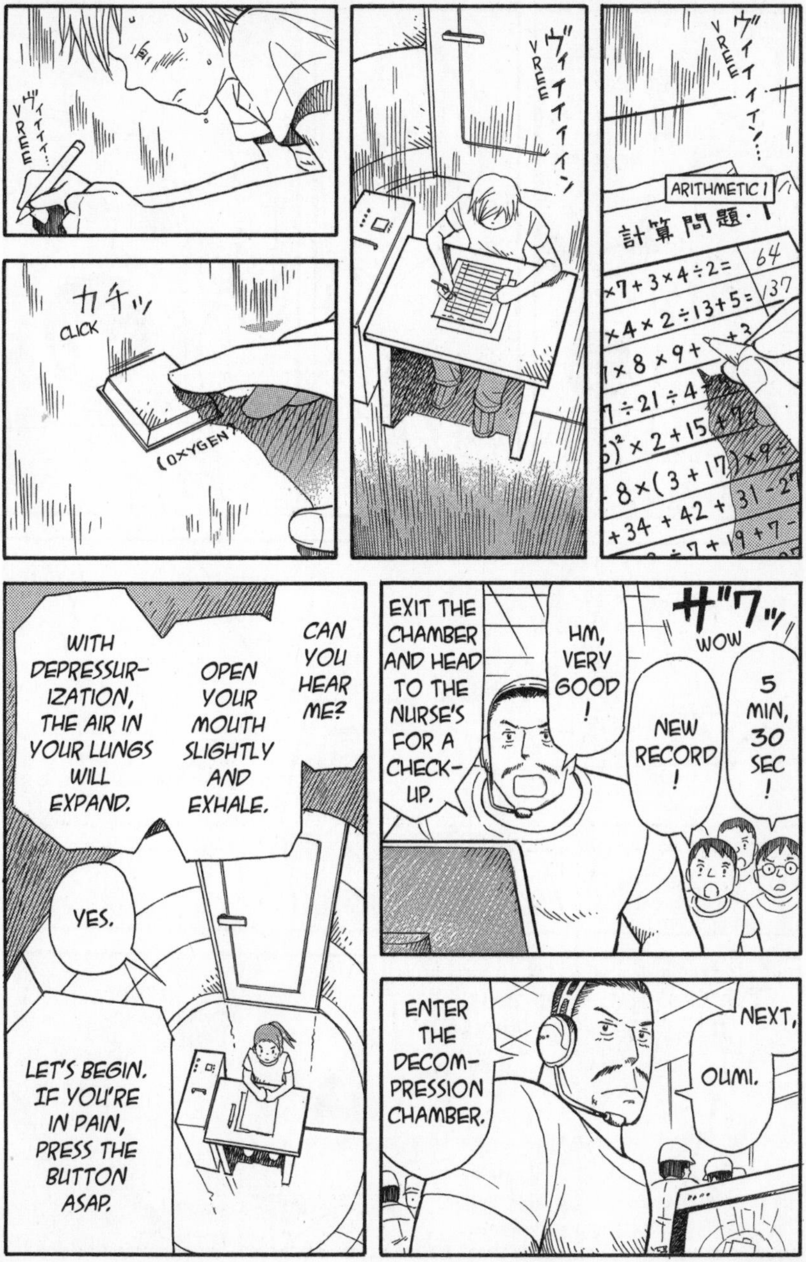
ヴィイイイン…
VREE
ARITHMETIC 1
計算問題・1
ヴィイイイイン
VREE
ヴィイイイ…
VREE…
カチッ
CLICK
(OXYGEN)
ザワッ
WOW
5 MIN, 30 SEC!
NEW RECORD!
HM, VERY GOOD!
EXIT THE CHAMBER AND HEAD TO THE NURSE'S FOR A CHECK-UP.
NEXT, OUMI.
ENTER THE DECOMPRESSION CHAMBER.
CAN YOU HEAR ME?
OPEN YOUR MOUTH SLIGHTLY AND EXHALE.
WITH DEPRESSURIZATION, THE AIR IN YOUR LUNGS WILL EXPAND.
YES.
LET'S BEGIN. IF YOU'RE IN PAIN, PRESS THE BUTTON ASAP.

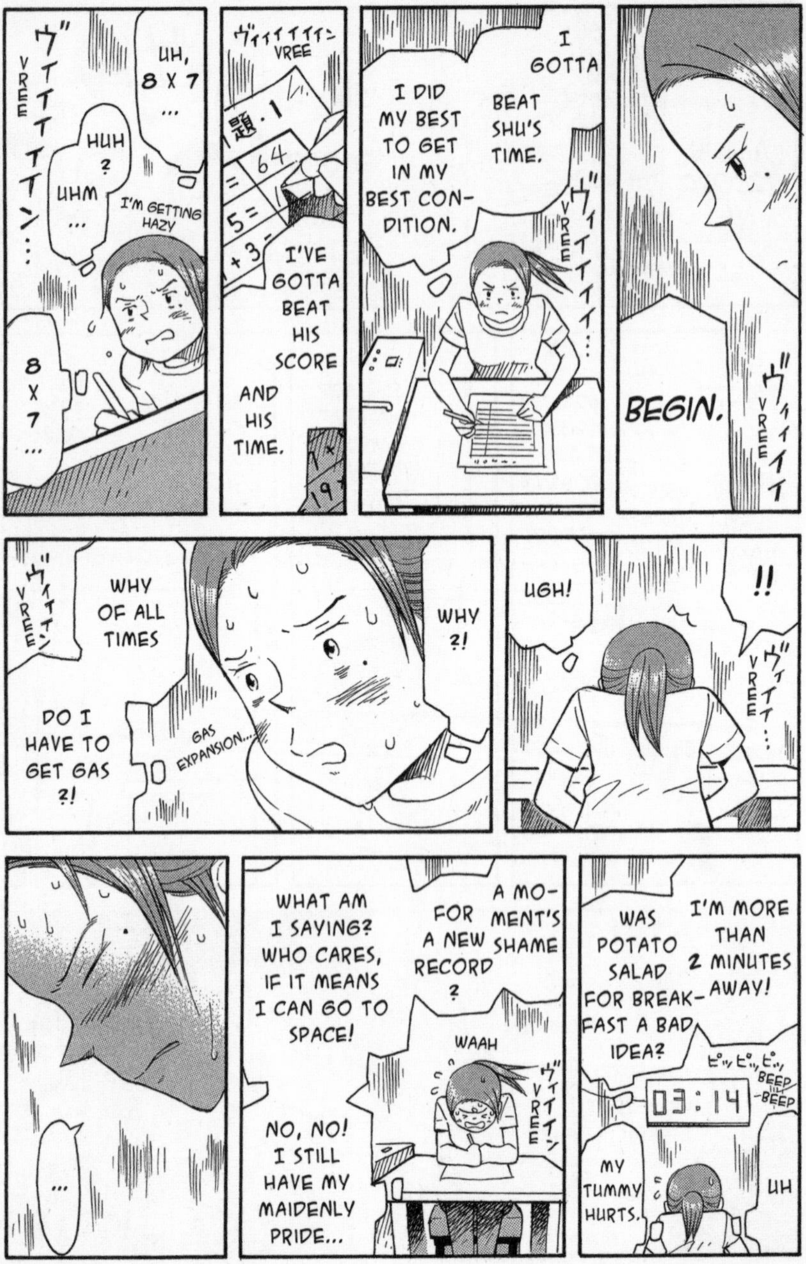
BEGIN.
VREE
ヴィィイイ
I GOTTA BEAT SHU'S TIME.
I DID MY BEST TO GET IN MY BEST CON-DITION.
VREE
ヴィィイイイ…
ヴィィイイイイン
VREE
I'VE GOTTA BEAT HIS SCORE
AND HIS TIME.
ヴィィイイイイン…
VREE
UH, 8 X 7 ...
HUH?
UHM ...
I'M GETTING HAZY
8 X 7 ...
!!
VREE
ヴィィイイ…
UGH!
WHY?!
WHY OF ALL TIMES
DO I HAVE TO GET GAS?!
GAS EXPANSION...
VREE
ヴィイイン
I'M MORE THAN 2 MINUTES AWAY!
WAS POTATO SALAD FOR BREAK-FAST A BAD IDEA?
ピッピッピッ
BEEP-BEEP-BEEP
03:14
UH
MY TUMMY HURTS.
A MO-MENT'S SHAME FOR A NEW RECORD?
WHAT AM I SAYING? WHO CARES, IF IT MEANS I CAN GO TO SPACE!
WAAH
VREE
ヴィイイン
NO, NO! I STILL HAVE MY MAIDENLY PRIDE...
...

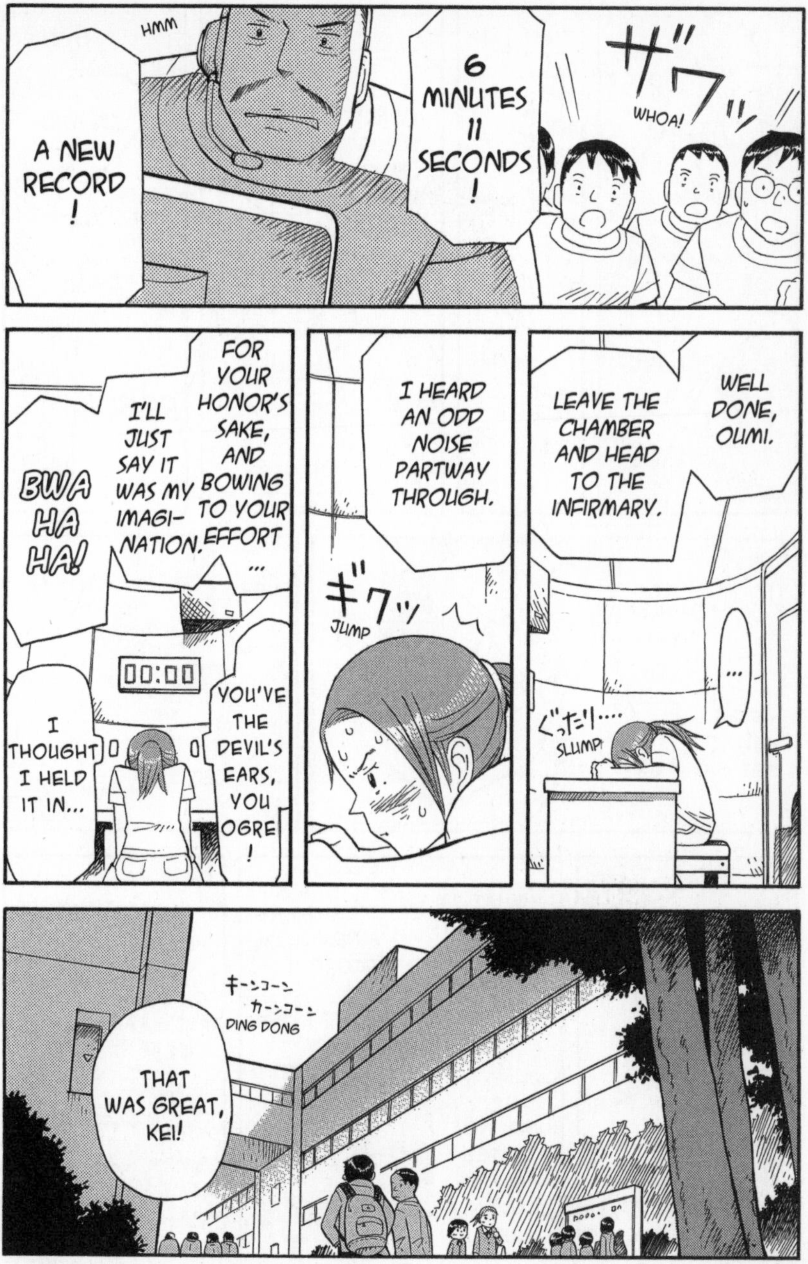
ザワッ
WHOA!
6 MINUTES 11 SECONDS!
HMM
A NEW RECORD!
WELL DONE, OUMI.
LEAVE THE CHAMBER AND HEAD TO THE INFIRMARY.
...
ぐったり….
SLUMP
I HEARD AN ODD NOISE PARTWAY THROUGH.
ギクッ
JUMP
FOR YOUR HONOR'S SAKE, AND BOWING TO YOUR EFFORT...
I'LL JUST SAY IT WAS MY IMAGINATION.
BWA HA HA!
00:00
YOU'VE THE DEVIL'S EARS, YOU OGRE!
I THOUGHT I HELD IT IN...
キーンコーン カーンコーン
DING DONG
THAT WAS GREAT, KEI!

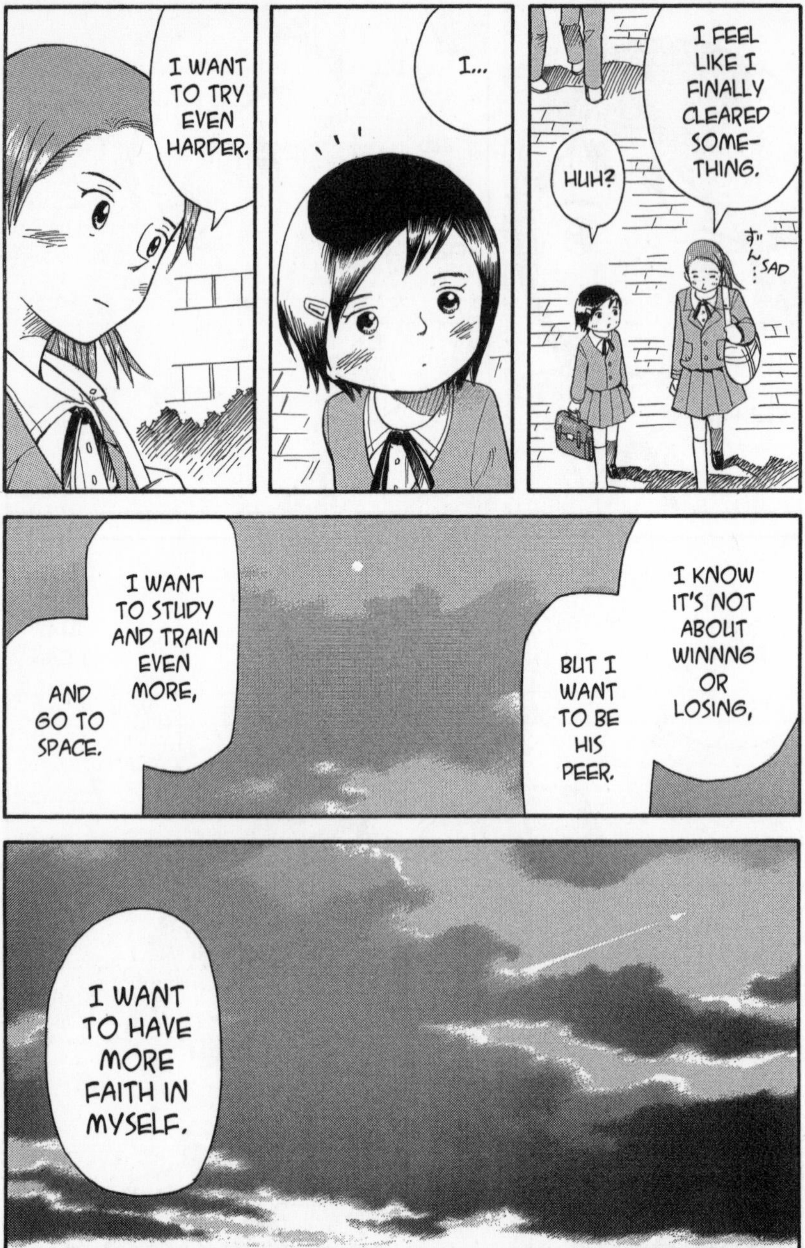
I FEEL LIKE I FINALLY CLEARED SOMETHING.
HUH?
ずん…SAD
I...
I WANT TO TRY EVEN HARDER.
I KNOW IT'S NOT ABOUT WINNNG OR LOSING,
BUT I WANT TO BE HIS PEER.
I WANT TO STUDY AND TRAIN EVEN MORE,
AND GO TO SPACE.
I WANT TO HAVE MORE FAITH IN MYSELF.

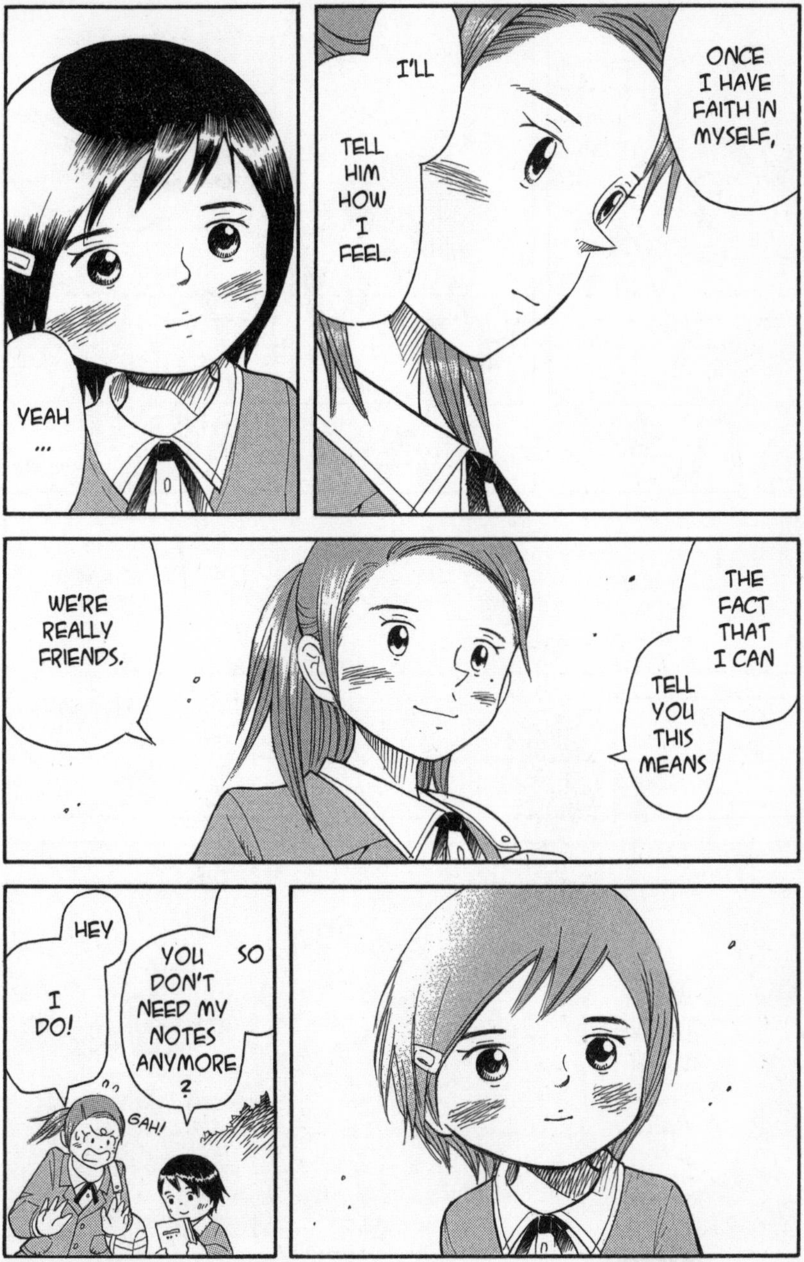
ONCE I HAVE FAITH IN MYSELF,
I'LL TELL HIM HOW I FEEL.
YEAH ...
THE FACT THAT I CAN TELL YOU THIS MEANS
WE'RE REALLY FRIENDS.
SO YOU DON'T NEED MY NOTES ANYMORE?
GAH!
HEY I DO!

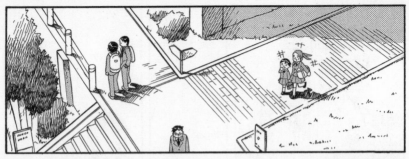

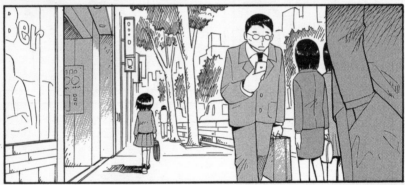

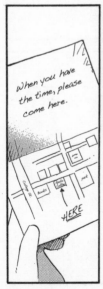

Ber
トントン
TUP TUP
HERE.
FOR YOU.
HUH?
When you have the time, please come here.
Books
Apollo Coffee
park
HERE

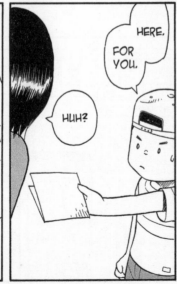

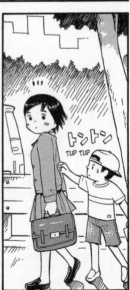

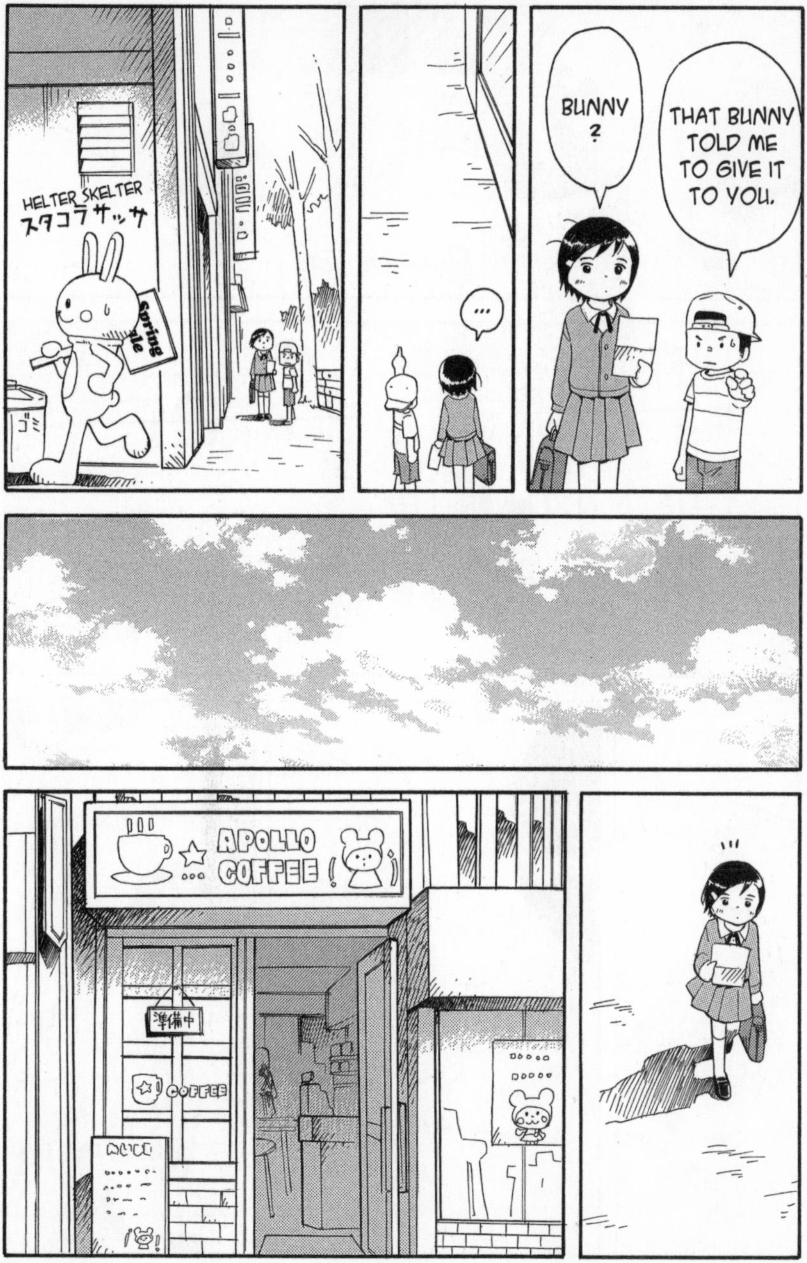
THAT BUNNY TOLD ME TO GIVE IT TO YOU.
BUNNY?
...
HELTER SKELTER
スタコラサッサ
Spring
ゴミ
APOLLO COFFEE
準備中
COFFEE

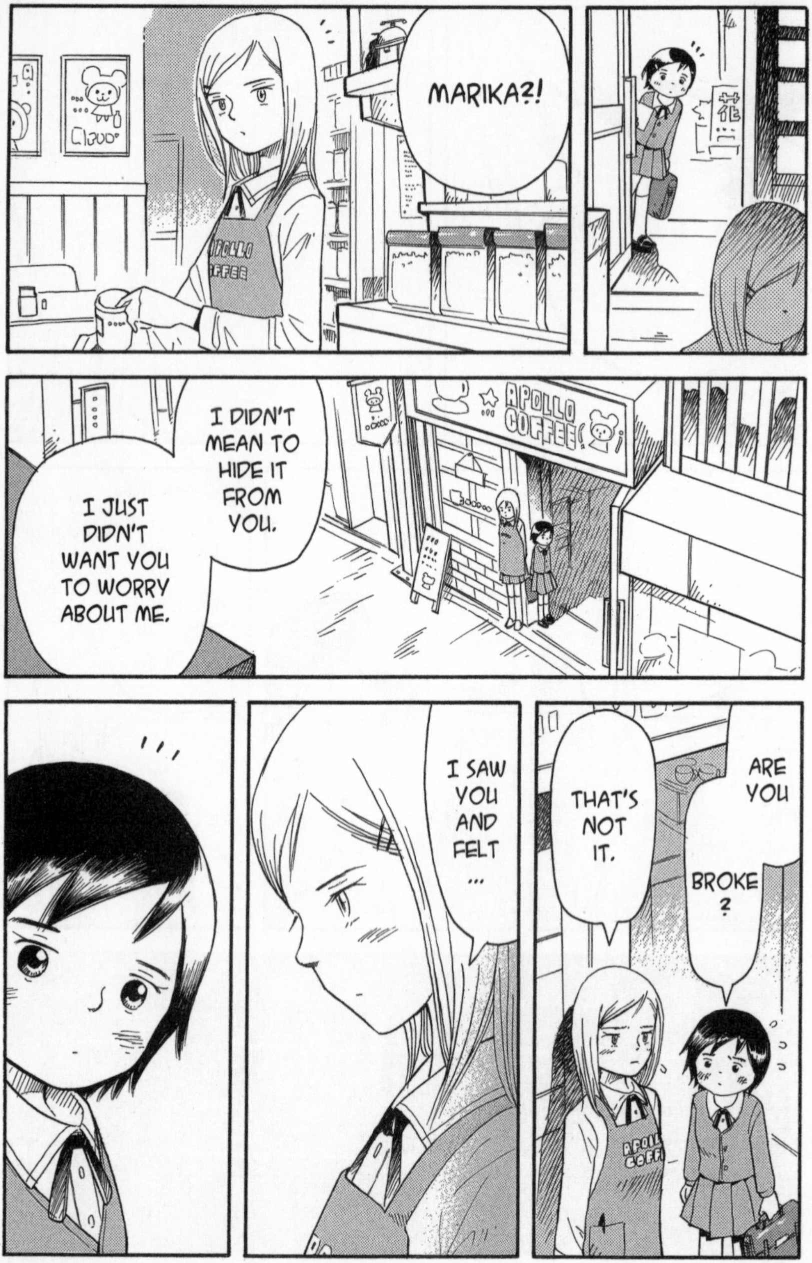

花
MARIKA?!
APOLLO COFFEE
I DIDN'T MEAN TO HIDE IT FROM YOU.
I JUST DIDN'T WANT YOU TO WORRY ABOUT ME.
ARE YOU BROKE?
THAT'S NOT IT.
I SAW YOU AND FELT ...

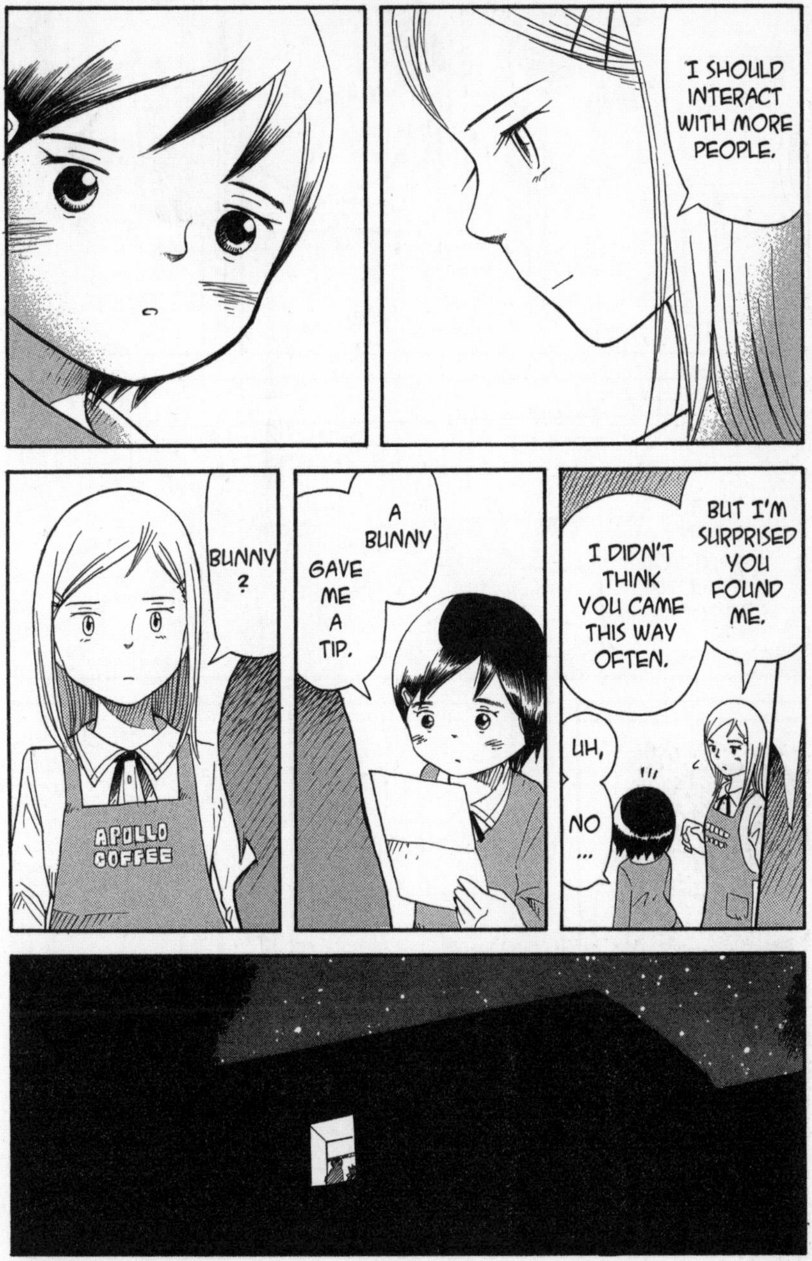
I SHOULD INTERACT WITH MORE PEOPLE.
BUT I'M SURPRISED YOU FOUND ME.
I DIDN'T THINK YOU CAME THIS WAY OFTEN.
UH, NO ...
A BUNNY GAVE ME A TIP.
BUNNY?
APOLLO COFFEE

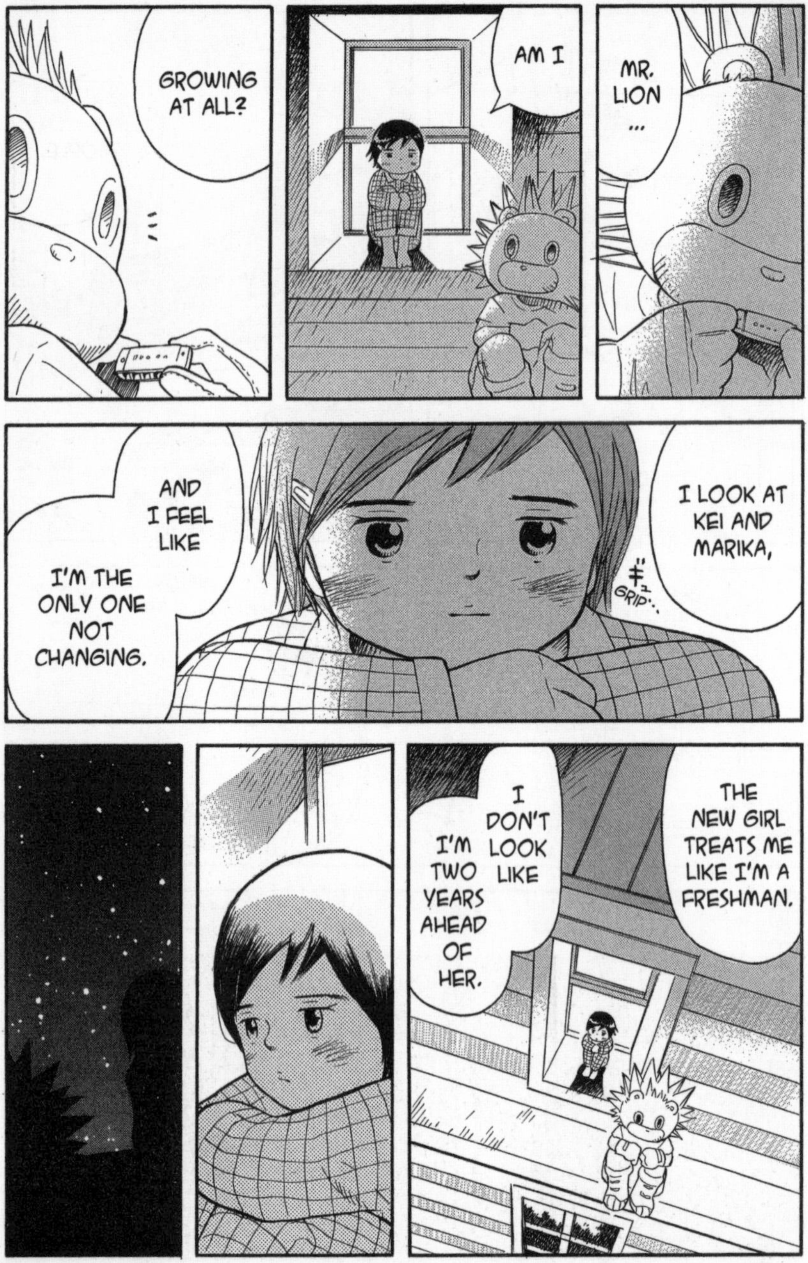
MR. LION ...
AM I
GROWING AT ALL?
I LOOK AT KEI AND MARIKA,
GRIP...
AND I FEEL LIKE
I'M THE ONLY ONE NOT CHANGING.
THE NEW GIRL TREATS ME LIKE I'M A FRESHMAN.
I DON'T LOOK LIKE
I'M TWO YEARS AHEAD OF HER.

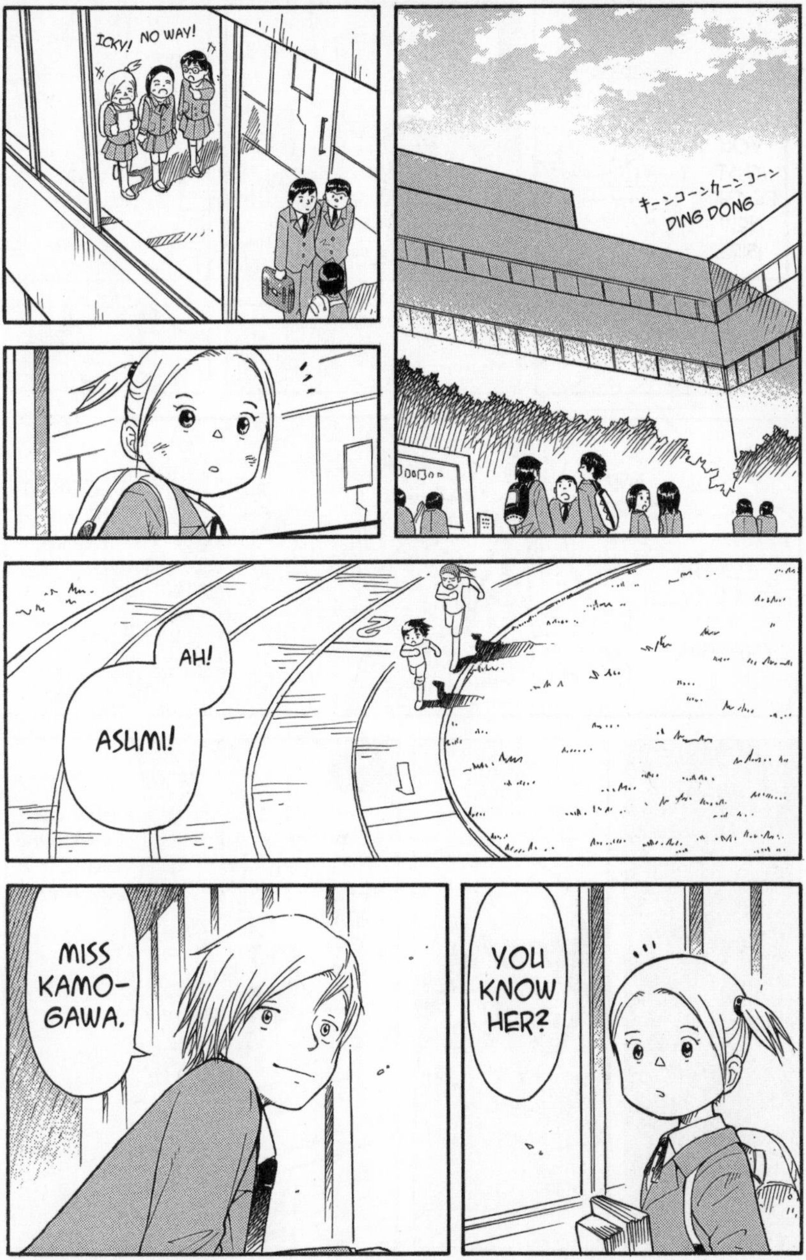

キーンコーンカーンコーン
DING DONG
NO WAY!
ICKY!
AH!
ASUMI!
YOU KNOW HER?
MISS KAMOGAWA.

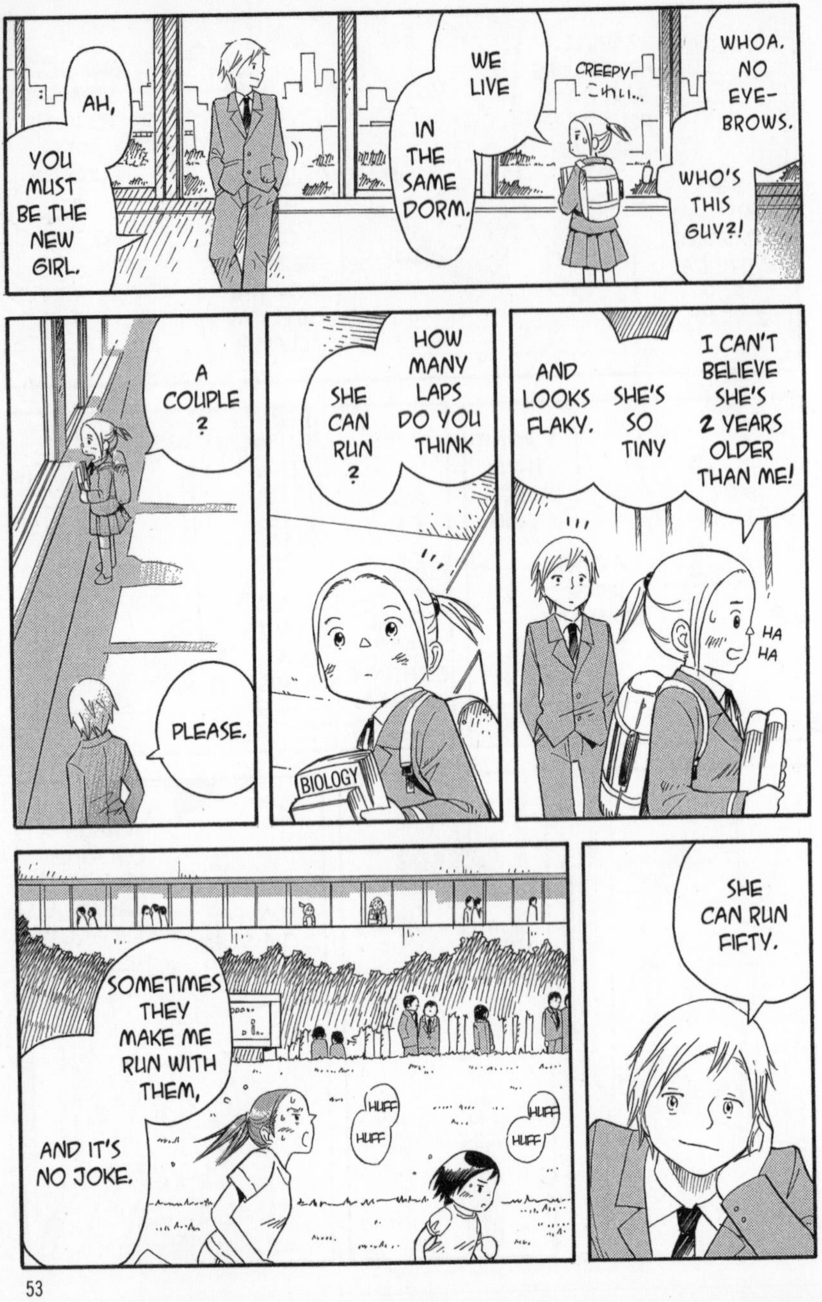
WHOA. NO EYE-BROWS.
WHO'S THIS GUY?!
CREEPY こわい...
WE LIVE IN THE SAME DORM.
AH, YOU MUST BE THE NEW GIRL.
I CAN'T BELIEVE SHE'S 2 YEARS OLDER THAN ME!
SHE'S SO TINY
AND LOOKS FLAKY.
HA HA
HOW MANY LAPS DO YOU THINK SHE CAN RUN?
A COUPLE?
PLEASE.
BIOLOGY
SHE CAN RUN FIFTY.
SOMETIMES THEY MAKE ME RUN WITH THEM,
HUFF
HUFF
HUFF
HUFF
AND IT'S NO JOKE.

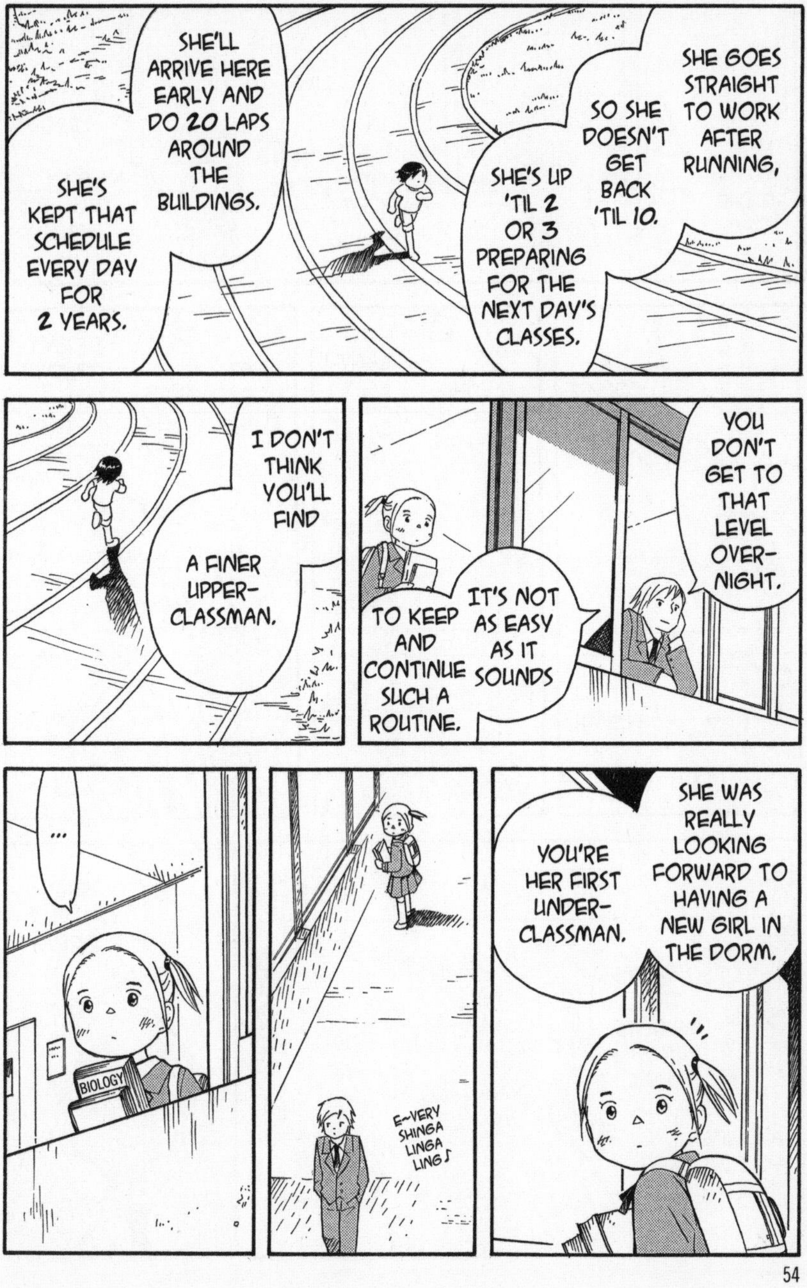
SHE GOES STRAIGHT TO WORK AFTER RUNNING,
SO SHE DOESN'T GET BACK 'TIL 10.
SHE'S UP 'TIL 2 OR 3 PREPARING FOR THE NEXT DAY'S CLASSES.
SHE'LL ARRIVE HERE EARLY AND DO 20 LAPS AROUND THE BUILDINGS.
SHE'S KEPT THAT SCHEDULE EVERY DAY FOR 2 YEARS.
YOU DON'T GET TO THAT LEVEL OVER-NIGHT.
IT'S NOT AS EASY AS IT SOUNDS
TO KEEP AND CONTINUE SUCH A ROUTINE.
I DON'T THINK YOU'LL FIND
A FINER UPPER-CLASSMAN.
SHE WAS REALLY LOOKING FORWARD TO HAVING A NEW GIRL IN THE DORM.
YOU'RE HER FIRST UNDER-CLASSMAN.
E~VERY SHINGA LINGA LING♪
...
BIOLOGY

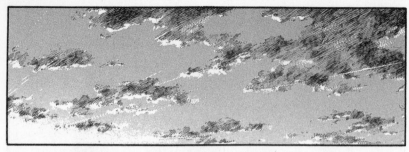

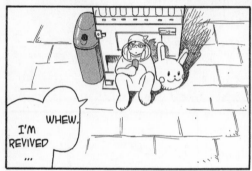

カッ KL
カッ KLI
カッ KLIK
カッ KLI
カッ KY
OPEN, DAMMIT!
WHEW. I'M REVIVED...
GAH!
GEEZ, WHAT TIMING...
カポッ POP
HEY! FUCCHY!
...

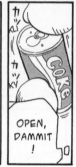

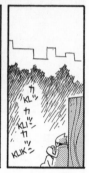

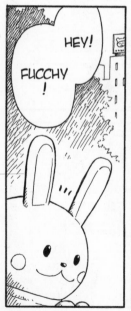

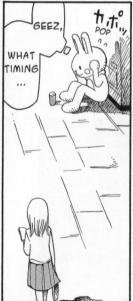

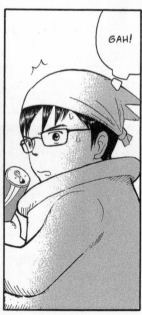

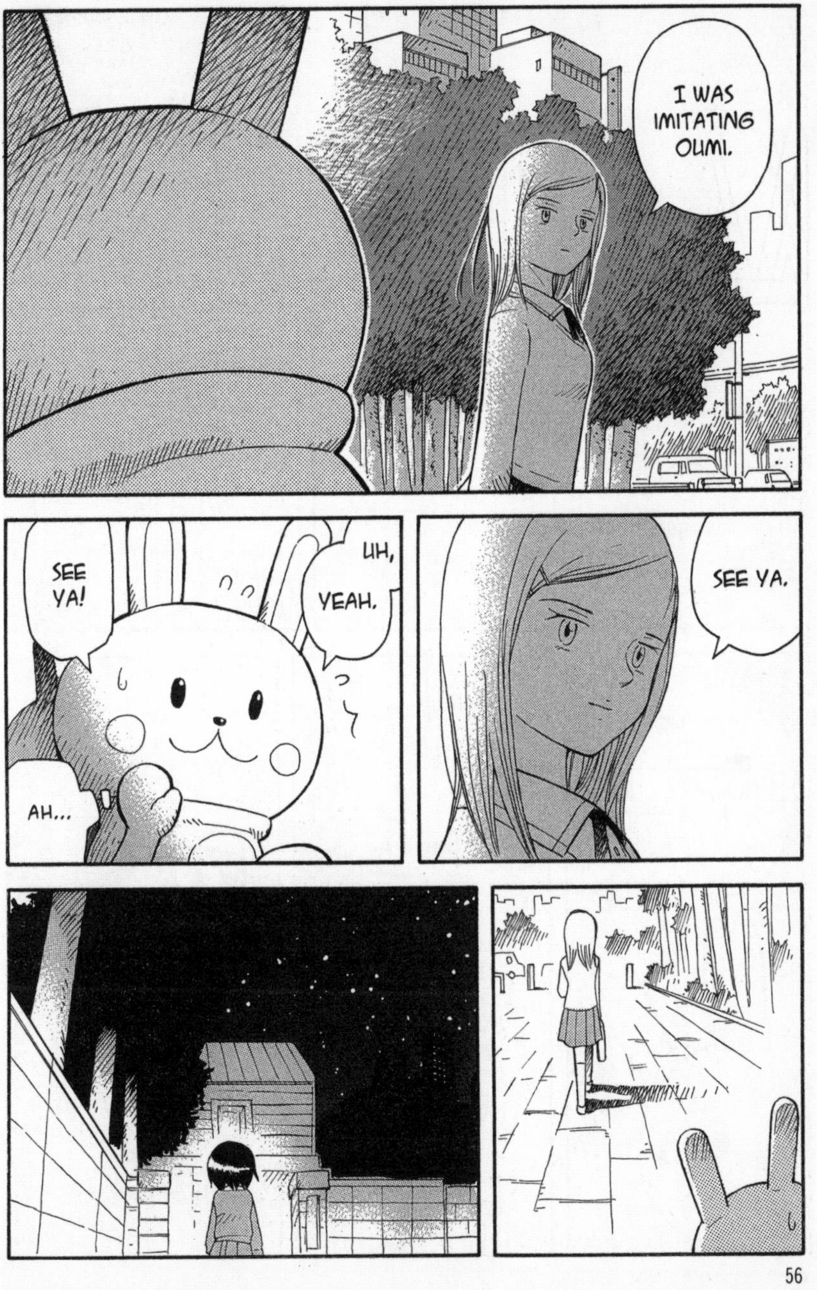
I WAS IMITATING OUMI.
SEE YA.
UH, YEAH.
SEE YA!
AH...

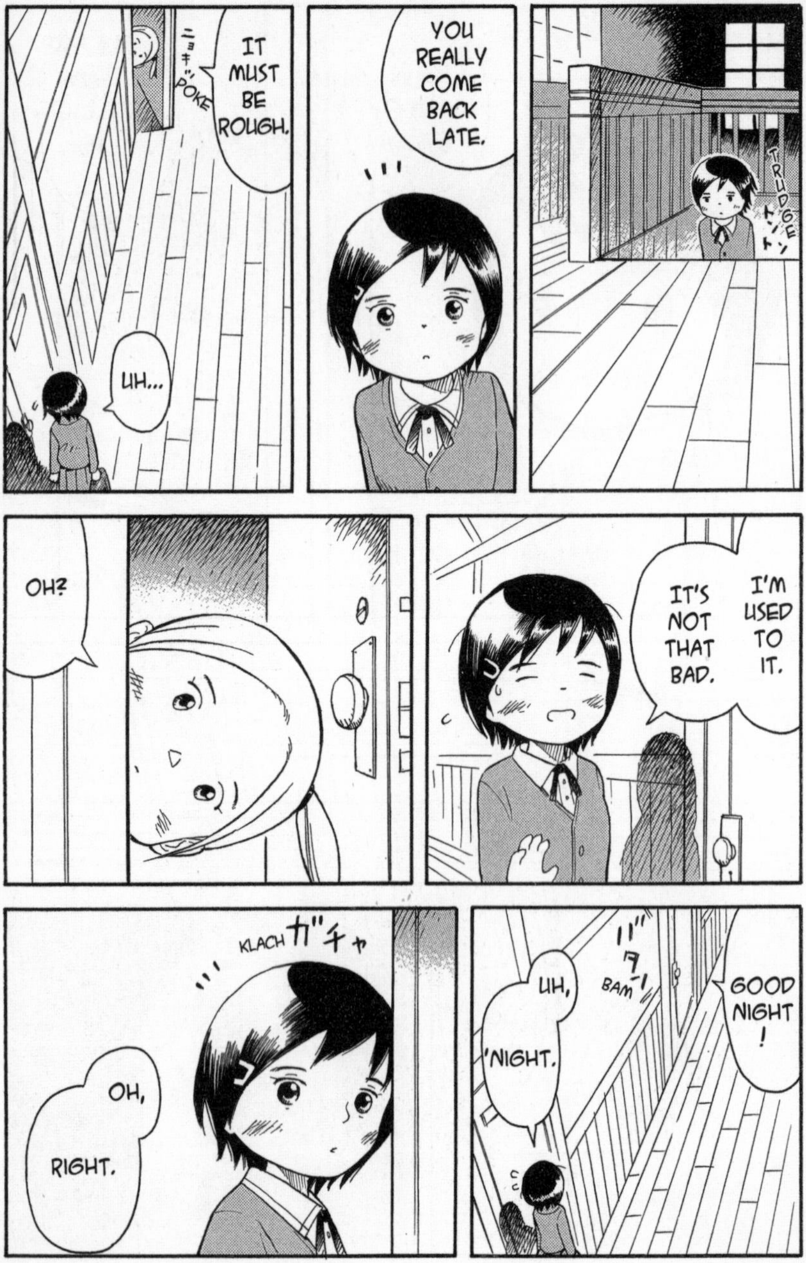
TRUDGE
YOU REALLY COME BACK LATE.
ニョキッ POKE
IT MUST BE ROUGH.
UH...
I'M USED TO IT.
IT'S NOT THAT BAD.
OH?
GOOD NIGHT!
バタン BAM
UH, 'NIGHT.
KLACH ガチャ
OH, RIGHT.

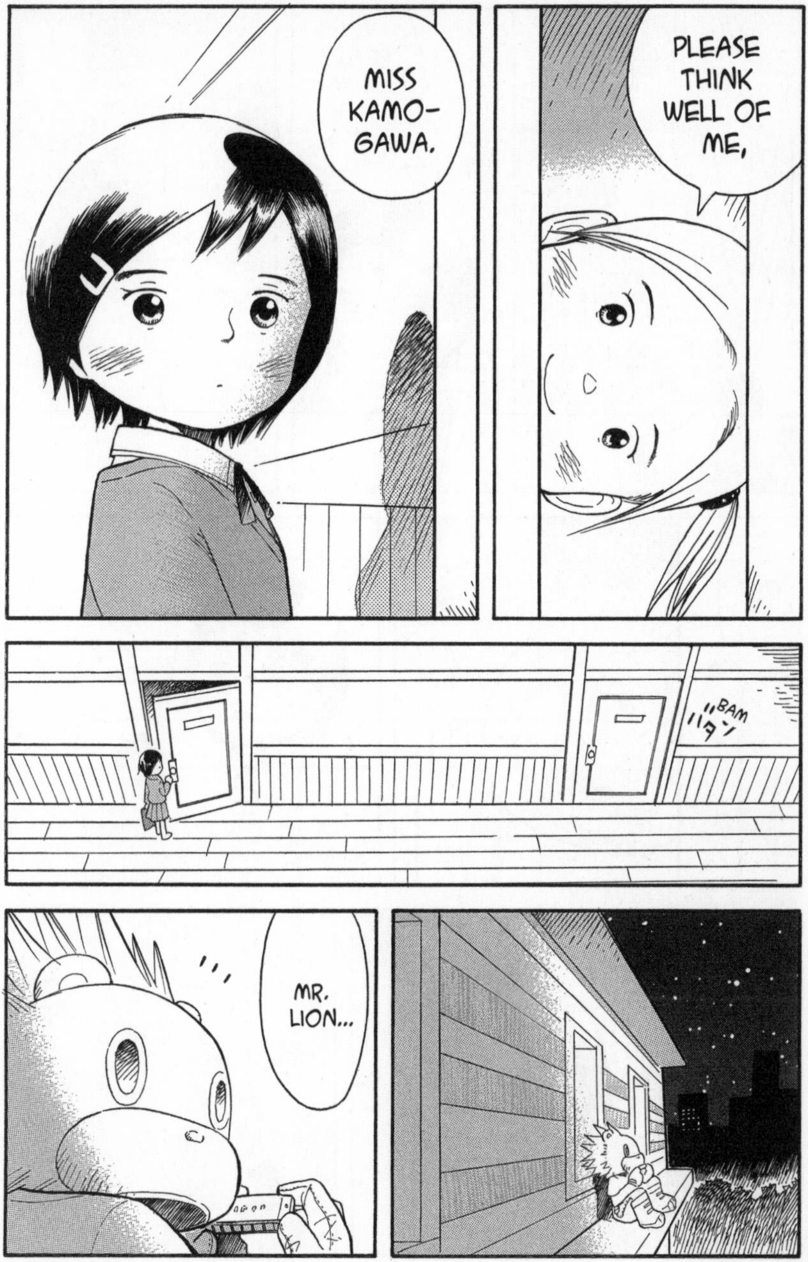
PLEASE THINK WELL OF ME,
MISS KAMO-GAWA.
BAM
バタン
MR. LION...

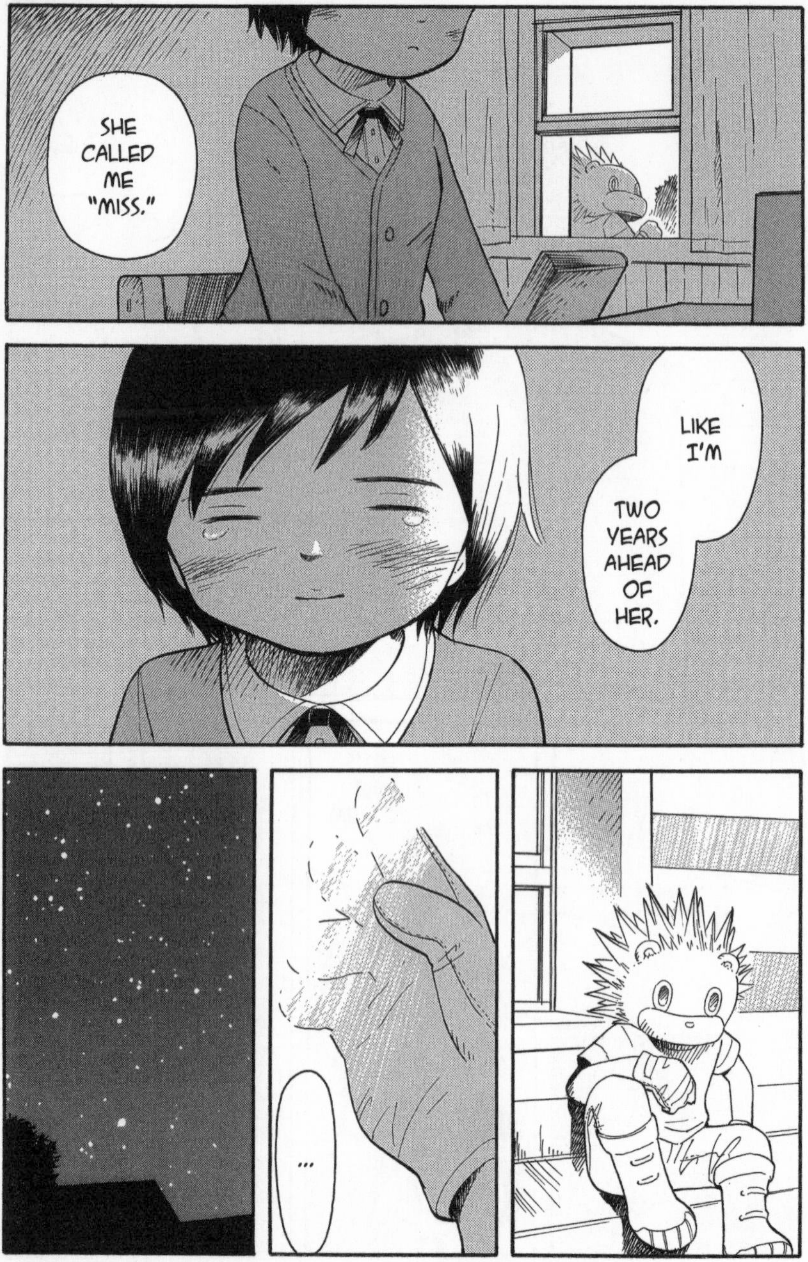
SHE CALLED ME "MISS."
LIKE I'M
TWO YEARS AHEAD OF HER.
...

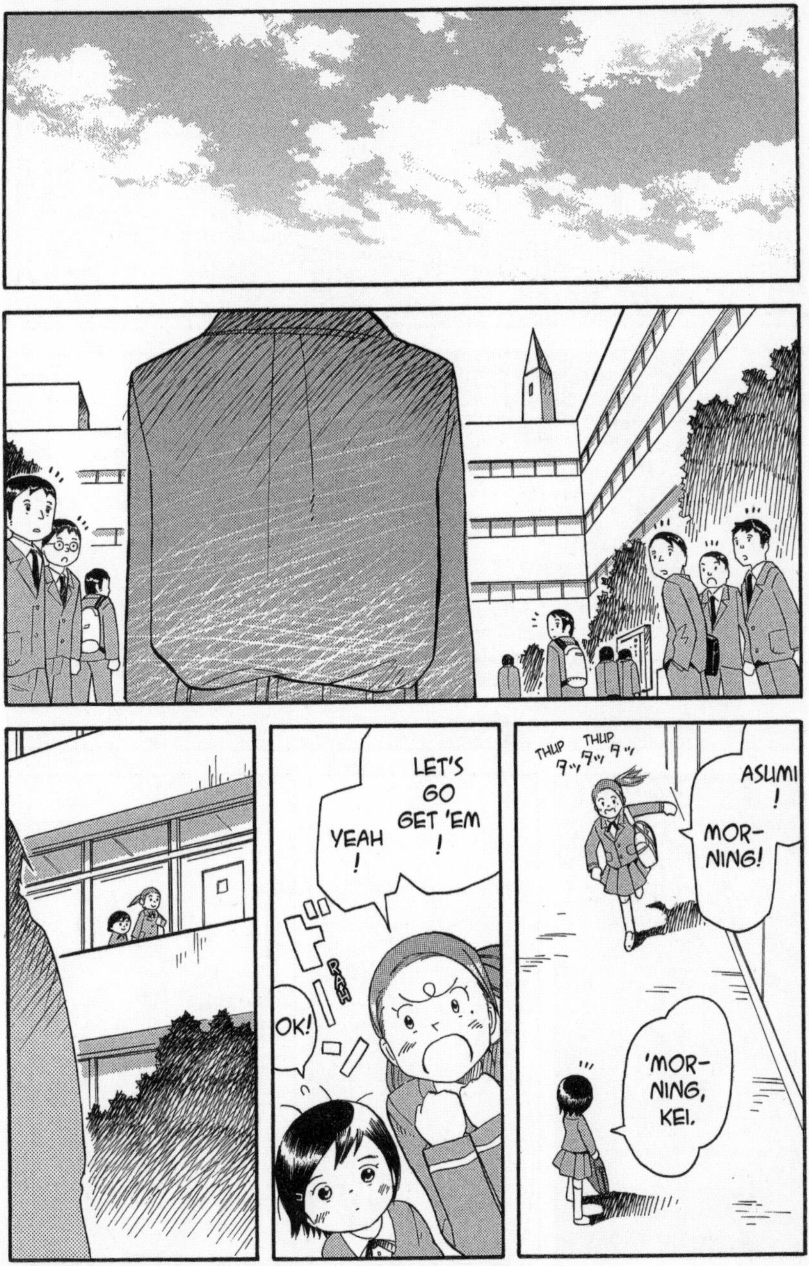
THUP タッ
THUP タッ タッ
ASUMI! MOR-NING!
'MOR-NING, KEI.
LET'S GO GET 'EM!
YEAH!
RAH
OK!

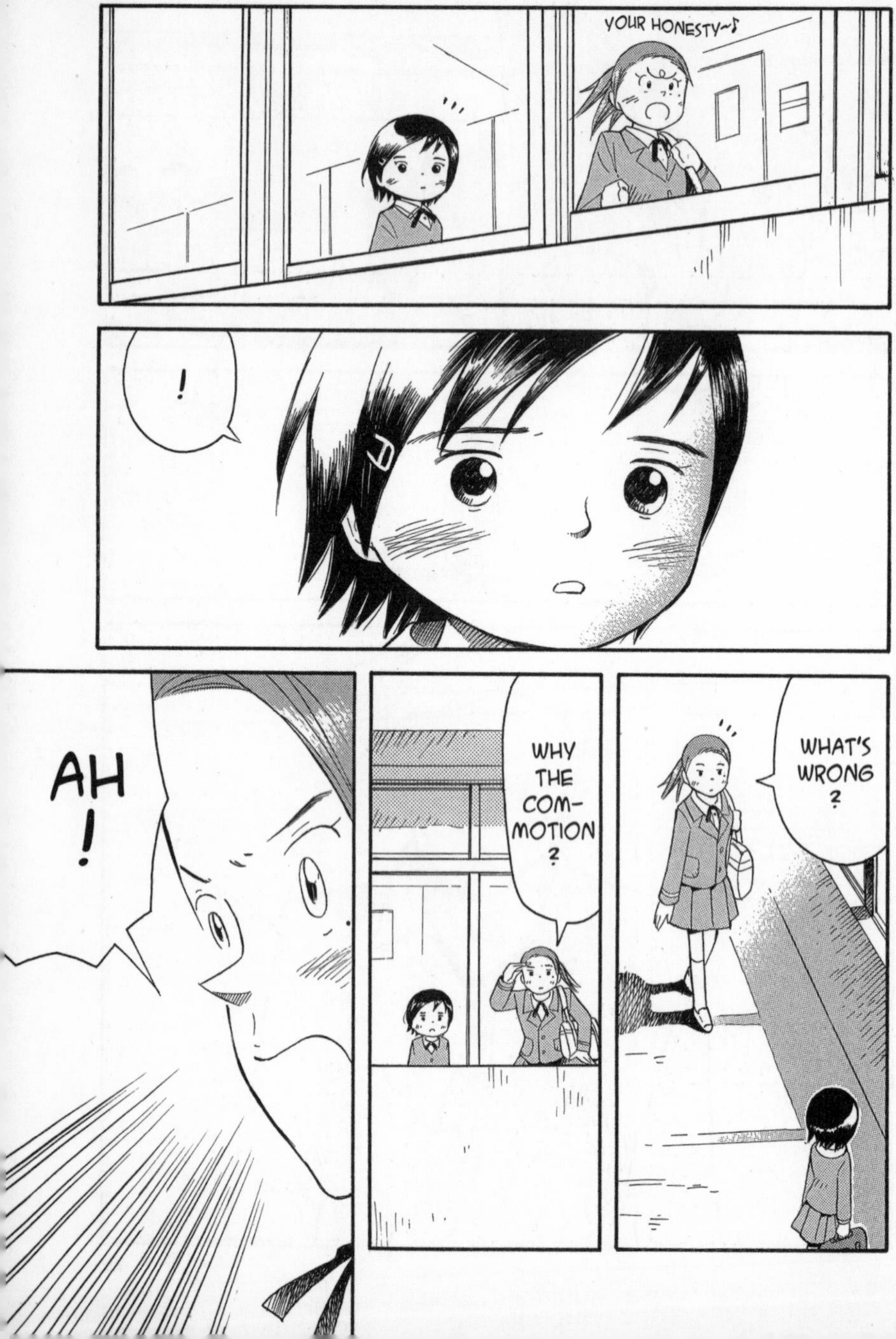
YOUR HONESTY~♪
!
WHAT'S WRONG?
WHY THE COM-MOTION?
AH!

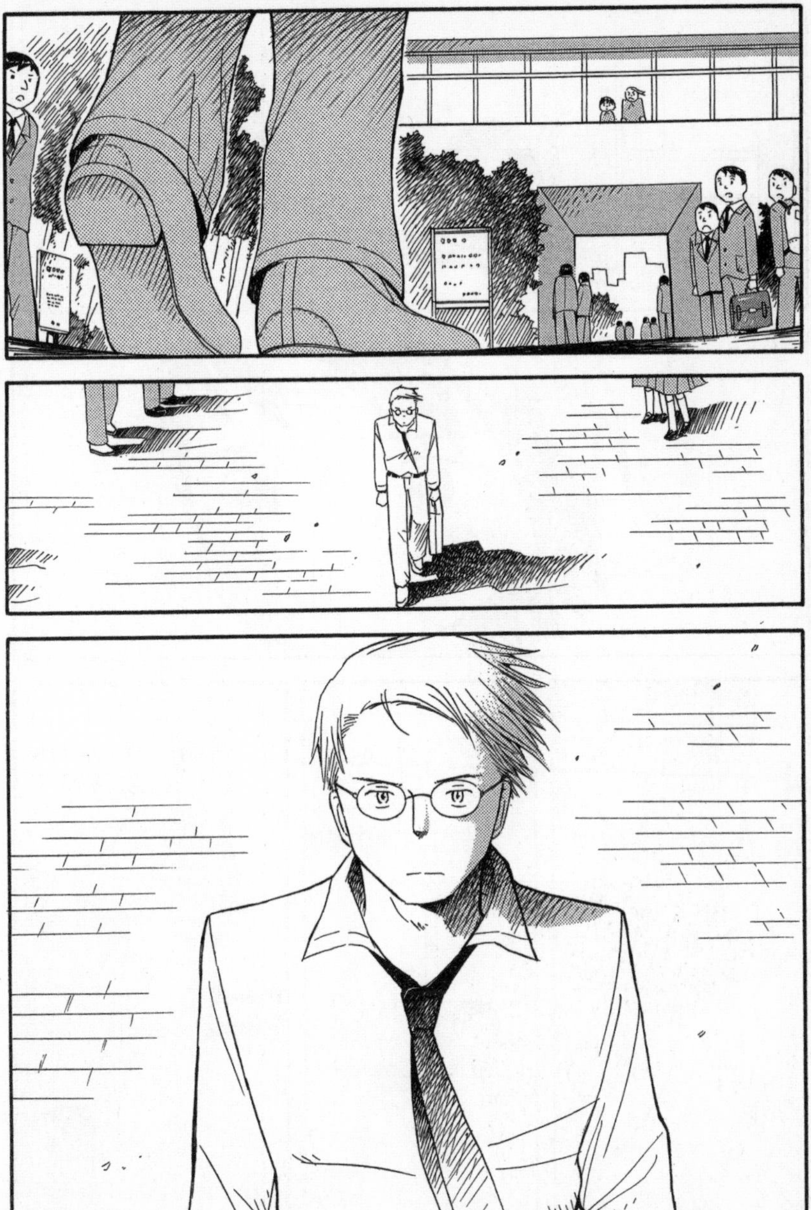

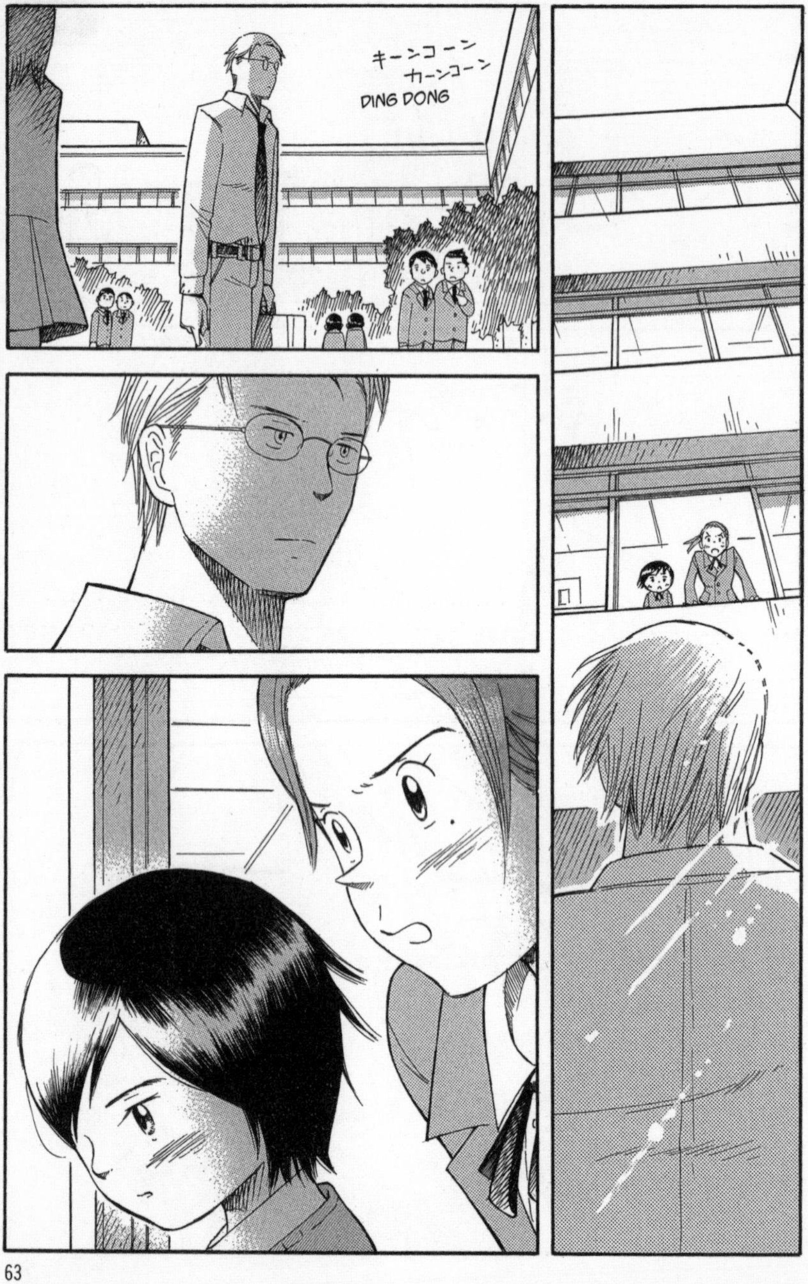
キーンコーン
カーンコーン
DING DONG

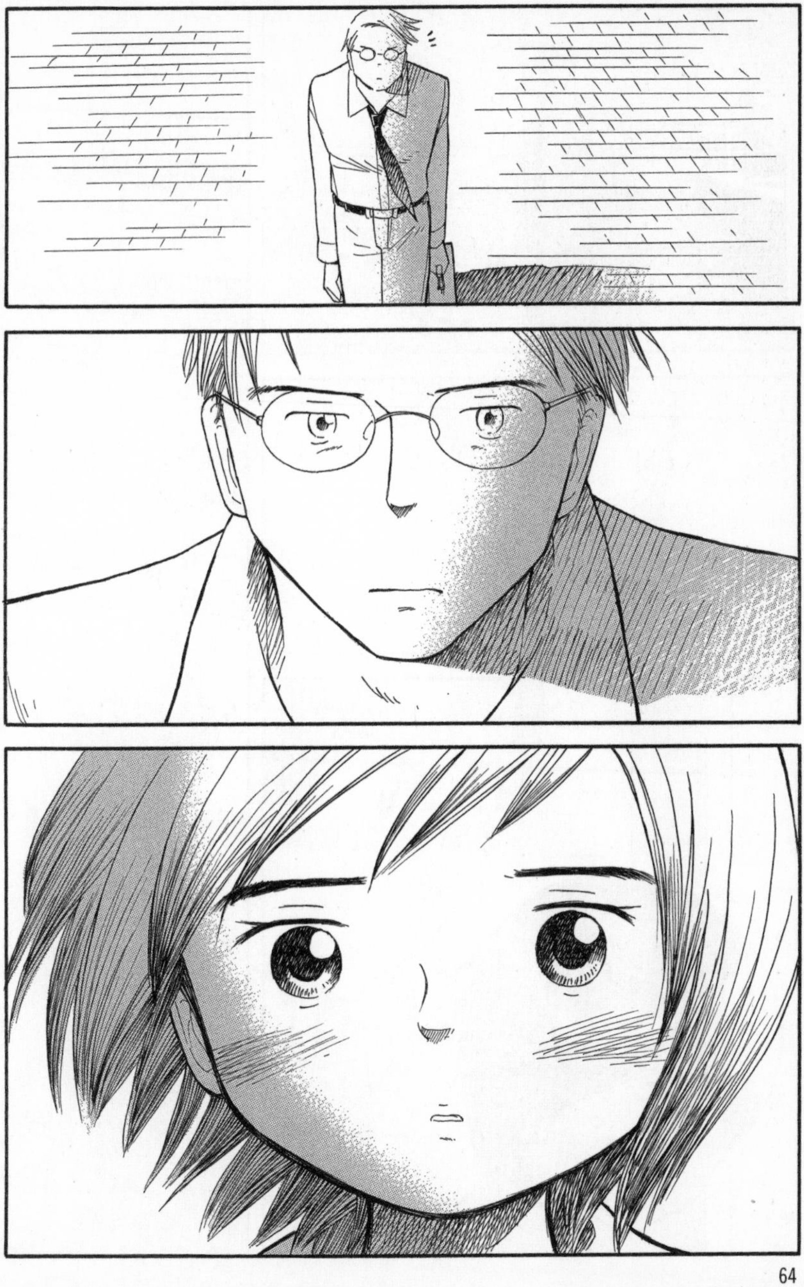

MISSION:49

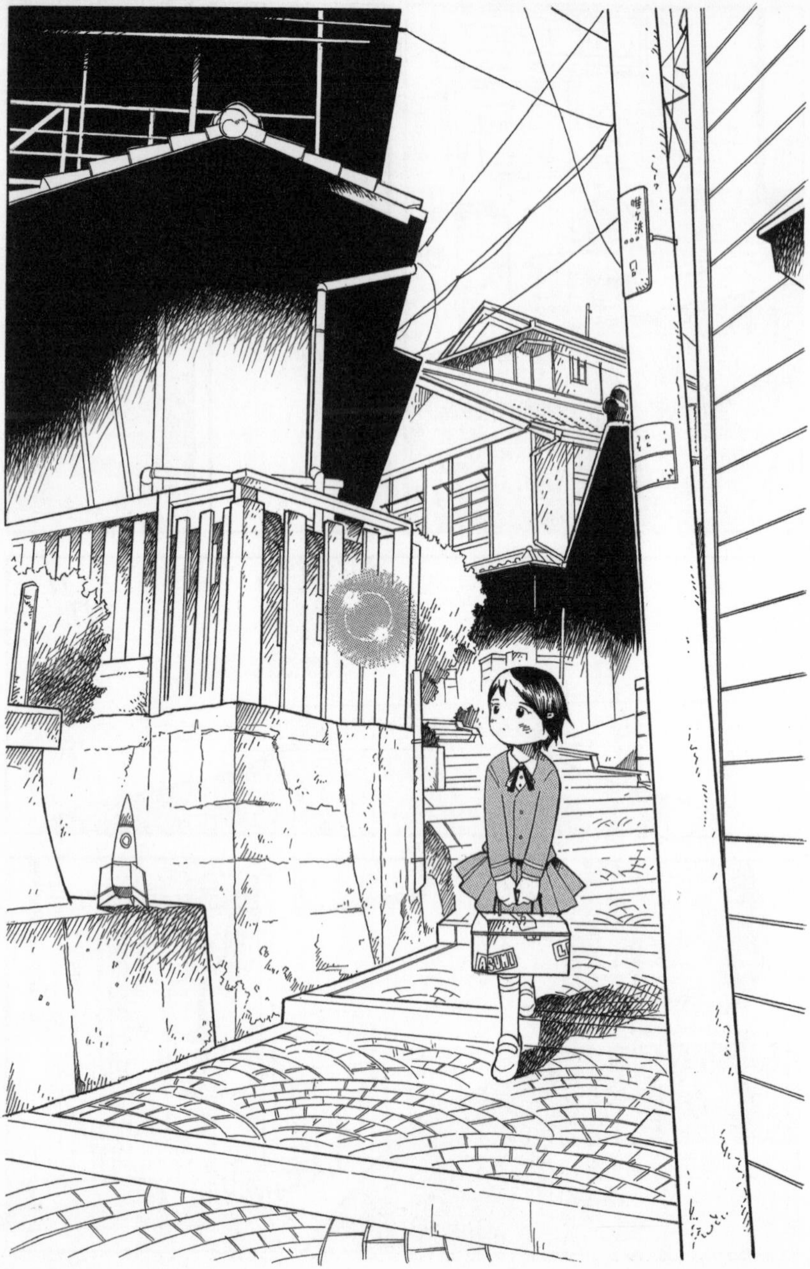

唯ケ浜
ASUMI

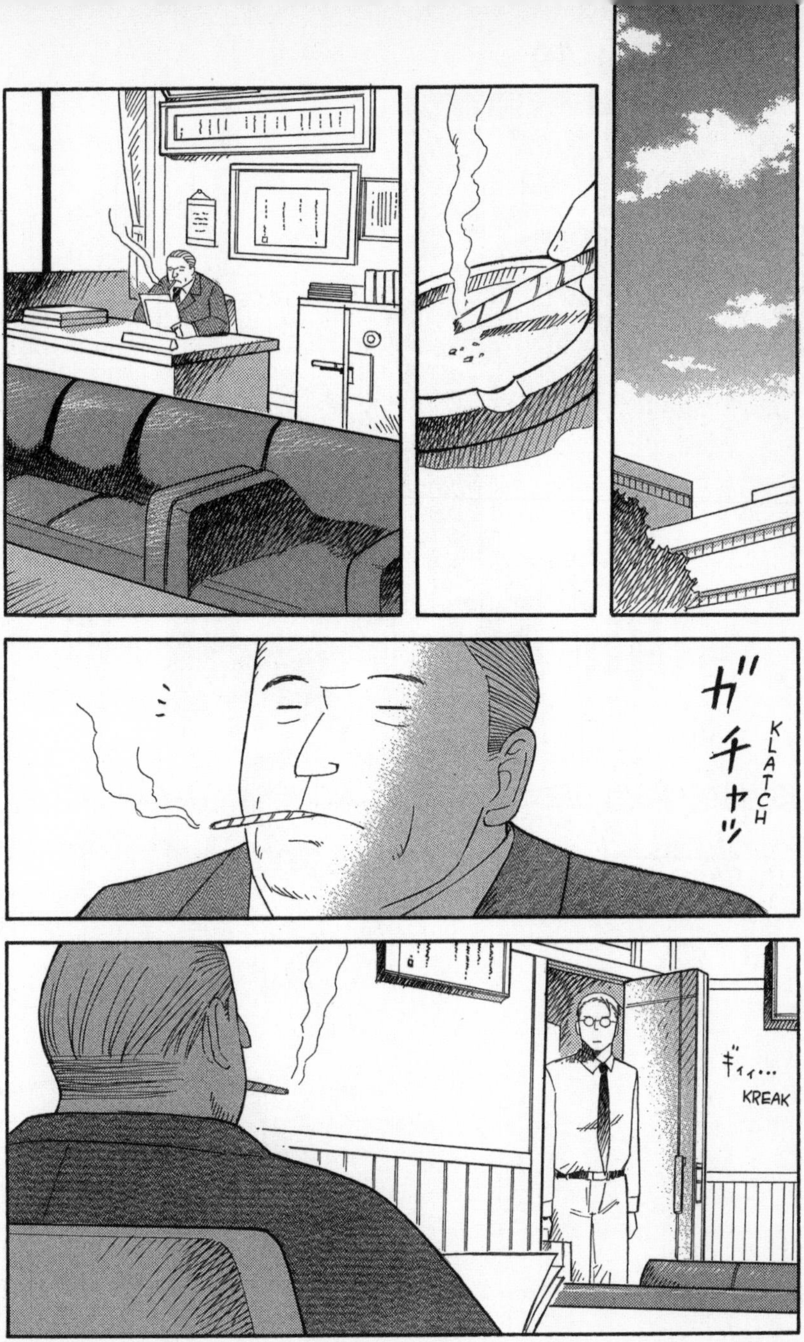
ガチャッ
KLATCH
ギィィ…
KREAK

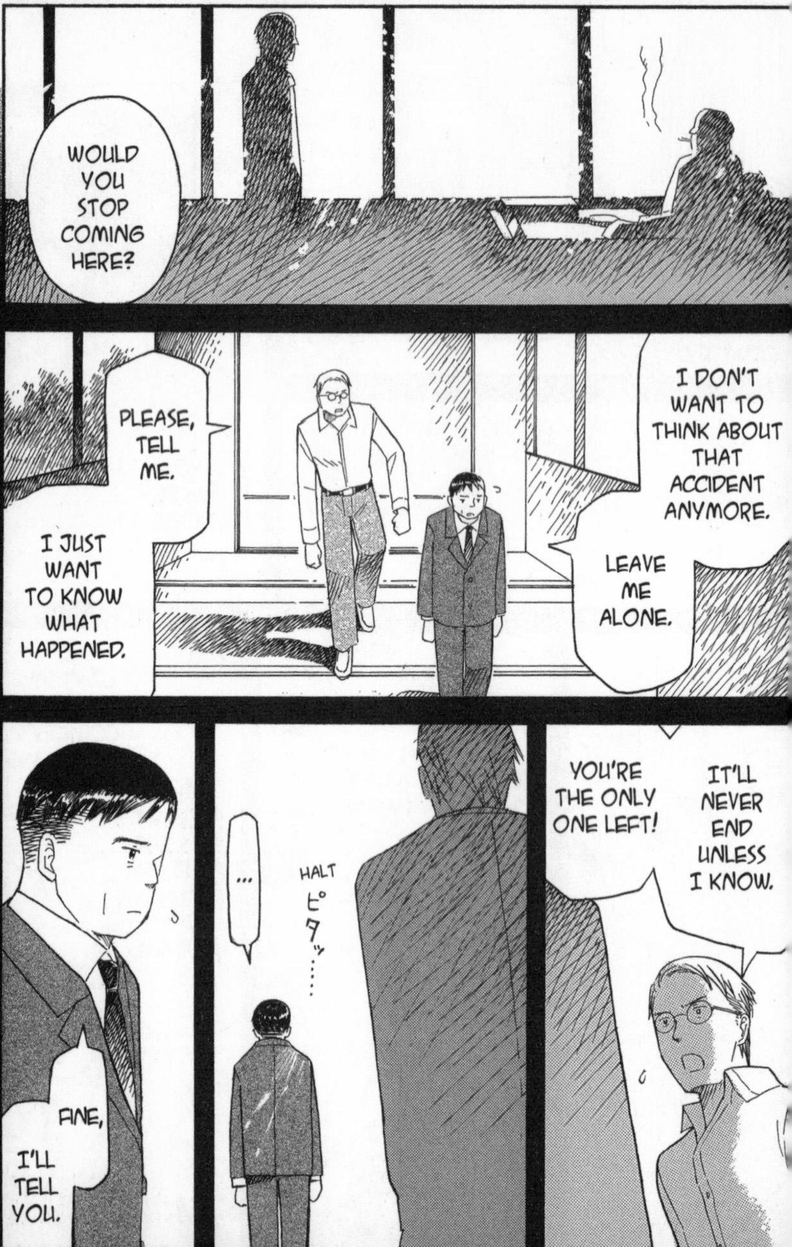
WOULD YOU STOP COMING HERE?
I DON'T WANT TO THINK ABOUT THAT ACCIDENT ANYMORE.
LEAVE ME ALONE.
PLEASE, TELL ME.
I JUST WANT TO KNOW WHAT HAPPENED.
IT'LL NEVER END UNLESS I KNOW.
YOU'RE THE ONLY ONE LEFT!
...
HALT
ピタッ……
FINE,
I'LL TELL YOU.

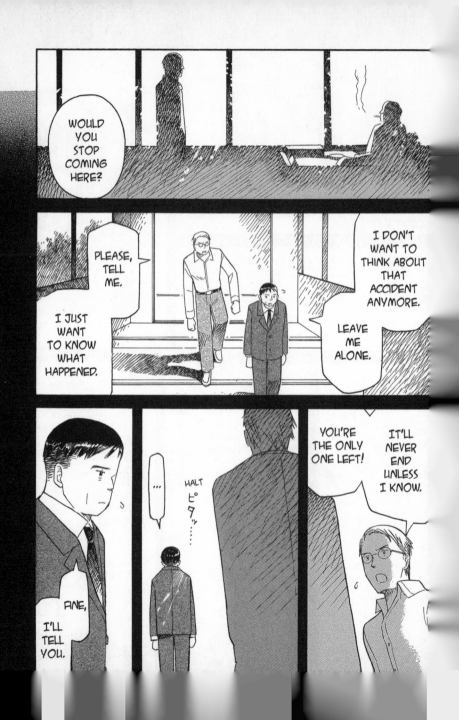

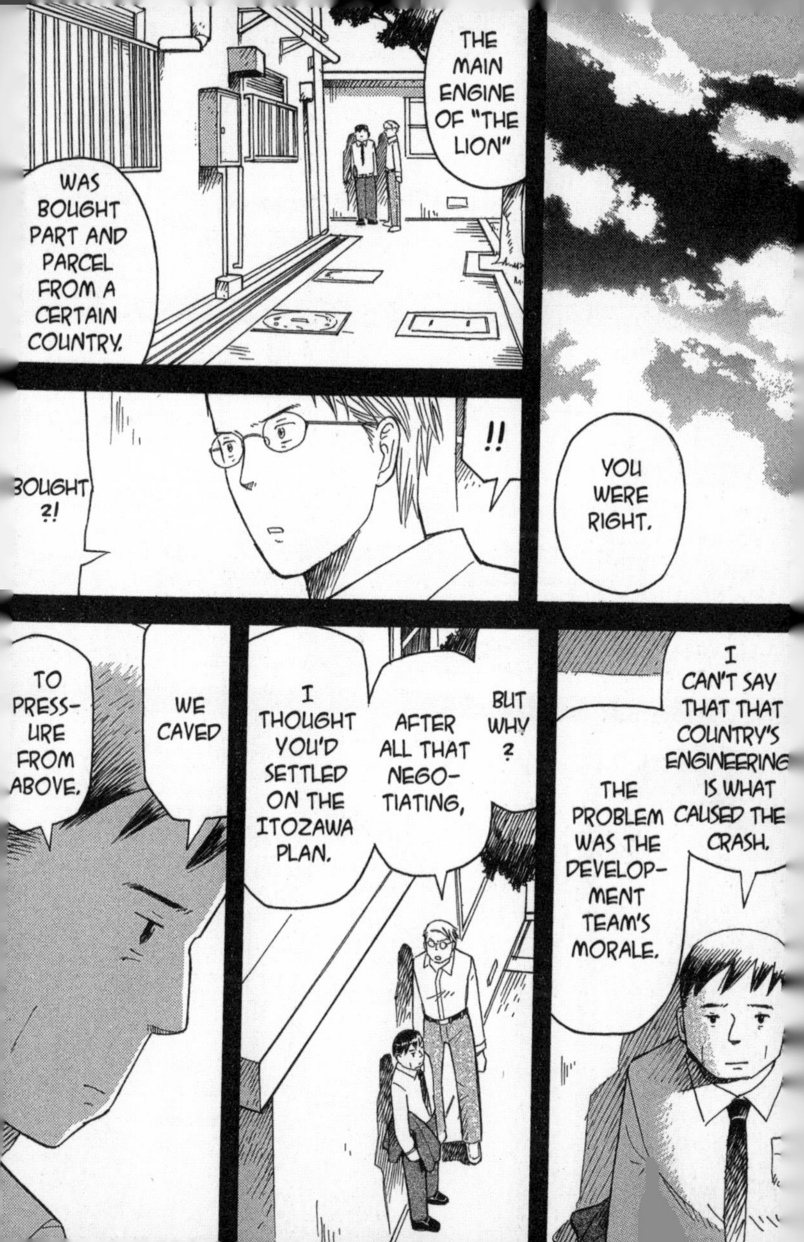
YOU WERE RIGHT.
THE MAIN ENGINE OF "THE LION"
WAS BOUGHT PART AND PARCEL FROM A CERTAIN COUNTRY.
!!
BOUGHT?!
I CAN'T SAY THAT THAT COUNTRY'S ENGINEERING IS WHAT CAUSED THE CRASH.
THE PROBLEM WAS THE DEVELOPMENT TEAM'S MORALE.
BUT WHY?
AFTER ALL THAT NEGOTIATING,
I THOUGHT YOU'D SETTLED ON THE ITOZAWA PLAN.
WE CAVED
TO PRESSURE FROM ABOVE.

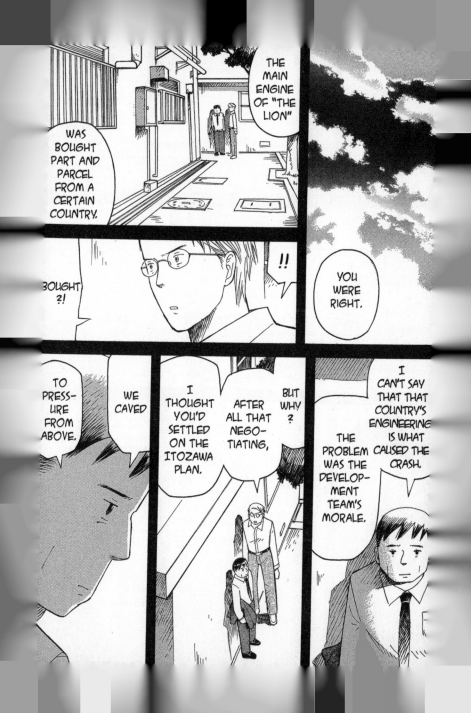

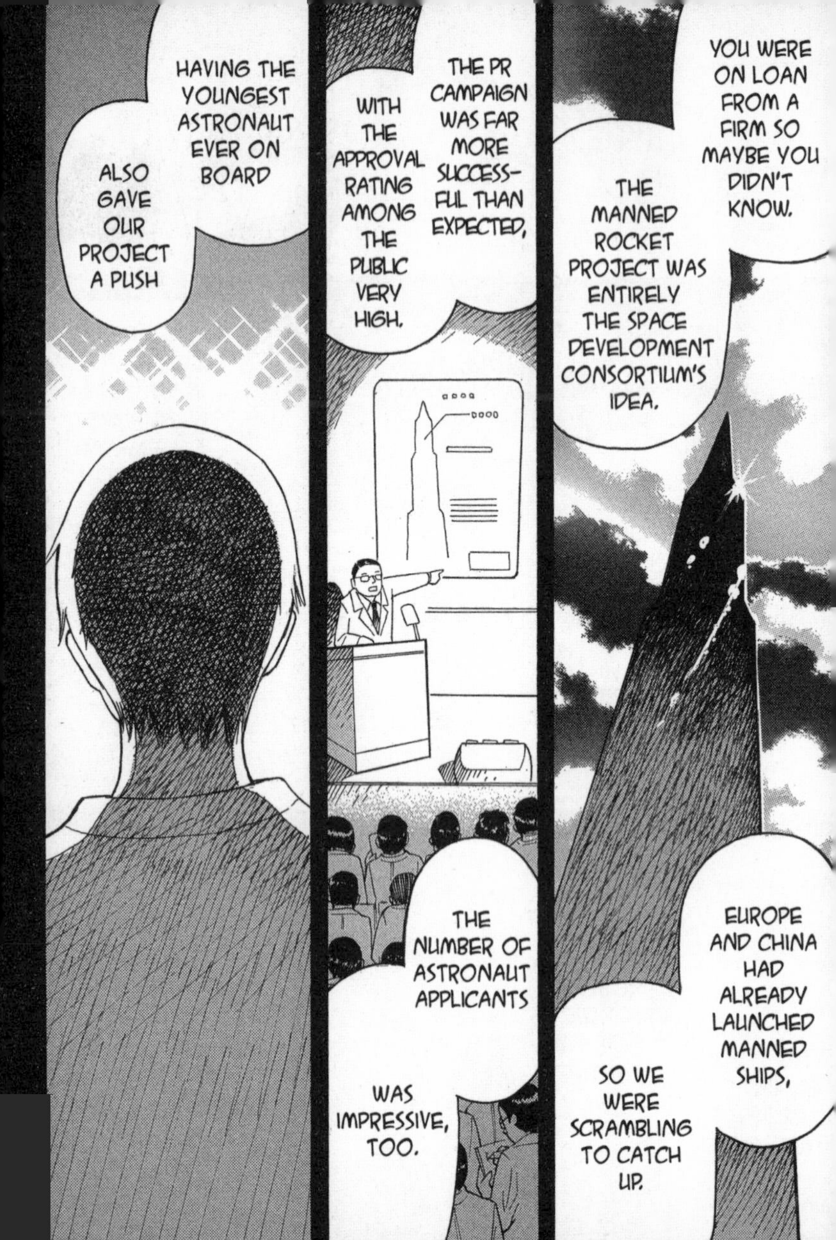
YOU WERE ON LOAN FROM A FIRM SO MAYBE YOU DIDN'T KNOW.
THE MANNED ROCKET PROJECT WAS ENTIRELY THE SPACE DEVELOPMENT CONSORTIUM'S IDEA.
EUROPE AND CHINA HAD ALREADY LAUNCHED MANNED SHIPS,
SO WE WERE SCRAMBLING TO CATCH UP.
THE PR CAMPAIGN WAS FAR MORE SUCCESS-FUL THAN EXPECTED,
WITH THE APPROVAL RATING AMONG THE PUBLIC VERY HIGH.
THE NUMBER OF ASTRONAUT APPLICANTS
WAS IMPRESSIVE, TOO.
HAVING THE YOUNGEST ASTRONAUT EVER ON BOARD
ALSO GAVE OUR PROJECT A PUSH

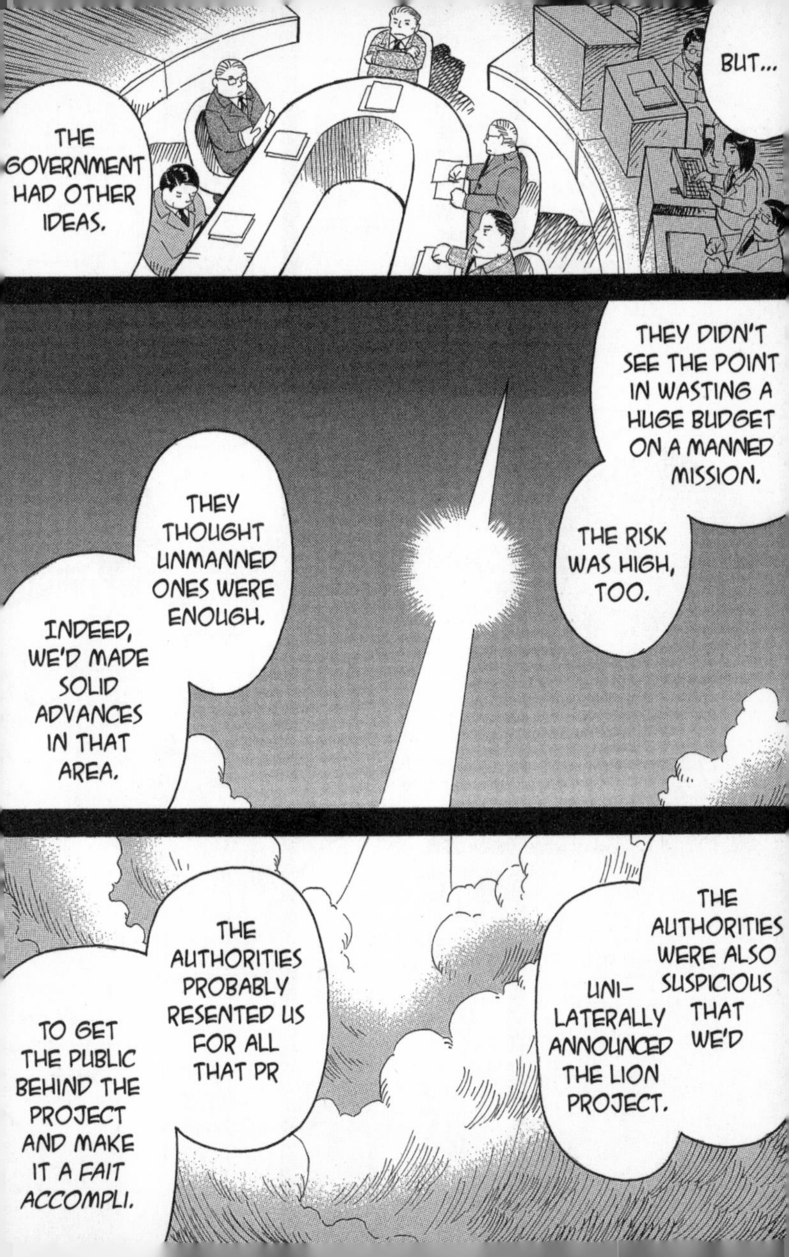
BUT...
THE GOVERNMENT HAD OTHER IDEAS.
THEY DIDN'T SEE THE POINT IN WASTING A HUGE BUDGET ON A MANNED MISSION.
THE RISK WAS HIGH, TOO.
THEY THOUGHT UNMANNED ONES WERE ENOUGH.
INDEED, WE'D MADE SOLID ADVANCES IN THAT AREA.
THE AUTHORITIES WERE ALSO SUSPICIOUS THAT WE'D
UNI-LATERALLY ANNOUNCED THE LION PROJECT.
THE AUTHORITIES PROBABLY RESENTED US FOR ALL THAT PR
TO GET THE PUBLIC BEHIND THE PROJECT AND MAKE IT A FAIT ACCOMPLI.

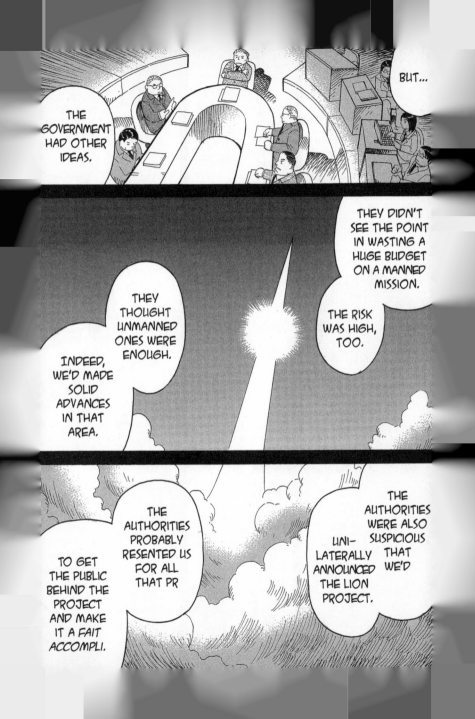

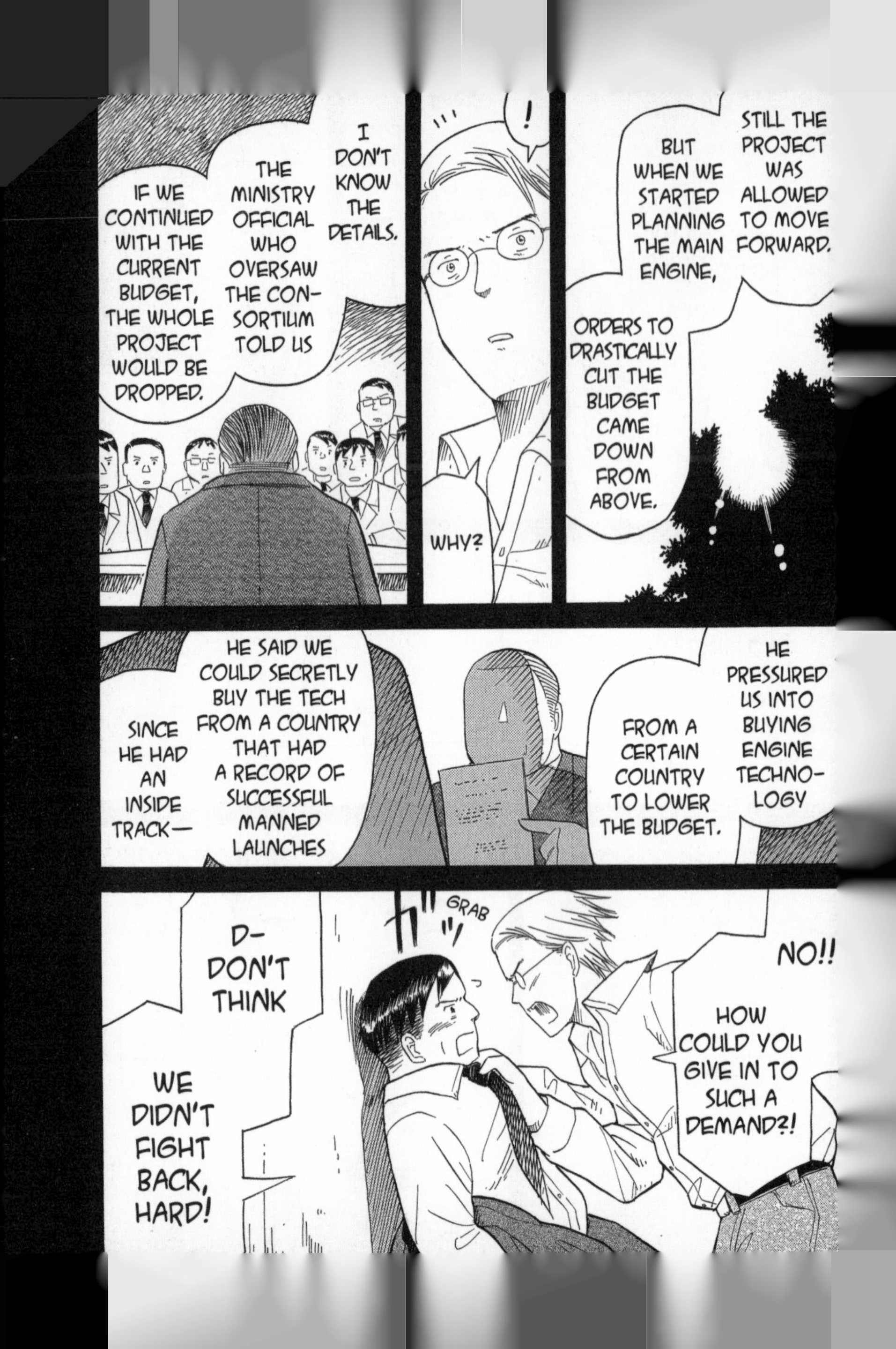
STILL THE PROJECT WAS ALLOWED TO MOVE FORWARD.
BUT WHEN WE STARTED PLANNING THE MAIN ENGINE,
ORDERS TO DRASTICALLY CUT THE BUDGET CAME DOWN FROM ABOVE.
!
WHY?
I DON'T KNOW THE DETAILS.
THE MINISTRY OFFICIAL WHO OVERSAW THE CONSORTIUM TOLD US
IF WE CONTINUED WITH THE CURRENT BUDGET, THE WHOLE PROJECT WOULD BE DROPPED.
HE PRESSURED US INTO BUYING ENGINE TECHNOLOGY
FROM A CERTAIN COUNTRY TO LOWER THE BUDGET.
HE SAID WE COULD SECRETLY BUY THE TECH FROM A COUNTRY THAT HAD A RECORD OF SUCCESSFUL MANNED LAUNCHES
SINCE HE HAD AN INSIDE TRACK—
NO!!
HOW COULD YOU GIVE IN TO SUCH A DEMAND?!
GRAB
D- DON'T THINK
WE DIDN'T FIGHT BACK, HARD!

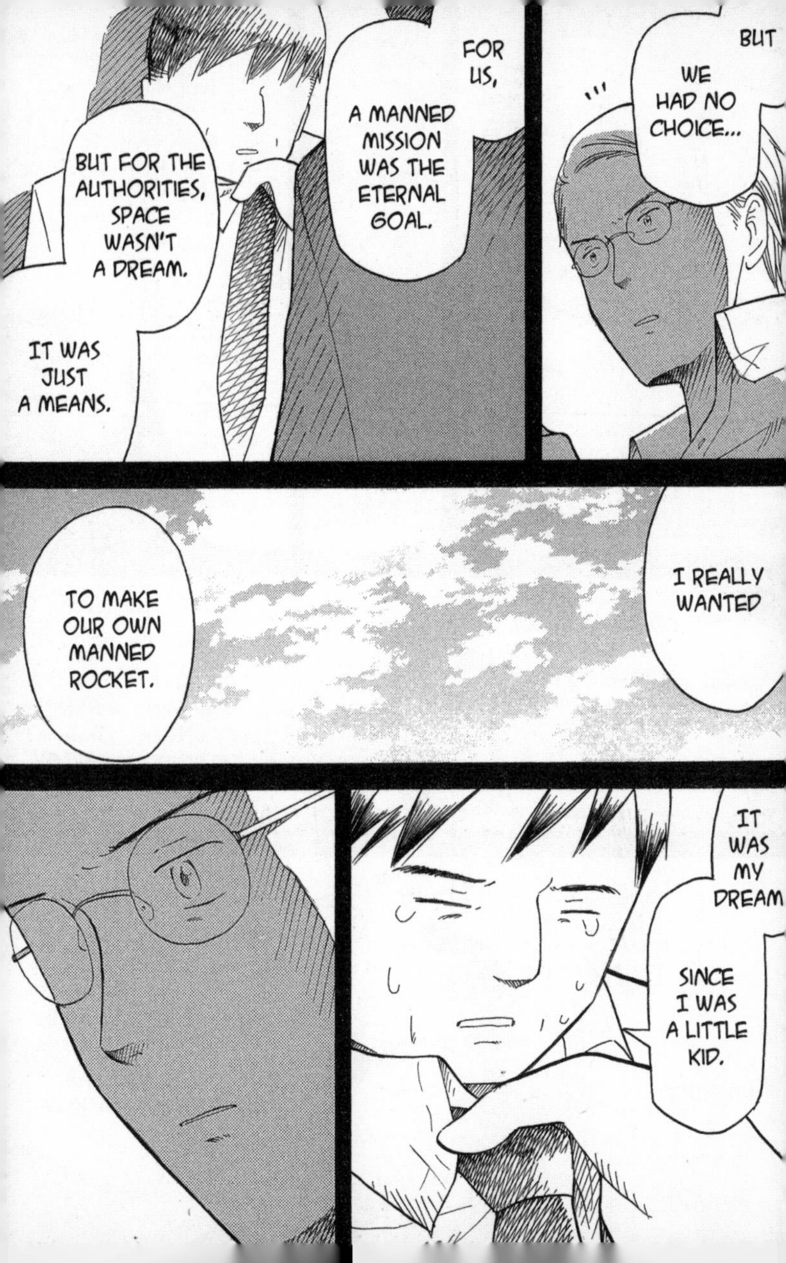
BUT
WE HAD NO CHOICE...
FOR US,
A MANNED MISSION WAS THE ETERNAL GOAL.
BUT FOR THE AUTHORITIES, SPACE WASN'T A DREAM.
IT WAS JUST A MEANS.
I REALLY WANTED
TO MAKE OUR OWN MANNED ROCKET.
IT WAS MY DREAM
SINCE I WAS A LITTLE KID.

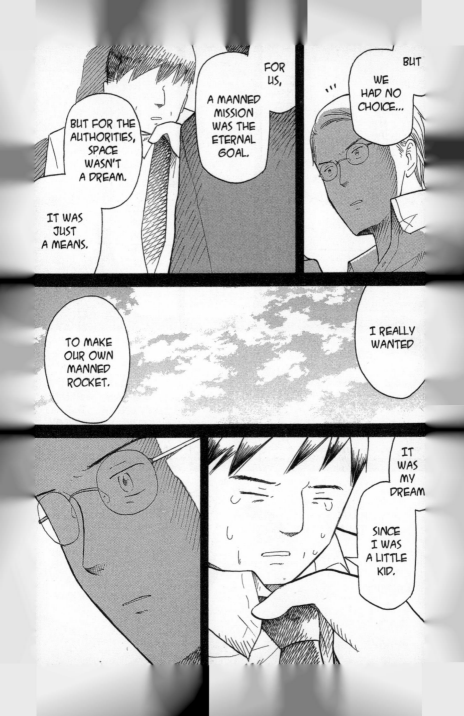

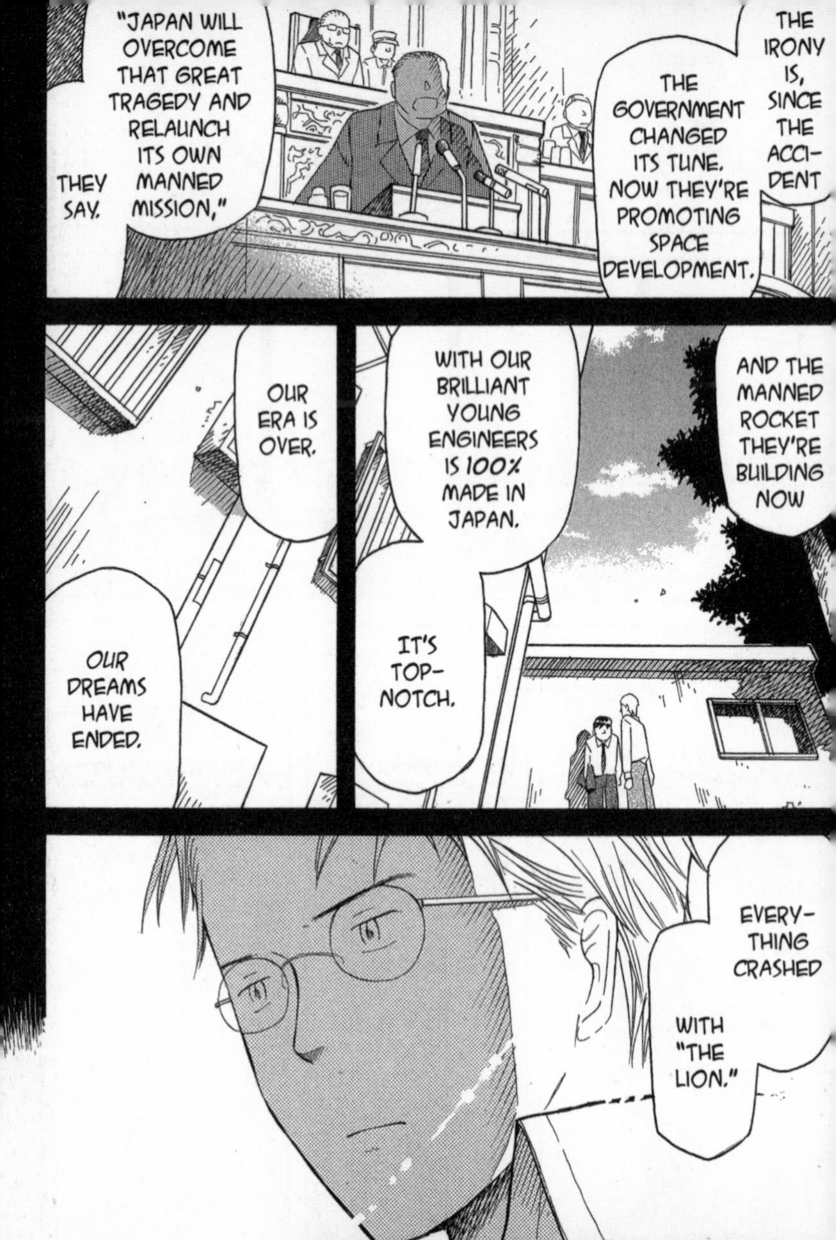
THE IRONY IS, SINCE THE ACCIDENT
THE GOVERNMENT CHANGED ITS TUNE. NOW THEY'RE PROMOTING SPACE DEVELOPMENT.
"JAPAN WILL OVERCOME THAT GREAT TRAGEDY AND RELAUNCH ITS OWN MANNED MISSION,"
THEY SAY.
AND THE MANNED ROCKET THEY'RE BUILDING NOW
WITH OUR BRILLIANT YOUNG ENGINEERS IS 100% MADE IN JAPAN.
IT'S TOP-NOTCH.
OUR ERA IS OVER.
OUR DREAMS HAVE ENDED.
EVERY-THING CRASHED
WITH "THE LION."

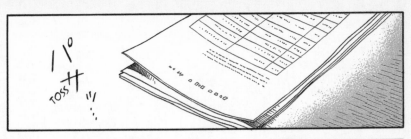

TOSS
YOU WERE INVOLVED WITH "THE LION."
I HEAR YOU WERE THE OFFICIAL WHO COERCED THEM
INTO USING FOREIGN ENGINE TECH.
WHAT A WAY TO PUT IT.
YOU CAME ALL THE WAY HERE TO SAY THAT,
DR. SANO?
THE ENGINEERS ON THE PROJECT WERE TOO GREEN.
I JUST WANTED TO HELP.
MY HANDS ARE CLEAN.
!

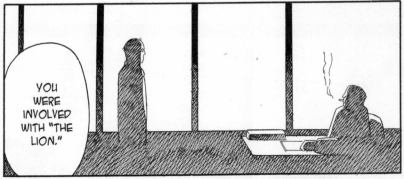

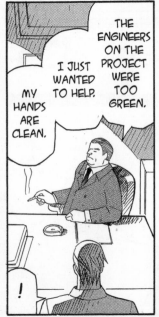

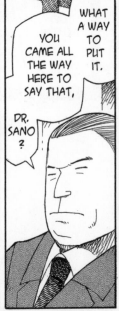

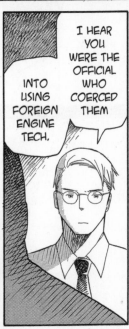

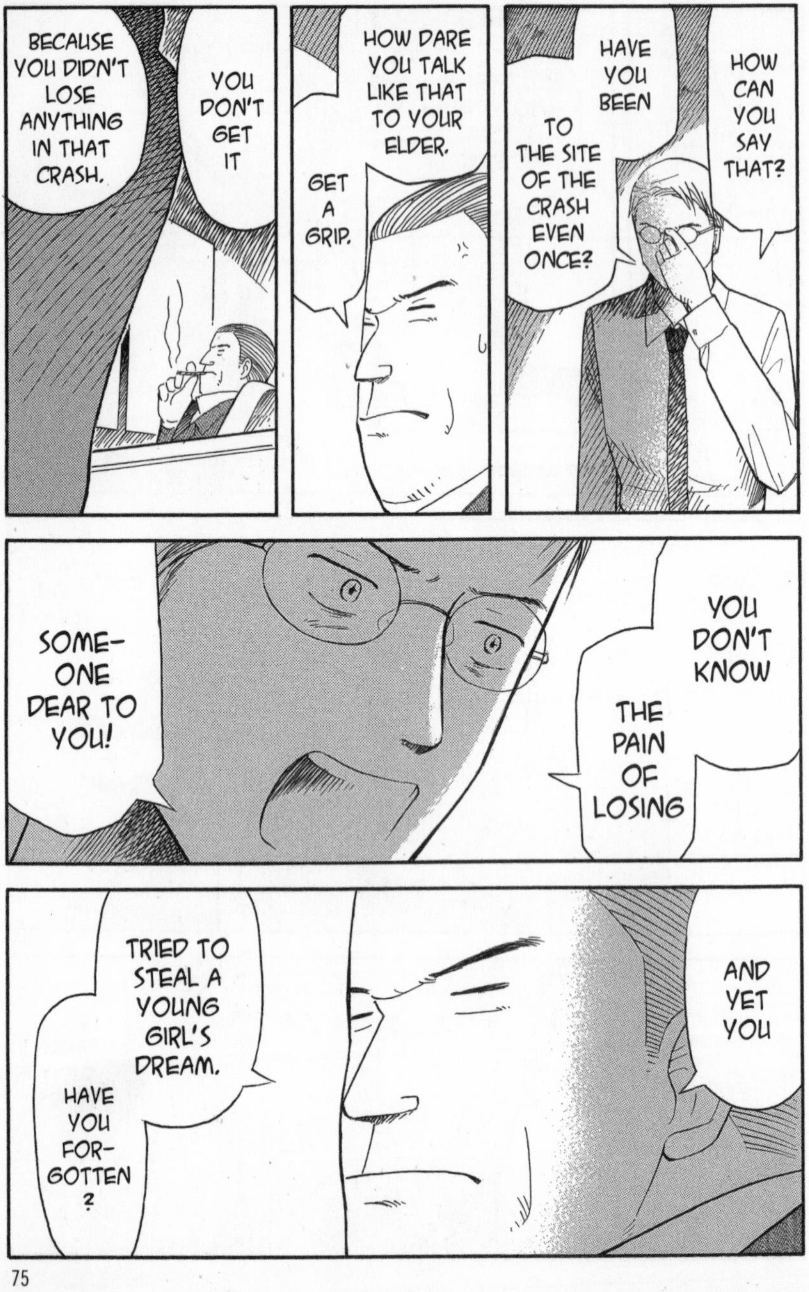
HOW CAN YOU SAY THAT?
HAVE YOU BEEN
TO THE SITE OF THE CRASH EVEN ONCE?
HOW DARE YOU TALK LIKE THAT TO YOUR ELDER.
GET A GRIP.
YOU DON'T GET IT
BECAUSE YOU DIDN'T LOSE ANYTHING IN THAT CRASH.
YOU DON'T KNOW
THE PAIN OF LOSING
SOME-ONE DEAR TO YOU!
AND YET YOU
TRIED TO STEAL A YOUNG GIRL'S DREAM.
HAVE YOU FOR-GOTTEN ?

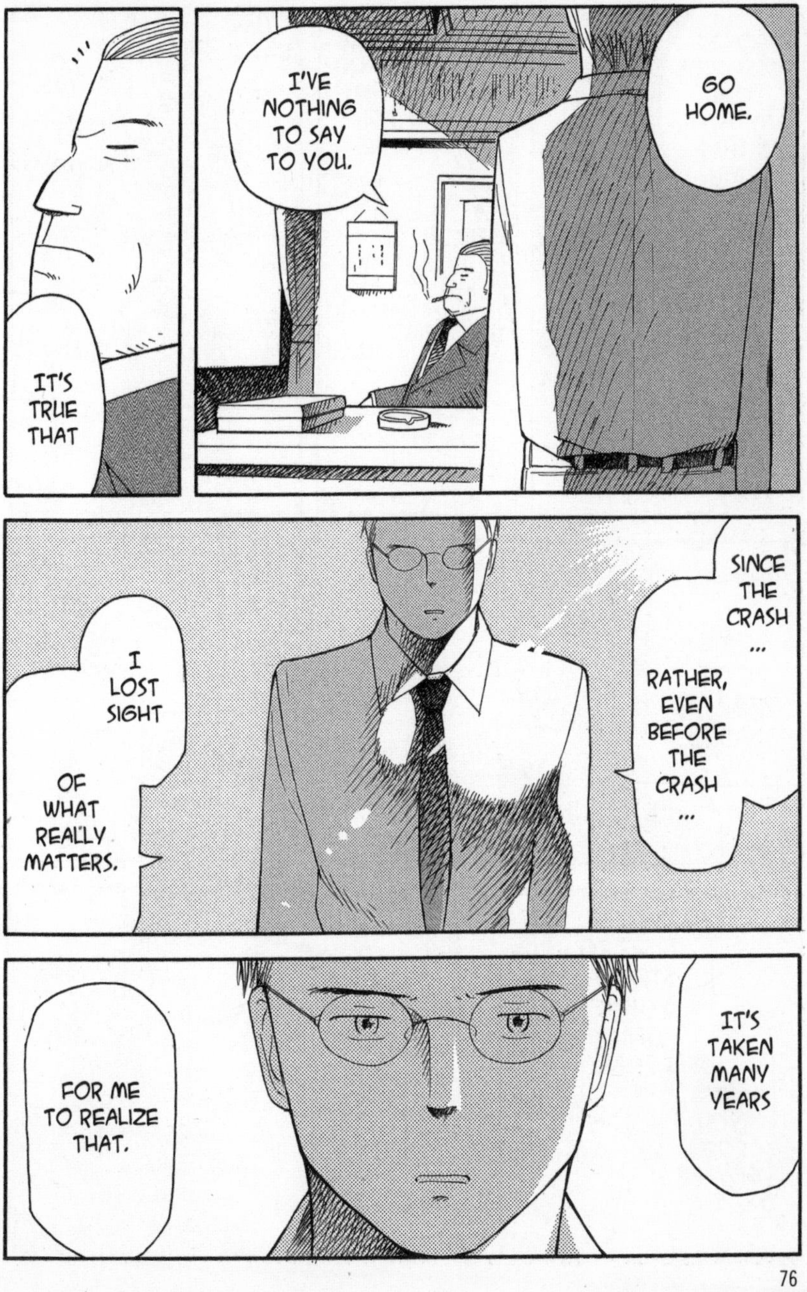
GO HOME.
I'VE NOTHING TO SAY TO YOU.
IT'S TRUE THAT
SINCE THE CRASH ...
RATHER, EVEN BEFORE THE CRASH ...
I LOST SIGHT
OF WHAT REALLY MATTERS.
IT'S TAKEN MANY YEARS
FOR ME TO REALIZE THAT.

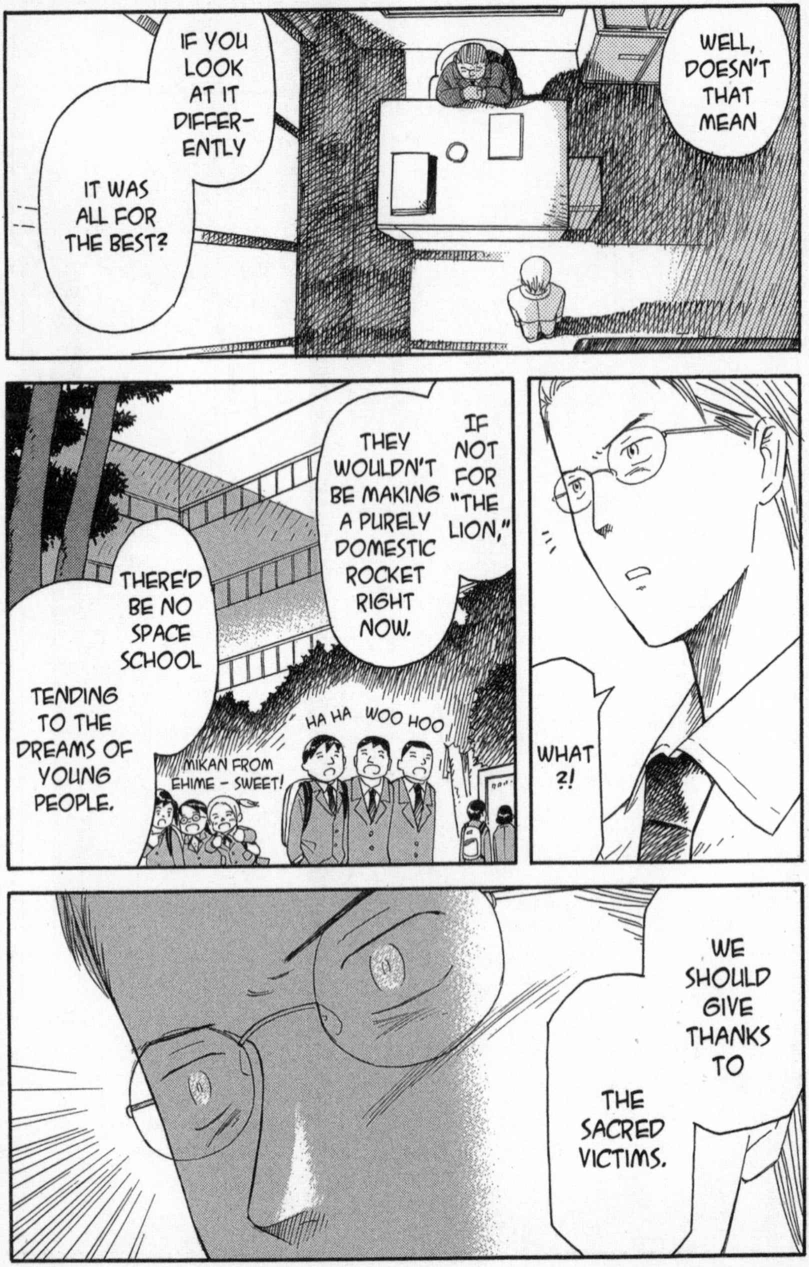
WELL, DOESN'T THAT MEAN
IF YOU LOOK AT IT DIFFER-ENTLY
IT WAS ALL FOR THE BEST?
WHAT?!
IF NOT FOR "THE LION,"
THEY WOULDN'T BE MAKING A PURELY DOMESTIC ROCKET RIGHT NOW.
THERE'D BE NO SPACE SCHOOL
TENDING TO THE DREAMS OF YOUNG PEOPLE.
HA HA WOO HOO
MIKAN FROM EHIME - SWEET!
WE SHOULD GIVE THANKS TO
THE SACRED VICTIMS.

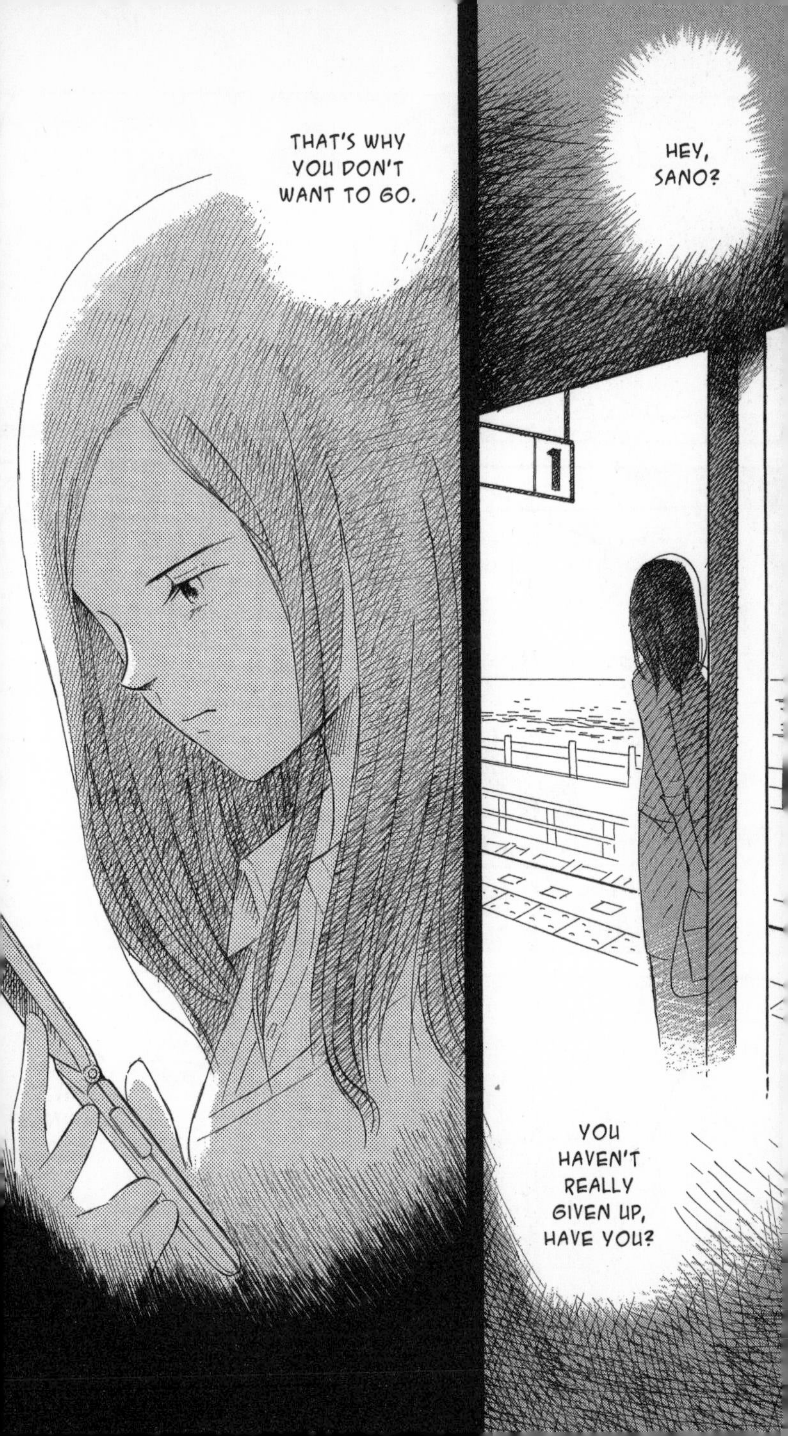
HEY, SANO?
YOU HAVEN'T REALLY GIVEN UP, HAVE YOU?
THAT'S WHY YOU DON'T WANT TO GO.

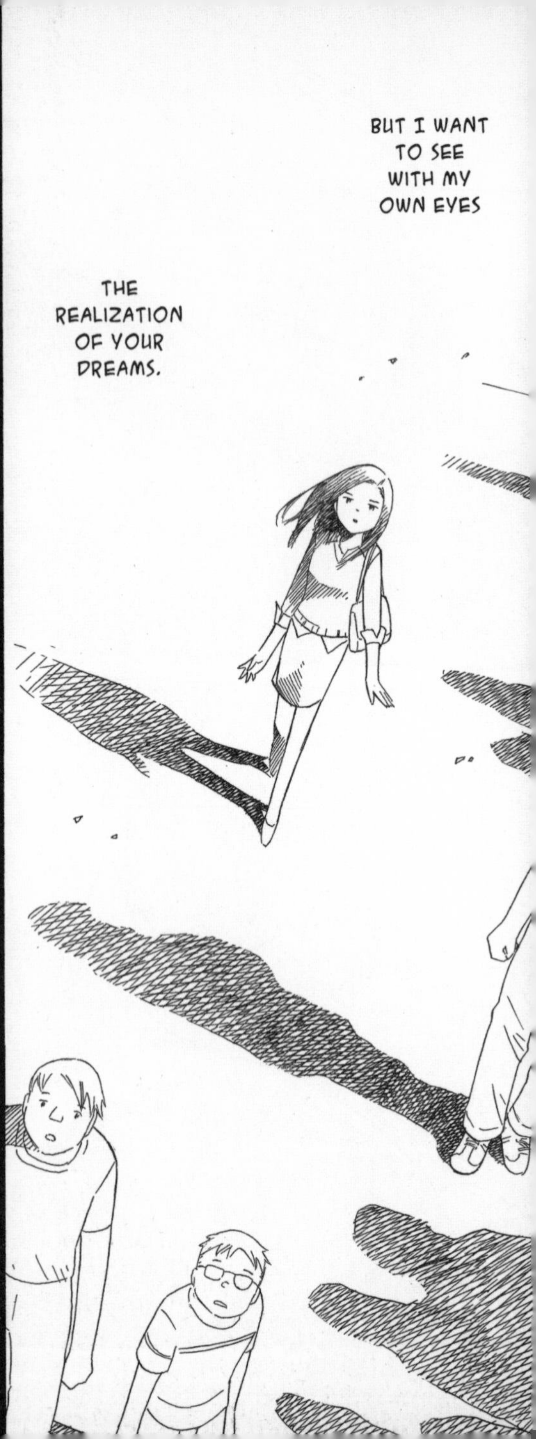
BUT I WANT TO SEE WITH MY OWN EYES
THE REALIZATION OF YOUR DREAMS.

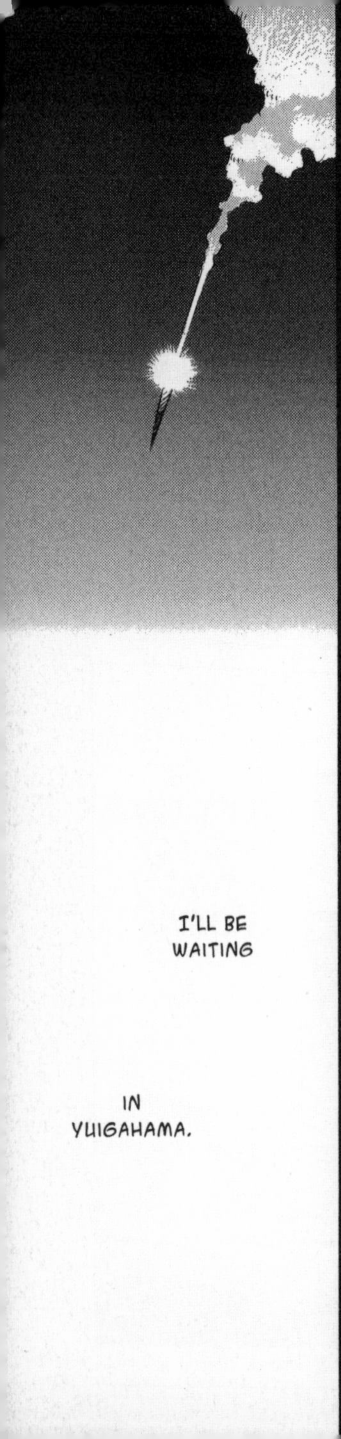
I'LL BE WAITING
IN YUIGAHAMA.

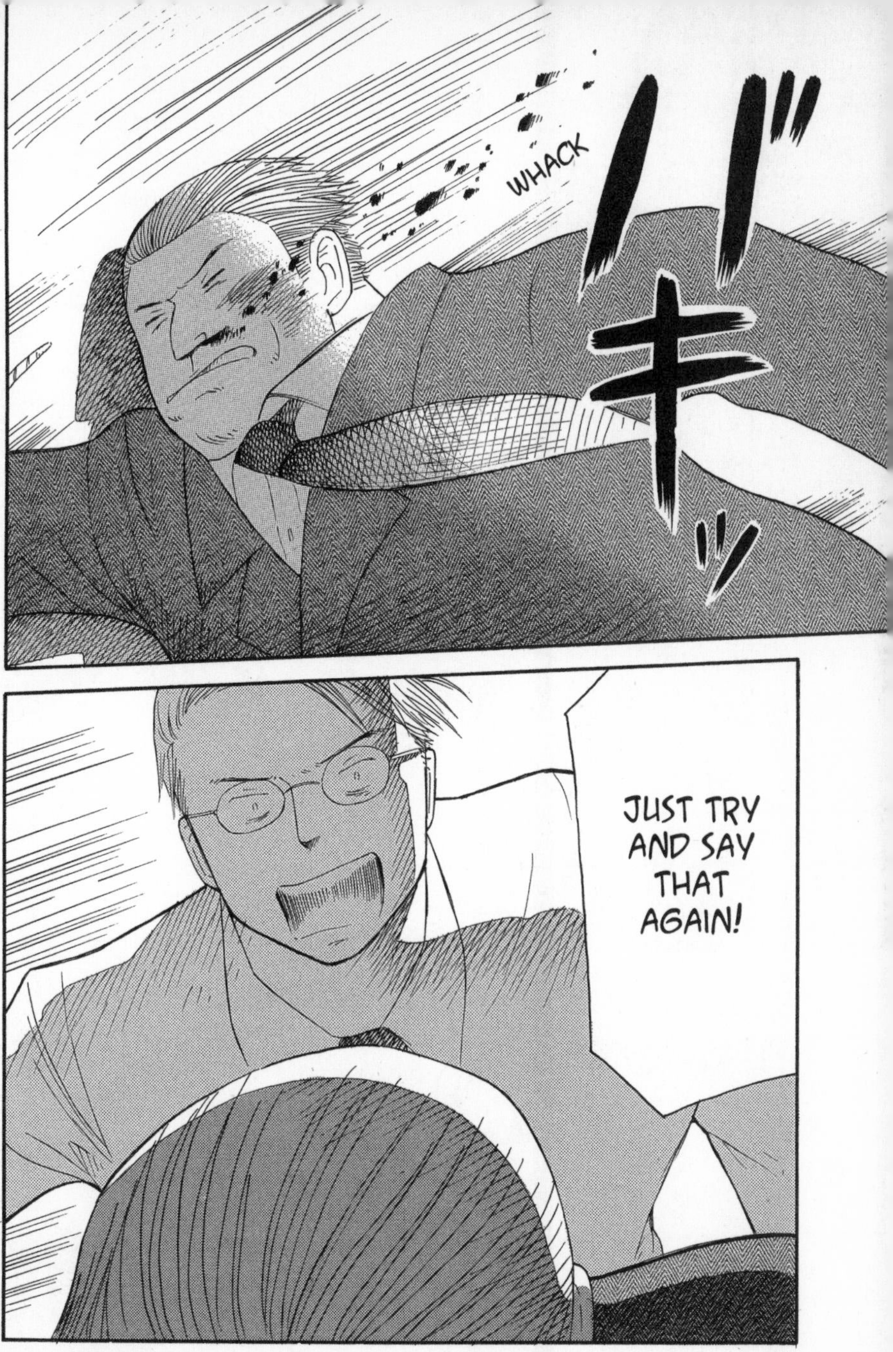
WHACK
JUST TRY AND SAY THAT AGAIN!

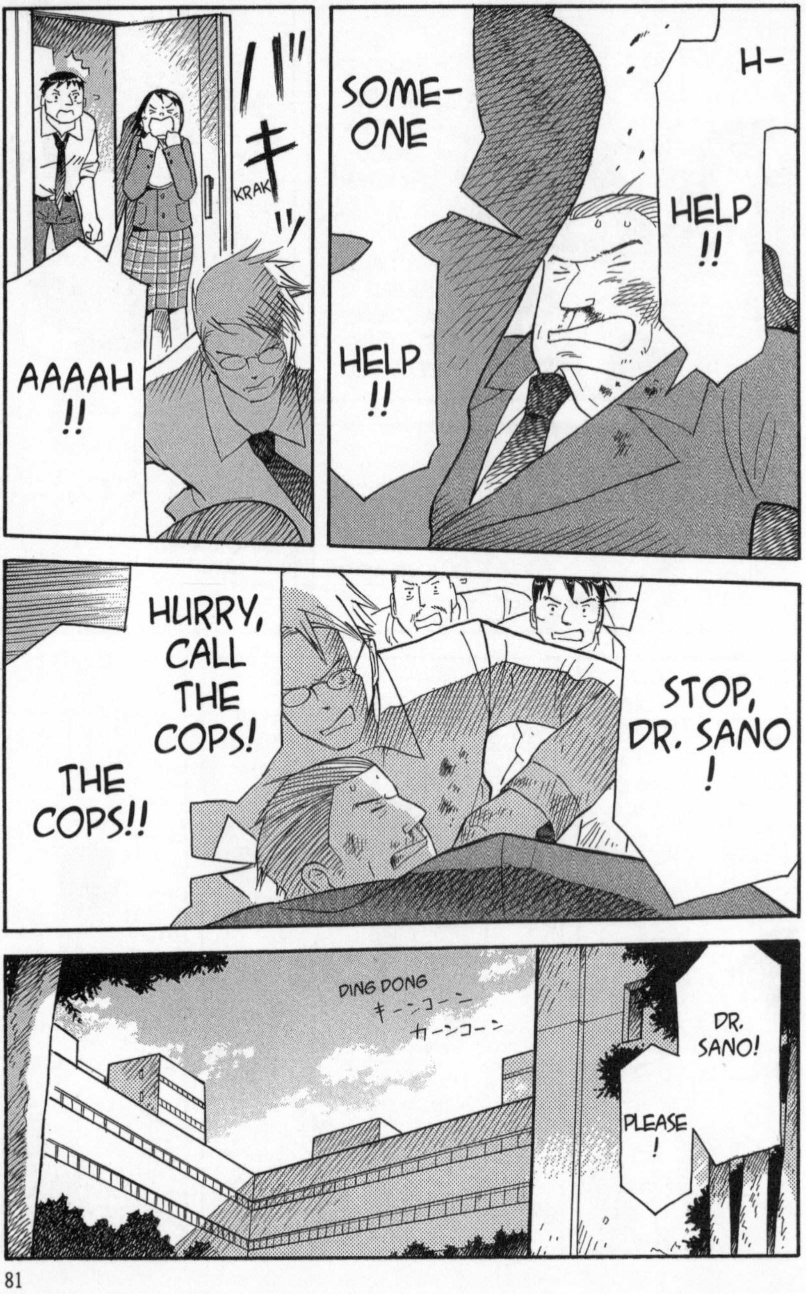
H-
HELP!!
SOME-ONE
HELP!!
バキッ
KRAK
AAAAH!!
STOP, DR. SANO!
HURRY, CALL THE COPS!
THE COPS!!
DR. SANO!
PLEASE!
DING DONG
キーンコーン
カーンコーン

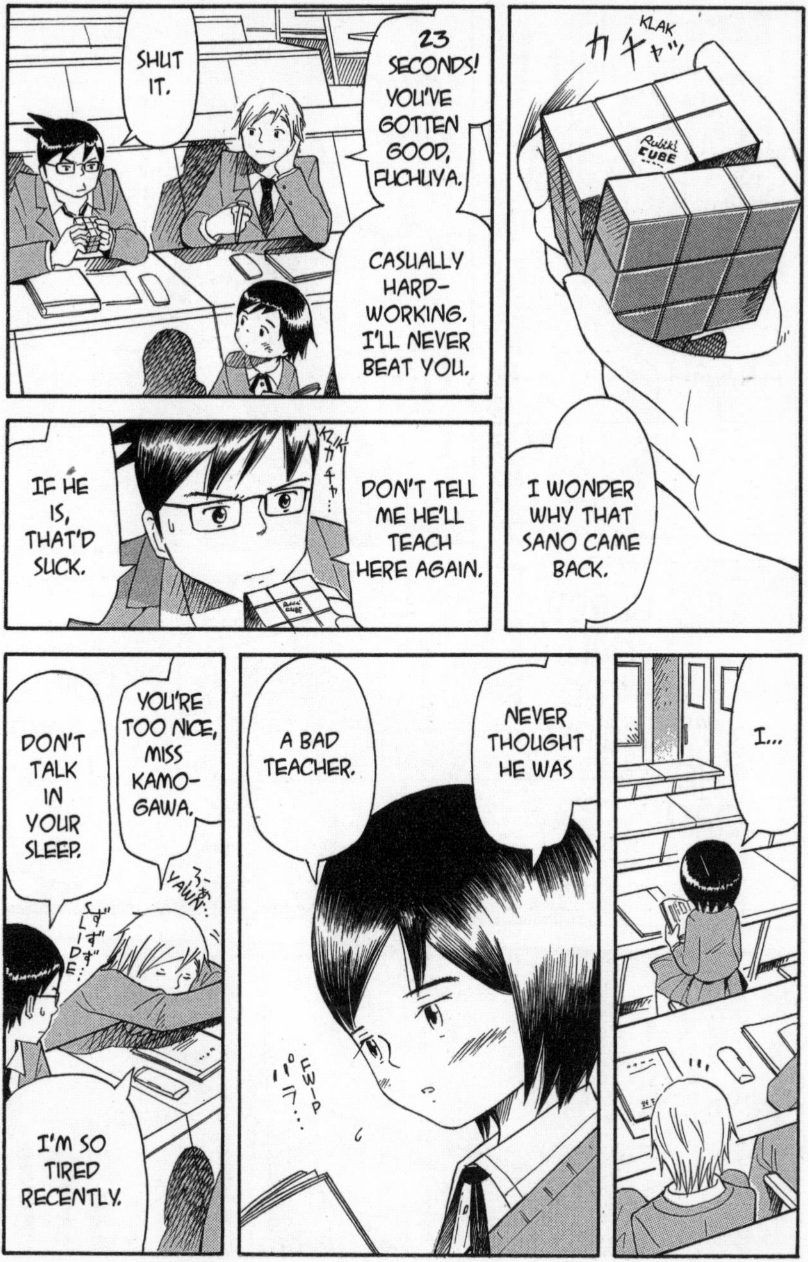
KLAK
I WONDER WHY THAT SANO CAME BACK.
23 SECONDS! YOU'VE GOTTEN GOOD, FUCHUYA.
CASUALLY HARD-WORKING. I'LL NEVER BEAT YOU.
SHUT IT.
KLIK
DON'T TELL ME HE'LL TEACH HERE AGAIN.
IF HE IS, THAT'D SUCK.
I...
NEVER THOUGHT HE WAS
A BAD TEACHER.
FWIP
YOU'RE TOO NICE, MISS KAMO-GAWA.
YAWN
DON'T TALK IN YOUR SLEEP.
SLIDE
I'M SO TIRED RECENTLY.

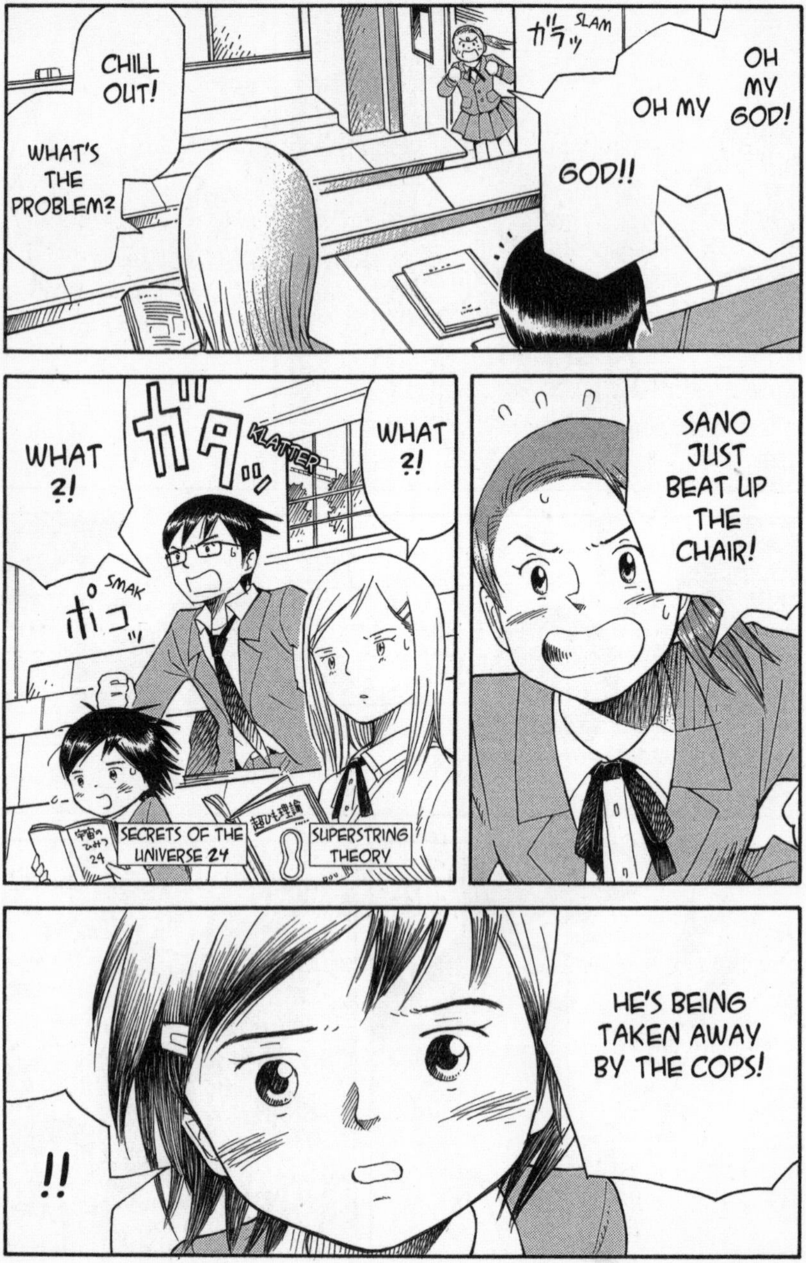

ガラッ SLAM
OH MY GOD!
OH MY GOD!!
CHILL OUT!
WHAT'S THE PROBLEM?
SANO JUST BEAT UP THE CHAIR!
WHAT?!
ガタッ KLATTER
WHAT?!
ポコッ SMAK
超ひも理論
SUPERSTRING THEORY
宇宙のひみつ 24
SECRETS OF THE UNIVERSE 24
HE'S BEING TAKEN AWAY BY THE COPS!
!!

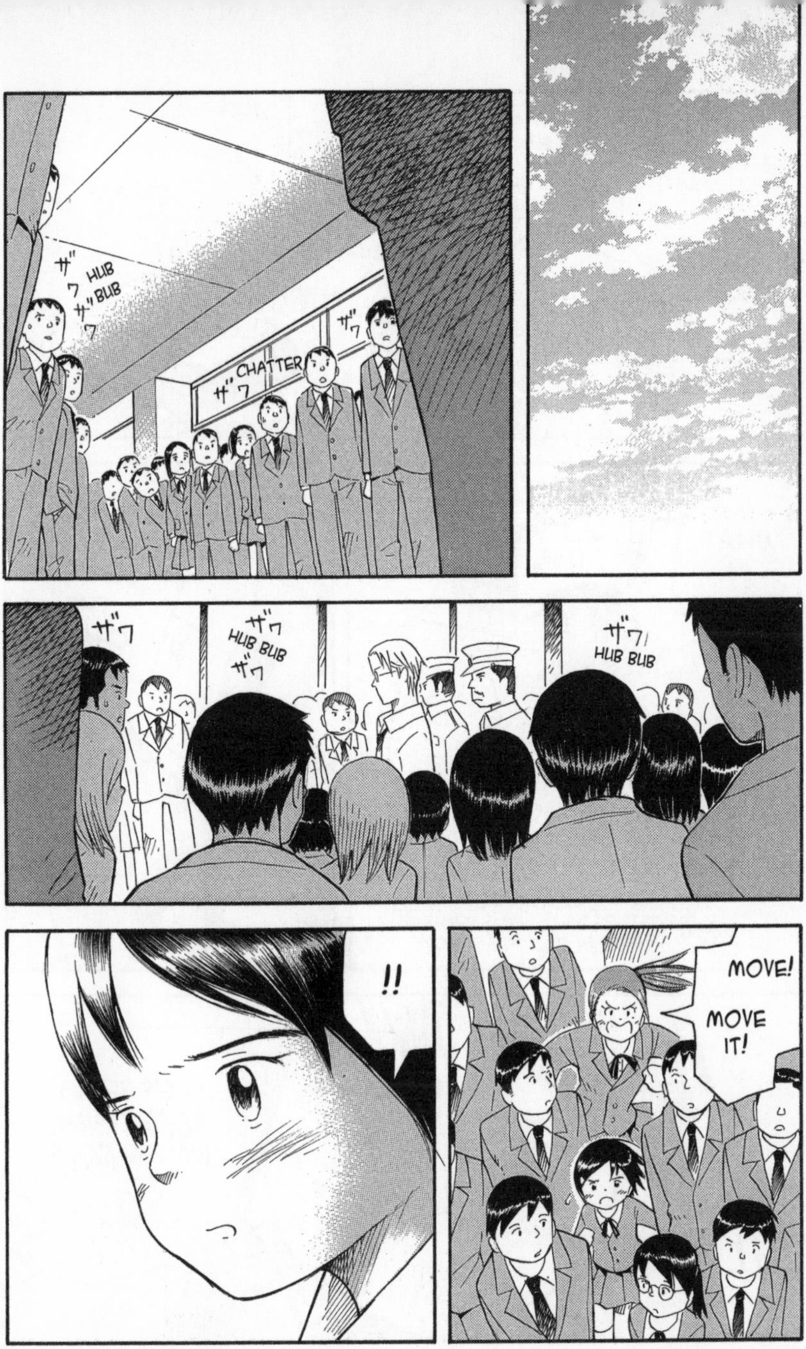
ザワ
ザワ
HUB BUB
ザワ
CHATTER
ザワ
ザワ!
HUB BUB
ザワ
HUB BUB
ザワ
ザワ
MOVE!
MOVE IT!
!!

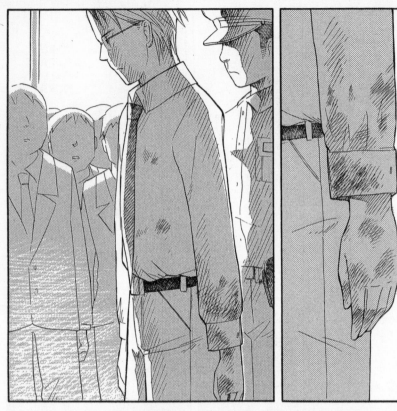

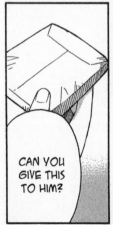

CAN YOU GIVE THIS TO HIM?

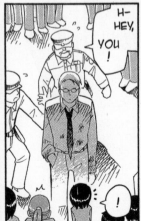

H— HEY, YOU!

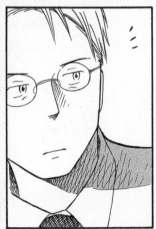

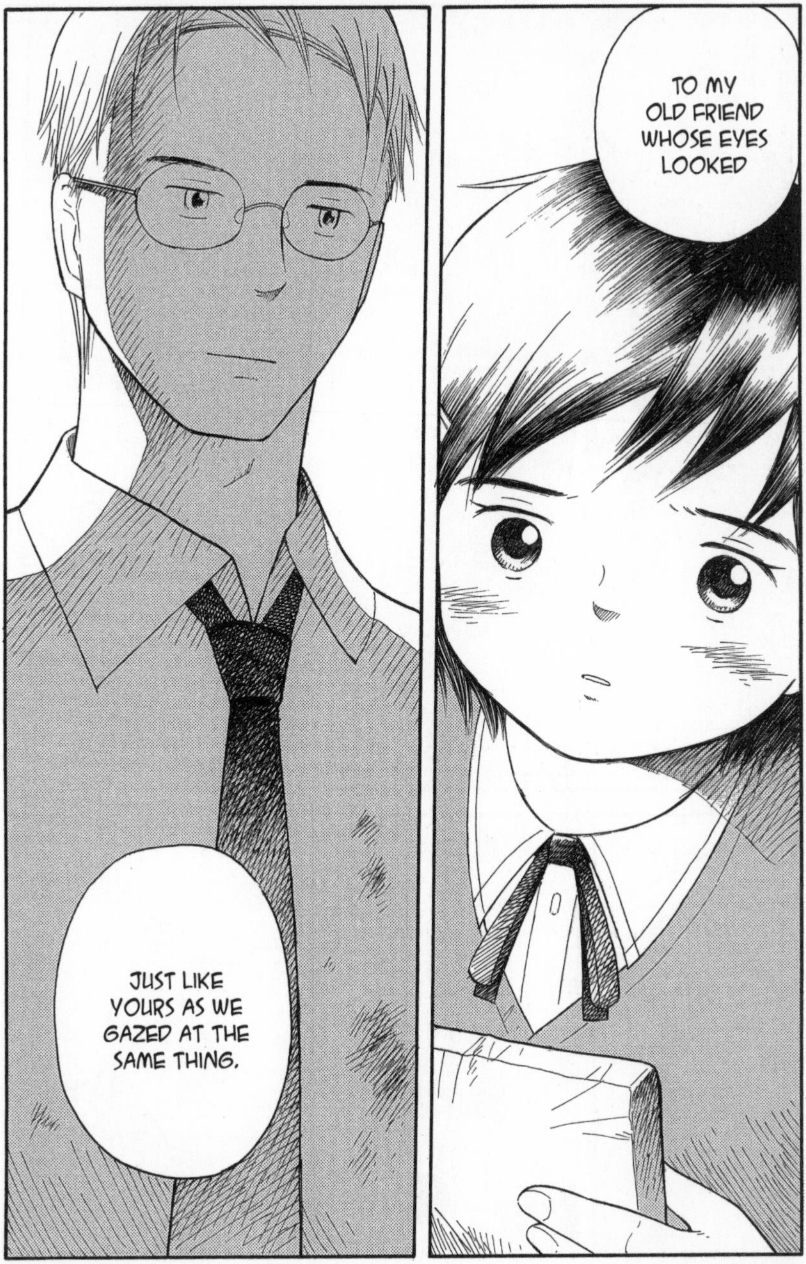
TO MY OLD FRIEND WHOSE EYES LOOKED
JUST LIKE YOURS AS WE GAZED AT THE SAME THING.

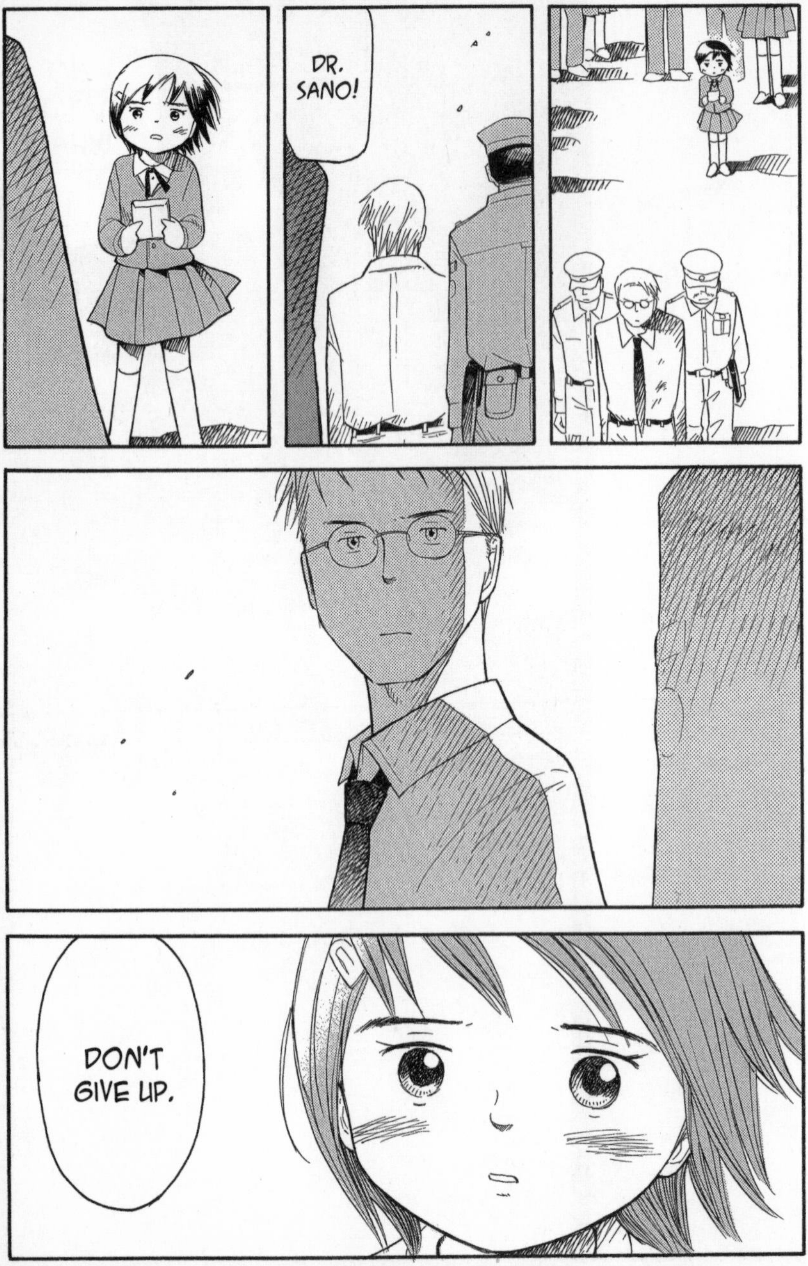
DR. SANO!
DON'T GIVE UP.

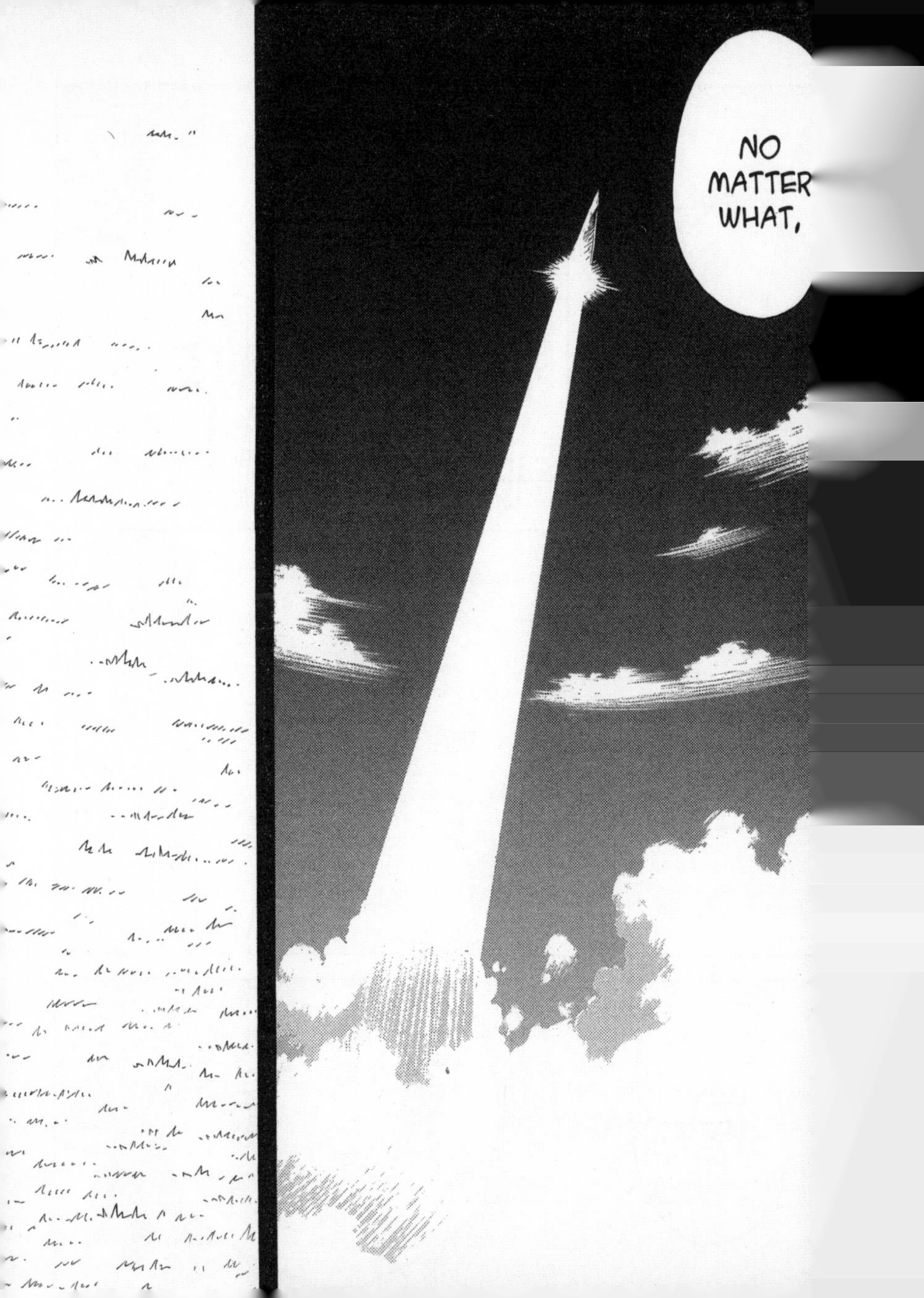
NO MATTER WHAT,

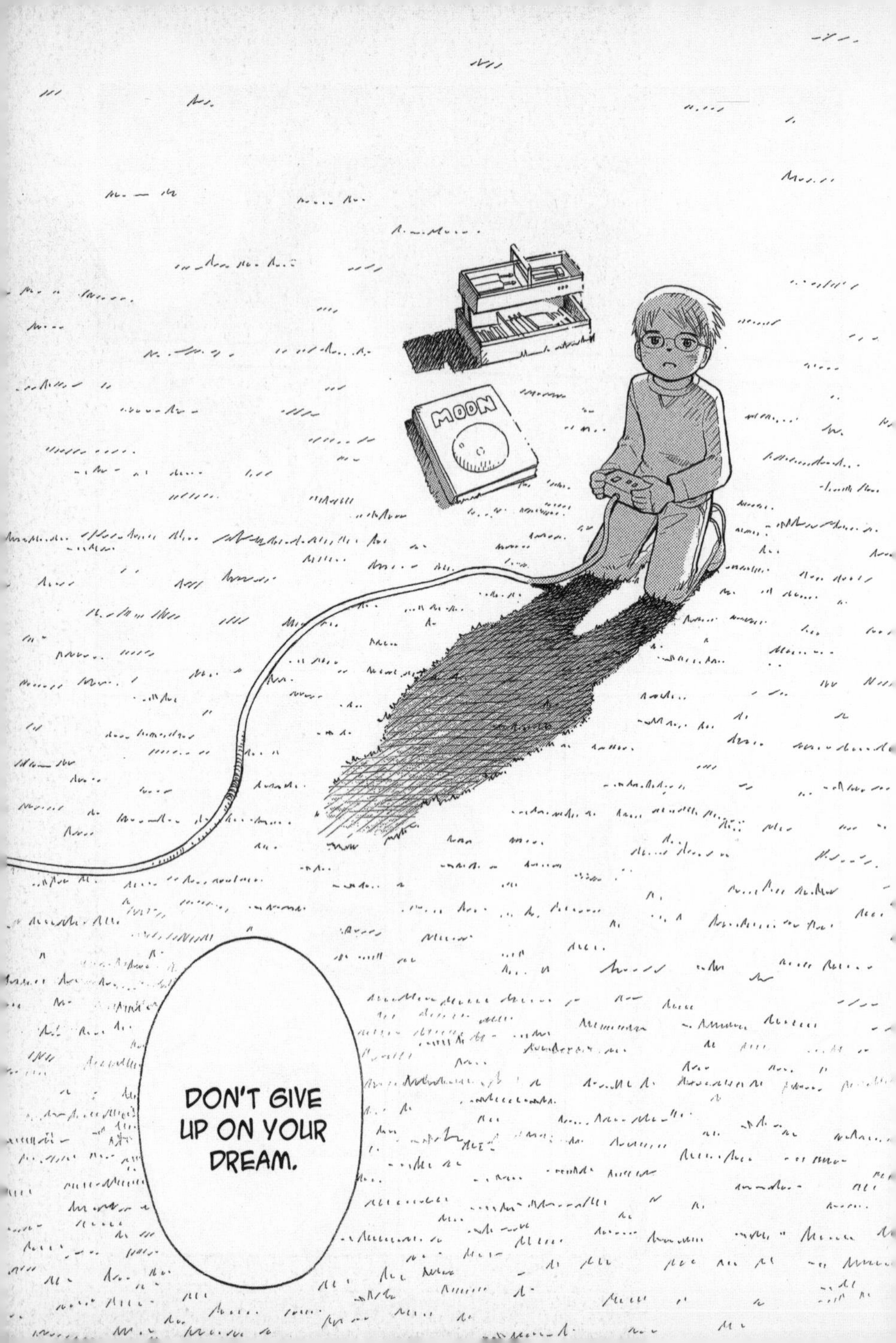
MOON
DON'T GIVE UP ON YOUR DREAM.

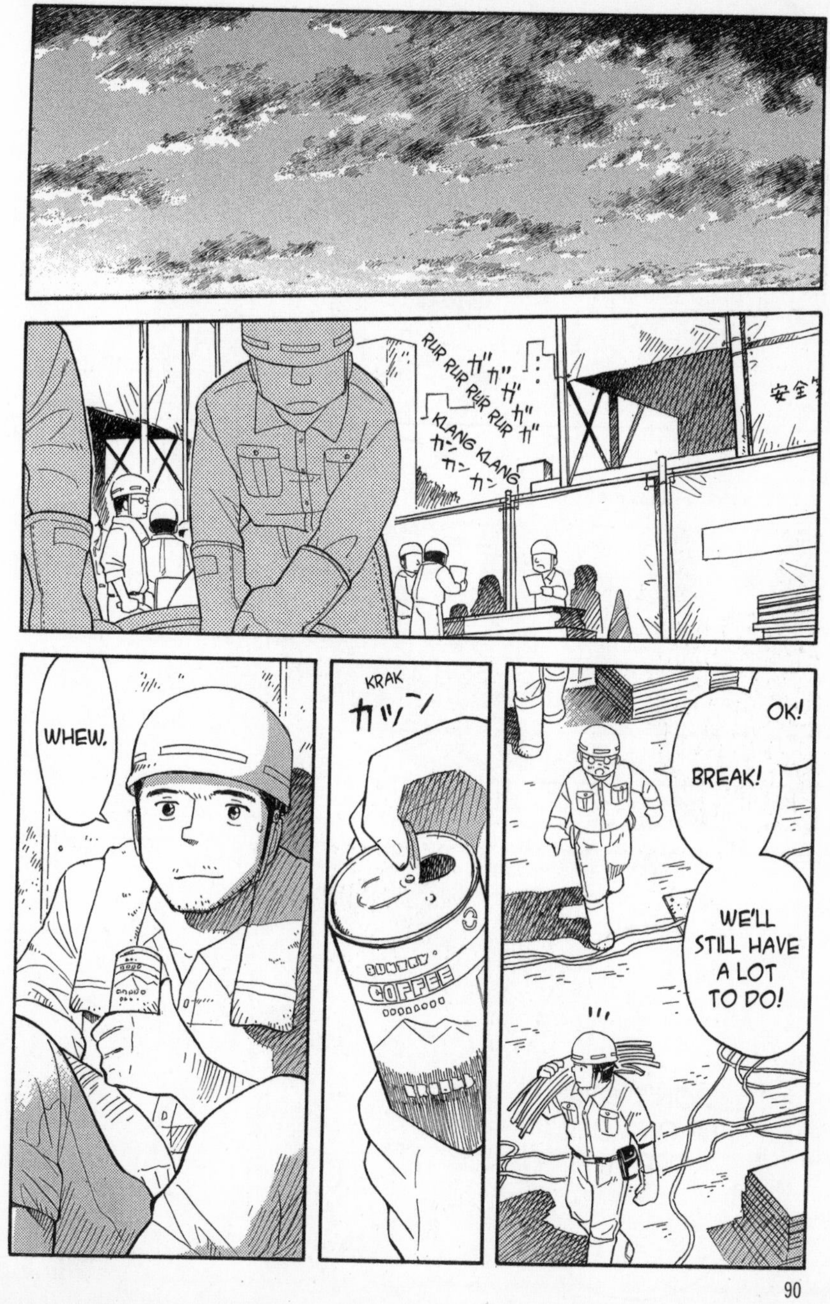
RUR RUR RUR RUR
ガガガガガ
KLANG KLANG
カンカンカン
安全
OK!
BREAK!
WE'LL STILL HAVE A LOT TO DO!
KRAK
カッン
COFFEE
WHEW.

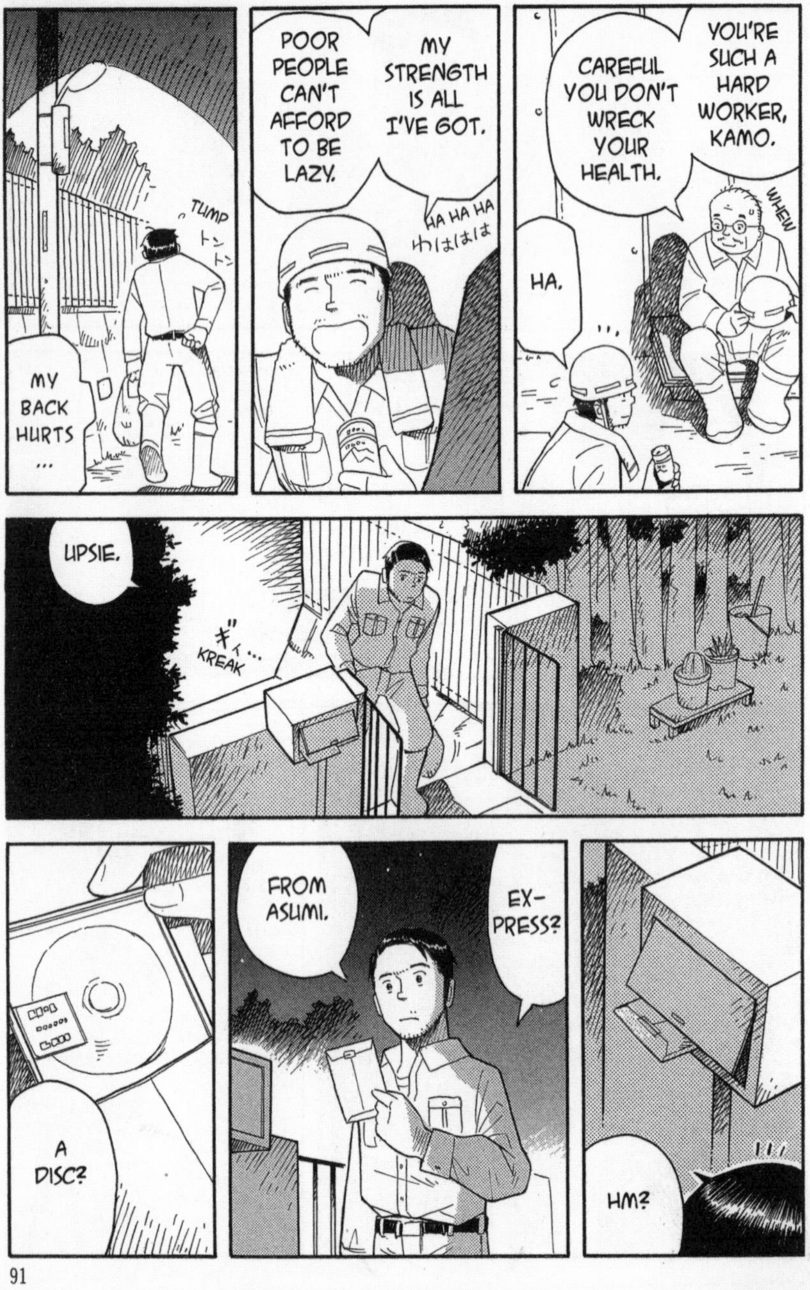
YOU'RE SUCH A HARD WORKER, KAMO.
CAREFUL YOU DON'T WRECK YOUR HEALTH.
WHEW
HA.
MY STRENGTH IS ALL I'VE GOT.
POOR PEOPLE CAN'T AFFORD TO BE LAZY.
HA HA HA
わははは
TUMP
トントン
MY BACK HURTS ...
UPSIE.
ギィ...
KREAK
HM?
EX-PRESS?
FROM ASUMI.
A DISC?

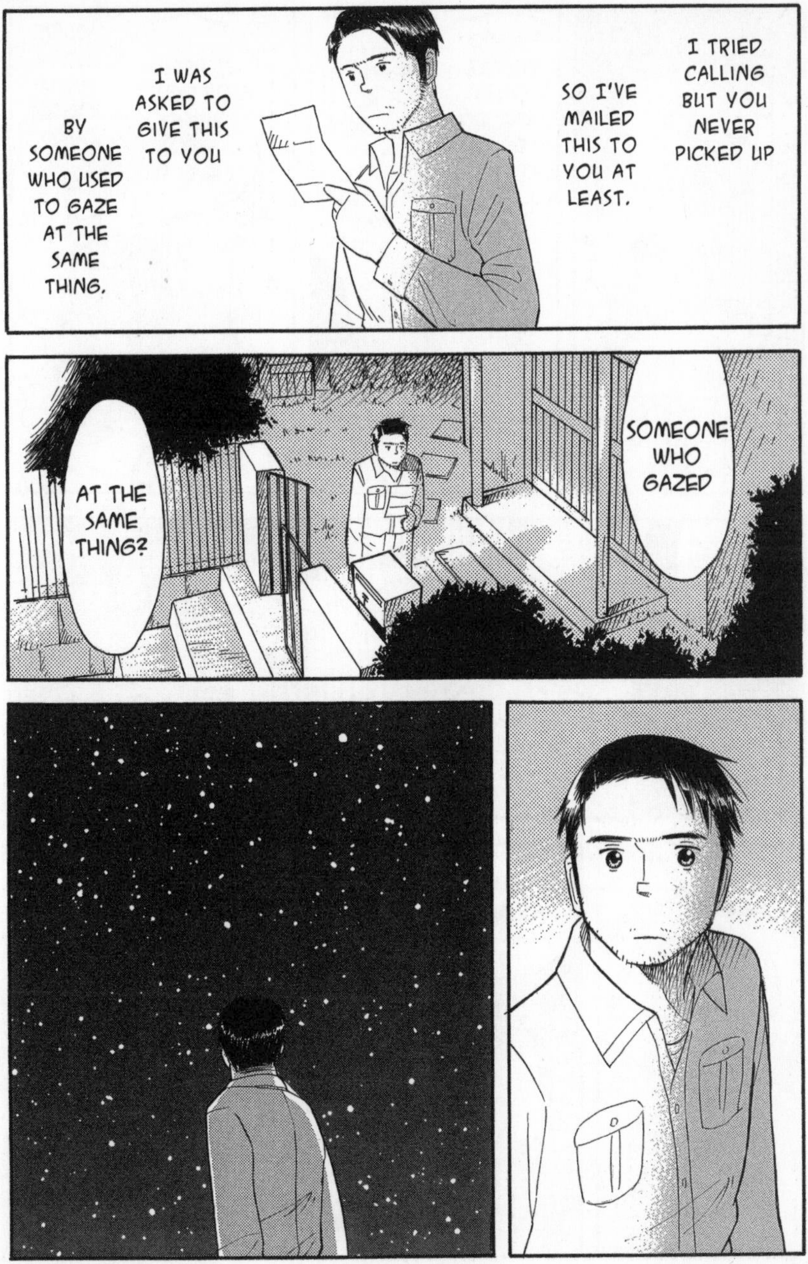
I TRIED CALLING BUT YOU NEVER PICKED UP
SO I'VE MAILED THIS TO YOU AT LEAST.
I WAS ASKED TO GIVE THIS TO YOU
BY SOMEONE WHO USED TO GAZE AT THE SAME THING.
SOMEONE WHO GAZED
AT THE SAME THING?

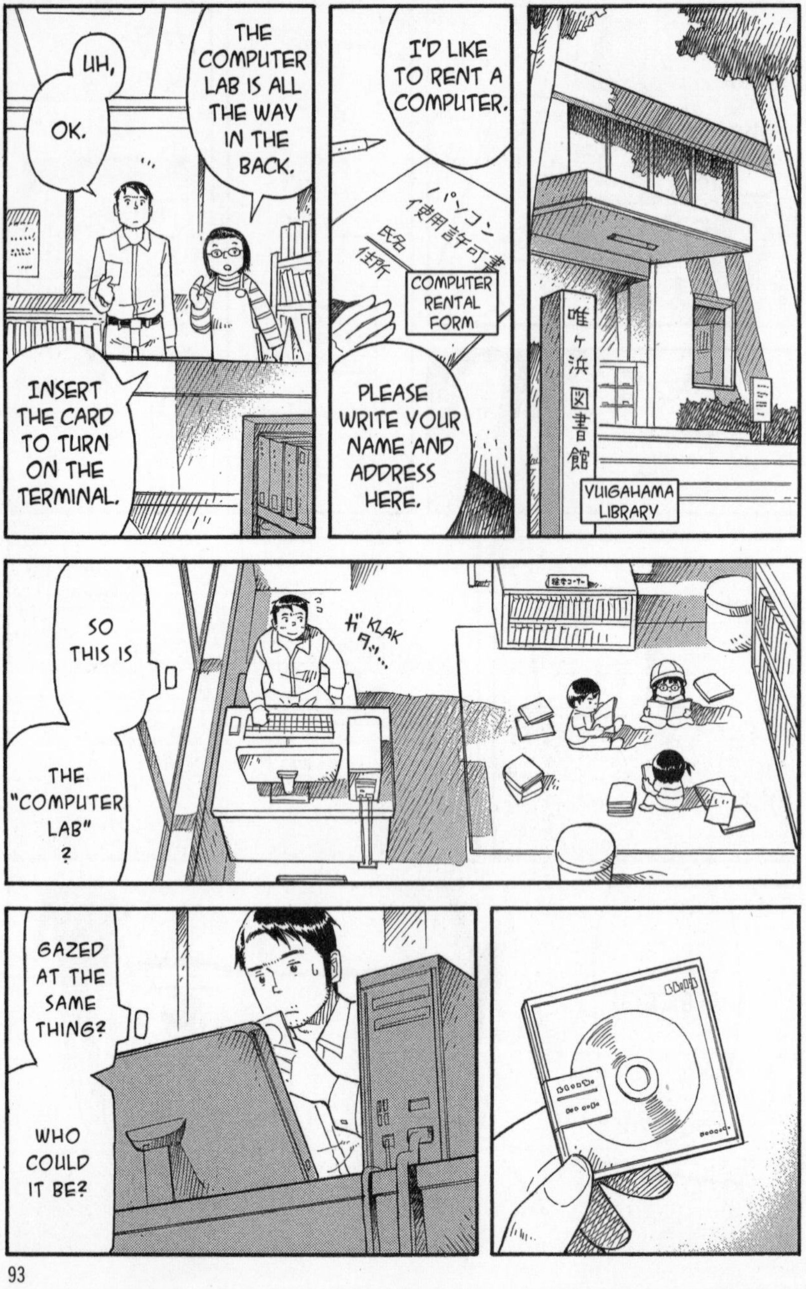
唯ヶ浜図書館
YUIGAHAMA LIBRARY
I'D LIKE TO RENT A COMPUTER.
パソコン使用許可書
氏名
住所
COMPUTER RENTAL FORM
PLEASE WRITE YOUR NAME AND ADDRESS HERE.
THE COMPUTER LAB IS ALL THE WAY IN THE BACK.
UH, OK.
INSERT THE CARD TO TURN ON THE TERMINAL.
KLAK
SO THIS IS THE "COMPUTER LAB"?
GAZED AT THE SAME THING?
WHO COULD IT BE?

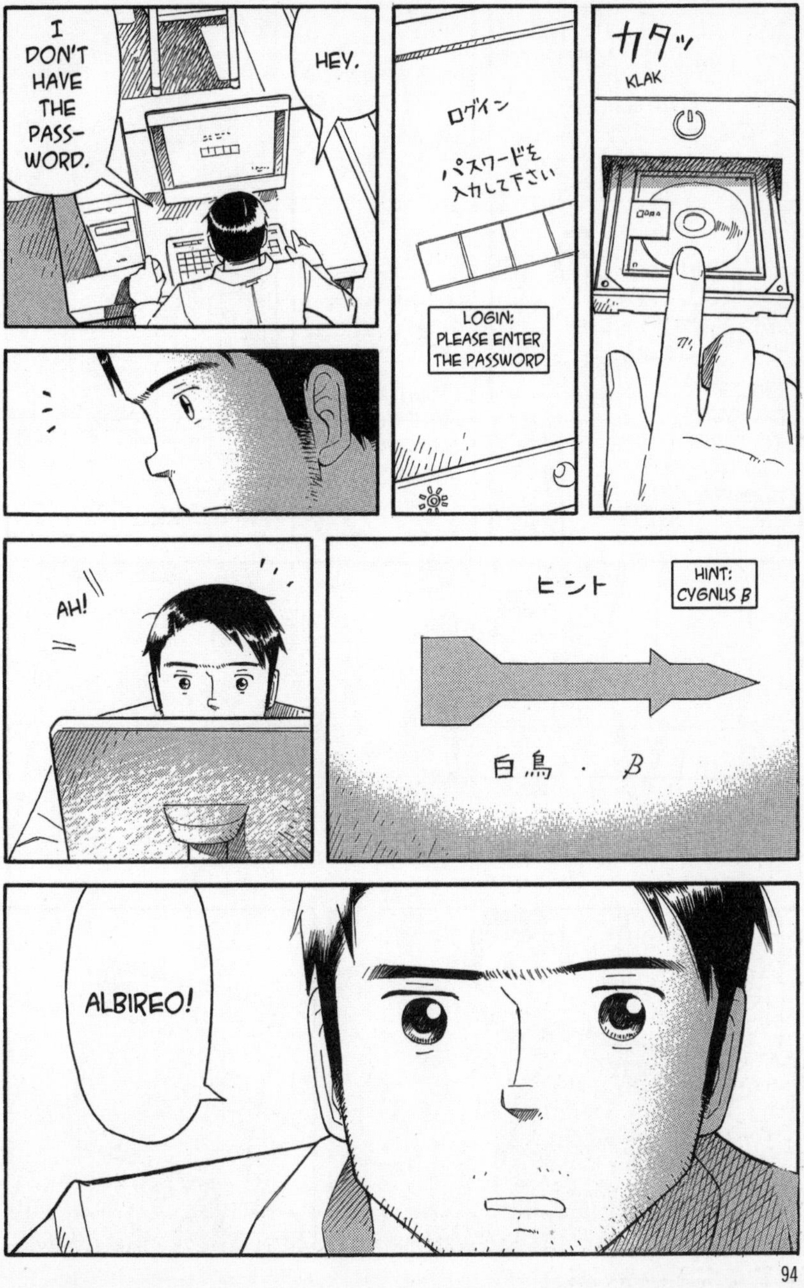
カタッ
KLAK
ログイン
パスワードを
入力して下さい
LOGIN: PLEASE ENTER THE PASSWORD
HEY.
I DON'T HAVE THE PASS-WORD.
ヒント
HINT: CYGNUS β
白鳥・β
AH!
ALBIREO!

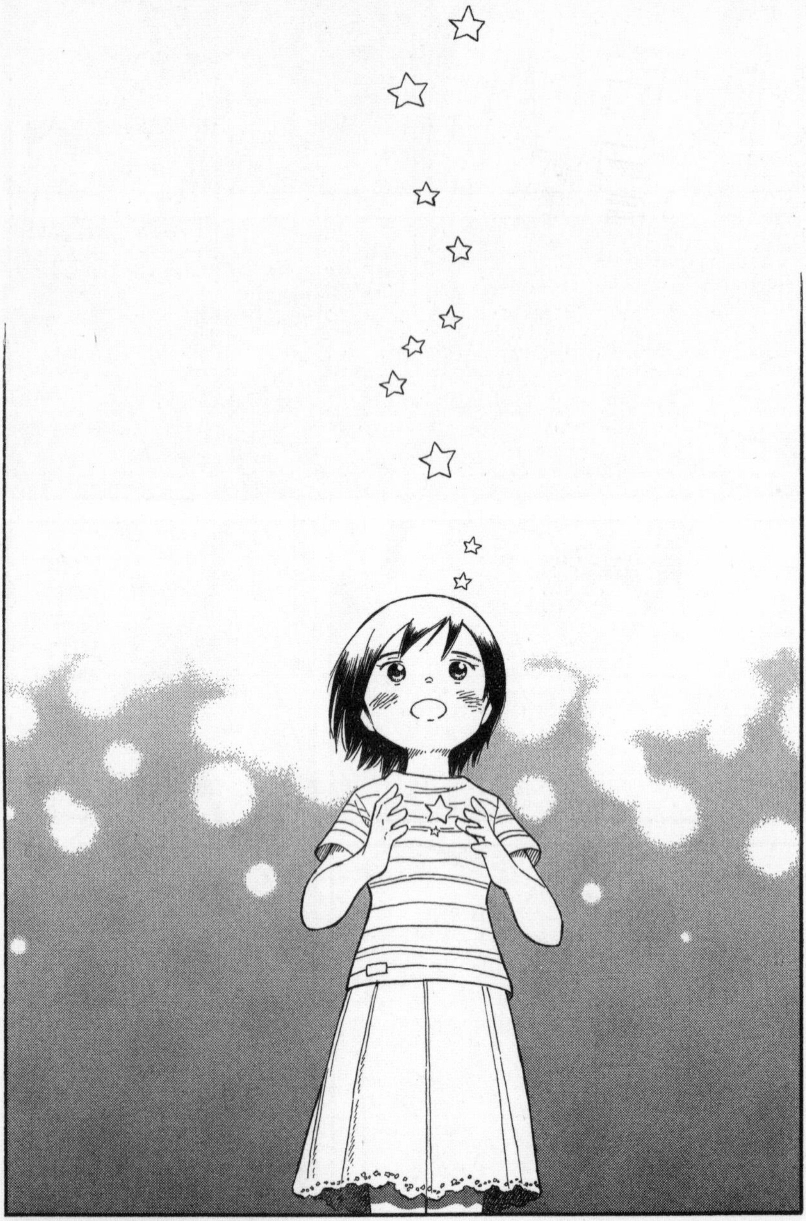

MISSION:50

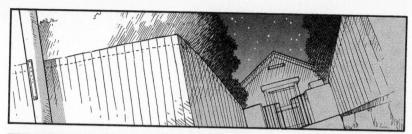

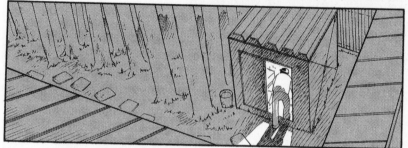

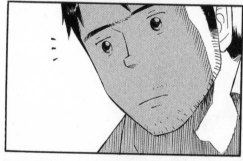

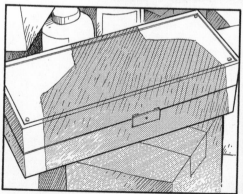

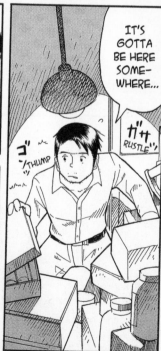

IT'S GOTTA BE HERE SOME- WHERE...

ガサ
RUSTLE

ゴン
THUMP

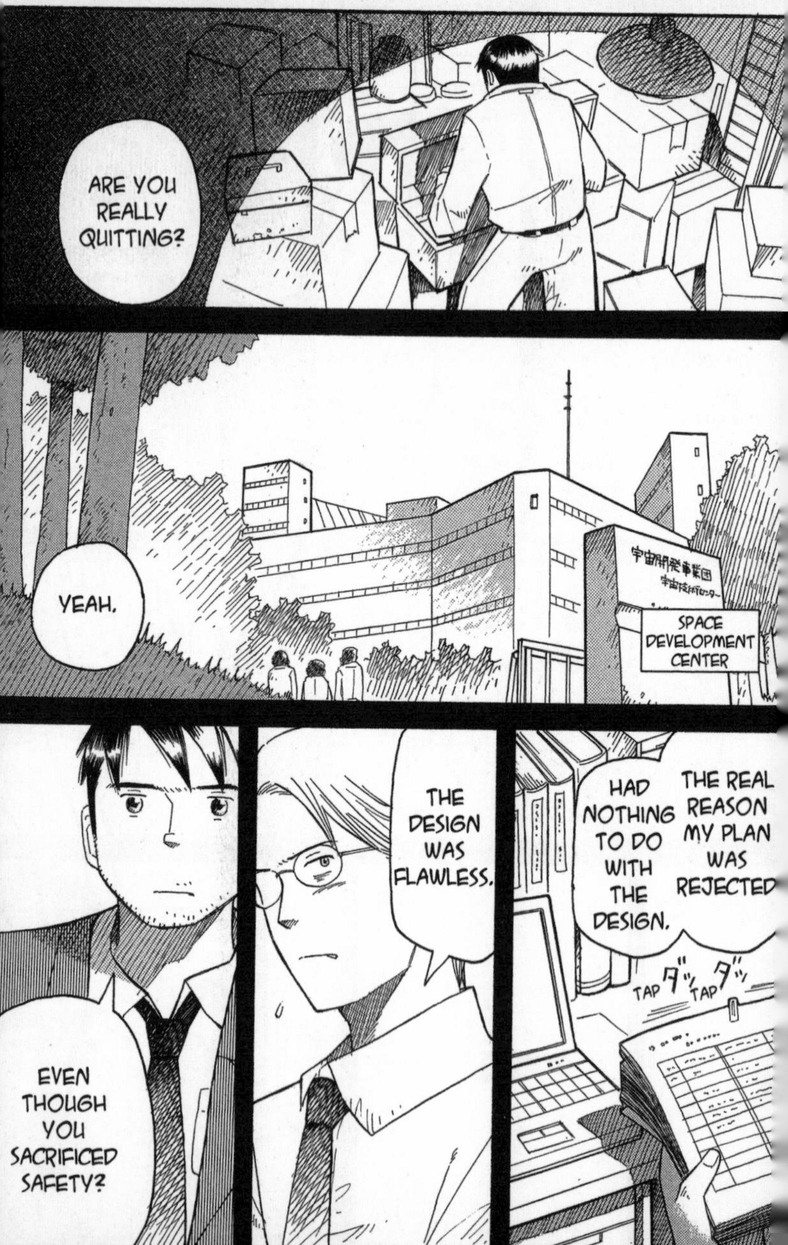
ARE YOU REALLY QUITTING?
YEAH.
宇宙開発事業団
SPACE DEVELOPMENT CENTER
THE REAL REASON MY PLAN WAS REJECTED
HAD NOTHING TO DO WITH THE DESIGN.
TAP ダッ TAP ダッ
THE DESIGN WAS FLAWLESS.
EVEN THOUGH YOU SACRIFICED SAFETY?

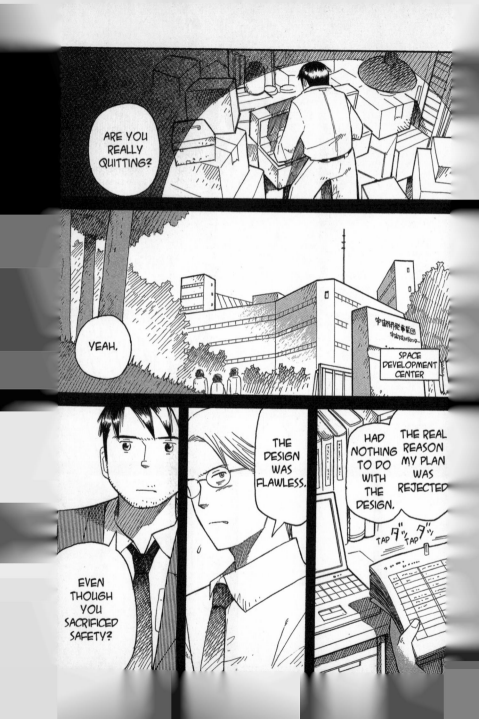

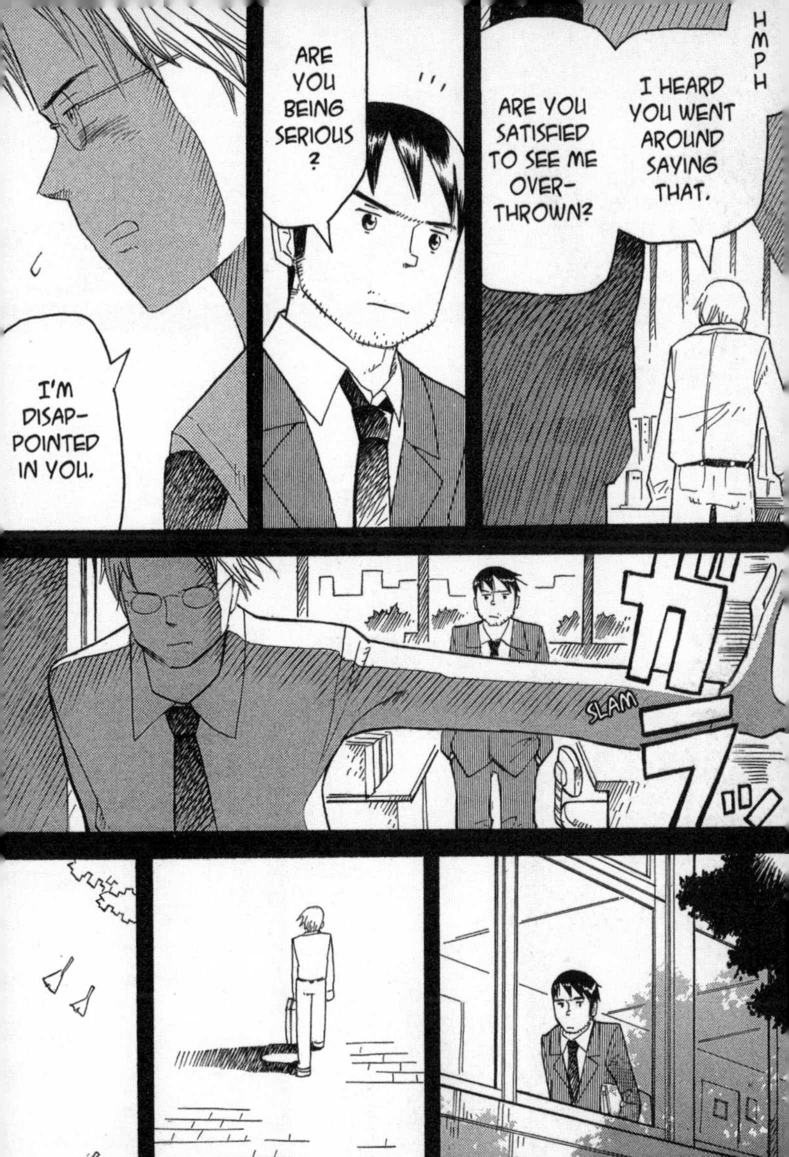
HMPH
I HEARD YOU WENT AROUND SAYING THAT.
ARE YOU SATISFIED TO SEE ME OVER-THROWN?
ARE YOU BEING SERIOUS?
I'M DISAP-POINTED IN YOU.
SLAM

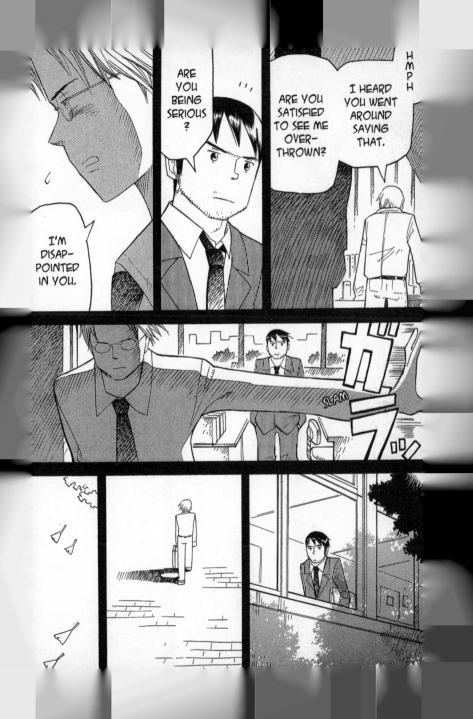

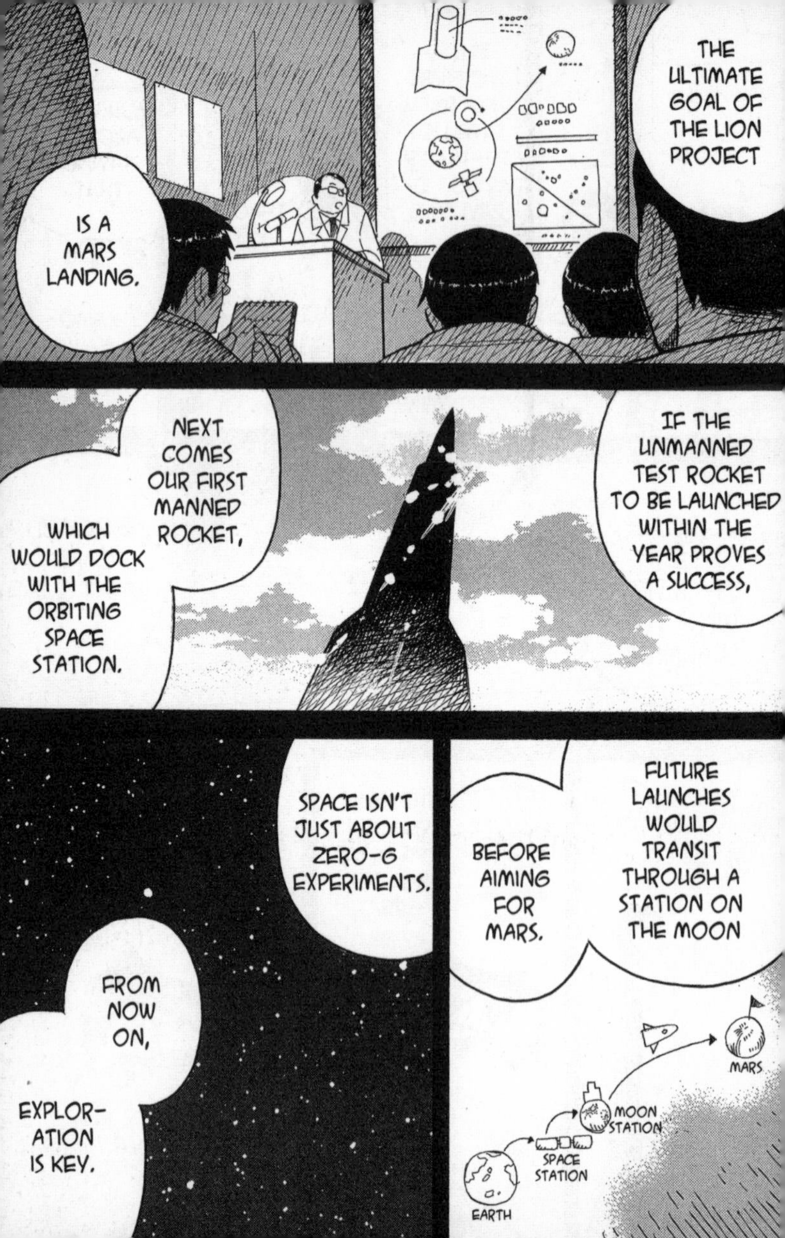
THE ULTIMATE GOAL OF THE LION PROJECT
IS A MARS LANDING.
IF THE UNMANNED TEST ROCKET TO BE LAUNCHED WITHIN THE YEAR PROVES A SUCCESS,
NEXT COMES OUR FIRST MANNED ROCKET,
WHICH WOULD DOCK WITH THE ORBITING SPACE STATION.
FUTURE LAUNCHES WOULD TRANSIT THROUGH A STATION ON THE MOON
BEFORE AIMING FOR MARS.
MARS
MOON STATION
SPACE STATION
EARTH
SPACE ISN'T JUST ABOUT ZERO-6 EXPERIMENTS.
FROM NOW ON,
EXPLOR-ATION IS KEY.

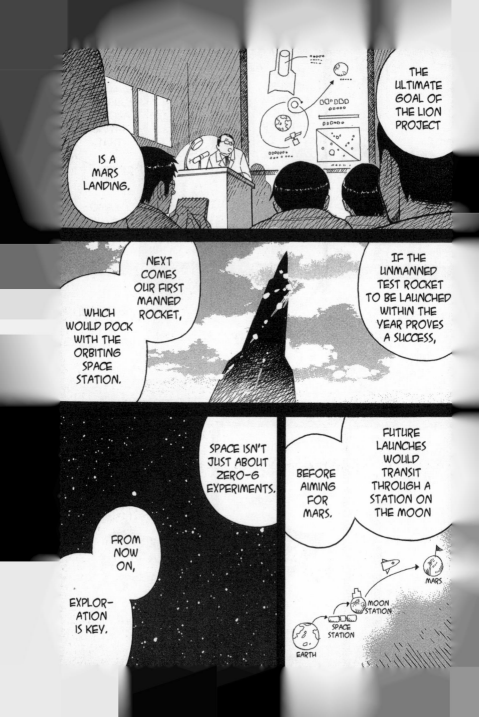

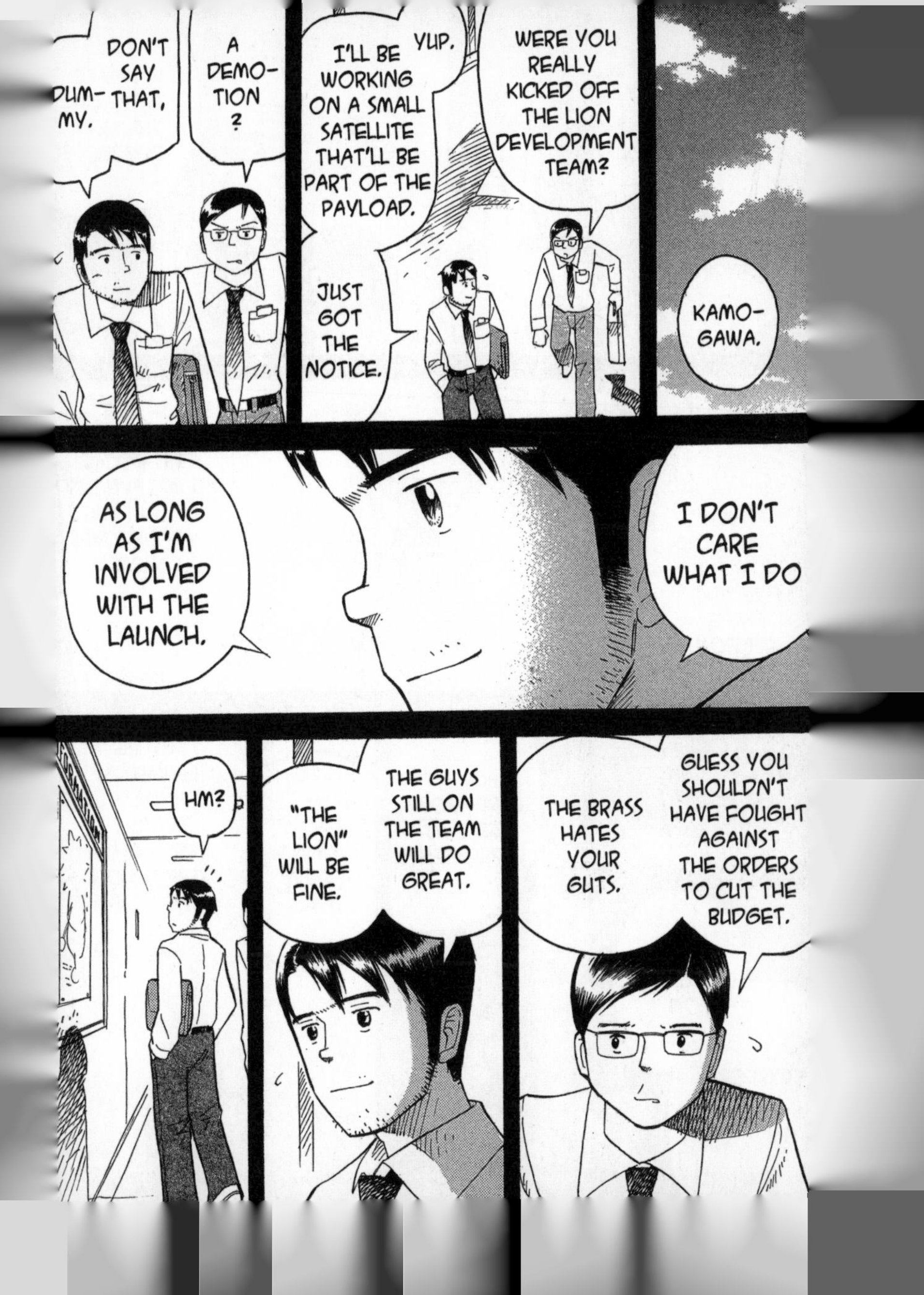
KAMO-GAWA.
WERE YOU REALLY KICKED OFF THE LION DEVELOPMENT TEAM?
YUP.
I'LL BE WORKING ON A SMALL SATELLITE THAT'LL BE PART OF THE PAYLOAD.
JUST GOT THE NOTICE.
A DEMO-TION?
DON'T SAY THAT, DUM-MY.
I DON'T CARE WHAT I DO
AS LONG AS I'M INVOLVED WITH THE LAUNCH.
GUESS YOU SHOULDN'T HAVE FOUGHT AGAINST THE ORDERS TO CUT THE BUDGET.
THE BRASS HATES YOUR GUTS.
THE GUYS STILL ON THE TEAM WILL DO GREAT.
"THE LION" WILL BE FINE.
HM?

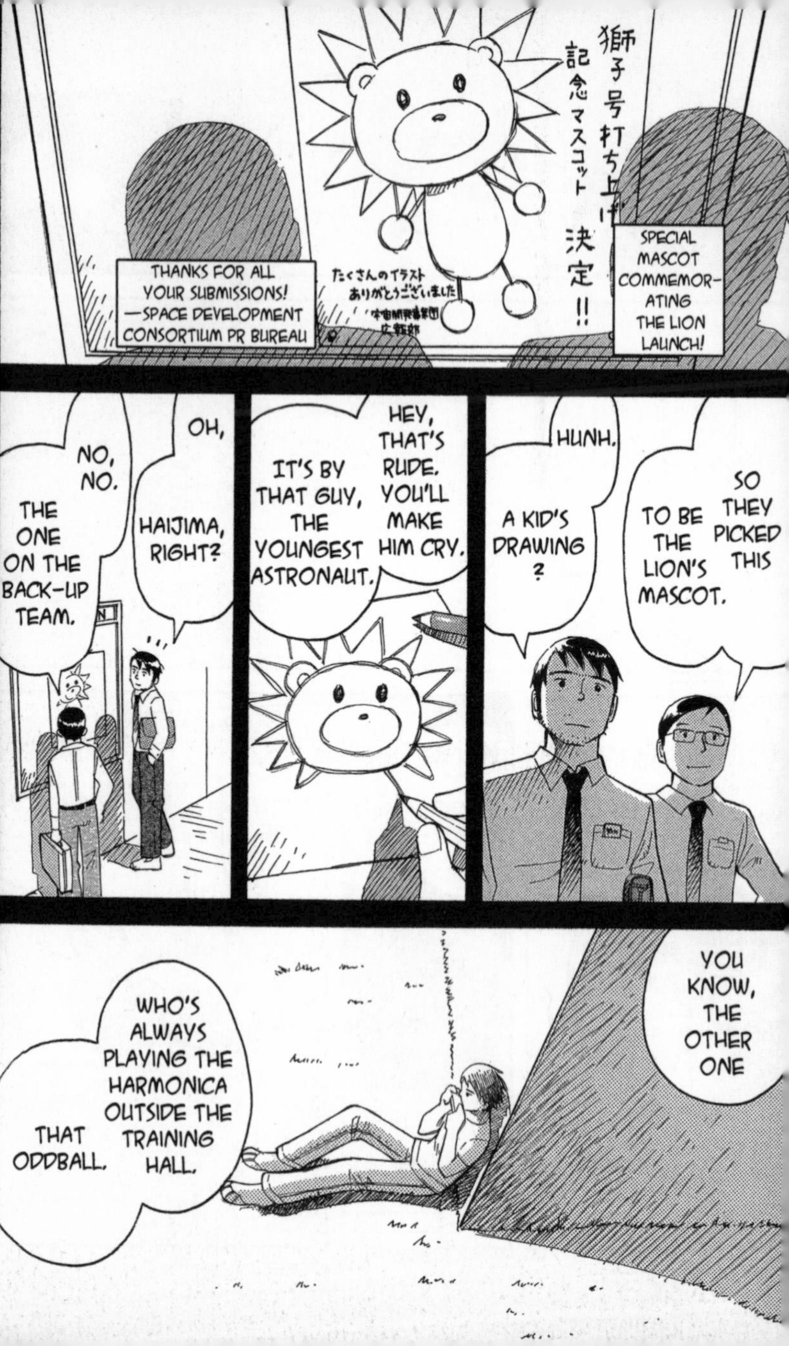
獅子号打ち上げ記念マスコット決定!!
SPECIAL MASCOT COMMEMORATING THE LION LAUNCH!
たくさんのイラストありがとうございました
THANKS FOR ALL YOUR SUBMISSIONS! —SPACE DEVELOPMENT CONSORTIUM PR BUREAU
SO THEY PICKED THIS TO BE THE LION'S MASCOT.
HUNH.
A KID'S DRAWING?
HEY, THAT'S RUDE. YOU'LL MAKE HIM CRY.
IT'S BY THAT GUY, THE YOUNGEST ASTRONAUT.
OH, HAIJIMA, RIGHT?
NO, NO. THE ONE ON THE BACK-UP TEAM.
YOU KNOW, THE OTHER ONE
WHO'S ALWAYS PLAYING THE HARMONICA OUTSIDE THE TRAINING HALL.
THAT ODDBALL.

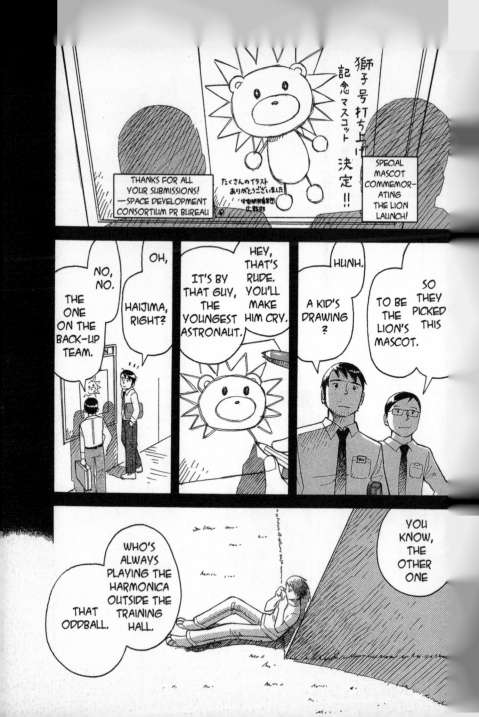

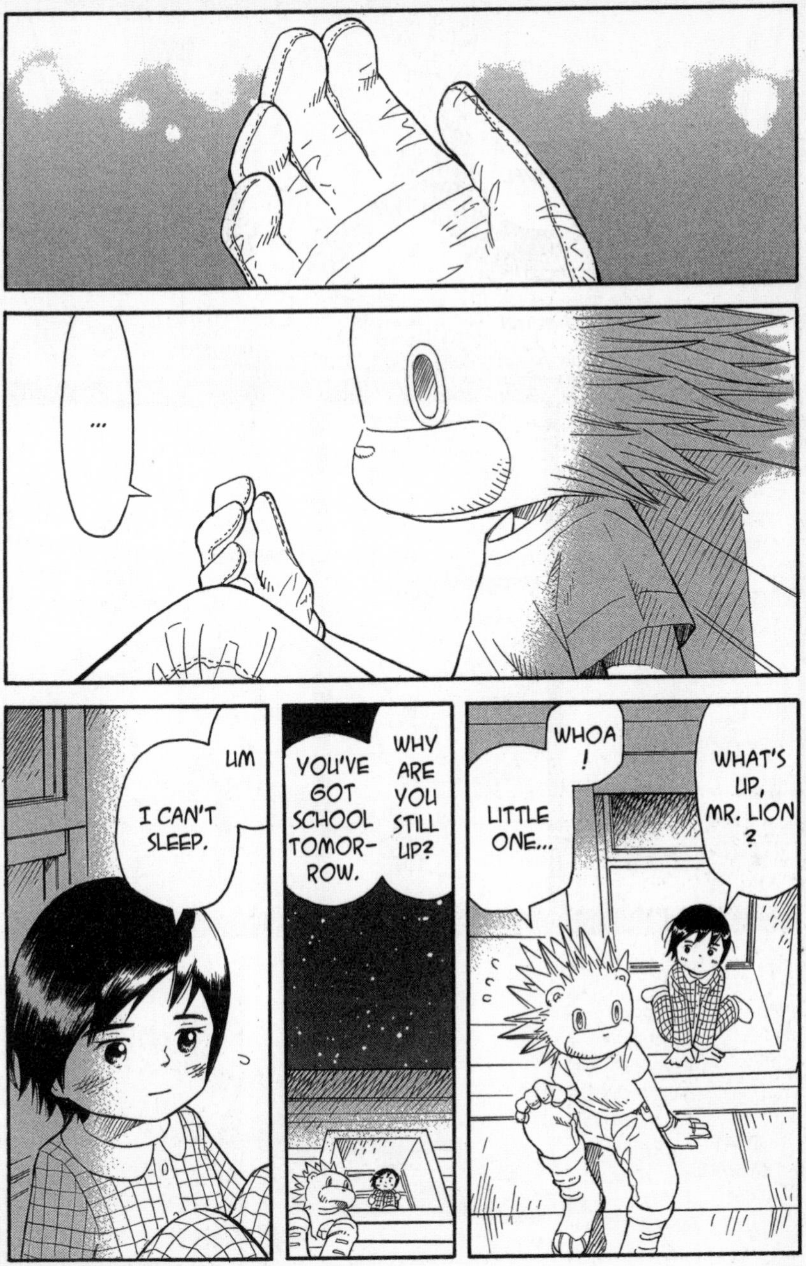
...
WHAT'S UP, MR. LION?
WHOA! LITTLE ONE...
WHY ARE YOU STILL UP? YOU'VE GOT SCHOOL TOMORROW.
UM I CAN'T SLEEP.

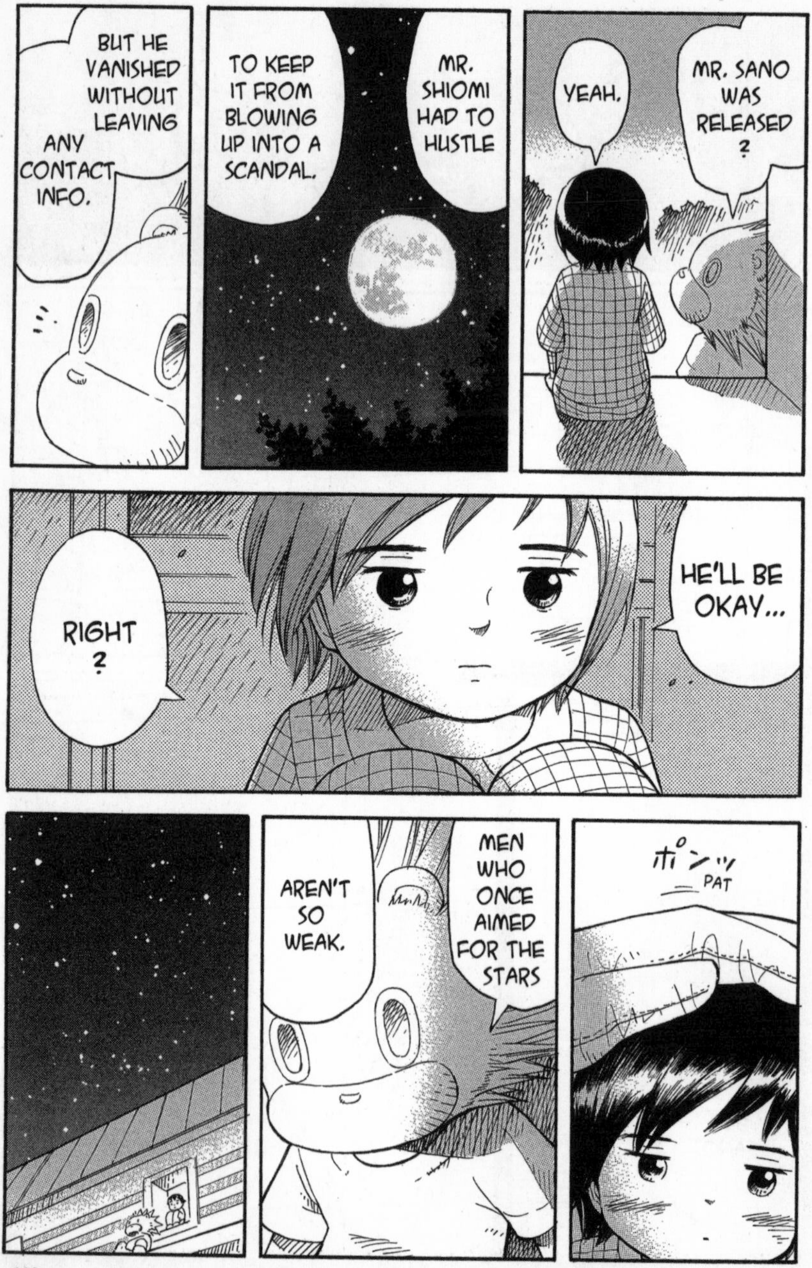
MR. SANO WAS RELEASED?
YEAH.
MR. SHIOMI HAD TO HUSTLE
TO KEEP IT FROM BLOWING UP INTO A SCANDAL.
BUT HE VANISHED WITHOUT LEAVING ANY CONTACT INFO.
HE'LL BE OKAY...
RIGHT?
ポンッ
PAT
MEN WHO ONCE AIMED FOR THE STARS
AREN'T SO WEAK.

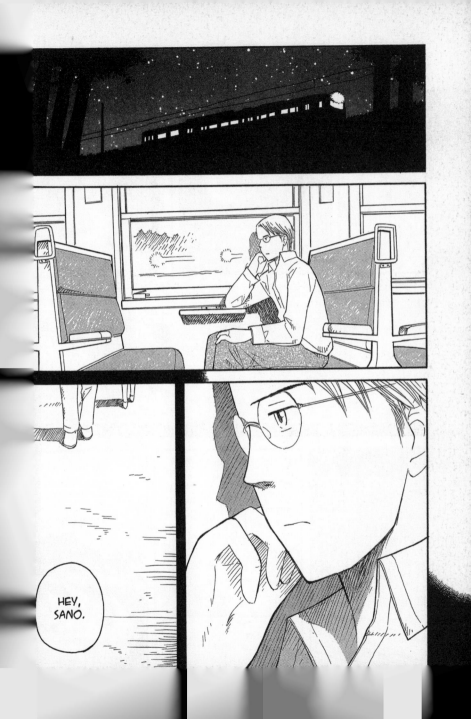

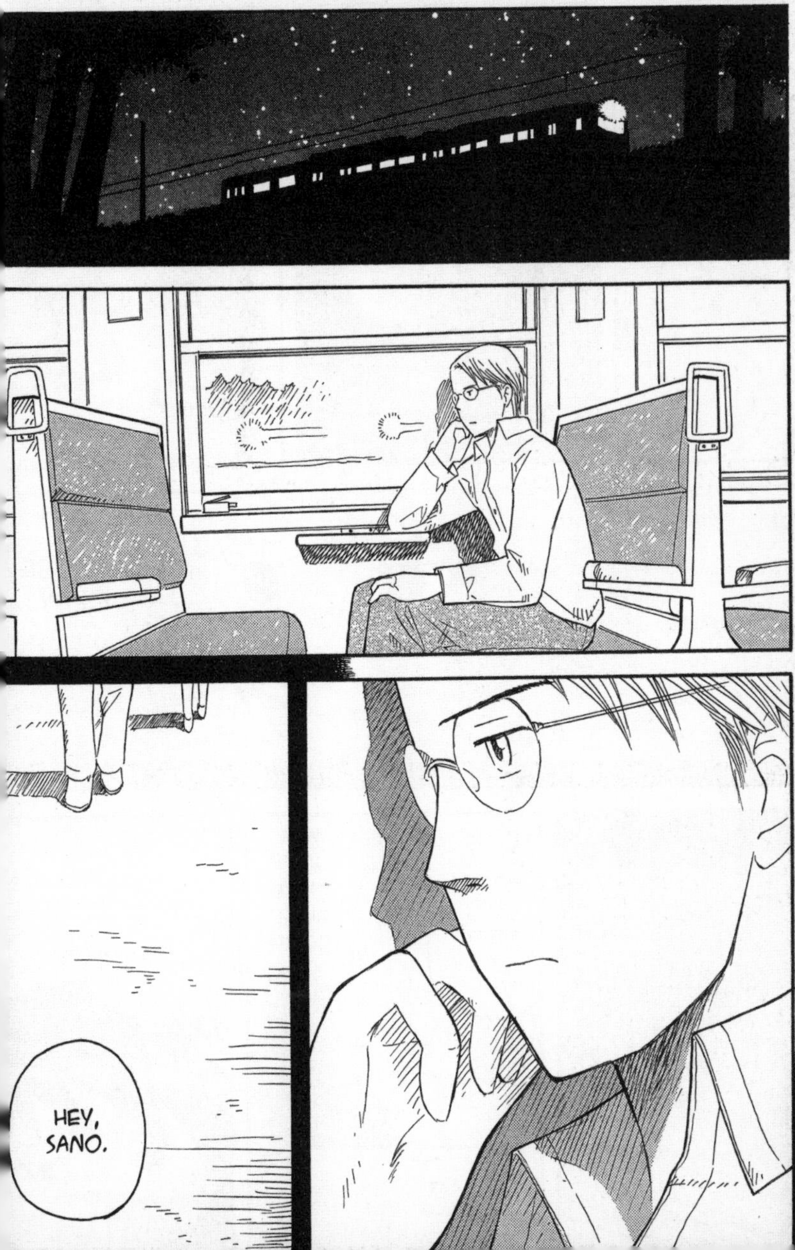
HEY, SANO.

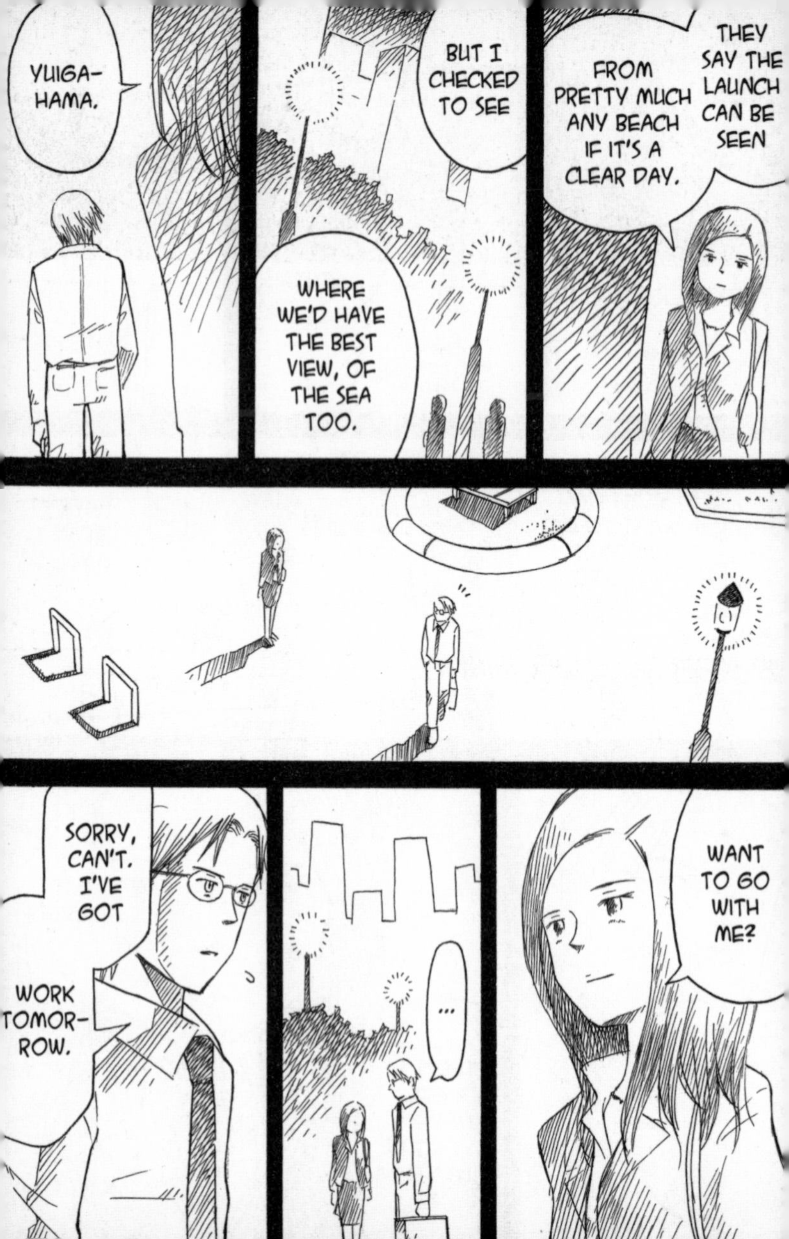
THEY SAY THE LAUNCH CAN BE SEEN
FROM PRETTY MUCH ANY BEACH IF IT'S A CLEAR DAY.
BUT I CHECKED TO SEE
WHERE WE'D HAVE THE BEST VIEW, OF THE SEA TOO.
YUIGA-HAMA.
WANT TO GO WITH ME?
...
SORRY, CAN'T. I'VE GOT
WORK TOMOR-ROW.

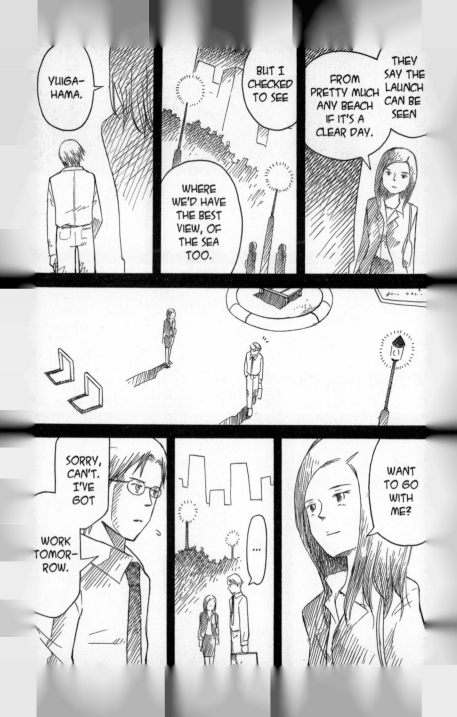

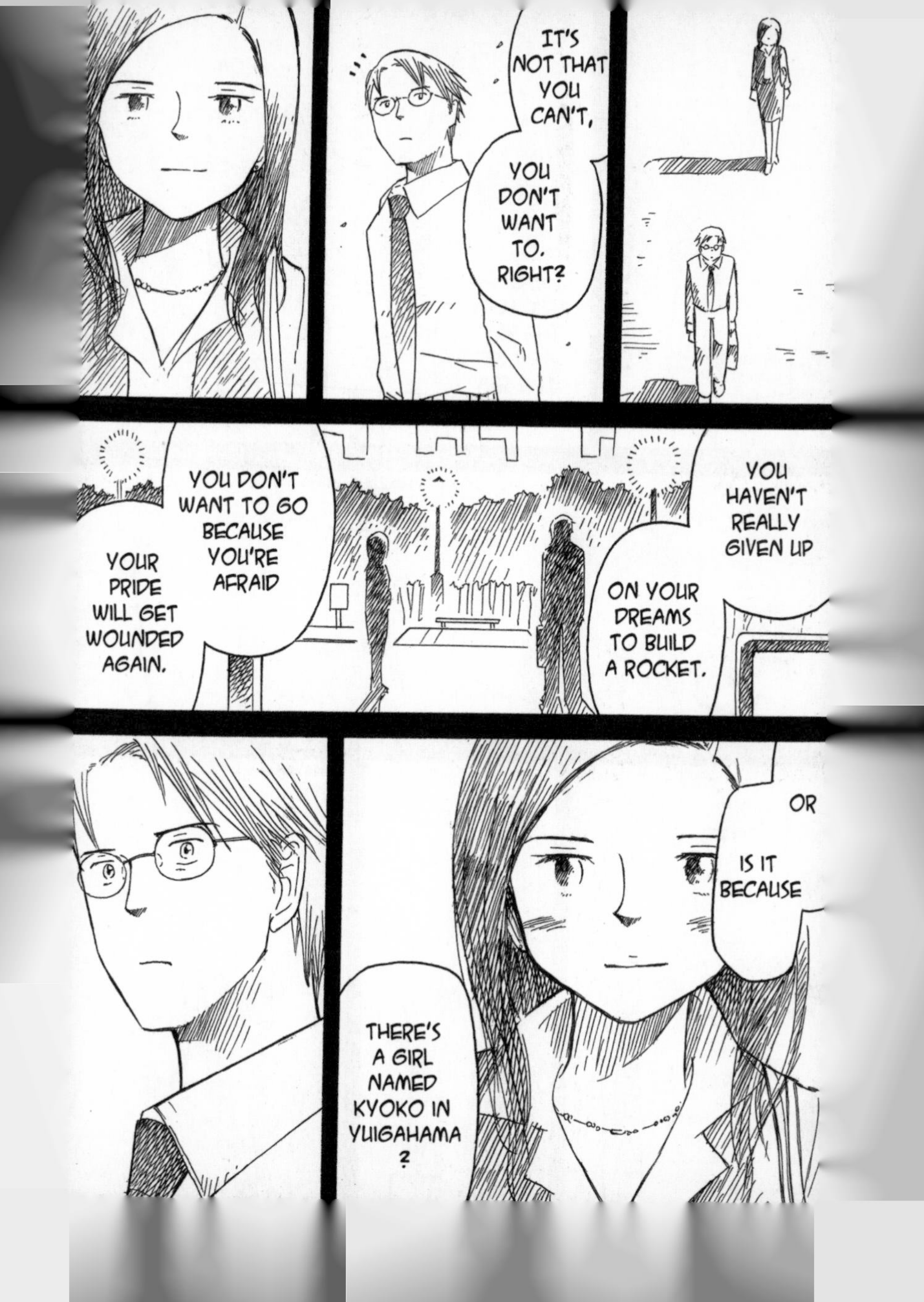
IT'S NOT THAT YOU CAN'T,
YOU DON'T WANT TO. RIGHT?
YOU HAVEN'T REALLY GIVEN UP
ON YOUR DREAMS TO BUILD A ROCKET.
YOU DON'T WANT TO GO BECAUSE YOU'RE AFRAID
YOUR PRIDE WILL GET WOUNDED AGAIN.
OR
IS IT BECAUSE
THERE'S A GIRL NAMED KYOKO IN YUIGAHAMA
?

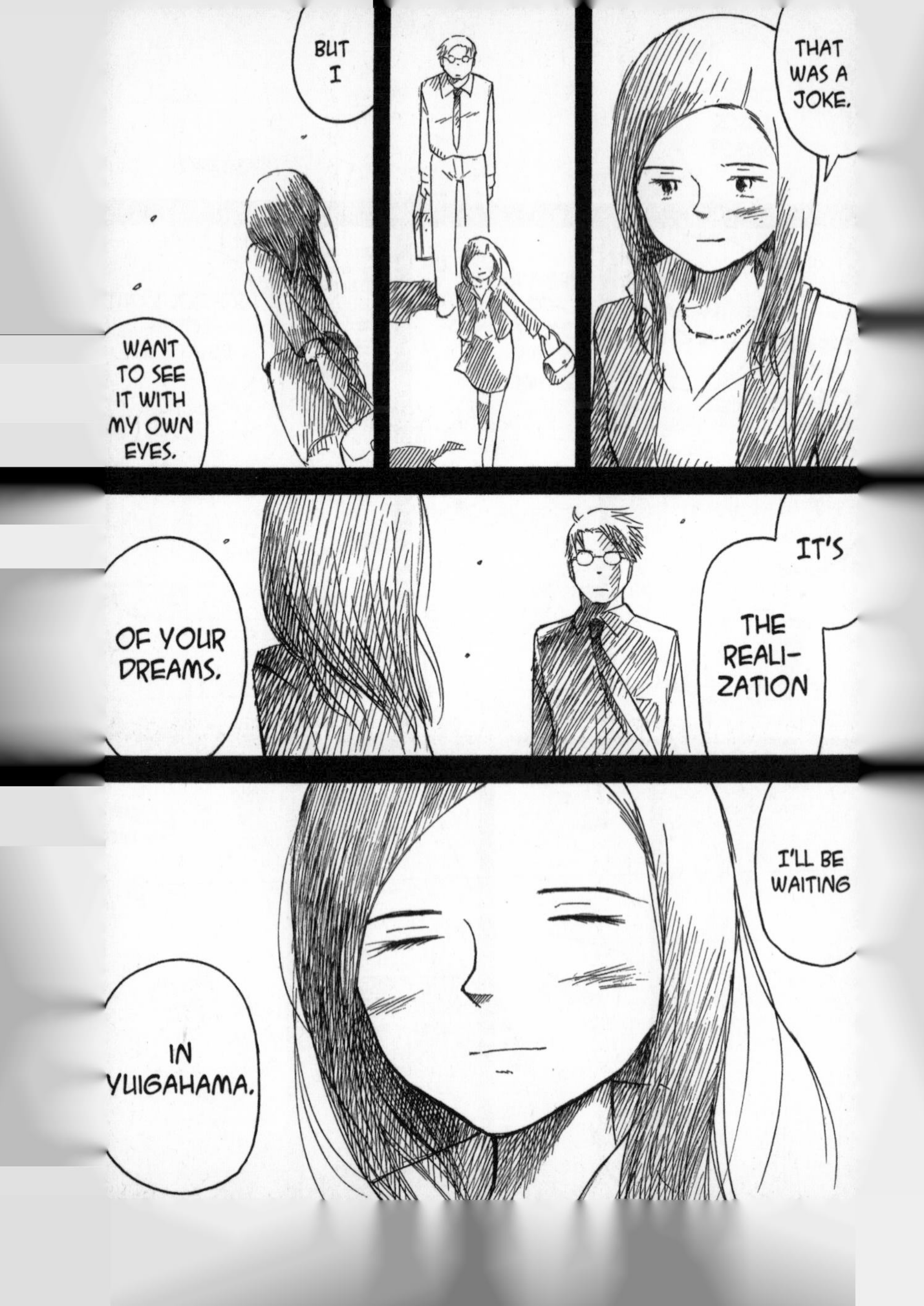
THAT WAS A JOKE.
BUT I
WANT TO SEE IT WITH MY OWN EYES.
IT'S
THE REALI-ZATION
OF YOUR DREAMS.
I'LL BE WAITING
IN YUIGAHAMA.

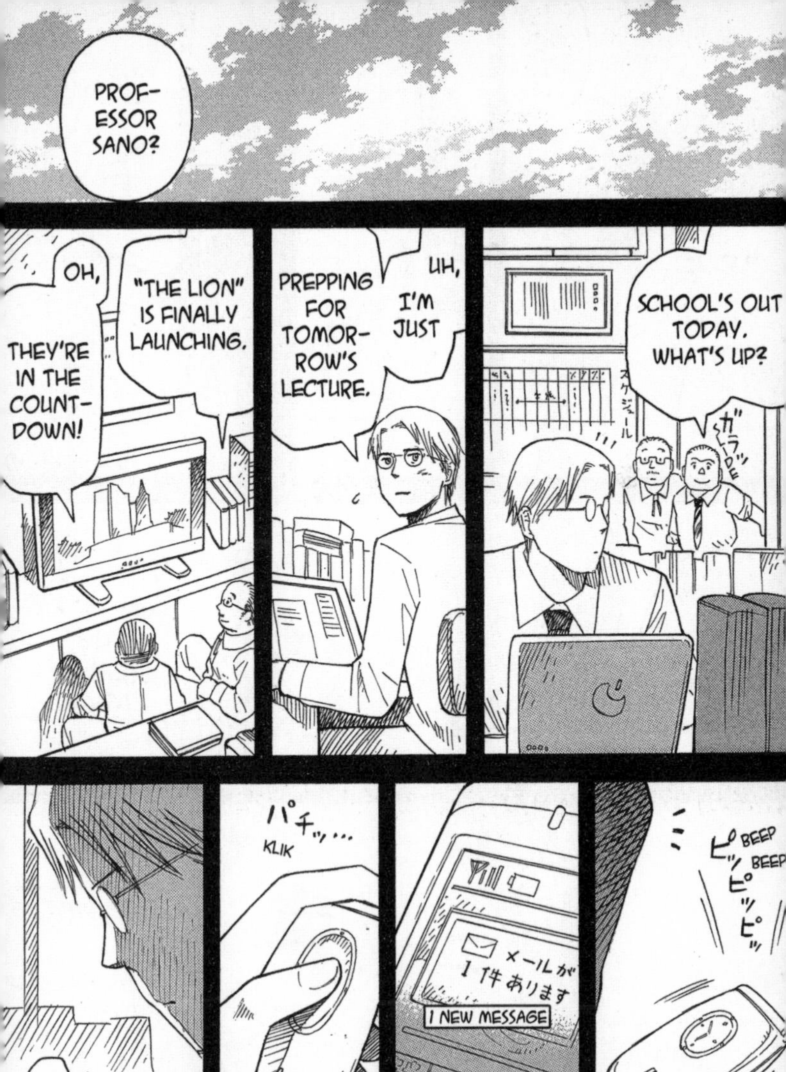
PROFESSOR SANO?
SCHOOL'S OUT TODAY. WHAT'S UP?
スケジュール
UH, I'M JUST
PREPPING FOR TOMORROW'S LECTURE.
OH, THEY'RE IN THE COUNTDOWN!
"THE LION" IS FINALLY LAUNCHING.
ピッピッピッ
BEEP BEEP
メールが1件あります
1 NEW MESSAGE
パチッ…
KLIK
...

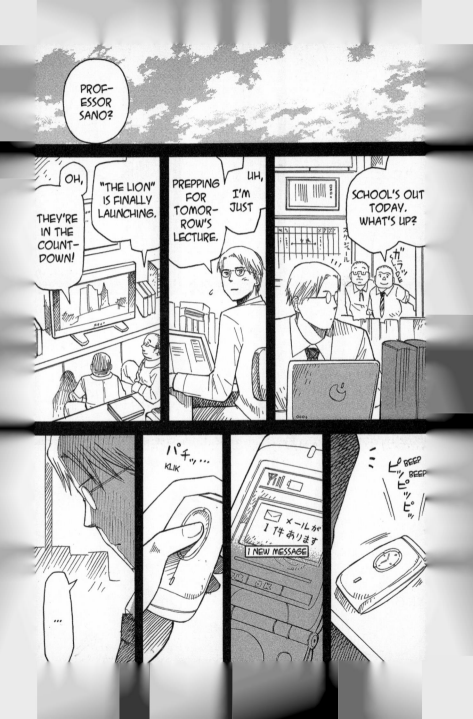

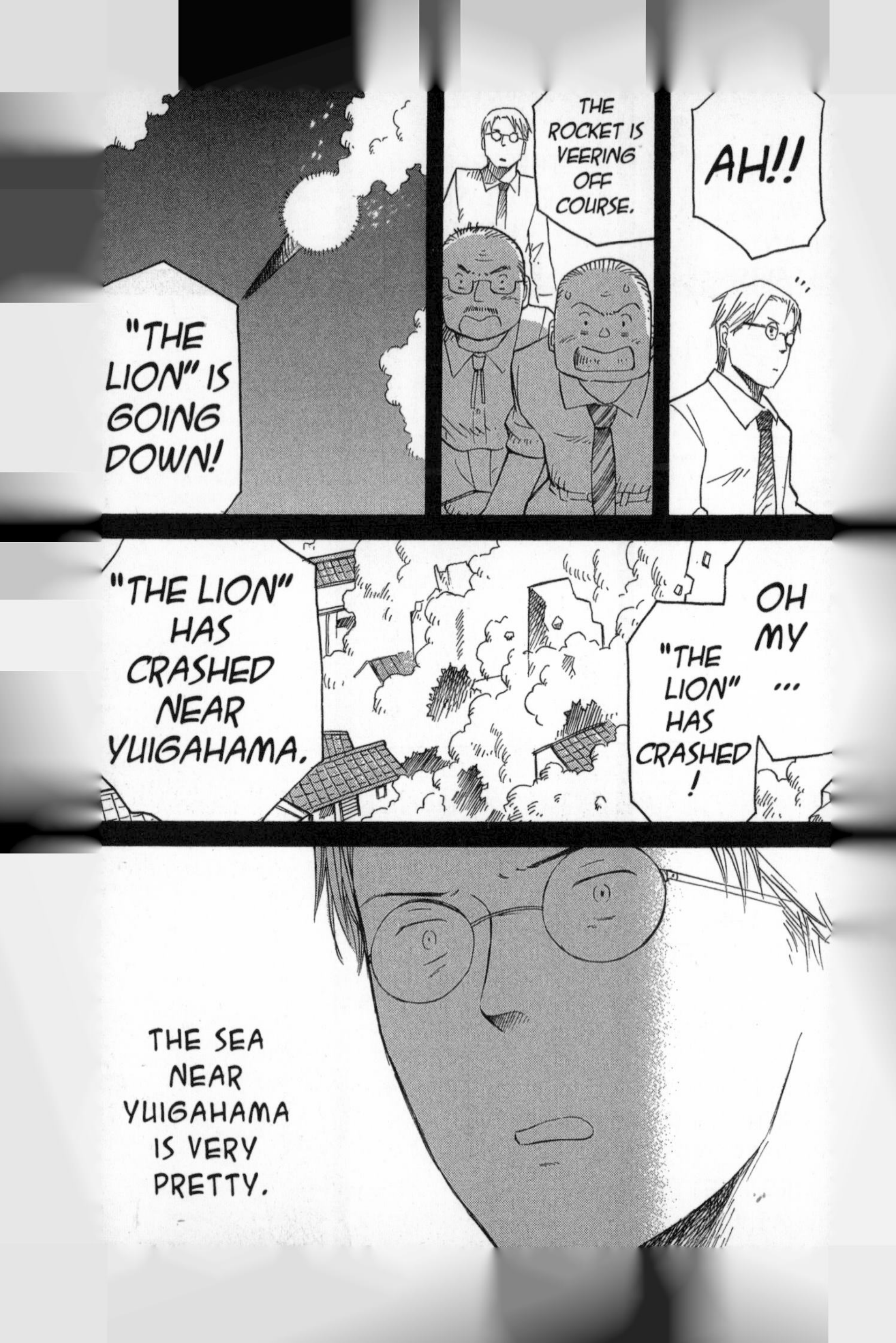
AH!!
THE ROCKET IS VEERING OFF COURSE.
"THE LION" IS GOING DOWN!
OH MY ...
"THE LION" HAS CRASHED!
"THE LION" HAS CRASHED NEAR YUIGAHAMA.
THE SEA NEAR YUIGAHAMA IS VERY PRETTY.

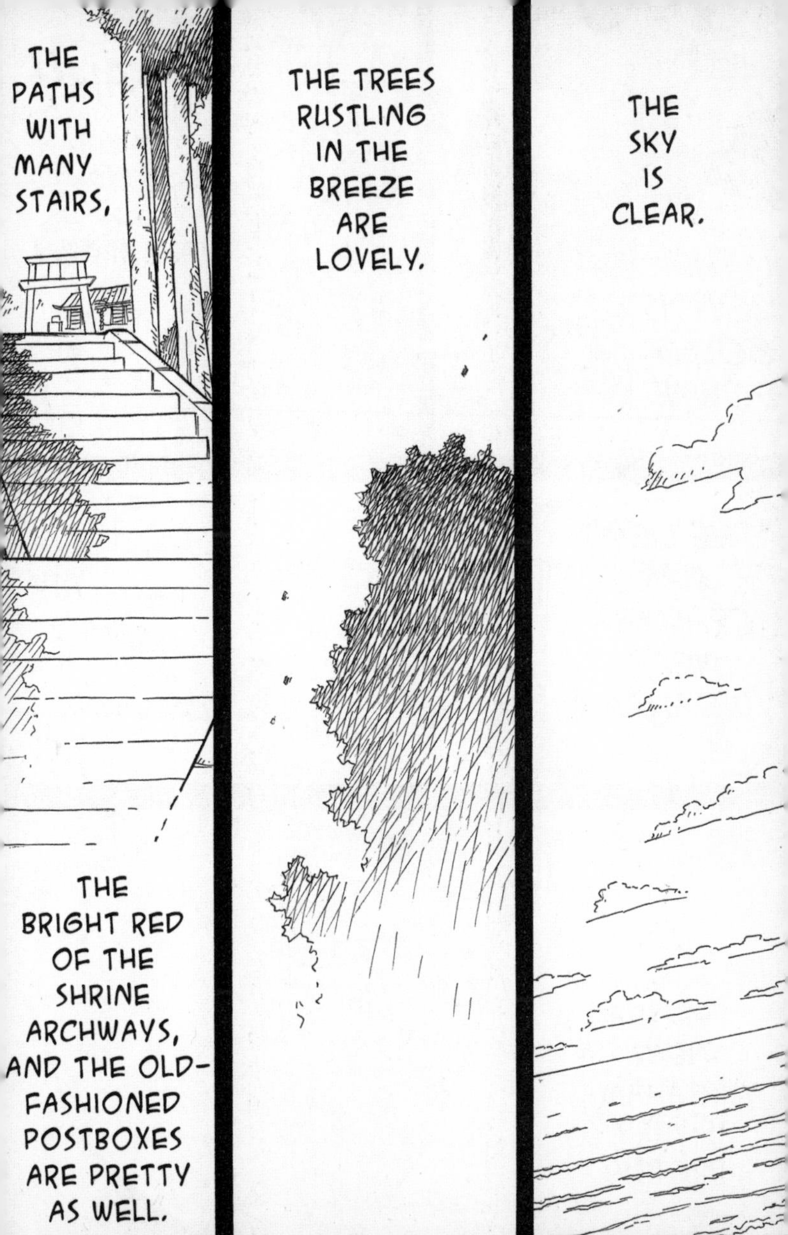
THE SKY IS CLEAR.
THE TREES RUSTLING IN THE BREEZE ARE LOVELY.
THE PATHS WITH MANY STAIRS,
THE BRIGHT RED OF THE SHRINE ARCHWAYS, AND THE OLD-FASHIONED POSTBOXES ARE PRETTY AS WELL.

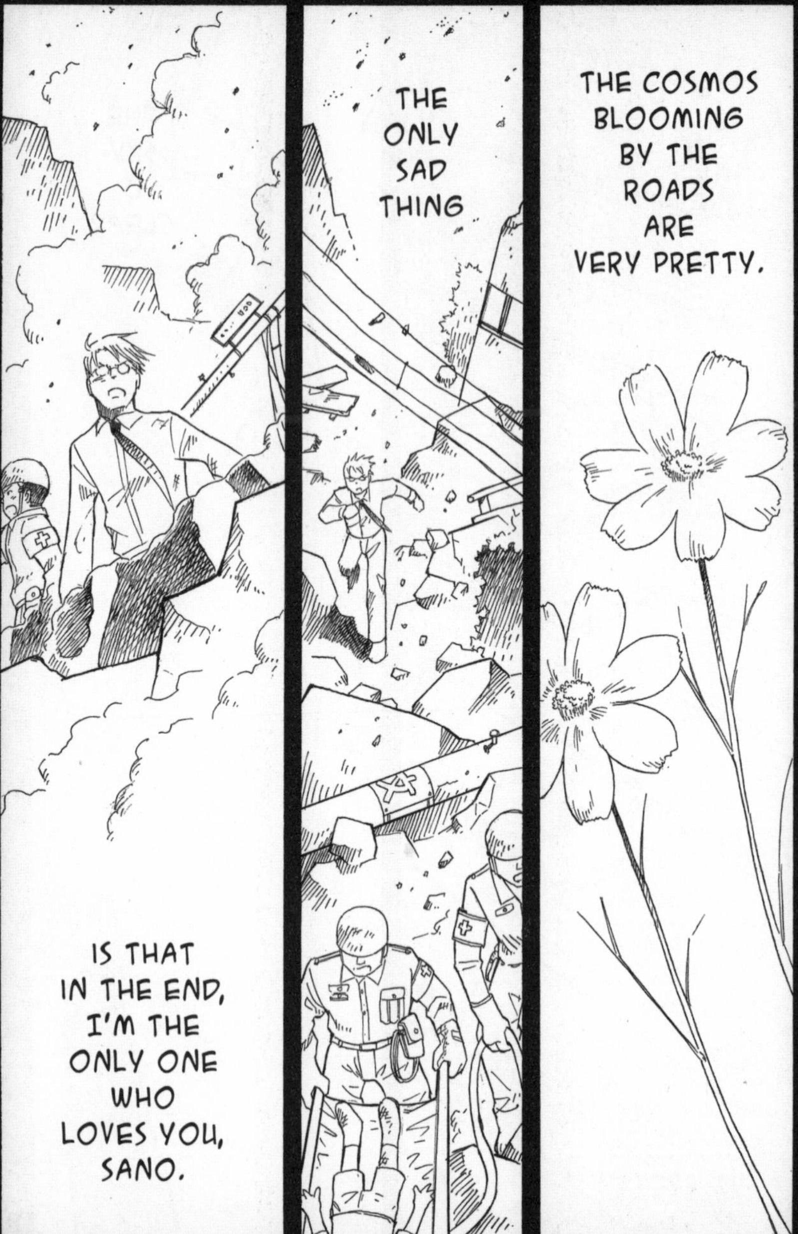
THE COSMOS BLOOMING BY THE ROADS ARE VERY PRETTY.
THE ONLY SAD THING
IS THAT IN THE END, I'M THE ONLY ONE WHO LOVES YOU, SANO.

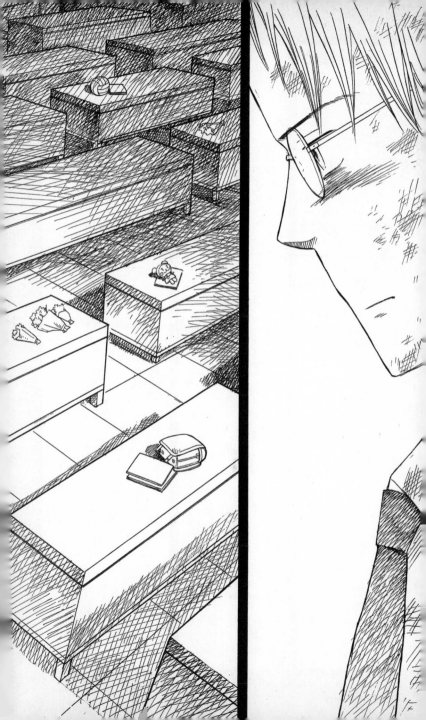

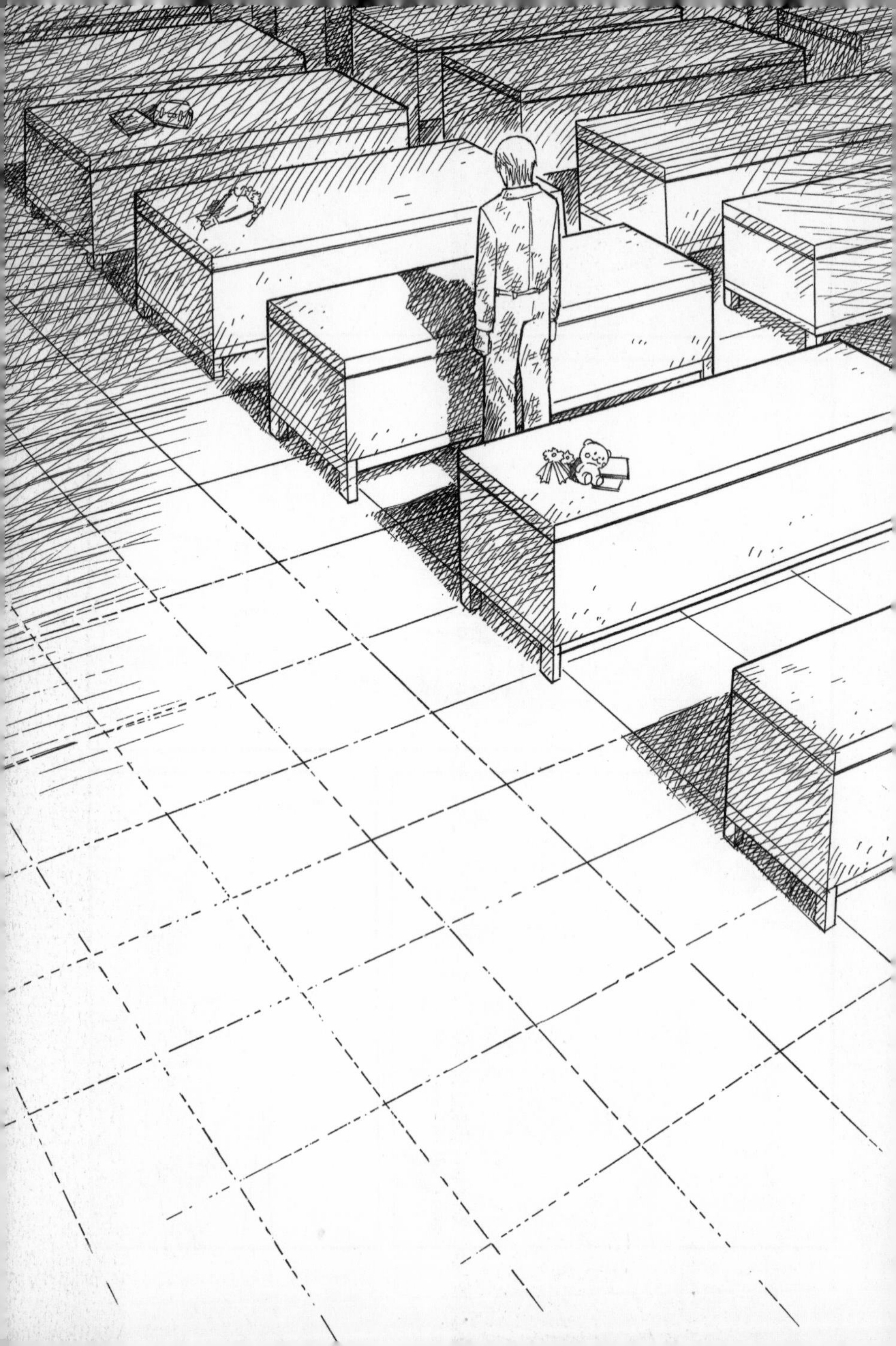

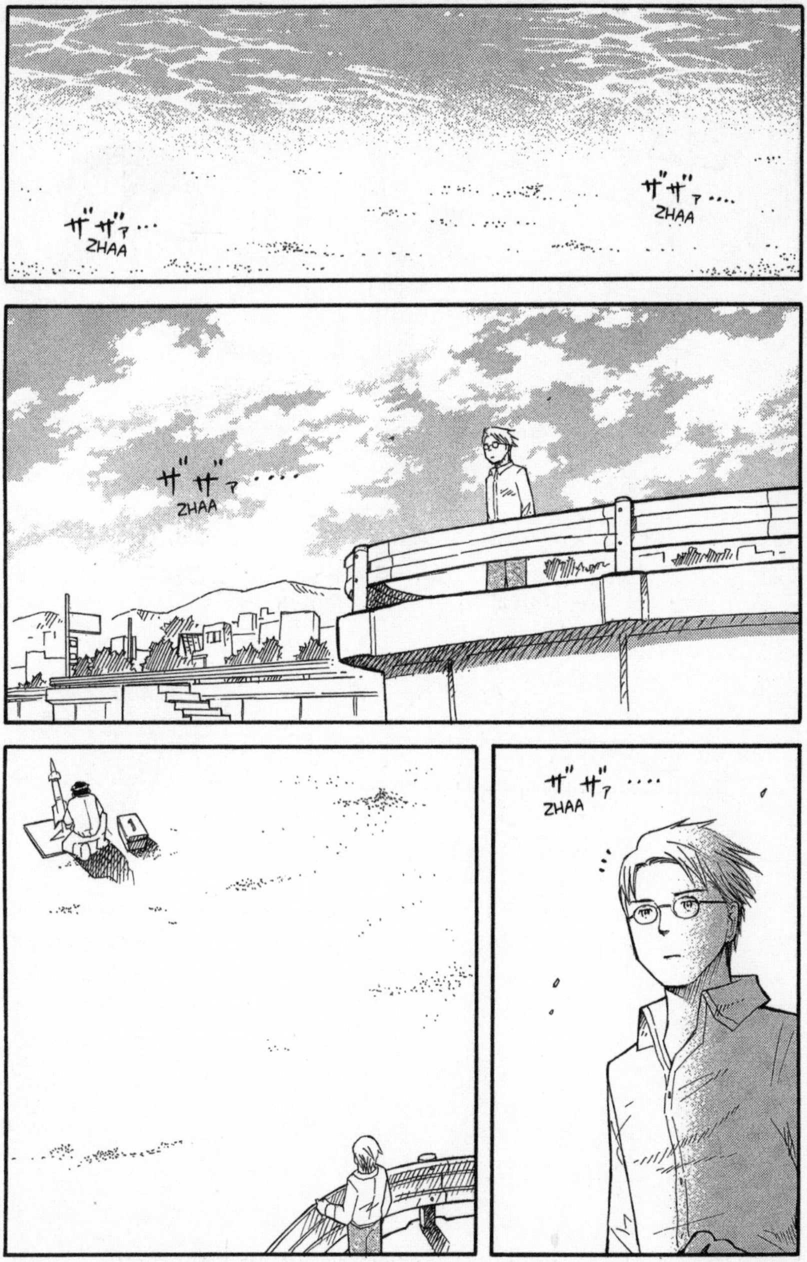
ザザァ….
ZHAA
ザザァ…
ZHAA
ザザァ….
ZHAA
ザザァ….
ZHAA

カチャ
KRIK
カチャ
KRIK
タッ
THUP
タッ
THUP
タッ
タッ
THUP
5
4
3
2
1
LIFT-OFF!

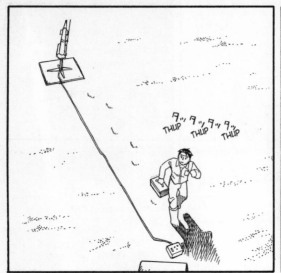

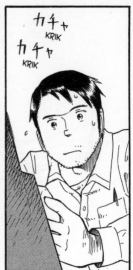

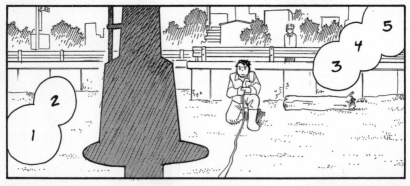

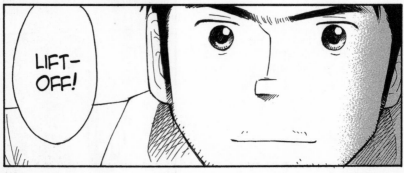

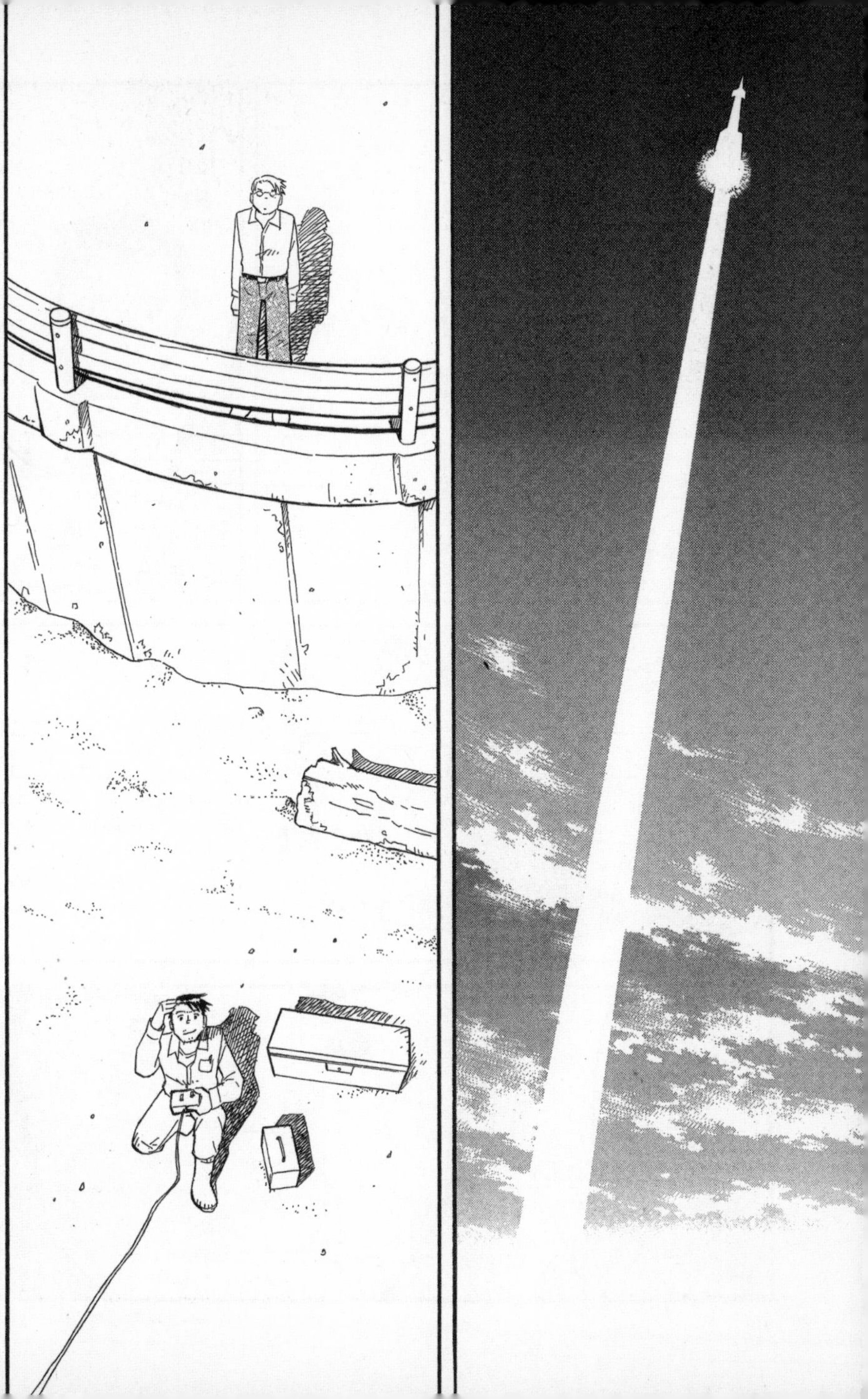

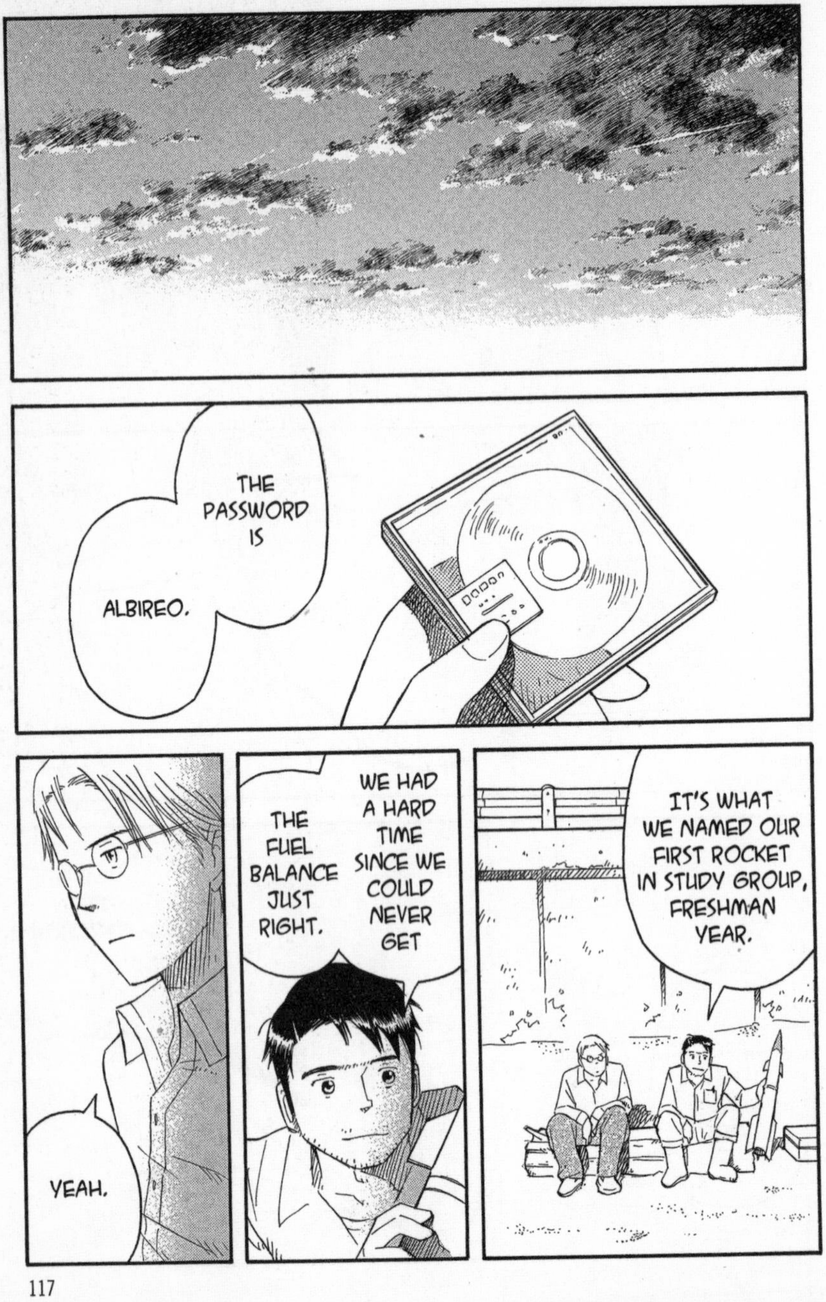
THE PASSWORD IS
ALBIREO.
IT'S WHAT WE NAMED OUR FIRST ROCKET IN STUDY GROUP, FRESHMAN YEAR.
WE HAD A HARD TIME SINCE WE COULD NEVER GET
THE FUEL BALANCE JUST RIGHT.
YEAH.

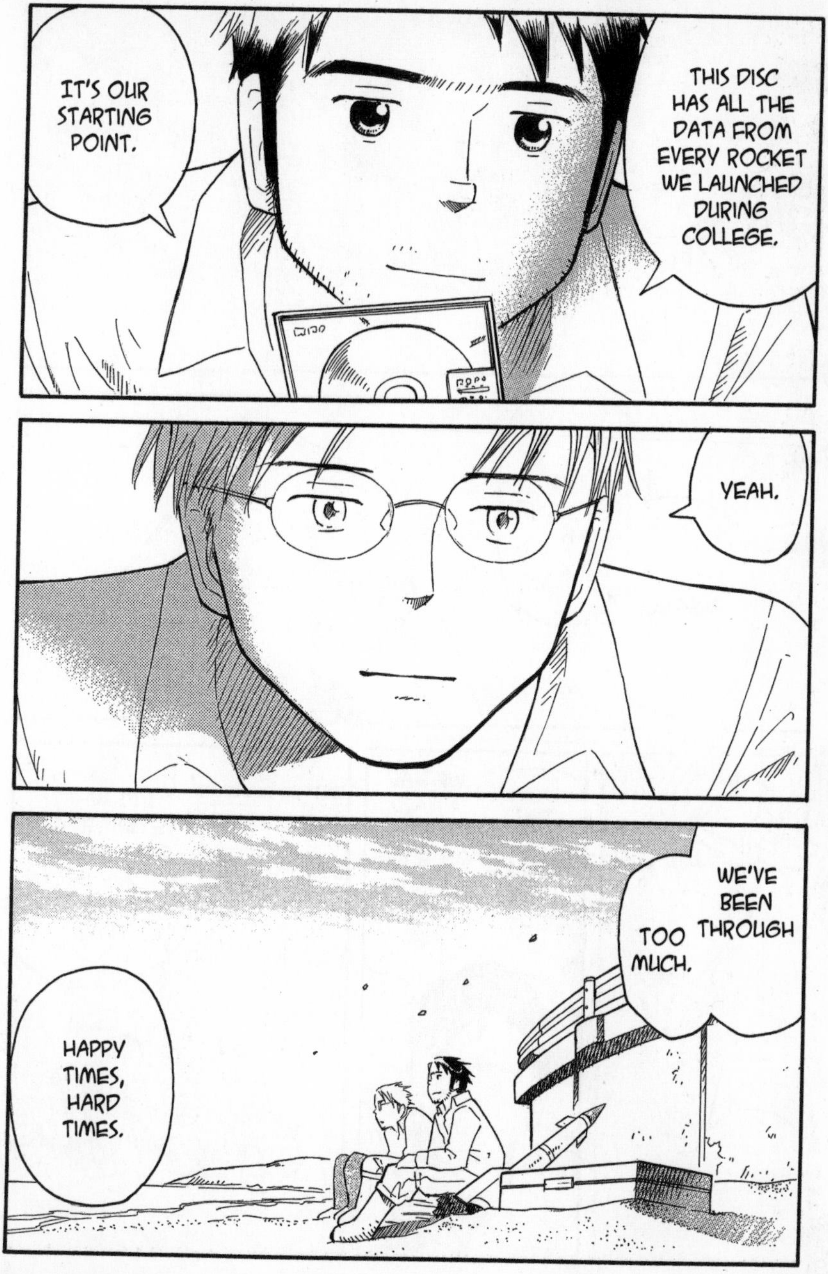
THIS DISC HAS ALL THE DATA FROM EVERY ROCKET WE LAUNCHED DURING COLLEGE.
IT'S OUR STARTING POINT.
YEAH.
WE'VE BEEN THROUGH TOO MUCH.
HAPPY TIMES, HARD TIMES.

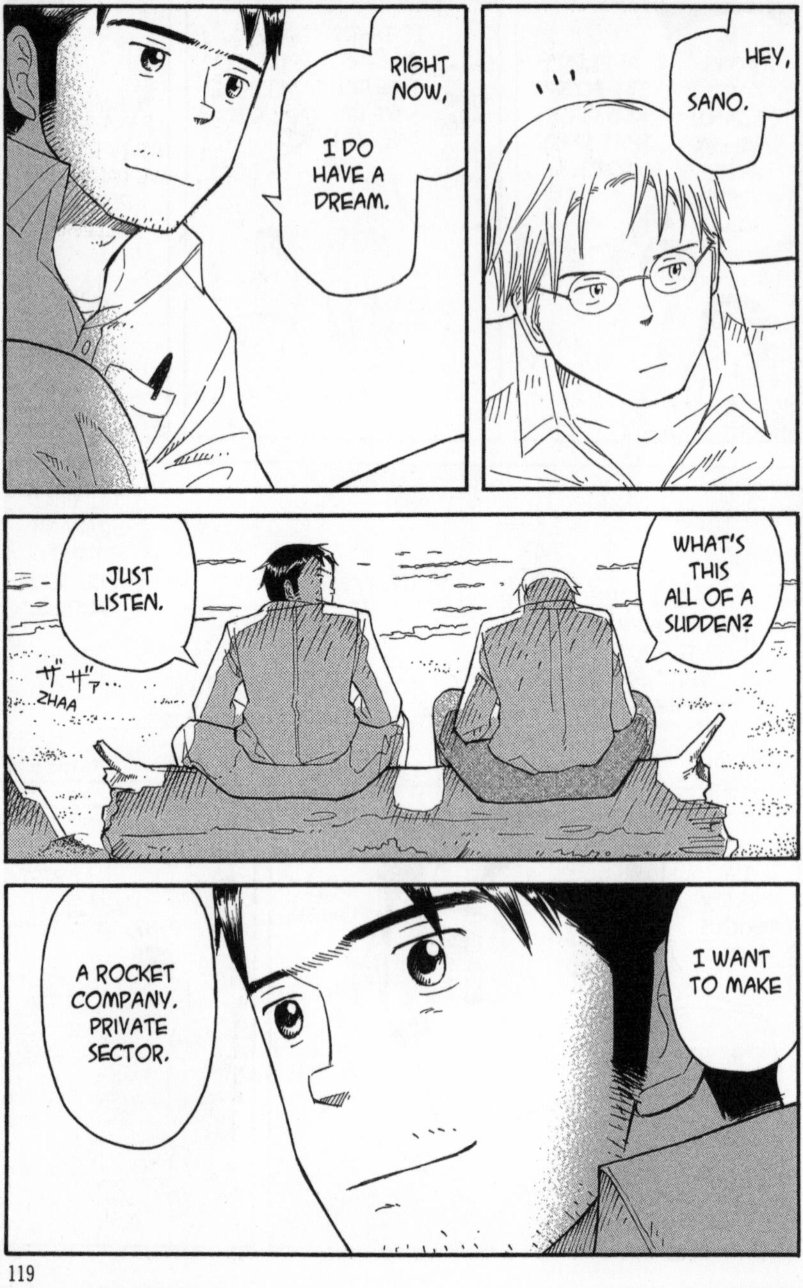
HEY, SANO.
RIGHT NOW,
I DO HAVE A DREAM.
WHAT'S THIS ALL OF A SUDDEN?
JUST LISTEN.
ザザァ…
ZHAA
I WANT TO MAKE
A ROCKET COMPANY. PRIVATE SECTOR.

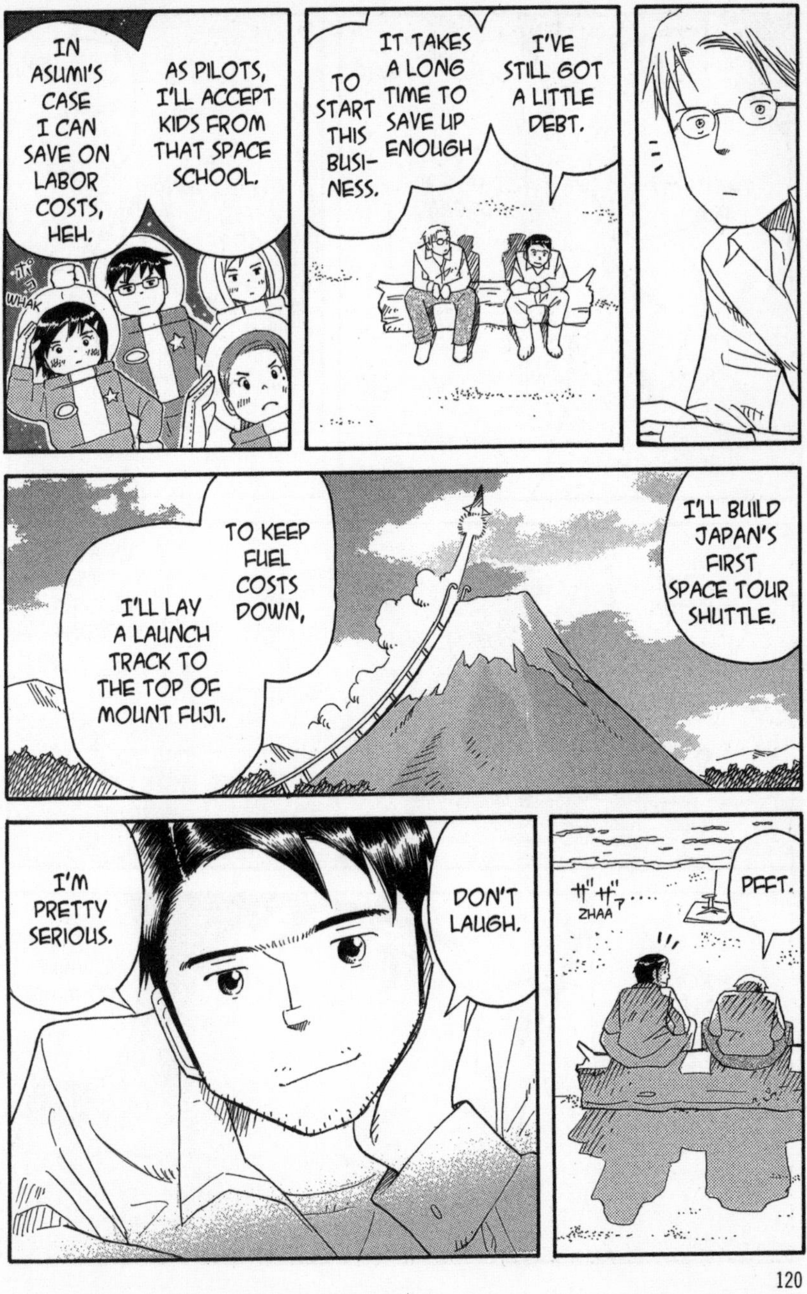
I'VE STILL GOT A LITTLE DEBT.
IT TAKES A LONG TIME TO SAVE UP ENOUGH
TO START THIS BUSI-NESS.
AS PILOTS, I'LL ACCEPT KIDS FROM THAT SPACE SCHOOL.
IN ASUMI'S CASE I CAN SAVE ON LABOR COSTS, HEH.
ポコ
WHAK
I'LL BUILD JAPAN'S FIRST SPACE TOUR SHUTTLE.
TO KEEP FUEL COSTS DOWN,
I'LL LAY A LAUNCH TRACK TO THE TOP OF MOUNT FUJI.
PFFT.
ザザァ…
ZHAA
DON'T LAUGH.
I'M PRETTY SERIOUS.

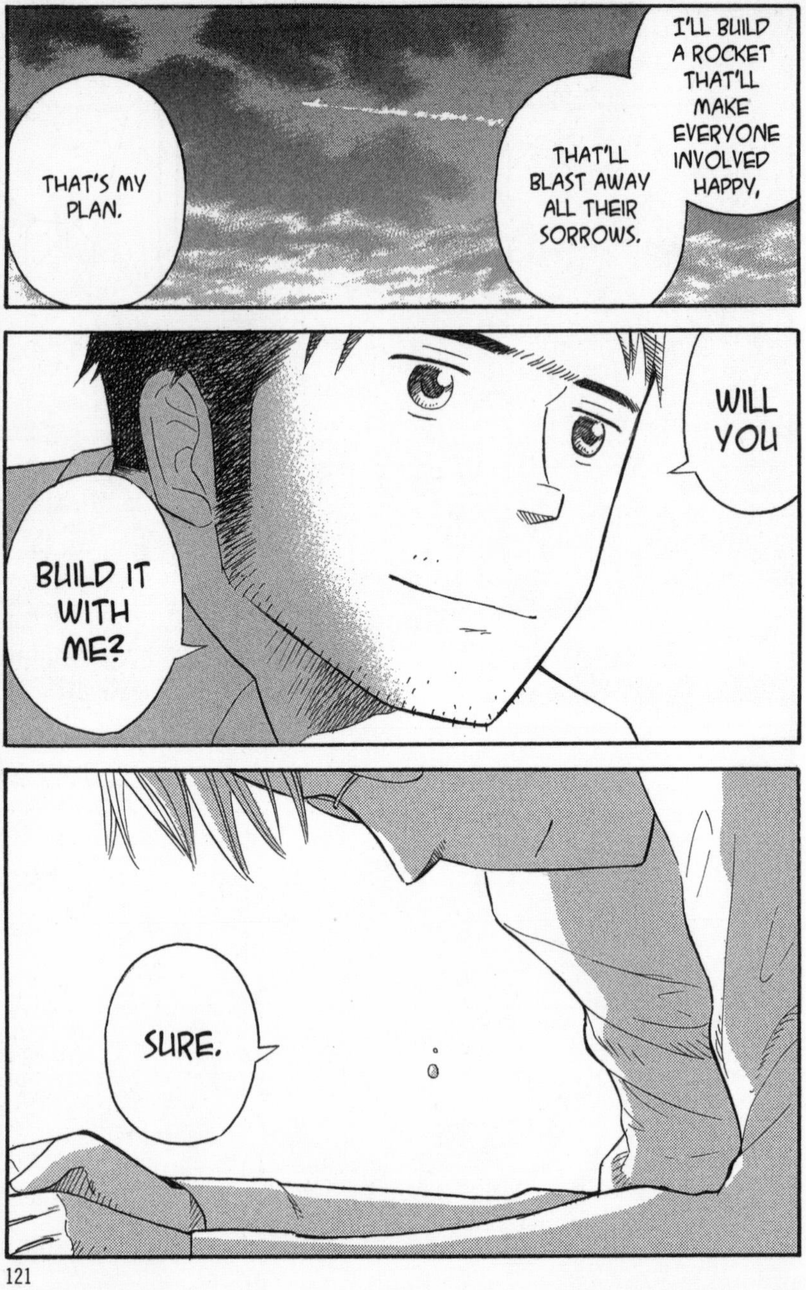
I'LL BUILD A ROCKET THAT'LL MAKE EVERYONE INVOLVED HAPPY,
THAT'LL BLAST AWAY ALL THEIR SORROWS.
THAT'S MY PLAN.
WILL YOU
BUILD IT WITH ME?
SURE.

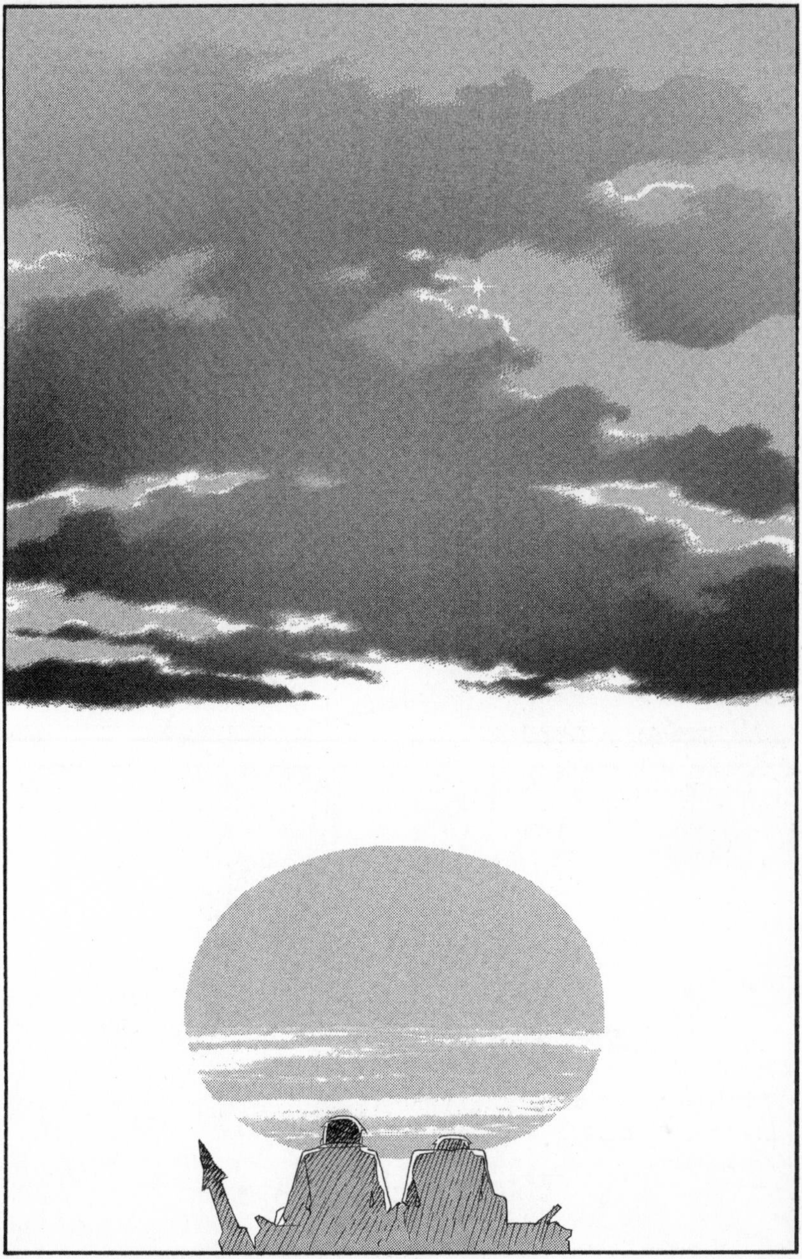

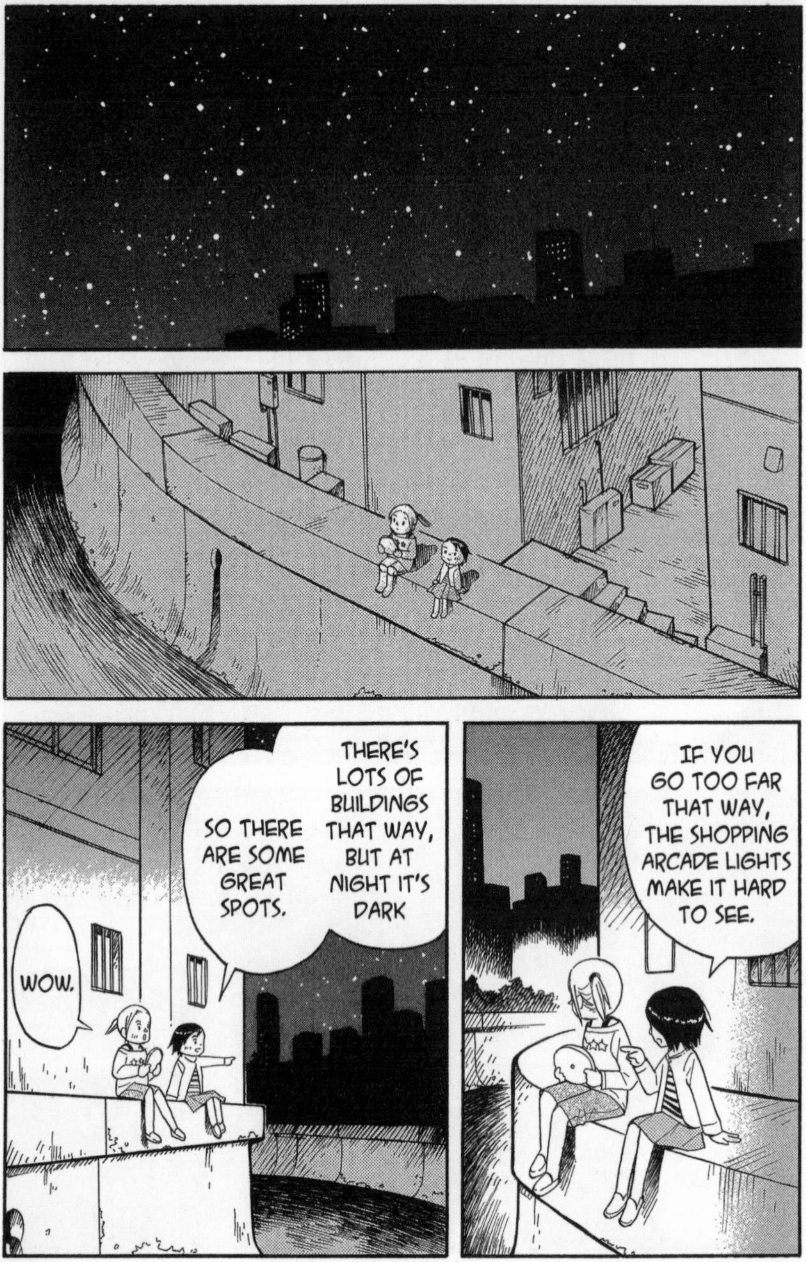
IF YOU GO TOO FAR THAT WAY, THE SHOPPING ARCADE LIGHTS MAKE IT HARD TO SEE.
THERE'S LOTS OF BUILDINGS THAT WAY, BUT AT NIGHT IT'S DARK
SO THERE ARE SOME GREAT SPOTS.
WOW.

SO THERE ARE GOOD SPOTS EVEN IN TOKYO IF YOU ONLY LOOK FOR THEM.
YUP.
I'LL TELL YOU THE OTHERS LATER.
MAYBE IT'LL BE EASIER TO REMEMBER THE CONSTEL-LATIONS IF I CAN
ONLY SEE THE BRIGHT STARS. TOO MANY CAN BE CONFUSING.
I LIKE TO TRY AND PICTURE THE STARS
I CAN'T SEE.
YOU CAN'T SEE IT,
BUT IT'S SHINING THERE.
A LOT OF STARS
ARE SHINING THERE.

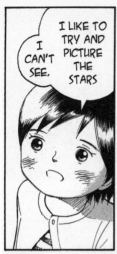

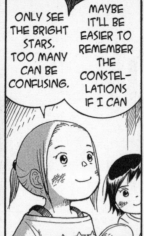

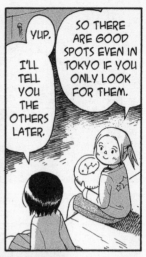

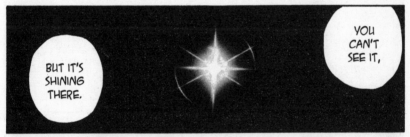

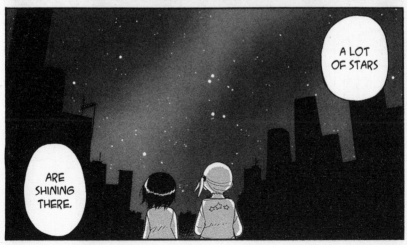

MISSION:51

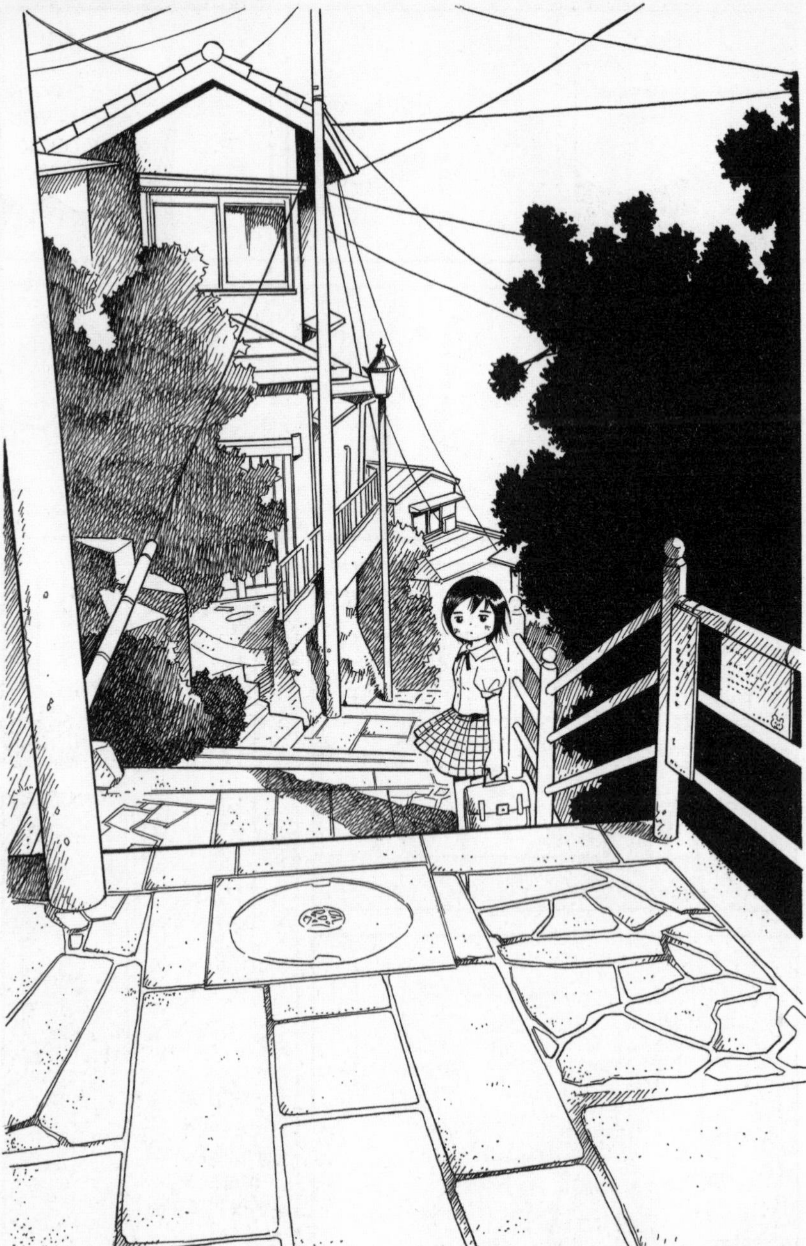

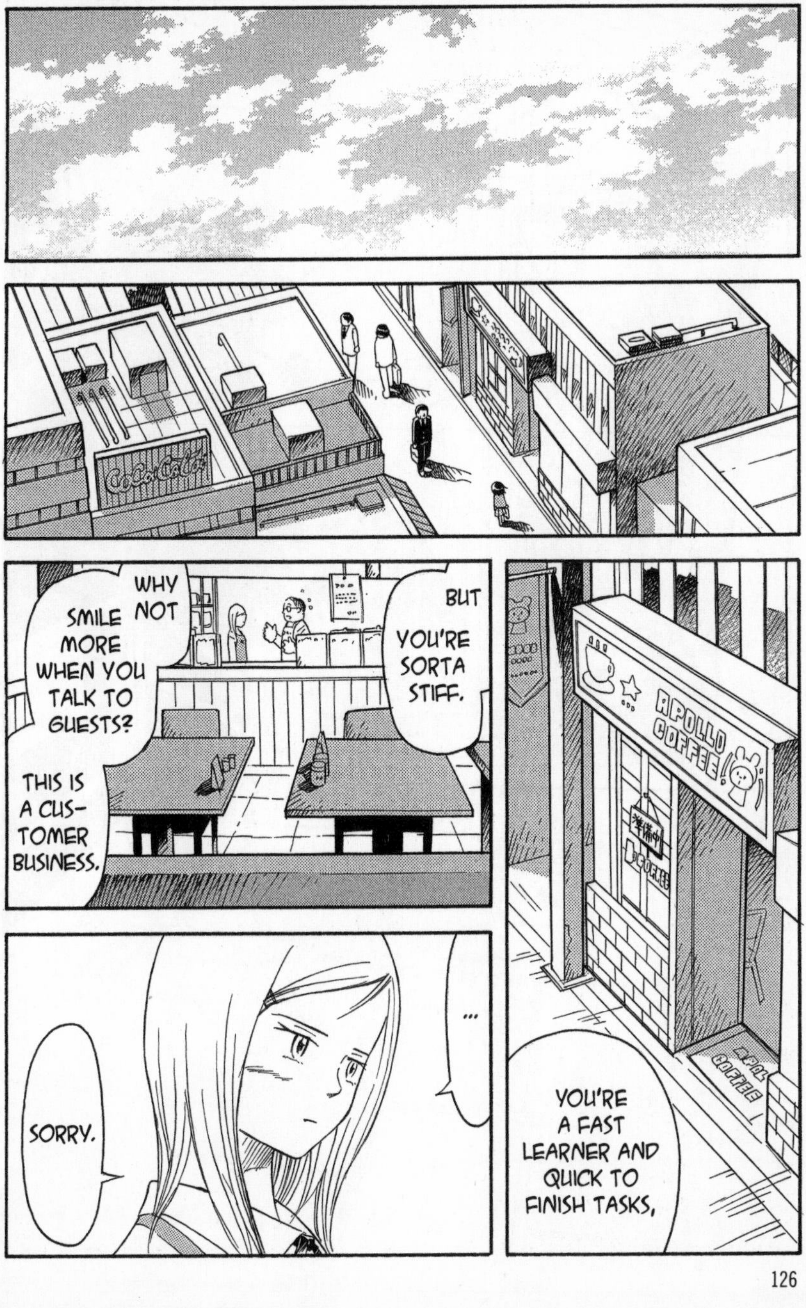
APOLLO COFFEE
準備中
YOU'RE A FAST LEARNER AND QUICK TO FINISH TASKS,
BUT YOU'RE SORTA STIFF.
WHY NOT SMILE MORE WHEN YOU TALK TO GUESTS?
THIS IS A CUS-TOMER BUSINESS.
...
SORRY.

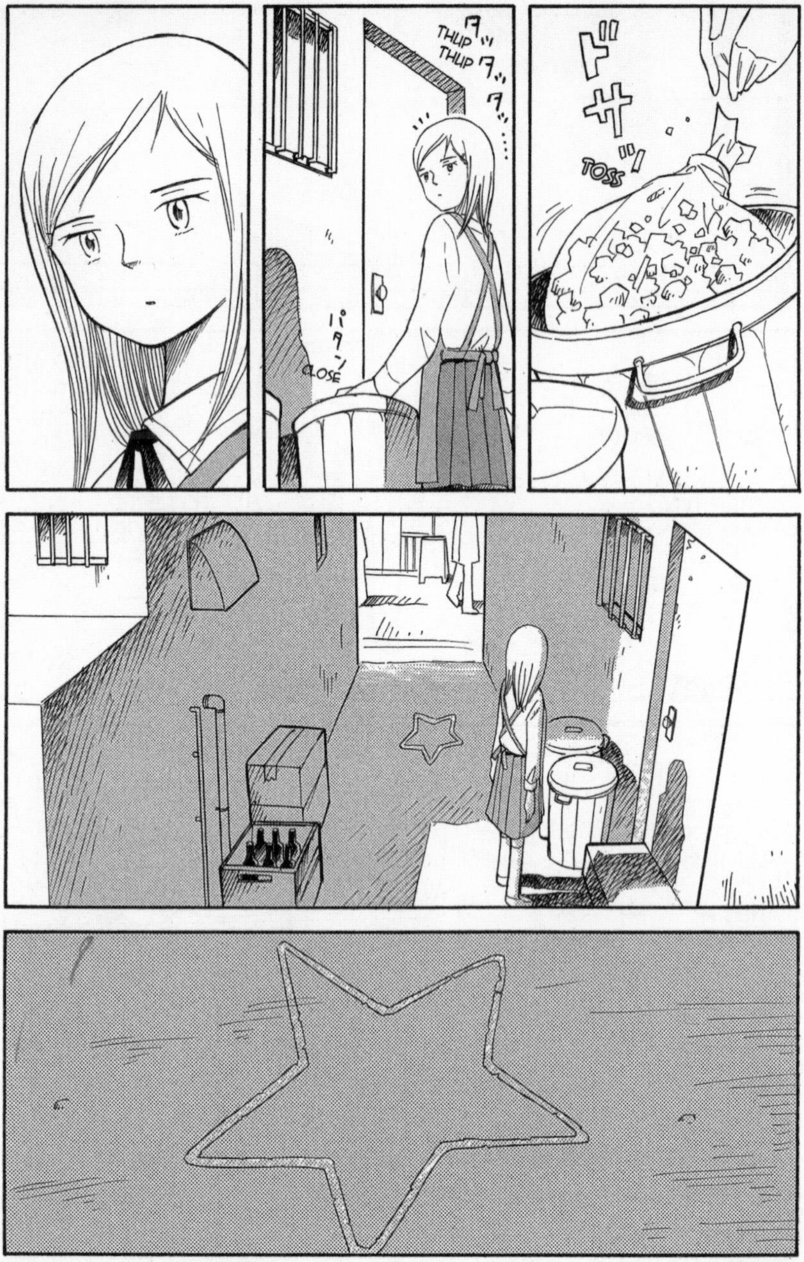
ドザッ
TOSS
タッ
THUP
タッ
THUP
タッ…
パタン
CLOSE

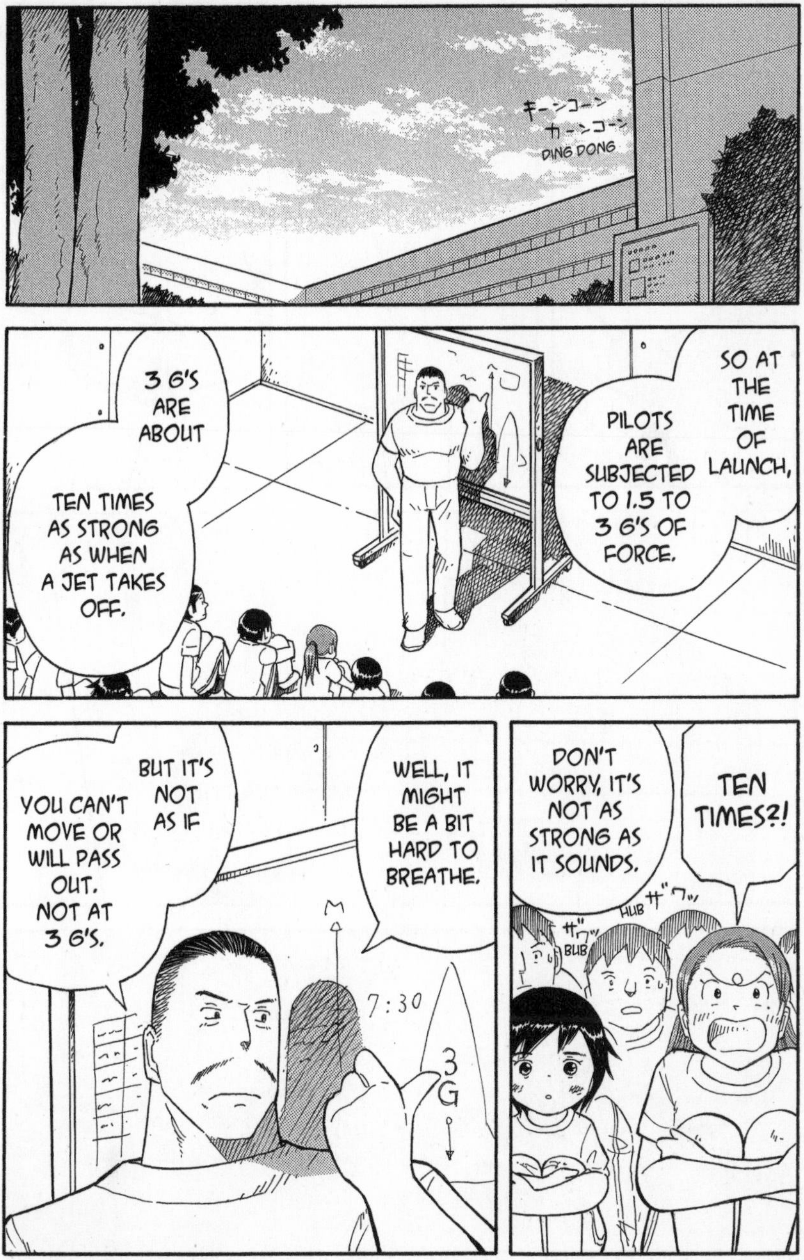
キーンコーン
カーンコーン
DING DONG
SO AT THE TIME OF LAUNCH,
PILOTS ARE SUBJECTED TO 1.5 TO 3 G'S OF FORCE.
3 G'S ARE ABOUT
TEN TIMES AS STRONG AS WHEN A JET TAKES OFF.
TEN TIMES?!
ザワッ
HUB
ザワッ
BUB
DON'T WORRY, IT'S NOT AS STRONG AS IT SOUNDS.
WELL, IT MIGHT BE A BIT HARD TO BREATHE.
BUT IT'S NOT AS IF
YOU CAN'T MOVE OR WILL PASS OUT. NOT AT 3 G'S.
7:30
3G

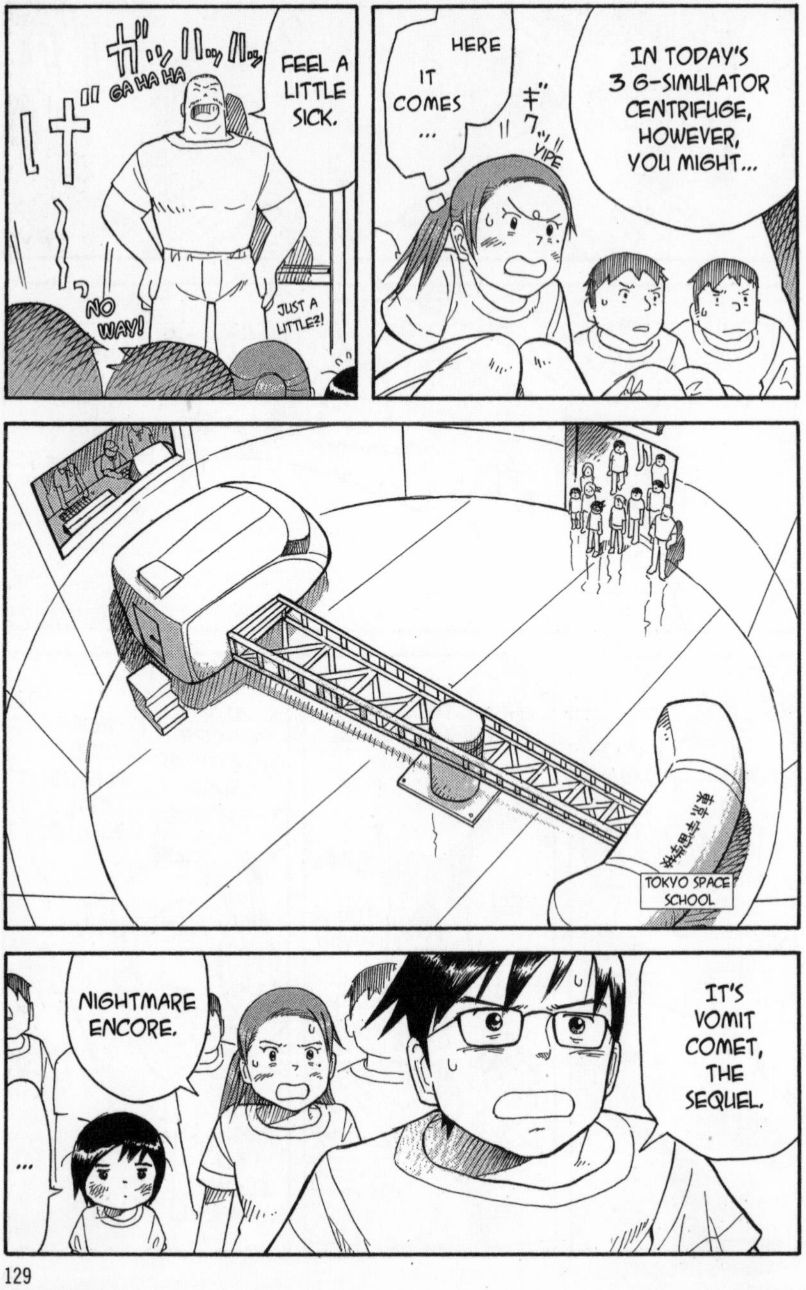
IN TODAY'S 3 G-SIMULATOR CENTRIFUGE, HOWEVER, YOU MIGHT...
HERE IT COMES ...
YIPE
FEEL A LITTLE SICK.
GA HA HA
NO WAY!
JUST A LITTLE?!
TOKYO SPACE SCHOOL
IT'S VOMIT COMET, THE SEQUEL.
NIGHTMARE ENCORE.
...

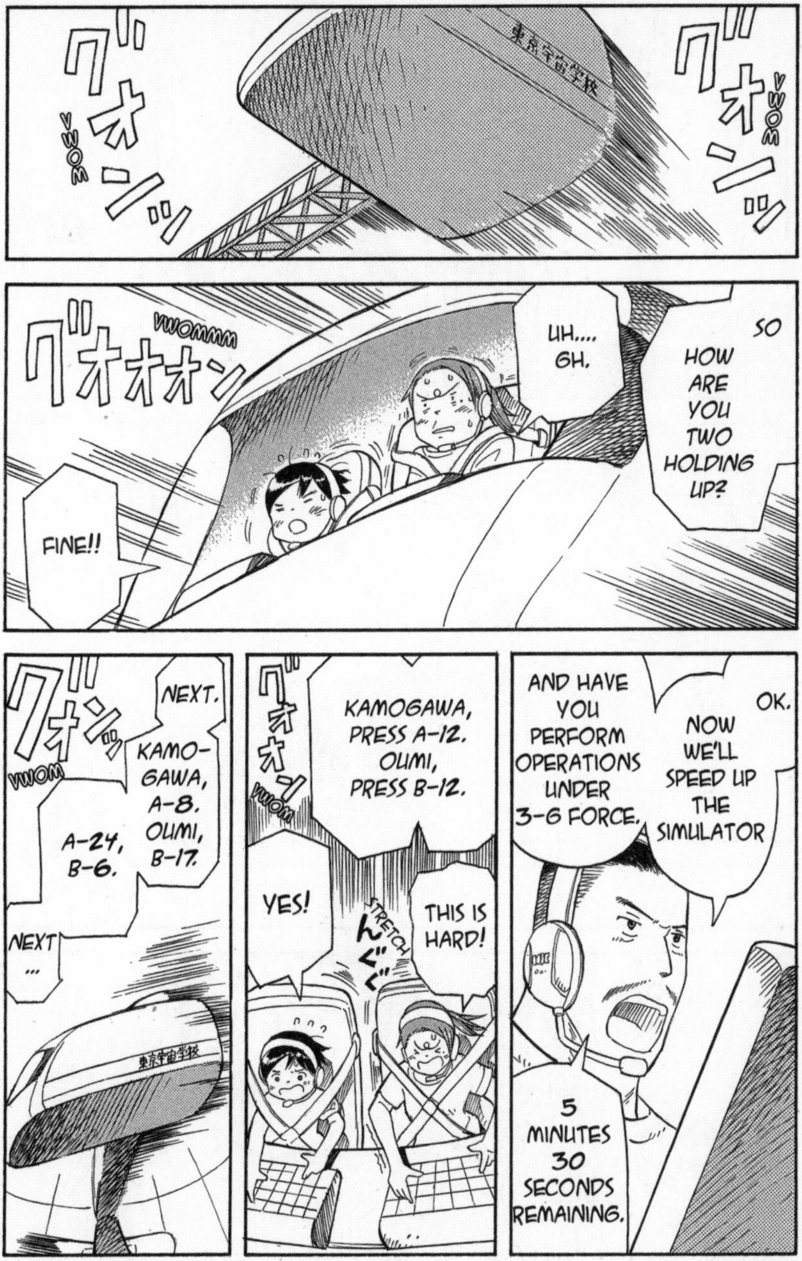
グオーンッ
VWOM
グオーンッ
VWOM
SO HOW ARE YOU TWO HOLDING UP?
UH.... GH.
グオオオン
VWOMMM
FINE!!
OK. NOW WE'LL SPEED UP THE SIMULATOR
AND HAVE YOU PERFORM OPERATIONS UNDER 3-6 FORCE.
5 MINUTES 30 SECONDS REMAINING.
KAMOGAWA, PRESS A-12. OUMI, PRESS B-12.
グオオン
VWOM
THIS IS HARD!
んぐぐ
STRETCH
YES!
NEXT.
KAMO-GAWA, A-8. OUMI, B-17.
A-24, B-6.
グォンッ
VWOM
NEXT ...

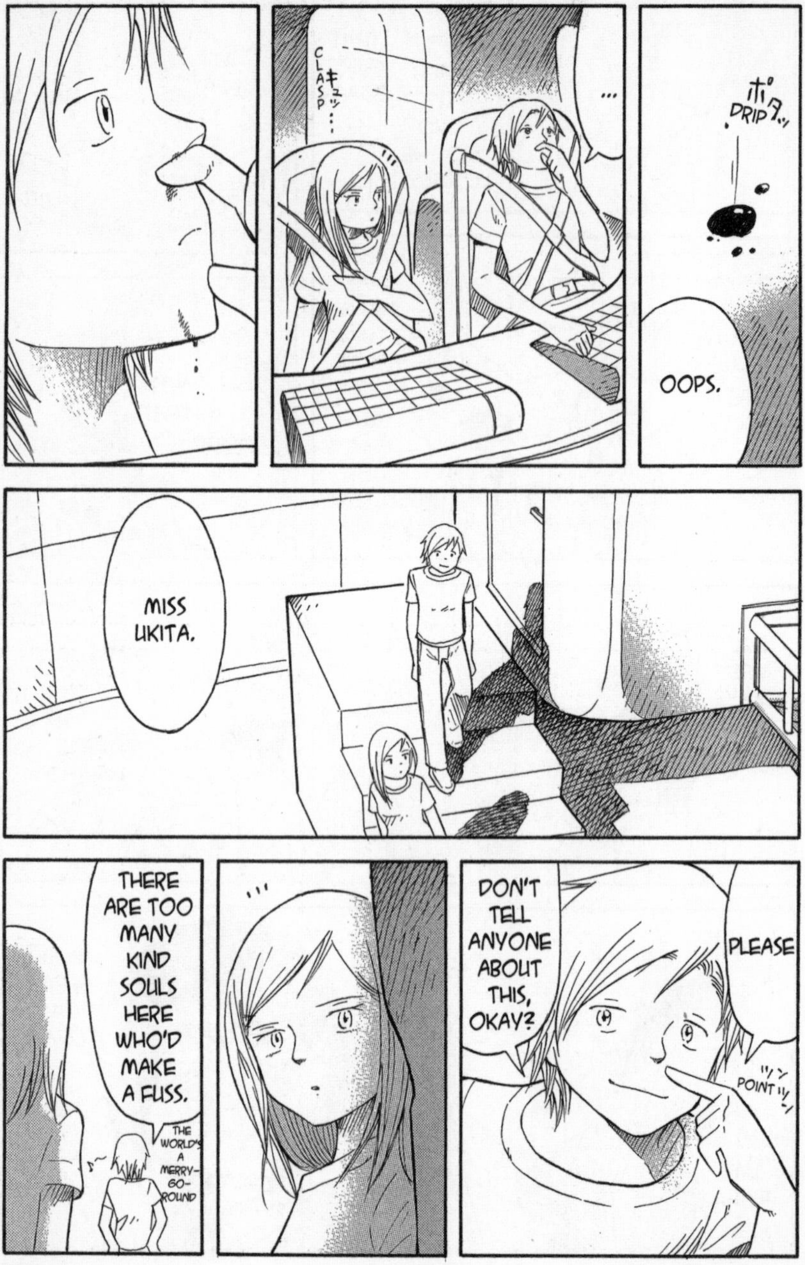
ポタッ
DRIP
OOPS.
...
キュッ...
CLASP
MISS UKITA.
PLEASE
DON'T TELL ANYONE ABOUT THIS, OKAY?
ツン
POINT
...
THERE ARE TOO MANY KIND SOULS HERE WHO'D MAKE A FUSS.
THE WORLD'S A MERRY-GO-ROUND

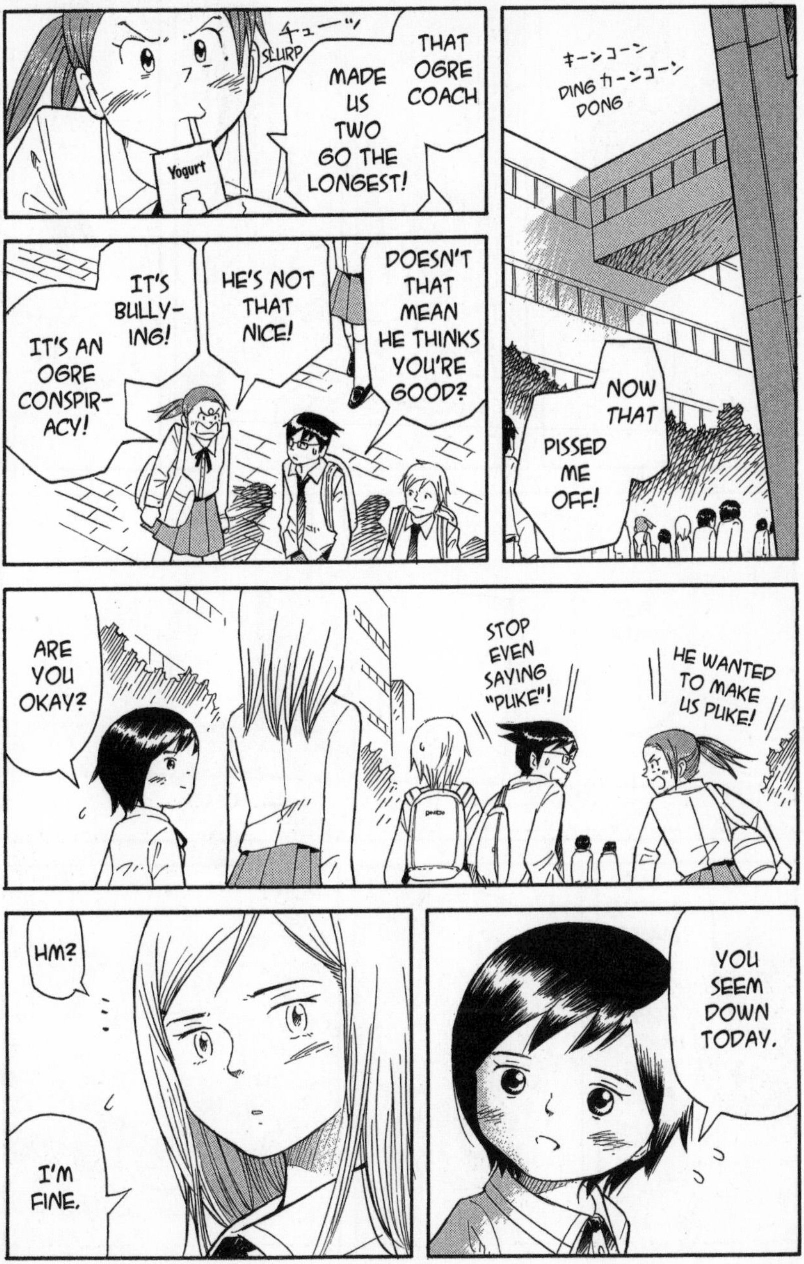
キーンコーン
カーンコーン
DING DONG
NOW THAT PISSED ME OFF!
チューッ
SLURP
THAT OGRE COACH MADE US TWO GO THE LONGEST!
Yogurt
DOESN'T THAT MEAN HE THINKS YOU'RE GOOD?
HE'S NOT THAT NICE!
IT'S BULLY-ING!
IT'S AN OGRE CONSPIR-ACY!
HE WANTED TO MAKE US PUKE!
STOP EVEN SAYING "PUKE"!
ARE YOU OKAY?
YOU SEEM DOWN TODAY.
HM?
I'M FINE.

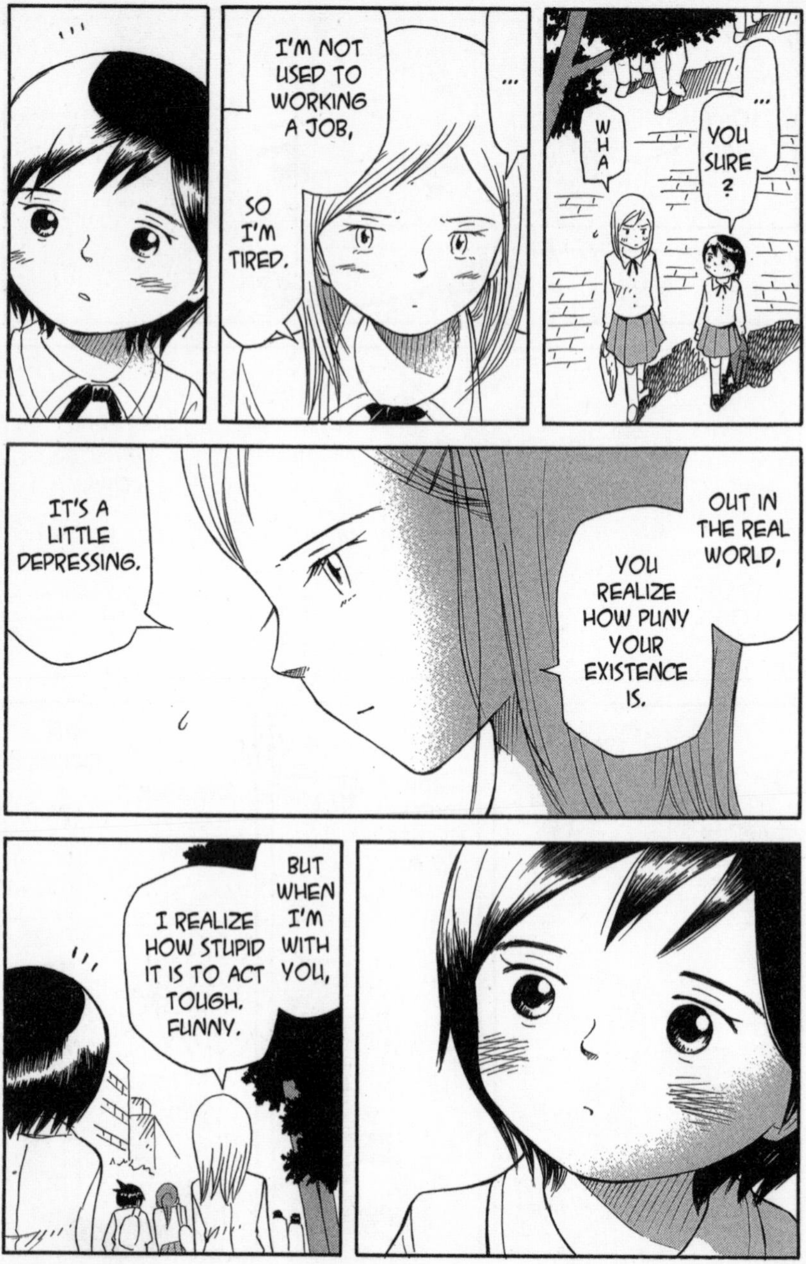

... YOU SURE?
WHA
...
I'M NOT USED TO WORKING A JOB,
SO I'M TIRED.
...
OUT IN THE REAL WORLD,
YOU REALIZE HOW PUNY YOUR EXISTENCE IS.
IT'S A LITTLE DEPRESSING.
BUT WHEN I'M WITH YOU,
I REALIZE HOW STUPID IT IS TO ACT TOUGH. FUNNY.
...

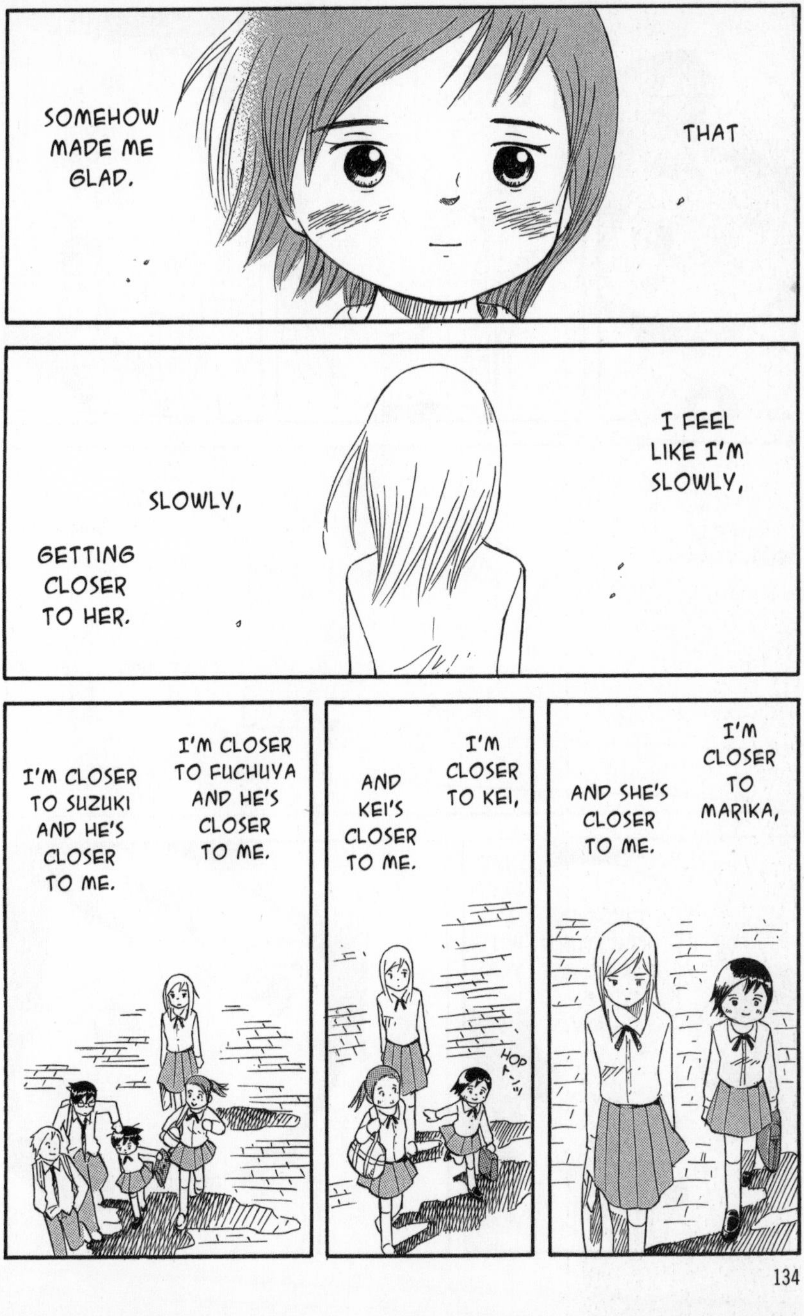
THAT
SOMEHOW MADE ME GLAD.
I FEEL LIKE I'M SLOWLY,
SLOWLY,
GETTING CLOSER TO HER.
I'M CLOSER TO MARIKA,
AND SHE'S CLOSER TO ME.
I'M CLOSER TO KEI,
AND KEI'S CLOSER TO ME.
HOP
I'M CLOSER TO FUCHUYA AND HE'S CLOSER TO ME.
I'M CLOSER TO SUZUKI AND HE'S CLOSER TO ME.

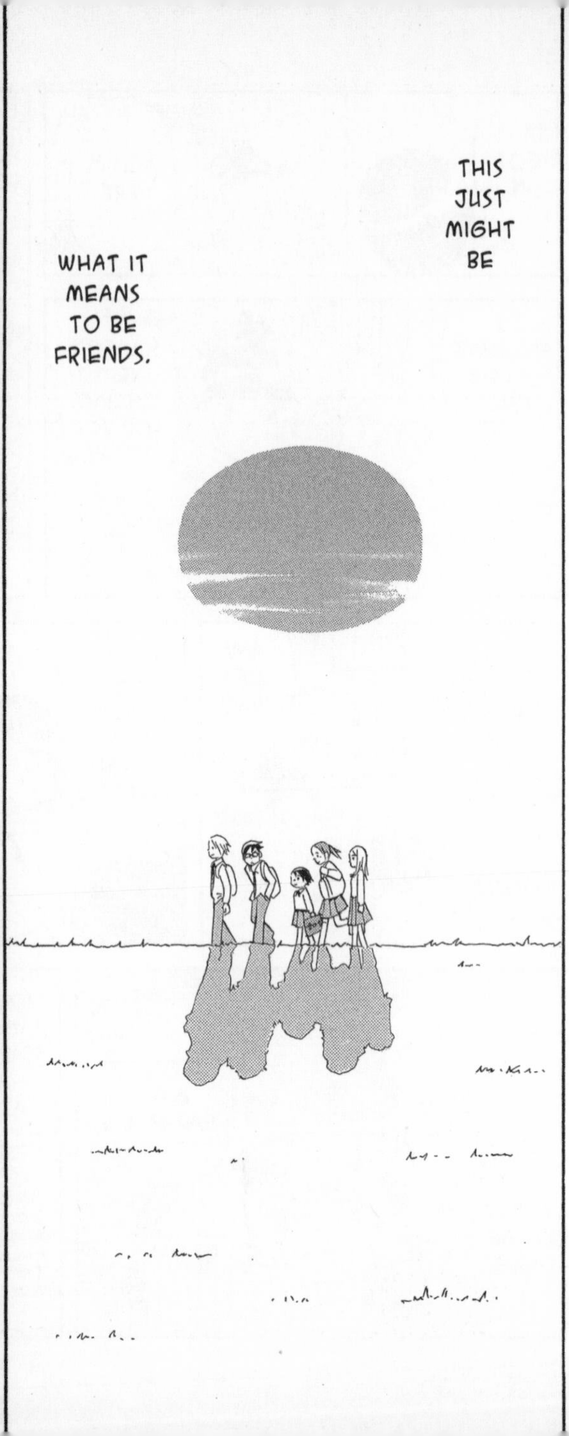
THIS JUST MIGHT BE
WHAT IT MEANS TO BE FRIENDS.
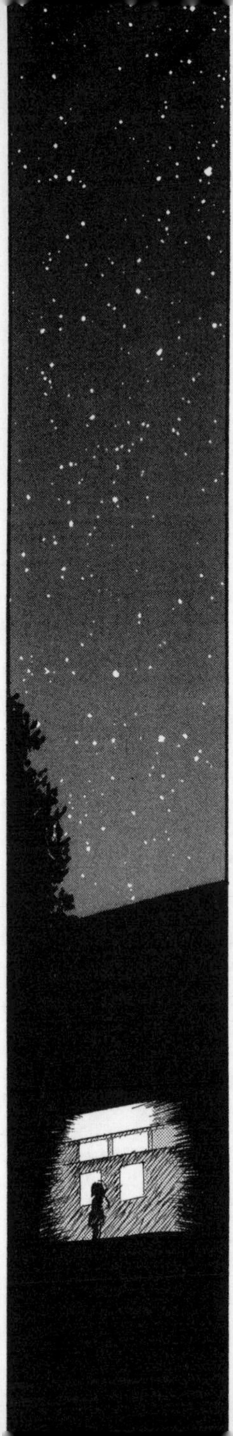

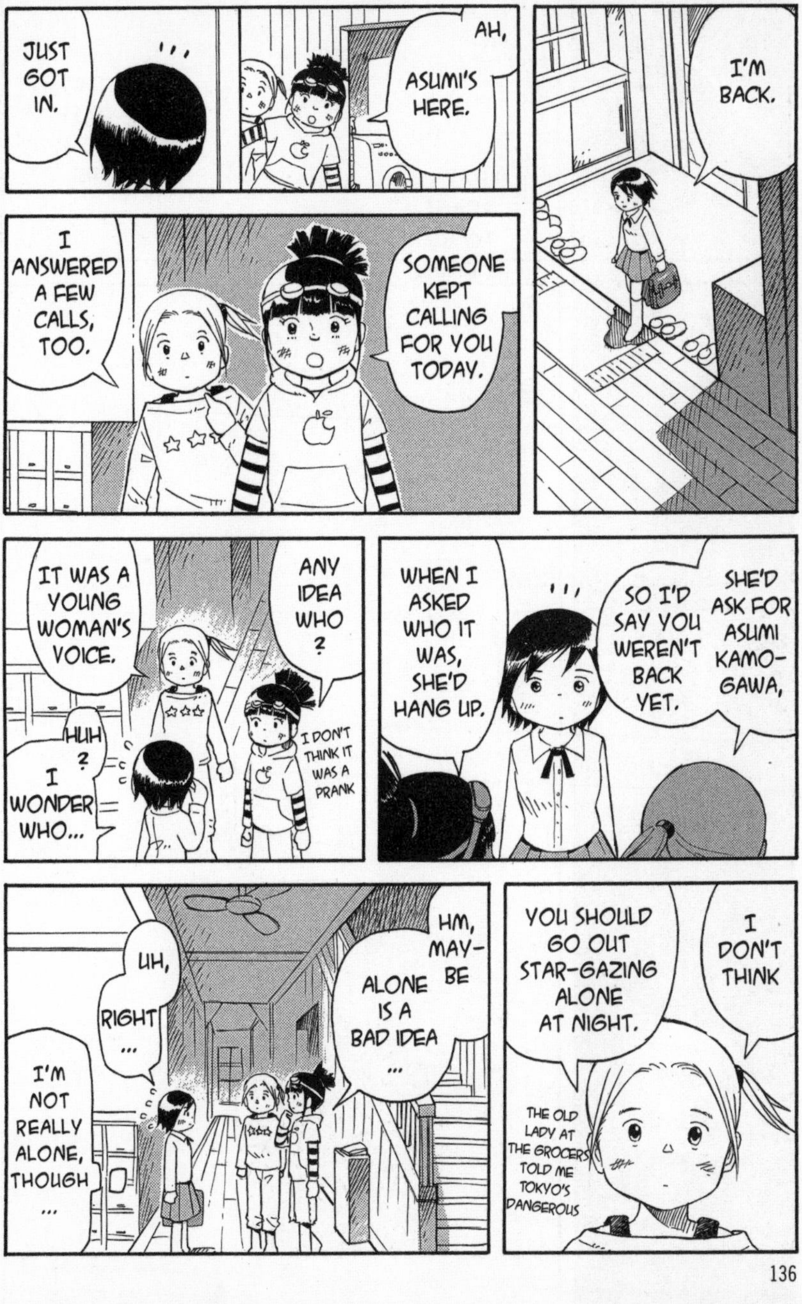
I'M BACK.
AH, ASUMI'S HERE.
JUST GOT IN.
SOMEONE KEPT CALLING FOR YOU TODAY.
I ANSWERED A FEW CALLS, TOO.
SHE'D ASK FOR ASUMI KAMO-GAWA,
SO I'D SAY YOU WEREN'T BACK YET.
WHEN I ASKED WHO IT WAS, SHE'D HANG UP.
ANY IDEA WHO?
IT WAS A YOUNG WOMAN'S VOICE.
I DON'T THINK IT WAS A PRANK
HUH?
I WONDER WHO...
I DON'T THINK
YOU SHOULD GO OUT STAR-GAZING ALONE AT NIGHT.
THE OLD LADY AT THE GROCERS TOLD ME TOKYO'S DANGEROUS
HM, MAY-BE
ALONE IS A BAD IDEA ...
UH,
RIGHT ...
I'M NOT REALLY ALONE, THOUGH ...

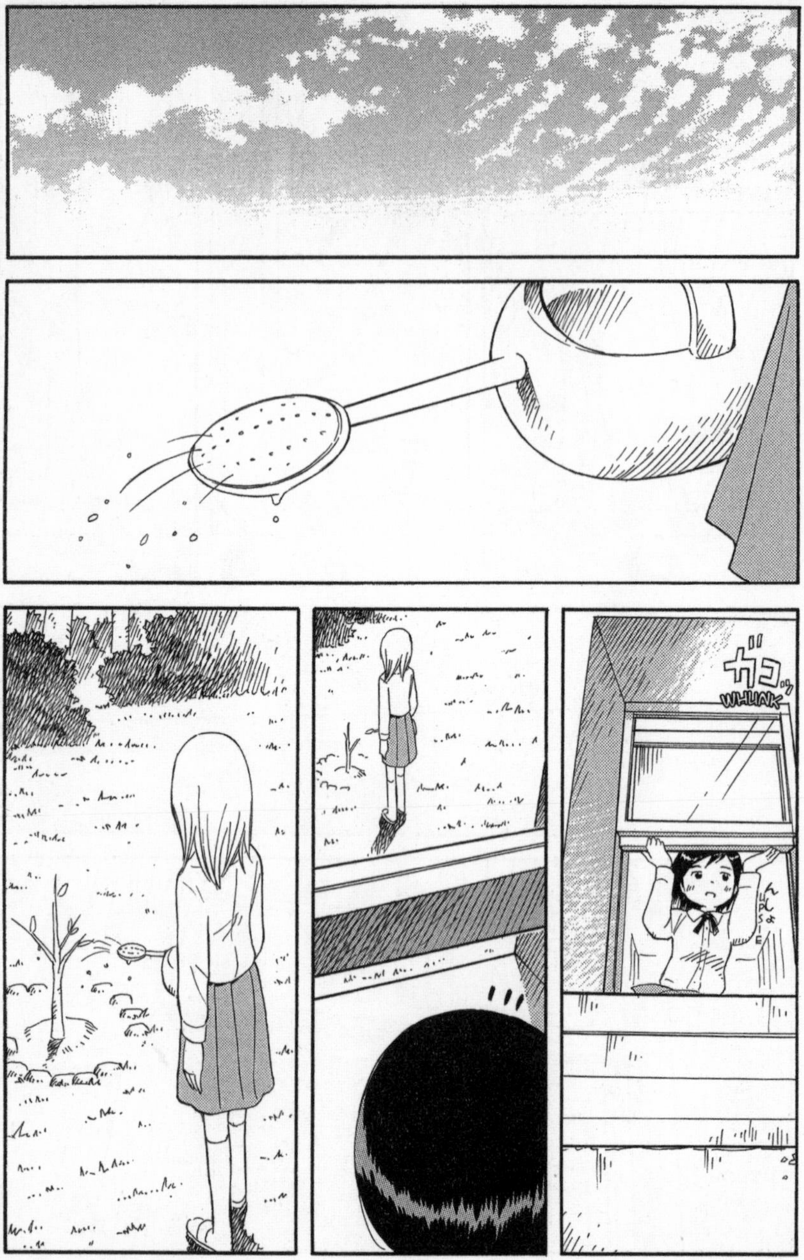
ガコッ
WHUNK
んしょ
UPSIE

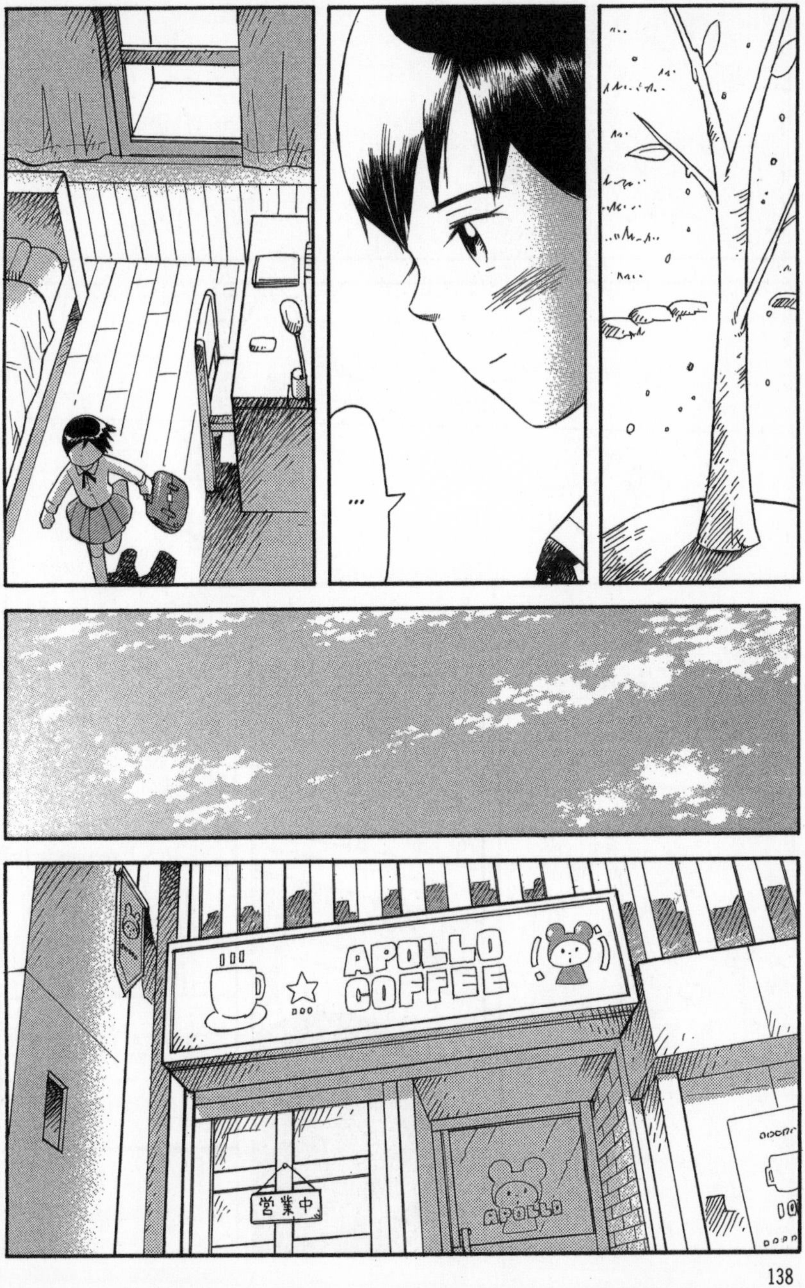
...
APOLLO COFFEE
営業中
APOLLO

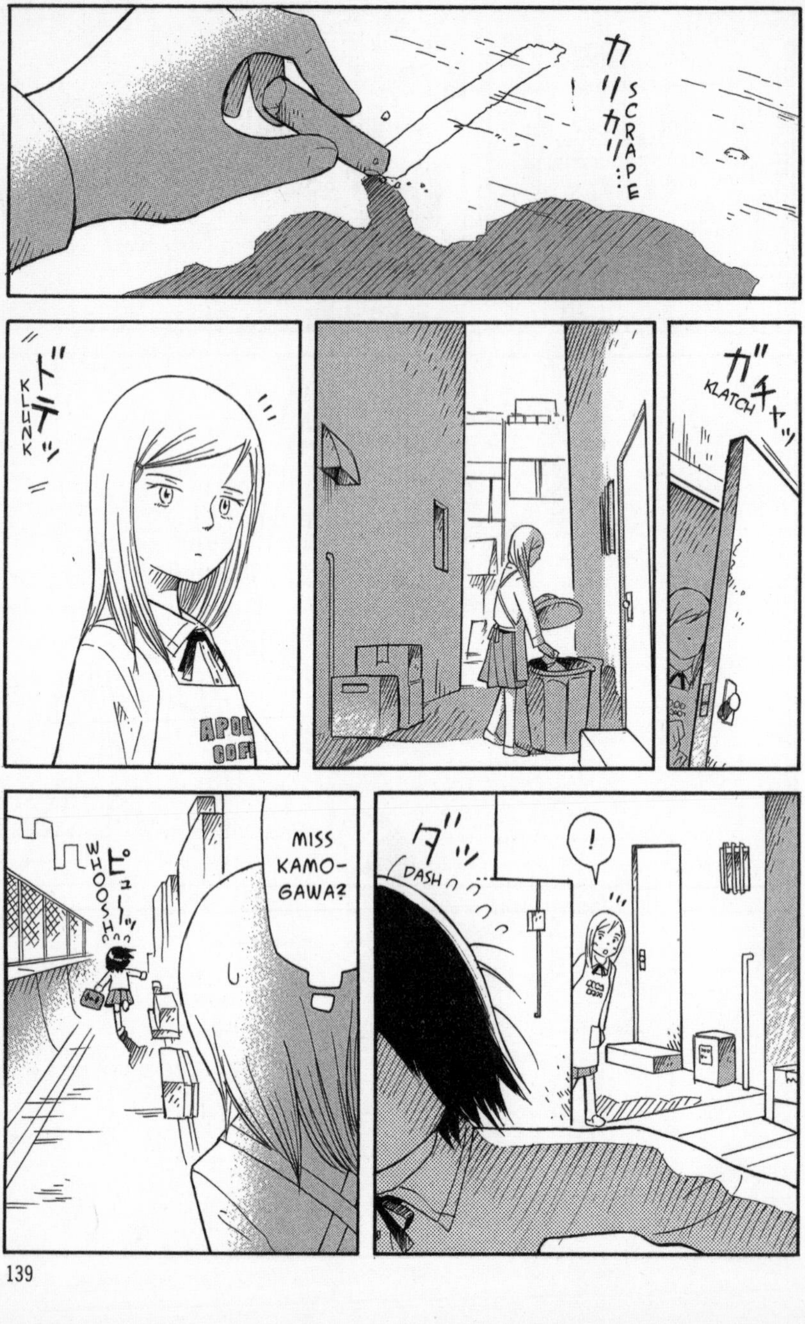
カリカリ…
SCRAPE
ガチャッ
KLATCH
ドテッ
KLUNK
ダッ
DASH
!
MISS KAMO-GAWA?
ピューッ
WHOOSH

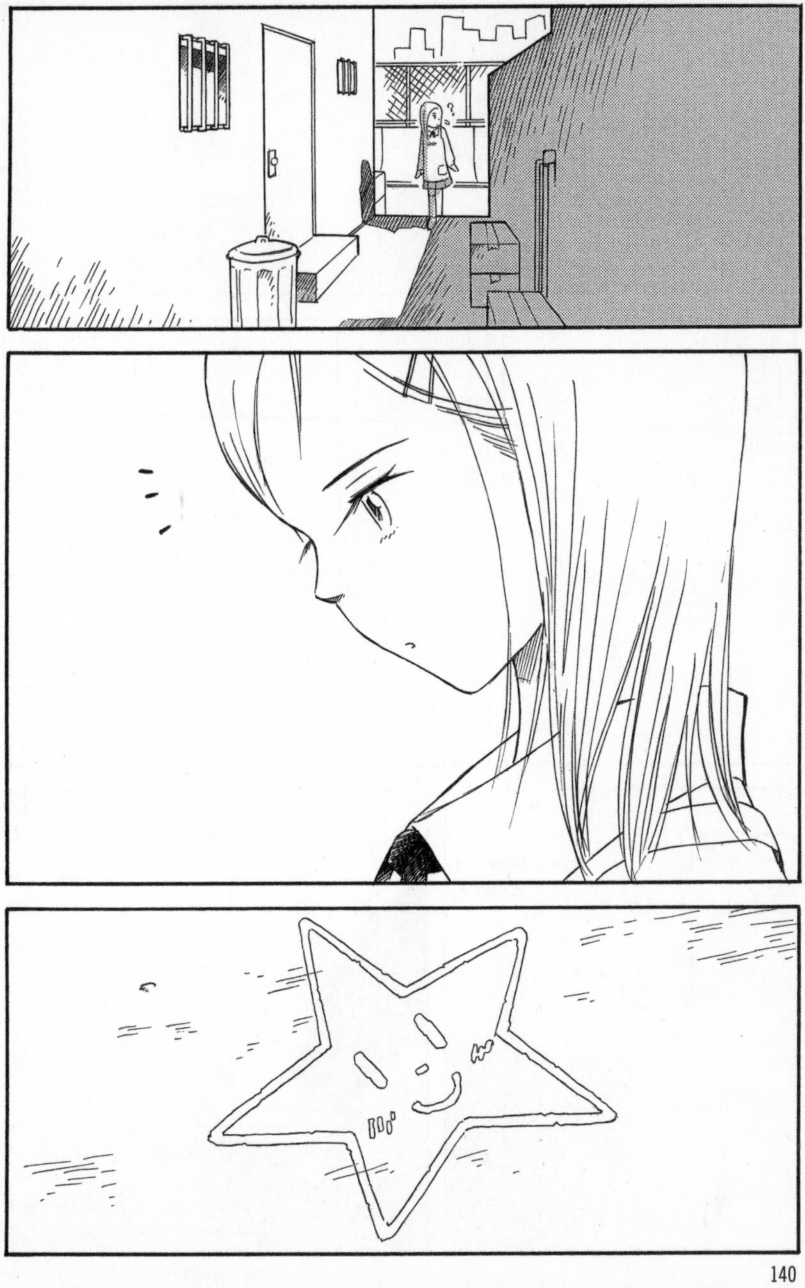

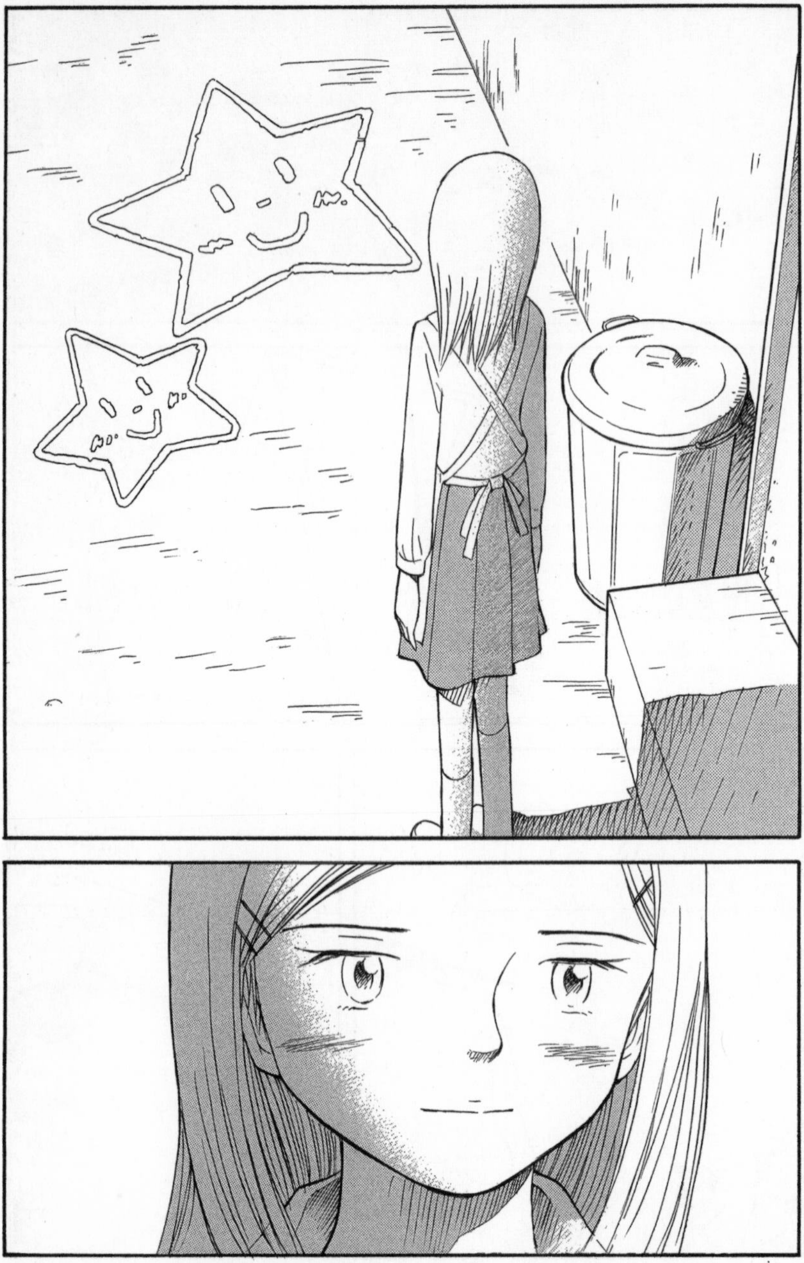

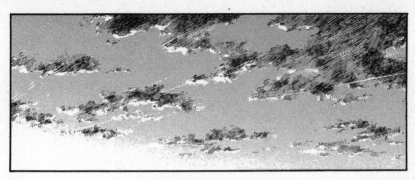

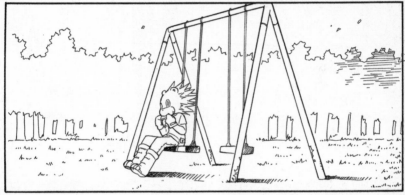

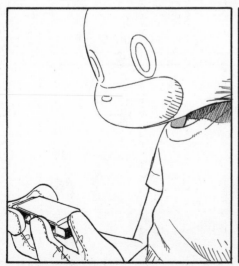

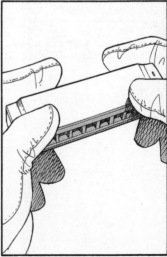

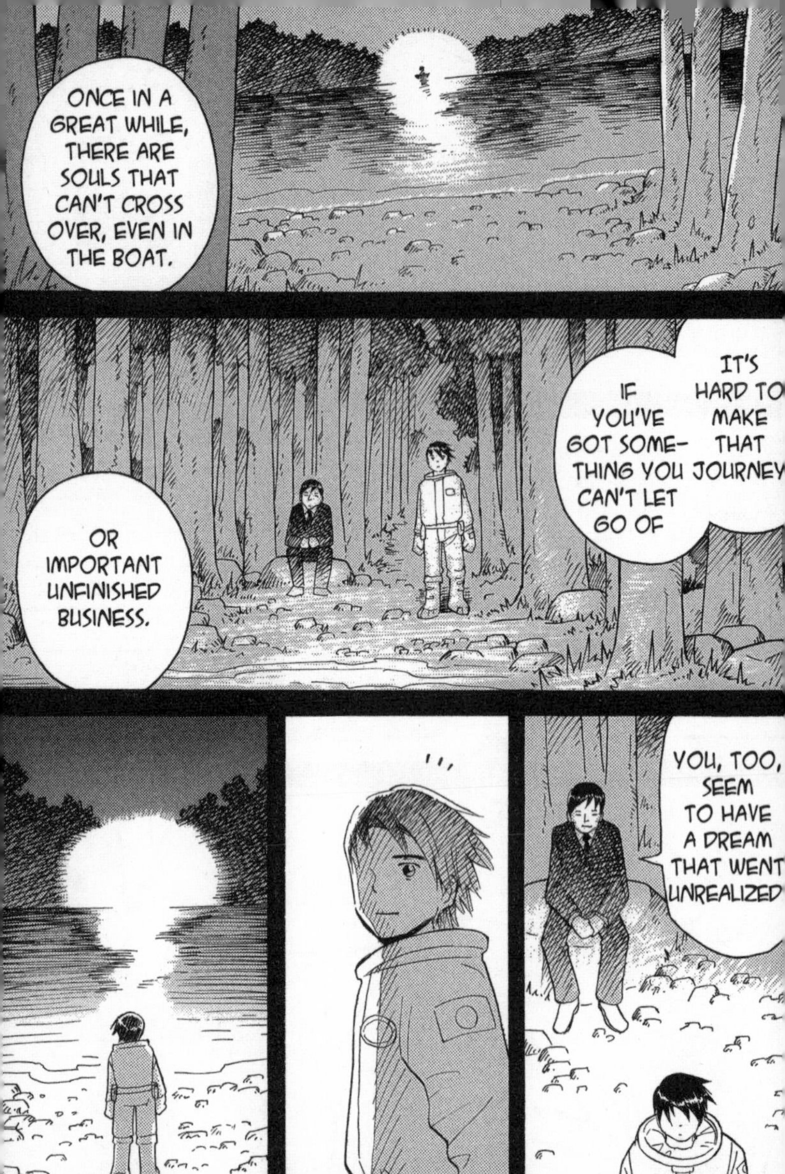
ONCE IN A GREAT WHILE, THERE ARE SOULS THAT CAN'T CROSS OVER, EVEN IN THE BOAT.
IT'S HARD TO MAKE THAT JOURNEY
IF YOU'VE GOT SOME-THING YOU CAN'T LET GO OF
OR IMPORTANT UNFINISHED BUSINESS.
YOU, TOO, SEEM TO HAVE A DREAM THAT WENT UNREALIZED

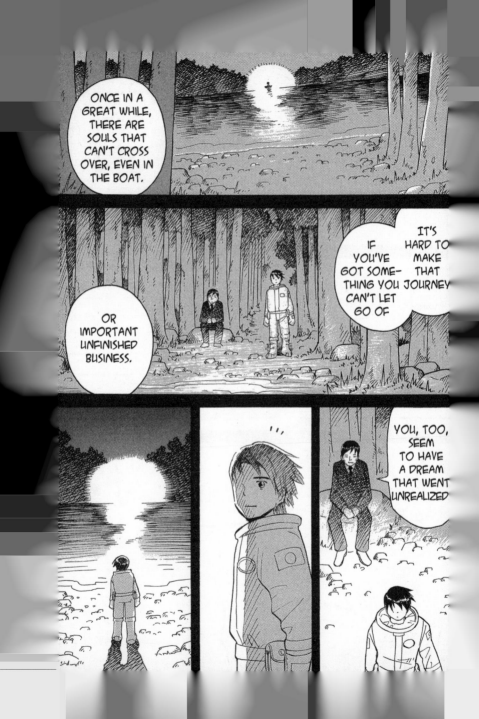

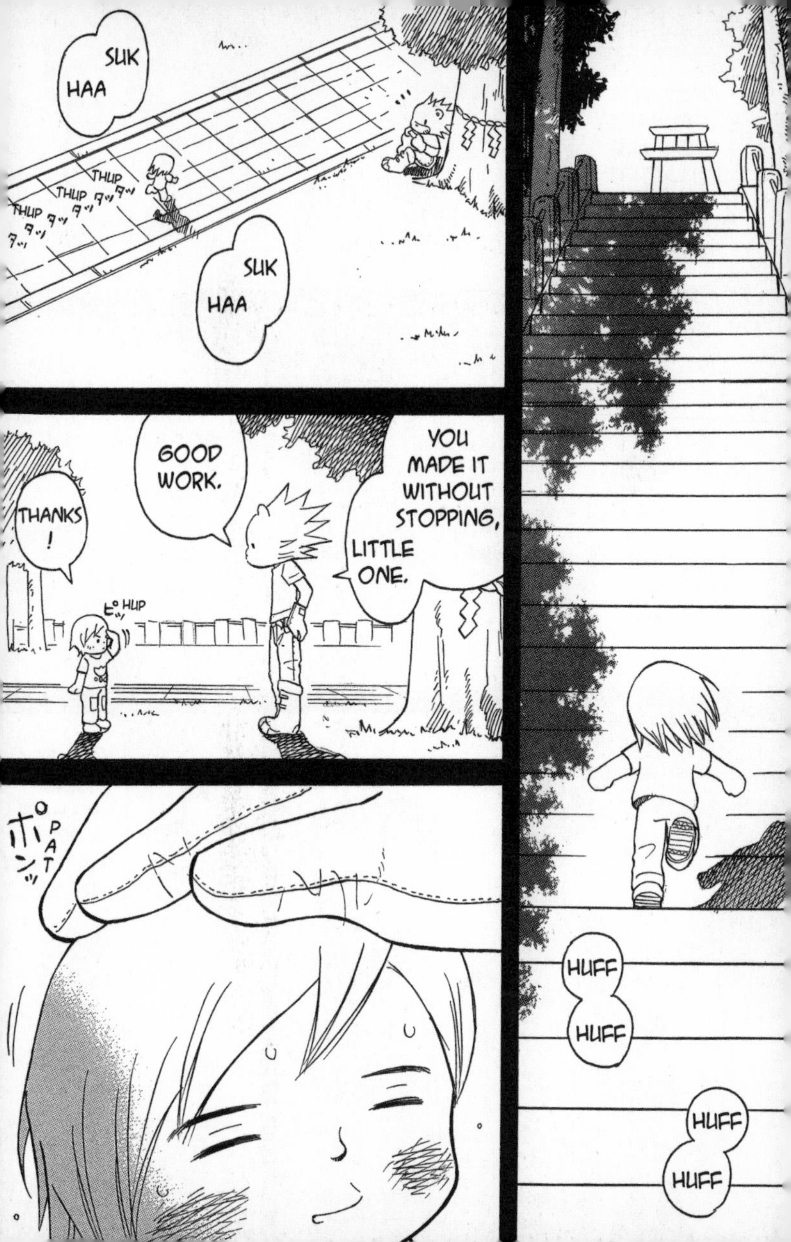
HUFF
HUFF
HUFF
HUFF
SUK HAA
THUP タッ THUP タッ THUP タッ
SUK HAA
YOU MADE IT WITHOUT STOPPING, LITTLE ONE.
GOOD WORK.
ピッ HUP
THANKS!
ポンッ PAT

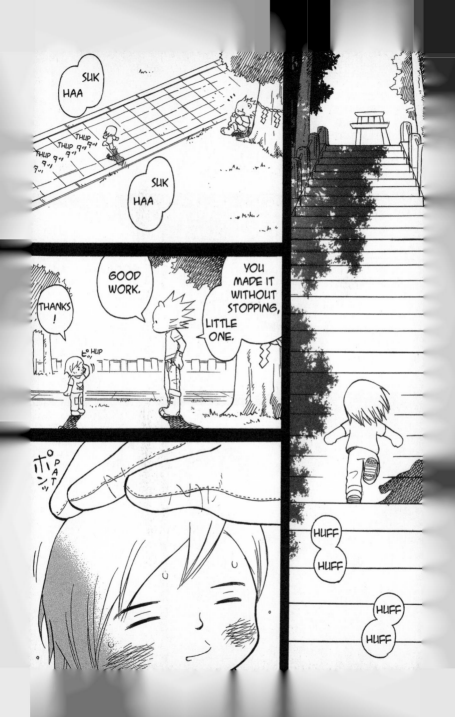

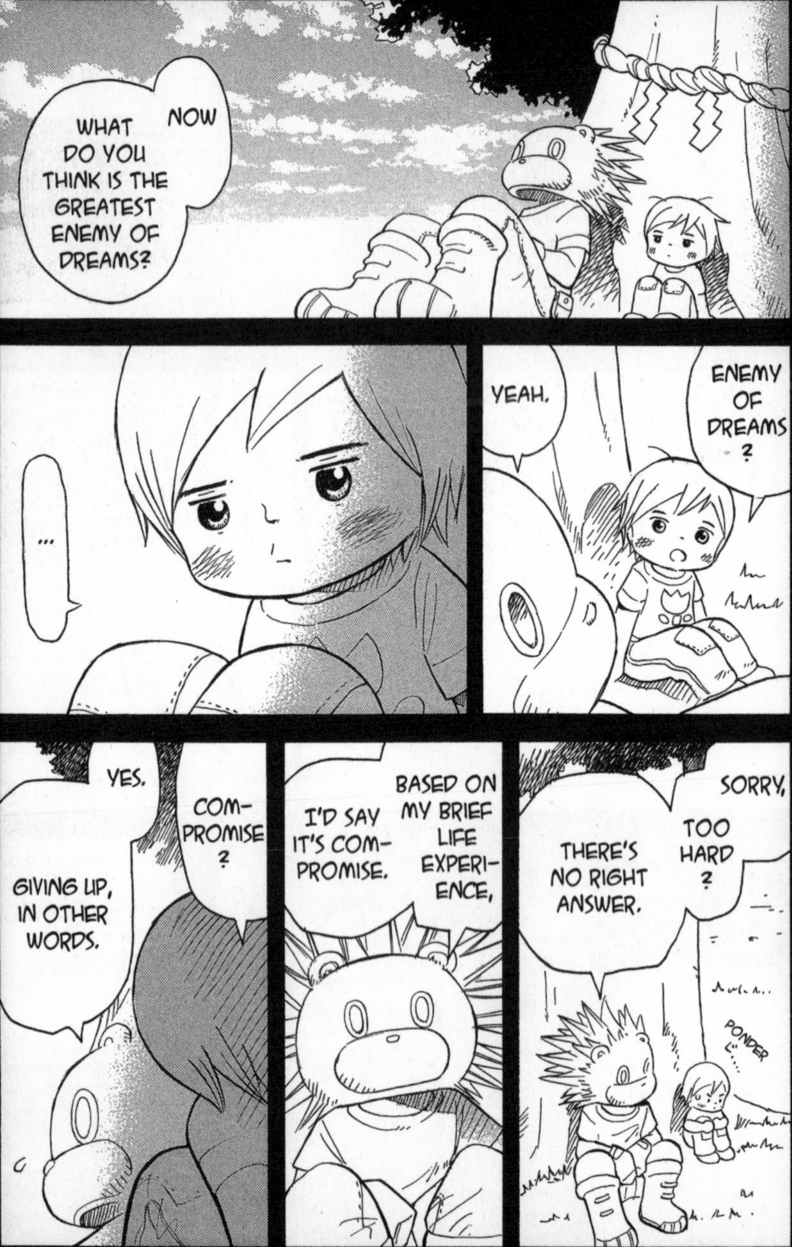
NOW WHAT DO YOU THINK IS THE GREATEST ENEMY OF DREAMS?
ENEMY OF DREAMS?
YEAH.
...
SORRY, TOO HARD?
THERE'S NO RIGHT ANSWER.
PONDER
BASED ON MY BRIEF LIFE EXPERI-ENCE,
I'D SAY IT'S COM-PROMISE.
COM-PROMISE?
YES.
GIVING UP, IN OTHER WORDS.

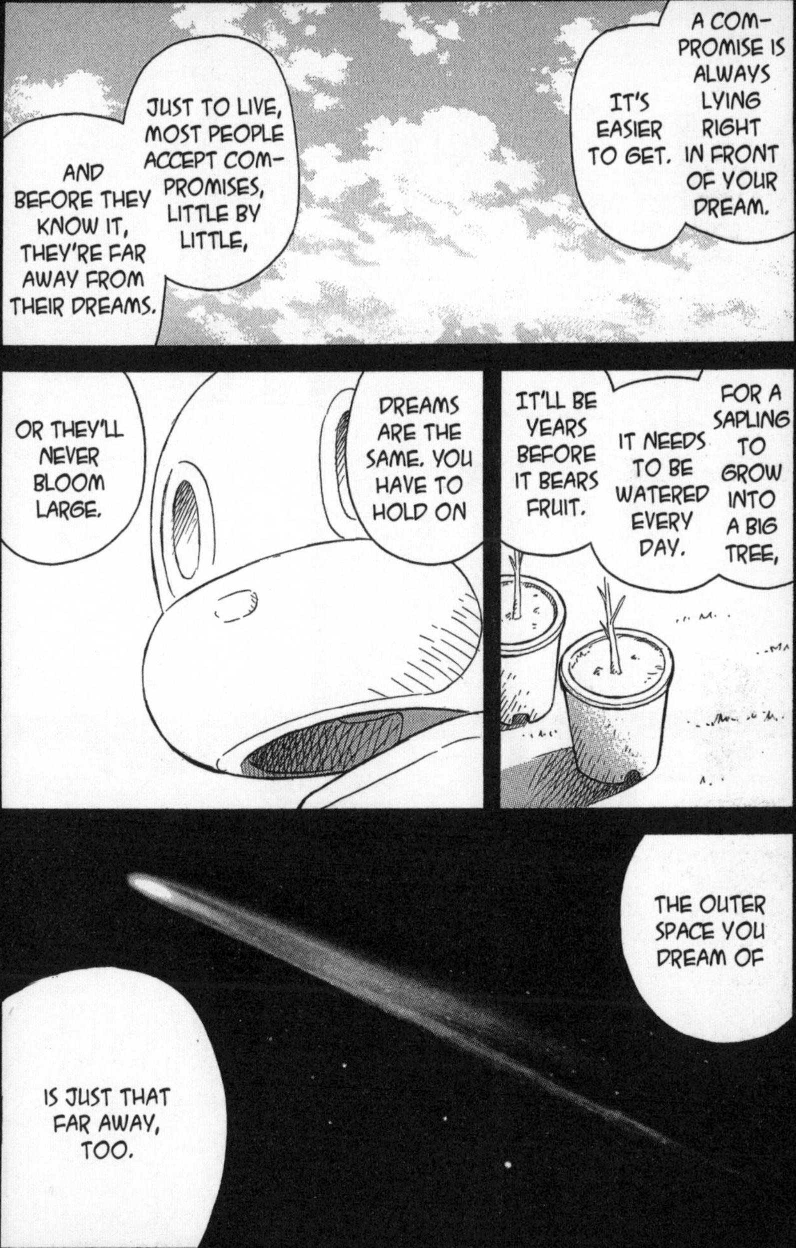
A COMPROMISE IS ALWAYS LYING RIGHT IN FRONT OF YOUR DREAM.
IT'S EASIER TO GET.
JUST TO LIVE, MOST PEOPLE ACCEPT COMPROMISES, LITTLE BY LITTLE,
AND BEFORE THEY KNOW IT, THEY'RE FAR AWAY FROM THEIR DREAMS.
FOR A SAPLING TO GROW INTO A BIG TREE,
IT NEEDS TO BE WATERED EVERY DAY.
IT'LL BE YEARS BEFORE IT BEARS FRUIT.
DREAMS ARE THE SAME. YOU HAVE TO HOLD ON
OR THEY'LL NEVER BLOOM LARGE.
THE OUTER SPACE YOU DREAM OF
IS JUST THAT FAR AWAY, TOO.

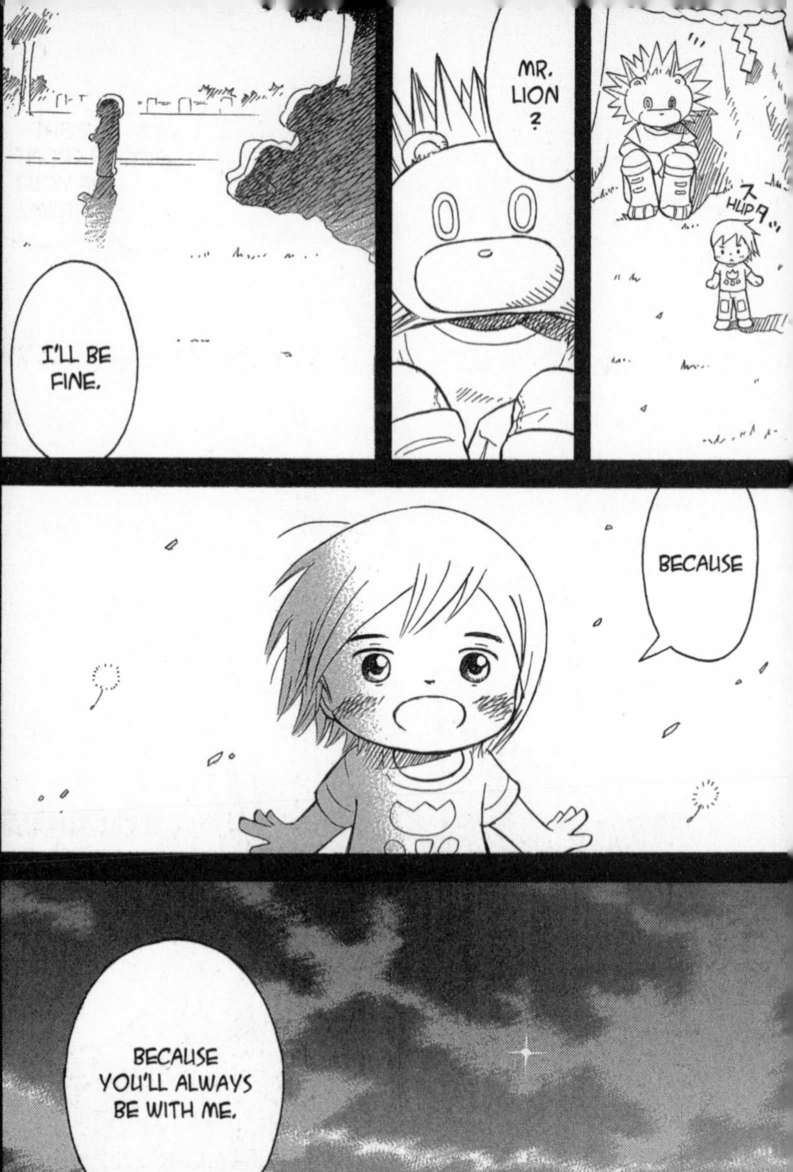
スタッ
HUP
MR. LION?
I'LL BE FINE.
BECAUSE
BECAUSE YOU'LL ALWAYS BE WITH ME.

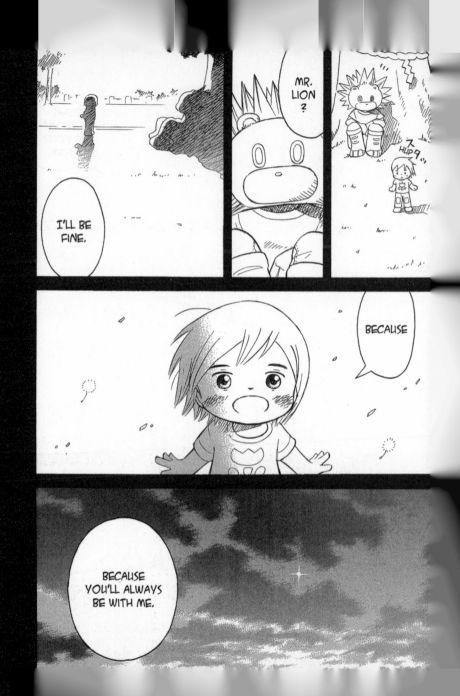

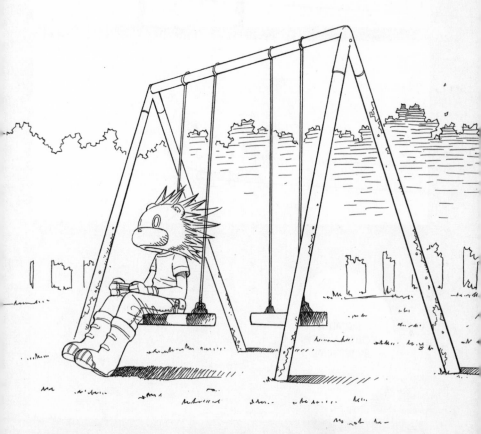

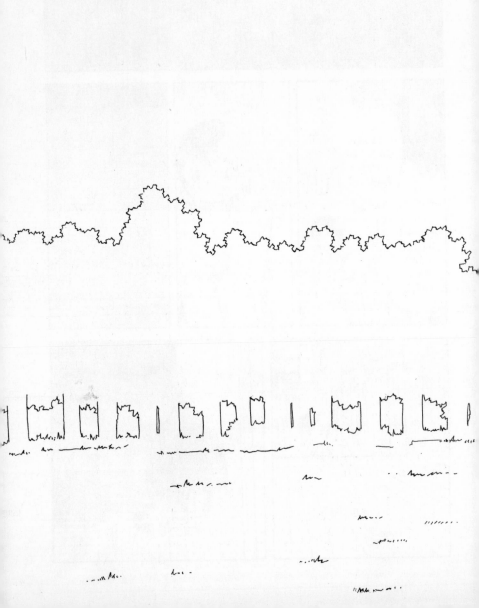

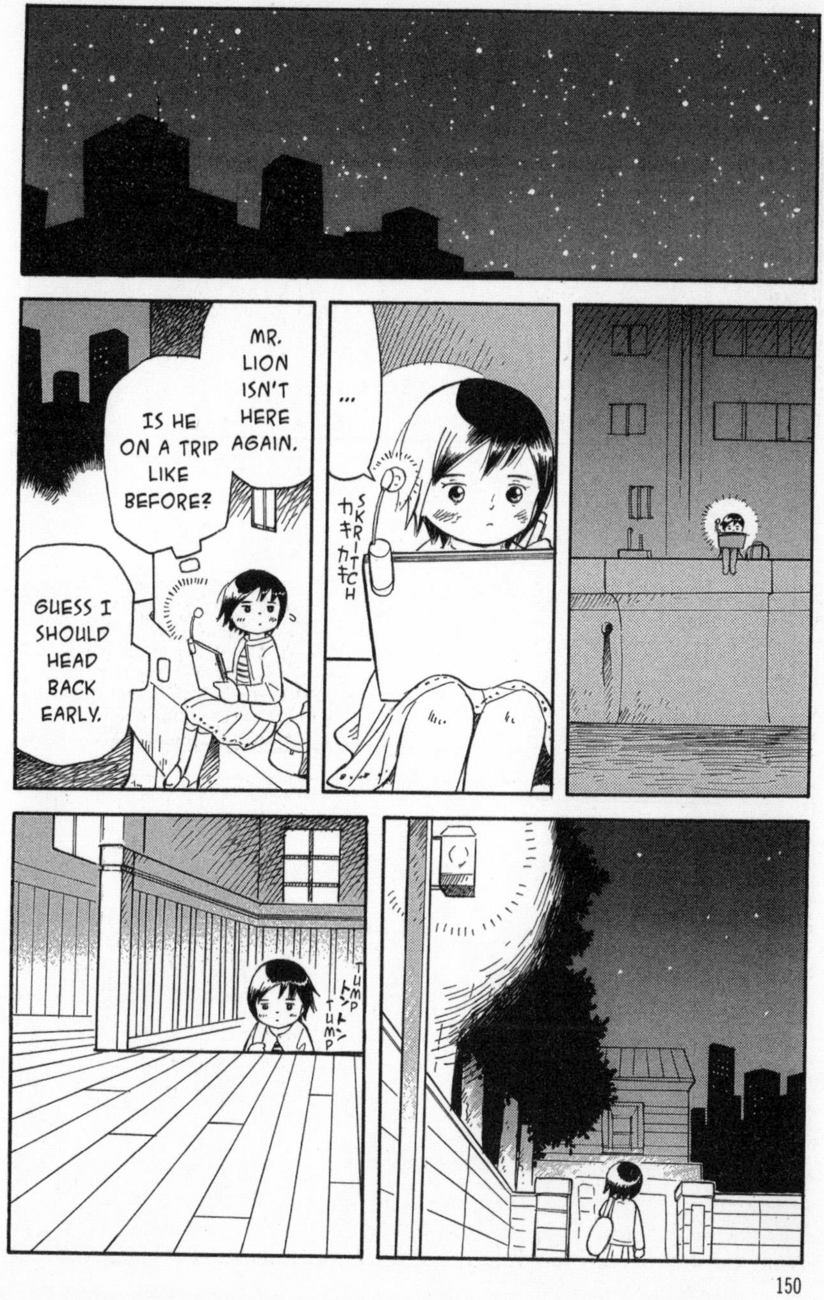
...
SKRITCH
カキカキ
MR. LION ISN'T HERE AGAIN.
IS HE ON A TRIP LIKE BEFORE?
GUESS I SHOULD HEAD BACK EARLY.
TUMP
トン
TUMP
トン

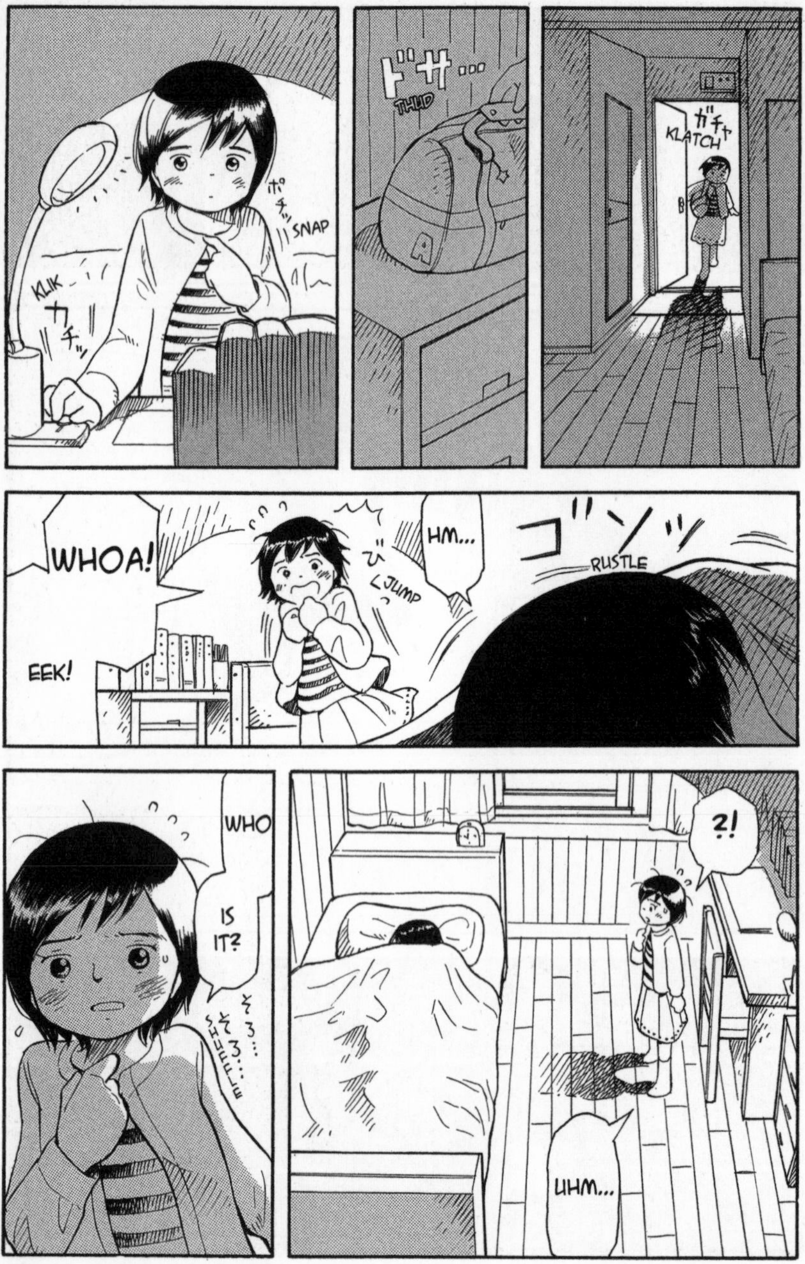
ガチャ
KLATCH
ドサ…
THUD
ポチッ
SNAP
KLIK
カチッ
ゴソッ
RUSTLE
HM...
びく
JUMP
WHOA!
EEK!
?!
UHM...
WHO IS IT?
そろそろ…
SHUFFLE

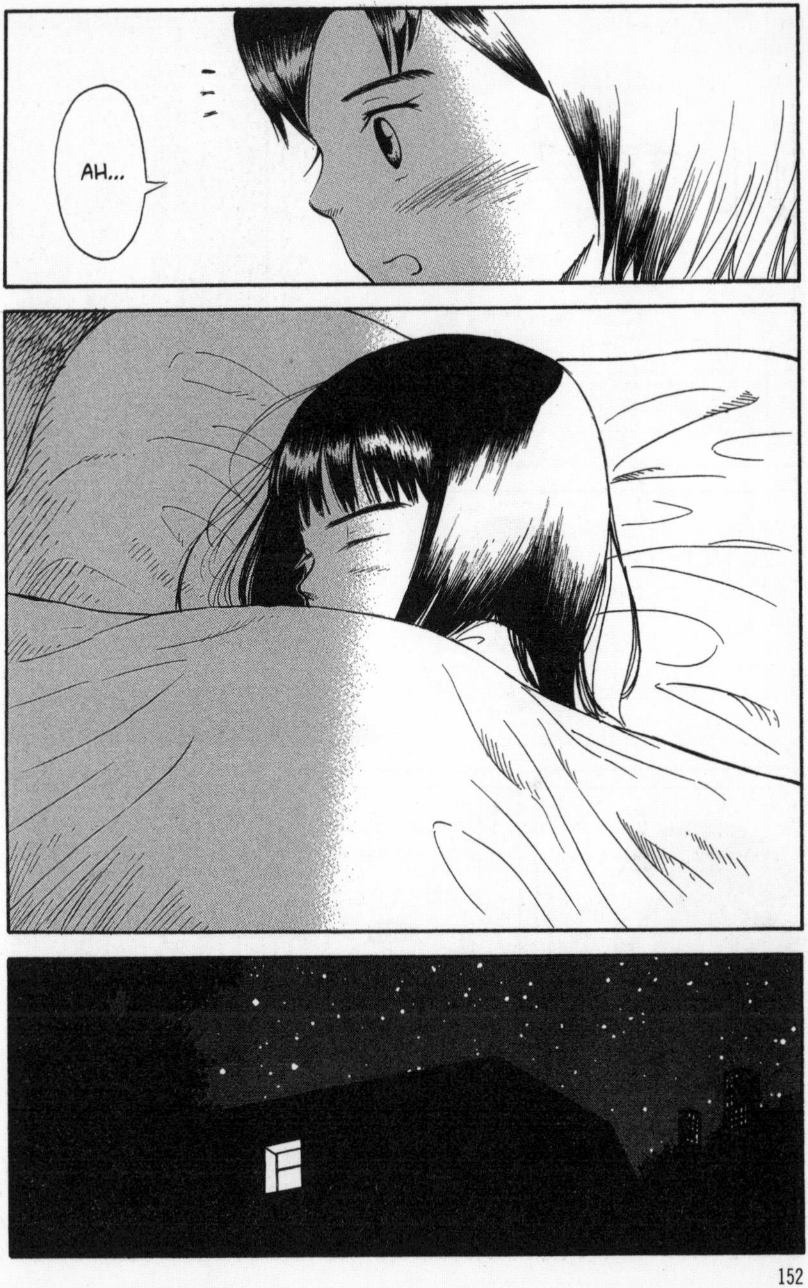
AH...

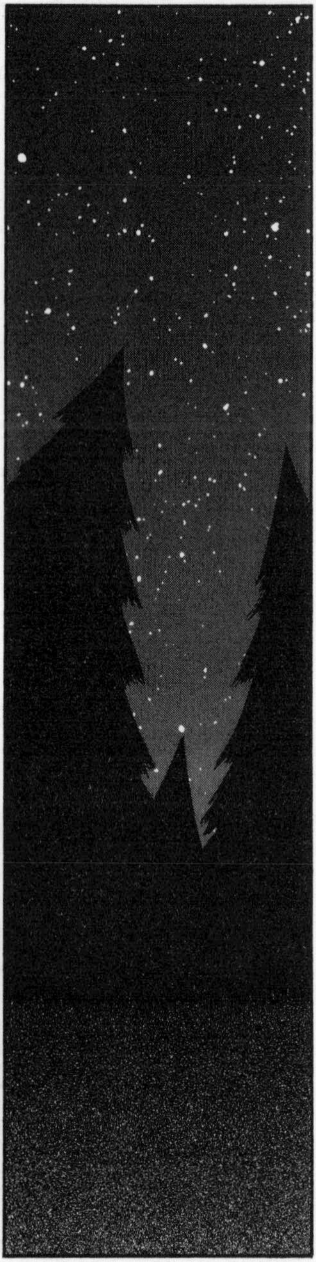

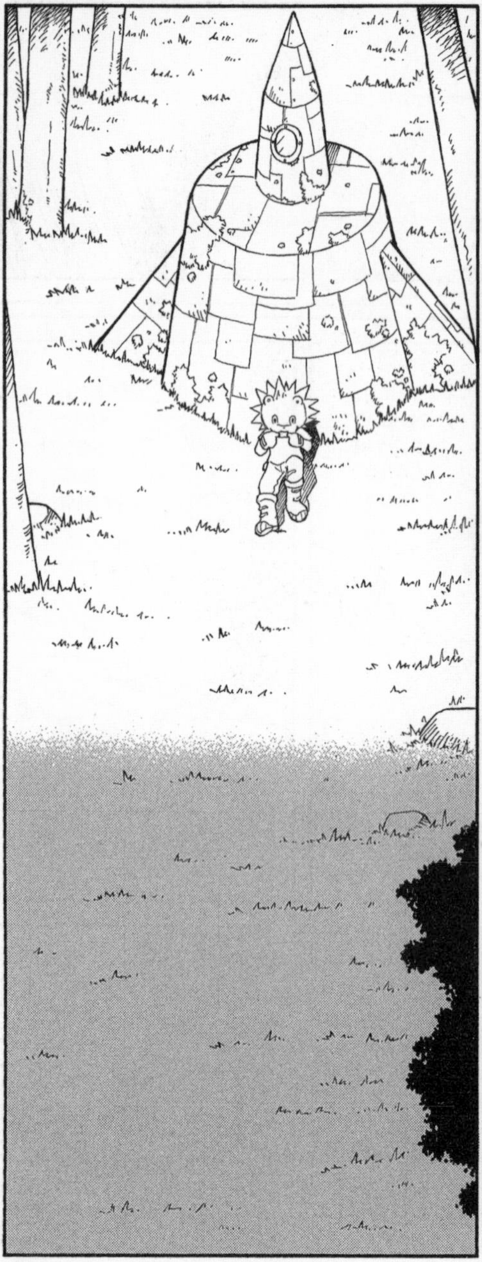

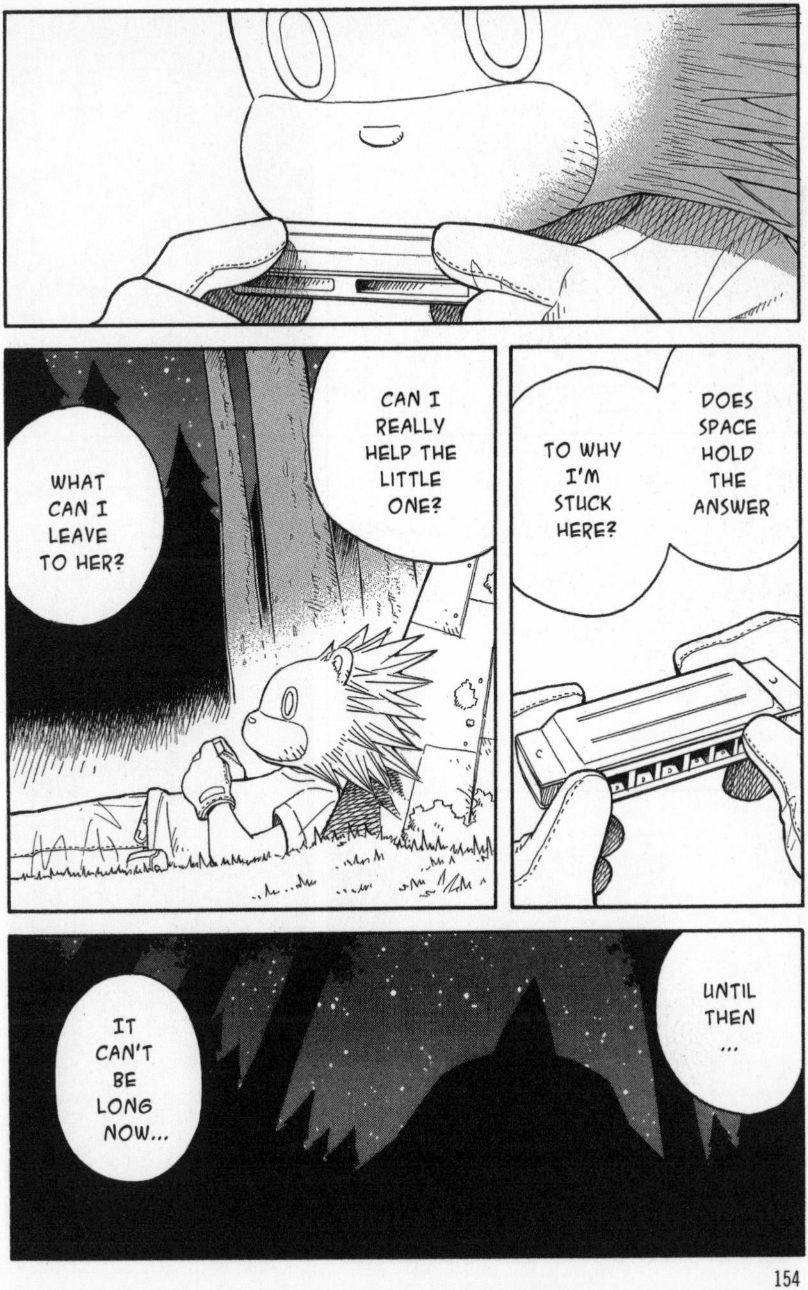
DOES SPACE HOLD THE ANSWER
TO WHY I'M STUCK HERE?
CAN I REALLY HELP THE LITTLE ONE?
WHAT CAN I LEAVE TO HER?
UNTIL THEN ...
IT CAN'T BE LONG NOW...

MISSION:52

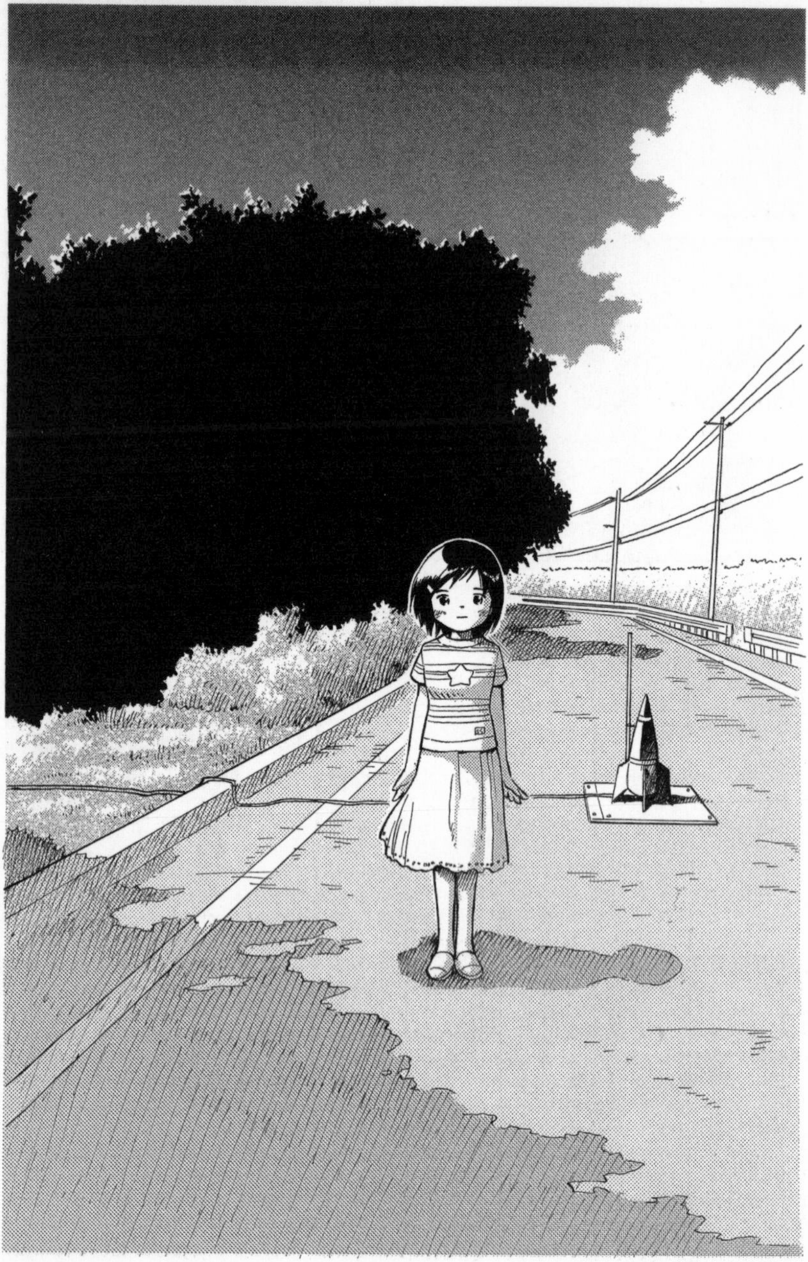

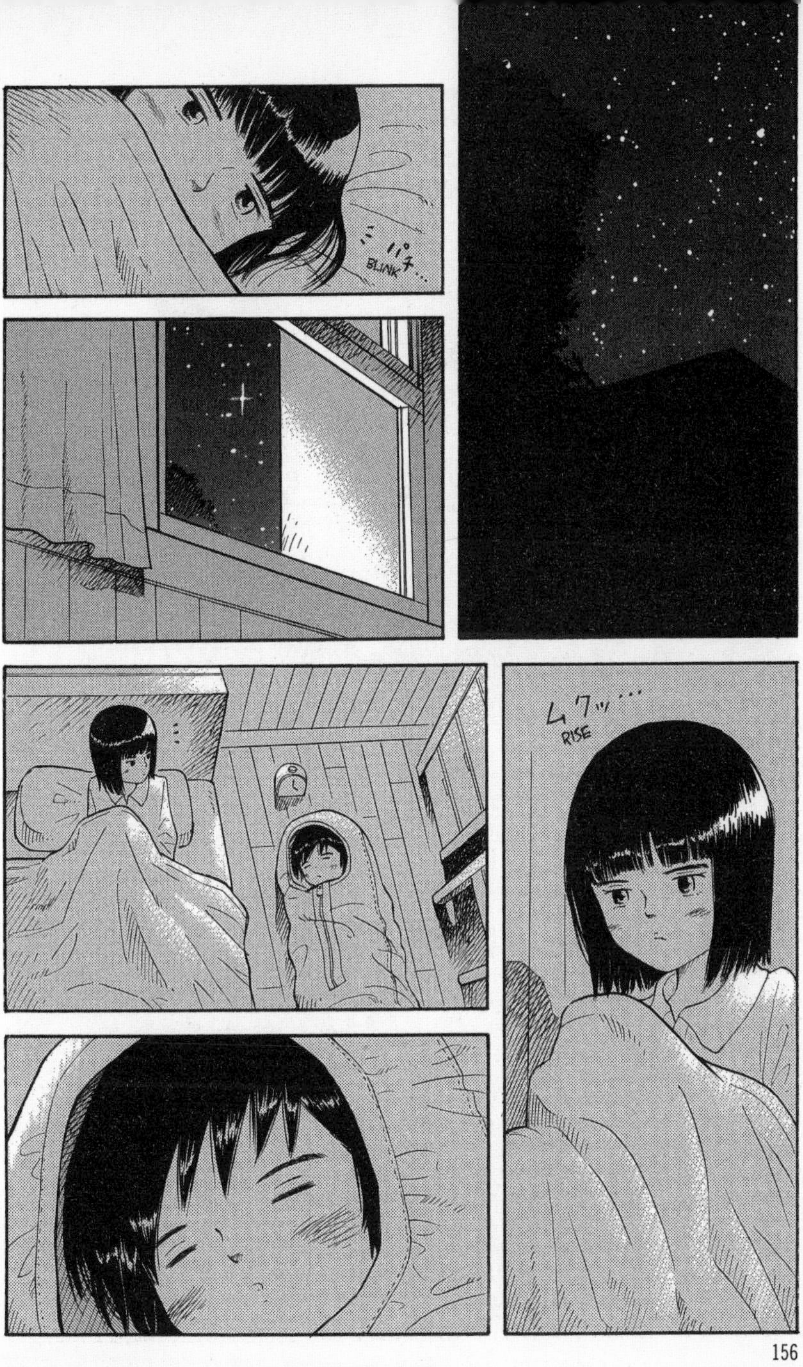
パチ…
BLINK…
ムクッ…
RISE

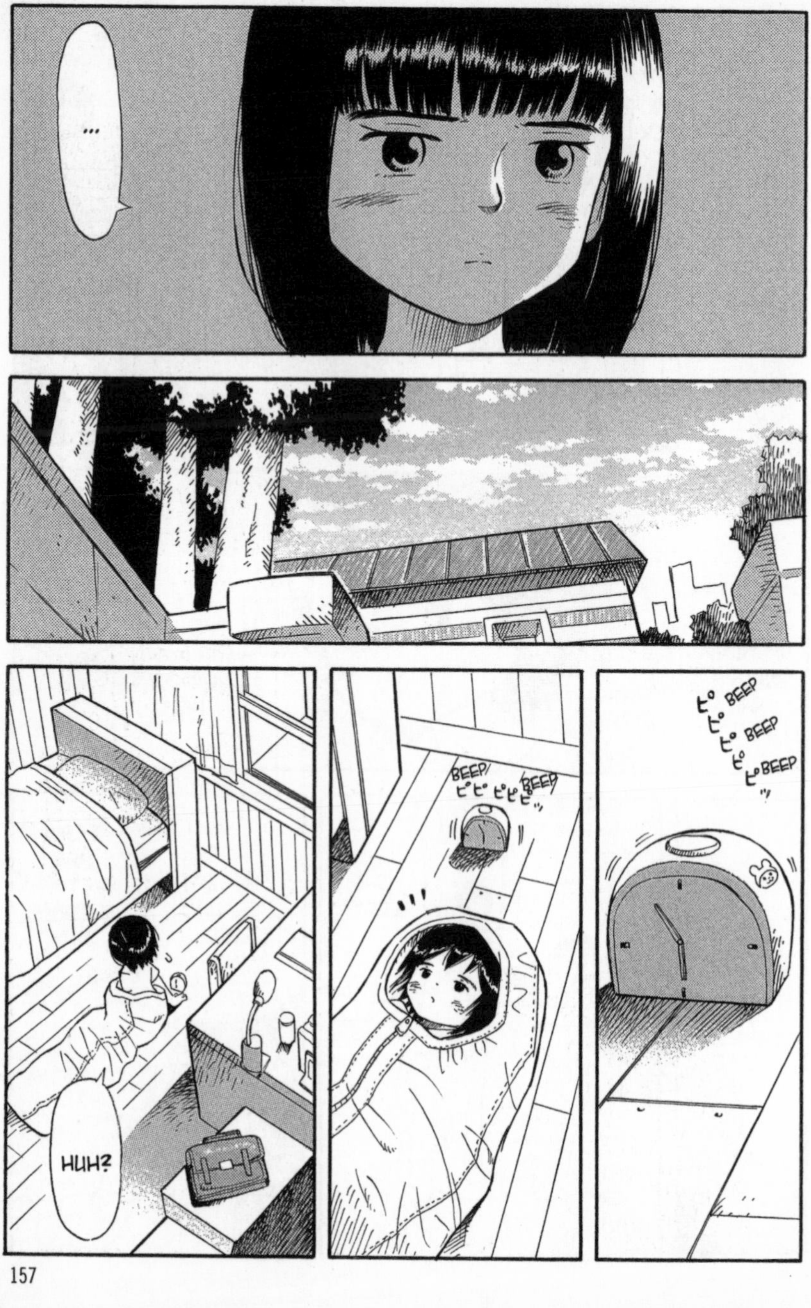
…
ピ BEEP
ピ BEEP
ピ BEEP
ピッ
BEEP BEEP
ピピ ピピピッ
HUH?

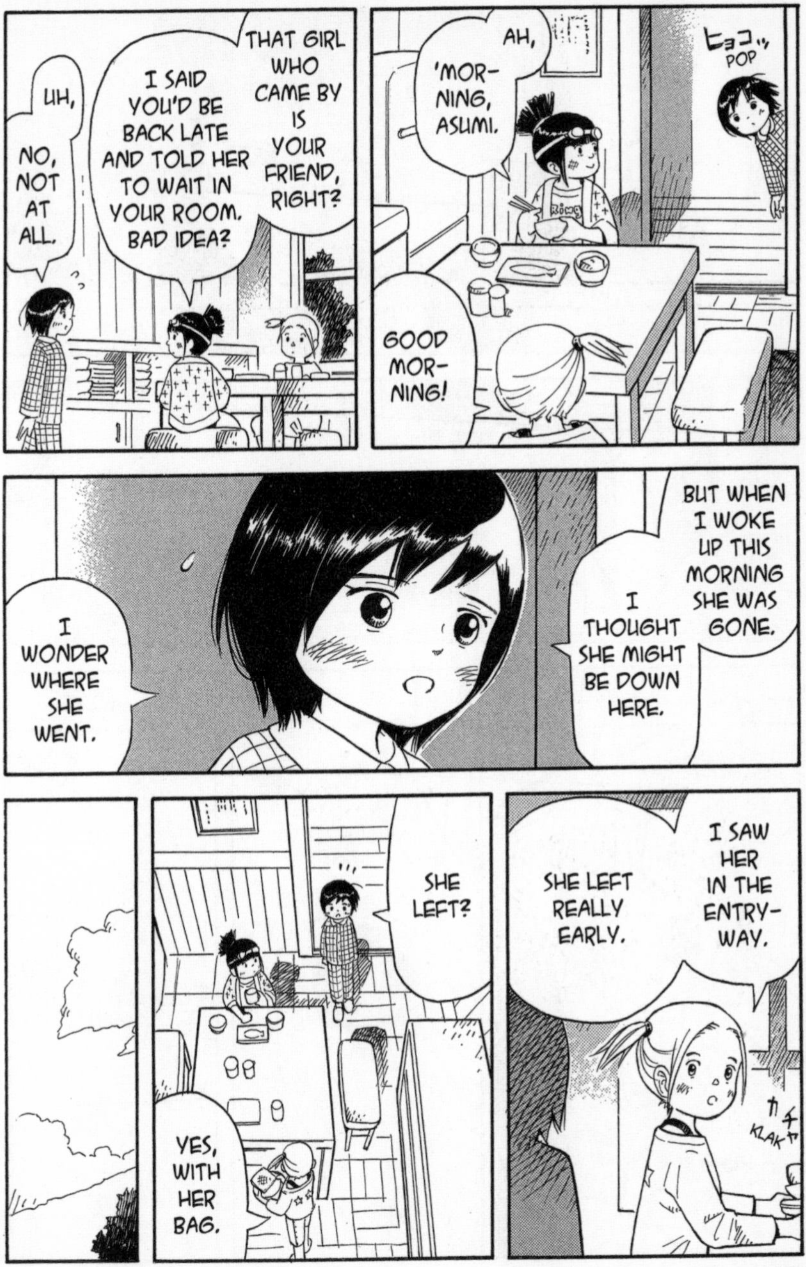
ヒョコッ
POP
AH, 'MOR-NING, ASUMI.
GOOD MOR-NING!
THAT GIRL WHO CAME BY IS YOUR FRIEND, RIGHT?
I SAID YOU'D BE BACK LATE AND TOLD HER TO WAIT IN YOUR ROOM. BAD IDEA?
UH,
NO, NOT AT ALL.
BUT WHEN I WOKE UP THIS MORNING SHE WAS GONE.
I THOUGHT SHE MIGHT BE DOWN HERE.
I WONDER WHERE SHE WENT.
I SAW HER IN THE ENTRY-WAY.
SHE LEFT REALLY EARLY.
カチャ
KLAK
SHE LEFT?
YES, WITH HER BAG.

キーンコーン
DING DONG
カーンコーン
HUFF
HUFF
HUFF
HUFF
HUFF
HUFF
HUFF
HUFF

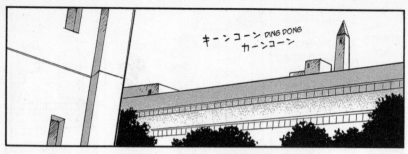

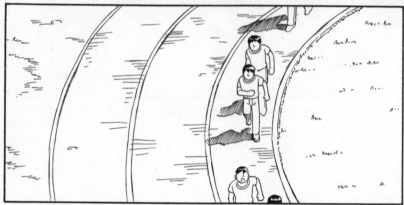

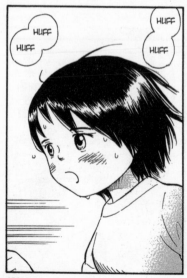

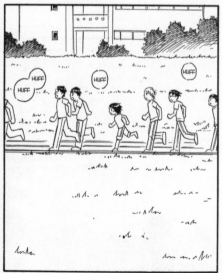

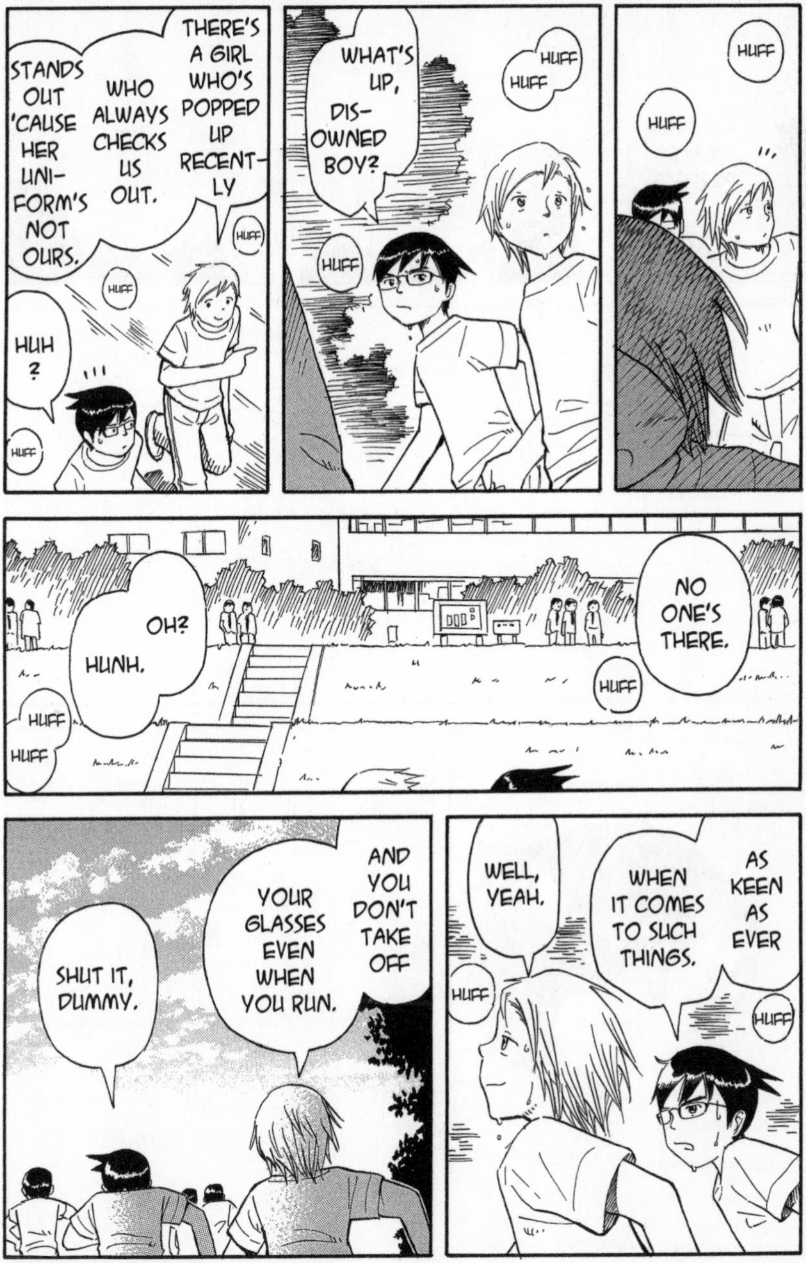
HUFF
HUFF
HUFF
WHAT'S UP, DIS-OWNED BOY?
HUFF
HUFF
HUFF
THERE'S A GIRL WHO'S POPPED UP RECENTLY WHO ALWAYS CHECKS US OUT. STANDS OUT 'CAUSE HER UNIFORM'S NOT OURS.
HUFF
HUFF
HUH?
HUFF
NO ONE'S THERE.
HUFF
OH? HUNH.
HUFF
HUFF
AS KEEN AS EVER WHEN IT COMES TO SUCH THINGS.
HUFF
WELL, YEAH.
HUFF
AND YOU DON'T TAKE OFF YOUR GLASSES EVEN WHEN YOU RUN.
SHUT IT, DUMMY.

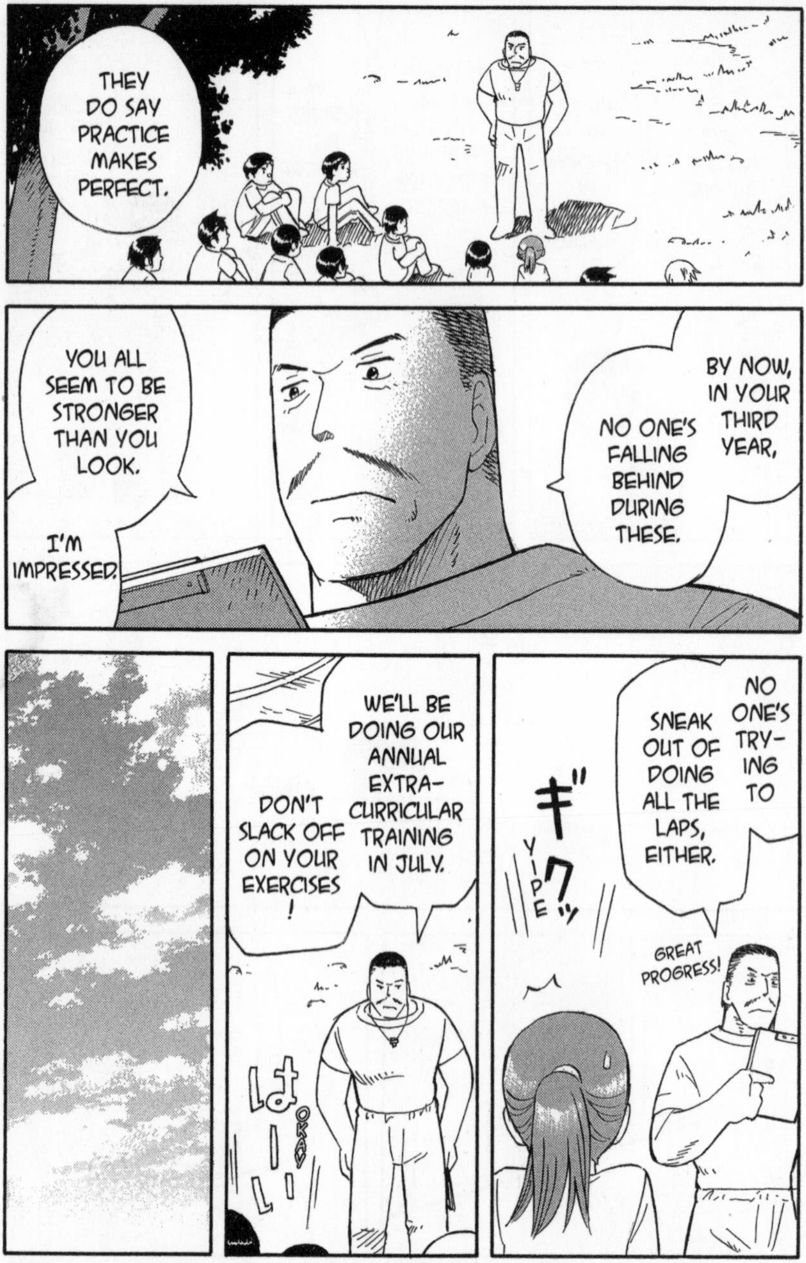
THEY DO SAY PRACTICE MAKES PERFECT.
BY NOW, IN YOUR THIRD YEAR,
NO ONE'S FALLING BEHIND DURING THESE.
YOU ALL SEEM TO BE STRONGER THAN YOU LOOK.
I'M IMPRESSED.
NO ONE'S TRYING TO SNEAK OUT OF DOING ALL THE LAPS, EITHER.
ギクッ
YIPE
GREAT PROGRESS!
WE'LL BE DOING OUR ANNUAL EXTRA-CURRICULAR TRAINING IN JULY.
DON'T SLACK OFF ON YOUR EXERCISES!
はーい
OKAY

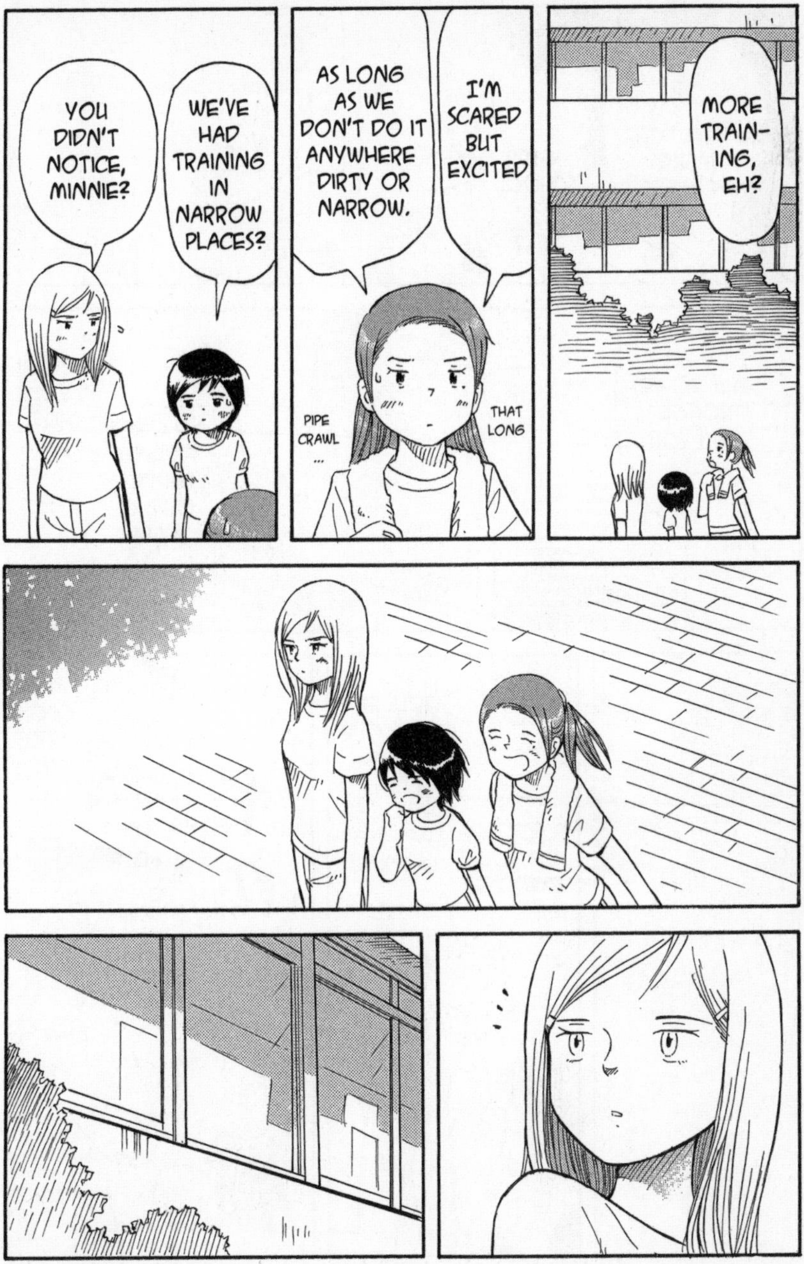
MORE TRAIN-ING, EH?
I'M SCARED BUT EXCITED
AS LONG AS WE DON'T DO IT ANYWHERE DIRTY OR NARROW.
THAT LONG
PIPE CRAWL ...
WE'VE HAD TRAINING IN NARROW PLACES?
YOU DIDN'T NOTICE, MINNIE?

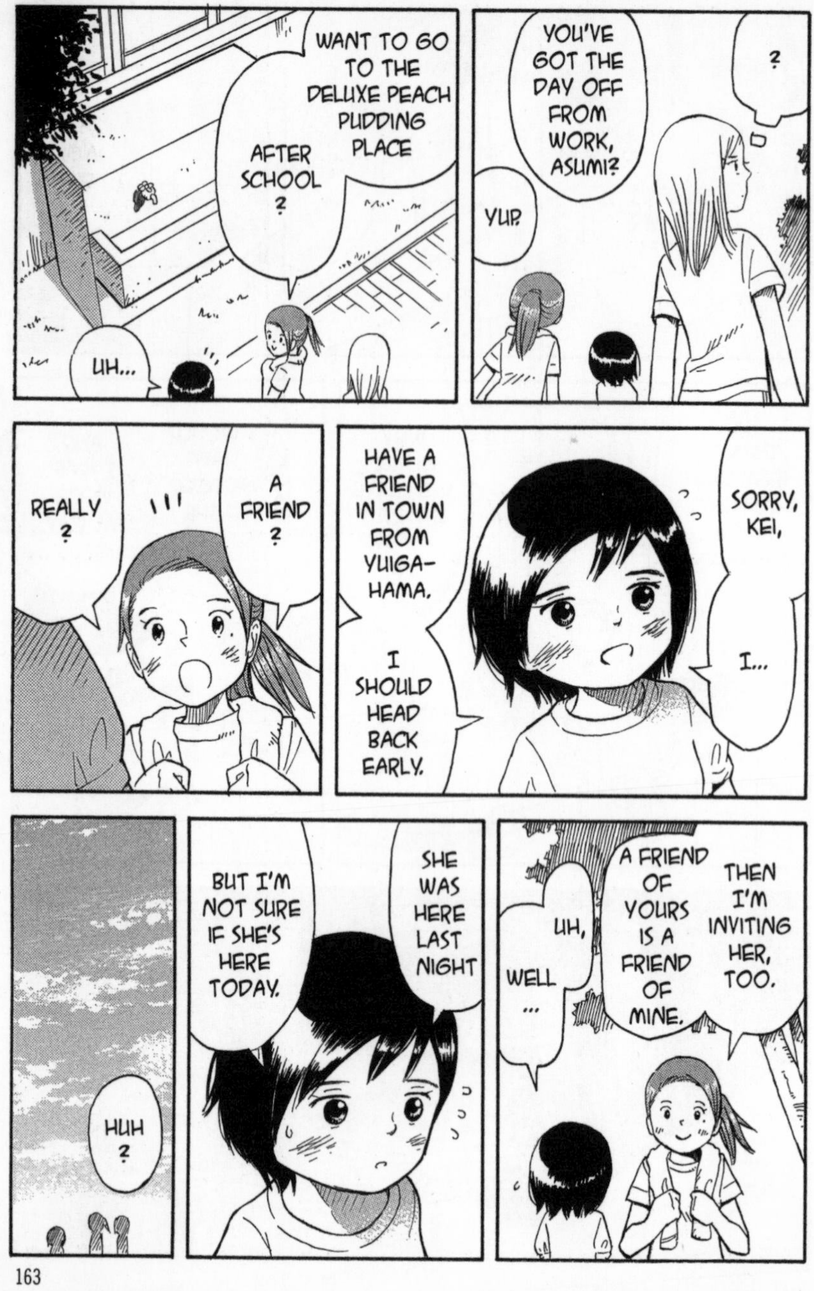
?
YOU'VE GOT THE DAY OFF FROM WORK, ASUMI?
YUP.
WANT TO GO TO THE DELUXE PEACH PUDDING PLACE
AFTER SCHOOL ?
UH...
SORRY, KEI,
I...
HAVE A FRIEND IN TOWN FROM YUIGA-HAMA.
I SHOULD HEAD BACK EARLY.
A FRIEND ?
REALLY ?
THEN I'M INVITING HER, TOO.
A FRIEND OF YOURS IS A FRIEND OF MINE.
UH,
WELL ...
SHE WAS HERE LAST NIGHT
BUT I'M NOT SURE IF SHE'S HERE TODAY.
HUH ?

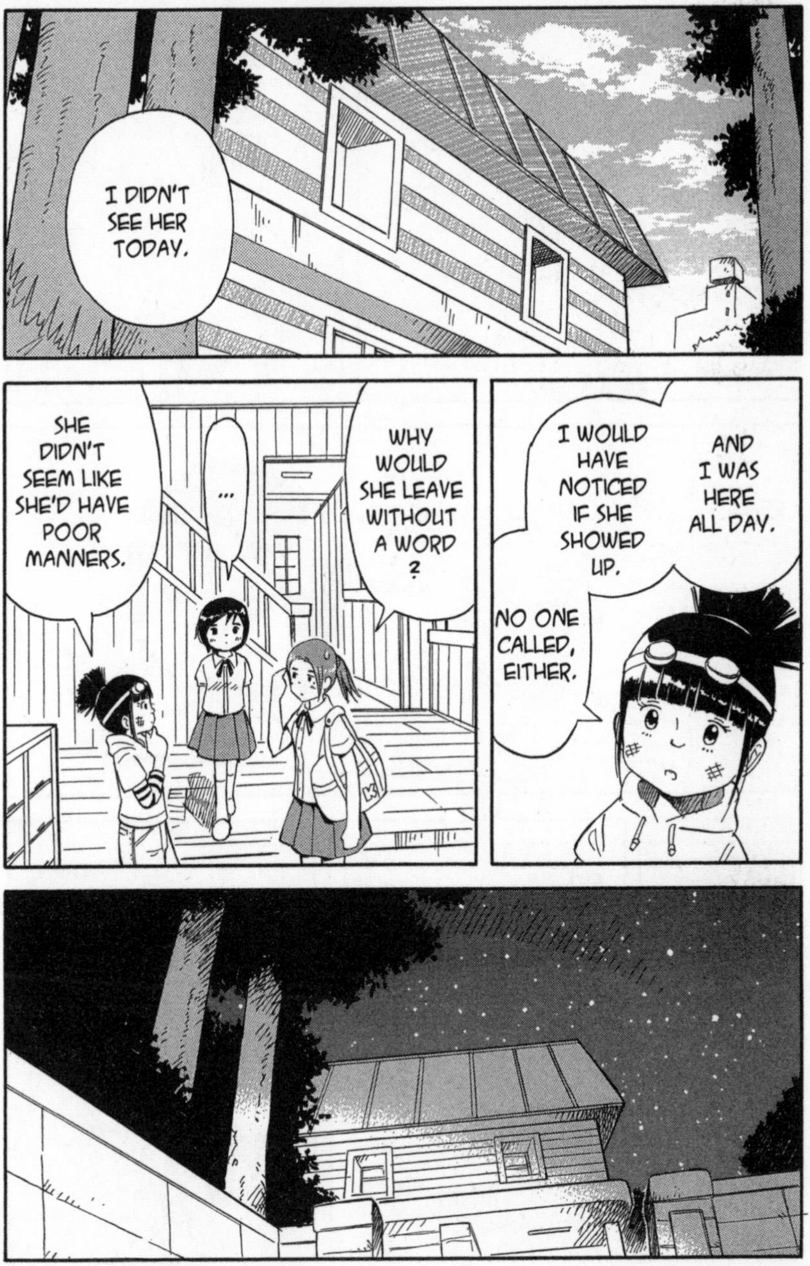
I DIDN'T SEE HER TODAY.
I WOULD HAVE NOTICED IF SHE SHOWED UP.
AND I WAS HERE ALL DAY.
NO ONE CALLED, EITHER.
WHY WOULD SHE LEAVE WITHOUT A WORD?
...
SHE DIDN'T SEEM LIKE SHE'D HAVE POOR MANNERS.

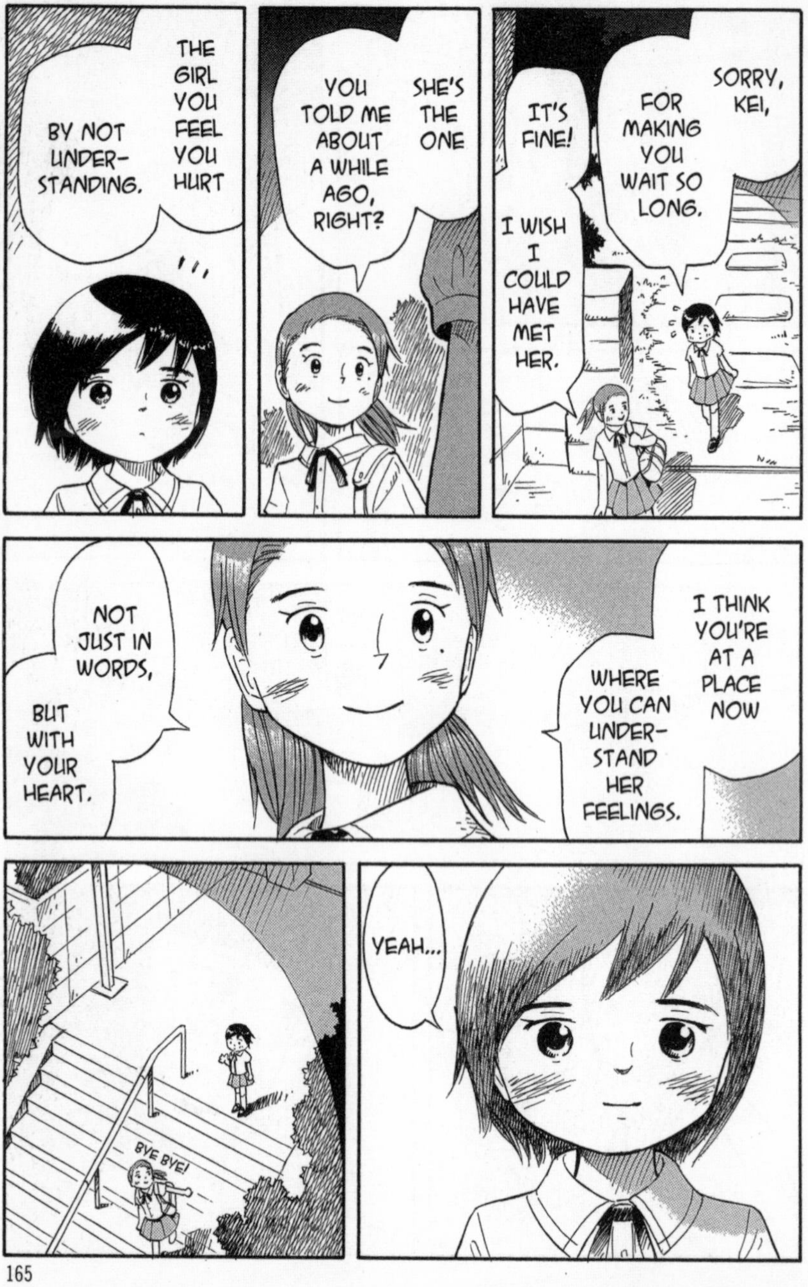
SORRY, KEI,
FOR MAKING YOU WAIT SO LONG.
IT'S FINE!
I WISH I COULD HAVE MET HER.
SHE'S THE ONE
YOU TOLD ME ABOUT A WHILE AGO, RIGHT?
THE GIRL YOU FEEL YOU HURT
BY NOT UNDER-STANDING.
I THINK YOU'RE AT A PLACE NOW
WHERE YOU CAN UNDER-STAND HER FEELINGS.
NOT JUST IN WORDS,
BUT WITH YOUR HEART.
YEAH...
BYE BYE!

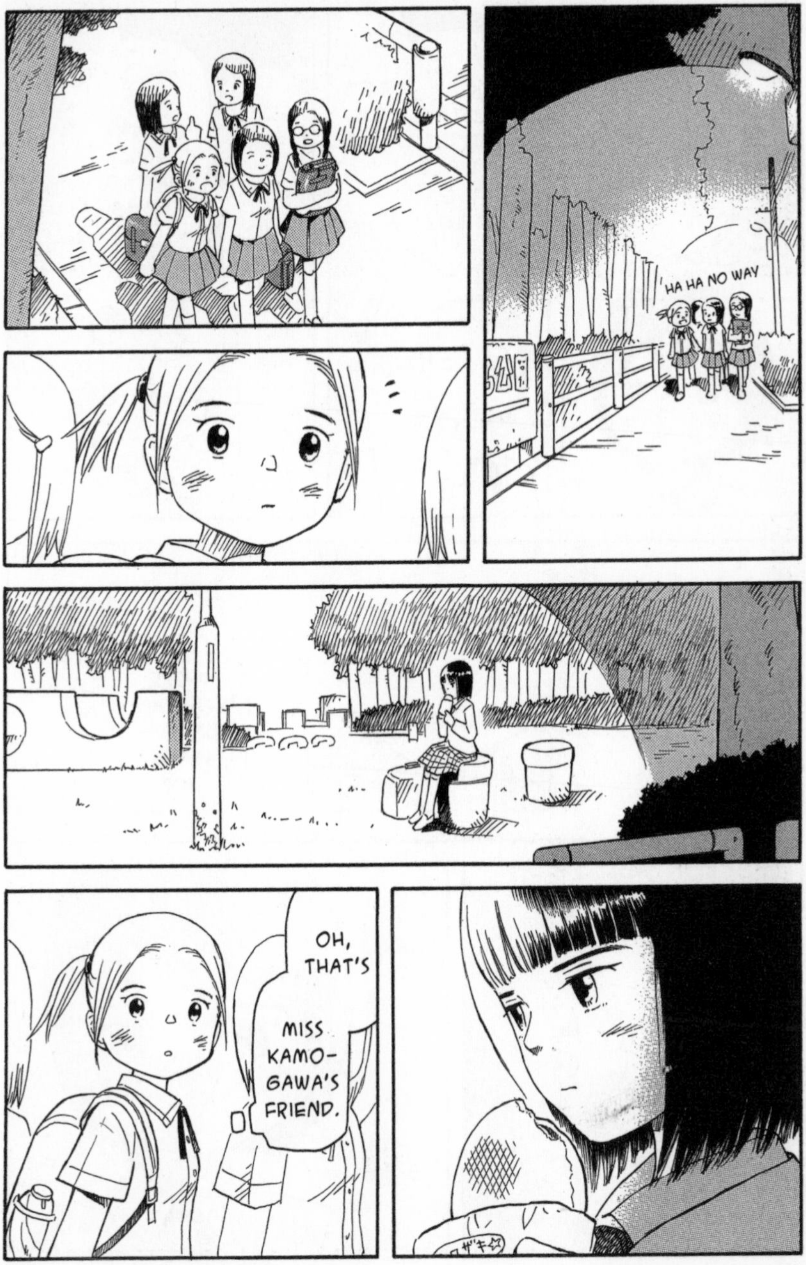
HA HA NO WAY
OH, THAT'S MISS KAMO-GAWA'S FRIEND.

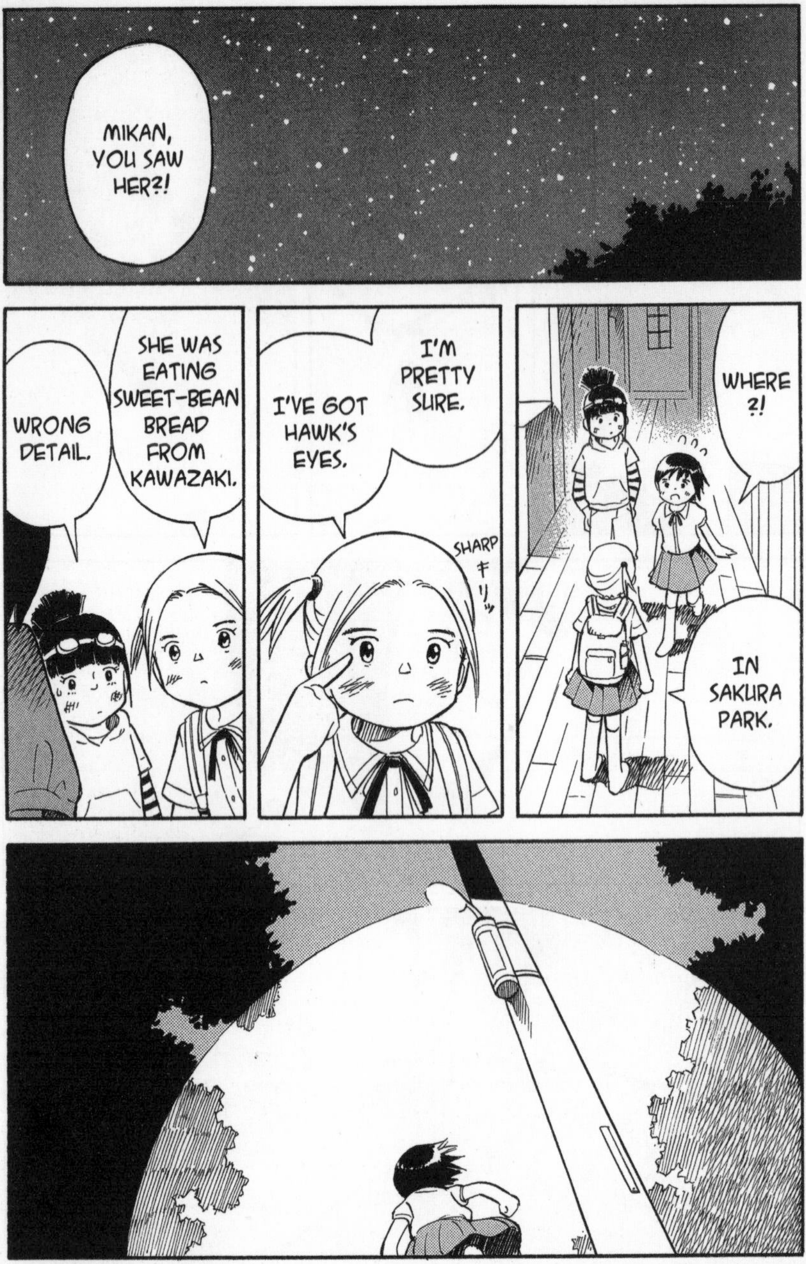

MIKAN, YOU SAW HER?!
WHERE ?!
IN SAKURA PARK.
I'M PRETTY SURE.
I'VE GOT HAWK'S EYES.
SHARP キリッ
SHE WAS EATING SWEET-BEAN BREAD FROM KAWAZAKI.
WRONG DETAIL.

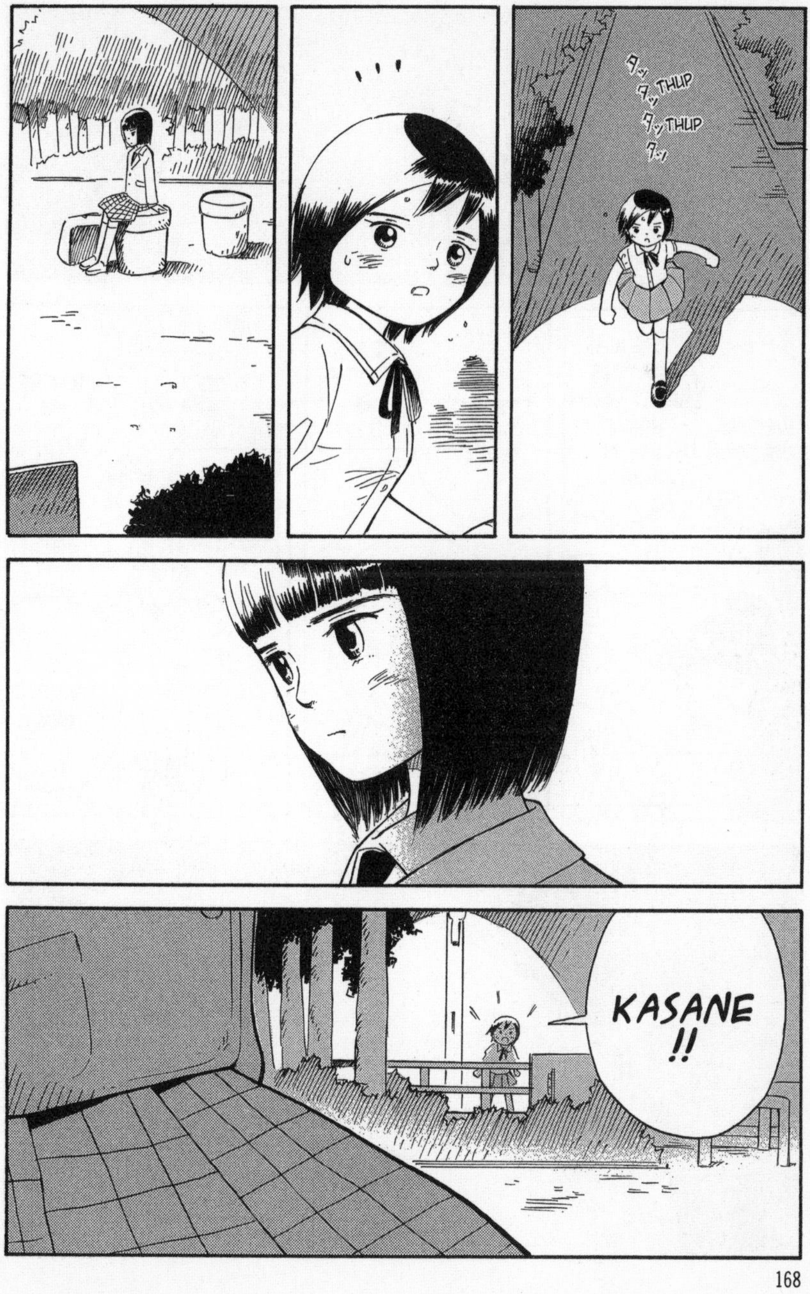
タッ
タッ THUP
タッ THUP
タッ
KASANE !!

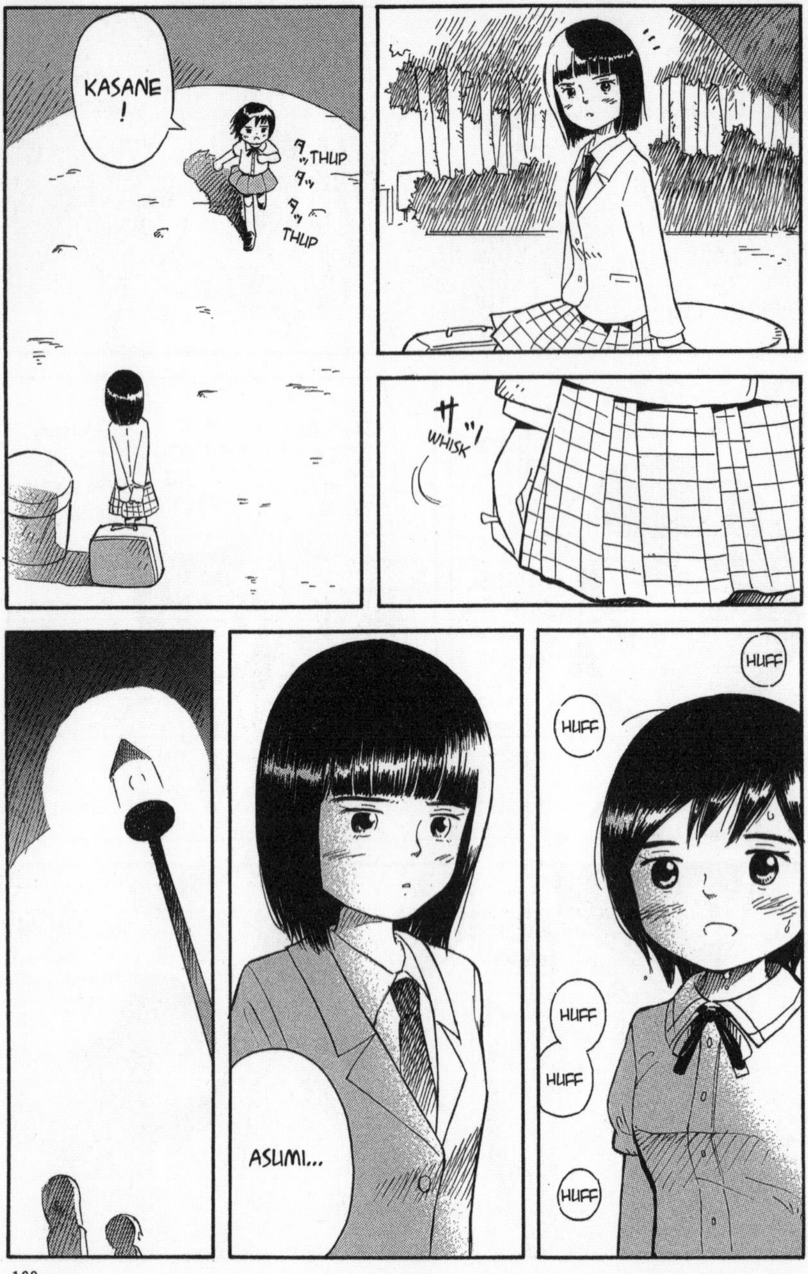
サッ WHISK
KASANE!
タッ THUP
タッ
タッ THUP
HUFF
HUFF
HUFF
HUFF
HUFF
ASUMI...

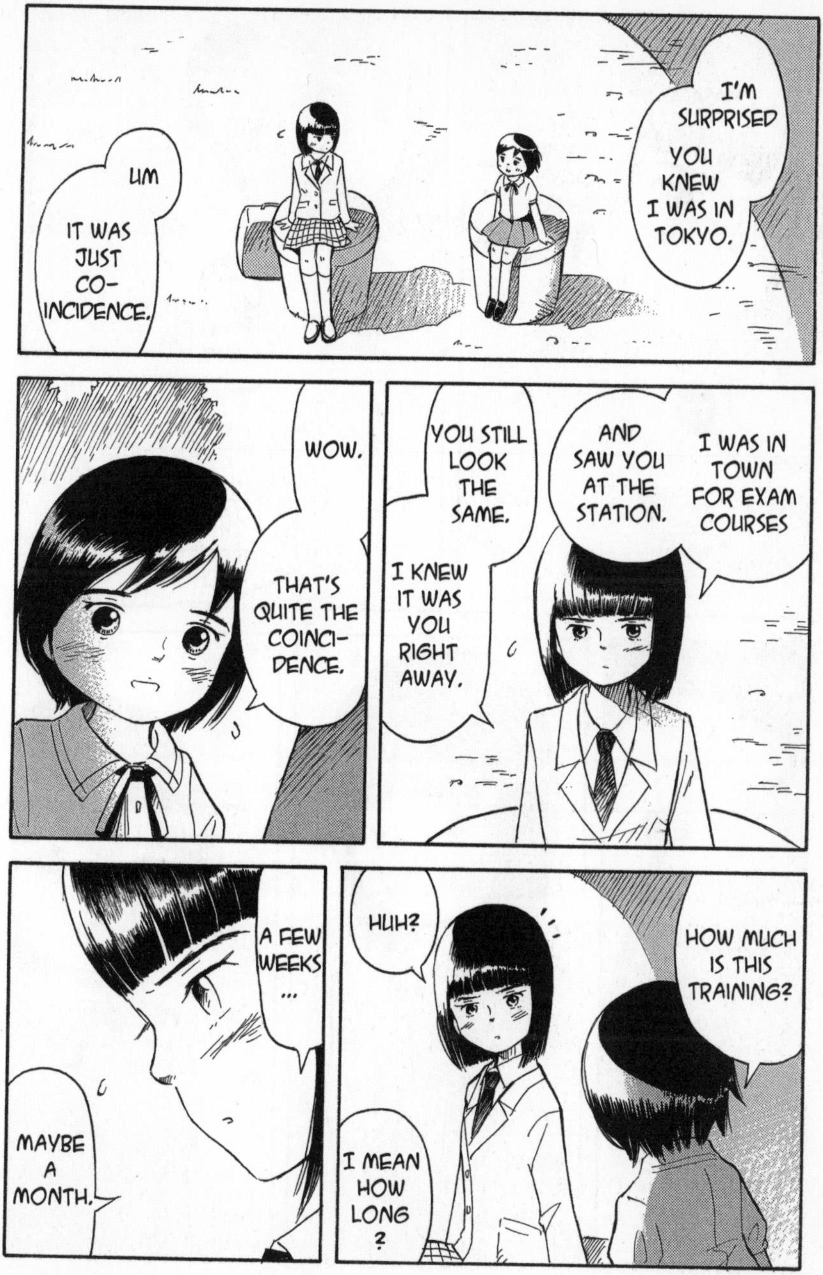
I'M SURPRISED YOU KNEW I WAS IN TOKYO.
UM
IT WAS JUST CO-INCIDENCE.
I WAS IN TOWN FOR EXAM COURSES
AND SAW YOU AT THE STATION.
YOU STILL LOOK THE SAME.
I KNEW IT WAS YOU RIGHT AWAY.
WOW.
THAT'S QUITE THE COINCI-DENCE.
HOW MUCH IS THIS TRAINING?
HUH?
I MEAN HOW LONG?
A FEW WEEKS...
MAYBE A MONTH.

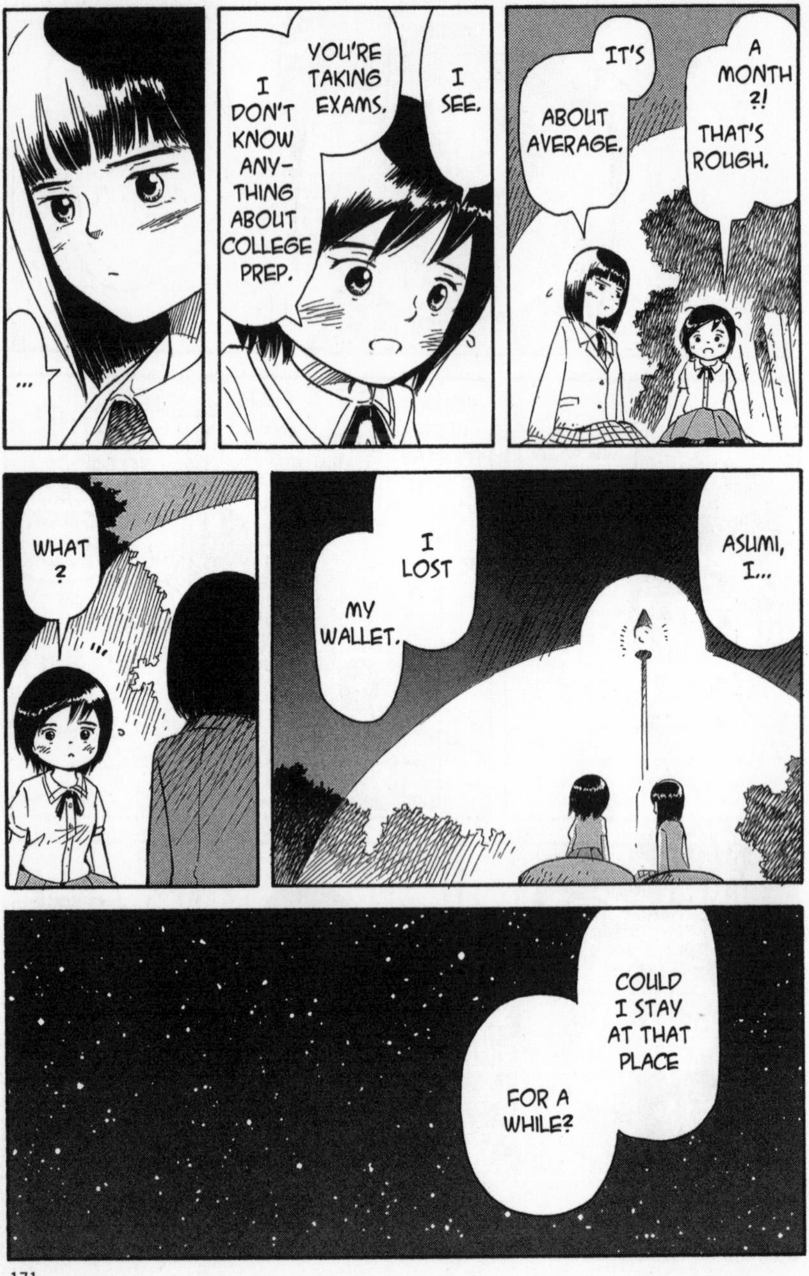

A MONTH?! THAT'S ROUGH.
IT'S ABOUT AVERAGE.
I SEE.
YOU'RE TAKING EXAMS.
I DON'T KNOW ANY-THING ABOUT COLLEGE PREP.
...
ASUMI, I...
I LOST MY WALLET.
WHAT?
...
COULD I STAY AT THAT PLACE FOR A WHILE?

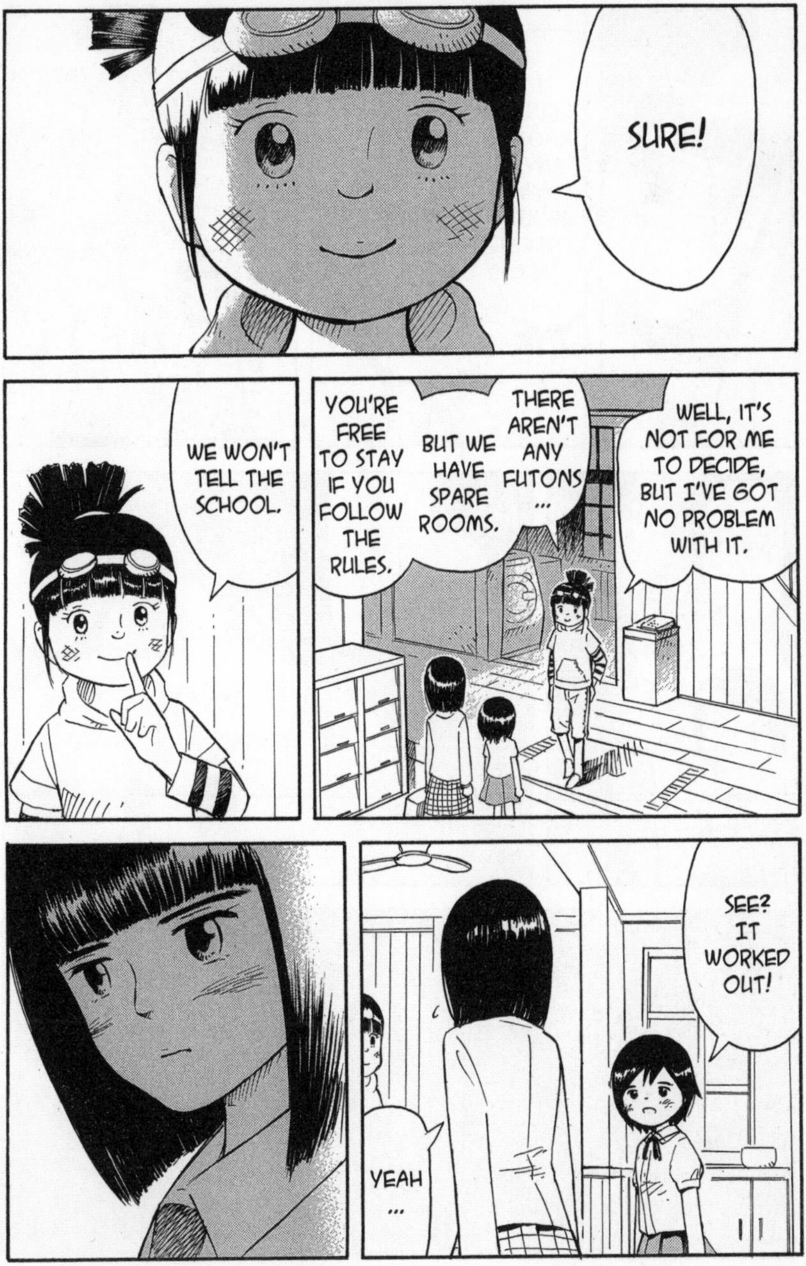
SURE!
WELL, IT'S NOT FOR ME TO DECIDE, BUT I'VE GOT NO PROBLEM WITH IT.
THERE AREN'T ANY FUTONS ...
BUT WE HAVE SPARE ROOMS.
YOU'RE FREE TO STAY IF YOU FOLLOW THE RULES.
WE WON'T TELL THE SCHOOL.
SEE? IT WORKED OUT!
YEAH ...

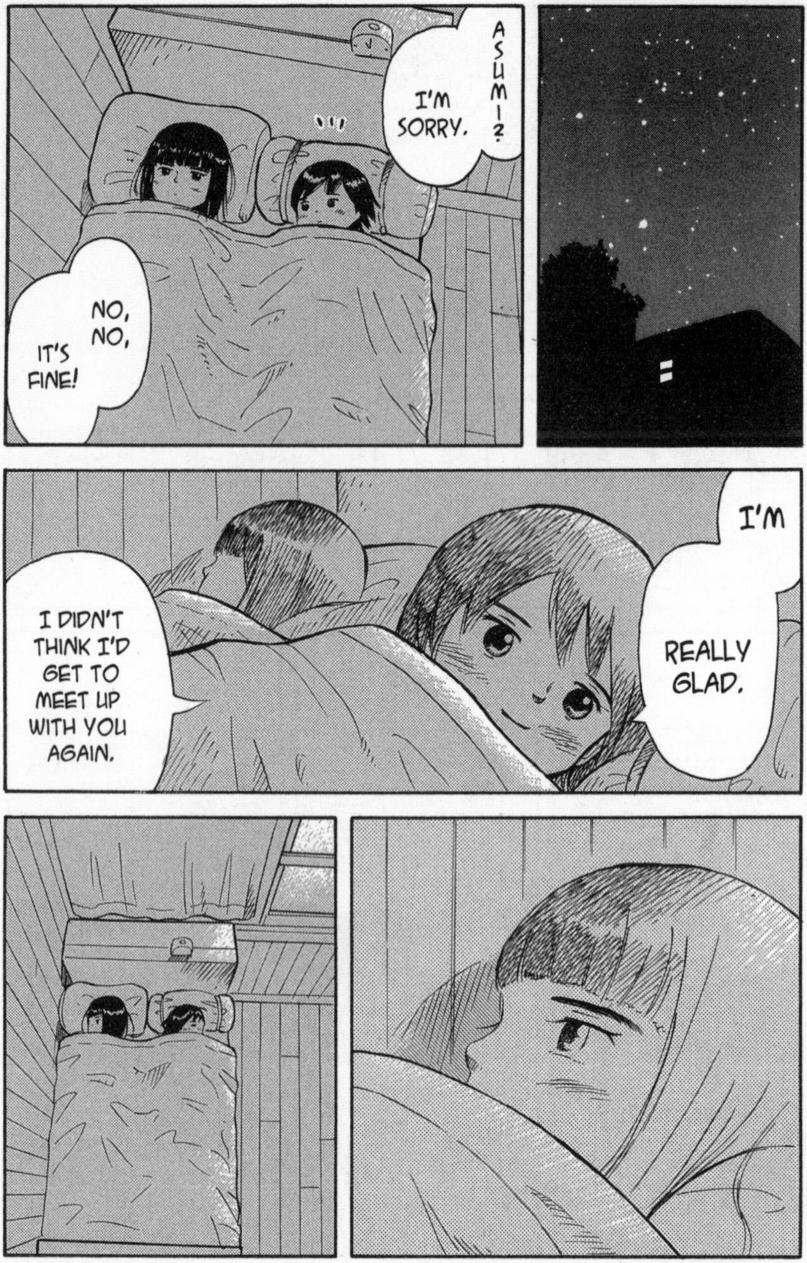
ASUMI?
I'M SORRY.
NO, NO, IT'S FINE!
I'M REALLY GLAD.
I DIDN'T THINK I'D GET TO MEET UP WITH YOU AGAIN.

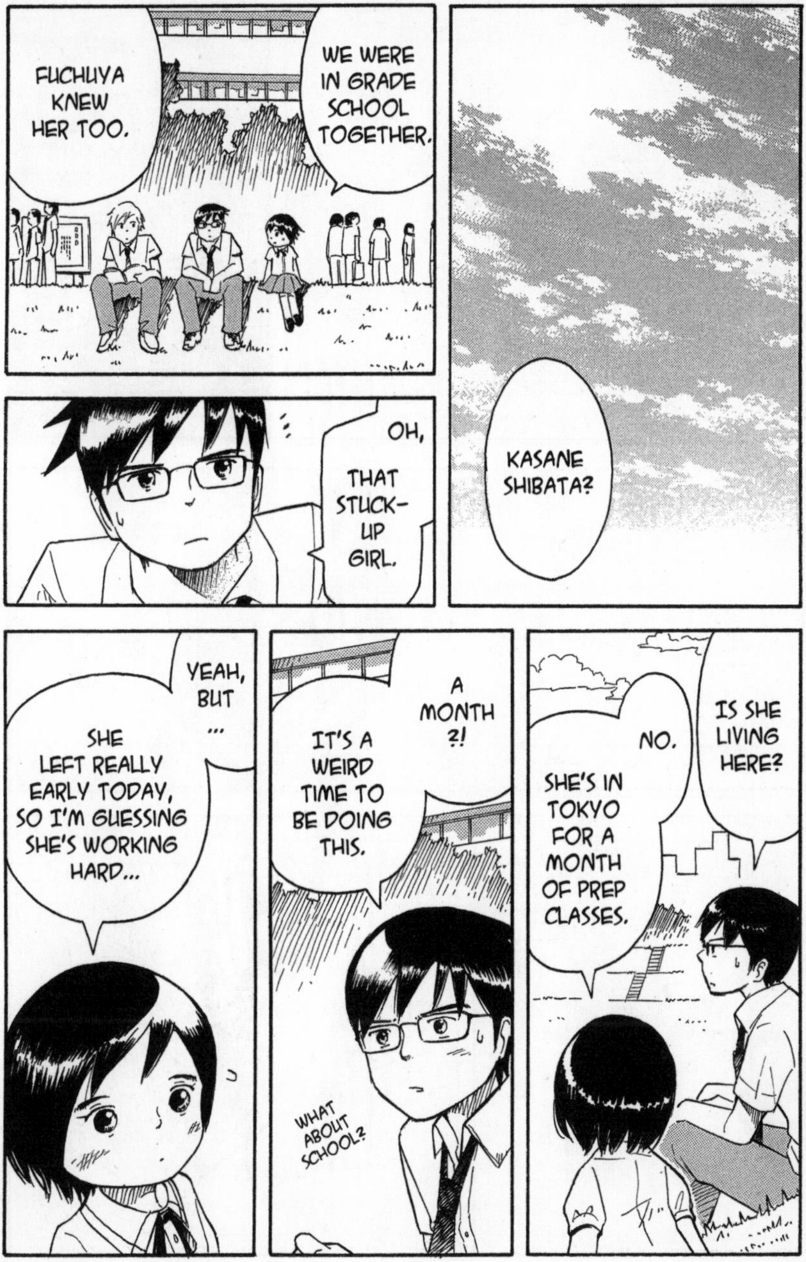
KASANE SHIBATA?
WE WERE IN GRADE SCHOOL TOGETHER.
FUCHUYA KNEW HER TOO.
OH, THAT STUCK-UP GIRL.
IS SHE LIVING HERE?
NO.
SHE'S IN TOKYO FOR A MONTH OF PREP CLASSES.
A MONTH?!
IT'S A WEIRD TIME TO BE DOING THIS.
WHAT ABOUT SCHOOL?
YEAH, BUT...
SHE LEFT REALLY EARLY TODAY, SO I'M GUESSING SHE'S WORKING HARD...

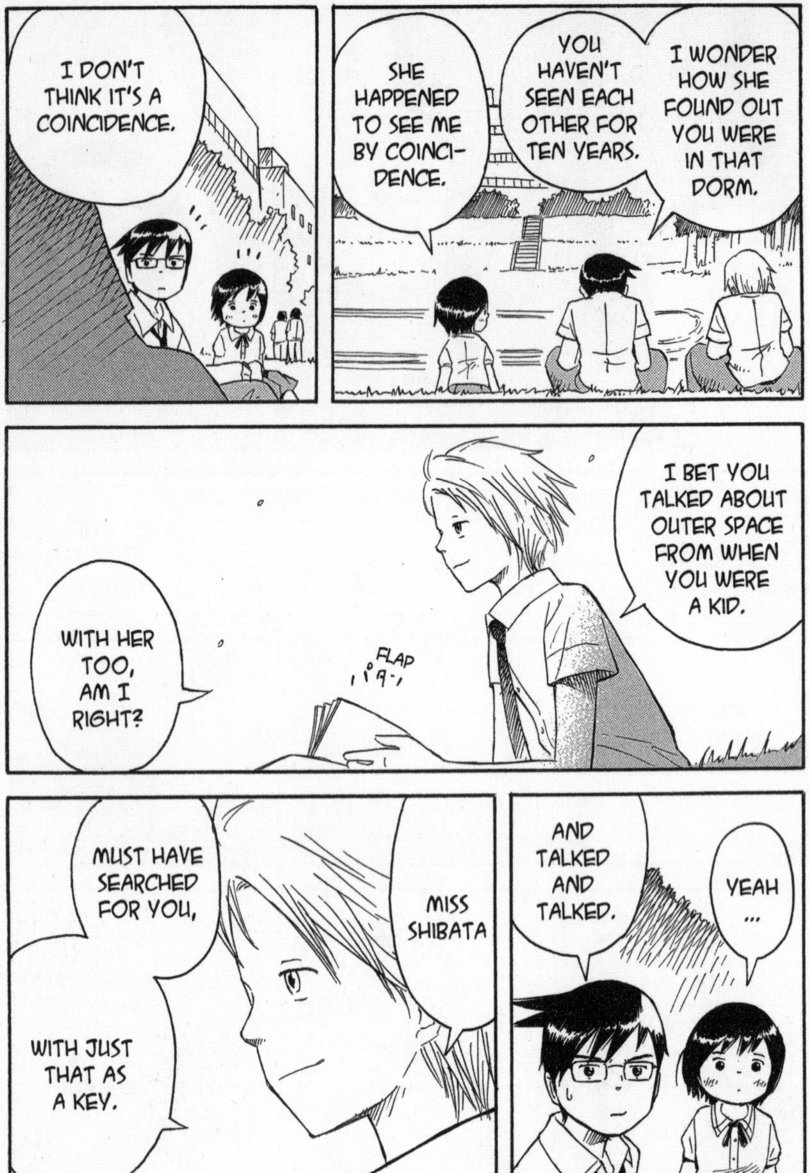
I WONDER HOW SHE FOUND OUT YOU WERE IN THAT DORM.
YOU HAVEN'T SEEN EACH OTHER FOR TEN YEARS.
SHE HAPPENED TO SEE ME BY COINCI-DENCE.
I DON'T THINK IT'S A COINCIDENCE.
I BET YOU TALKED ABOUT OUTER SPACE FROM WHEN YOU WERE A KID.
FLAP
WITH HER TOO, AM I RIGHT?
YEAH ...
AND TALKED AND TALKED.
MISS SHIBATA
MUST HAVE SEARCHED FOR YOU,
WITH JUST THAT AS A KEY.

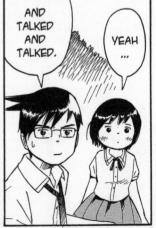

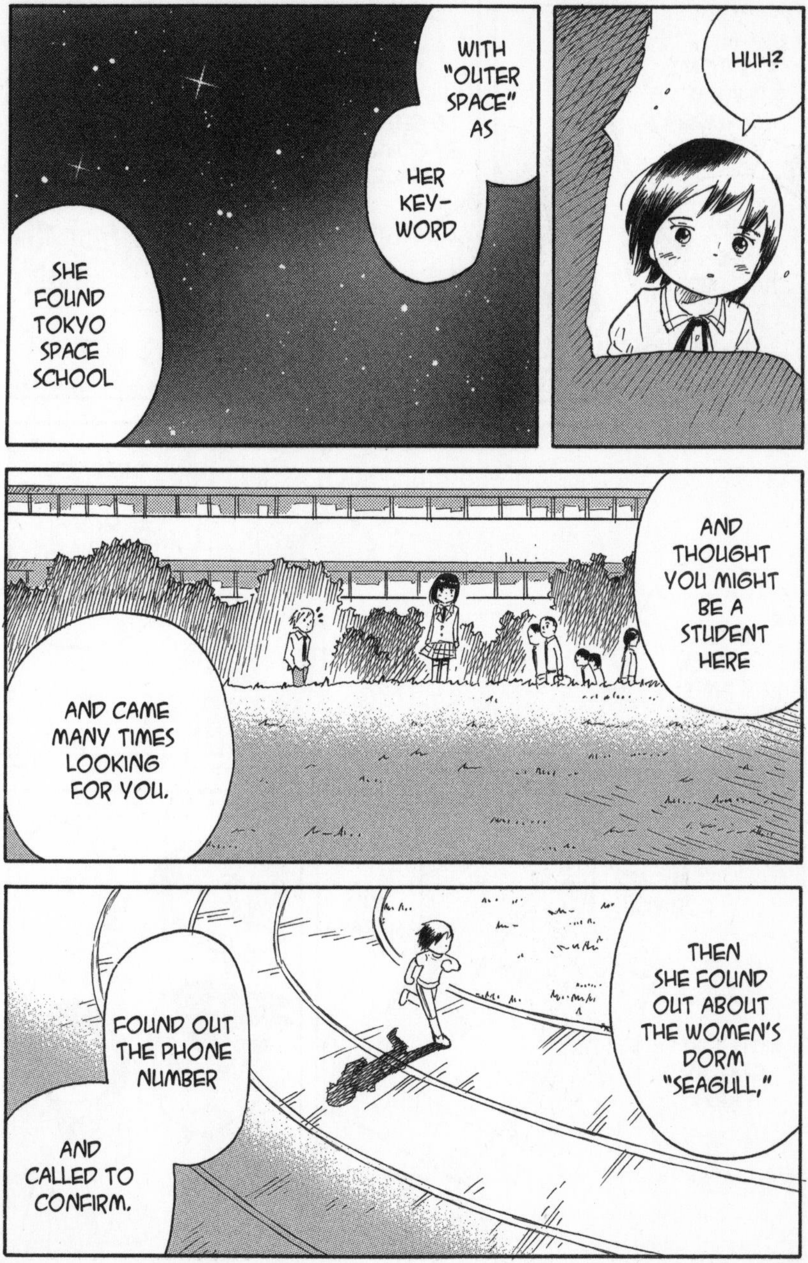
HUH?
WITH "OUTER SPACE" AS HER KEY-WORD
SHE FOUND TOKYO SPACE SCHOOL
AND THOUGHT YOU MIGHT BE A STUDENT HERE
AND CAME MANY TIMES LOOKING FOR YOU.
THEN SHE FOUND OUT ABOUT THE WOMEN'S DORM "SEAGULL,"
FOUND OUT THE PHONE NUMBER
AND CALLED TO CONFIRM.

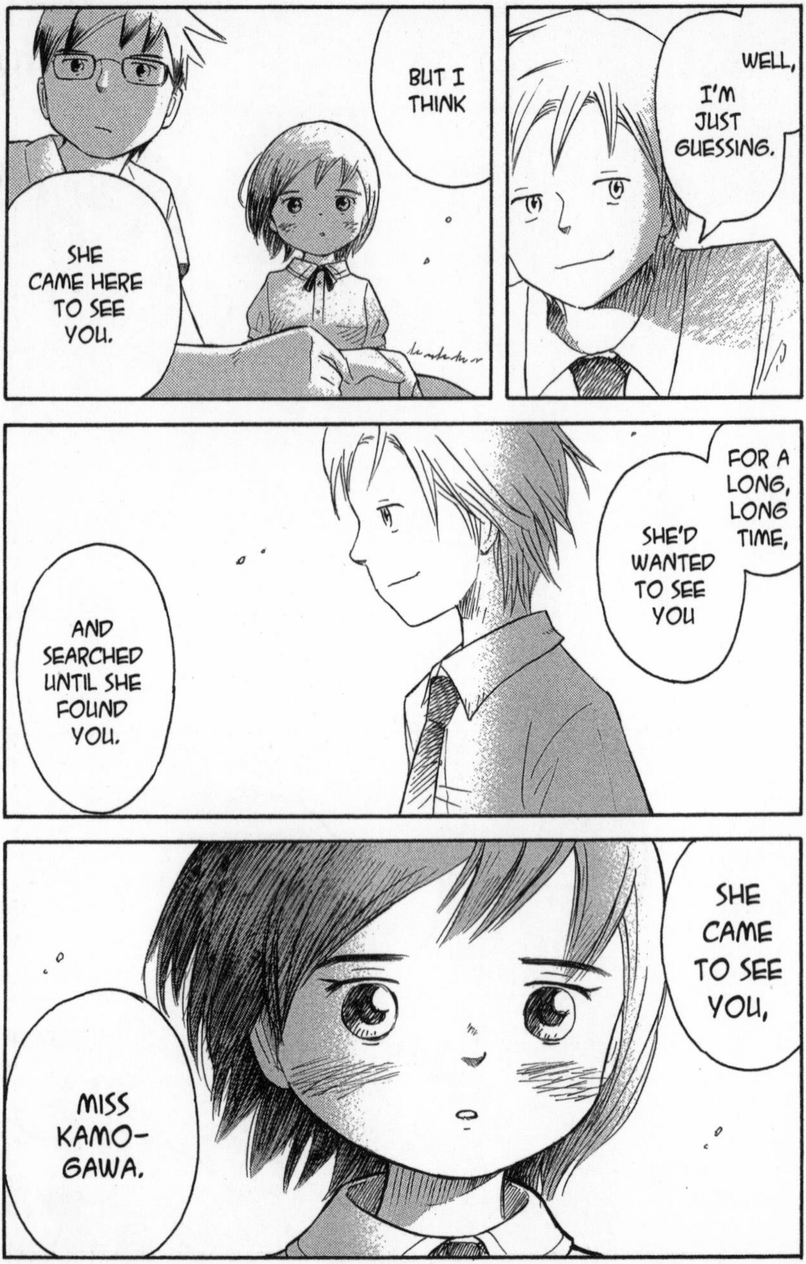
WELL, I'M JUST GUESSING.
BUT I THINK
SHE CAME HERE TO SEE YOU.
FOR A LONG, LONG TIME,
SHE'D WANTED TO SEE YOU
AND SEARCHED UNTIL SHE FOUND YOU.
SHE CAME TO SEE YOU,
MISS KAMO-GAWA.

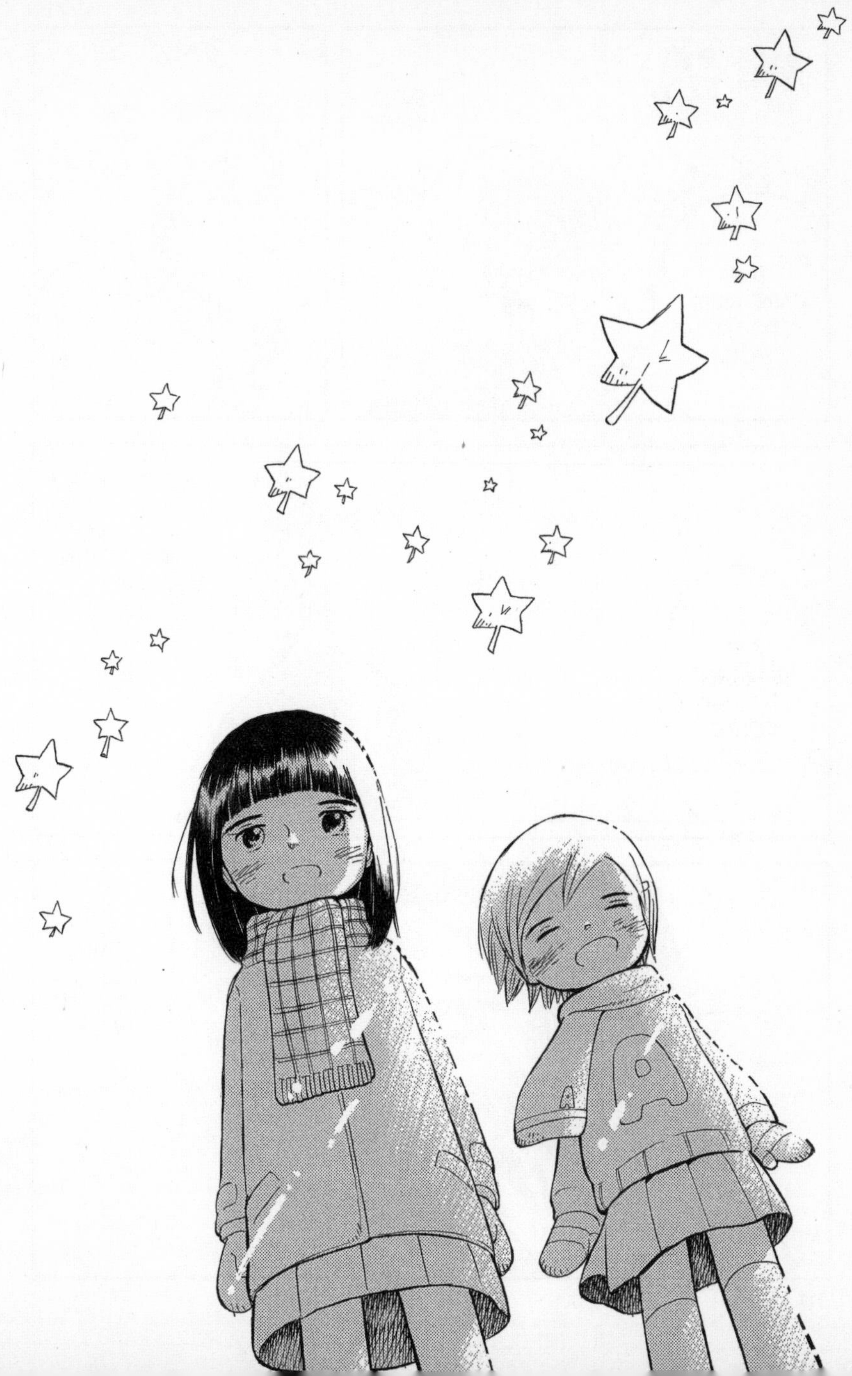

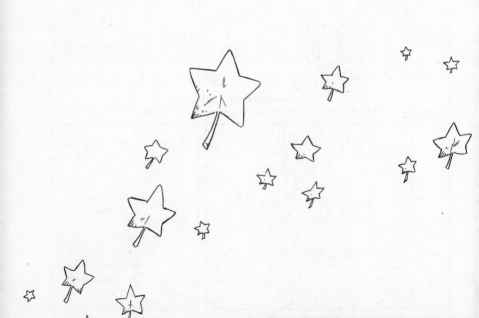

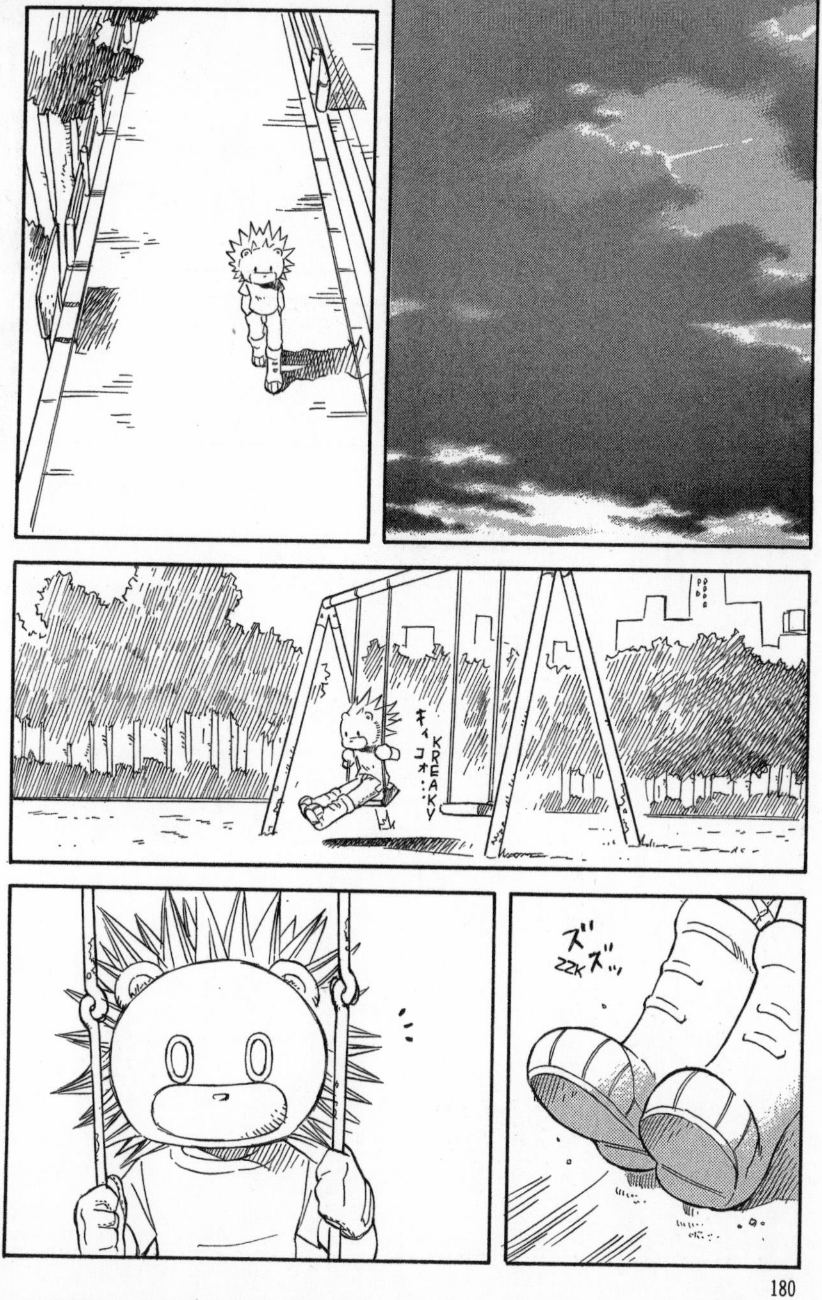
キィコォ…
KREAKY
ズズッ
ZZK

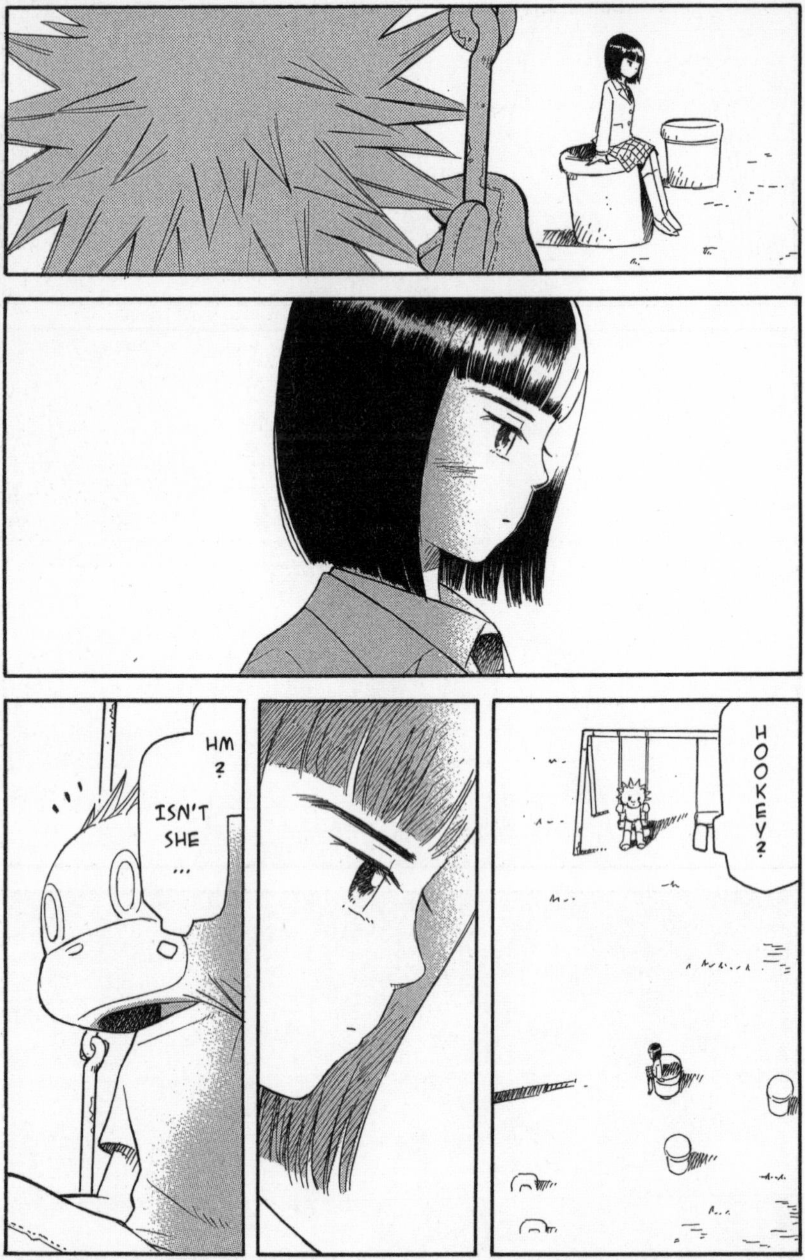
HOOKEY?
HM? ISN'T SHE ...

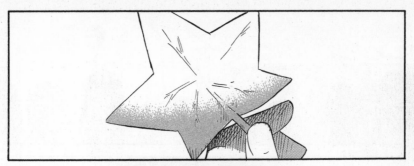

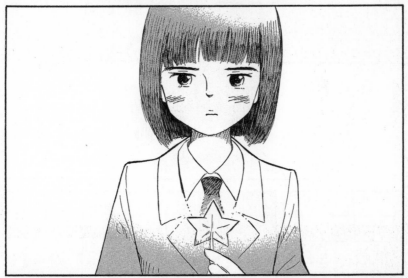

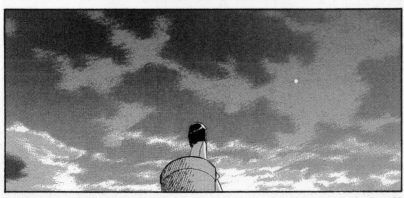

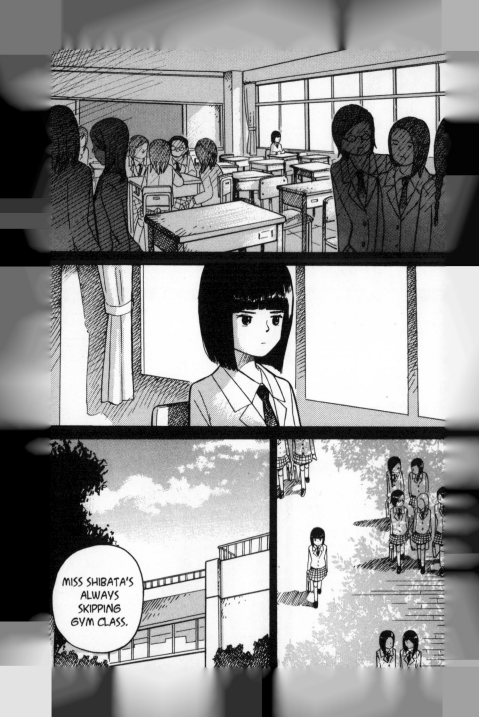

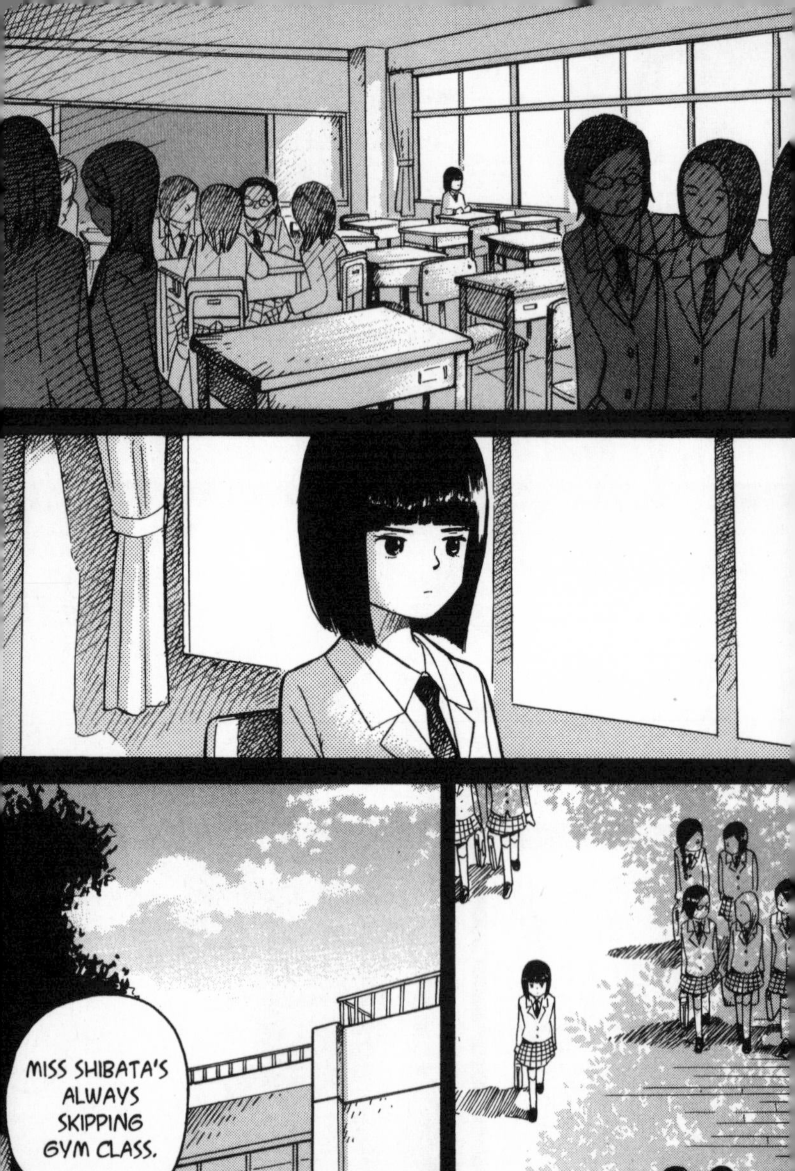
MISS SHIBATA'S ALWAYS SKIPPING GYM CLASS.

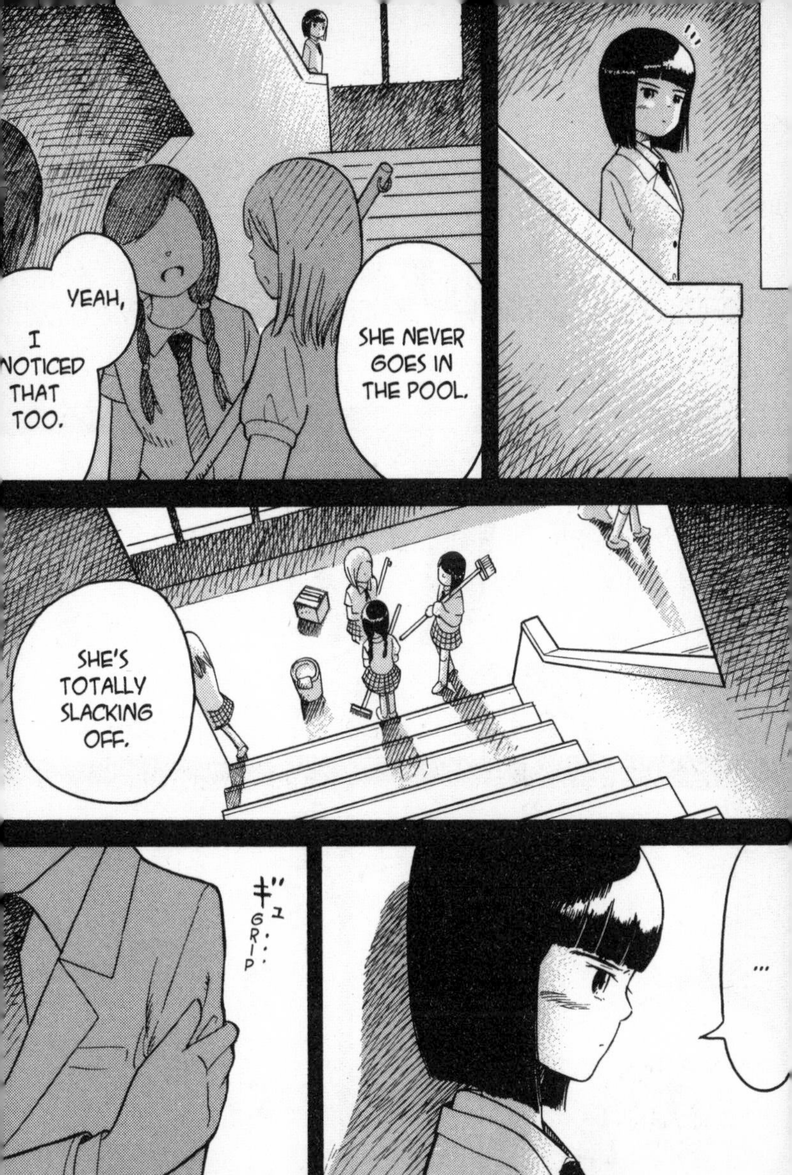
SHE NEVER GOES IN THE POOL.
YEAH, I NOTICED THAT TOO.
SHE'S TOTALLY SLACKING OFF.
...
ギュ
GRIP

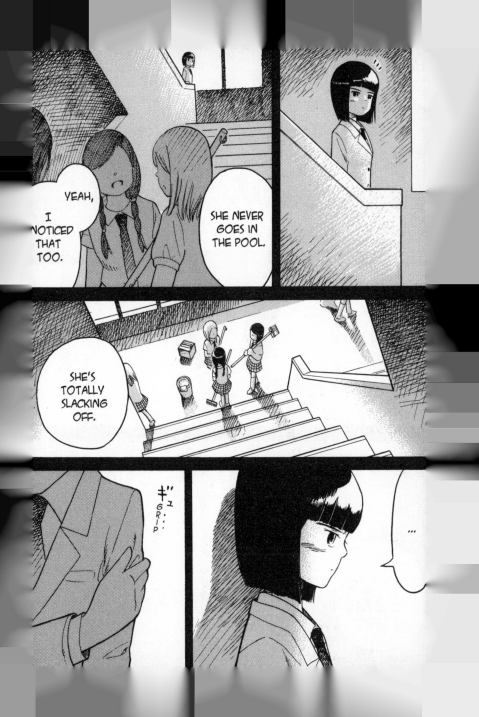

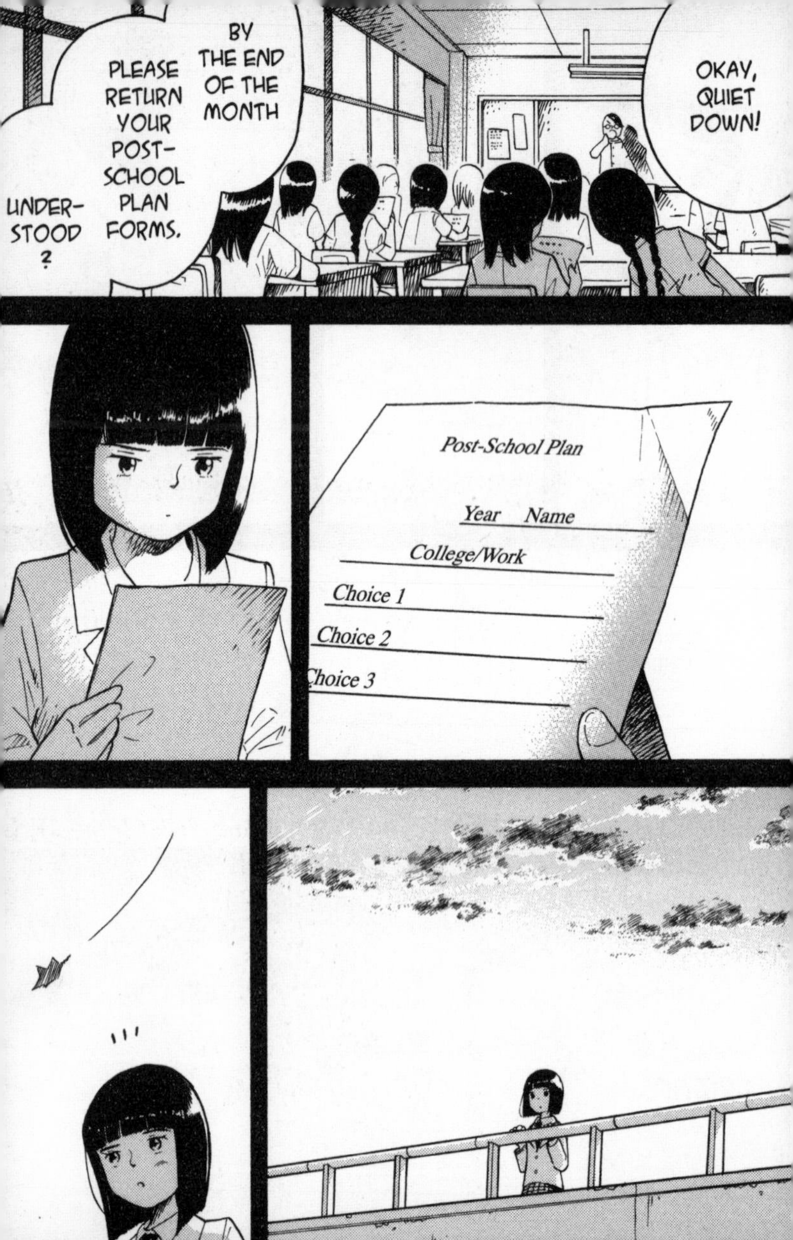
OKAY, QUIET DOWN!
BY THE END OF THE MONTH PLEASE RETURN YOUR POST-SCHOOL PLAN FORMS.
UNDER-STOOD?
Post-School Plan
Year Name
College/Work
Choice 1
Choice 2
Choice 3

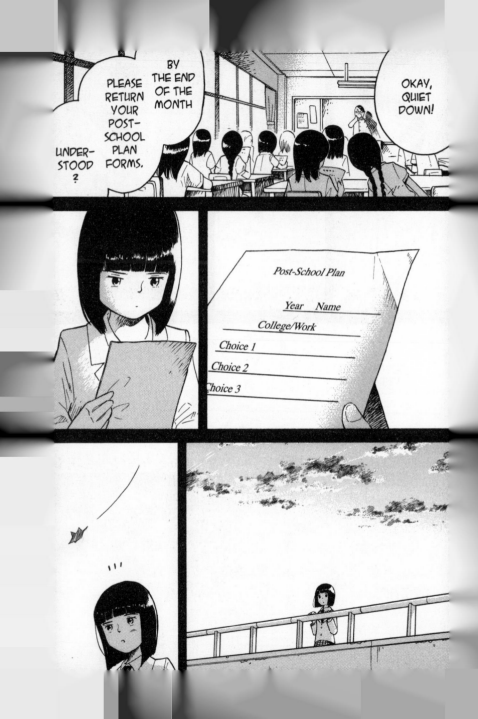

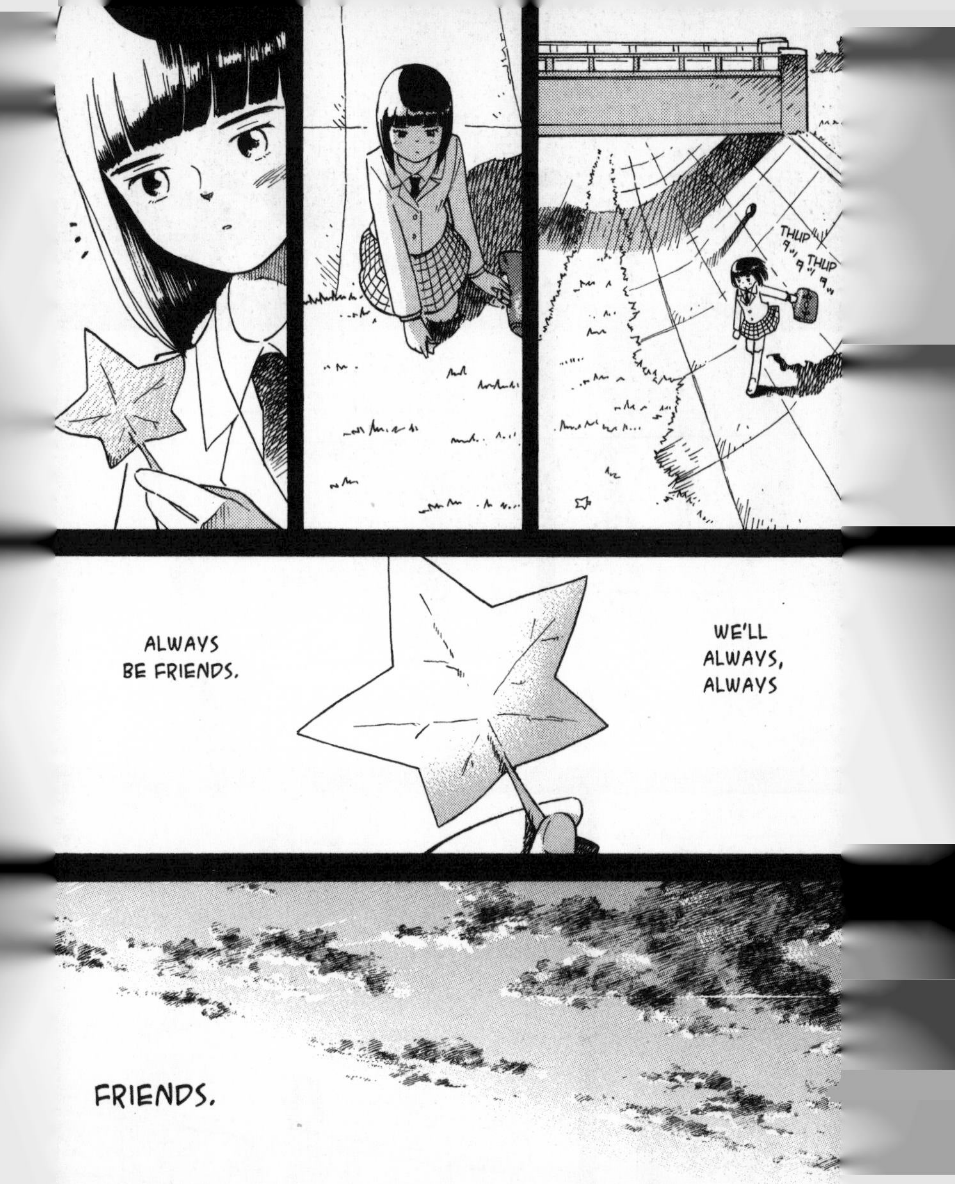
THUP
THUP
WE'LL ALWAYS, ALWAYS
ALWAYS BE FRIENDS.
FRIENDS.

MISSION:53

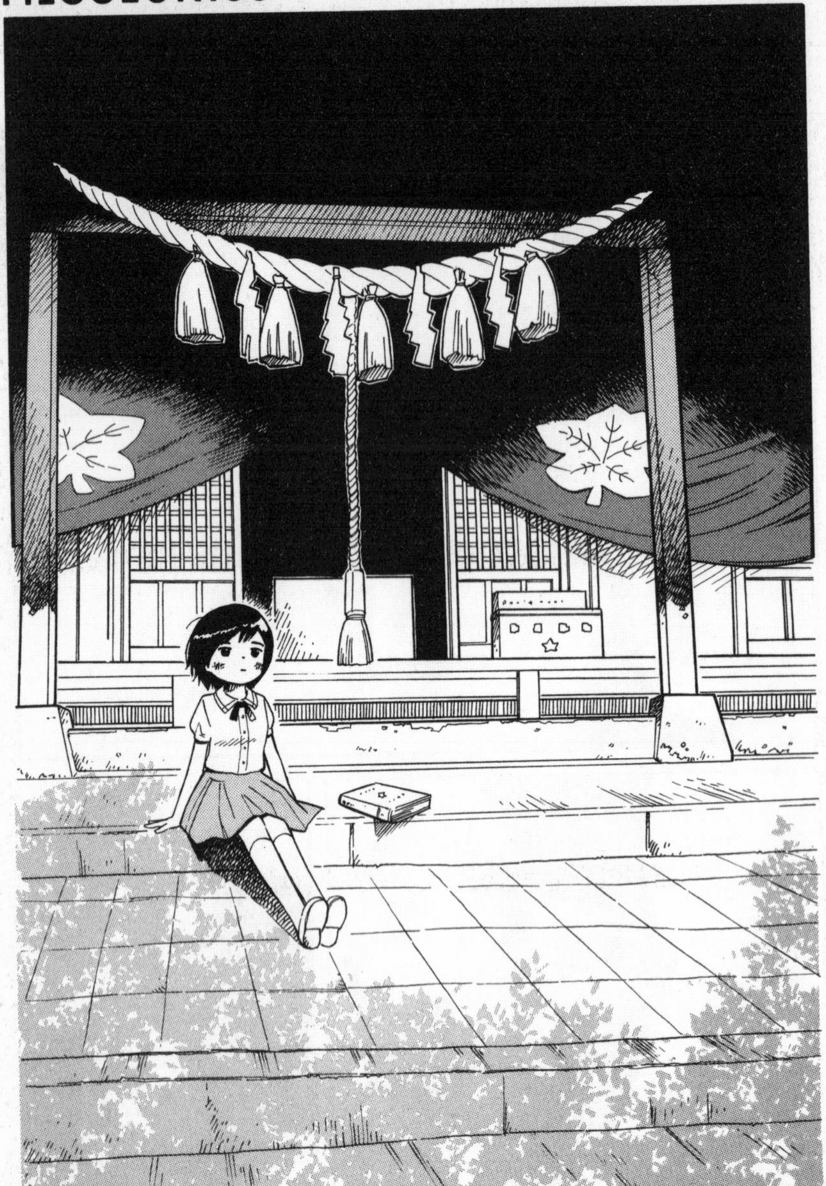

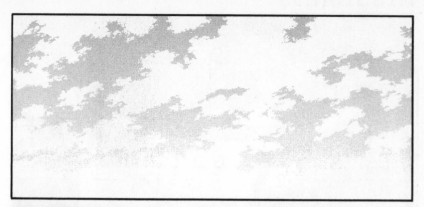

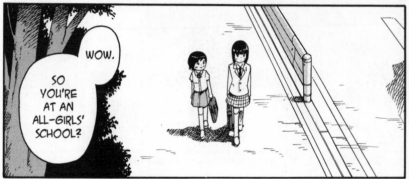

WOW.
SO YOU'RE AT AN ALL-GIRLS' SCHOOL?
IS IT FUN?
HUH?
YEAH SUPER FUN.
SINCE THERE'S NO BOYS, WE'RE A LOT MORE FREE.

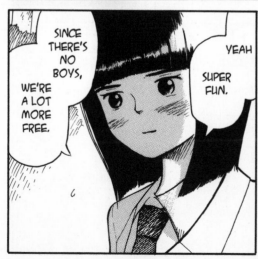

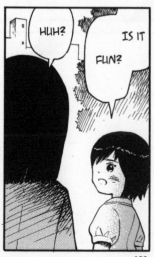

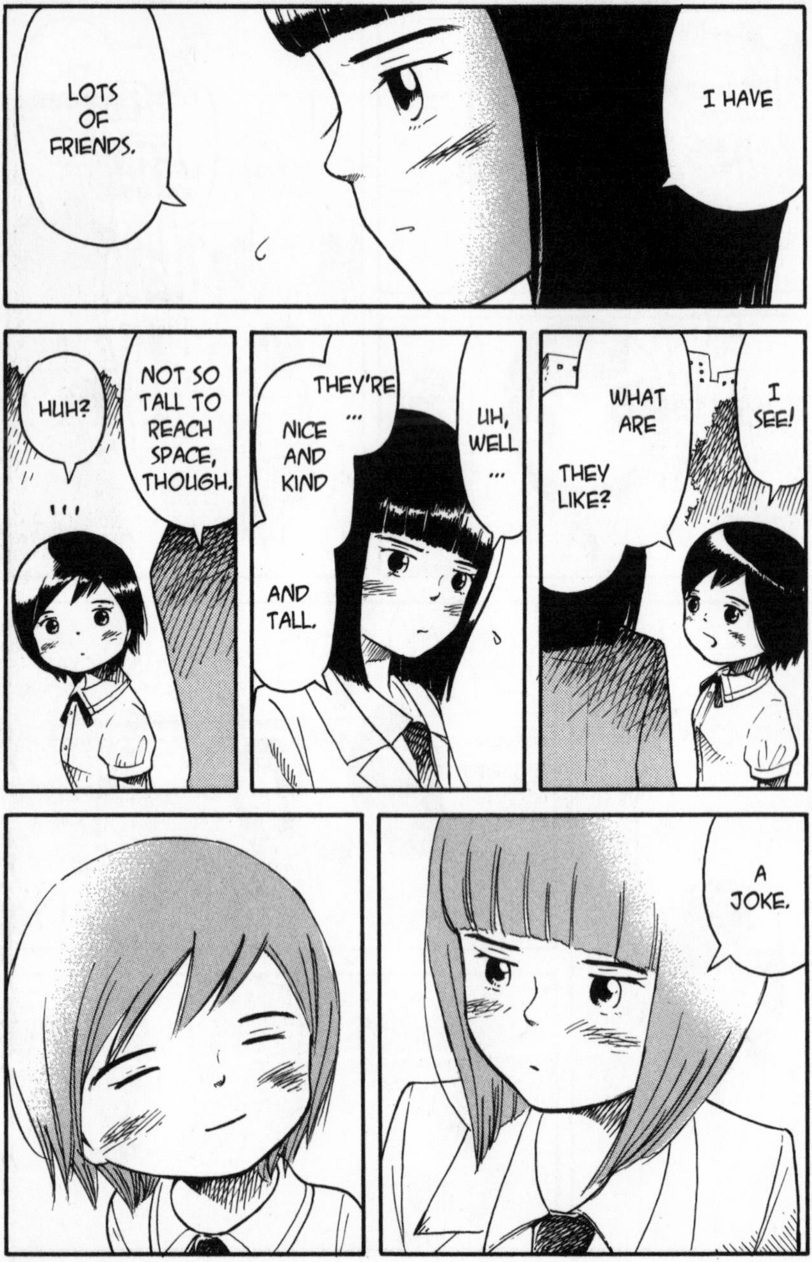
I HAVE
LOTS OF FRIENDS.
I SEE!
WHAT ARE THEY LIKE?
UH, WELL ...
THEY'RE ... NICE AND KIND
AND TALL.
NOT SO TALL TO REACH SPACE, THOUGH.
HUH?
A JOKE.

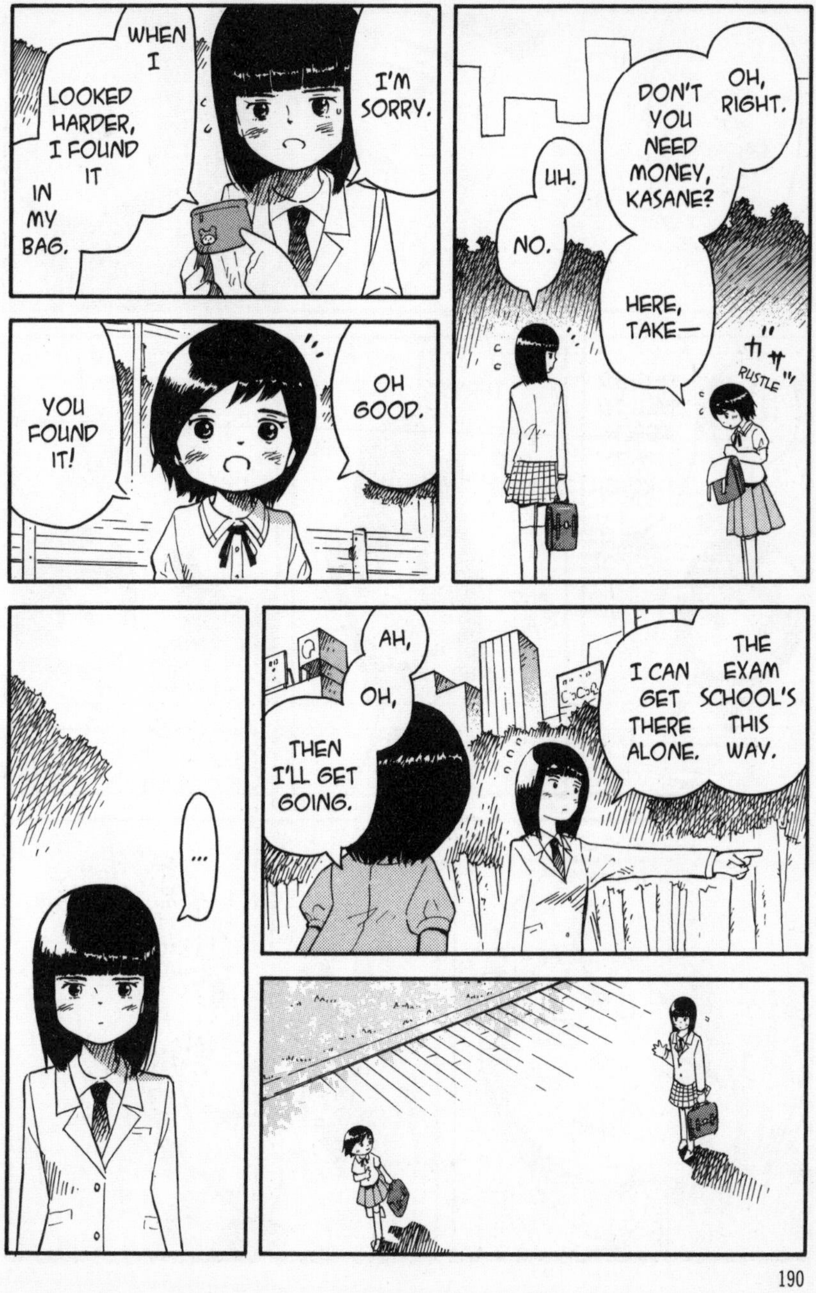
OH, RIGHT.
DON'T YOU NEED MONEY, KASANE?
UH.
NO.
HERE, TAKE—
RUSTLE
I'M SORRY.
WHEN I LOOKED HARDER, I FOUND IT IN MY BAG.
OH GOOD.
YOU FOUND IT!
THE EXAM SCHOOL'S THIS WAY.
I CAN GET THERE ALONE.
AH, OH, THEN I'LL GET GOING.
...

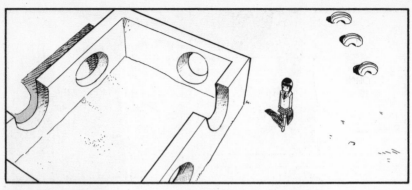

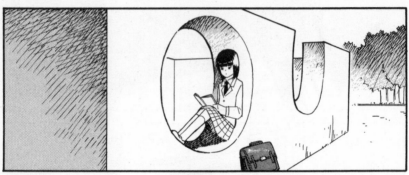

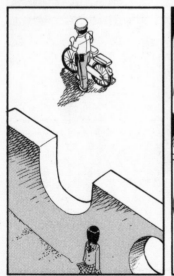

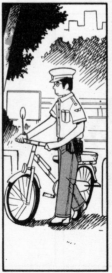

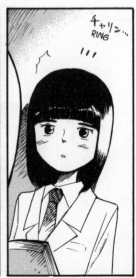

チャリン…
RING

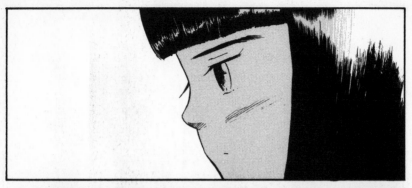

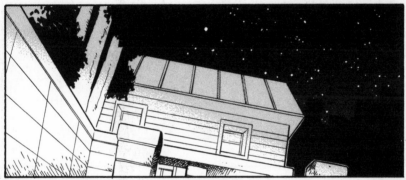

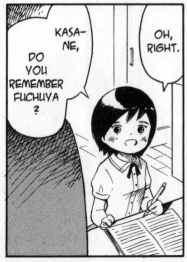

KASA-
NE,

DO
YOU
REMEMBER
FUCHUYA
?

OH,
RIGHT.

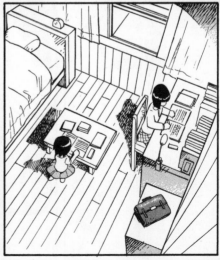

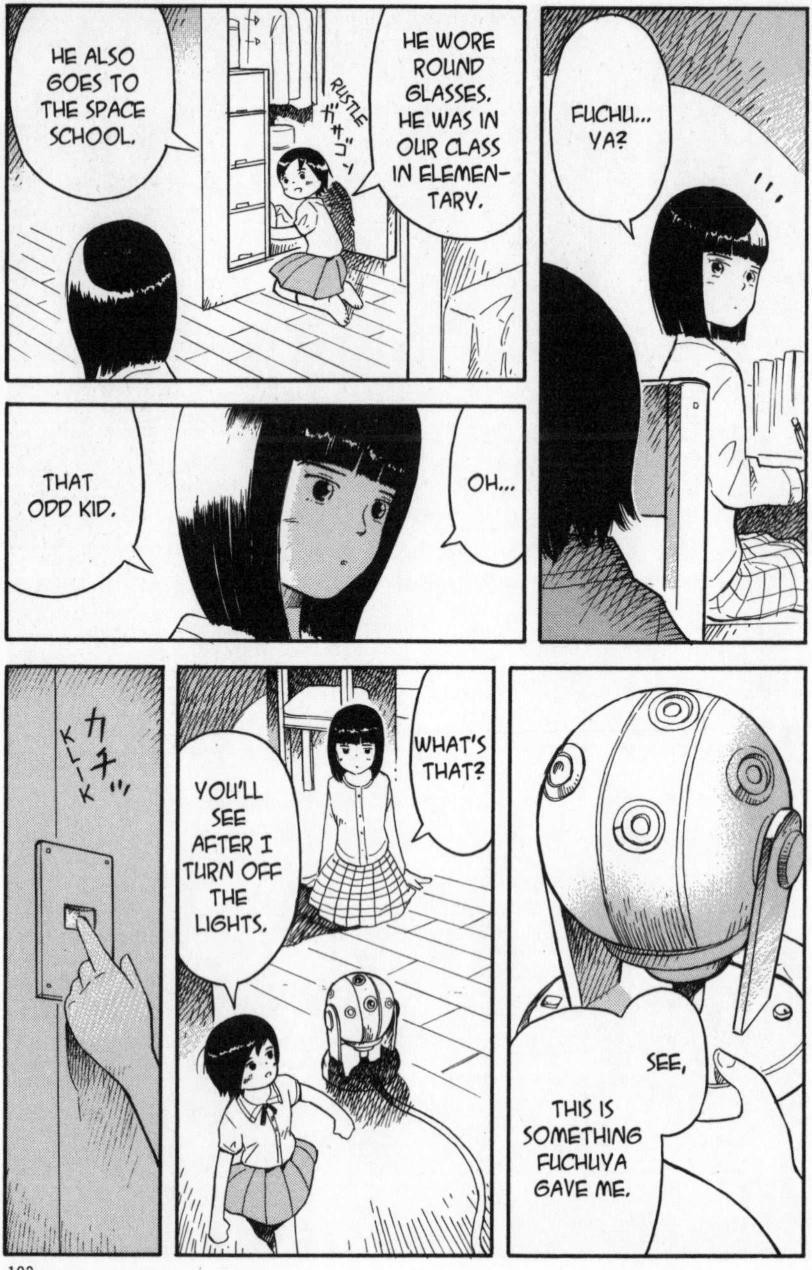

FUCHU... YA?
HE WORE ROUND GLASSES. HE WAS IN OUR CLASS IN ELEMENTARY.
RUSTLE
HE ALSO GOES TO THE SPACE SCHOOL.
OH...
THAT ODD KID.
SEE,
THIS IS SOMETHING FUCHUYA GAVE ME.
WHAT'S THAT?
YOU'LL SEE AFTER I TURN OFF THE LIGHTS.
KLIK

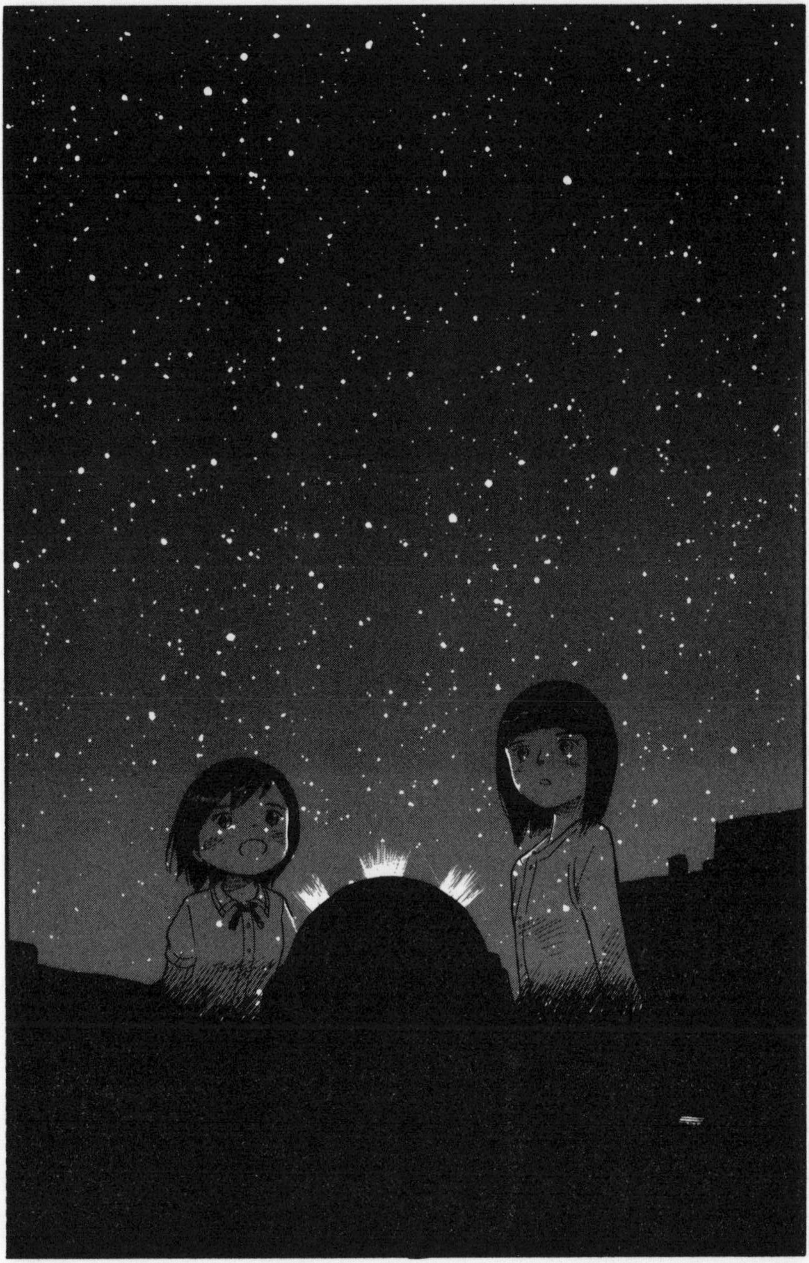

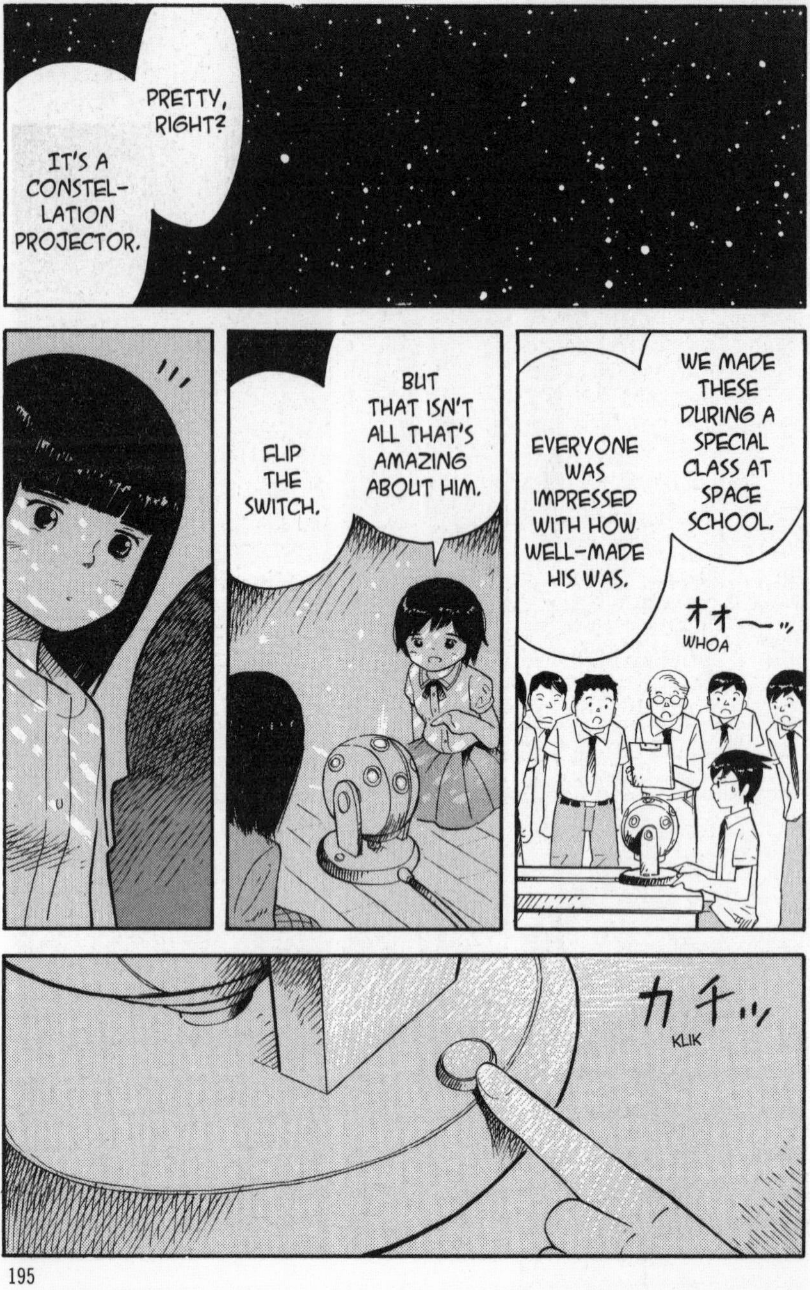
PRETTY, RIGHT?
IT'S A CONSTEL-LATION PROJECTOR.
WE MADE THESE DURING A SPECIAL CLASS AT SPACE SCHOOL.
EVERYONE WAS IMPRESSED WITH HOW WELL-MADE HIS WAS.
オオ～ッ
WHOA
BUT THAT ISN'T ALL THAT'S AMAZING ABOUT HIM.
FLIP THE SWITCH.
カチッ
KLIK

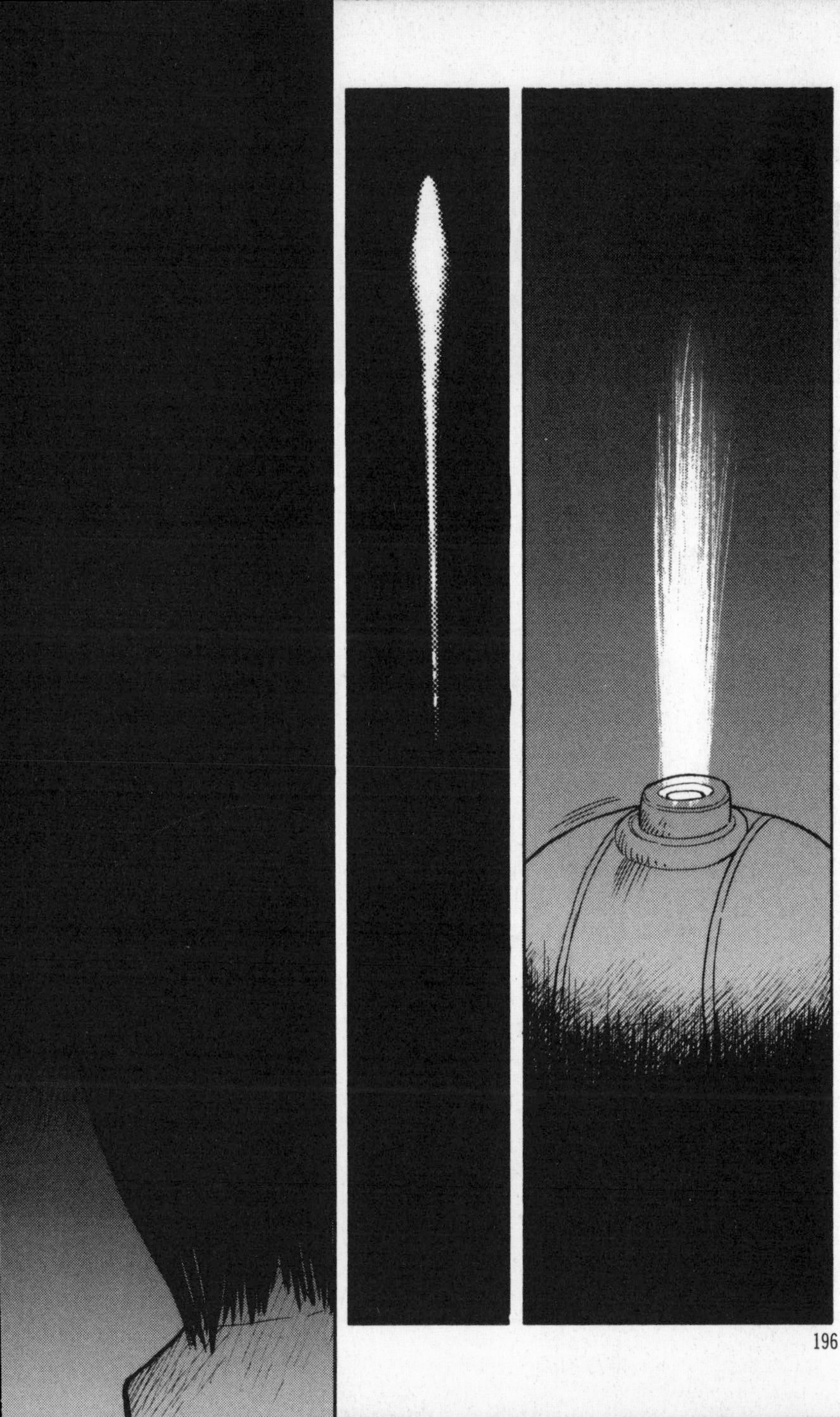

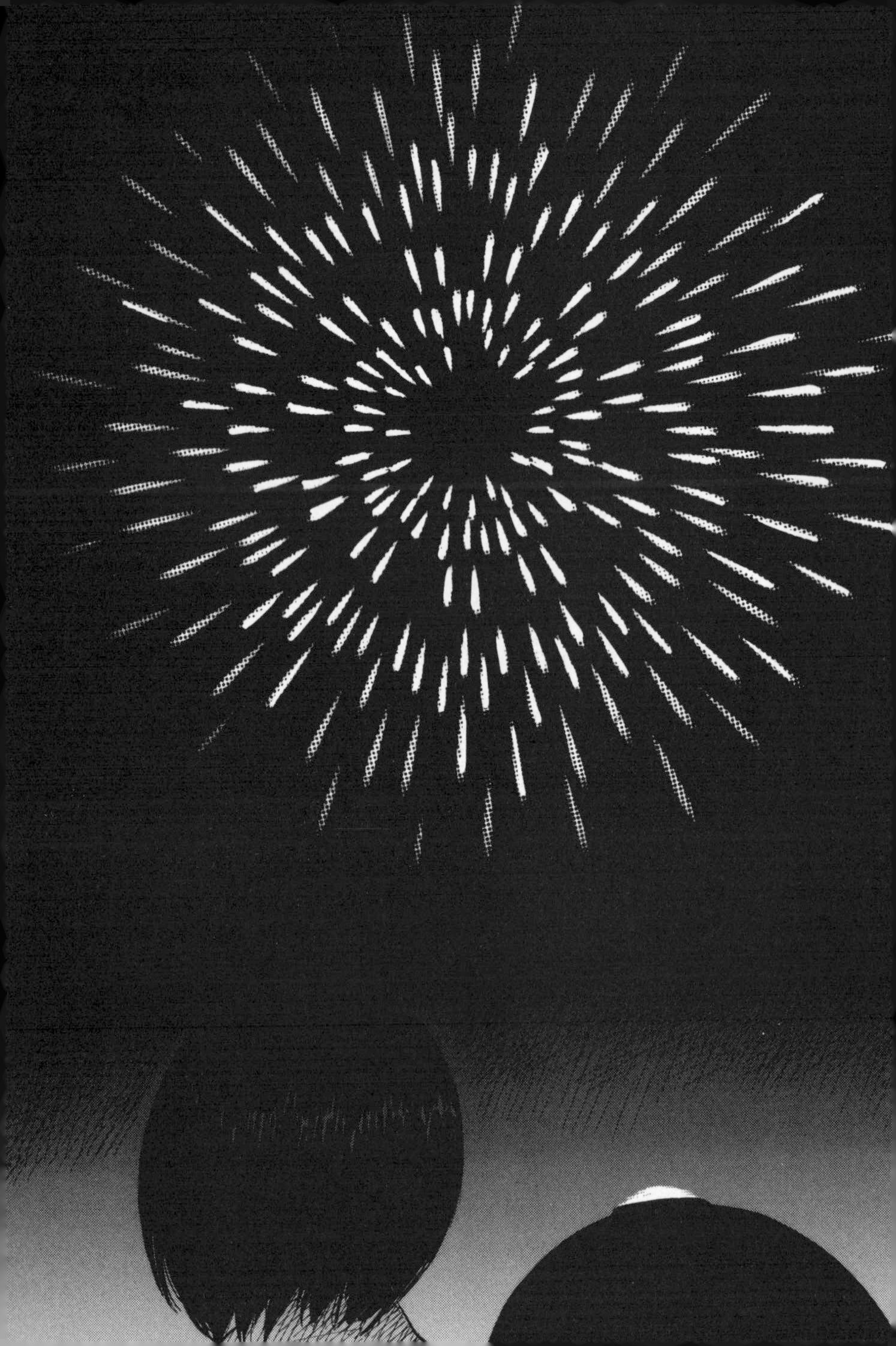

WHEN I WATCH THIS
I'M REMINDED OF YUIGAHAMA'S FIREWORKS.
IT GIVES ME COURAGE.
AND SO DOES LOOKING AT
SO MANY STARS.

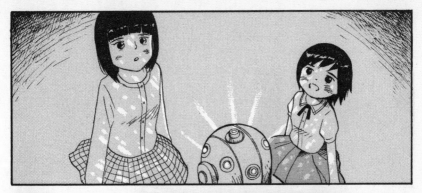

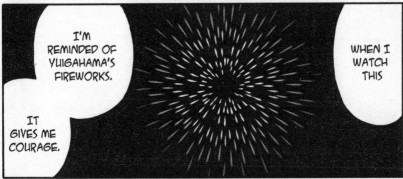

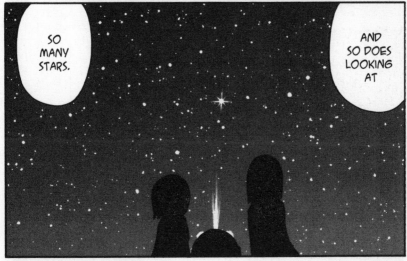

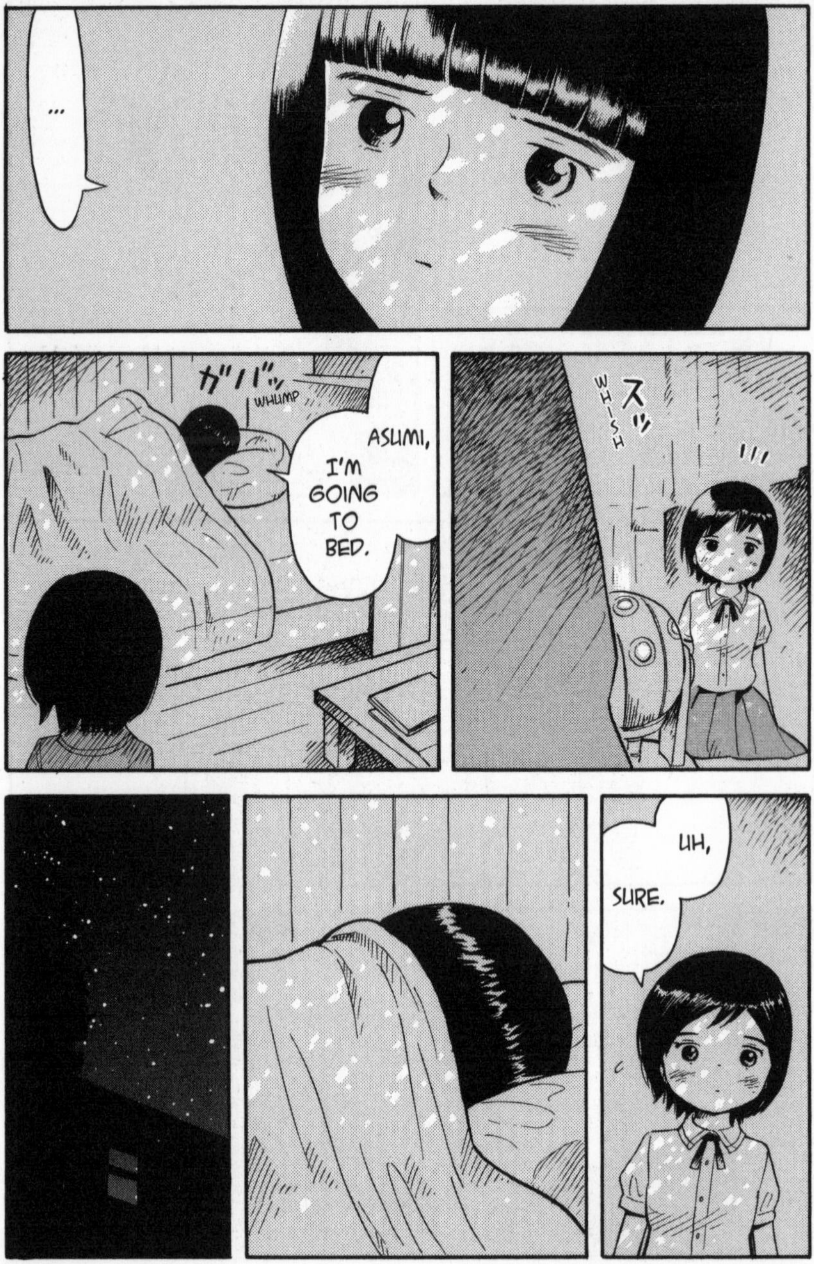
...
スッ
WHISH
ガバッ
WHUMP
ASUMI, I'M GOING TO BED.
UH, SURE.

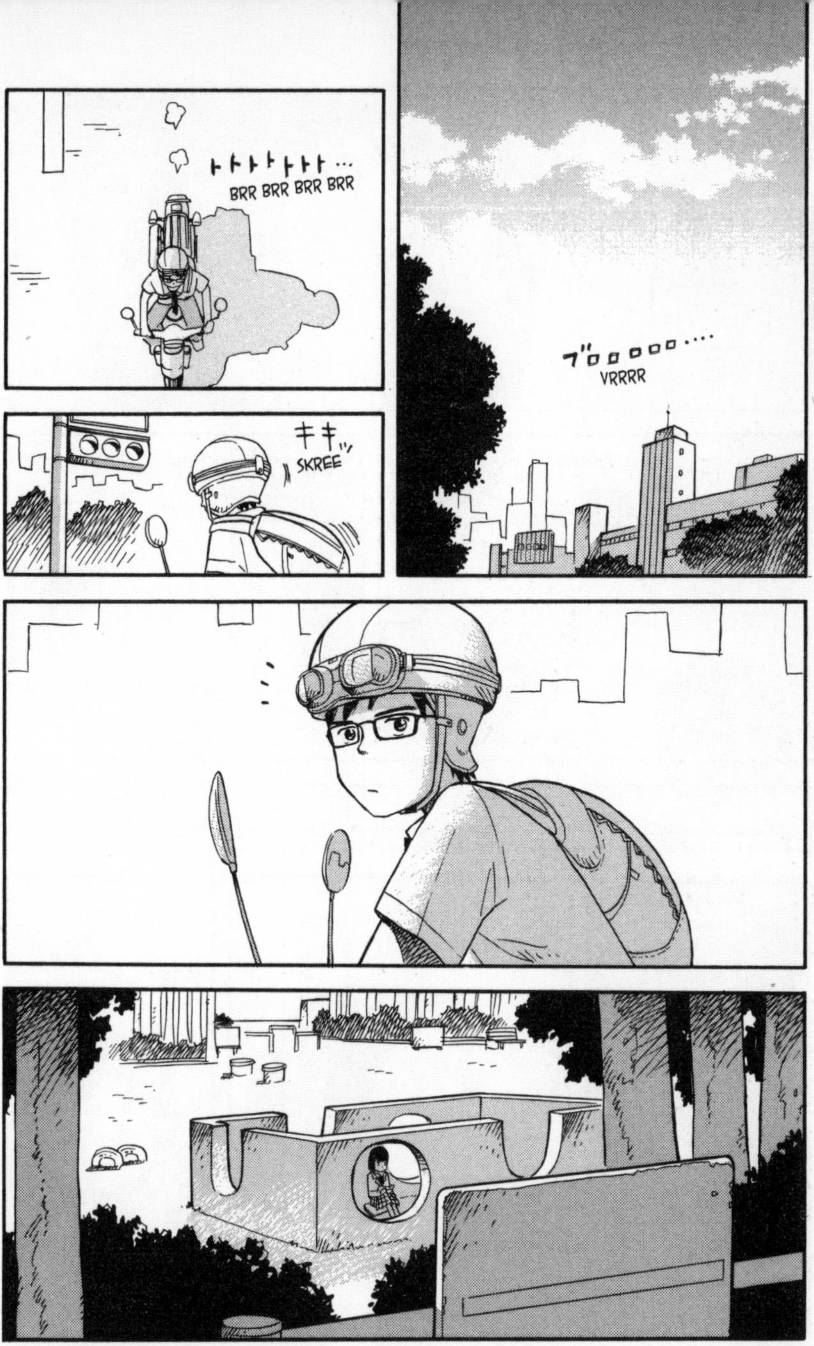
ブロロロロロ….
VRRRR
トトトトトトト…
BRR BRR BRR BRR
キキッ
SKREE

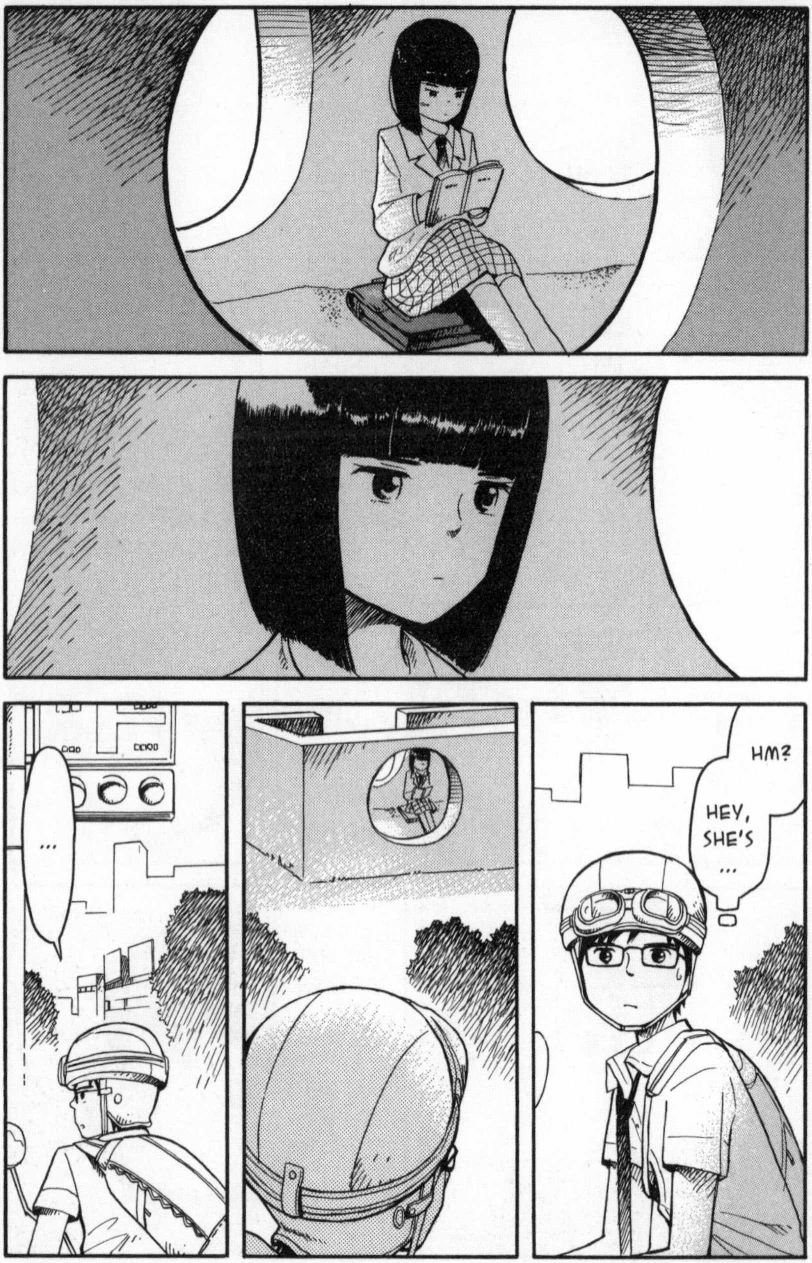
HM?
HEY, SHE'S ...
...

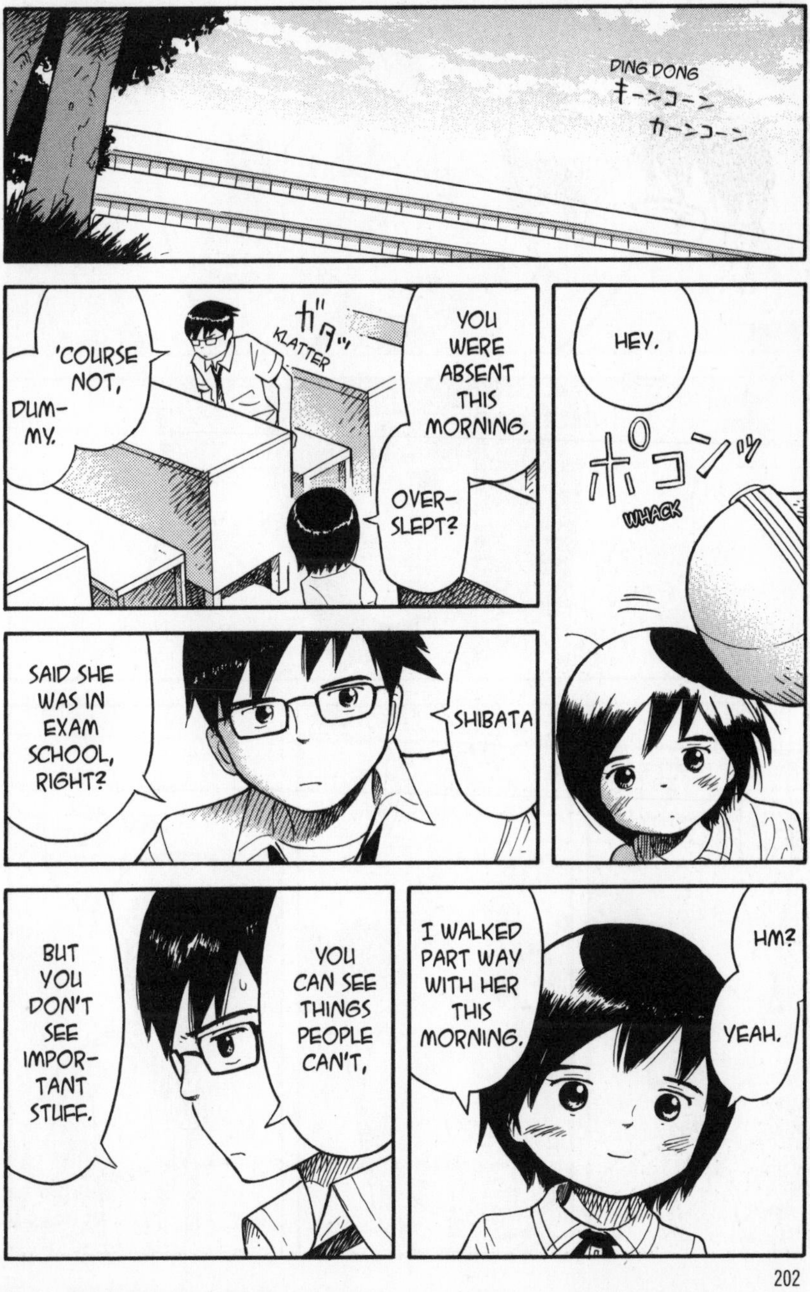
DING DONG
キーンコーン
カーンコーン
HEY.
ポコンッ
WHACK
YOU WERE ABSENT THIS MORNING.
ガタッ
KLATTER
OVER-SLEPT?
'COURSE NOT, DUM-MY.
SHIBATA
SAID SHE WAS IN EXAM SCHOOL, RIGHT?
HM?
YEAH.
I WALKED PART WAY WITH HER THIS MORNING.
YOU CAN SEE THINGS PEOPLE CAN'T,
BUT YOU DON'T SEE IMPOR-TANT STUFF.

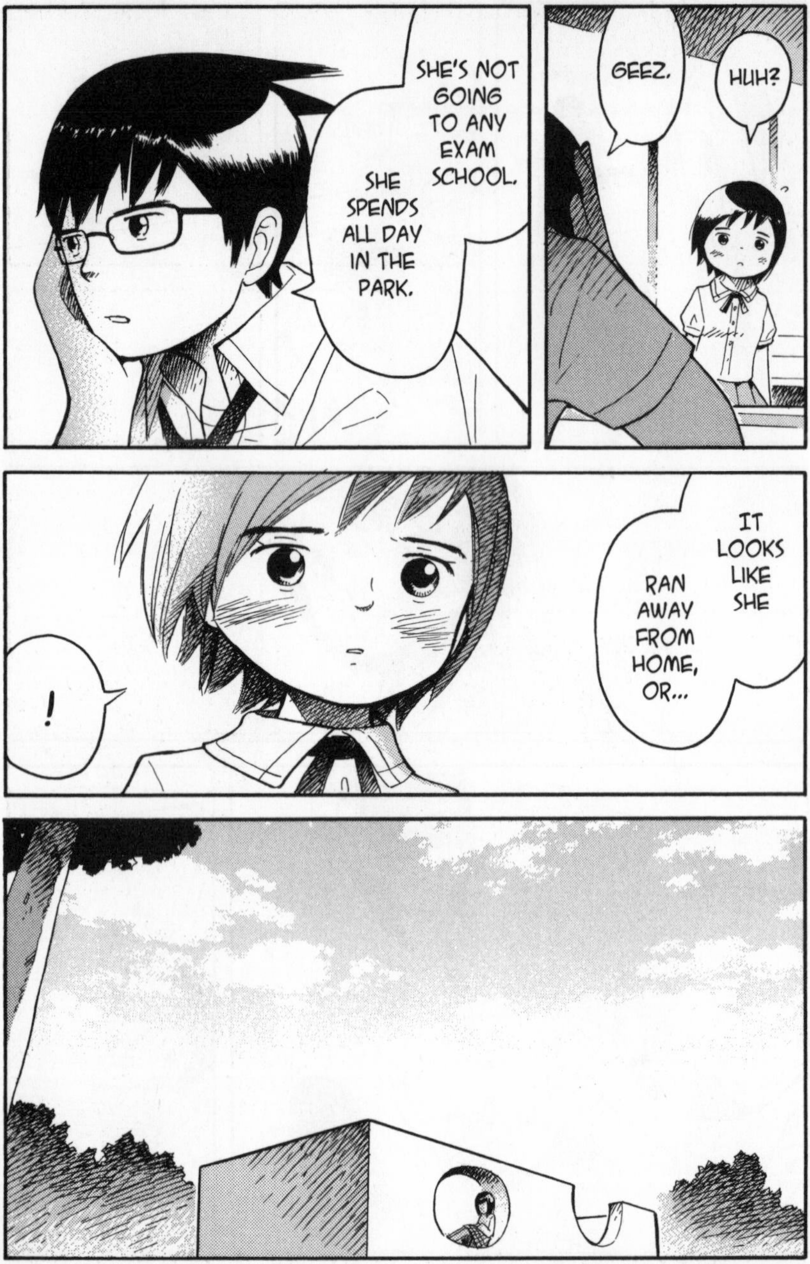
GEEZ.
HUH?
SHE'S NOT GOING TO ANY EXAM SCHOOL.
SHE SPENDS ALL DAY IN THE PARK.
IT LOOKS LIKE SHE RAN AWAY FROM HOME, OR...
!

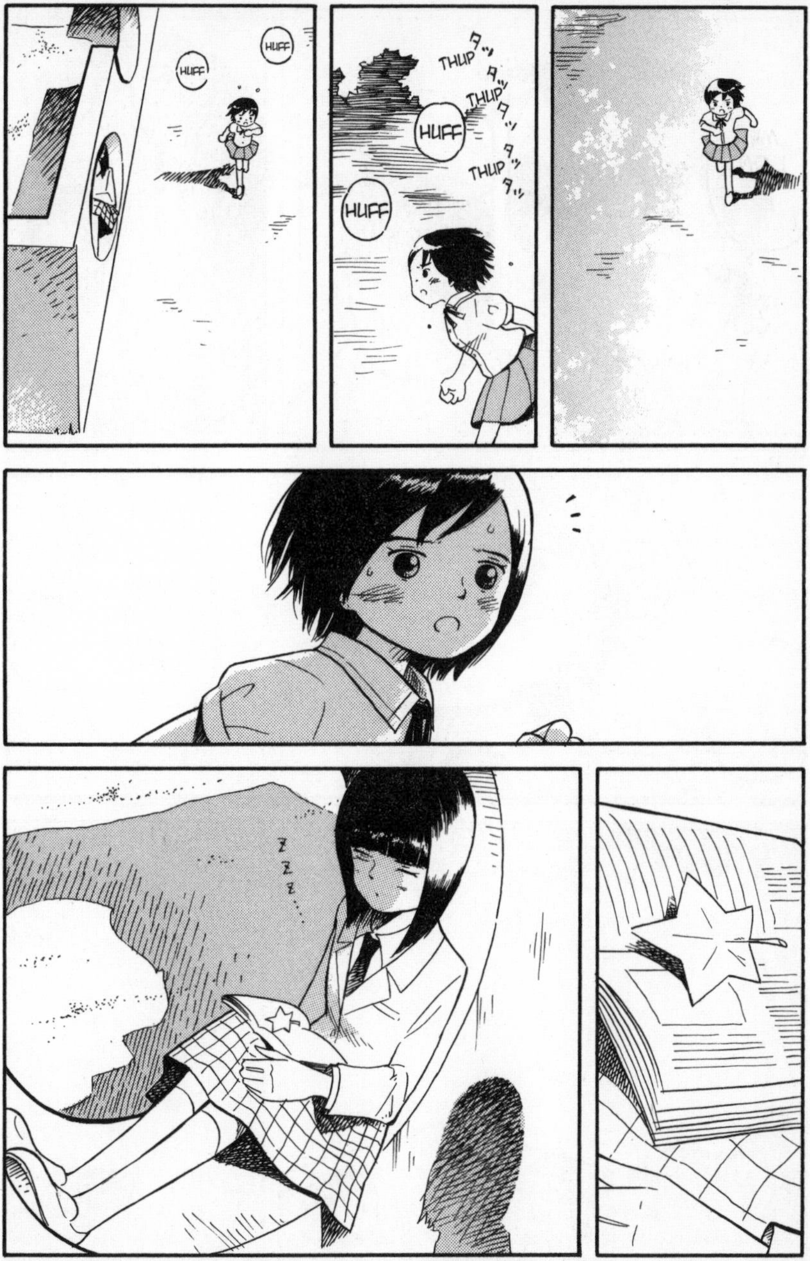
THUP
タッ
タッ
THUP
タッ
タッ
THUP
タッ
タッ
HUFF
HUFF
HUFF
HUFF
Z
Z
Z...

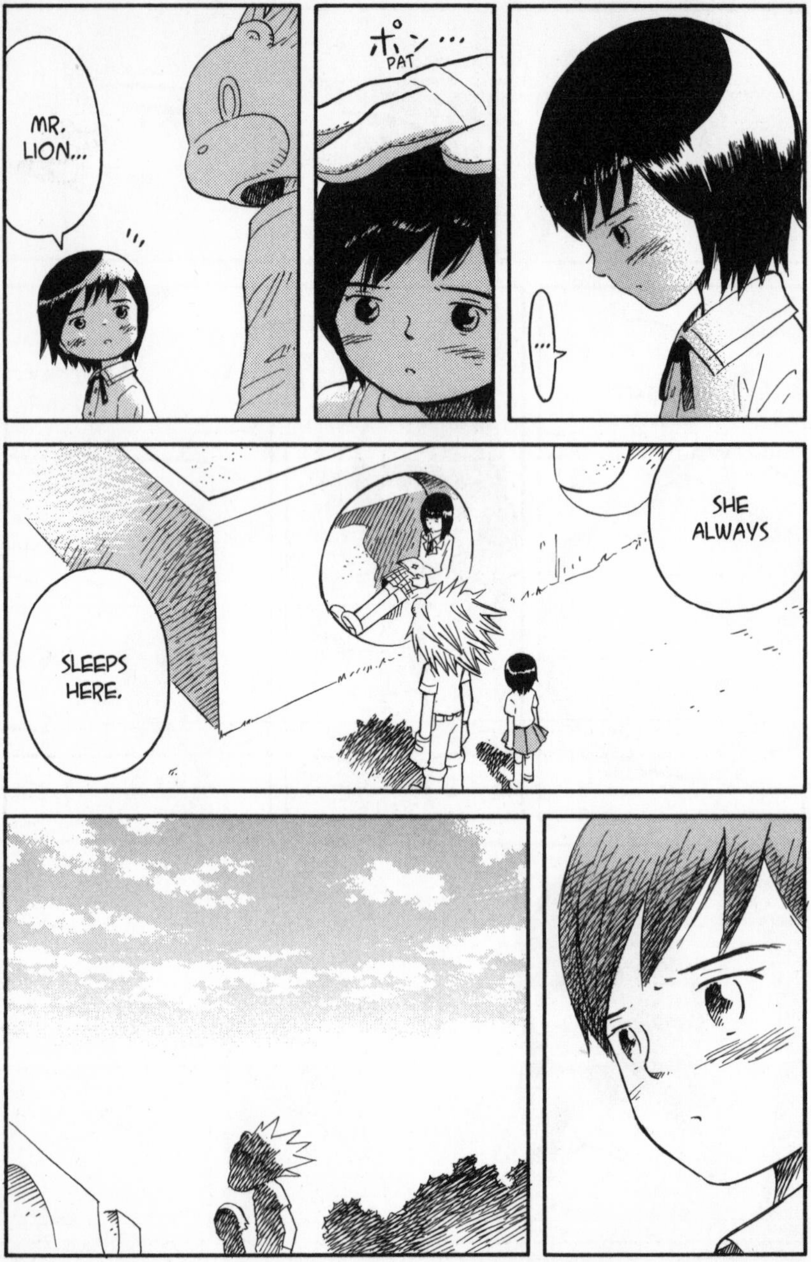
...
ポン...
PAT
MR. LION...
SHE ALWAYS
SLEEPS HERE.

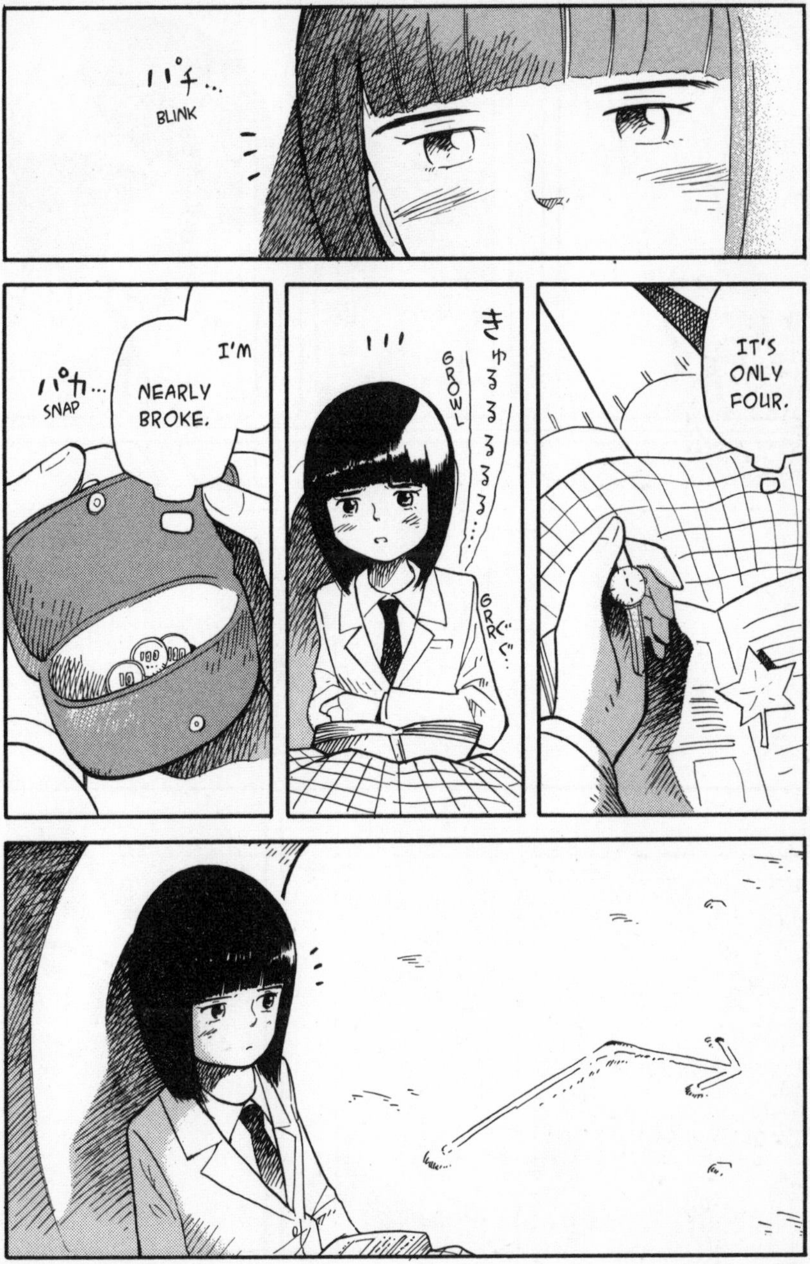
パチ…
BLINK
IT'S ONLY FOUR.
きゅるるるるる…
GROWL
ぐぐ
GRR
パカ…
SNAP
I'M NEARLY BROKE.

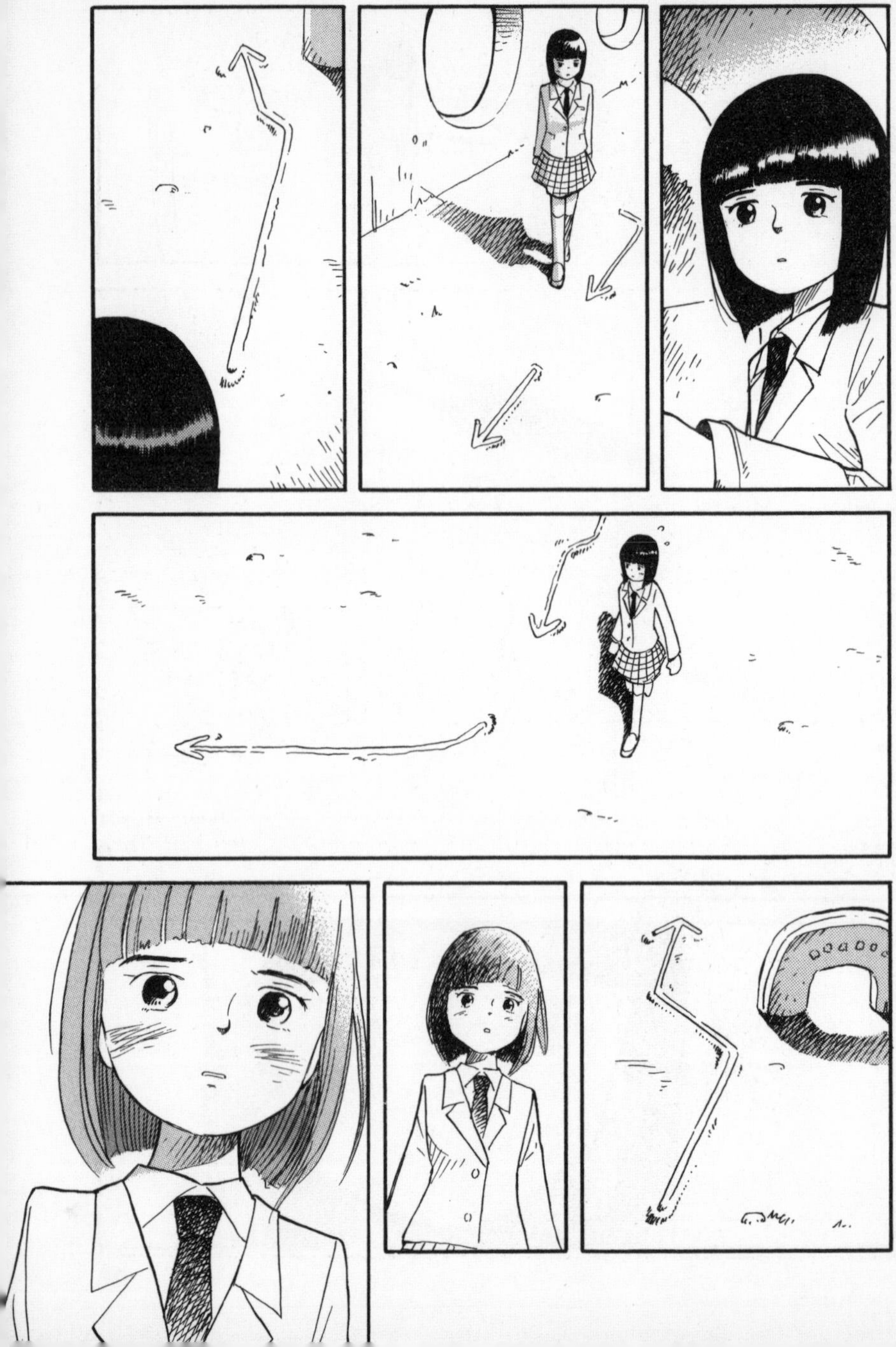

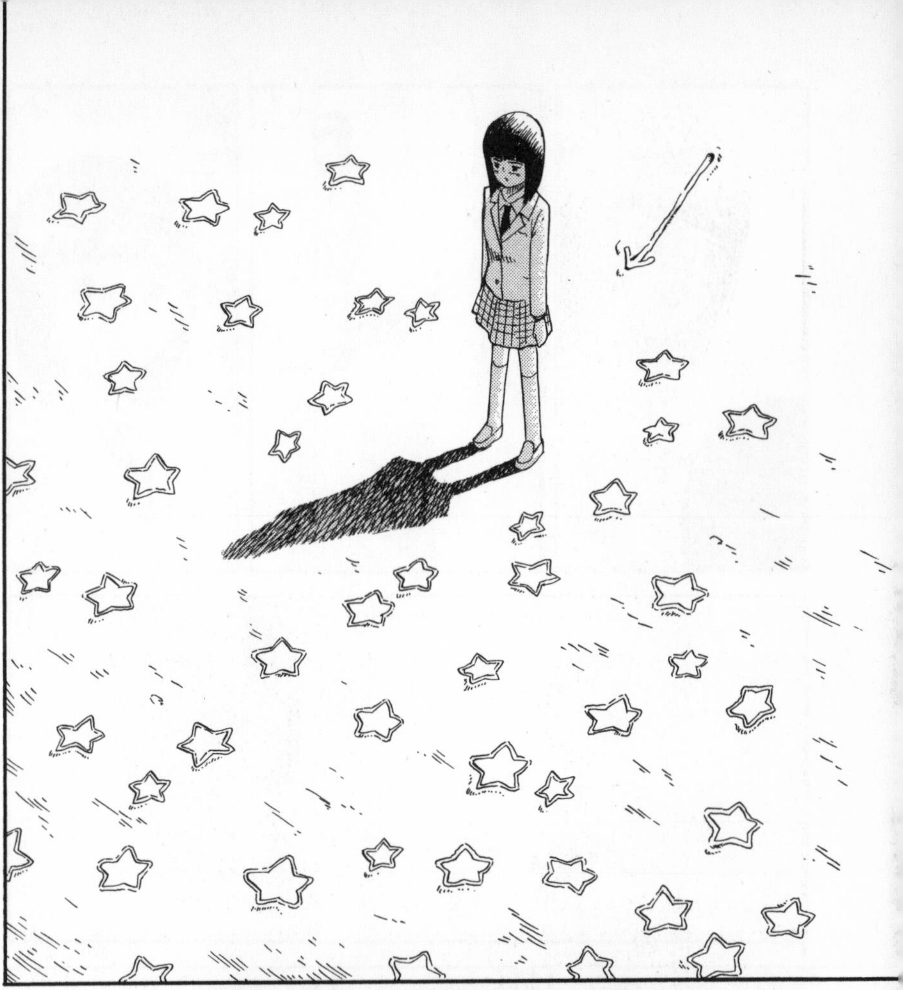

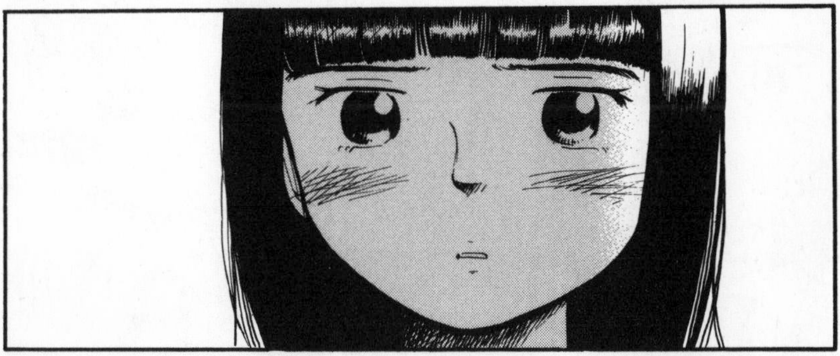

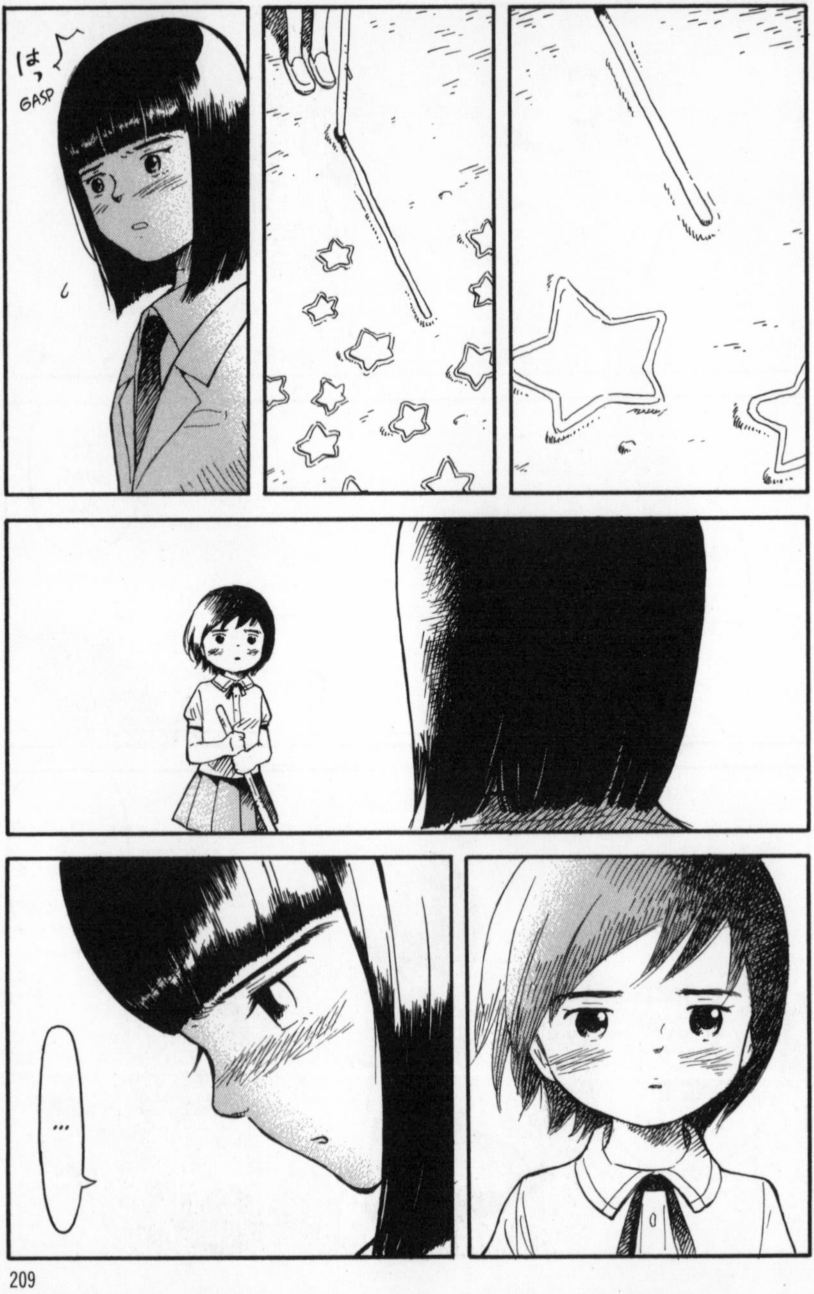
はっ
GASP
...

I LIED.
IT WAS ALL
A LIE.
I ACTUALLY
DON'T ENJOY SCHOOL ONE BIT.

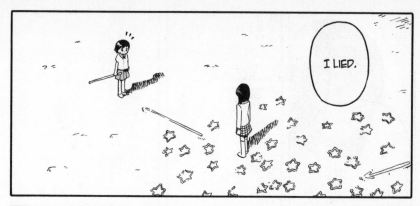

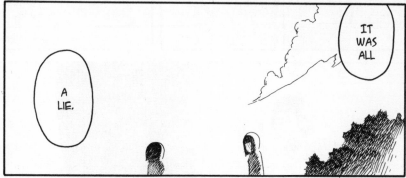

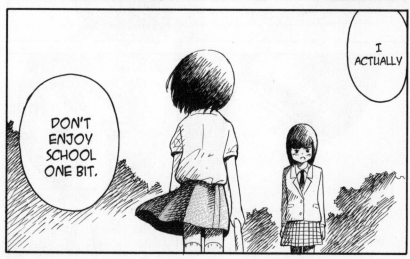

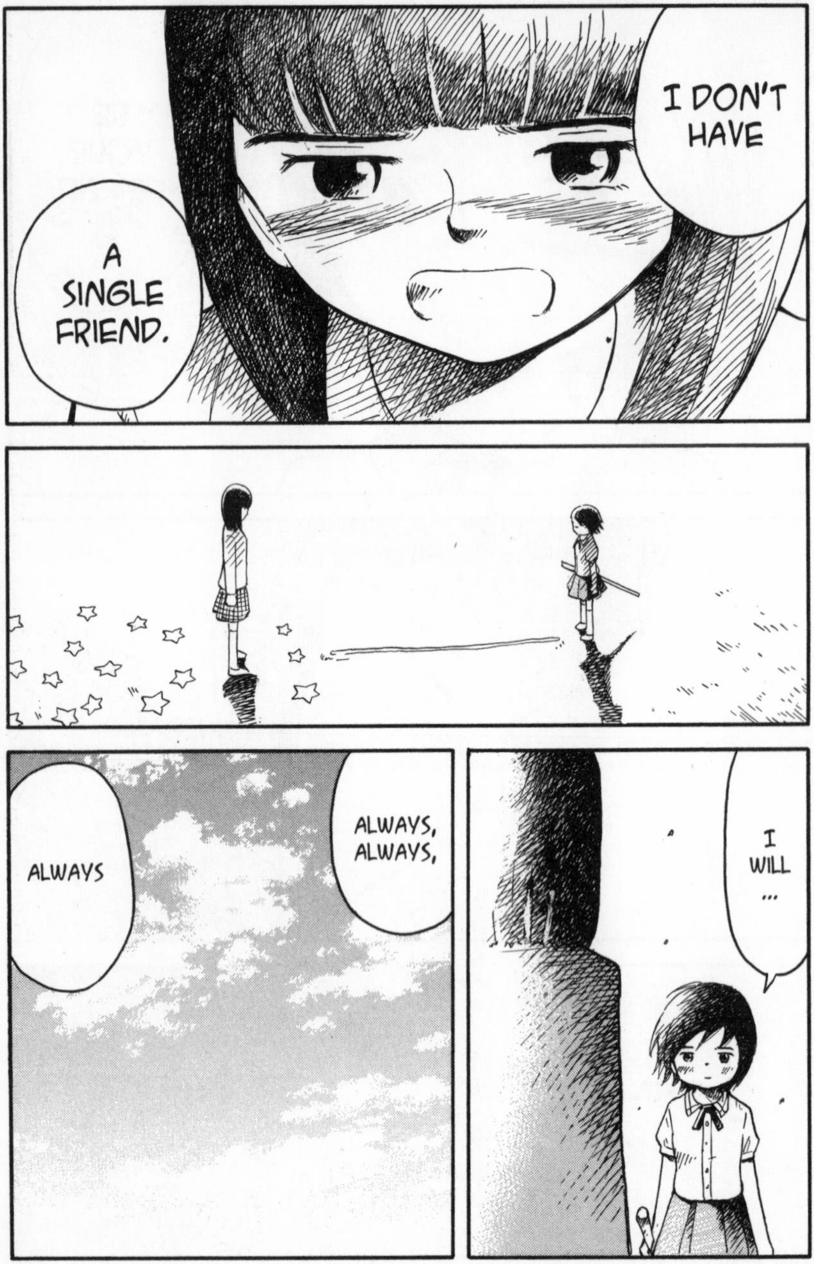
I DON'T HAVE
A SINGLE FRIEND.
I WILL ...
ALWAYS, ALWAYS,
ALWAYS

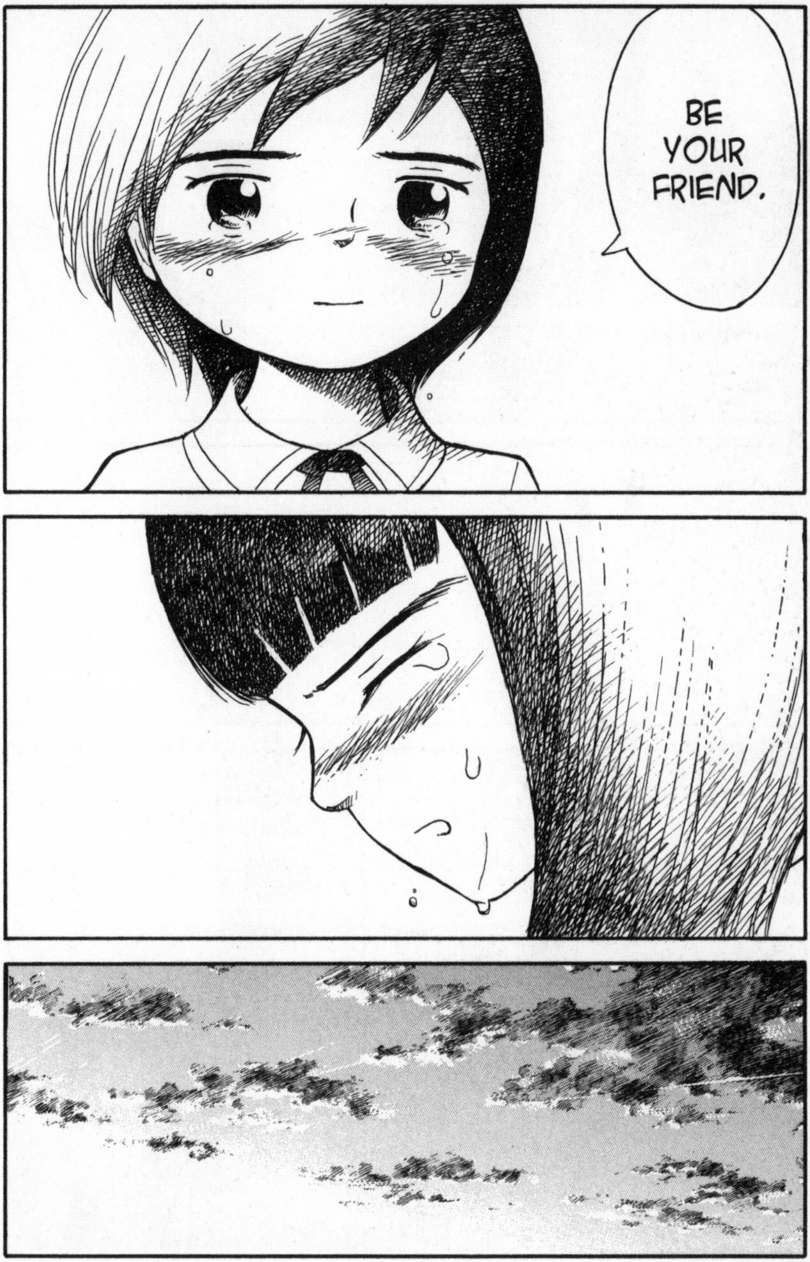
BE YOUR FRIEND.

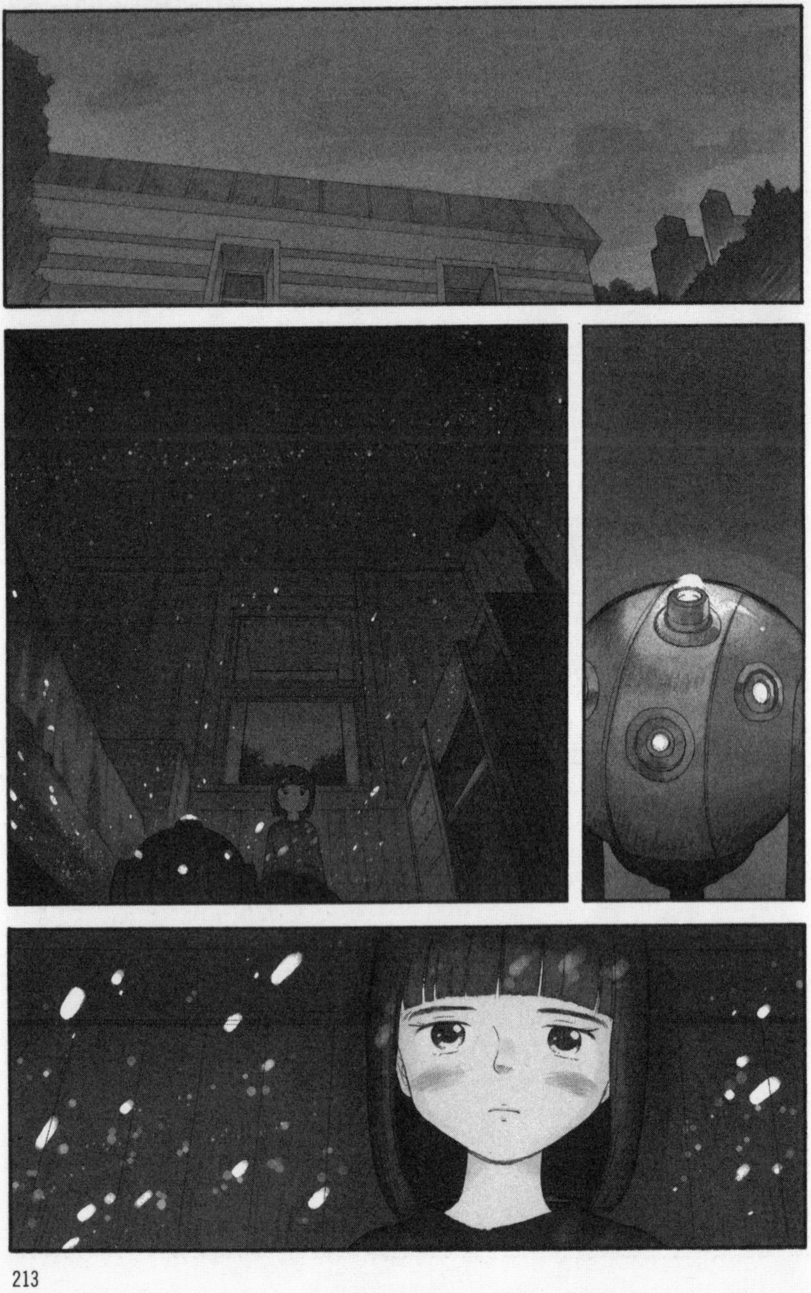

MISSION:54

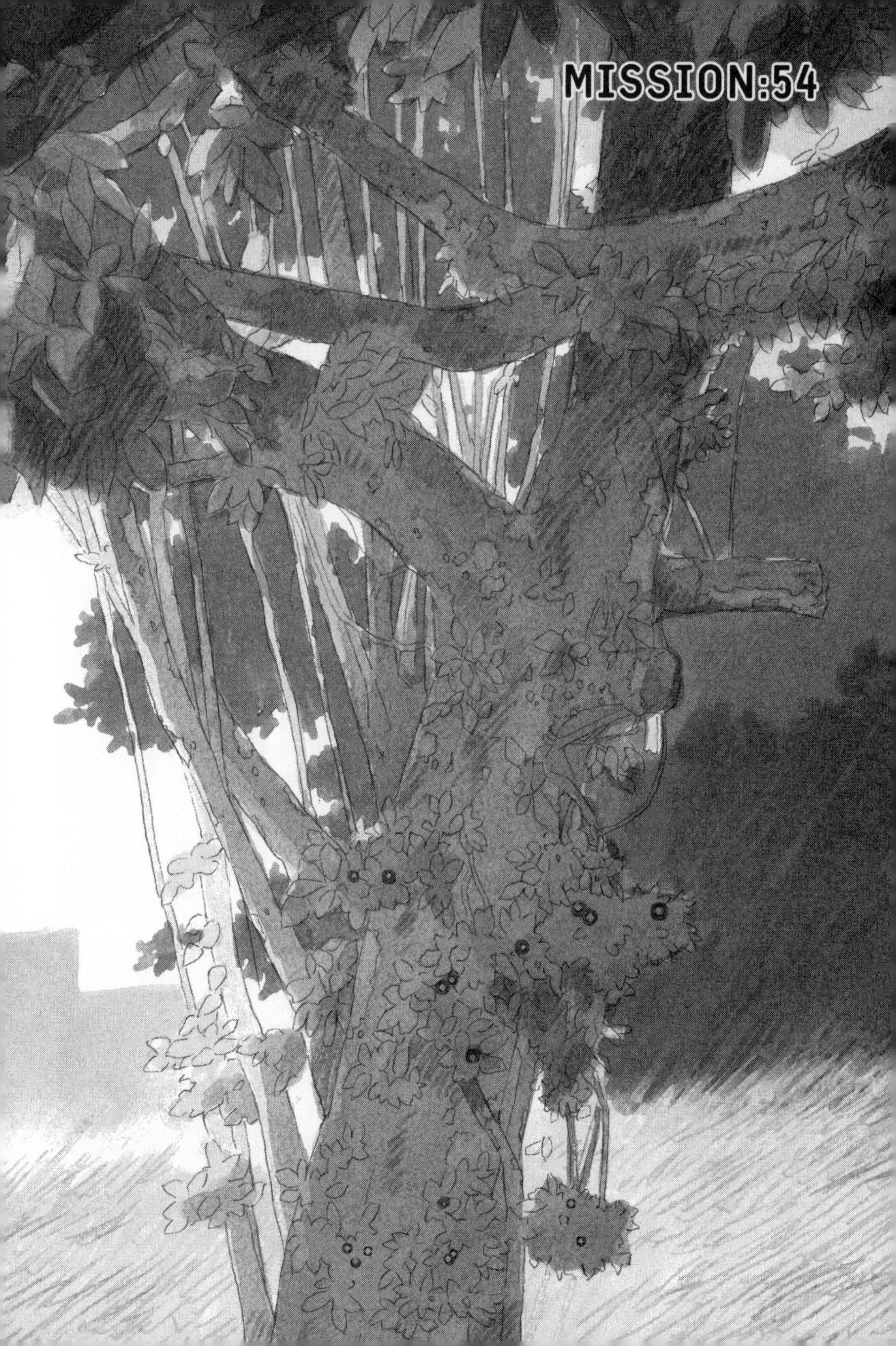

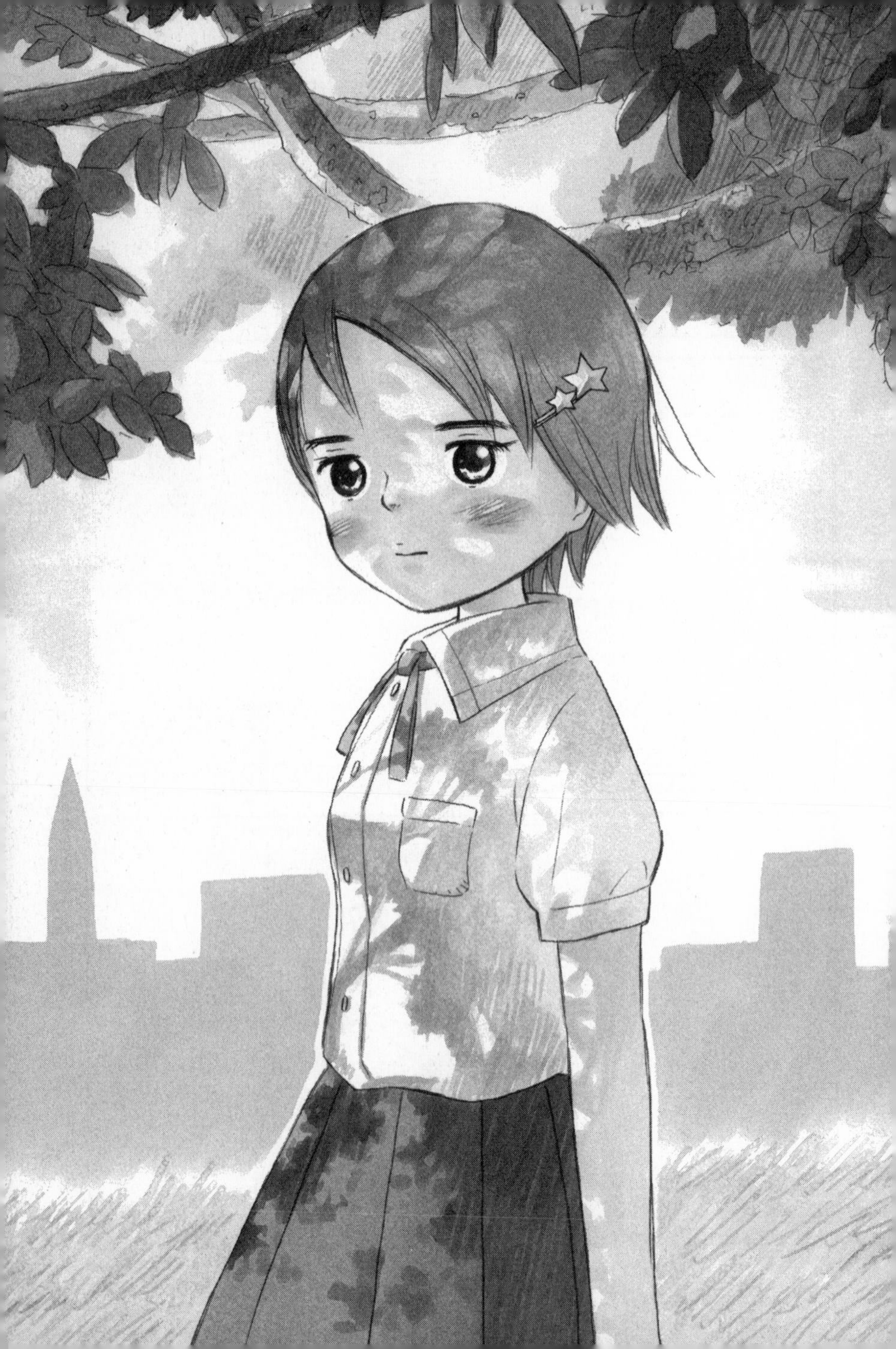

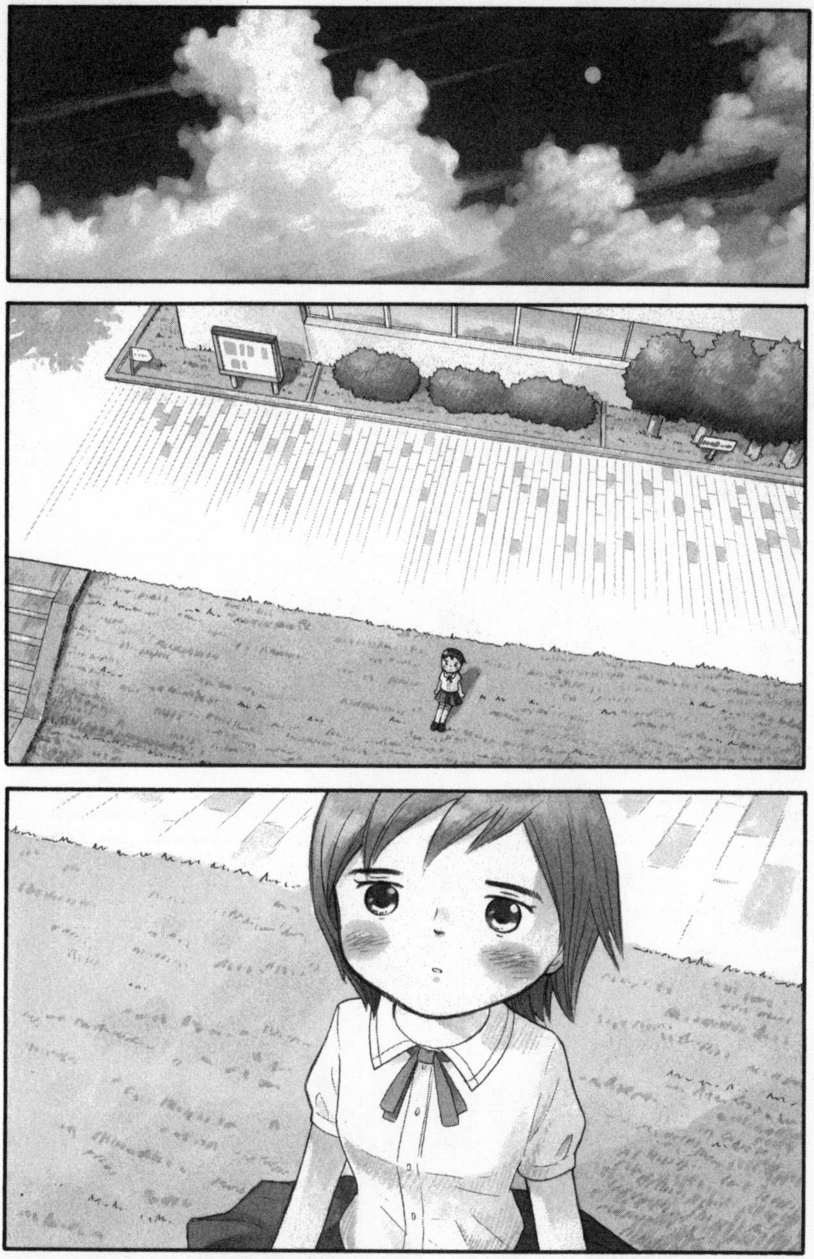

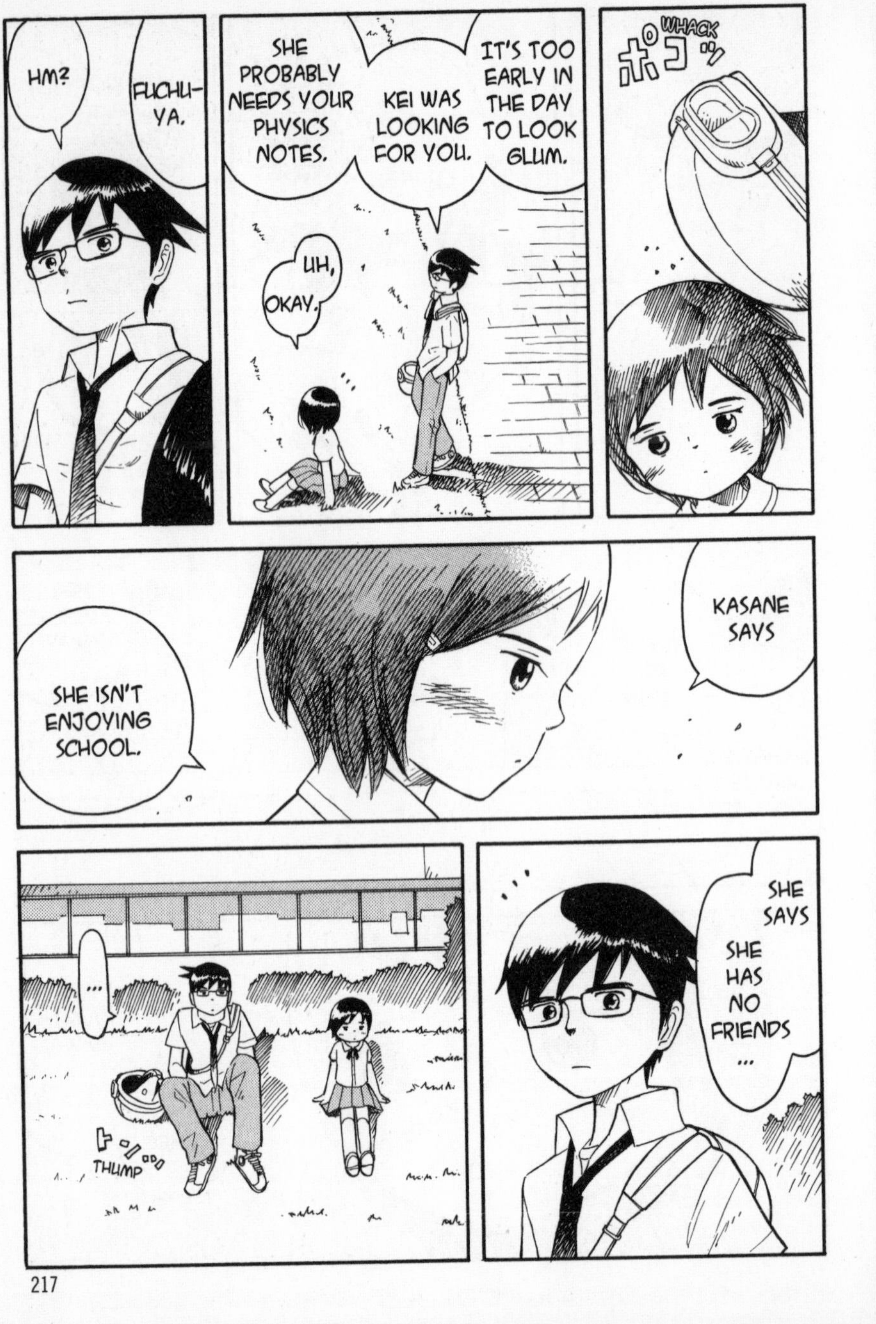

WHACK
ポコッ
IT'S TOO EARLY IN THE DAY TO LOOK GLUM.
KEI WAS LOOKING FOR YOU.
SHE PROBABLY NEEDS YOUR PHYSICS NOTES.
UH, OKAY.
FUCHU-YA.
HM?
KASANE SAYS
SHE ISN'T ENJOYING SCHOOL.
SHE SAYS SHE HAS NO FRIENDS ...
...
THUMP

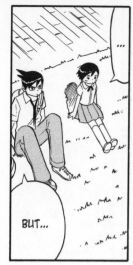

TSK
THAT'S NOT SOMETHING YOU CAN HELP HER WITH.
SHE HAS TO FIGURE IT OUT FOR HERSELF
IF SHE WANTS THINGS TO CHANGE.
...
BUT...
HER RUNNING AWAY
MIGHT BE A SIGN
THAT SHE WANTS TO CHANGE.
YOU, KAMO-GAWA,
JUST KEEP BEING FRIENDLY TO HER.

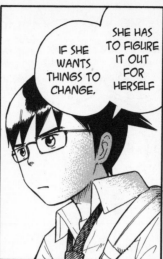

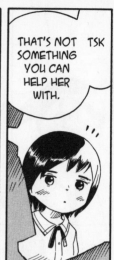

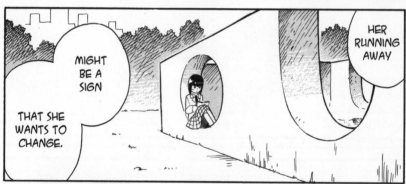

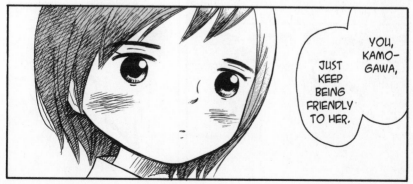

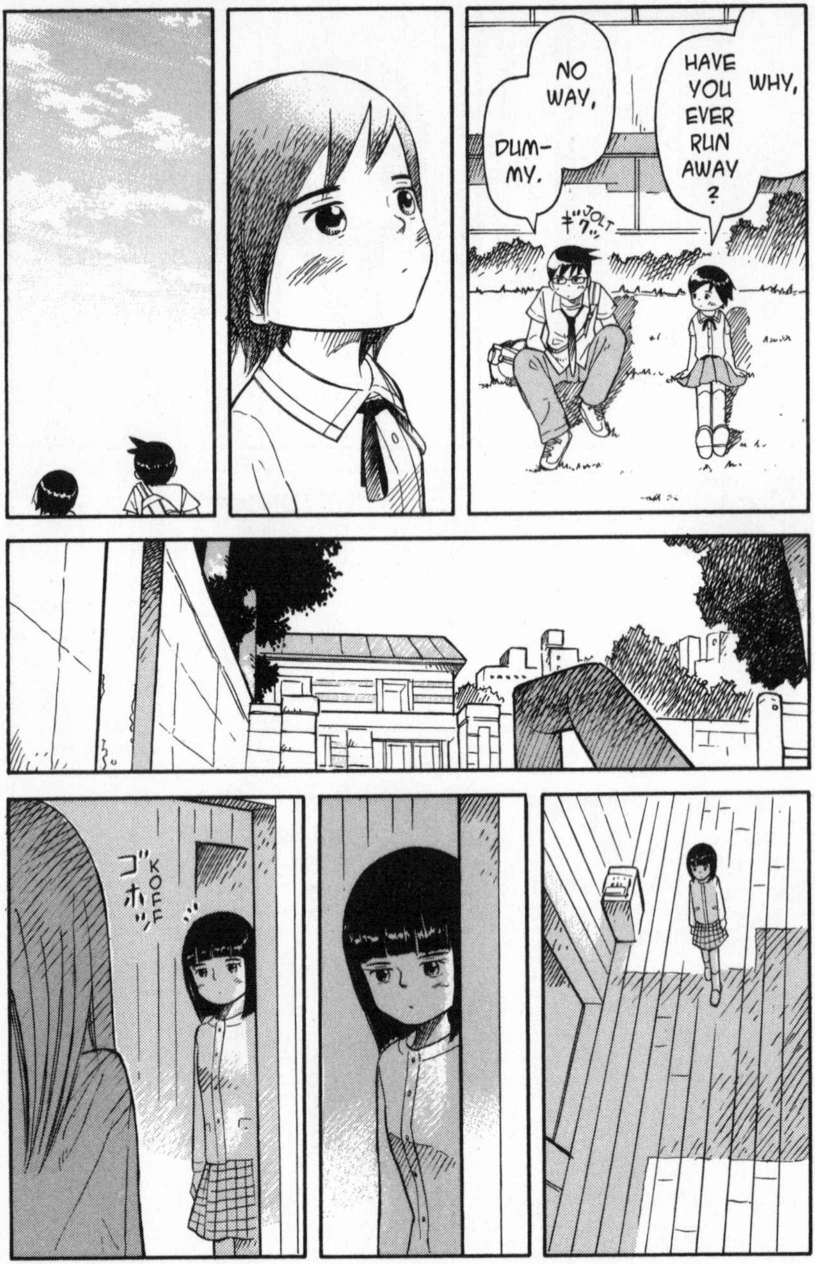
WHY,
HAVE YOU EVER RUN AWAY?
JOLT
NO WAY, DUMMY.
KOFF

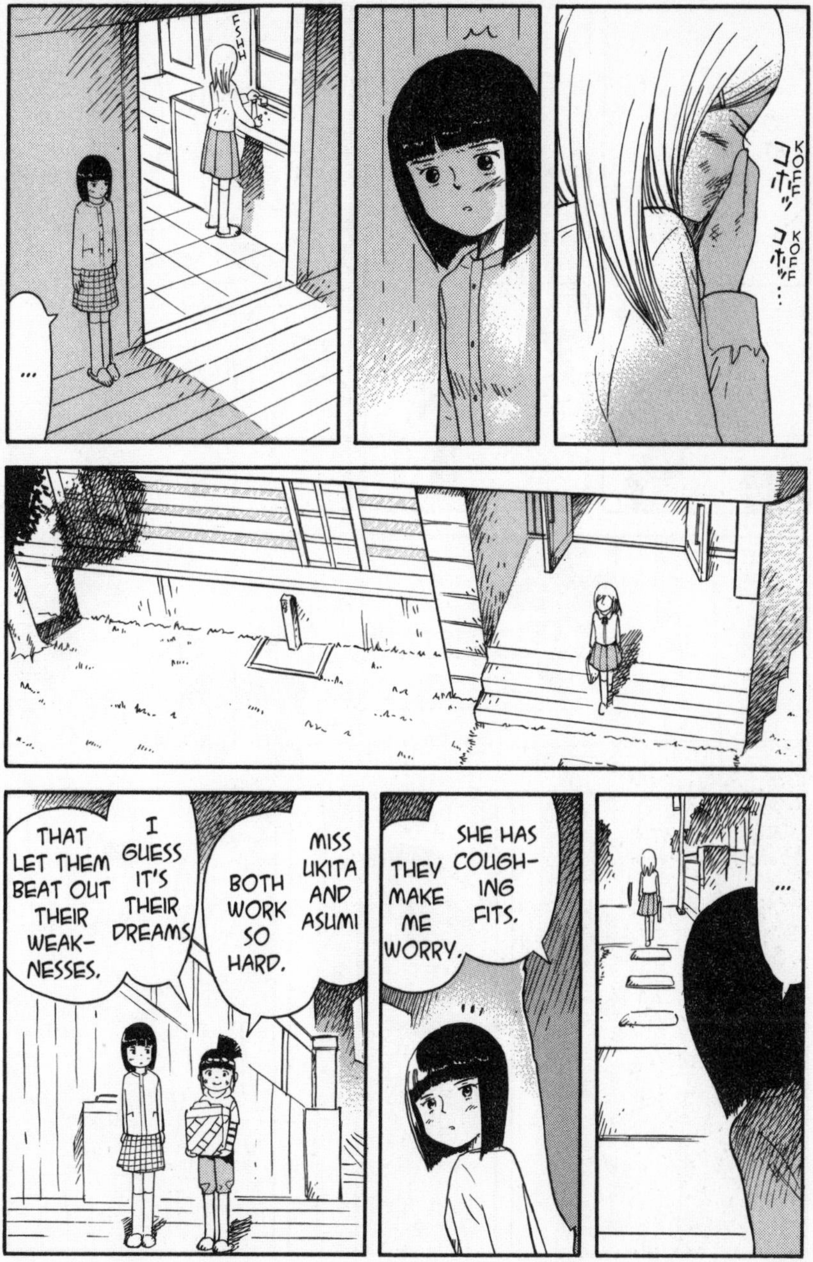
KOFF
コホッ
KOFF
コホッ…
FSHH
...
...
SHE HAS COUGH-ING FITS.
THEY MAKE ME WORRY.
MISS UKITA AND ASUMI
BOTH WORK SO HARD.
I GUESS IT'S THEIR DREAMS
THAT LET THEM BEAT OUT THEIR WEAK-NESSES.

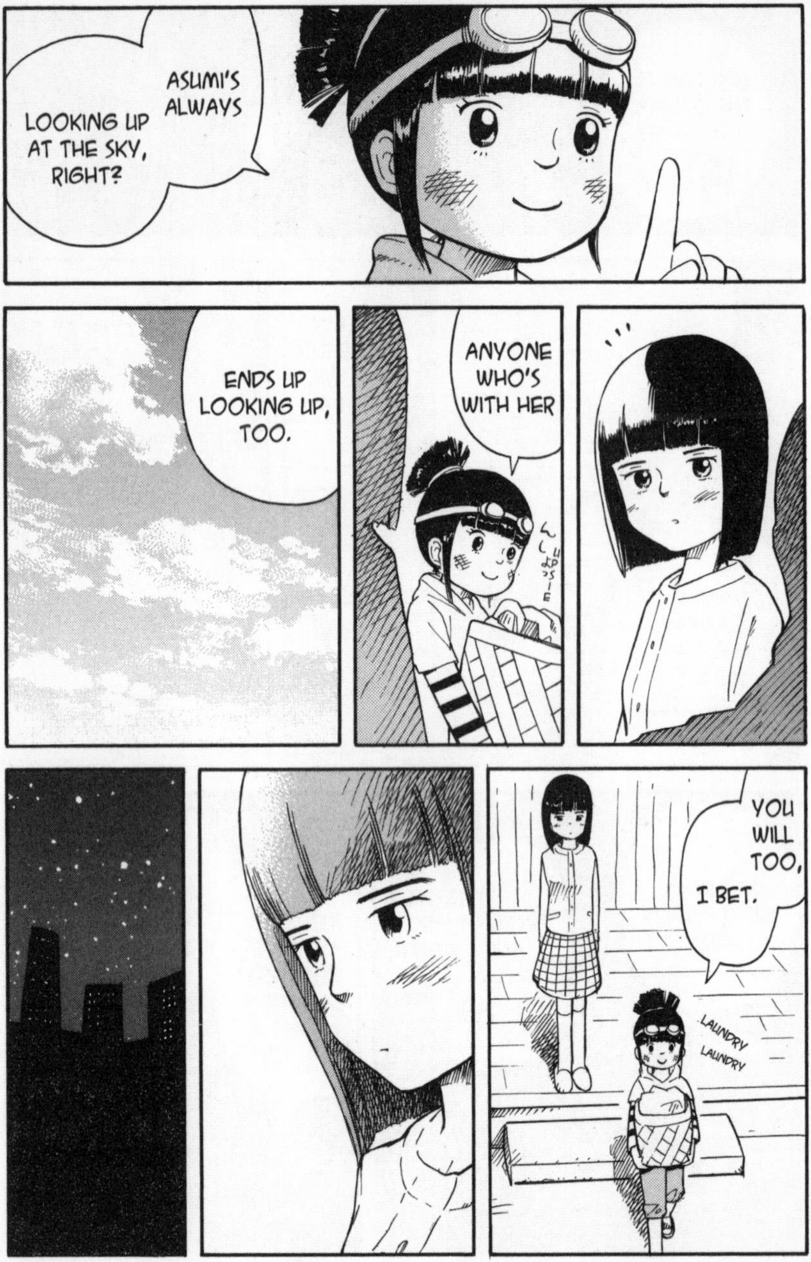
ASUMI'S ALWAYS
LOOKING UP AT THE SKY, RIGHT?
ANYONE WHO'S WITH HER
ENDS UP LOOKING UP, TOO.
YOU WILL TOO, I BET.
LAUNDRY
LAUNDRY

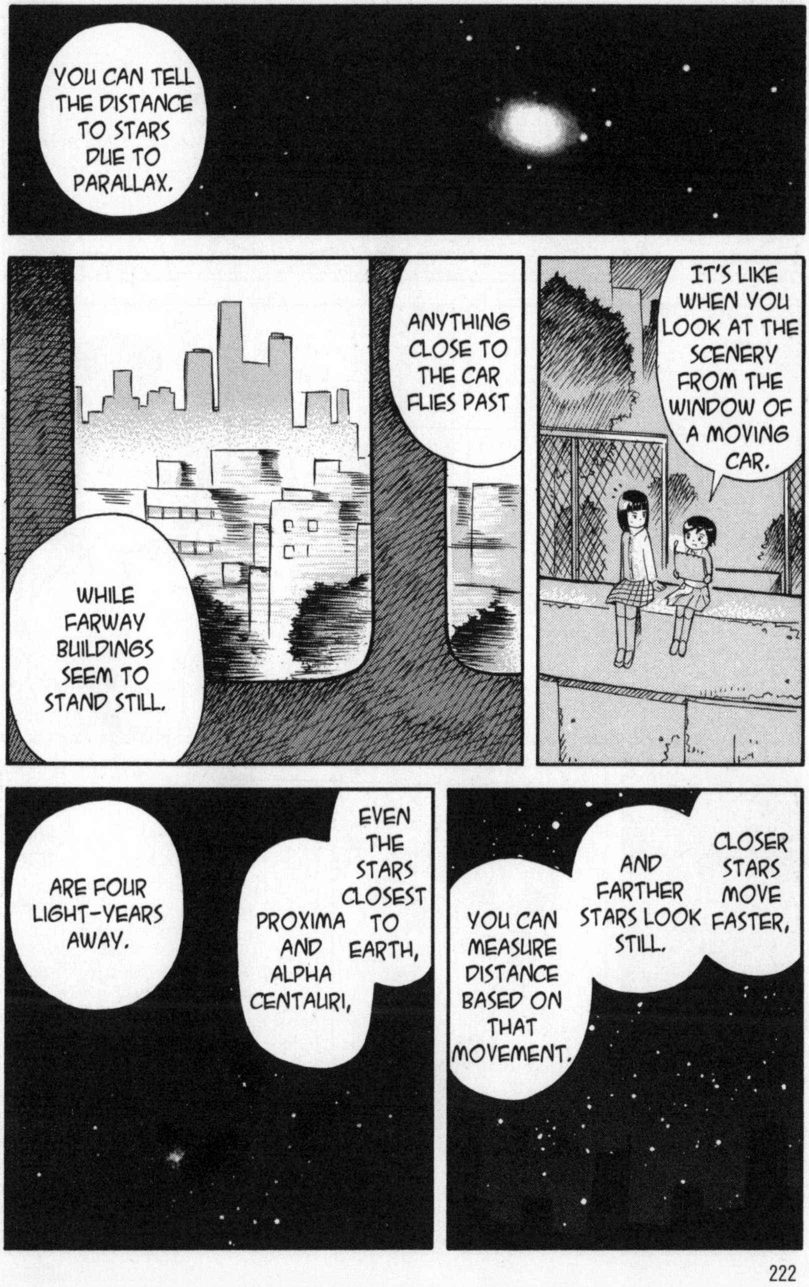
YOU CAN TELL THE DISTANCE TO STARS DUE TO PARALLAX.
IT'S LIKE WHEN YOU LOOK AT THE SCENERY FROM THE WINDOW OF A MOVING CAR.
ANYTHING CLOSE TO THE CAR FLIES PAST
WHILE FARWAY BUILDINGS SEEM TO STAND STILL.
CLOSER STARS MOVE FASTER,
AND FARTHER STARS LOOK STILL.
YOU CAN MEASURE DISTANCE BASED ON THAT MOVEMENT.
EVEN THE STARS CLOSEST TO EARTH,
PROXIMA AND ALPHA CENTAURI,
ARE FOUR LIGHT-YEARS AWAY.

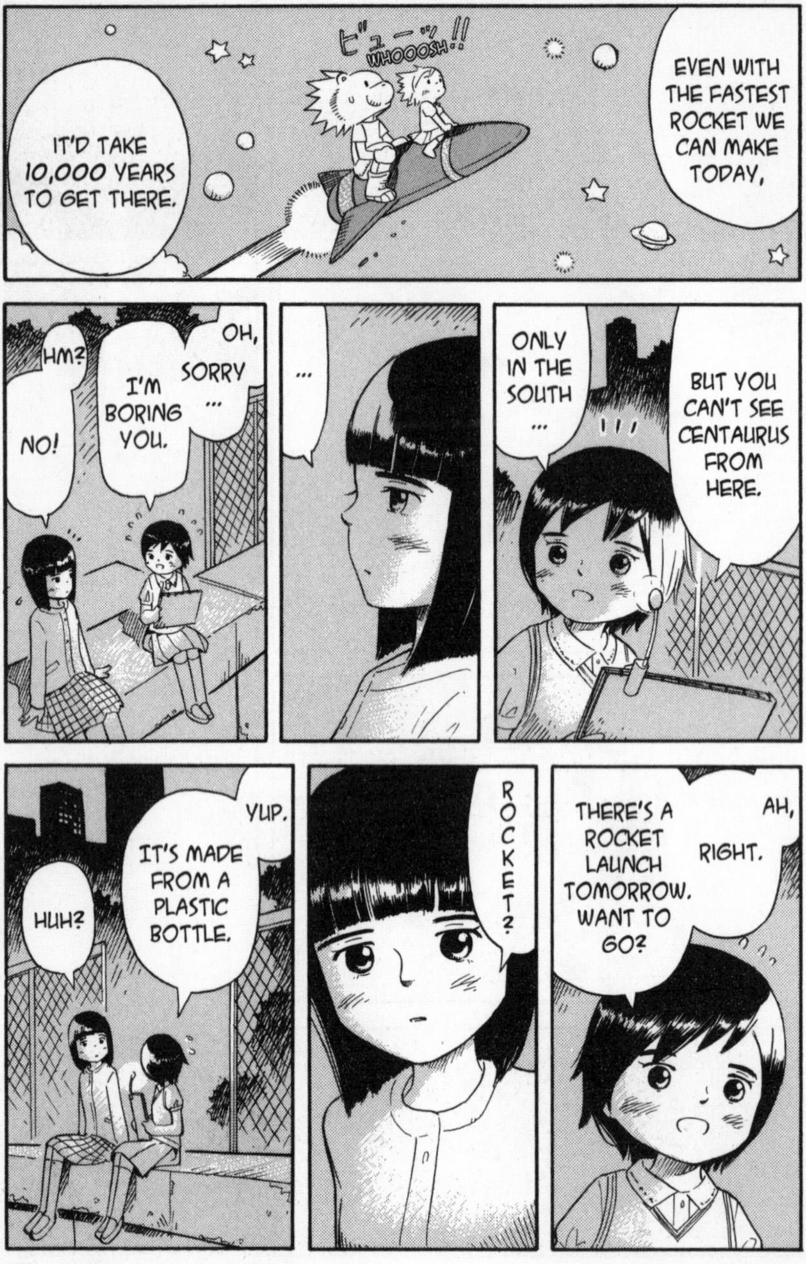
EVEN WITH THE FASTEST ROCKET WE CAN MAKE TODAY,
ビューッ!!
WHOOOSH!!
IT'D TAKE 10,000 YEARS TO GET THERE.
BUT YOU CAN'T SEE CENTAURUS FROM HERE.
ONLY IN THE SOUTH ...
...
OH, SORRY ...
I'M BORING YOU.
HM?
NO!
AH, RIGHT.
THERE'S A ROCKET LAUNCH TOMORROW. WANT TO GO?
ROCKET?
YUP.
IT'S MADE FROM A PLASTIC BOTTLE.
HUH?

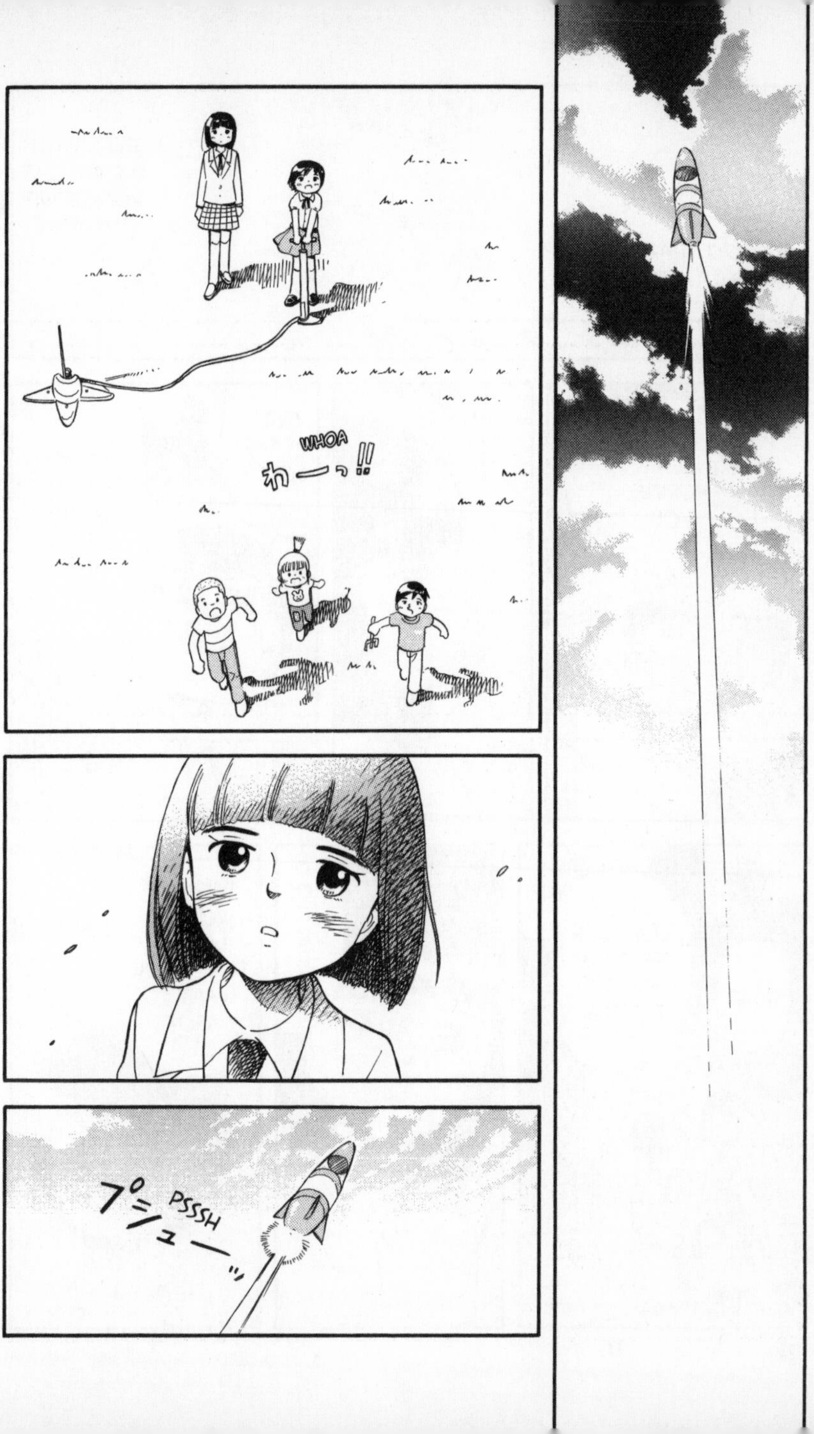

WHOA
わーっ!!
PSSSH
プシューーッ

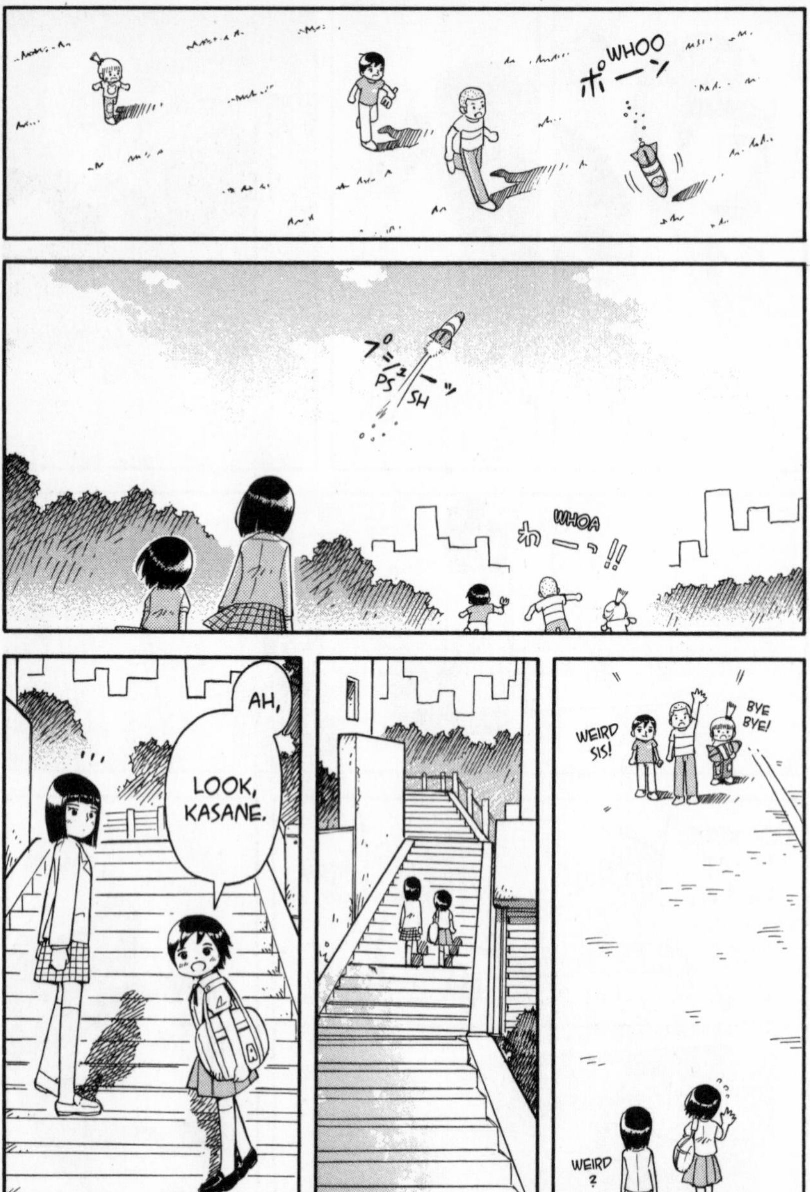

ポーン
WHOO
プシューッ
PSSH
わーっ!!
WHOA
BYE BYE!
WEIRD SIS!
WEIRD ?
AH, LOOK, KASANE.

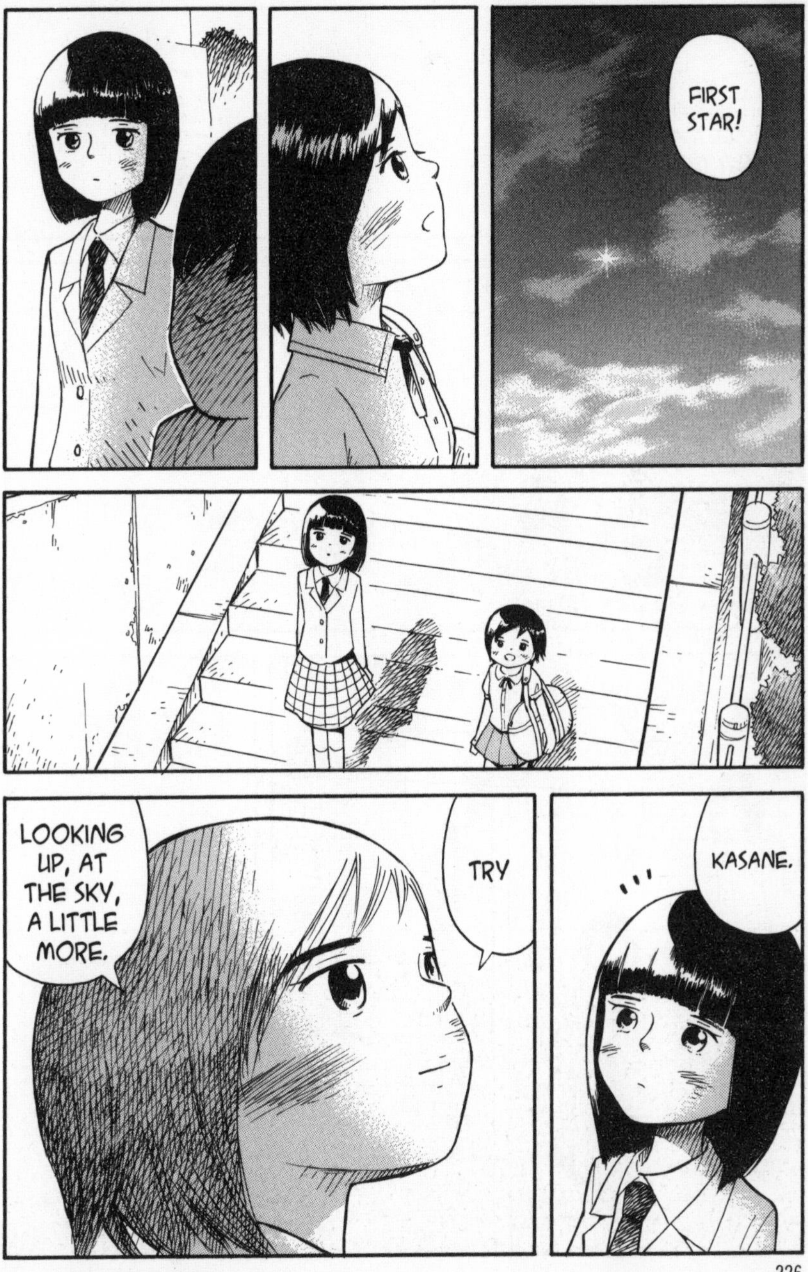
FIRST STAR!
KASANE.
...
TRY
LOOKING UP, AT THE SKY, A LITTLE MORE.

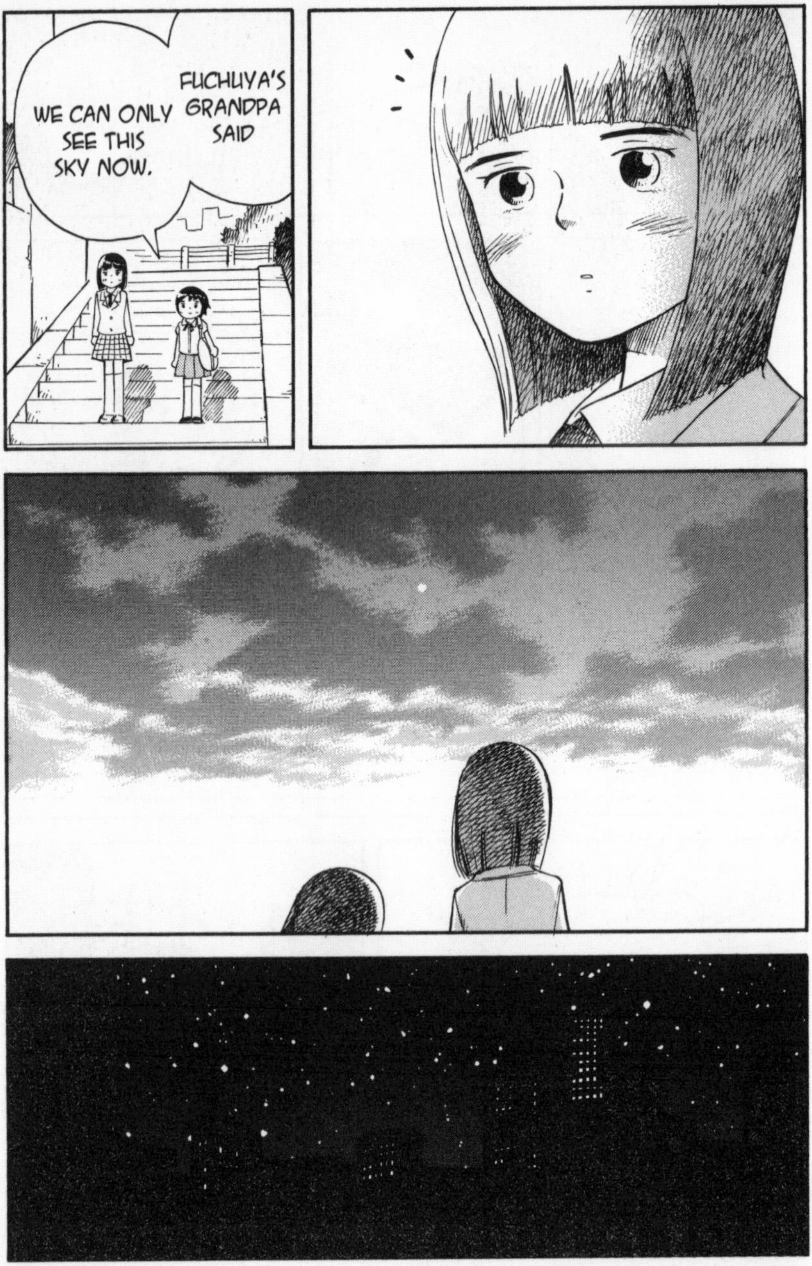
FUCHUYA'S GRANDPA SAID
WE CAN ONLY SEE THIS SKY NOW.

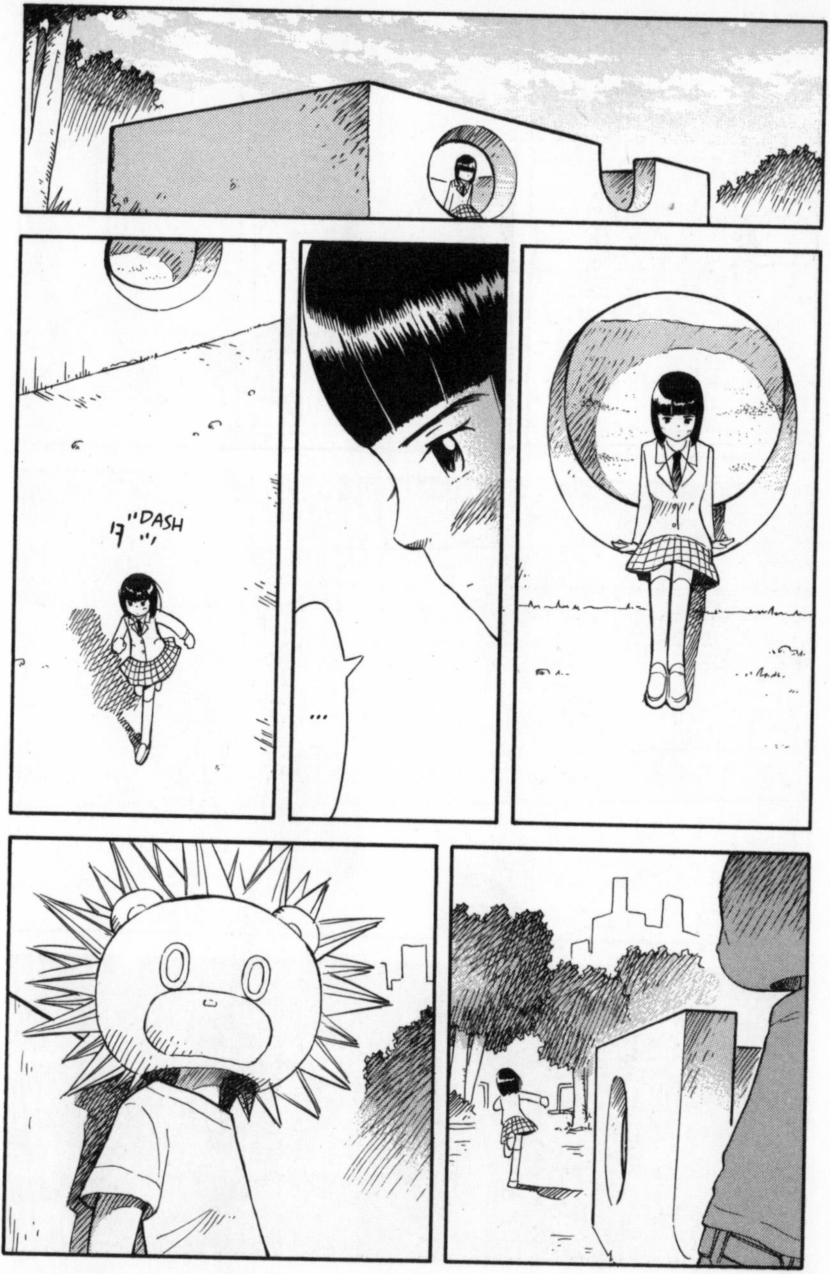
...
DASH

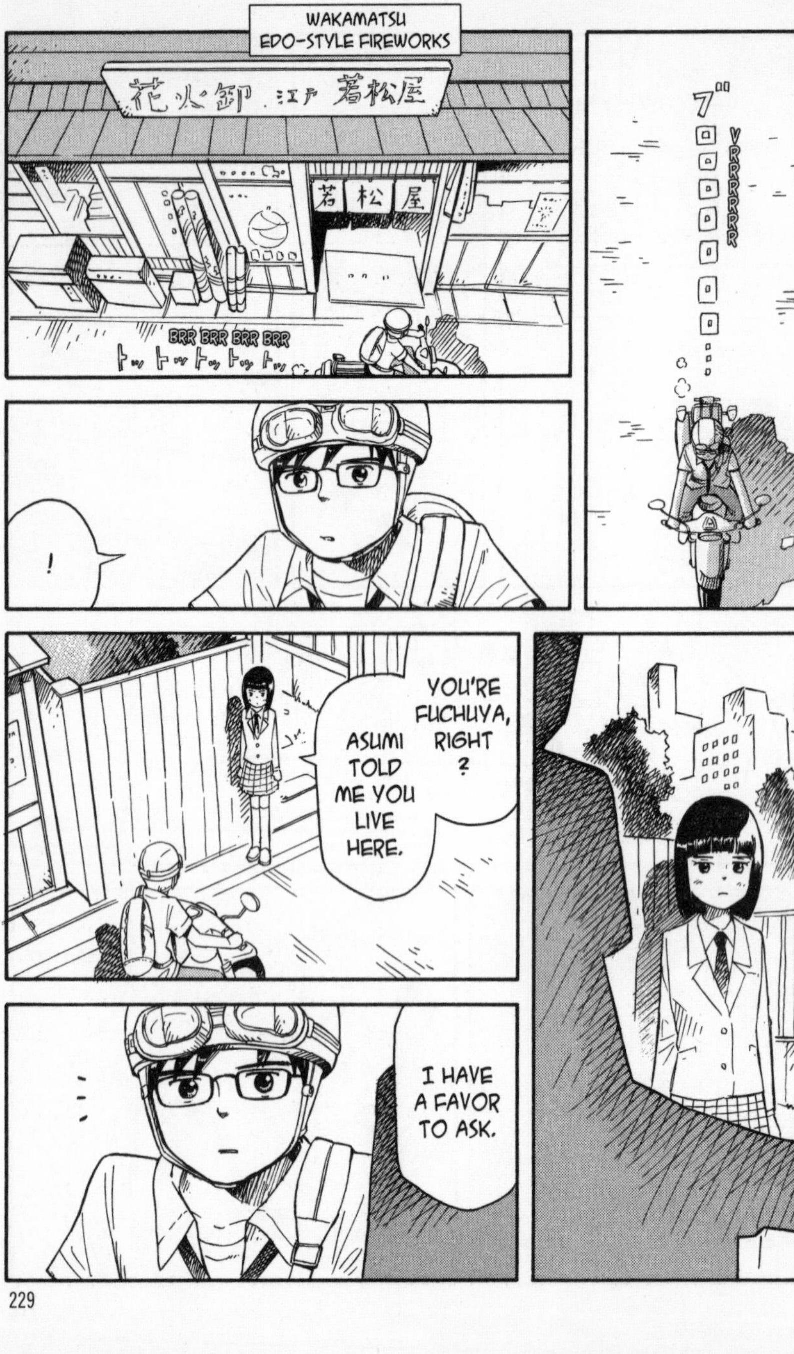
VRRRRRRR
WAKAMATSU EDO-STYLE FIREWORKS
若松屋
BRR BRR BRR BRR
!
YOU'RE FUCHUYA, RIGHT?
ASUMI TOLD ME YOU LIVE HERE.
I HAVE A FAVOR TO ASK.

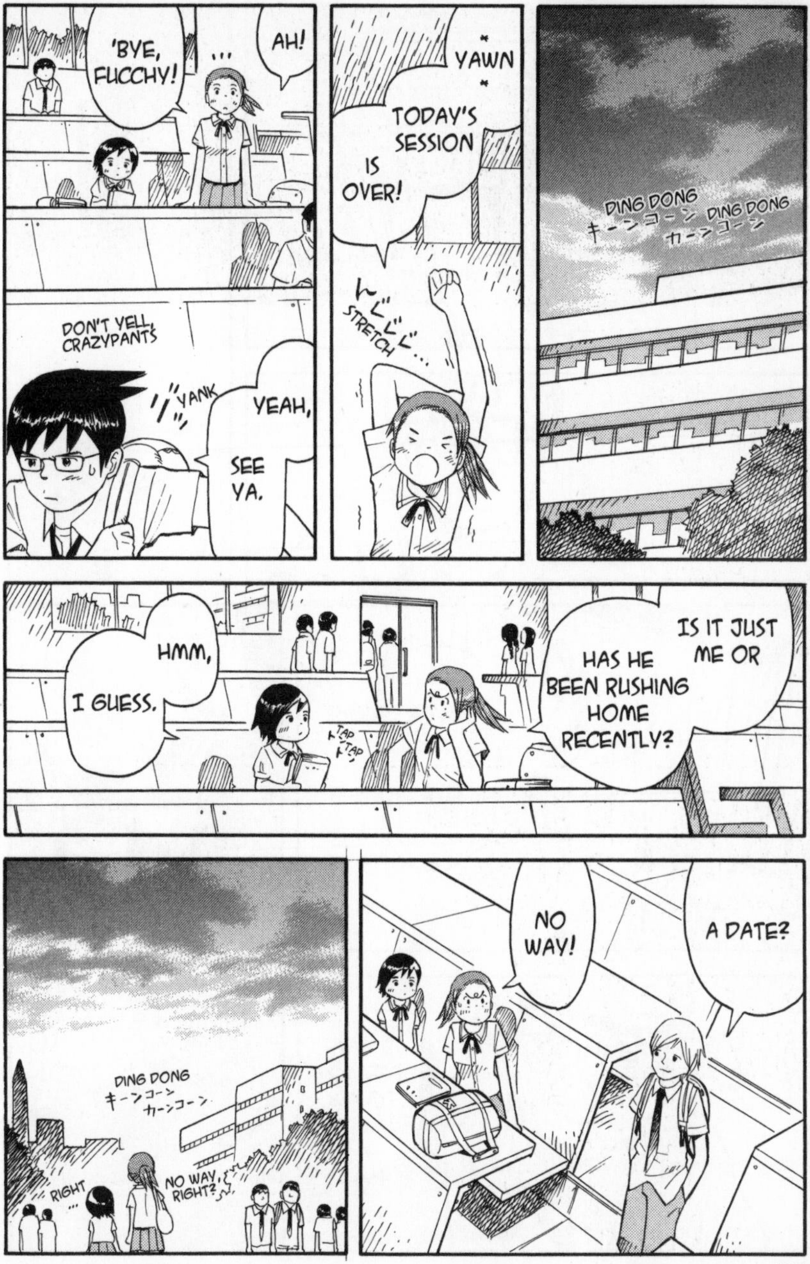
DING DONG
キーンコーン
DING DONG
カーンコーン
YAWN
TODAY'S SESSION
IS OVER!
んじじじ…
STRETCH
'BYE, FUCCHY!
...
AH!
YEAH,
SEE YA.
YANK
DON'T YELL, CRAZYPANTS
IS IT JUST ME OR
HAS HE BEEN RUSHING HOME RECENTLY?
TAP TAP
HMM,
I GUESS.
A DATE?
NO WAY!
DING DONG
キーンコーン
カーンコーン
NO WAY, RIGHT?
RIGHT ...

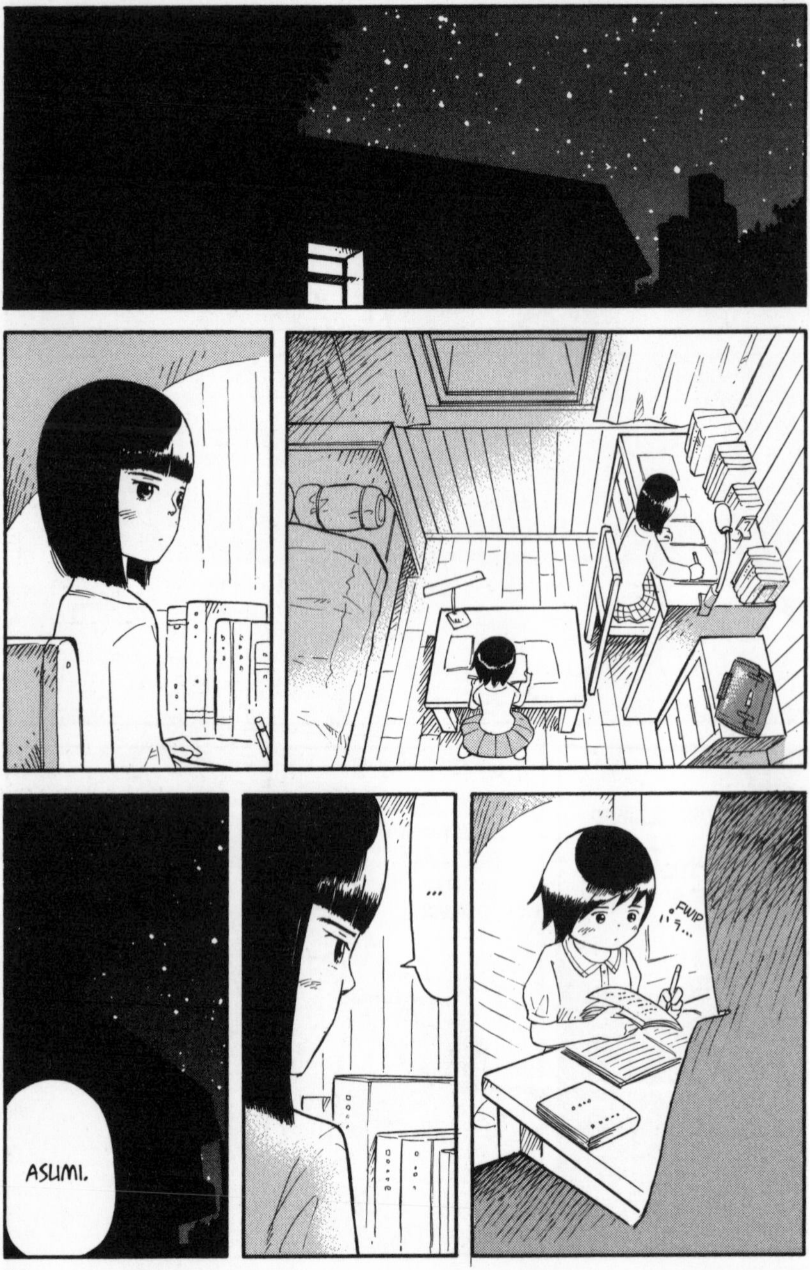
FWIP
パラ...
...
ASUMI.

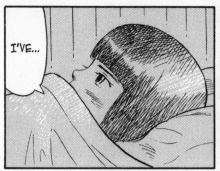

I'VE...
ALWAYS RUN AWAY,
'TIL NOW.
AS SOON AS I SEE A WALL,
ANYTHING THE LEAST BIT HARD OR AWFUL,
I'VE BLAMED IT ALL ON "THE LION" AND RUN AWAY.

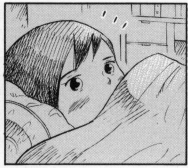

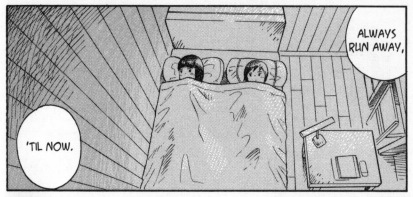

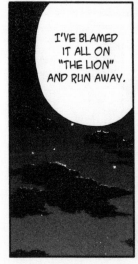

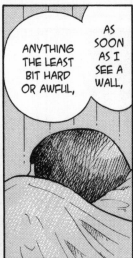

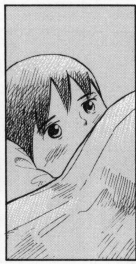

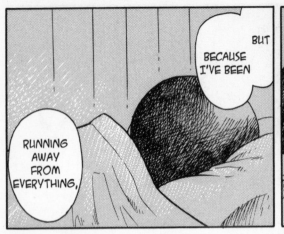

BUT BECAUSE I'VE BEEN
RUNNING AWAY FROM EVERYTHING,
I'VE ENDED UP
HAVING NO DREAMS AND NOTHING I WANT TO DO.
WHEN I THINK
THAT I'LL ALWAYS LIVE LIKE THAT,
I GET SCARED.
POST-SCHOOL PLAN
進路志
年 組 氏名
I COULDN'T TAKE IT,
SO I RAN AWAY FROM HOME.

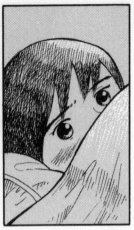

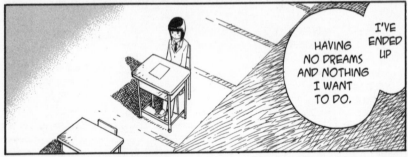

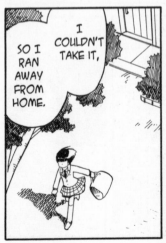

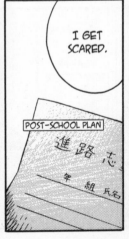

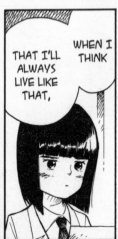

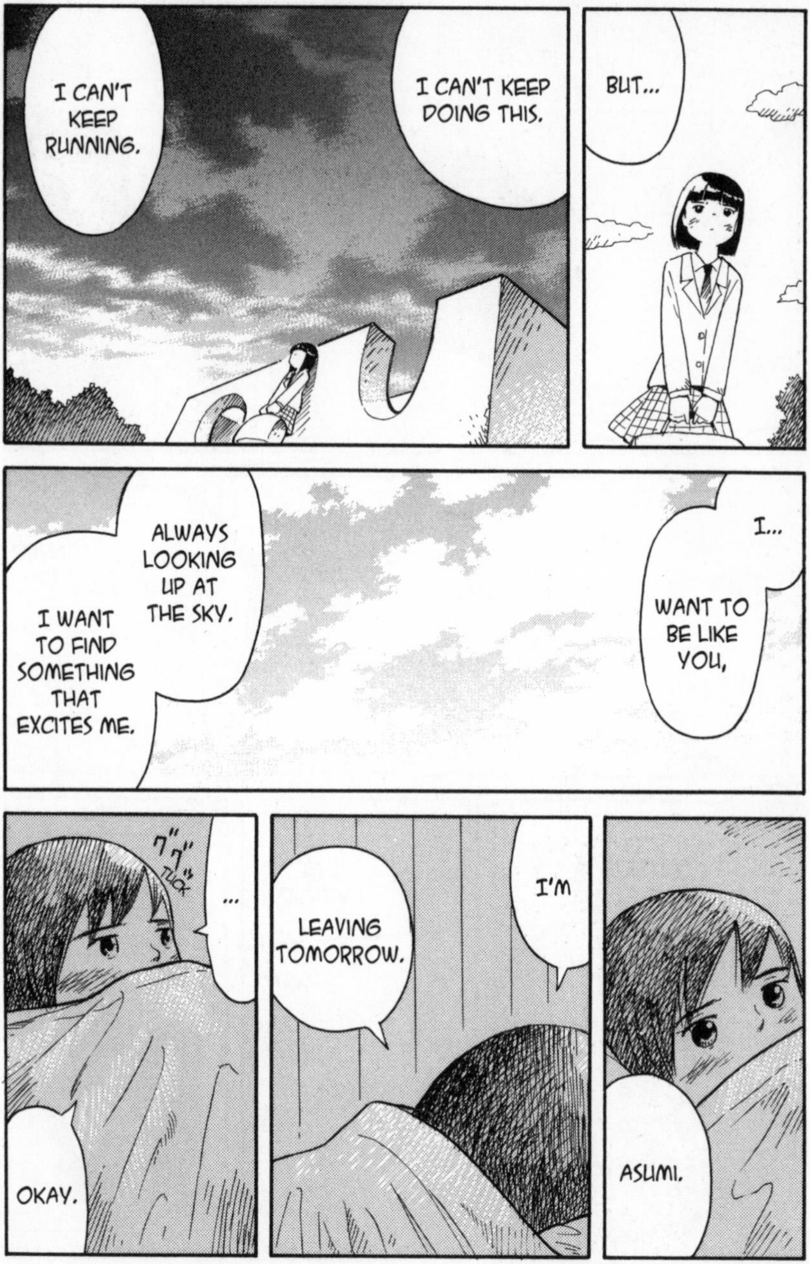
BUT...
I CAN'T KEEP DOING THIS.
I CAN'T KEEP RUNNING.
I...
WANT TO BE LIKE YOU,
ALWAYS LOOKING UP AT THE SKY.
I WANT TO FIND SOMETHING THAT EXCITES ME.
ASUMI.
I'M
LEAVING TOMORROW.
...
TUCK
OKAY.

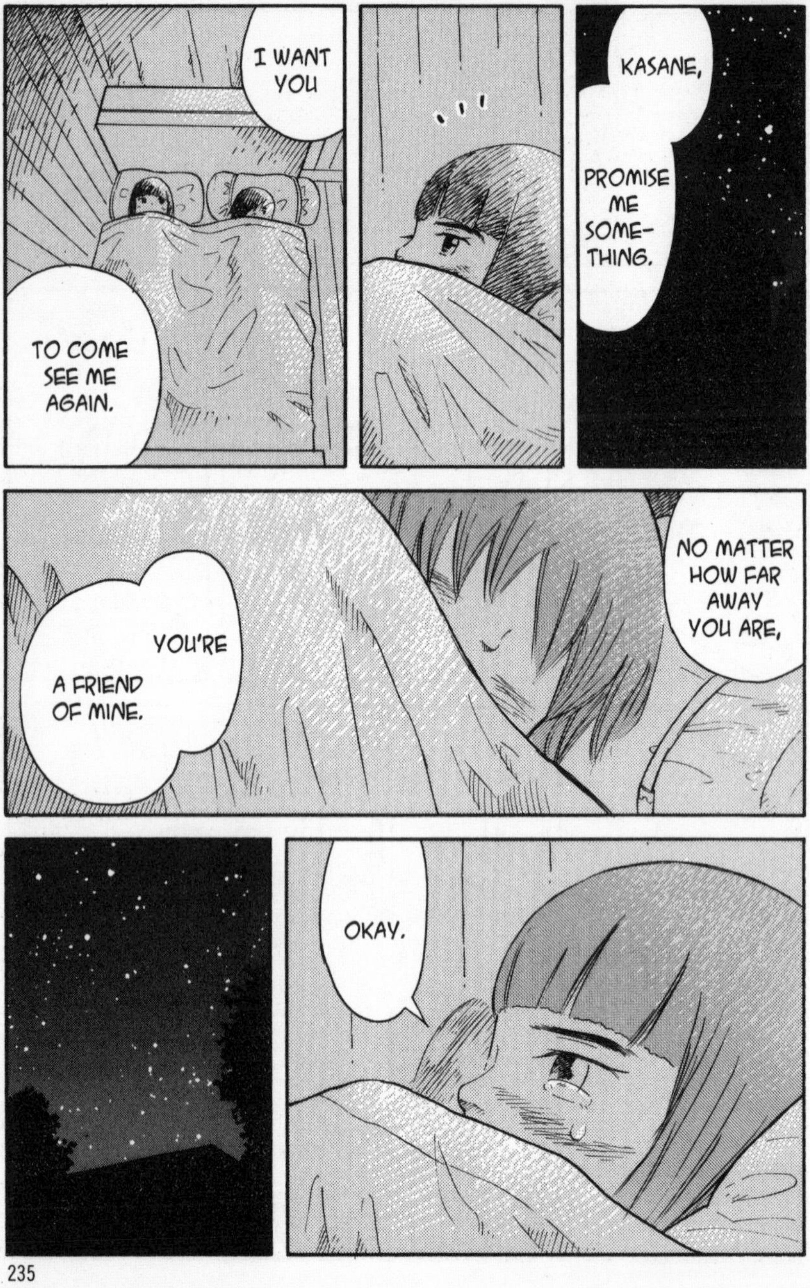
KASANE,
PROMISE ME SOME-THING.
...
I WANT YOU
TO COME SEE ME AGAIN.
NO MATTER HOW FAR AWAY YOU ARE,
YOU'RE
A FRIEND OF MINE.
OKAY.

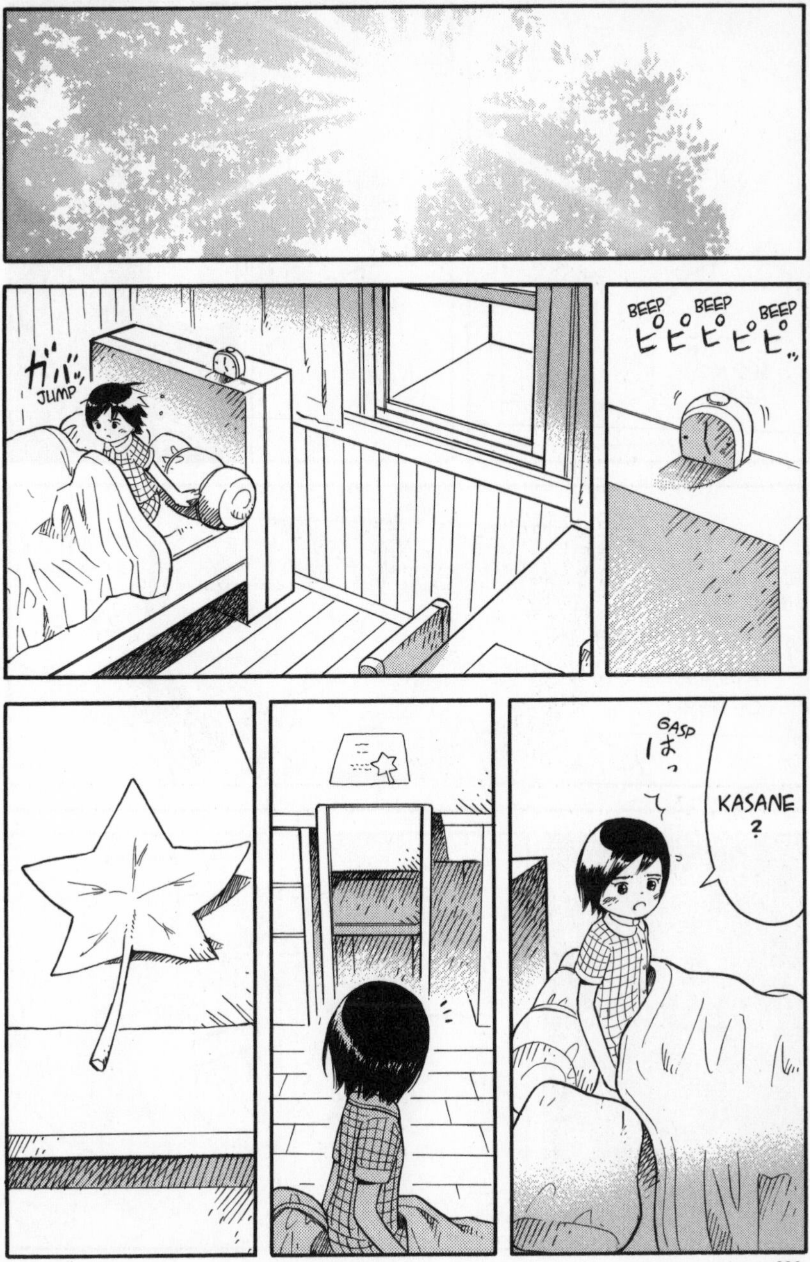
BEEP BEEP BEEP
ピピピピピッ
ガバ
JUMP
GASP
はっ
KASANE
?

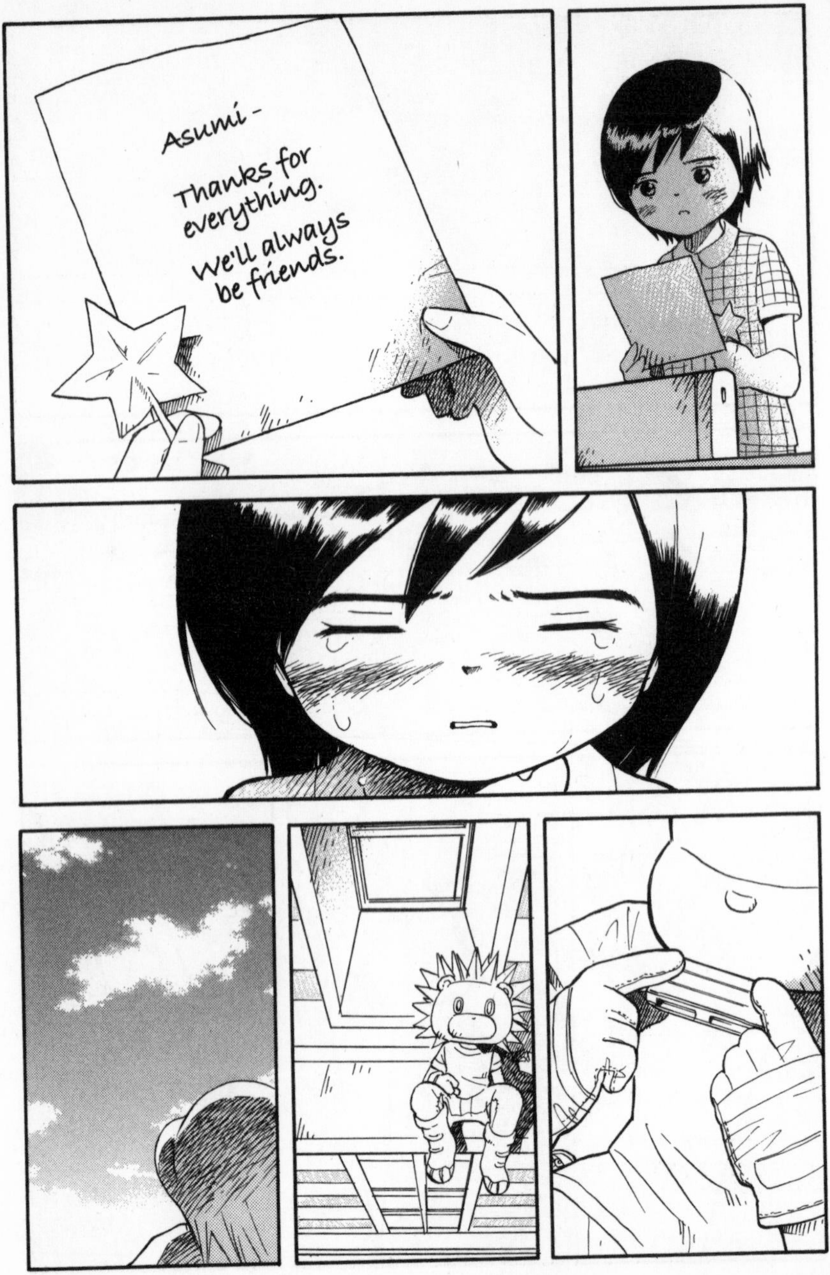
Asumi -
Thanks for everything.
We'll always be friends.

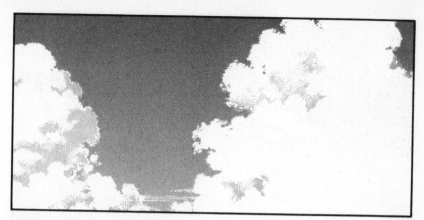

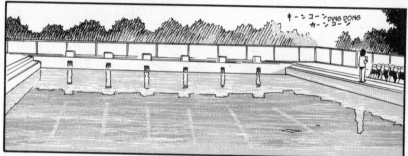

キーンコーン DING DONG
カーンコーン

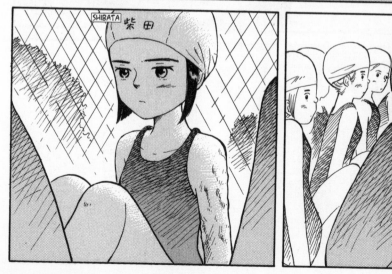

SHIBATA 柴田

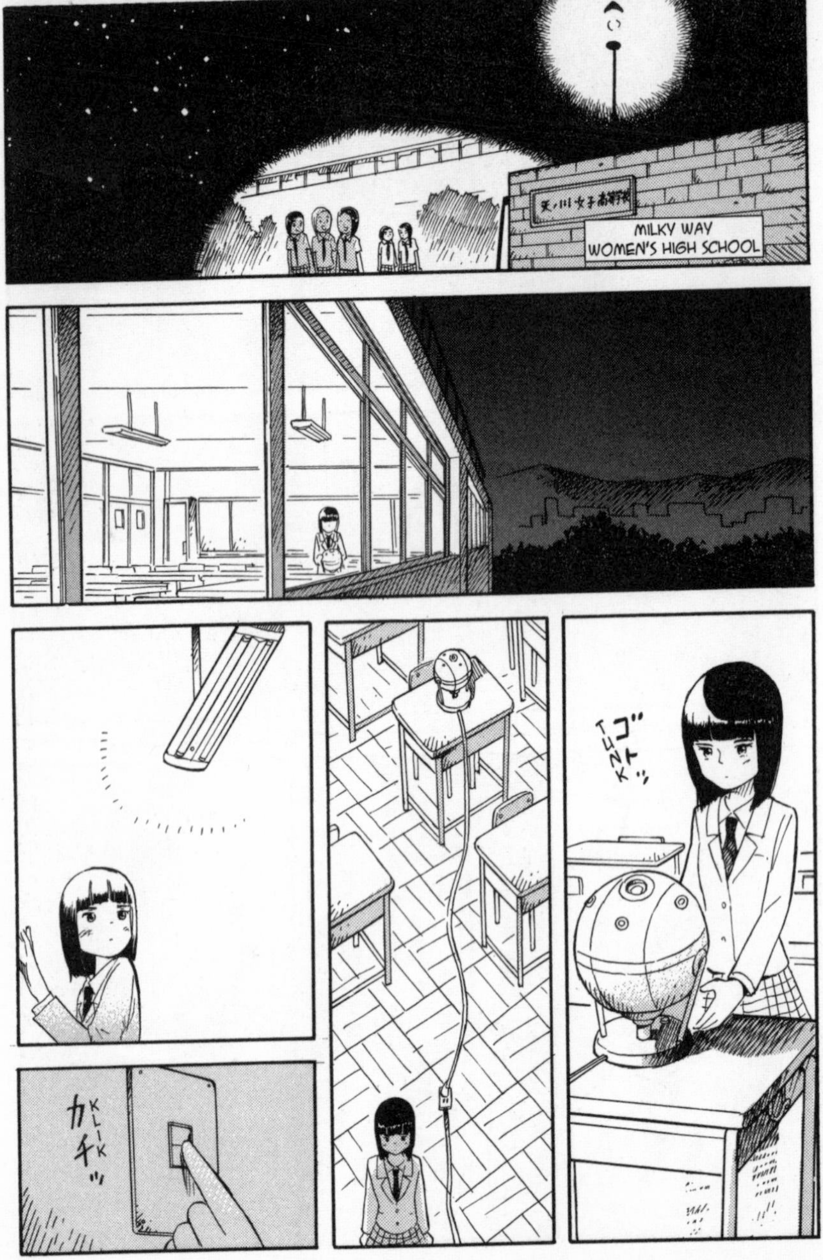
MILKY WAY
WOMEN'S HIGH SCHOOL
ゴトッ
TUNK
カチッ
KLIK

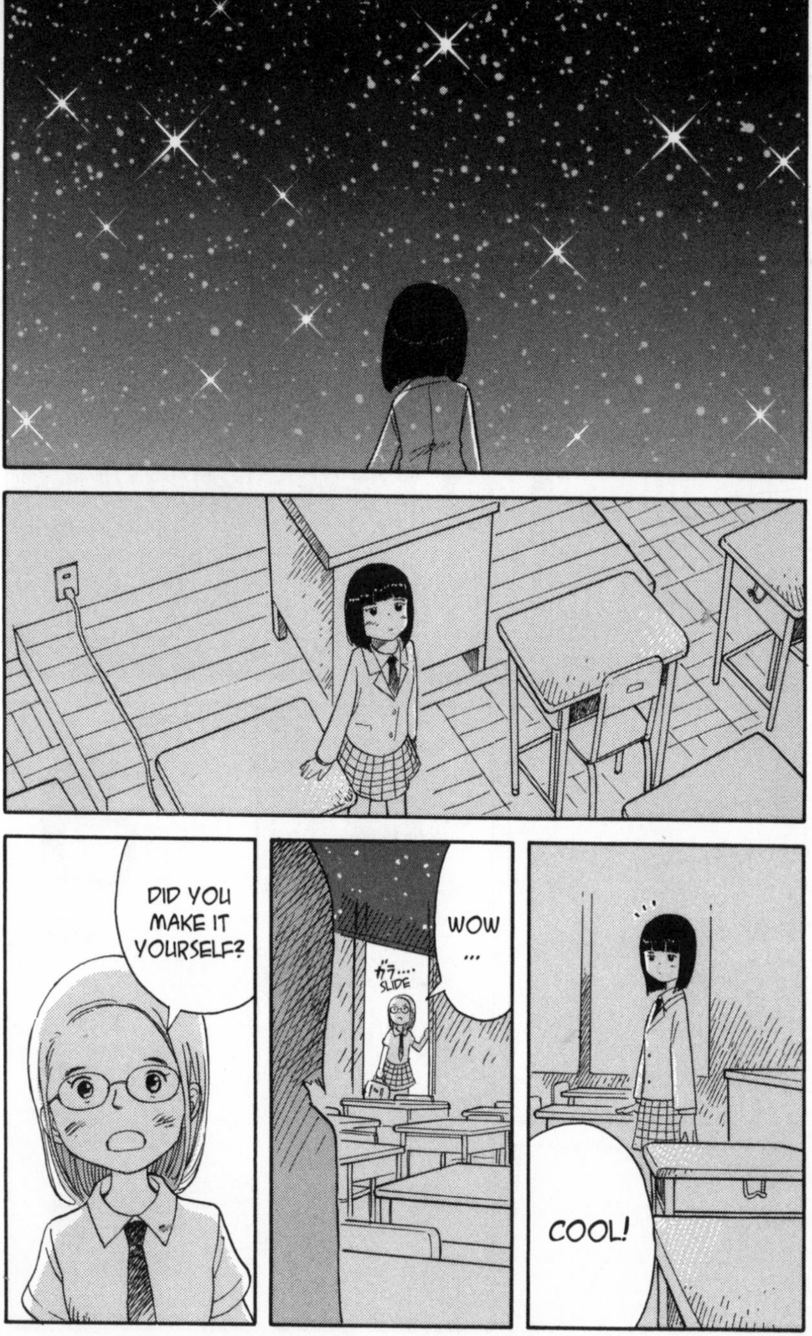
COOL!
WOW ...
ガラ....
SLIDE
DID YOU MAKE IT YOURSELF?

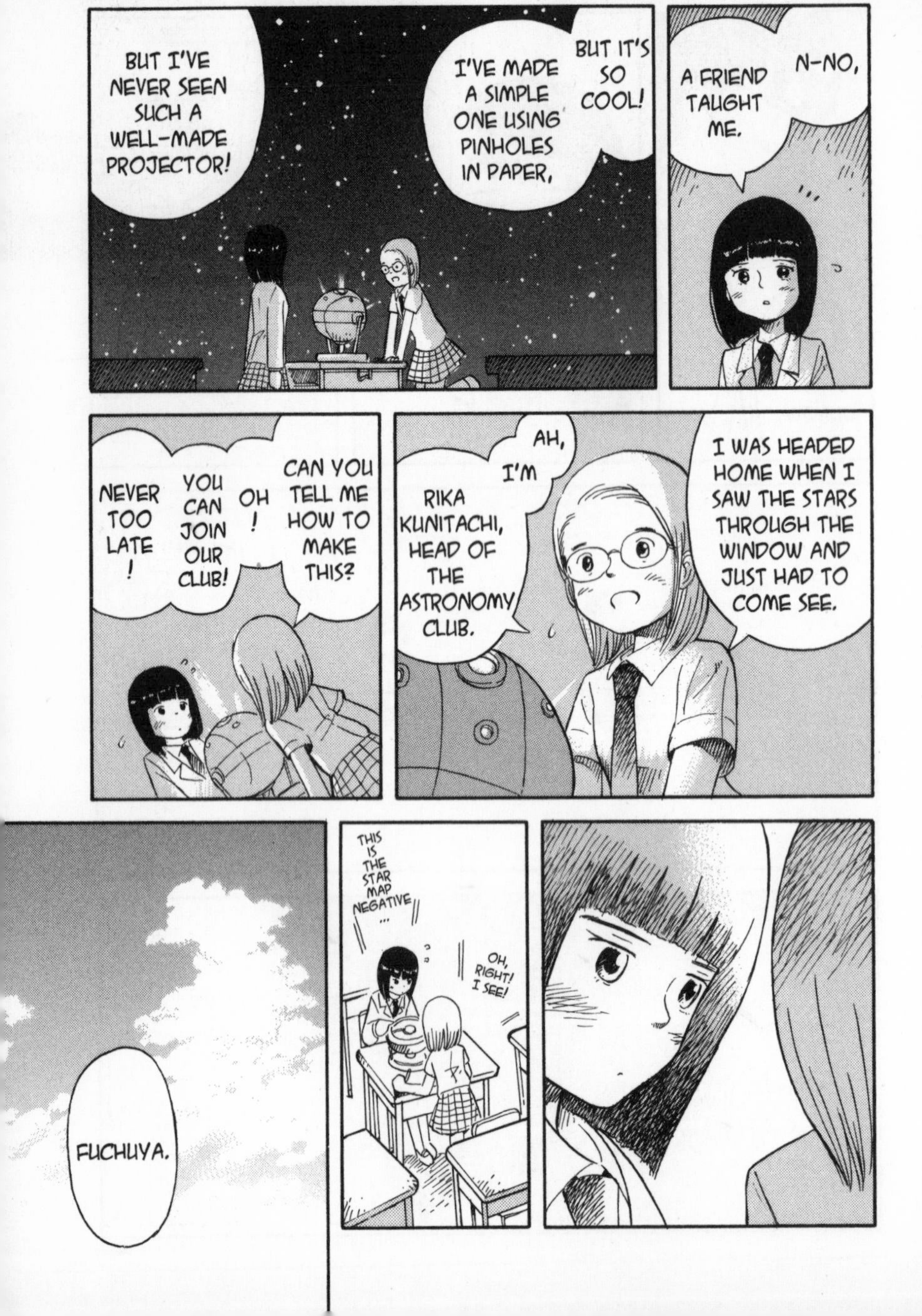
N-NO,
A FRIEND TAUGHT ME.
BUT IT'S SO COOL!
I'VE MADE A SIMPLE ONE USING PINHOLES IN PAPER,
BUT I'VE NEVER SEEN SUCH A WELL-MADE PROJECTOR!
I WAS HEADED HOME WHEN I SAW THE STARS THROUGH THE WINDOW AND JUST HAD TO COME SEE.
AH, I'M RIKA KUNITACHI, HEAD OF THE ASTRONOMY CLUB.
CAN YOU TELL ME HOW TO MAKE THIS?
OH!
YOU CAN JOIN OUR CLUB!
NEVER TOO LATE!
THIS IS THE STAR MAP NEGATIVE...
OH, RIGHT! I SEE!
FUCHUYA.

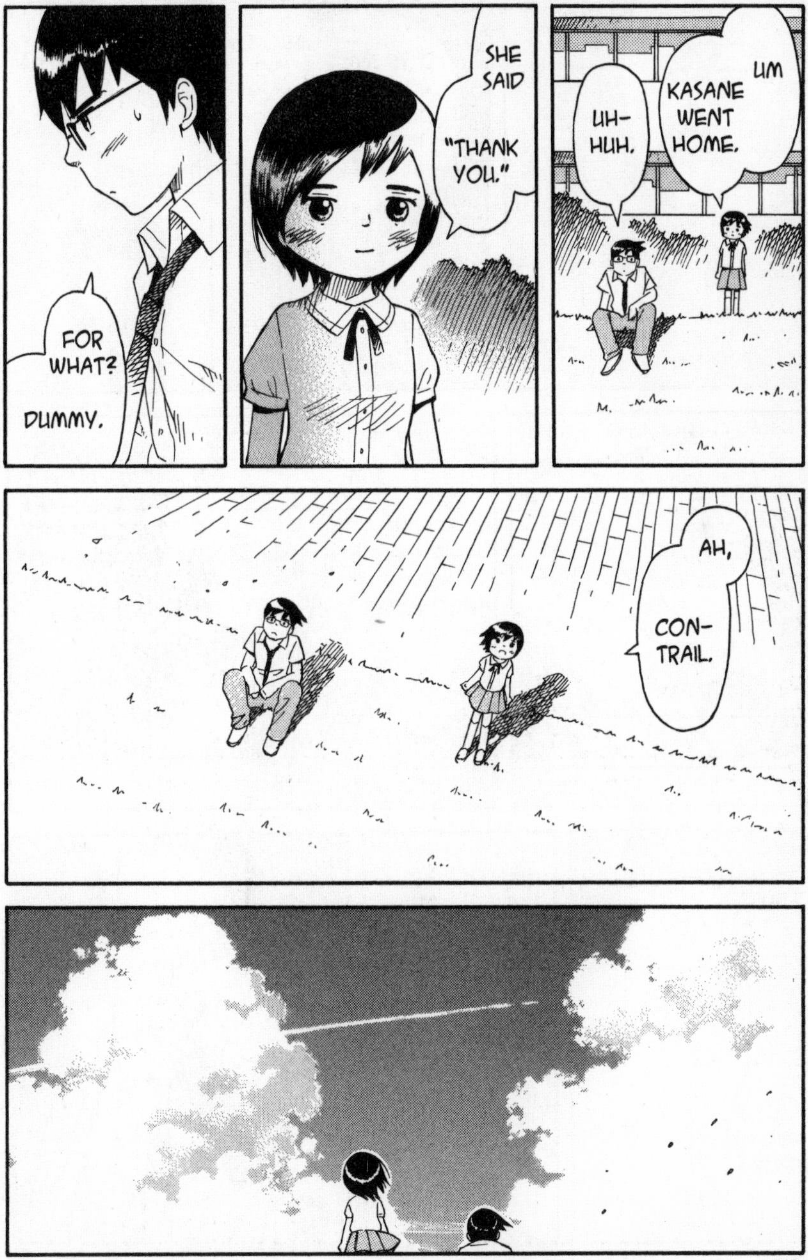
UM
KASANE WENT HOME.
UH-HUH.
SHE SAID
"THANK YOU."
FOR WHAT?
DUMMY.
AH,
CON-TRAIL.

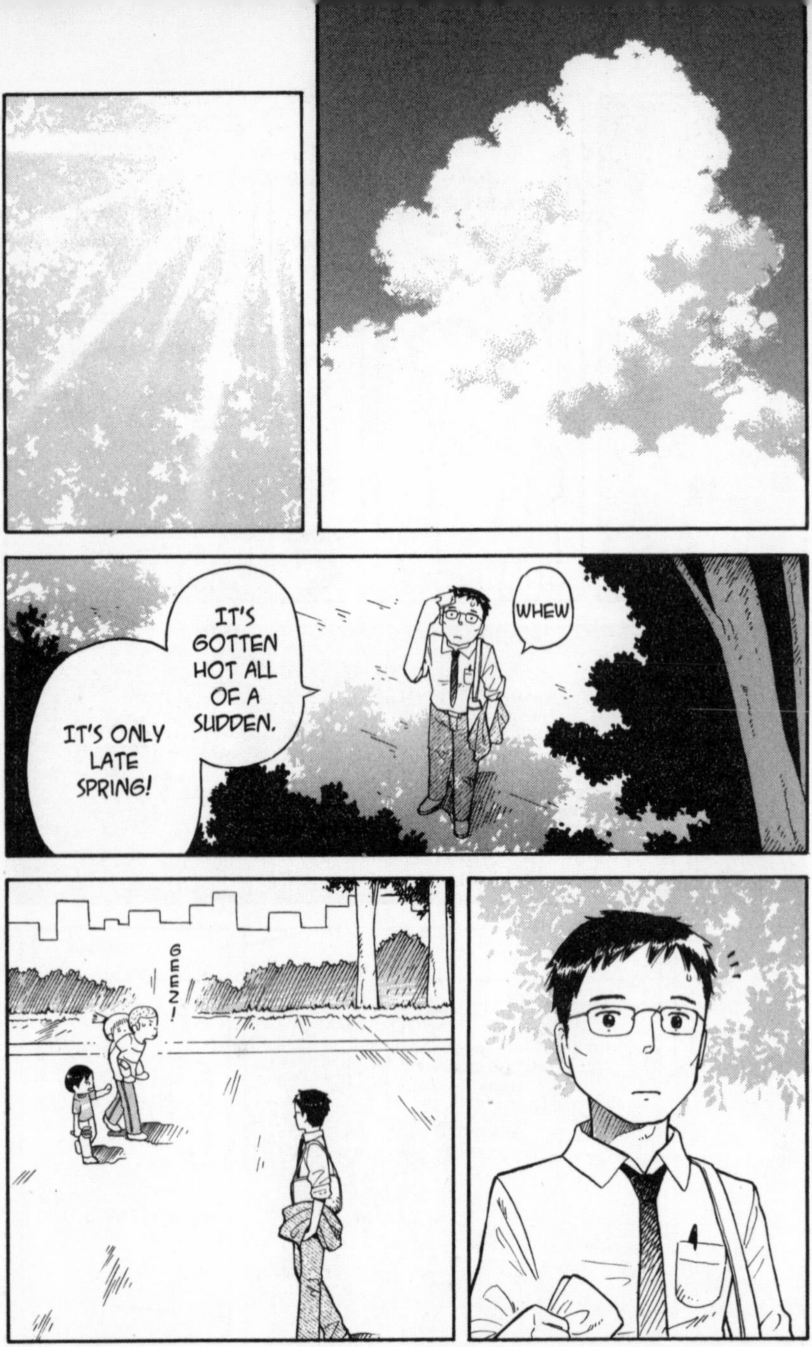
WHEW
IT'S GOTTEN HOT ALL OF A SUDDEN.
IT'S ONLY LATE SPRING!
GEEZ!

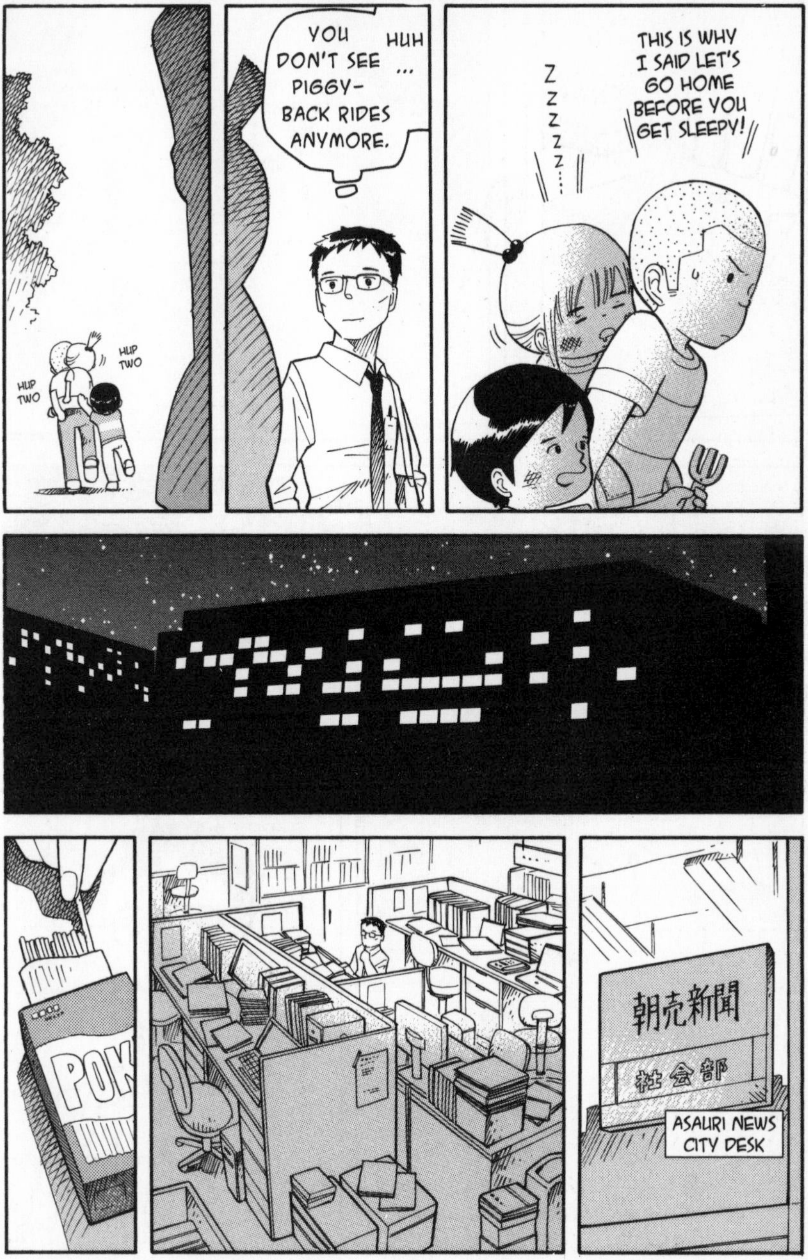
THIS IS WHY I SAID LET'S GO HOME BEFORE YOU GET SLEEPY!
ZZZZZ…
HUH …
YOU DON'T SEE PIGGY-BACK RIDES ANYMORE.
HUP TWO
HUP TWO
朝売新聞
社会部
ASAURI NEWS CITY DESK
POK

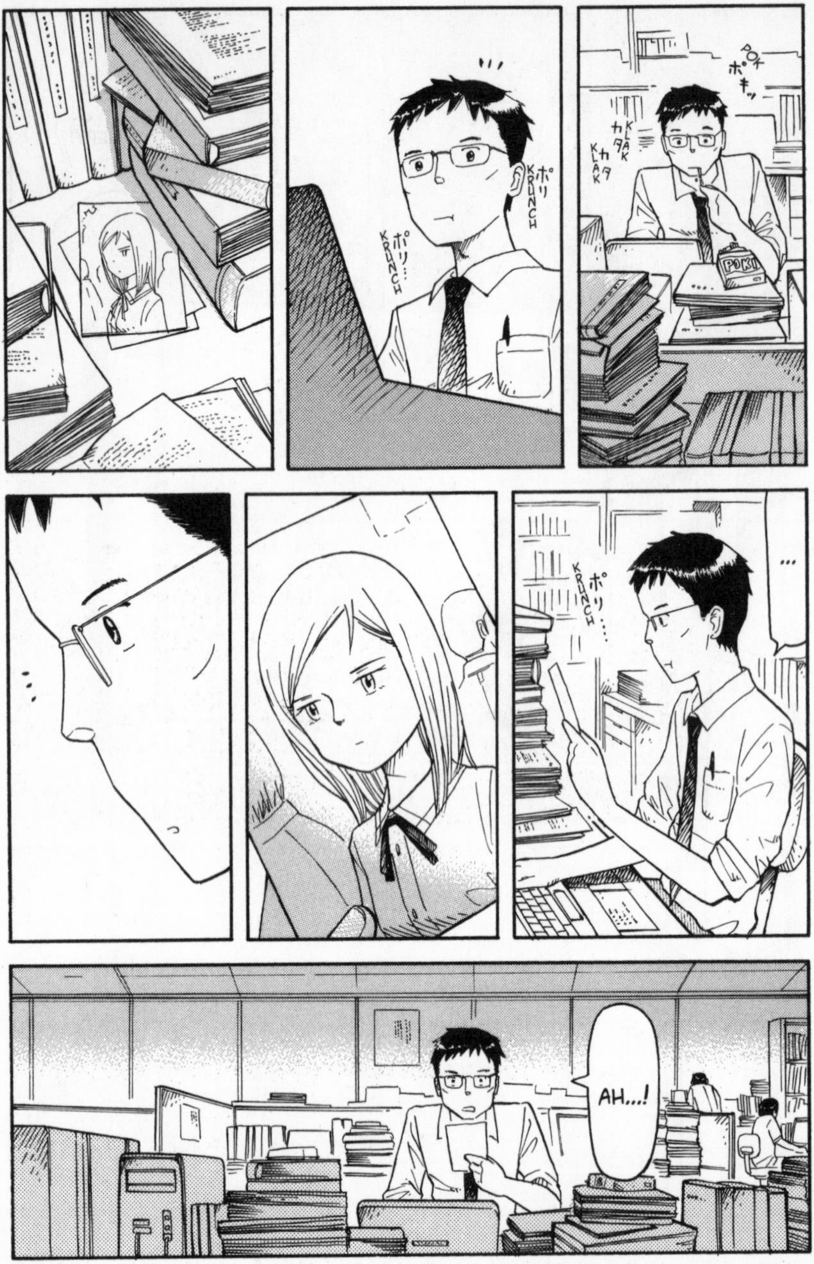
POK
ポキッ
KLAK
カタ
KLAK
カタ
POKI
ポリ
KRUNCH
ポリ…
KRUNCH
…
ポリ……
KRUNCH
AH...!

MISSION:55

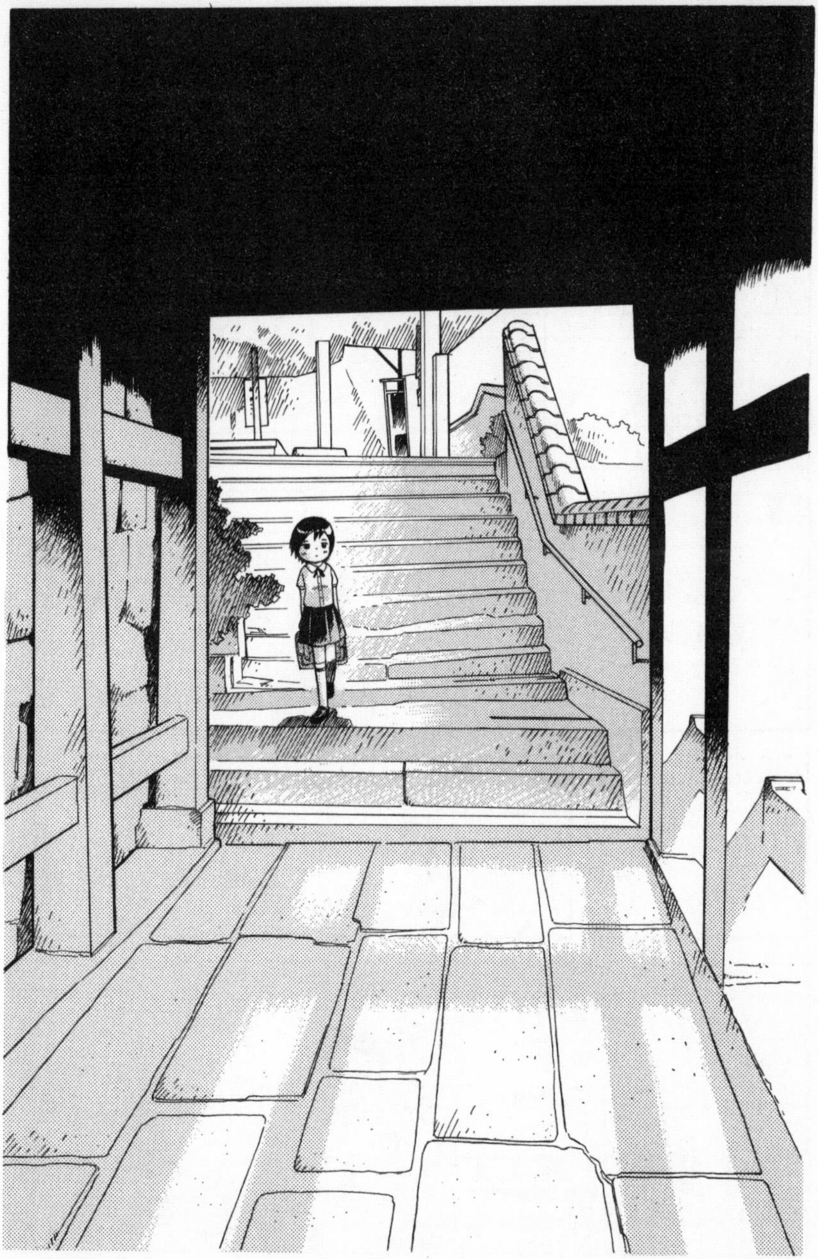

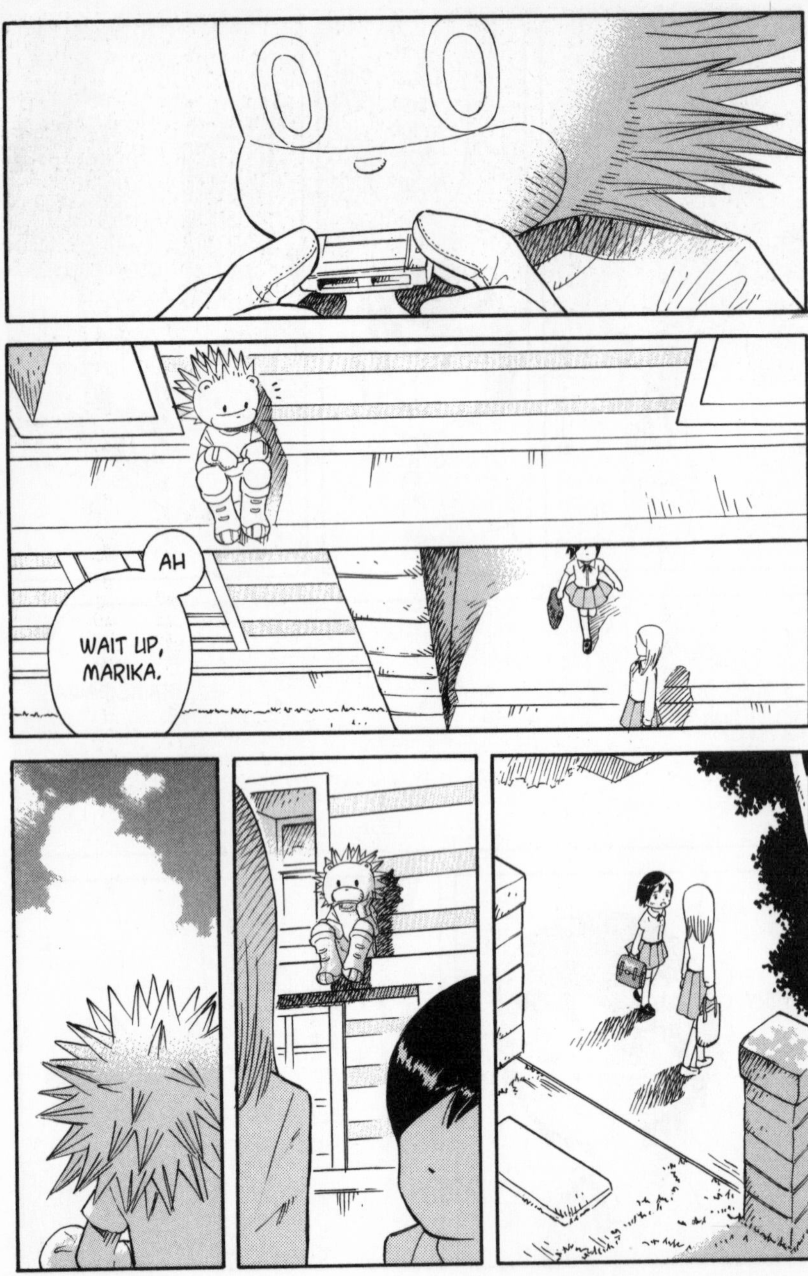
AH
WAIT UP, MARIKA.

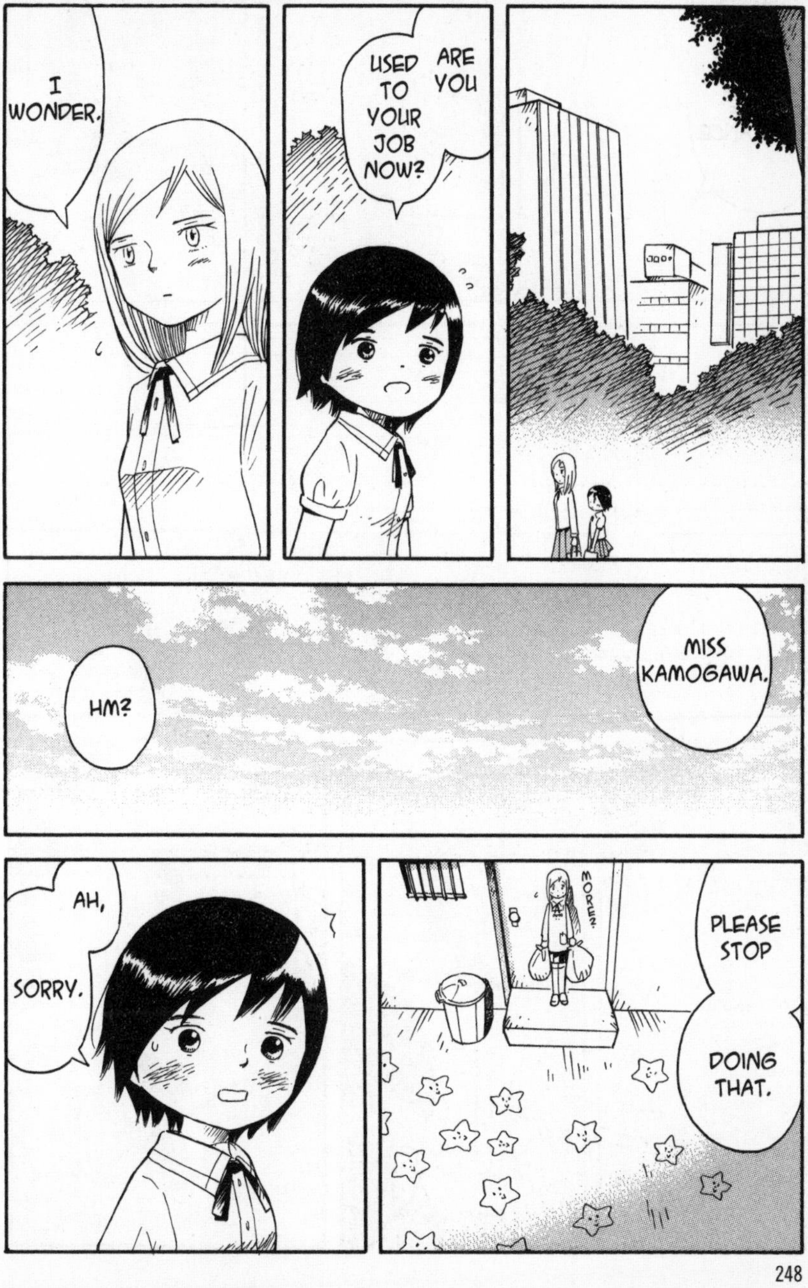
ARE YOU USED TO YOUR JOB NOW?
I WONDER.
MISS KAMOGAWA.
HM?
PLEASE STOP DOING THAT.
AH, SORRY.

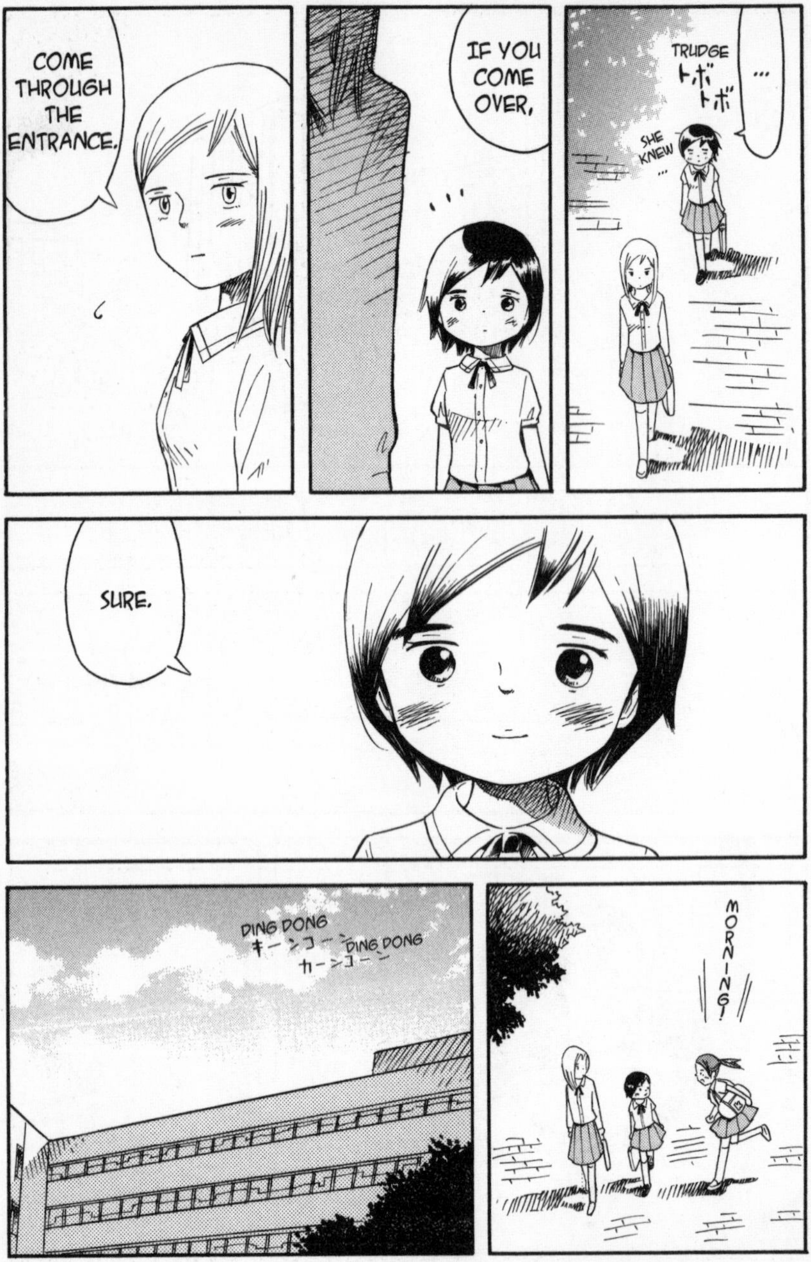
...
TRUDGE トボトボ
SHE KNEW ...
IF YOU COME OVER,
COME THROUGH THE ENTRANCE.
SURE.
MORNING!
DING DONG キーンコーン
DING DONG カーンコーン

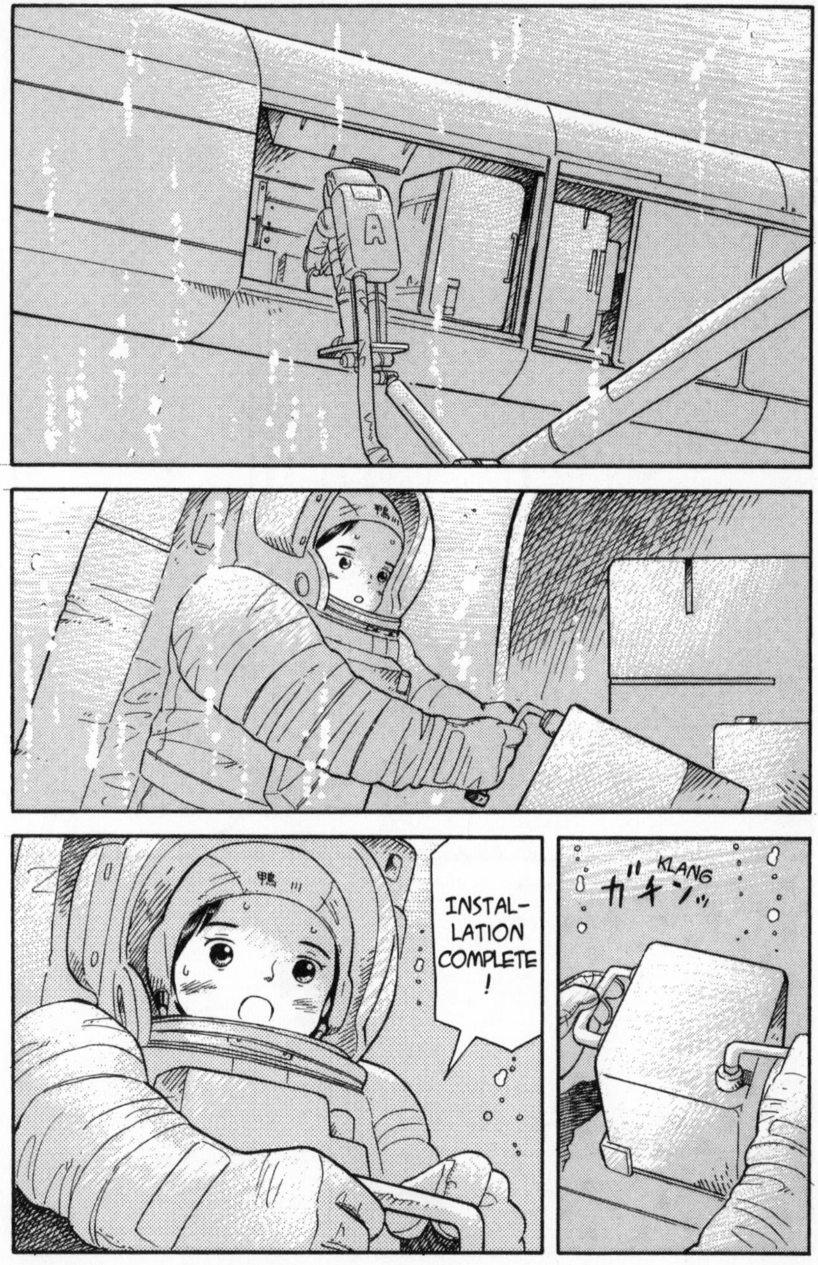
KLANG
ガキンッ
INSTAL-
LATION
COMPLETE
!

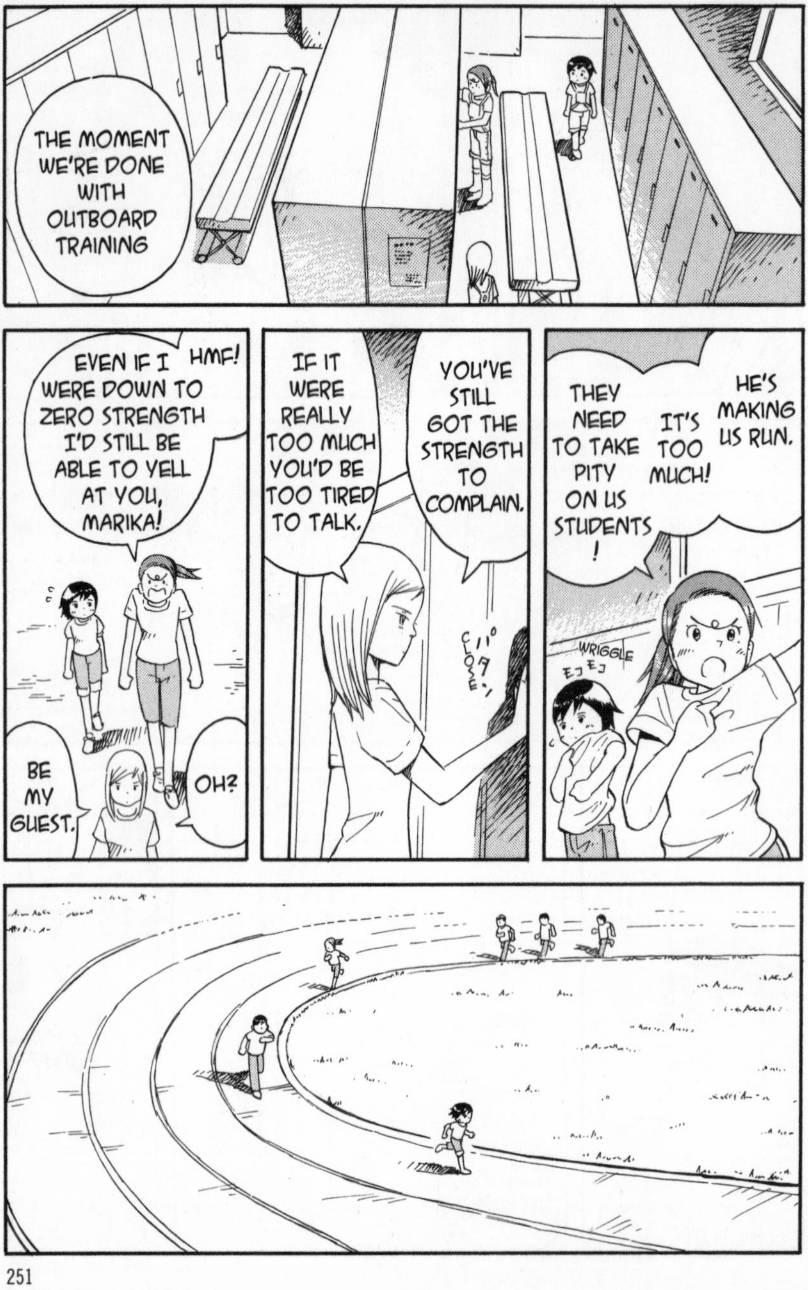
THE MOMENT WE'RE DONE WITH OUTBOARD TRAINING
HE'S MAKING US RUN.
IT'S TOO MUCH!
THEY NEED TO TAKE PITY ON US STUDENTS!
WRIGGLE
YOU'VE STILL GOT THE STRENGTH TO COMPLAIN.
IF IT WERE REALLY TOO MUCH YOU'D BE TOO TIRED TO TALK.
CLOSE
HMF!
EVEN IF I WERE DOWN TO ZERO STRENGTH I'D STILL BE ABLE TO YELL AT YOU, MARIKA!
OH?
BE MY GUEST.

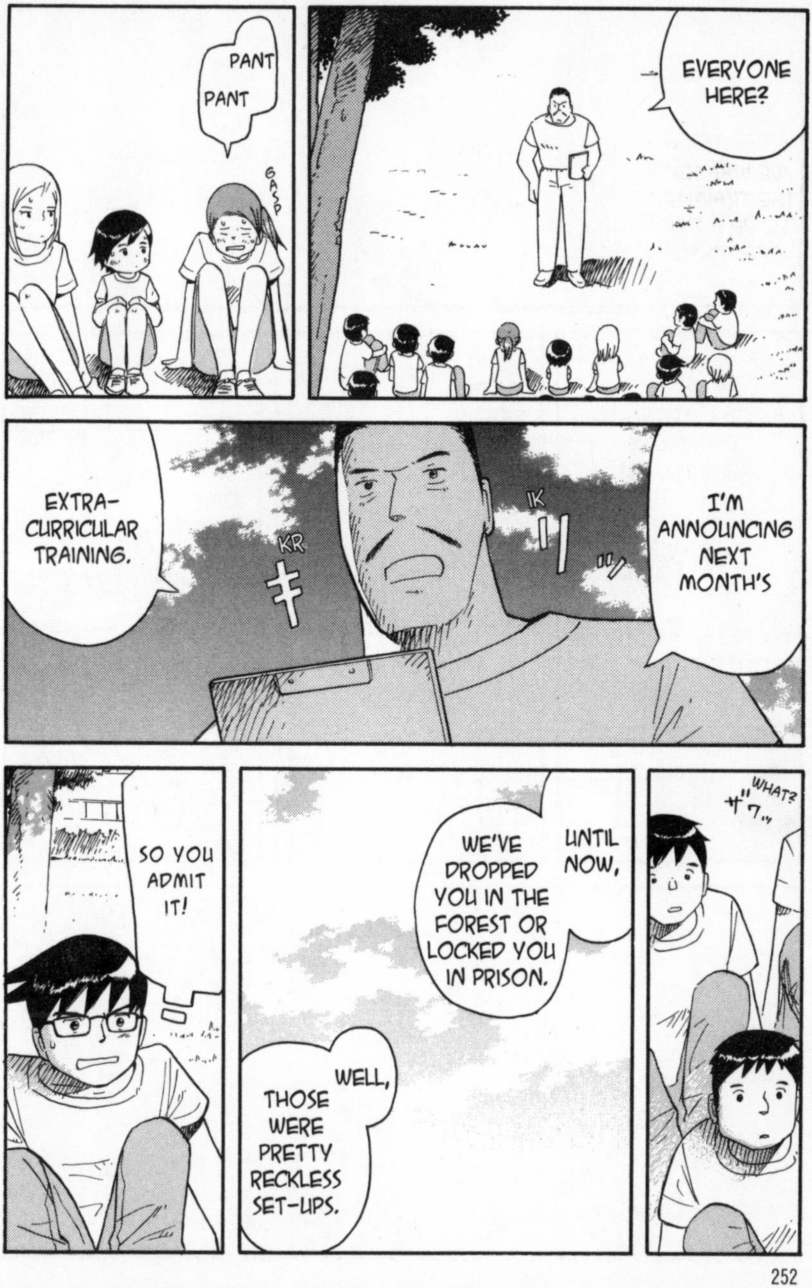
EVERYONE HERE?
PANT
PANT
GASP
I'M ANNOUNCING NEXT MONTH'S
IK
KR
EXTRA-CURRICULAR TRAINING.
WHAT?
UNTIL NOW,
WE'VE DROPPED YOU IN THE FOREST OR LOCKED YOU IN PRISON.
WELL,
THOSE WERE PRETTY RECKLESS SET-UPS.
SO YOU ADMIT IT!

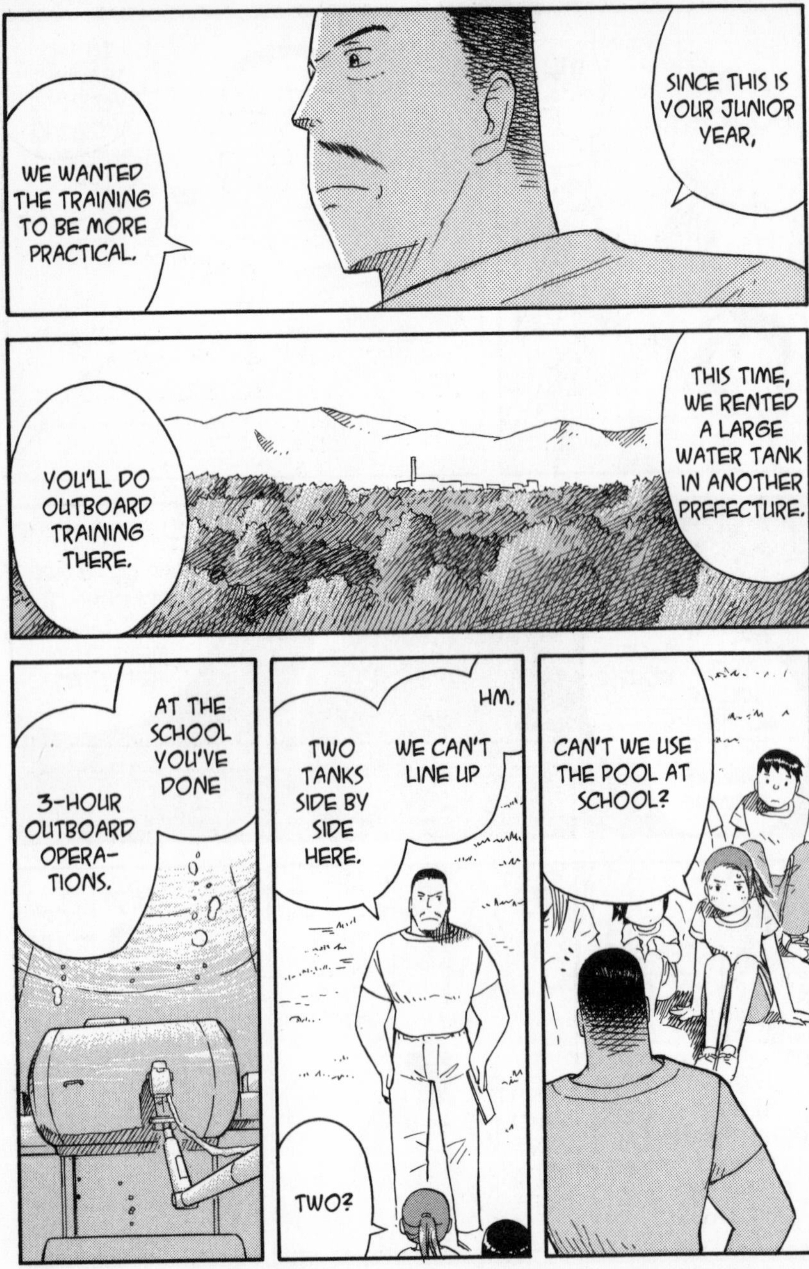
SINCE THIS IS YOUR JUNIOR YEAR,
WE WANTED THE TRAINING TO BE MORE PRACTICAL.
THIS TIME, WE RENTED A LARGE WATER TANK IN ANOTHER PREFECTURE.
YOU'LL DO OUTBOARD TRAINING THERE.
CAN'T WE USE THE POOL AT SCHOOL?
HM.
WE CAN'T LINE UP
TWO TANKS SIDE BY SIDE HERE.
TWO?
AT THE SCHOOL YOU'VE DONE
3-HOUR OUTBOARD OPERA-TIONS.

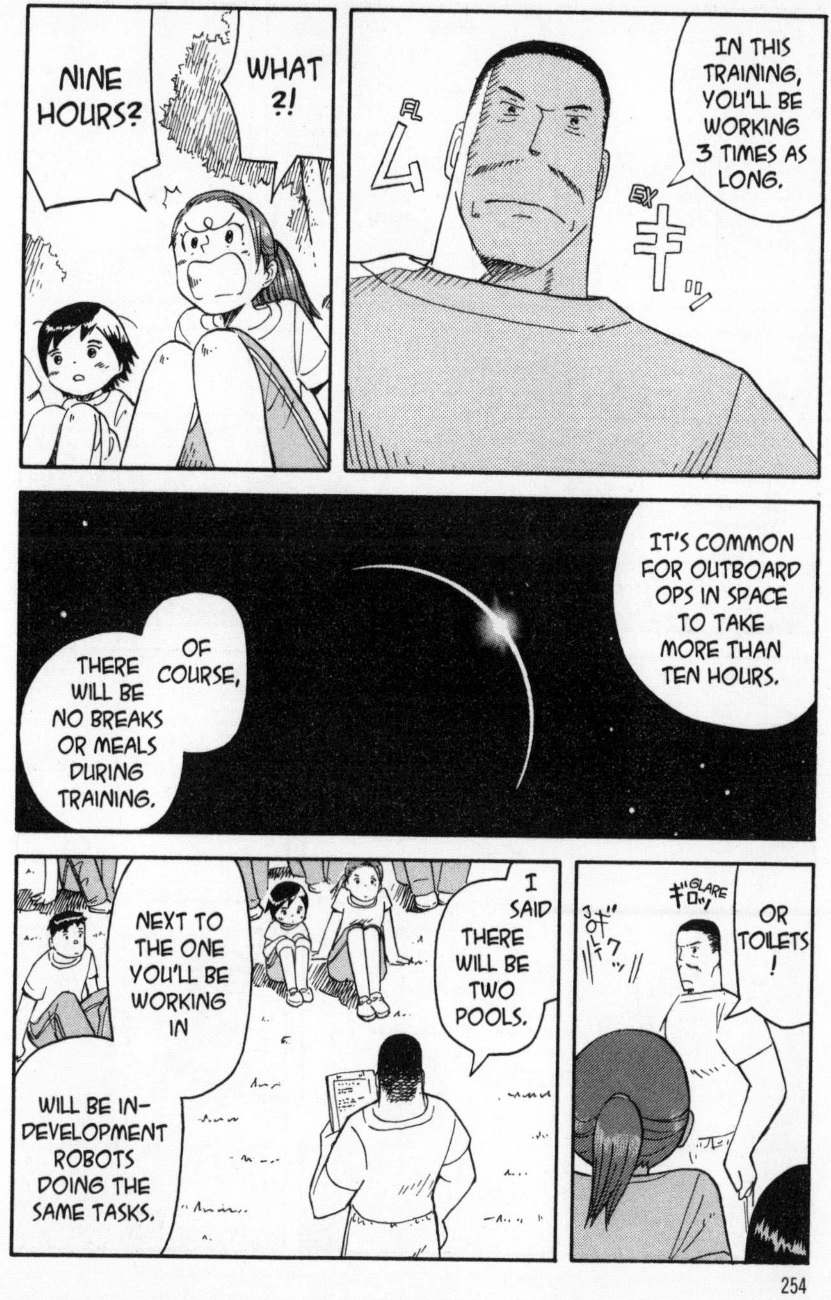
IN THIS TRAINING, YOU'LL BE WORKING 3 TIMES AS LONG.
WHAT ?!
NINE HOURS?
IT'S COMMON FOR OUTBOARD OPS IN SPACE TO TAKE MORE THAN TEN HOURS.
OF COURSE, THERE WILL BE NO BREAKS OR MEALS DURING TRAINING.
GLARE
OR TOILETS !
I SAID THERE WILL BE TWO POOLS.
NEXT TO THE ONE YOU'LL BE WORKING IN
WILL BE IN-DEVELOPMENT ROBOTS DOING THE SAME TASKS.

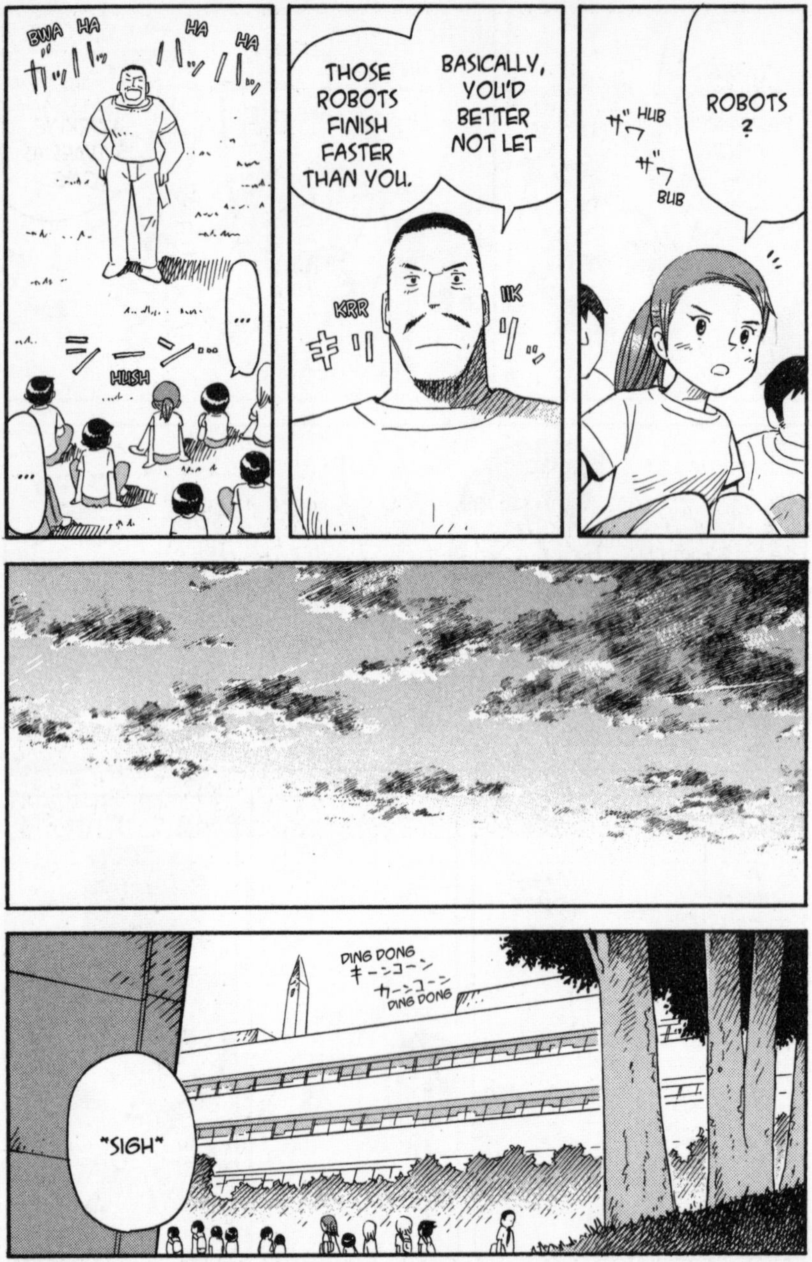
ROBOTS?
HUB ザワ
ザワ BUB
BASICALLY, YOU'D BETTER NOT LET
THOSE ROBOTS FINISH FASTER THAN YOU.
KRR キリ
IIK
BWA HA
HA
HA
...
HUSH シーン...
...
DING DONG キーンコーン
カーンコーン DING DONG
SIGH

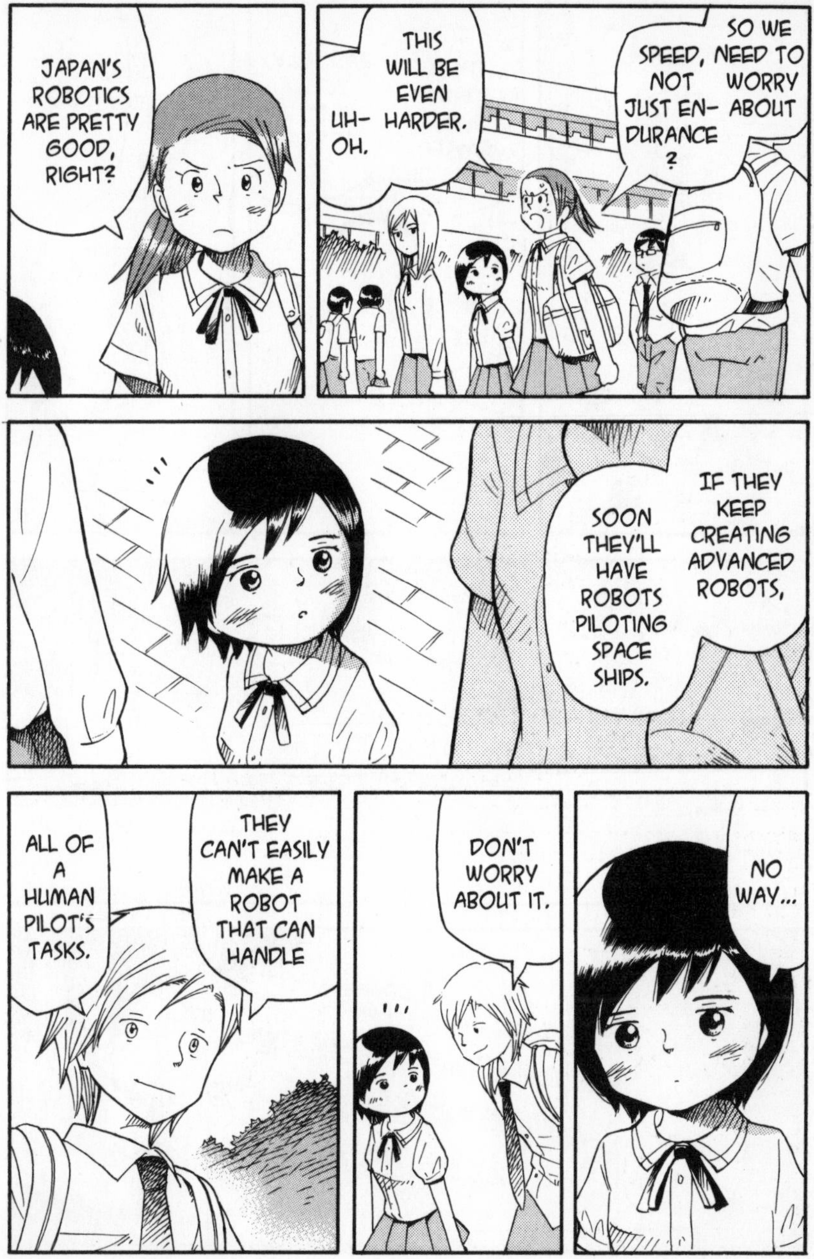
SO WE NEED TO WORRY ABOUT SPEED, NOT JUST EN-DURANCE?
THIS WILL BE EVEN HARDER.
UH-OH.
JAPAN'S ROBOTICS ARE PRETTY GOOD, RIGHT?
IF THEY KEEP CREATING ADVANCED ROBOTS,
SOON THEY'LL HAVE ROBOTS PILOTING SPACE SHIPS.
NO WAY...
DON'T WORRY ABOUT IT.
THEY CAN'T EASILY MAKE A ROBOT THAT CAN HANDLE
ALL OF A HUMAN PILOT'S TASKS.

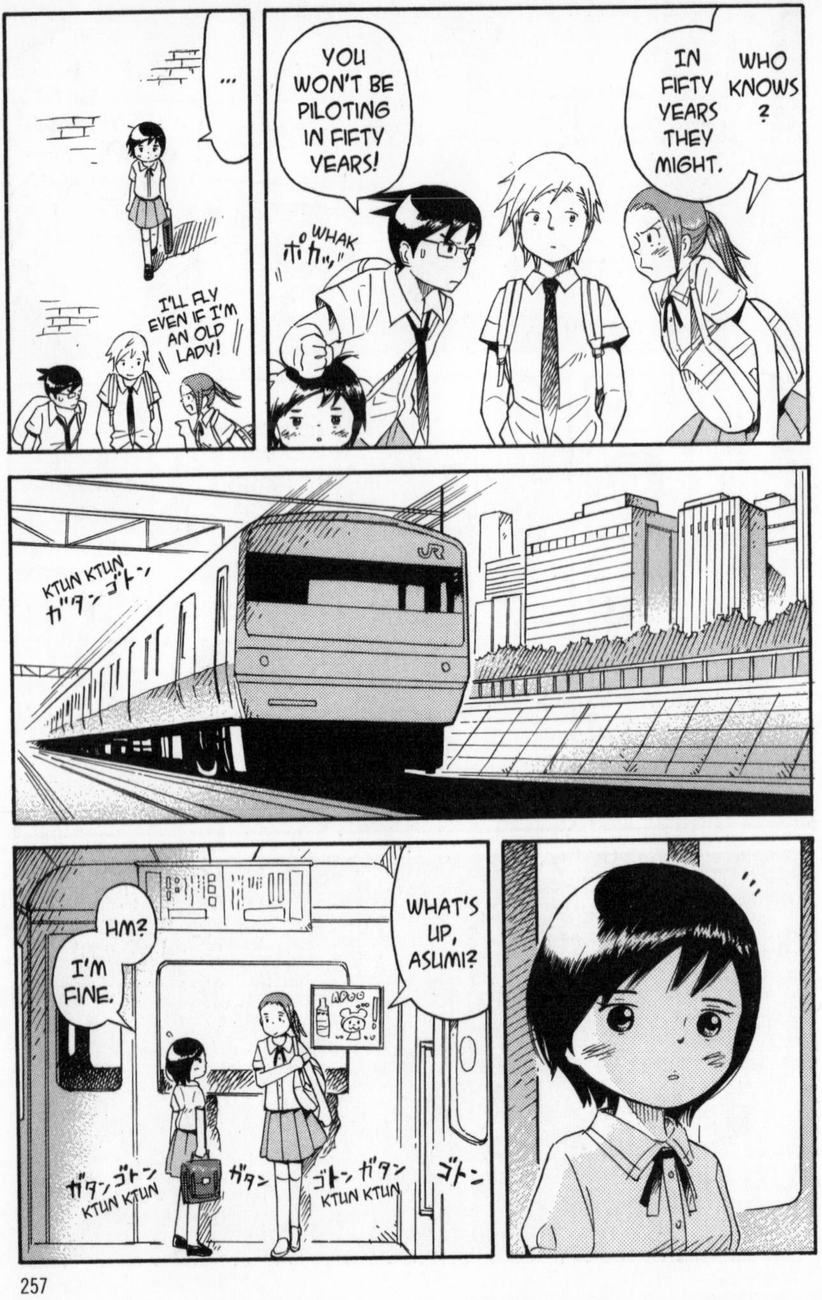
WHO KNOWS? IN FIFTY YEARS THEY MIGHT.
YOU WON'T BE PILOTING IN FIFTY YEARS!
WHAK ポカッ
...
I'LL FLY EVEN IF I'M AN OLD LADY!
KTUN KTUN ガタンゴトン
WHAT'S UP, ASUMI?
HM? I'M FINE.
ゴトン
ゴトンガタン KTUN KTUN
ガタン
ガタンゴトン KTUN KTUN

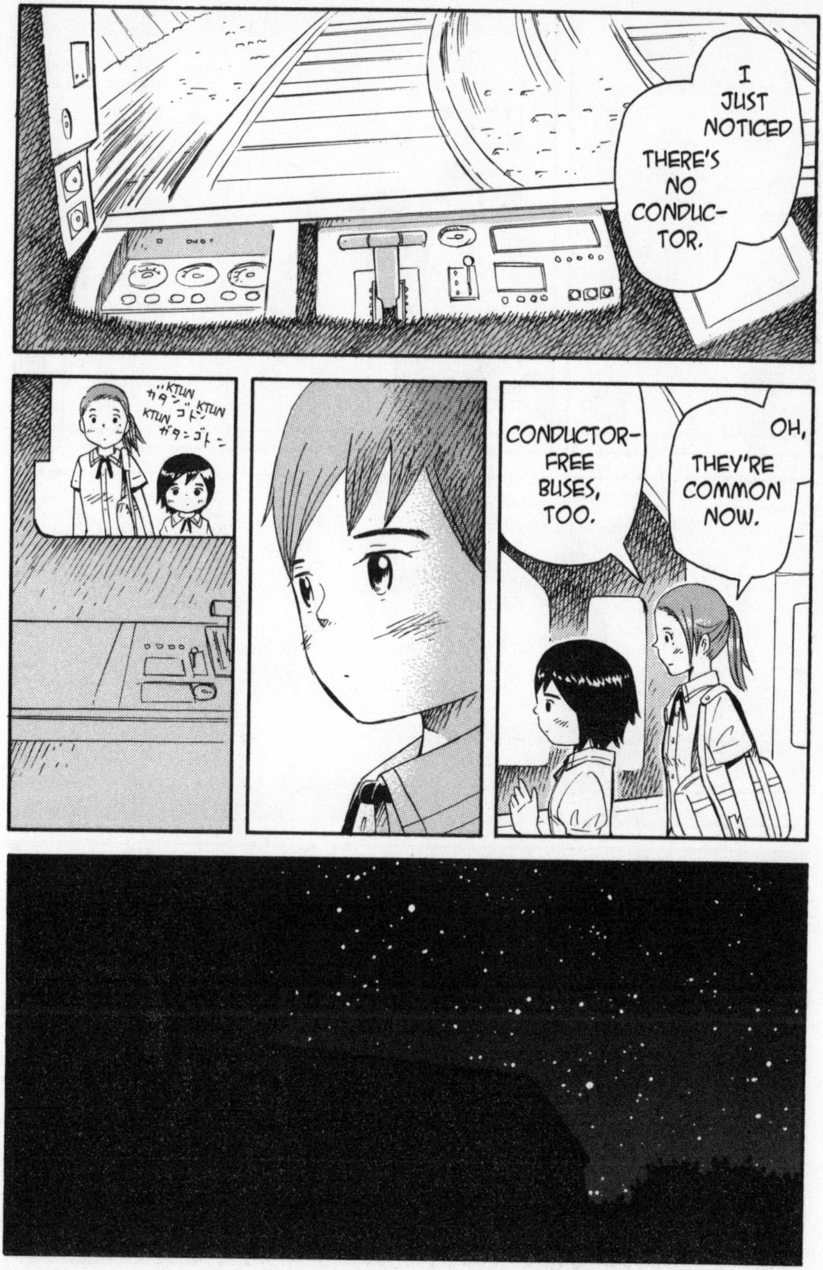
I JUST NOTICED THERE'S NO CONDUCTOR.
OH, THEY'RE COMMON NOW.
CONDUCTOR-FREE BUSES, TOO.
KTUN ガタンゴトン
KTUN ガタンゴトン
KTUN

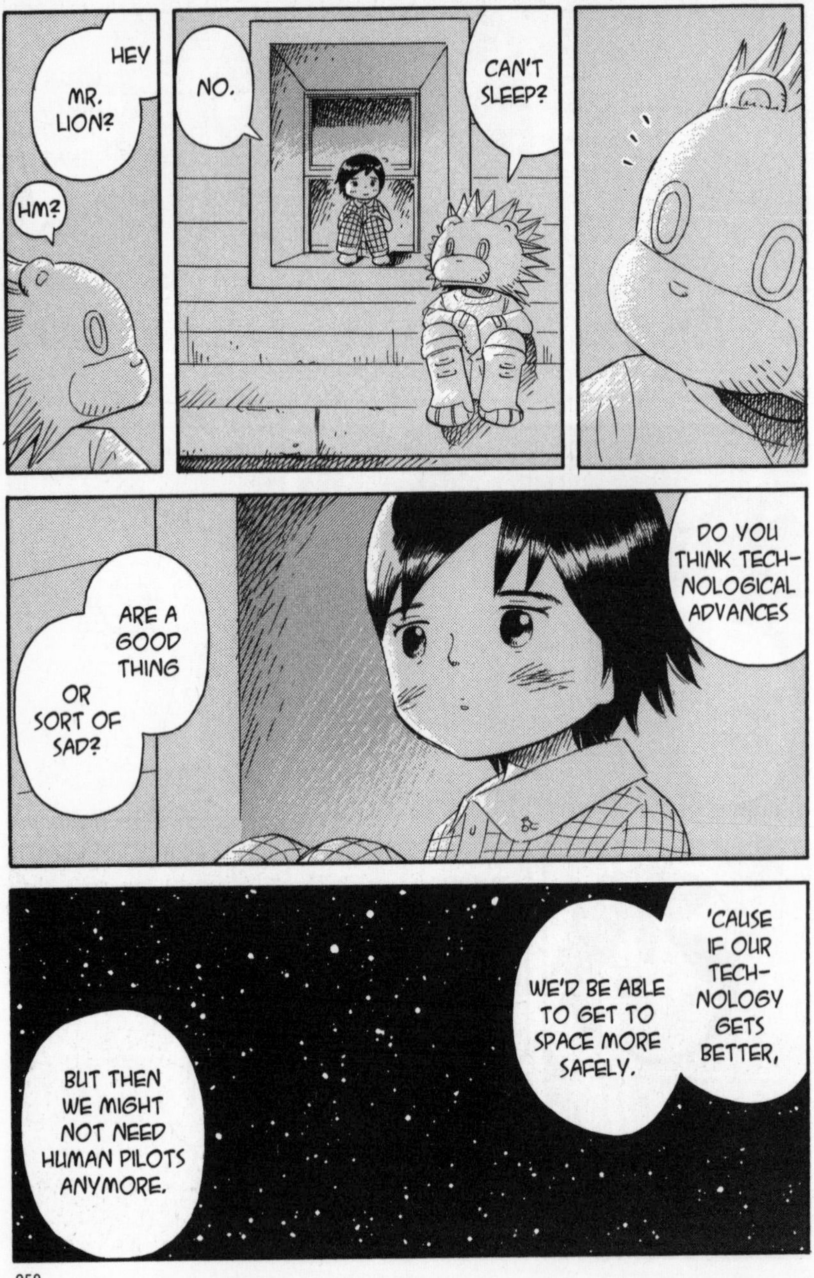
CAN'T SLEEP?
NO.
HEY MR. LION?
HM?
DO YOU THINK TECHNOLOGICAL ADVANCES
ARE A GOOD THING OR SORT OF SAD?
'CAUSE IF OUR TECHNOLOGY GETS BETTER,
WE'D BE ABLE TO GET TO SPACE MORE SAFELY.
BUT THEN WE MIGHT NOT NEED HUMAN PILOTS ANYMORE.

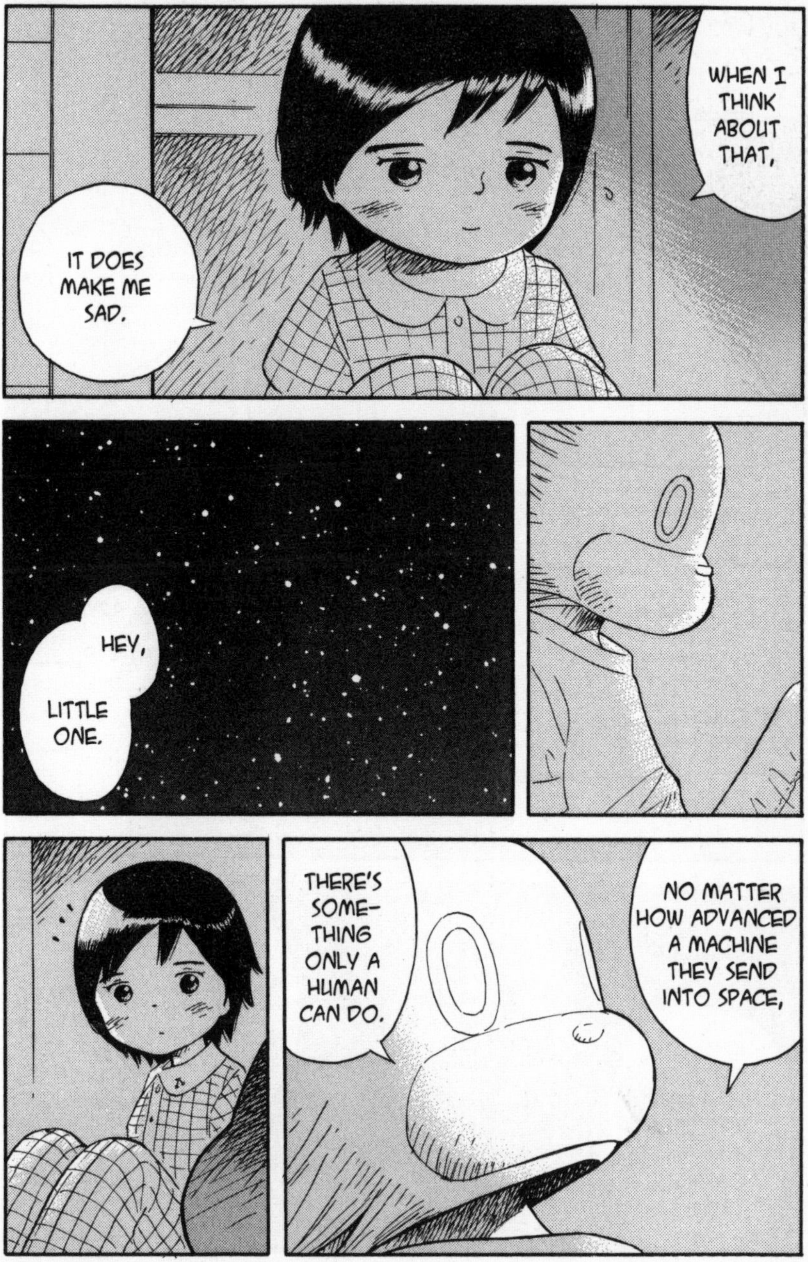
WHEN I THINK ABOUT THAT,
IT DOES MAKE ME SAD.
HEY,
LITTLE ONE.
NO MATTER HOW ADVANCED A MACHINE THEY SEND INTO SPACE,
THERE'S SOME-THING ONLY A HUMAN CAN DO.

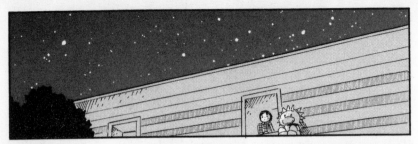

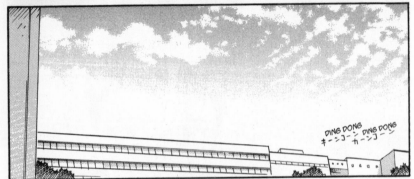

DING DONG
キーンコーン DING DONG
カーンコーン

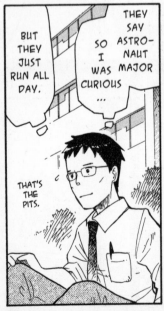

THEY SAY ASTRONAUT MAJOR

SO I WAS CURIOUS...

BUT THEY JUST RUN ALL DAY.

THAT'S THE PITS.

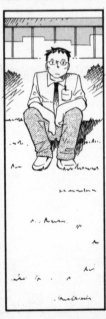

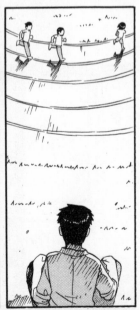

261

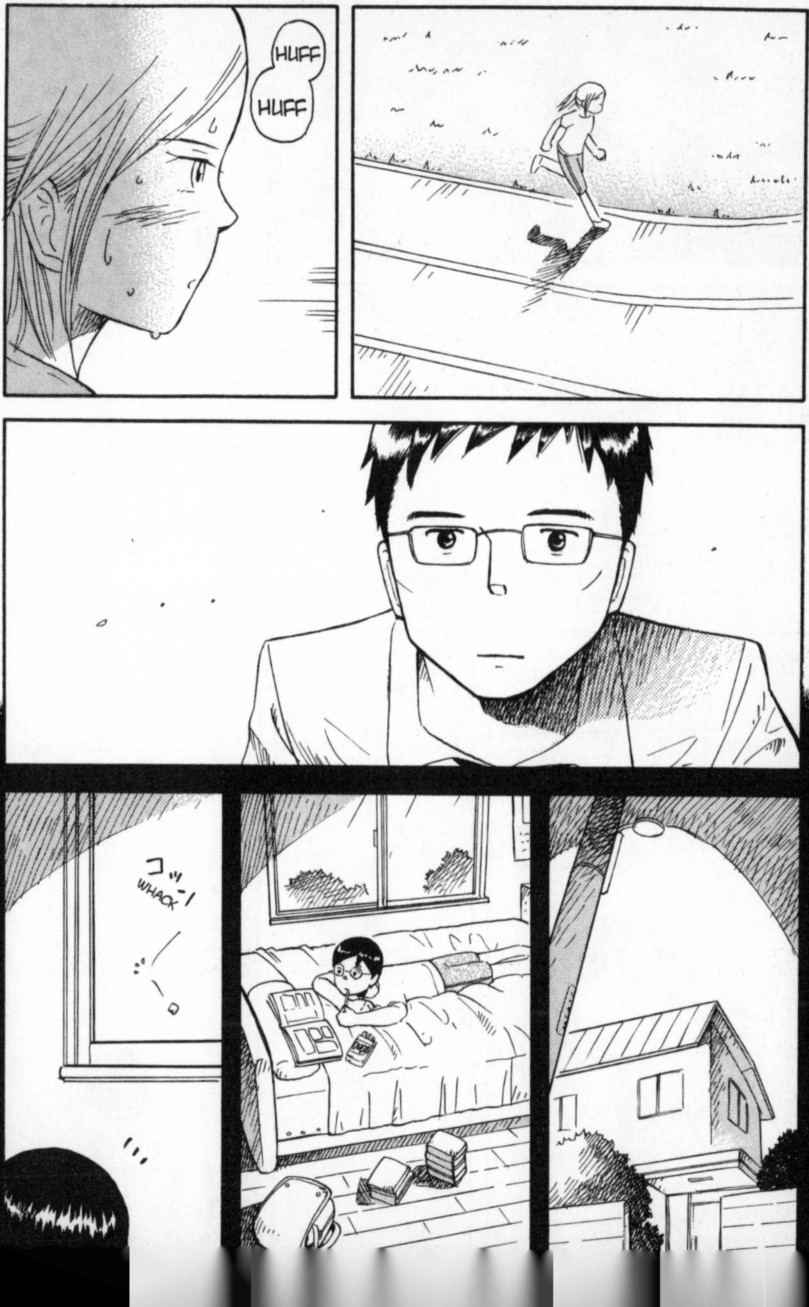
HUFF
HUFF
コッ
WHACK

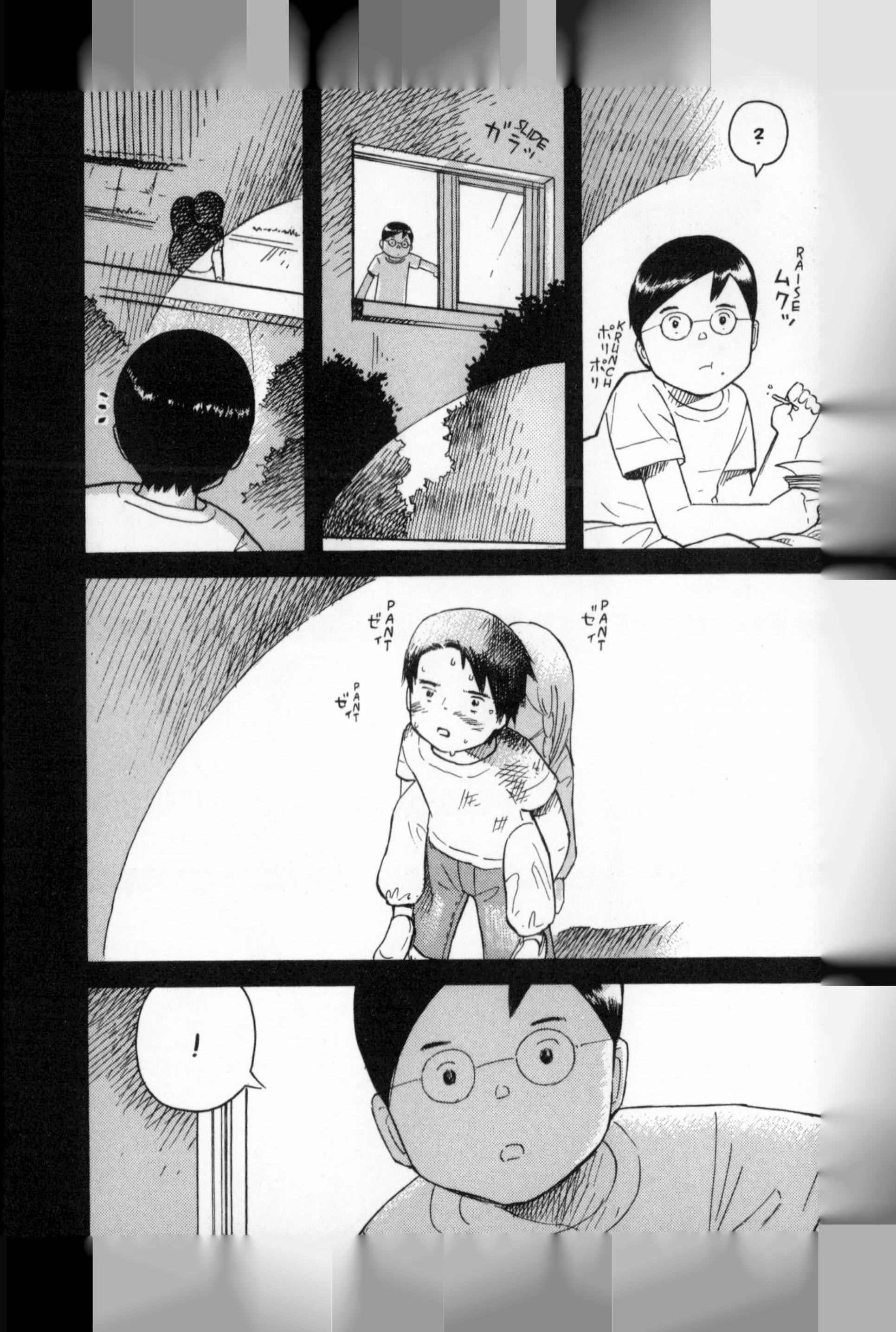
?
ムクッ RAISE
ポリポリ KRUNCH
ガラッ SLIDE
ゼィ PANT
ゼィ PANT
ゼィ PANT
!

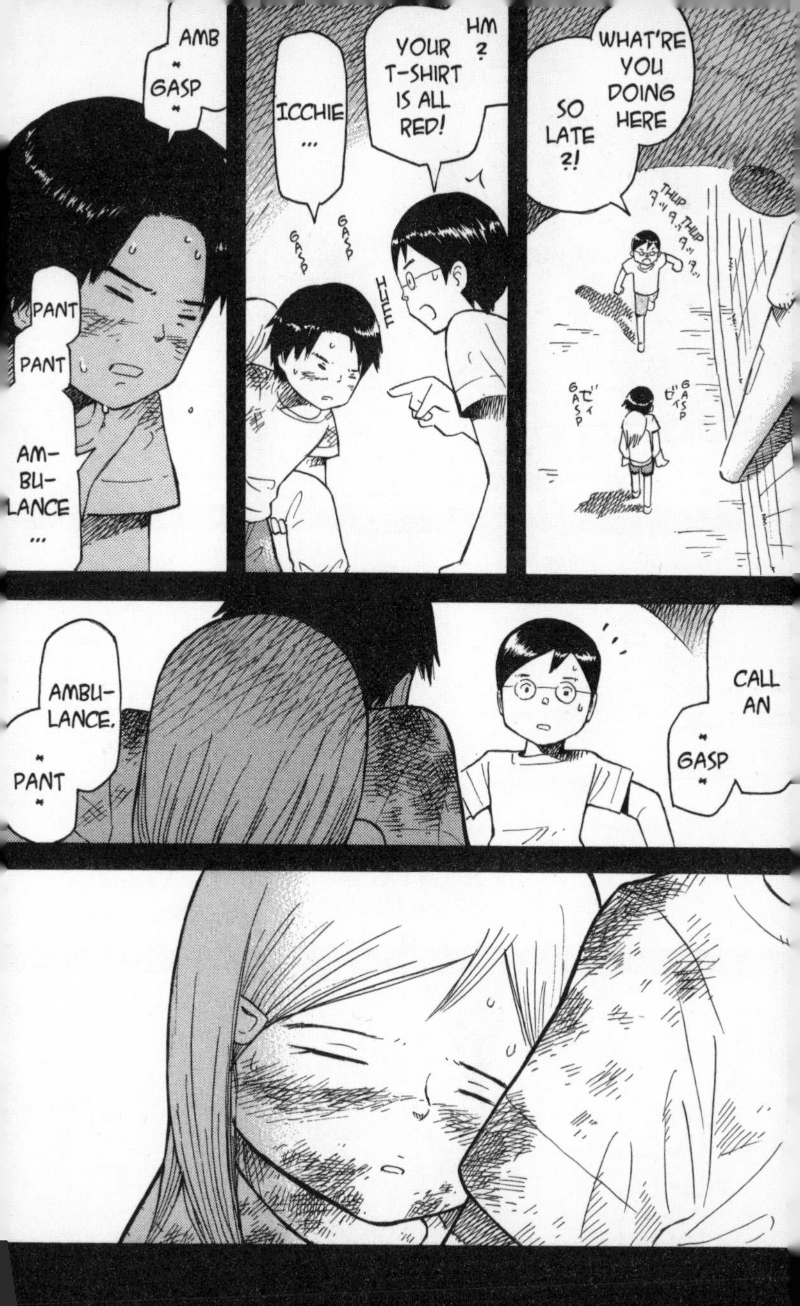
WHAT'RE YOU DOING HERE SO LATE ?!
THUP THUP
GASP GASP
HM ?
YOUR T-SHIRT IS ALL RED!
ICCHIE ...
GASP GASP
HUFF
AMB *GASP*
PANT
PANT
AM-BU-LANCE ...
CALL AN *GASP*
AMBU-LANCE. *PANT*

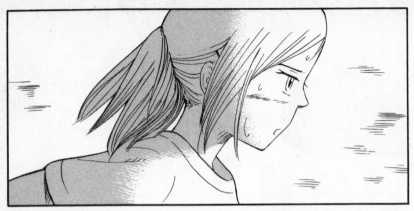

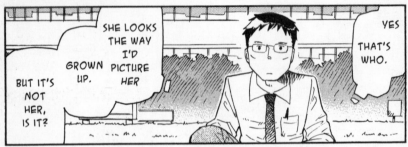

SHE LOOKS THE WAY I'D PICTURE HER GROWN UP.

BUT IT'S NOT HER, IS IT?

YES THAT'S WHO.

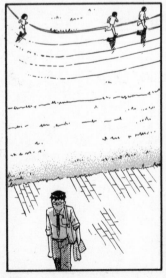

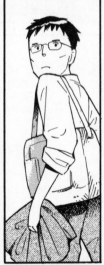

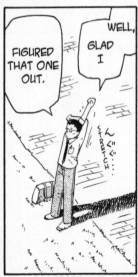

WELL, GLAD I

FIGURED THAT ONE OUT.

STRETCH

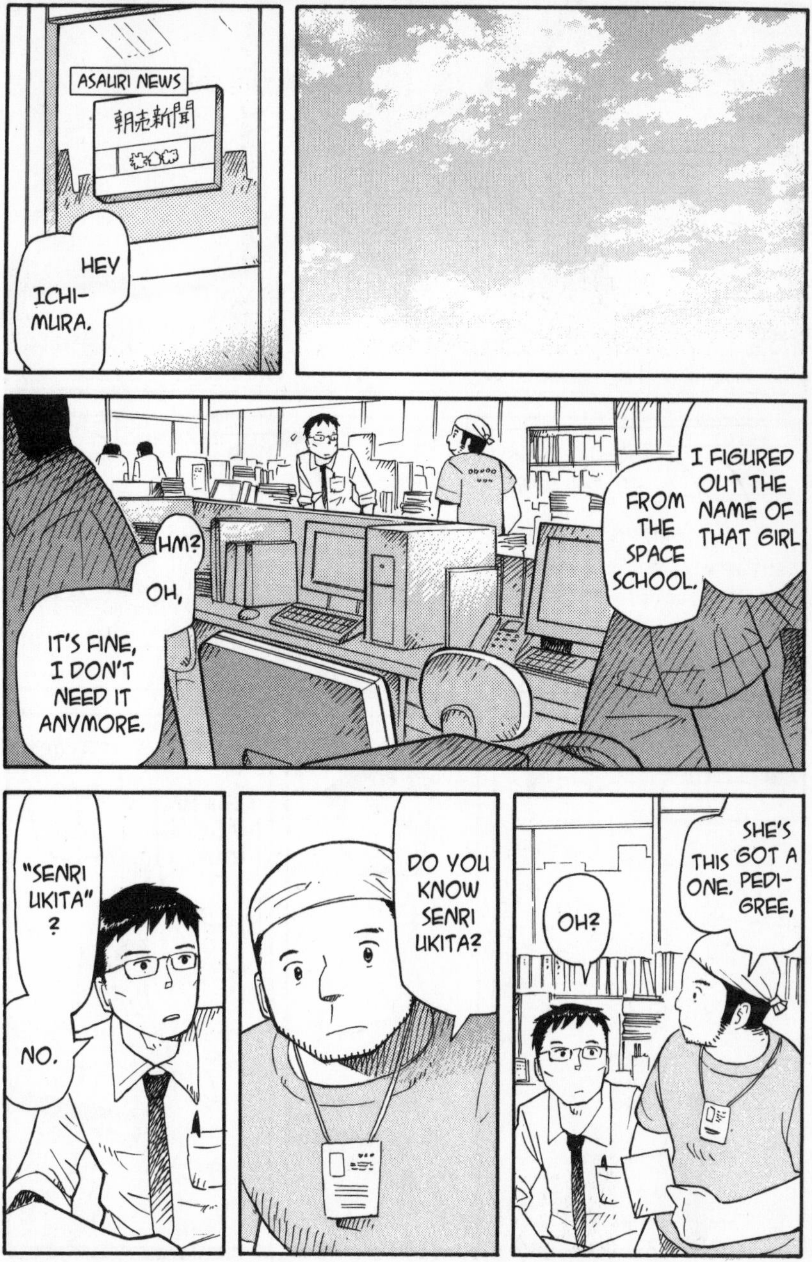
ASAURI NEWS
朝売新聞
HEY ICHIMURA.
I FIGURED OUT THE NAME OF THAT GIRL FROM THE SPACE SCHOOL.
HM?
OH,
IT'S FINE, I DON'T NEED IT ANYMORE.
SHE'S GOT A PEDIGREE, THIS ONE.
OH?
DO YOU KNOW SENRI UKITA?
"SENRI UKITA"?
NO.

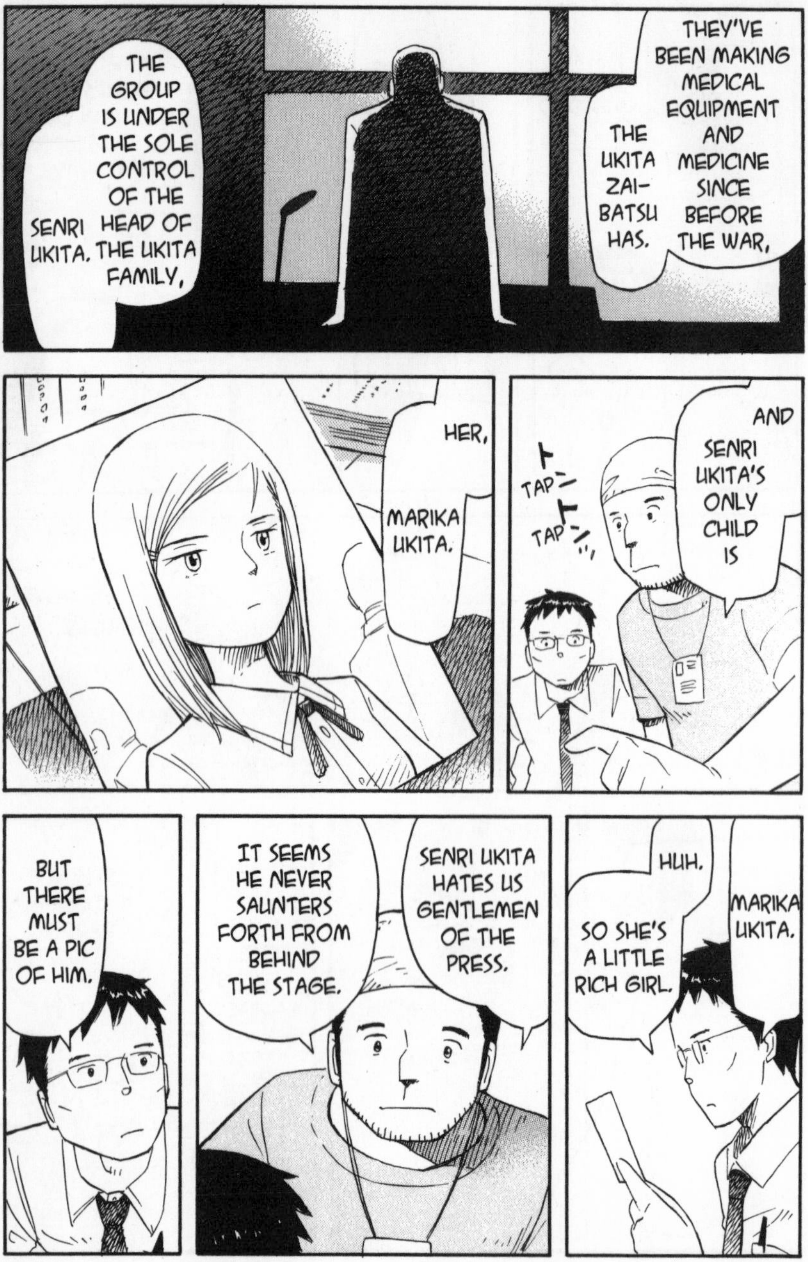
THEY'VE BEEN MAKING MEDICAL EQUIPMENT AND MEDICINE SINCE BEFORE THE WAR, THE UKITA ZAI-BATSU HAS.
THE GROUP IS UNDER THE SOLE CONTROL OF THE HEAD OF THE UKITA FAMILY, SENRI UKITA.
AND SENRI UKITA'S ONLY CHILD IS
TAP
TAP
HER, MARIKA UKITA.
MARIKA UKITA.
HUH.
SO SHE'S A LITTLE RICH GIRL.
SENRI UKITA HATES US GENTLEMEN OF THE PRESS.
IT SEEMS HE NEVER SAUNTERS FORTH FROM BEHIND THE STAGE.
BUT THERE MUST BE A PIC OF HIM.

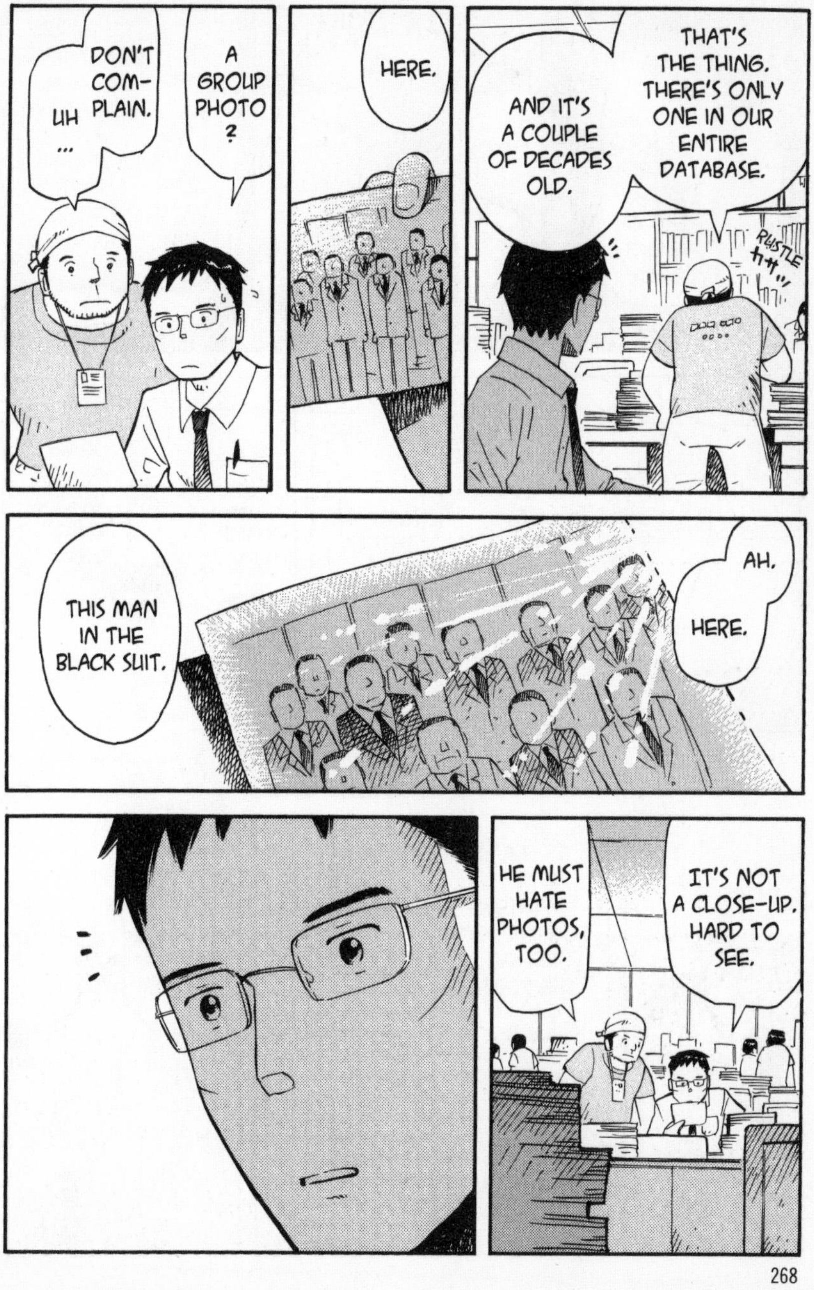
THAT'S THE THING. THERE'S ONLY ONE IN OUR ENTIRE DATABASE.
AND IT'S A COUPLE OF DECADES OLD.
RUSTLE
HERE.
A GROUP PHOTO?
DON'T COM-PLAIN.
UH ...
AH. HERE.
THIS MAN IN THE BLACK SUIT.
IT'S NOT A CLOSE-UP. HARD TO SEE.
HE MUST HATE PHOTOS, TOO.

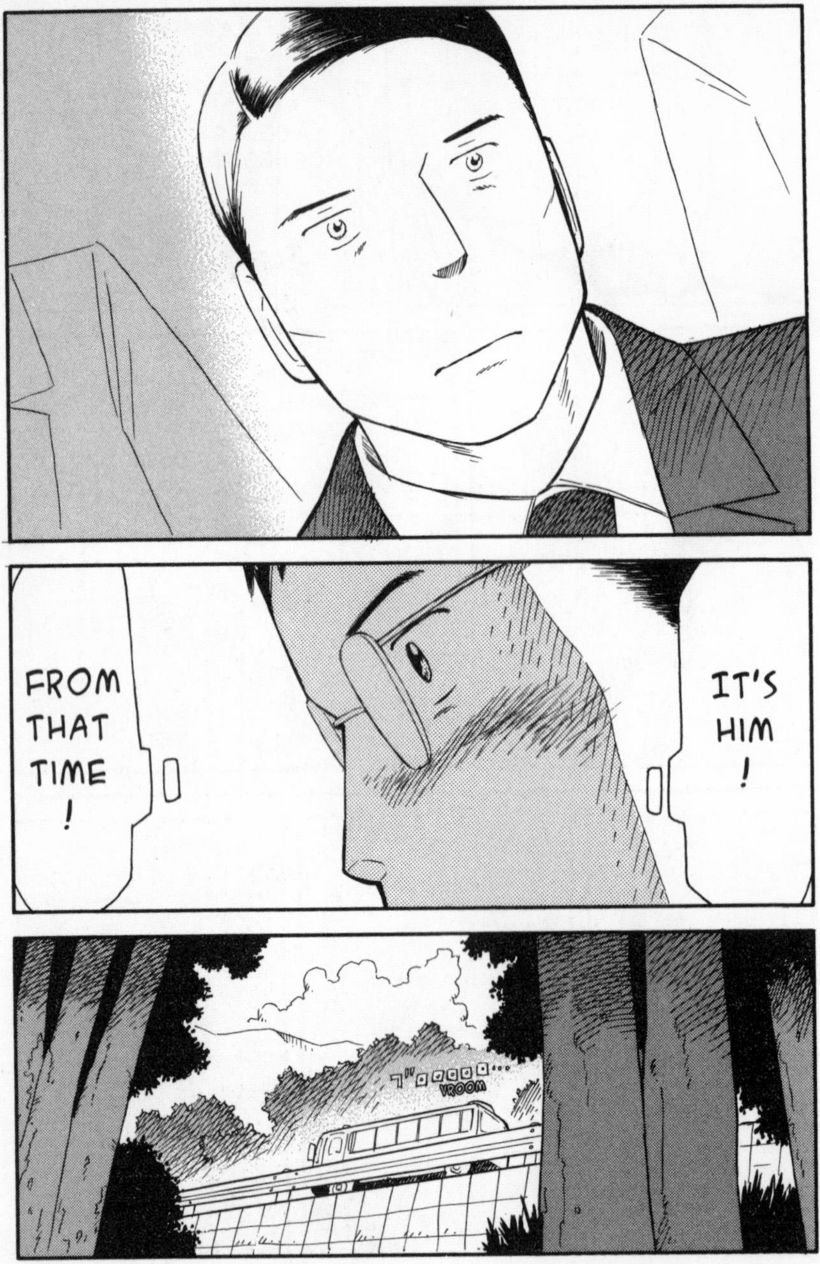
IT'S HIM!
FROM THAT TIME!
ブロロロロロ…
VROOM

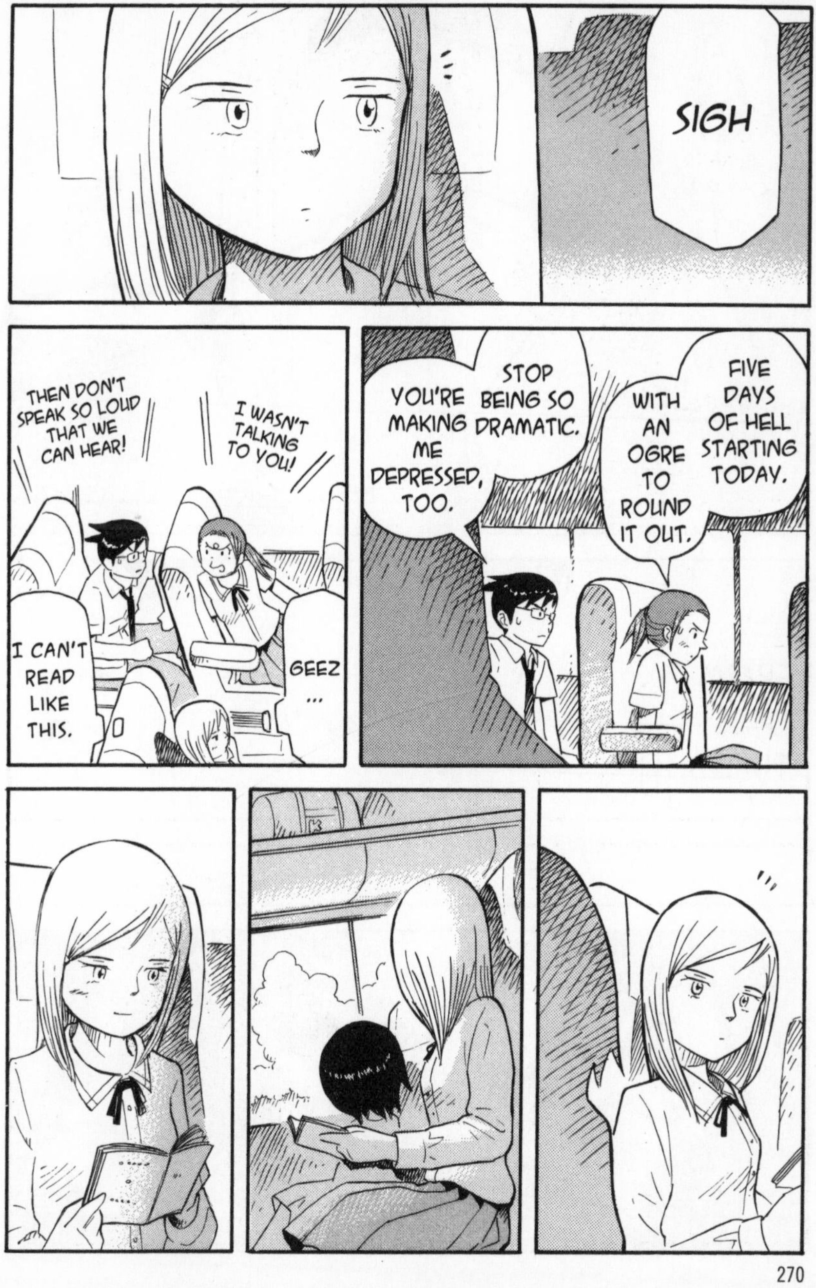
SIGH
FIVE DAYS OF HELL STARTING TODAY.
WITH AN OGRE TO ROUND IT OUT.
STOP BEING SO DRAMATIC.
YOU'RE MAKING ME DEPRESSED, TOO.
I WASN'T TALKING TO YOU!
THEN DON'T SPEAK SO LOUD THAT WE CAN HEAR!
GEEZ ...
I CAN'T READ LIKE THIS.

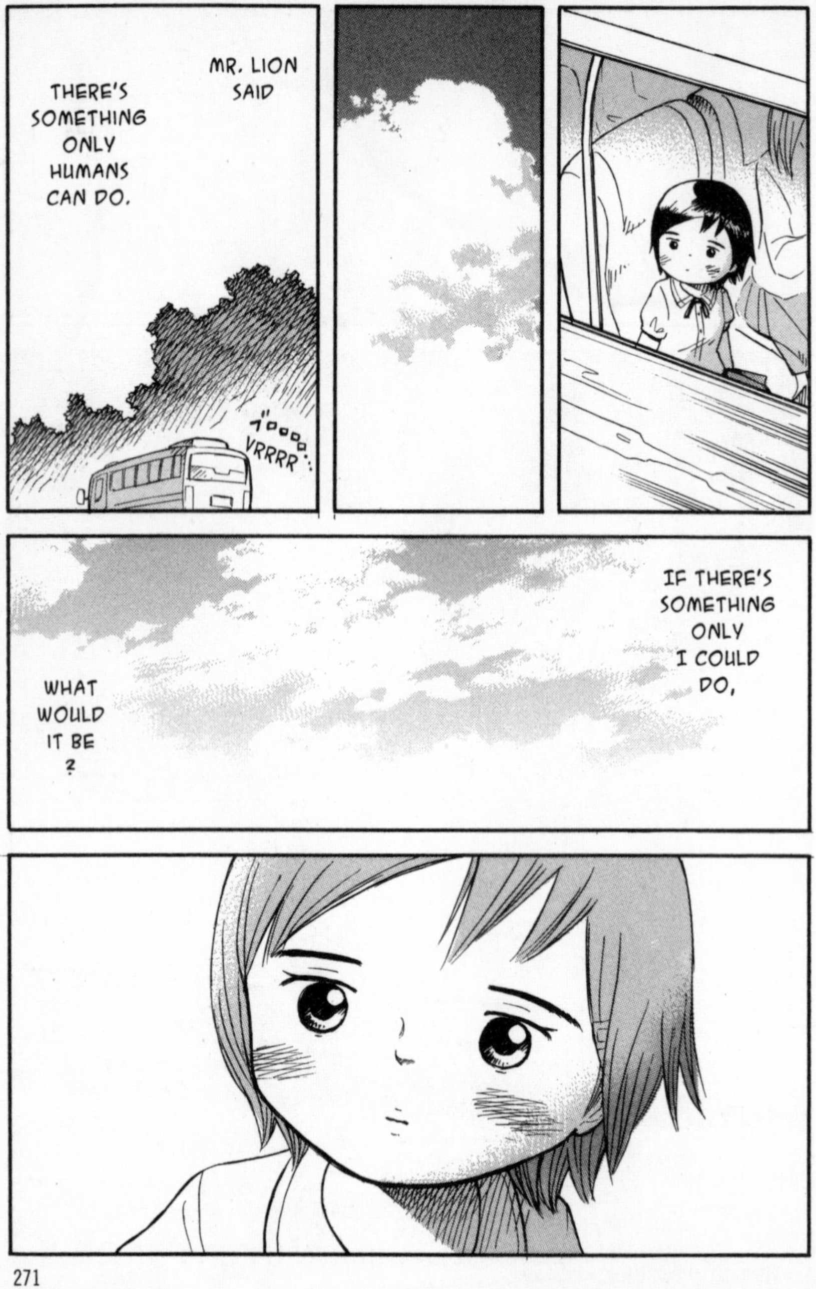
MR. LION SAID
THERE'S SOMETHING ONLY HUMANS CAN DO.
VRRRR
IF THERE'S SOMETHING ONLY I COULD DO,
WHAT WOULD IT BE?

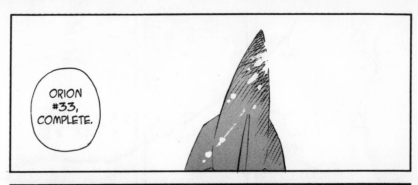

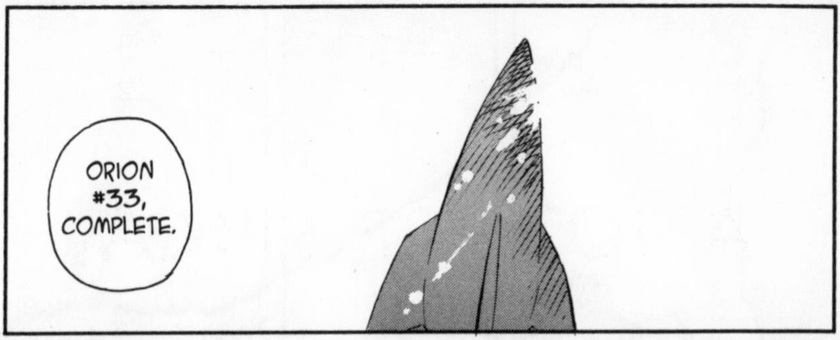
ORION #33, COMPLETE.

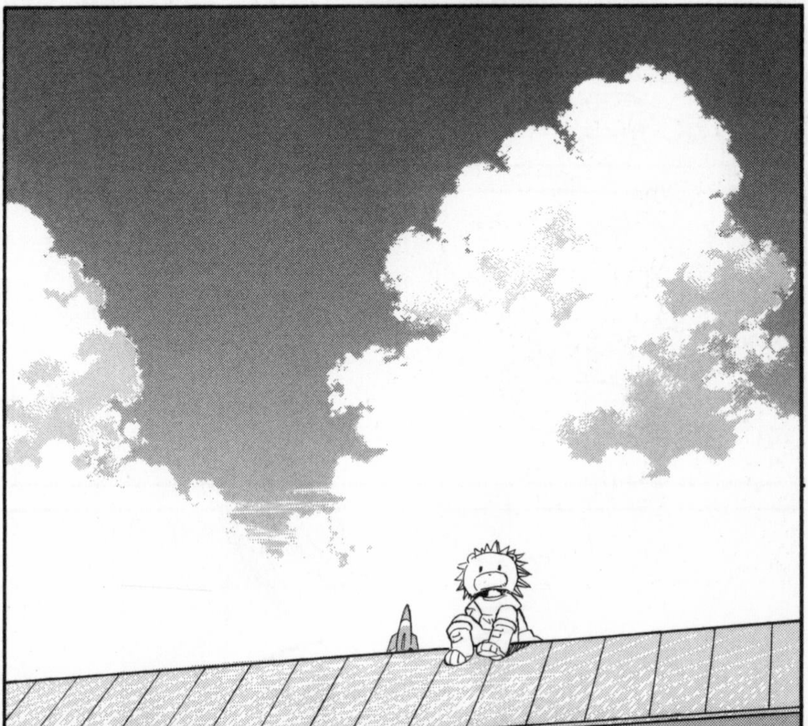

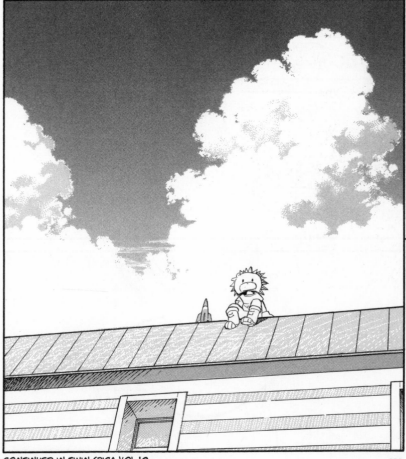

CONTINUED IN TWIN SPICA VOL.10

ANOTHER SPICA

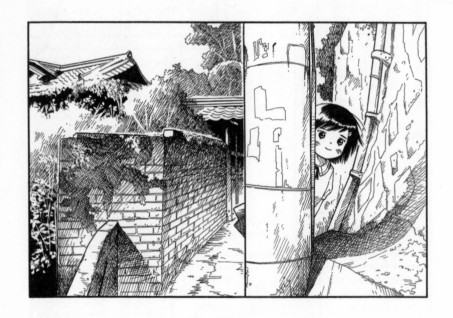

KOU YAGINUMA

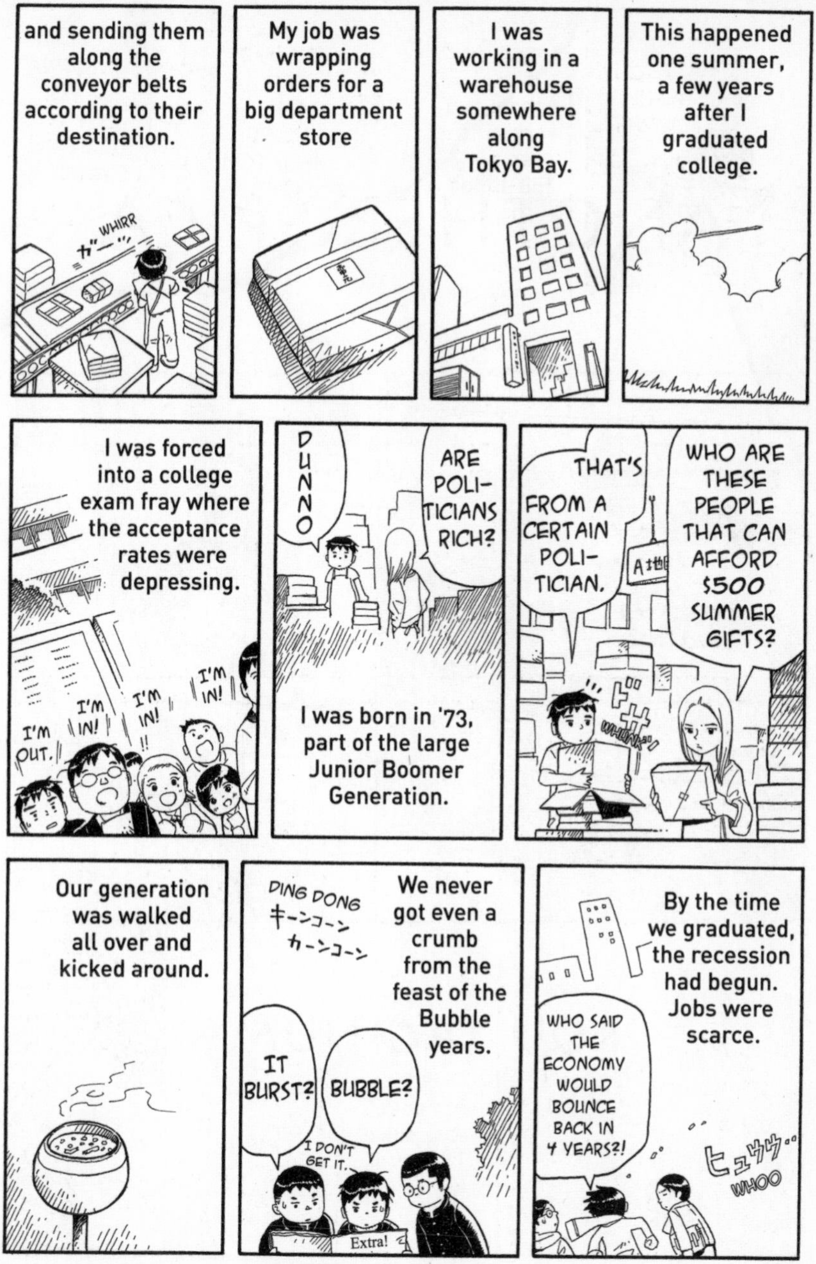
This happened one summer, a few years after I graduated college.
I was working in a warehouse somewhere along Tokyo Bay.
My job was wrapping orders for a big department store
and sending them along the conveyor belts according to their destination.
WHIRR
WHO ARE THESE PEOPLE THAT CAN AFFORD $500 SUMMER GIFTS?
THAT'S FROM A CERTAIN POLITICIAN.
WHUNK
ARE POLITICIANS RICH?
DUNNO
I was born in '73, part of the large Junior Boomer Generation.
I was forced into a college exam fray where the acceptance rates were depressing.
I'M IN!
I'M IN!
I'M IN!
I'M OUT.
By the time we graduated, the recession had begun. Jobs were scarce.
WHO SAID THE ECONOMY WOULD BOUNCE BACK IN 4 YEARS?!
WHOO
We never got even a crumb from the feast of the Bubble years.
DING DONG
キーンコーン
カーンコーン
BUBBLE?
IT BURST?
I DON'T GET IT.
Extra!
Our generation was walked all over and kicked around.

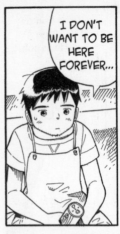

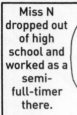

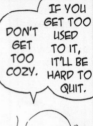

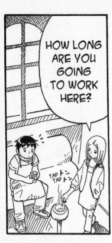

HOW LONG ARE YOU GOING TO WORK HERE?
TAP トン TAP トン
IF YOU GET TOO USED TO IT, IT'LL BE HARD TO QUIT.
DON'T GET TOO COZY.
Miss N dropped out of high school and worked as a semi-full-timer there.
We were the same age, yet she always spoke politely to me.
I DON'T WANT TO BE HERE FOREVER...
WANT ONE?
UH,
THANKS.
WELL?
I MEAN NO THANKS.
I'd just started to look forward to going to work there and was at a loss about what I really wanted to do.
I got the call
one night that summer.
YES
THIS IS YAGI-NUMA.
UH...
YAGI-NUMA?
DO YOU REMEMBER ME?
It was the girl who dumped me in school.
HUH?!
It'd been years since I'd heard her voice.
I was dumbfounded, completely taken off-guard.
I honestly can't remember a thing I said.
AH,
UH,
BEEN A WHILE.
HM?
NO,
UH,
HUH?
UH,
HUH.

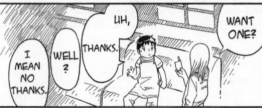

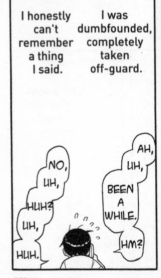

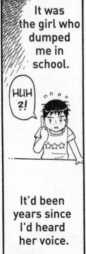

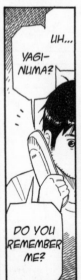

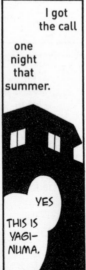

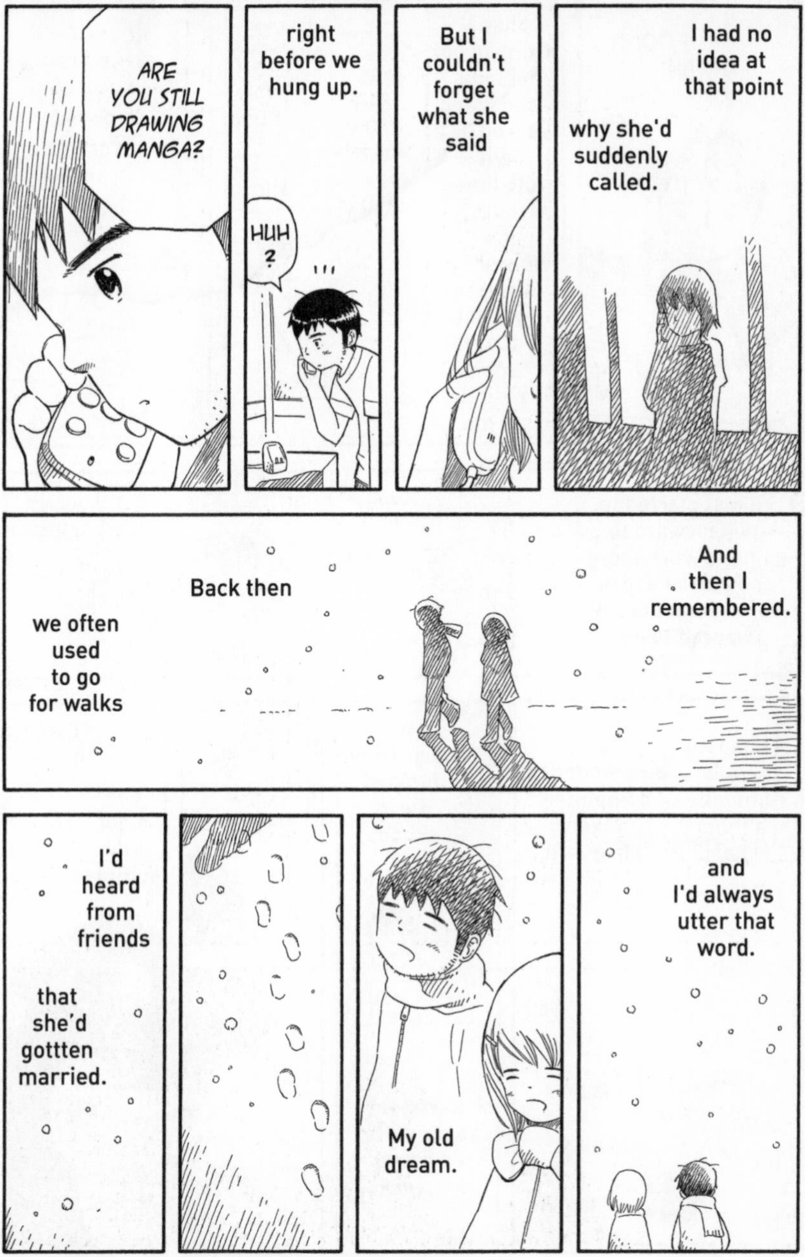
I had no idea at that point
why she'd suddenly called.
But I couldn't forget what she said
right before we hung up.
HUH ?
ARE YOU STILL DRAWING MANGA?
And then I remembered.
Back then
we often used to go for walks
and I'd always utter that word.
My old dream.
I'd heard from friends
that she'd gottten married.

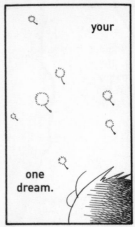

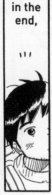

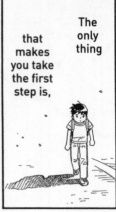

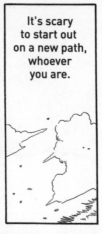

It's scary to start out on a new path, whoever you are.
The only thing
that makes you take the first step is,
in the end,
your
one dream.
SO YOU'RE QUITTING THIS PLACE?
UH, YES.
AH...
I SEE, I SEE.
I'd started to fall for Miss N.
I never told her that.
The next summer:

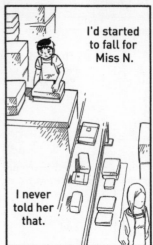

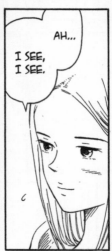

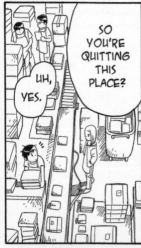

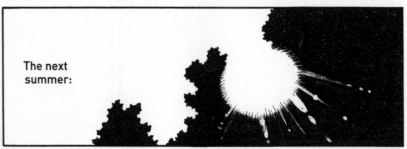

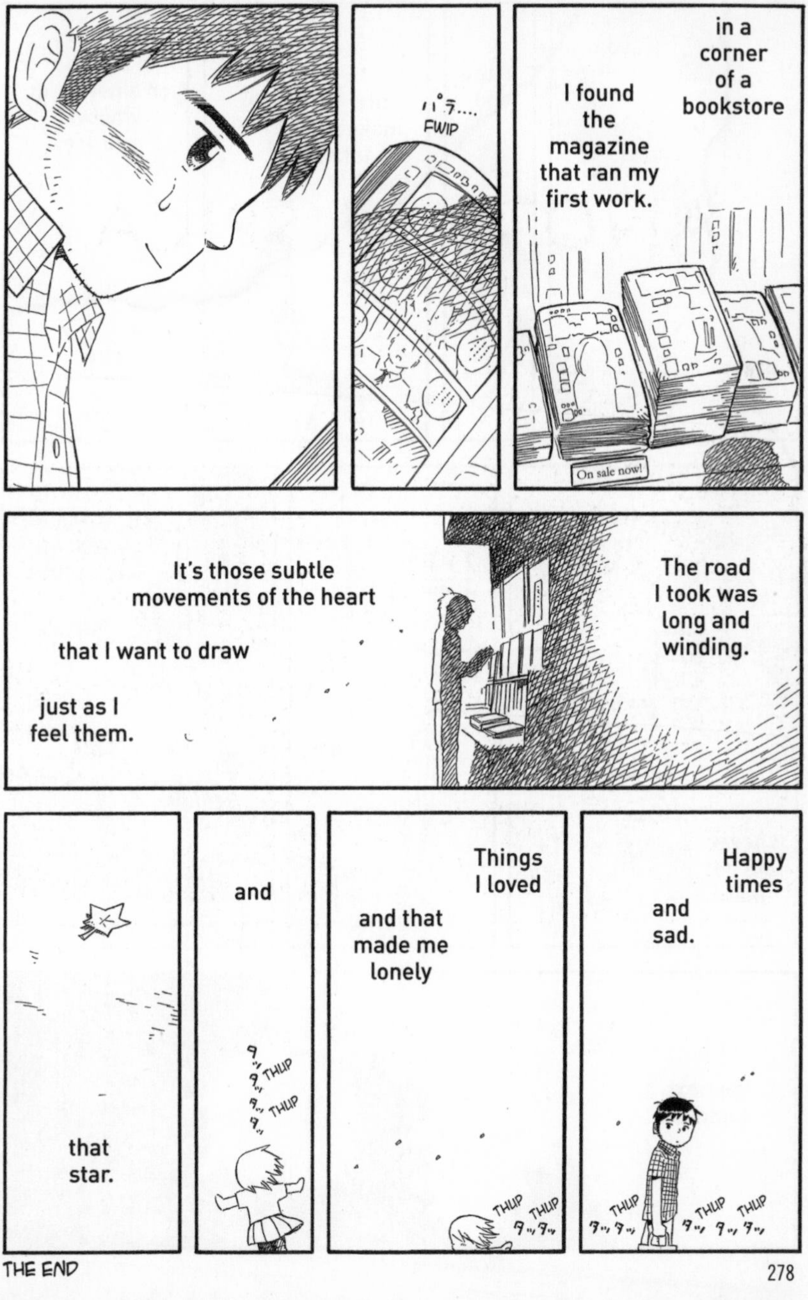
in a corner of a bookstore
I found the magazine that ran my first work.
On sale now!
パラ....
FWIP
The road I took was long and winding.
It's those subtle movements of the heart
that I want to draw
just as I feel them.
Happy times
and sad.
タッ タッ
THUP
タッ タッ タッ
THUP THUP
Things I loved
and that made me lonely
タッ タッ
THUP THUP
and
タッ
THUP
タッ
タッ
THUP
タッ
that star.

THE END

ANOTHER SPICA

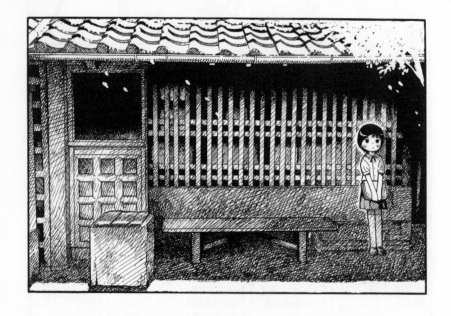

KOU YAGINUMA

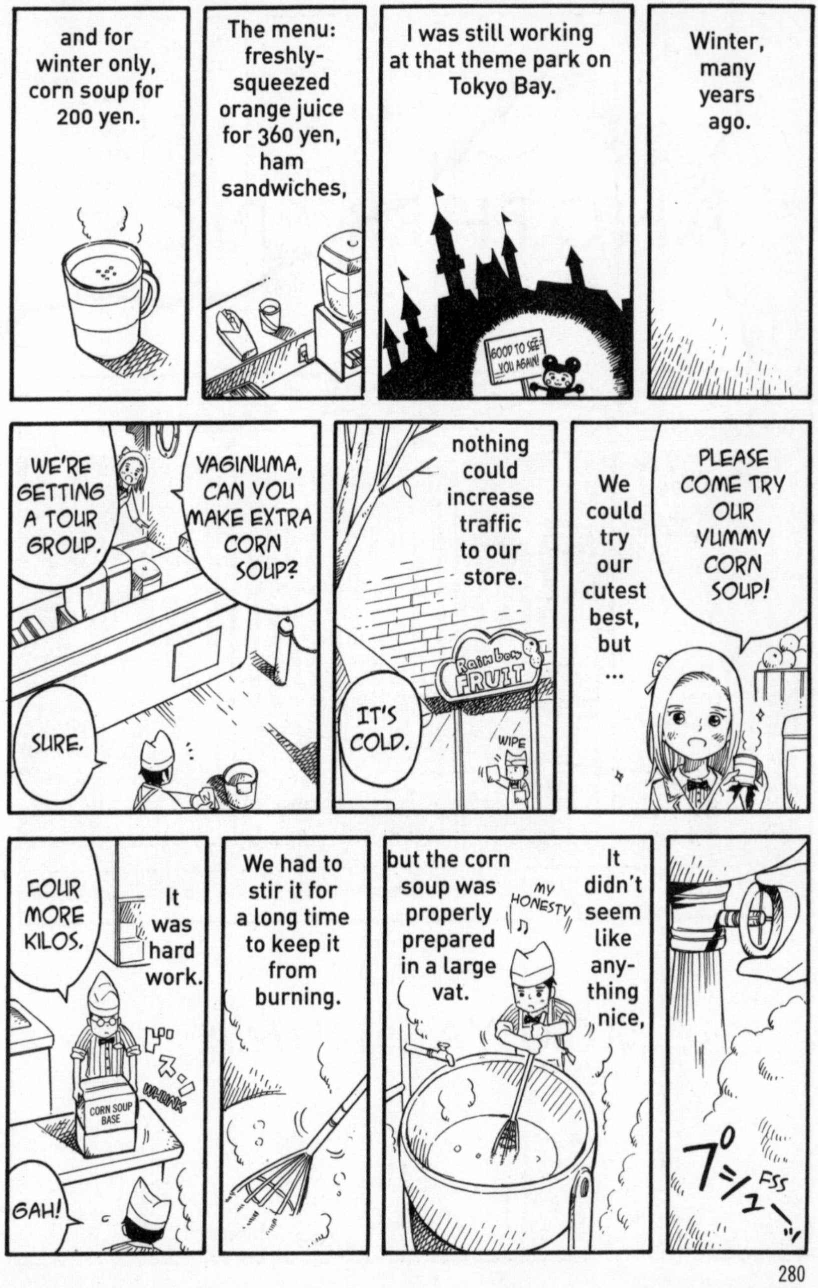
Winter, many years ago.
I was still working at that theme park on Tokyo Bay.
GOOD TO SEE YOU AGAIN!
The menu: freshly-squeezed orange juice for 360 yen, ham sandwiches,
and for winter only, corn soup for 200 yen.
PLEASE COME TRY OUR YUMMY CORN SOUP!
We could try our cutest best, but ...
nothing could increase traffic to our store.
Rainbow FRUIT
IT'S COLD.
WIPE
YAGINUMA, CAN YOU MAKE EXTRA CORN SOUP?
WE'RE GETTING A TOUR GROUP.
SURE.
FSS
It didn't seem like anything nice,
but the corn soup was properly prepared in a large vat.
MY HONESTY ♪
We had to stir it for a long time to keep it from burning.
It was hard work.
FOUR MORE KILOS.
WHUNK
CORN SOUP BASE
GAH!

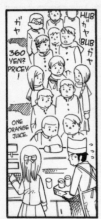

ガラ
ROLL
ガラガラ
ROLL
THE GROUP IS A MIDDLE SCHOOL FIELD TRIP.
FINALLY DONE
HUH.
ガラガラ
ROLL
ガラガラ
ROLL
I'LL LEAVE 'EM TO YOU.
'NIGHT!
HEY, WAIT!!
HEY!
I NEED HELP!
GIMME A BREAK!
UH, BE RIGHT THERE.
HUB
ガヤ
BUB
ガヤ
ガヤ
360 YEN? PRICEY!
ONE ORANGE JUICE.
ガヤ
BUB
ガヤ
HUB
WHAT'RE YOU HAVING?
HAM SANDWICH
It hadn't been all fun and games, but I used to be that age too.
In geography, my teacher asked,
"What's the mountain range that runs north-south across Eurasia?"
YAGINUMA,
PLEASE ANSWER.
ギクッ
YIPE
URALA RANGE
World Map
...I answered.
For a while, everyone called me "Urala."
HEY URALA.
ガ
NO...
There was a time when delinquents ganged up on me,
shoving a razor blade in my face.
YAGINUMA,
DON'T GET TOO COCKY,
Even though I'd never said anything to her, a girl I had a crush on
HERE, YAGINUMA.
Sorry, I'm not interested.
pre-emptively dumped me.
My junior high days
were filled with boo-hoos.
DING DONG
キンコン
カンコン

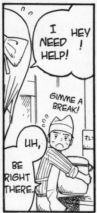

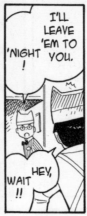

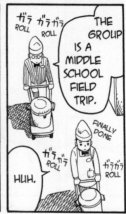

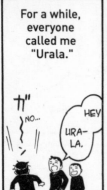

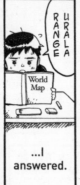

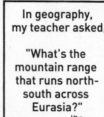

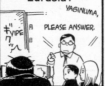

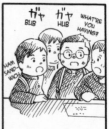

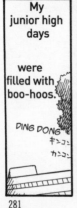

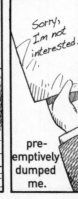

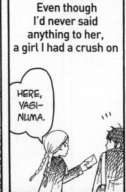

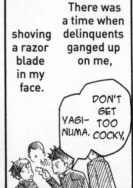

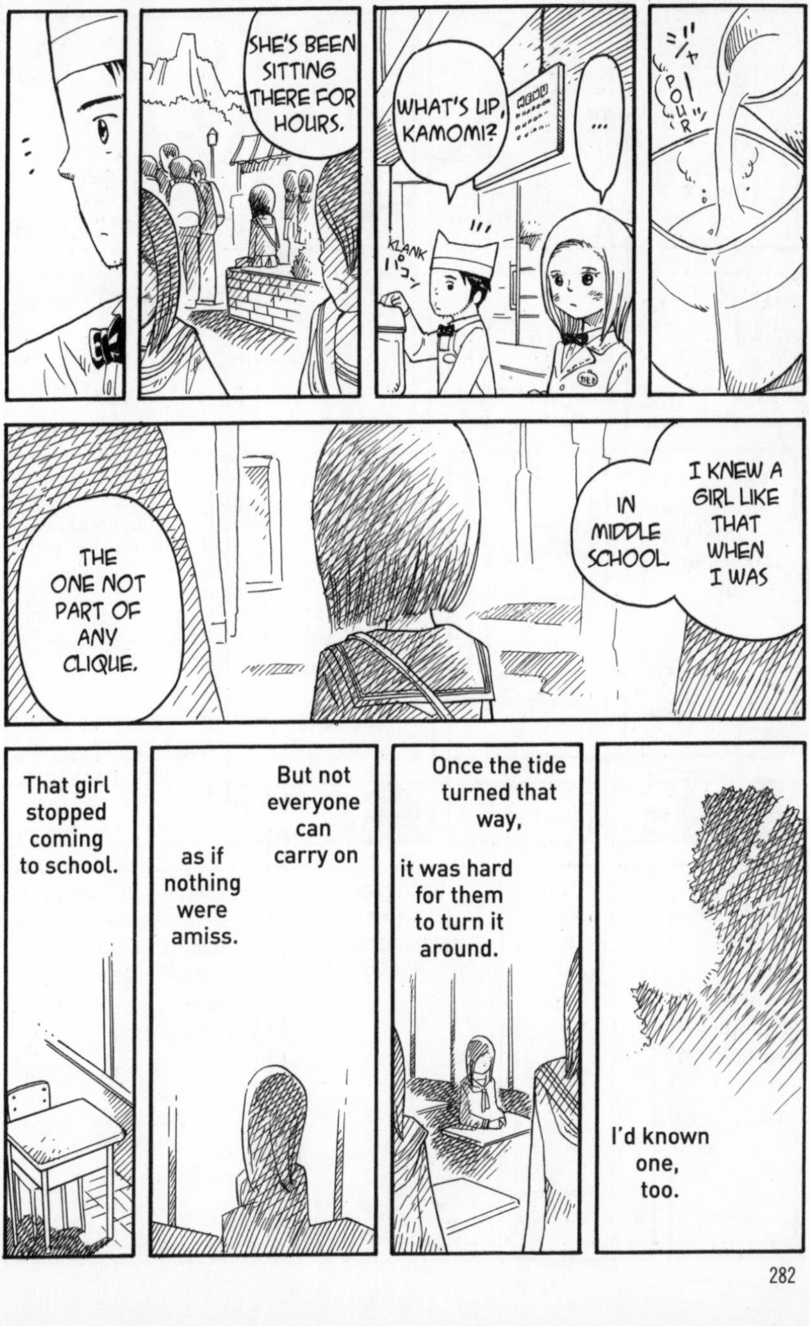
POUR
...
WHAT'S UP, KAMOMI?
KLANK
パコッ
SHE'S BEEN SITTING THERE FOR HOURS.
I KNEW A GIRL LIKE THAT WHEN I WAS
IN MIDDLE SCHOOL.
THE ONE NOT PART OF ANY CLIQUE.
I'd known one, too.
Once the tide turned that way,
it was hard for them to turn it around.
But not everyone can carry on
as if nothing were amiss.
That girl stopped coming to school.

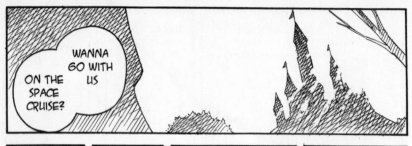

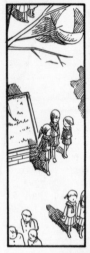

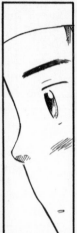

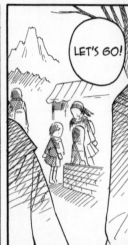

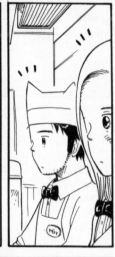

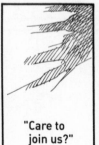

WANNA GO WITH US ON THE SPACE CRUISE?
LET'S GO!
I'M GLAD!
YEAH.
I felt like
crying a little.
They did what we couldn't do.
Just saying the words,
"Care to join us?"

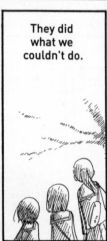

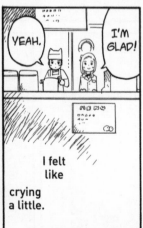

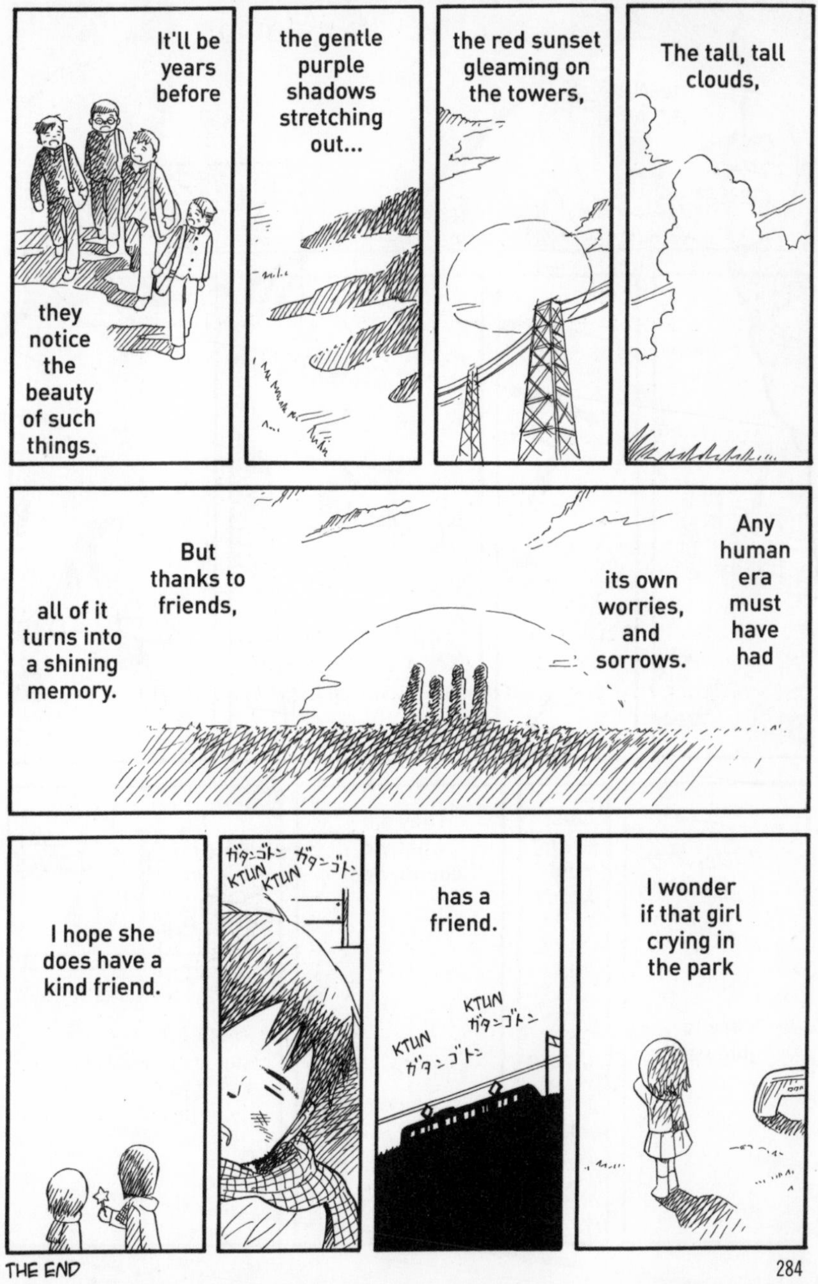
The tall, tall clouds,
the red sunset gleaming on the towers,
the gentle purple shadows stretching out...
It'll be years before
they notice the beauty of such things.
Any human era must have had
its own worries, and sorrows.
But thanks to friends,
all of it turns into a shining memory.
I wonder if that girl crying in the park
has a friend.
KTUN ガタンゴトン
KTUN ガタンゴトン
ガタンゴトン ガタンゴトン
KTUN KTUN
I hope she does have a kind friend.

THE END

Notes on the Translation

P. 13

HE IS THE ELDEST SON OF FORMER CHIEF CABINET SECRETARY, DIET MEMBER HARUO SUZUKI.
SHU IS CURRENTLY A JUNIOR AT THE TOKYO SPACE SCHOOL...

"Chief Cabinet Secretary" is an important administration post that has no immediate American counterpart, combining as it does elements of the functions of White House Chief of Staff, White House Press Secretary, and Vice President. It is considered a stepping stone to an eventual premiership.

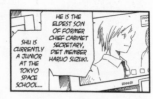

P. 38, 39

I'M MIKAN TOKUSHIMA. I'LL BE LIVING HERE.
NICE TO MEET YOU,
MISS SAKA-SHITA!
ペコッ
BOW
MIKAN FROM EHIME
I'M RINGO SAKASHITA. NICE TO MEET YOU.
あははははは、
HA HA HA
NICE TO MEET YOU.
"APPLE" AND "ORANGE"... YOU'LL HAVE TO BE THE NEXT R.A.!
NOT WHAT I EXPECT-ED...

Tokushima and Ehime are both prefectures on Shikoku, the smallest of Japan's four major islands. While Tokushima also produces "mikan" or oranges, it is Ehime that is known for them. Resident advisor Sakashita, whose first name "Ringo" means apple, jokes about their fruitful meeting on the next page. (There is no Japanese expression about how the two can't be compared.)

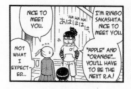

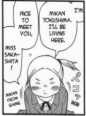

P. 267

THEY'VE BEEN MAKING MEDICAL EQUIPMENT AND MEDICINE SINCE BEFORE THE WAR,
THE UKITA ZAI-BATSU HAS.

A "zaibatsu" is a conglomerate of firms owned by a family; the Mitsubishi Group is an example. After World War II, American occupation forces initially moved to disband zaibatsu for having wielded excessive influence. This policy, however, was reversed for anti-Communist reasons, in particular due to the Korean War, which rendered indispensable the logistical support that zaibatsu were capable of providing.

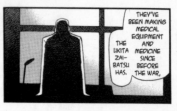

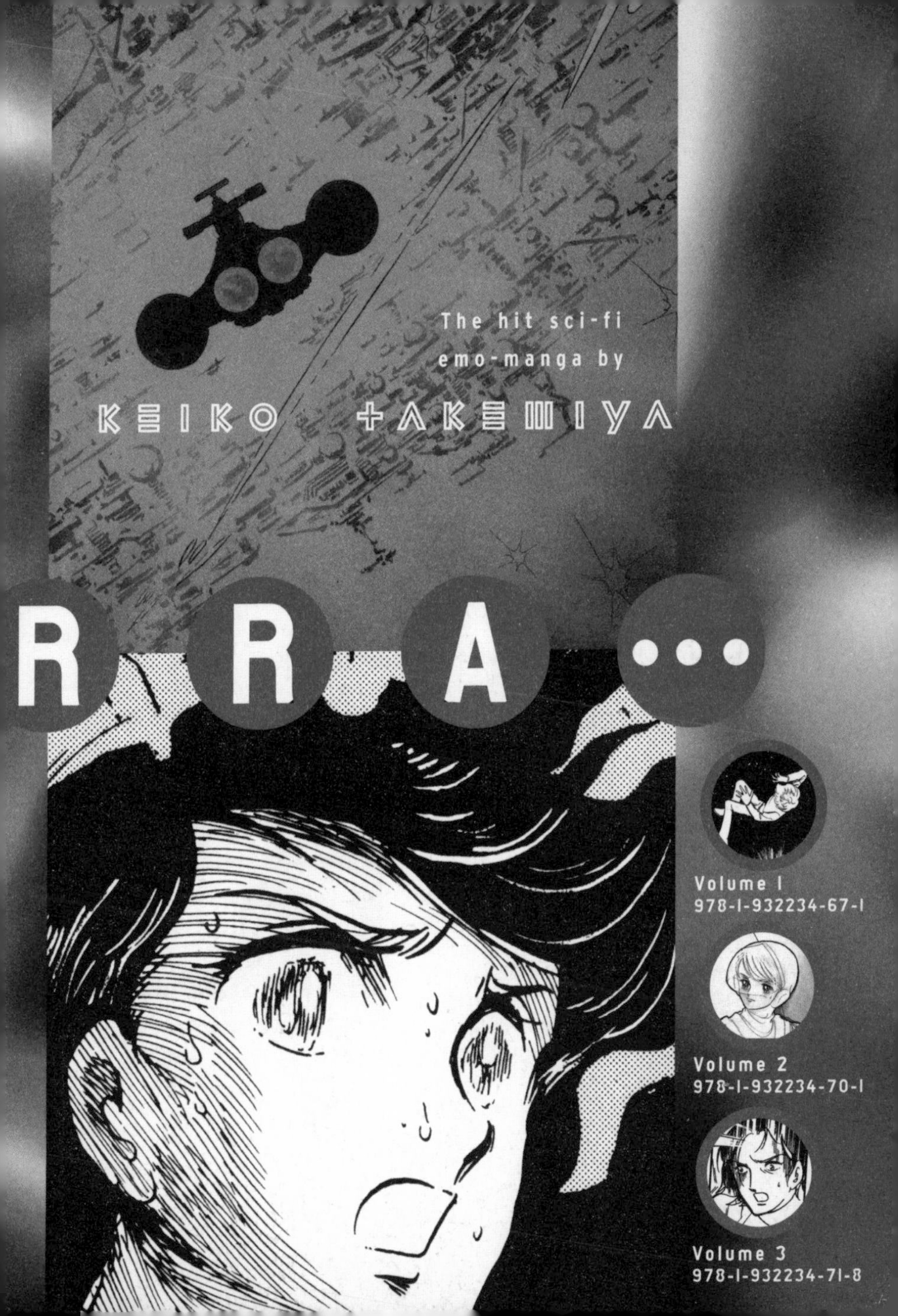

The hit sci-fi
emo-manga by
KEIKO TAKEMIYA
RRA...
Volume 1
978-1-932234-67-1
Volume 2
978-1-932234-70-1
Volume 3
978-1-932234-71-8

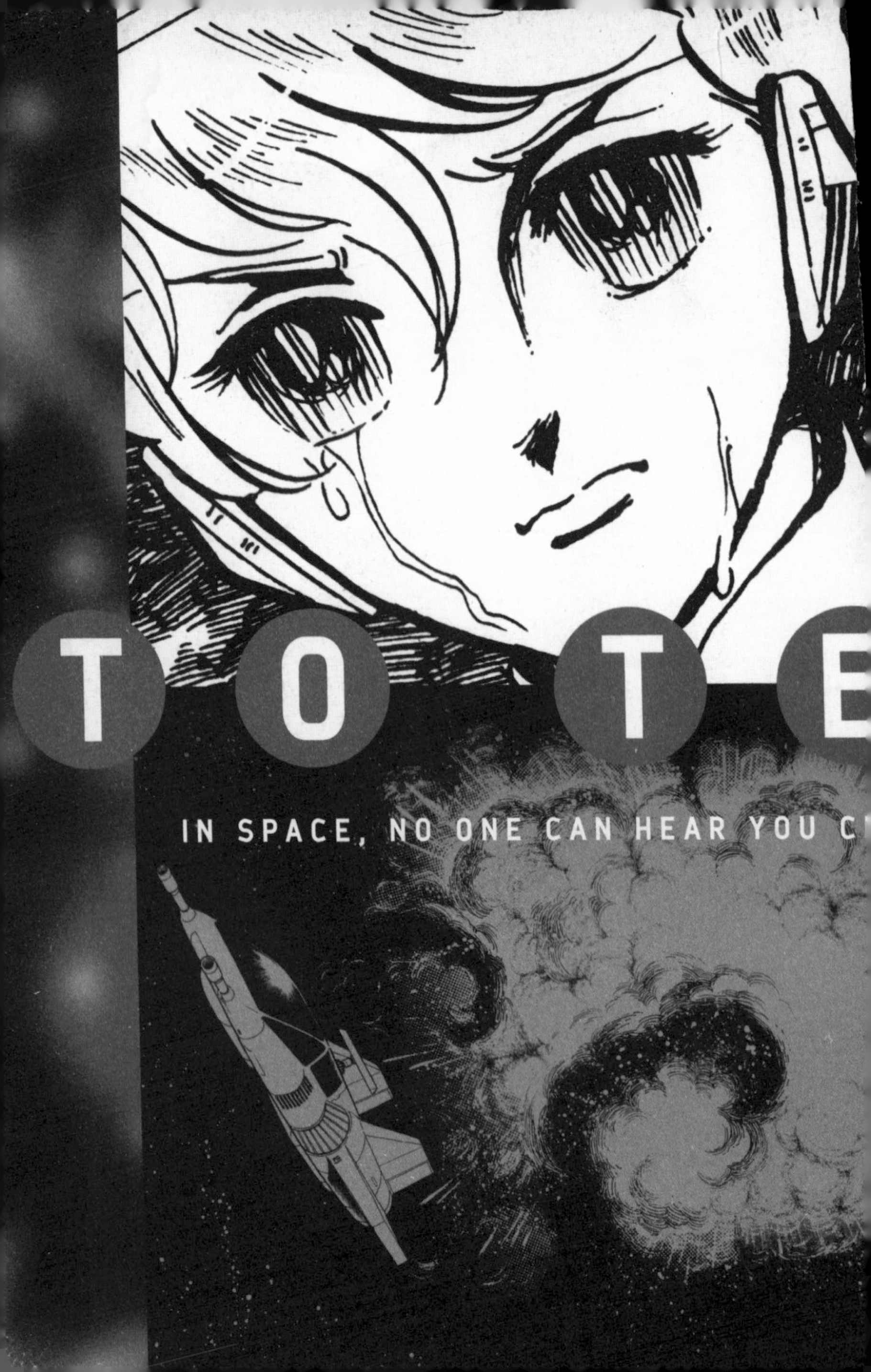
T O T E
IN SPACE, NO ONE CAN HEAR YOU

Production - Hiroko Mizuno
           Glen Isip
           Tomoe Tsutsumi
           Nicole Dochych
           Jill Rittymanee

Originally published in Japanese as *Futatsu no Supika 10, 11*
by MEDIA FACTORY, Inc., Tokyo 2006
Futatsu no Supika first serialized in Gekkan Comic Flapper,
MEDIA FACTORY, Inc., 2001-2009

This is a work of fiction.

ISBN: 978-1-935654-23-0

Manufactured in Canada

First Edition

Vertical, Inc.
451 Park Avenue South, 7th Floor
New York, NY 10016
www.vertical-inc.com